Aging

CONCEPTS AND CONTROVERSIES

Sociology for a New Century *A Pine Forge Press Series*
edited by Charles C. Ragin, Wendy Griswold, and Larry Griffin

Sociology for a New Century brings the best current scholarship to today's students in a series of short texts authored by leaders of a new generation of social scientists. Each book addresses its subject from a comparative, historical, global perspective, and, in doing so, connects social science to the wider concerns of students seeking to make sense of our dramatically changing world.

Social Psychology and Social Institutions
Denise D. Bielby and William T. Bielby

Global Transitions: Emerging Patterns of Inequality
York Bradshaw and Michael Wallace

Schools and Societies   *Steven Brint*

The Social Ecology of Natural Resources and Development
Stephen G. Bunker

How Societies Change   *Daniel Chirot*

Ethnic Dynamics in the Modern World   *Stephen Cornell*

The Sociology of Childhood   *William A. Corsaro*

Cultures and Societies in a Changing World   *Wendy Griswold*

Crime and Disrepute   *John Hagan*

Racism and the Modern World   *Wilmot James*

Gods in the Global Village   *Lester Kurtz*

Waves of Democracy   *John Markoff*

A Global View of Development   *Philip McMichael*

Health and Society   *Bernice Pescosolido*

Organizations in a World Economy   *Walter W. Powell*

Constructing Social Research   *Charles C. Ragin*

Women, Men, and Work   *Barbara Reskin and Irene Padavic*

Cities in a World Economy   *Saskia Sassen*

M. E. Henry

Aging

CONCEPTS AND CONTROVERSIES

Harry R. Moody

Brookdale Center on Aging
Hunter College

PINE FORGE PRESS
Thousand Oaks, California
London • New Delhi

For information address:

 Pine Forge Press
A Sage Publications Company
2455 Teller Road
Thousand Oaks, California 91320
(805) 499-4224
Internet: sdr@pfp.sagepub.com

Administrative Assistant: Mary Sutton
Editor: Janet Brown
Production Editor: Diane S. Foster
Designer: Lisa S. Mirski
Copy Editor: Janet Brown
Typesetter: Christina M. Hill
Cover: Paula Shuhert
Print Buyer: Anna Chin
Printer: Malloy Lithographing, Inc.
Photo credits: Part opening photos reprinted by permission of Marianne Gontarz, photographer.

Printed in the United States of America

Library of Congress Cataloging-in-Publication Data

Moody, Harry R.
    Aging: concepts and controversies / Harry R. Moody
        p.   cm. — (The Pine Forge Press social science library)
    Includes bibliographical references and index.
    ISBN 0-8039-9013-8 (pbk. : alk. paper)
        1. Gerontology—United States.   2. Aging—United States.
    I. Title. II. Series.
    HQ1064.U5M665   1994
    305.26′0973—dc20

                                                                    93-37727

94 95 96 97 98 10 9 8 7 6 5 4 3 2

ABOUT THE AUTHOR

Harry R. Moody is a graduate of Yale University and received his Ph.D. in philosophy from Columbia University. He has taught philosophy at Columbia University, Hunter College, New York University, and the University of California at Santa Cruz. For the past 15 years he has been at the Brookdale Center on Aging of Hunter College in the City University of New York, where he is Deputy Director. Earlier, at the National Council on Aging in Washington, DC, he served as Co-Director of its National Policy Center. He is the author of over 70 articles and two books: *Abundance of Life: Human Development Policies for an Aging Society* (Columbia University Press, 1988) and *Ethics in an Aging Society* (Johns Hopkins University Press, 1992). He is Co-Editor of the newsletter, *Aging and the Human Spirit,* which is devoted to the search for meaning in later life. He became involved in the field of gerontology in 1971 while teaching humanities in senior centers. He is known for his work in older adult education and he currently serves as Vice-Chairman of the Board of ELDERHOSTEL. He has also been active in the field of biomedical ethics and is an Adjunct Associate of the Hastings Center, Briar Cliff, New York.

ABOUT THE PUBLISHER

Pine Forge Press is a new educational publisher, dedicated to publishing innovative books and software throughout the social sciences. On this and any other of our publications, we welcome your comments and suggestions. Please call or write us at

Pine Forge Press
A Sage Publications Company
2455 Teller Road
Thousand Oaks, CA 91320
(805) 499-4224
Internet: sdr@pfp.sagepub.com

Brief Contents

BASIC CONCEPTS AGING, HEALTH CARE, AND SOCIETY / 1

CONTROVERSY 1 **Why Do We Grow Old? / 35**

Does aging come about because of inborn biological limits for the human species? Some biologists believe that without raising maximum life span we can now postpone the illnesses and disabilities of old age. Others reply that deeper understanding of the biology of aging is needed to understand why we grow old or whether it is possible to raise the maximum human life span.

CONTROVERSY 2 **Should We Ration Health Care on Grounds of Age? / 71**

How do we respond to the rising cost of health care in an aging society? Some have urged that health care costs should be rationed on the basis of age; that is, priority should be given to quality of life rather than extending survival for those who have lived a full life span. But critics argue that such a plan is deeply misguided and that better alternatives are needed.

CONTROVERSY 3 **Should People Have the Choice to End Their Lives? / 99**

People today have the option of refusing medical treatment even if it means loss of life. But some would go further and permit direct killing or assisted suicide on behalf of those who want to end their lives. Critics worry that to permit direct killing would profoundly change our society in dangerous ways.

Detailed Contents

Preface

Becoming acquainted with a new discipline is never an easy task because it requires two elements that do not always easily go together. On the one hand, a good introduction requires learning facts—key ideas, technical terms, and major findings that have stood the test of time. On the other hand, a good introduction requires learning to think in new ways: to evaluate issues and evidence and to recognize the limits of knowledge, and to separate facts from values when it comes to applying what we know to the world around us.

Aging: Concepts and Controversies conveys both these contrasting elements to the introductory student. On the one hand, it presents key ideas from the field of gerontology. But, more important, it aims to strengthen the student's capacity for critical thinking about issues in the study of aging.

For most college students, gerontology will be a brand-new field of study with a special challenge of its own. Unlike history or chemistry, it is not a subject typically studied in secondary school. Moreover, gerontology is a multidisciplinary field. The natural sciences, the social and behavioral sciences, and the humanities are all important for understanding what human aging has been or might become in the future. Thus this book draws on concepts from biology, economics, philosophy, sociology, and psychology as well as many other disciplines.

This interdisciplinary mix can make the study of gerontology intellectually exciting. But the very scale of the enterprise conceals a pitfall. With such a vast range of disciplines and ideas to draw on, the temptation is to try to encompass as much as possible between two covers of a textbook. Then, as the semester begins, we hope that, against all odds, students will assimilate some modest portion of the facts assembled between the covers.

That hope is often disappointed, and the disappointment is keenly felt by faculty who are searching for a better way to interest students in the field of aging. The problem is that fact- and research-oriented approaches to the subject are important for students already committed to gerontological study; however, for many more students who have a more *general* interest in both individual and societal aging, we need a different approach.

Hence *Aging: Concepts and Controversies* is written from an entirely different perspective. It consciously focuses on issues of interest to all of us as citizens and as educated human beings, not just as potential gerontologists

---

or professional service providers. As we move into a new century, as an increasingly age-conscious society, we all have a stake in better understanding the subject. This book, in short, presents gerontology as central to a good general education.

This book takes a similarly broad view toward what aging is all about. From the opening chapter, students are encouraged to see aging not as a fixed period of life but as a process beginning at birth and extending over the entire life course. This open-ended quality of human aging is a theme woven throughout the book: from biological experiments to extend the life span to difficult choices about allocation of health care resources. The social and economic conditions of an aging society will mean new dilemmas about rights and responsibilities ascribed to old age in a world where we increasingly come to see aging as a social construction rather than a natural or unalterable fact of the human condition.

Because the possibilities for how we might age both as individuals and as a society are multiple, it requires new thinking to grasp the central issues at stake. The fundamental aim of this book is to help students see gerontology as a domain for critical thinking. That aim is what has dictated the basic pedagogical design of the book: namely, its focus on controversies and questions rather than exhorting students to adopt a "correct" view about aging or older people. The readings are selected to accentuate contrast and conflict, to stimulate the student to think more deeply about what is at stake in the debates presented here. In the end, there is no "right answer" to these debates. But there *is* a body of knowledge indispensable for reaching their resolution in theory or in practice.

That is why *Aging: Concepts and Controversies* presents gerontology's most important empirical findings supported by current research. That is the purpose of the three major "essays" around which the book's controversies or "debates" are organized. The "facts" and basic concepts of gerontology are offered in these essays to help students make sense of the controversies, understand their origin, engage in critical thinking, and, finally, develop their own views. As students become engaged in the debates, they will appreciate the justification for having the factual background necessary to make responsible judgments and interpretations. My *introductions* to each controversy and the *questions* I have written to conclude them also reinforce this important link between factual knowledge and interpretation/reflection, which is at the heart of this book.

This book, then, can best be seen as a textbook constructed to provide drama and compelling interest for the reader. It is structured so as to encourage a style of teaching and learning that is more than conveying facts and methods. Other, more specific features of the book reinforce this pedagogical approach: The "Focus on Practice" sections demonstrate the relevance of the *controversies* to care and human services work in our society; the Appendix offers guidance on researching and writing term papers on aging; and key terms/ideas are glossed in the index.

Whether students reading this book go on to specialized professional work or whether they never take another course in gerontology, my aim is directed squarely at issues of compelling human importance, now and in the future. By returning again and again to those questions of perennial human interest, it is my hope that both teachers and students will find new excitement in questions that properly concern us all at any age.

Acknowledgments

I want to acknowledge the contributions of some of the people who made this book possible. First and foremost is Steve Rutter, President of Pine Forge Press, who originally conceived the idea for the book and who had faith that I could finish the job. At Hunter College I have been blessed with wonderful colleagues at the Brookdale Center on Aging: above all, Rose Dobrof, Director of the Center, and Sam Sadin and Pat Gilberto, Deputy Directors. They will certainly recognize in this book some familiar issues we've debated from time to time.

Let me also thank the academic colleagues around the country from whom I have learned so much both from their writing and through personal relationships over a period of many years: Andy Achenbaum, Ed Ansello, Scott Bass, Bob Binstock, James Birren, Daniel Callahan, Tom Cole, Brian Hofland, Martha Holstein, Rob Hudson, Rosalie Kane, Bob Kastenbaum, Eric Kingston, Ron Manheimer, Bernice Neugarten, Jack and Matilda Riley, and Fernando Torres-Gil. I remain especially grateful to Alan Pifer and Lydia Bronte, for the generous opportunity to be involved in the Carnegie Corporation's Aging Society Project.

Among the reviewers and commentators on this book, let me single out Lynne Hodgson for special praise. I am also grateful to those who read the manuscript at different stages of development:

Linda Breytspraak, *University of Missouri, Kansas City*
David Eaton, *Illinois State University*
Gail E. Eisen, *The University of Michigan*
Susan B. Eve, *University of North Texas*
Karen Frederick, *St. Anselm's College*
Davis Gardner, *University of Kentucky*
Lynne G. Hodgson, *Quinnipiac College*
Dale Lund, *University of Utah*
Richard Machemer, *St. John Fisher College*
Tom MacLachlan, *North Shore Community College*
Leslie A. Morgan, *University of Maryland*
Carolyn C. Rizza, *Slippery Rock University*
Karen Roberto, *University of Northern Colorado*
Dena Shenk, *University of North Carolina at Charlotte*

Let me not forget my two faithful research assistants, Jonathan Mazer and Ethel Levy, whose labors in the library enabled me to get this project under way.

I want to acknowledge the help and support of my always patient family: my wife Elizabeth, and my children, Carolyn Maryam and Roger Habib. Finally, I owe a personal debt to the greatest gerontology teacher I ever had, Lawrence Morris, whose old age and death remains an illuminating example of the life cycle completed.

Prologue: America as an Aging Society

It is no secret that the number of people over age 65 in the United States is growing rapidly, a phenomenon recognized as the "graying of America." The numbers are staggering. There has been a 30-fold increase in older people in the United States since 1870: from 1 million up to nearly 32 million in 1990—a number now bigger than the entire population of Canada. During the past two decades, the 65+ group has been increasing twice as fast as the rest of the population.

As a result, the U.S. population looks different than it did earlier this century. In 1900 only 4% of the population was over the age of 65. Today, that figure has jumped to 13%. And the pace of growth will continue in the next two decades, as the **baby boom generation** moves into the ranks of senior citizens. The proportion over 65 will increase in the future to 20% by the year 2030. This rate of growth in the older population is unprecedented in human history. When the baby boomers begin to retire, about one in five Americans will be eligible for Social Security and Medicare, as opposed to just over one in eight today.

We usually think of aging as strictly an individual matter. But we can also speak of a whole population "aging" or growing older, although to speak that way is to speak in terms of a metaphor. In literal terms, only organisms, not populations, grow older. Still, metaphorical or not, there's no doubt about a key trend in contemporary society: that is, the rise in the average age of the population or an increase in the proportion of the population made up of people over age 65. This change in the demographic structure of the population can be defined as **population aging.**

For purposes of comparison, we can note that in 1900 the percentage of children and teenagers in the population was 40%—a relatively "young" population. By 1990 that proportion of youth had dropped to 24%. By contrast, seniors increased from 4% in 1900 to 13% in 1990 with larger increases still to come. In fact, during the next several decades, overall population growth in the United States will be concentrated among middle-aged and older Americans. The number aged 50 or more is projected to increase 76% by the year 2020. Those under age 50 will actually decrease by 1%—in effect, the rate remaining flat for the next few decades.

Population aging also shows up as an increase in the average or median age of the entire population: that is, the age for which half the population is older and half the population is younger. The median age of the U.S. population in 1820 was only 17 years; by 1900 it had risen to 23 and by 1990, to 33 years. It is estimated that by the turn of the century the median age of the American population will be 36; by 2030 it will rise to 42 years. This shift, too, is another measure of the dramatic impact of population aging.

It is clear, then, that populations "age" for reasons different than individuals do, and the reasons have to do with demographic trends. In the first place, population aging can occur because birthrates decline. The result is that there is a smaller proportion of children in the population and so the average age of the population will go up. But population aging can also come about because of improvements in life expectancy: people living longer on average. Finally, the process of population aging can be augmented for a time because of a large group of people—in technical language, a birth **cohort**—who were born during a particular period: for example, the baby boom generation born between 1946 and 1964. Baby boomers are now in middle age and, early in the next century, they will enter old age. At least for a period of time, they will dramatically hasten the aging of the American population.

Thus trends in birthrates, death rates, and the flow of cohorts all contribute to population aging. What makes matters confusing is that *all three trends* can be happening at once, as they have been in America in recent decades (Hauser, 1976). Population aging, then, is more complex than it seems. Casual observers sometimes suggest that the American population is aging just because people are living longer. But that impression isn't quite accurate because it fails to take into account multiple trends defined by demographic factors including birth (fertility), death (mortality), and migration rates.

But a demographic description does not explain the reason these trends happen in the first place. One logical question is this: Why has this process of population aging occurred? The rising proportion of older people in the population can be explained by **demographic transition theory,** which points to the connection between population growth and the economic process of industrialization. In preindustrial societies, there is a generally stable population because both birthrates and death rates remain high. With industrialization, death rates tend to fall while birthrates remain high for a period, and thus the population grows. But at a certain point, at least in advanced industrial societies, birthrates begin to fall in line with death rates. Eventually, when the rate of fertility is exactly balanced by the rate of mortality, we have a condition of stability known as zero population growth.

The industrial revolution of the nineteenth century brought improved agricultural production, improved standards of living, and therefore an increase in population size. At the same time, there came a shift in the age structure of the population, known to demographers as the demographic transition. This was a shift away from a population with high fertility and high mortality to one having low fertility and low mortality. That population pattern is what we see today in America, in Europe, and in Japan. The result in all industrialized societies has been population aging: a change in the age distribution of the population.

Most developing countries in the Third World—in Africa, Asia, and Latin America—still have fertility rates and death rates that are much higher than those in advanced industrialized countries. For the United States in 1800, as for most Third World countries today, that population distribution can be represented as a population pyramid: many births (high fertility) and relatively few people surviving to old age (high mortality). For countries that are approaching zero population growth, that pyramid becomes replaced by a cylinder: Each cohort becomes approximately the same in size.

As we have seen, the increased number of older people is only part of the cause of population aging. It is important to remember that overall population aging has actually been brought about much more by declines in fertility than by reductions in mortality. The trend toward declining fertility in America actually can be traced back to the early nineteenth century, so the process of population aging has causes that date back a long time. Finally, to complete the demographic picture, we would need to point to other factors that influence population size and composition, such as improvements in the chance of survival of people at different ages or the impact of immigration into the United States, largely by younger people. But one conclusion is inescapable. Today's increased proportion of people over 65 springs from causes that are deeply rooted in American society. Population aging is a long-range trend that will characterize our society into the twenty-first century. It is a fact we all will cope with for the rest of our lives.

But how is American society coping with population aging? And how are the major institutions of society—government, the economy, the family—coping with the aging of a large number of individuals? The answer, in simplified terms, is rooted in the basic difference between individual and population aging. As human beings, we are all quite familiar with individual aging. It is therefore not surprising that as a society we have devised many policies and practices to take into account changes that predictably occur in the later years: for example, retirement pensions, medical interventions for chronic illness, and familiar government programs such as Social Security and Medicare.

Whether it involves changes in biological functioning or changes in work roles, individual aging is tangible and undeniable: a pattern we observe well enough in our parents and family members, not to mention in ourselves. But population aging is more subtle and less easily observed. We have many institutional policies and programs to deal with individual aging. But our society is just beginning to wrestle with the controversies generated by the population aging trends now emerging, with the prospect of even more dramatic debate and change in the decades ahead. The fact that these demographic changes are so significant and are stimulating so much ferment in our society's fundamental institutions is one important reason that this book is organized by *controversies* as well as by the facts and basic concepts that lie behind them.

Our society's response to population aging can best be summed up in the aphorism that generals prepare for the "next" war by fighting the "old" one over again. That is to say, in our individual and our social planning, we tend to do the same thing, to look back to past experience to guide our thinking about the future. Thus, when the railroad was first introduced, it was dubbed "the iron horse." But it wasn't a horse at all, and the changes that rail transport brought to society were revolutionary, beyond anything that could be expected by looking to the past.

The same holds true for population aging. We cannot anticipate the changes that will be brought about by population aging by looking backward because population aging is historically unprecedented among the world's societies. Moreover, we cannot confuse population aging with the process of individual aging. An aging society, after all, is not like an individual with a fixed life span. Why is it that people are so often fearful when they begin to think about America's future as an aging society? Part of the reason is surely that many of us are locked into images of decline that are based on prejudice or simply on outdated impressions of what individual aging entails. Because our social institutions have responded to aging as a problem, we tend to see only losses and to overlook opportunities in the process of aging.

An important fact to remember is that the solutions to yesterday's problems may not give us creative solutions to new challenges we face today. For example, Social Security has proven to be a vital program that protects older Americans from the threat of poverty in old age. But Social Security was never designed to help promote second careers or new forms of productivity among older people. We may need to think in new ways about pensions and retirement in the future. Similarly, Medicare has proved to be an important, though expensive means of guaranteeing access to medical care for older people. But it was never designed to address the problem of long-term care for elderly people who need help to remain in their own homes. Finally, as the sheer number of people over 65 increases, America as a society will need to consider what institutions and policies are best able to provide for the needs of this growing population.

Social gerontologist Matilda Riley has pointed out that our failure to think deeply about population aging is a weakness in gerontology as a discipline. Gerontologists know more about individual aging than about opportunity structures over the whole life course. A good example is the way the life course itself has been shaped, with transitions between education, work, and retirement. These transitions do not seem to prepare us well for an aging society in the future. In effect, we have a "cultural lag" in facing the future. We know that in this century the age of leaving the workforce to retire has been gradually going down, while the age for leaving schooling has been going up. Riley points out that, if we were to project these trends into the future, sometime in the twenty-first century people would leave college at age 38 and immediately enter retirement! This scenario, of course, is not serious. But it does make a serious point. We must not take current trends and simply project them into the future.

Part of the problem is that we have less knowledge than we ought to have about the interaction between individual lives and the wider society. During the twentieth century, nearly three decades have been added to human life expectancy. Now nearly one third of adult life is spent in retirement. The population of people over 65 is healthier and better educated than ever before. Yet opportunity structures are lacking to integrate this older population into major institutions of society such as education or the workplace. Where will we find a blueprint for what an aging society of the future might look like? The blueprint must be constructed. Today, we grow old very differently compared with our grandparents, so it does little good to look backward as we anticipate the twenty-first century.

The challenge is to change our way of anticipating the future by thinking critically about assumptions we otherwise take for granted. This task of critical thinking may actually be more difficult in gerontology than in other fields, because of the familiarity of aging itself. Revolutionary changes have taken place in the twentieth century, but most of us tend to assume that aging and the human life course have remained the same. In spite of our commonsense perceptions, however, history and social science tell us that the process of aging is not something fixed or given but is a changeable construction and subject to interpretation.

Taking a more critical and thoughtful stance, we know that the basic structures of the life course—the "stages of life"—have been viewed very differently by different societies. Even in our own society, the experience of growing older is not uniform but means very different things to individuals depending on their gender, race, or ethnicity. From this perspective, a societal "given" like retirement turns out to be less than a century old and now is in the process of being reexamined and redefined. And in this century, life expectancy in America has risen from 47 years to 75 years. Even in the biology of aging, scientists are engaged in serious debate about whether it is possible to extend the maximum human life span from what we have known in the past.

In short, wherever we look, in biology, economics, the social and behavioral sciences, or public policy, we see that "aging," despite its familiarity, cannot be taken as a given or fixed fact about human life. Both individual aging and population aging are socially and historically constructed, subject to interpretation, and therefore open to controversy, debate, and change. What aging will mean for us in the twenty-first century is not something to be predicted merely by extrapolating from the present and the past.

Still less can the study of aging consist of an accumulation of facts to be assimilated by us as if knowing these facts could somehow prepare us for the future. The changes are too far-reaching for that approach. What we need most of all is to see facts about individual and population aging in a wider context: to understand that facts and theories are subject to interpretation and revision. That is the second major reason much of the study of aging in this book is presented in the form of controversy and debate, offering all of us an opportunity to reflect on and construct an old age worthy of "our future selves."

Aging, Health Care, and Society

Five hundred years ago, the Spanish explorer Ponce de León embarked on a journey to the new world in search of the fountain of youth. He never found it. Instead, he discovered what is today Florida, the state with the largest percentage of elderly people.

Ponce de León might have smiled at the irony of how his discovery turned out. But discoveries often have a way of turning out differently than expected. When we think about medical advances in our time, things also have turned out unexpectedly. For instance, people are living longer today, but is the prolongation of life into old age always a benefit? Or have recent gains in human life expectancy instead been a prolongation of decrepitude and frailty? Will further medical advances only make matters worse? This question was raised nearly three centuries ago by Jonathan Swift in his satirical novel *Gulliver's Travels*.

The Challenge of Longevity: The Case of the Struldbruggs

Swift describes a voyage to the fictional country of Luggnagg, where his hero, Lemuel Gulliver, meets a strange group of beings, the "Struldbruggs," who are a race condemned to immortality. It turns out that for the Struldbruggs unlimited life span has not proved the blessing it promised to be. Longevity has come but without good health. Their existence is a dismal prolongation of senescence and decay, a nightmare like unlimited existence in a nursing home, as Swift describes them:

> They were the most mortifying sight I ever beheld. . . . Besides the usual deformities in extreme old age, they acquired an additional ghastliness in proportion to their number of years, which is not to be described.
>
> The diseases they were subject to still continue without increasing or diminishing. In talking they forget the common appellation of things, and the names of persons, even of those who are their nearest friends and relations. . . . The least miserable among them appear to be those who turn to dotage, and entirely lose their memories.

Swift's description of the Struldbruggs raises a question, still of compelling interest in thinking about aging, biology, and health care:

> The question therefore [is] not whether a man would choose to be always in the prime of youth, attended with prosperity and health, but how he would pass a perpetual life under all the usual disadvantages which old age brings along with it.

No doubt Swift has exaggerated to make his point. Aging cannot be equated with disease. To speak of the "usual disadvantages" of old age misses the positive development of aging in our time. Today, we all see countless examples of older people who are *not* sick or debilitated but who maintain health and vigor into their later years. Yet Swift's vision does come back to haunt us. A visit to a nursing home today is apt to provoke the question: Is this what medical science has produced? What shall we do, as individuals and as a society, in response to a condition of extreme frailty that is, too often, the very last stage of life? Several answers have been put forth in response.

Biomedical advances. There are those who believe that biology will save us from the problem. They argue that biomedical researchers can meet the challenge of longevity by developing techniques for delaying the onset of debilitating conditions in old age. In effect, they hope to postpone sickness until a final, brief period of life and so eliminate prolonged dependency. Other biologists believe that we can make good on Ponce de León's dream and discover a fountain of youth by altering the fundamental biological mechanism that makes us grow old. Whether by delaying illness or by actually preventing biological aging, the scientific optimists believe the "Struldbrugg" problem can eventually be solved.

Rationing health care. Their optimism is not shared by all. Others believe that hard choices are called for, and they doubt that biology will save us from making those choices. We do better, it is said, to acknowledge the biological limits rather than hope for a technological fix for the problems that often come with aging. In this spirit, ethicist Daniel Callahan wants to reject high-tech medical care used to prolong life for the very old. Instead, he believes, we do better to ration health care on the basis of age. He recommends forgoing life-extending treatment once elderly people have lived out a full and natural life span.

Providing long-term care. If more and more of the population live into advanced old age, we will see growing numbers of frail, chronically ill elderly in need of long-term care, at home or in institutions. Without unexpected biomedical advances, growing numbers will suffer from joint diseases, dementia, and other chronic disorders that keep them from living independently. In that case, long-term care will loom even larger in the future than it does today. Opinions differ about who should bear the cost of that care, but paying the bill for longevity is already a serious challenge to society.

Self-determined death. Neither prolonged debilitation nor rationing of health care is popular with most Americans. But growing numbers today do feel that decline and a diminished quality of life might be sufficient reasons for ending one's own life. Those who hold this view usually reject the idea of society setting limits but would instead leave the choice about dying up to the individual. Advocates of this idea believe that deliberate termination of treatment must be more openly recognized by law and should be actively supported by health care services.

So here we have four different answers to the Struldbrugg dilemma: hoping for a medical breakthrough, making tough cost-cutting decisions, providing long-term care, or permitting individuals to end life. All are ways of coping with the prospect of a prolonged period of frailty and dependency at the end of life. The options considered here are not mutually exclusive. But each raises profound questions about our values: Are the old less valued than the young? Where will we find the resources to take care of the frail elderly? Could scientific breakthroughs in the biology of aging have unforeseen consequences for society, either for good or for ill?

These questions have no easy answers. Indeed, they are at the center of the major debates examined in this book. The biology of longevity, the economics of health care, and the right to die are all related. By appreciating some key facts about biology, economics, and death and dying, we can better approach the debates surrounding these critical issues.

Biology of Aging

Oliver Wendell Holmes in his poem the "Wonderful One Hoss Shay" invokes a memorable image of longevity and mortality:

> Have you heard of the wonderful one-hoss shay,
> That was built in such a logical way
> It ran a hundred years to a day . . . ?

The wonderful "one-hoss shay," we learn, was built in such a way that every part of it "aged" at the same rate and therefore didn't wear out until, all at once, the whole thing fell apart at the same time. So, exactly a century after the carriage was produced, the village parson was driving this marvelous machine down the street, when

> What do you think the parson found,
> When he got up and stared around?
> The poor old chaise in a heap or mound,
> As if it had been to the mill and ground!
> You see, of course, if you're not a dunce,
> How it went to pieces all at once,—
> All at once, and nothing first,—
> Just as bubbles do when they burst.

Compression of Morbidity

The wonderful one-horse shay is the perfect image of an optimistic hope about aging. According to most biologists, the maximum human life span is fixed at something like 120 years. We may not yet be able to surpass that limit but our goal should be to eliminate the signs and symptoms of aging that appear well before the maximum age. The proper aim of medicine and public policy therefore would be to intervene, perhaps even slow down the rate of aging, so that more and more of us can remain healthy up to the very end of life. Sickness or **morbidity** would then be compressed into the last few years or months of life. At the end, the body would simply "fall apart" all at once, like the wonderful one-horse shay (Avorn, 1986).

According to the **compression of morbidity** theory, we should aim for a healthy old age followed by rapid decline and death. The scenario sounds good. But is it feasible? Do our health care practices and policies promote that scenario? And will it solve the problems we see around us already?

A difficulty arises from the fact that contemporary medical practice in the United States is based on a strategy of curing disease, not promoting health. This familiar strategy has led to the conquest of many killer diseases, such as smallpox and polio, thus permitting a greater portion of the population to reach old age. In recent decades, a drop in **mortality** from heart disease has permitted an ever larger proportion of people to survive into advanced old age (Paffenbarger, 1979). The net effect of these interventions has been to raise average life expectancy in America from 47 years in 1900 to 75 years today.

But gains in life expectancy are not the same as a change in maximum life span. **Life expectancy**, or expected years of life from birth, has risen; but **life span**—the maximum possible length of life—has not changed at all. The causes of maximum life span and of aging itself still remain unknown. Biological investigation suggests that maximum life span is genetically determined, and therefore fixed, for each species (Schneider, 1978). Medical research has not focused on the underlying process of biological aging, which remains mysterious and complex in its causes (Medawar, 1952).

Normal Aging

In a broad sense, we might say that aging begins at birth but we normally associate it with changes that come after maturity. In fact, aging as a biological process can be defined as all those time-dependent, irreversible changes that lead to progressive loss of functional capacity after the point of maturity. **Primary aging** would describe those changes that occur over time independent of any specific disease or trauma to the body, while **secondary aging** would describe disabilities resulting from forces such as disease.

Today, gerontologists often use the term **normal aging** to describe this underlying time-dependent process characteristic of each species. Following Strehler (1977), we can say that biological aging in itself comprises changes that (a) involve functional decline, such as respiratory function, visual function, and so on; (b) take place sequentially or after maturity; (c) are intrinsic within the body rather than brought about by the outside environment; and (d) are universal and characteristic of each species. These biological changes, then, are what constitute normal aging.

Normal aging is not a disease but eventually leads to functional declines and involves increased susceptibility to death from specific diseases. For example, decline in short-term memory, wrinkled skin, and gray hair are signs of normal aging. But they are not symptoms of disease and need not result in greater susceptibility to death. Recent research has focused on aging and changes in the immune system of the body. The strength of the immune function begins to decline after puberty and with advanced age comes a propensity to autoimmune disorders, such as arthritis, as well as higher rates of cancer.

Increasingly, biologists have come to believe that the process of aging is controlled at the most basic level of organic life. The key to prolonging the human life span or reversing the process of aging may lie in the strands of the molecule called DNA, which is the basis for heredity in the living cell. All evidence suggests that the maximum human life span, programmed into us by our genes, is around 120 years. But if the control of that upper limit lies in the molecular structure of our genes, then why wouldn't it be possible to alter the structure and thus modify the maximum upper bound of life?

The organic process of life is a delicate balance between forces that wear down structures—that lead to cell death, for instance—and forces that repair damage at the molecular and cellular level. This balance is maintained by the structure and metabolism of each living thing over time. But over time the balance begins to shift, and damage occurs faster than it can be repaired. Even oxygen, the essential element required by energy transformation in living organisms, can become a destructive force when it produces a class of oxygen molecules known as free radicals, which have been implicated in many processes of biological aging (Harman, 1956; Armstrong et al., 1984).

Functional Capacity and Chronological Age

At the biological level, aging seems to result from changes in molecular, cellular, tissue, and whole organism function. The simplest way to study the effects of aging at these levels would be to compare younger and older organisms and note the differences. Such studies employ a cross-sectional methodology; that is, they look at physical function at different ages but at a single point in time. The general conclusion from such studies of human beings would suggests that most physiological functions decline after approximately age 30.

There are weaknesses in using a purely **cross-sectional design** study to measure changes presumably brought about by aging. For one thing, it is hard to be sure we have taken into account changes in all the possible variables that might affect what is going on. A contrasting methodological approach is a **longitudinal design,** in which the same individuals are followed over a long period of time to measure changes in physical function at different ages. This approach also has problems; for instance, with human beings, we need to look at influences from a changing external environment. Further, carrying out longitudinal studies is expensive and not easy for long-lived organisms, whether human or animal. But the results can be of great importance.

One of the most successful of these investigations is the Baltimore Longitudinal Study, sponsored by the National Institute on Aging and now directed by Dr. James Fozard (Shock et al., 1984). The Baltimore study has turned up important evidence about the difference between normal aging and disease. An important focus of the Baltimore Study has been **biomarkers.** These are biological indicators that can predict one or another feature of the process of aging; biomarkers can be defined as specific physiological or functional processes that may remain stable but often decline with chronological age (Shock, 1962; Masoro, 1981). Such biomarkers include excretory function in the kidney and the behavior of the immune system. In the Baltimore Longitudinal Study of Aging, scientists looked at 24 distinct physiological functions, and research on biomarkers is actively under way today (Sprott and Roth, 1992).

Many changes in physical function have been documented, some of them familiar. For instance, with increased age, height tends to diminish while weight increases; hair becomes thinner and skin tends to wrinkle. Another change is the loss in vital capacity, or the maximum breathing capacity of the lungs. With aging, both respiratory and kidney function decrease. But this decline chiefly results in a loss of **reserve capacity,** or the ability of the body to recover from assaults and withstand peak-load demands: for example, during physical exertion. It is important to note, however, that diminished reserve capacity may not have any discernible impact on normal activities of daily living (Masoro, 1981). For instance, not having the reserves to run a marathon race is probably irrelevant to most activities of daily life. Further, a key finding from these longitudinal studies is that chronological age in itself is not a good predictor of **functional age** or the diminished loss of organ functions. In other words, people of the same chronological age differ dramatically in their functional age.

We sometimes think of "aging" or senescence as a process applying to the whole organism. Yet physiological studies show that different organ systems age at different rates. For example, white blood cells die and are replaced within 10 days, while red blood cells last 120 days. But the stem cells that produce all blood cells reveal none of the signs of aging at all. Cells in the brain last as long as the body lives, never replicating but maintaining themselves. But apart from these long-living cells, cells and tissues of the body at the smallest scale are constantly subjected to damage and repair.

Aging Versus Longevity

Is it possible that longevity is determined by specific biological processes that are separate and different than those that bring about what we see as aging? This question is important because it might turn out that maximum life span is determined by factors much simpler than whatever produces time-dependent declines of aging. We might wonder whether it would be desirable to increase maximum life span if the effects of aging were left unchanged: What would it be like if people started to show symptoms of aging, as they do now, say, in their 60s or 70s, but then continued to live, under decrepitude, until 130 or 140, instead of 80 or 90? That would be what happened to the Struldbruggs.

It seems likely that longevity, or maximum life span for a species, is genetically determined. But it remains an open question whether the decremental changes we know as aging are also thus determined. Sacher, Cutler, and other scientists have argued that natural selection may have promoted longevity-assurance genes (Sacher, 1978). In other words, evolution may have brought it about that we live as long as we do but not necessarily that we have the signs and symptoms of aging that we do. It is possible, for example, that genes having a favorable influence early in life could have a harmful influence later on.

We might conjecture that whatever genes determine maximum life span are also linked to genetic factors that forestall degenerative diseases of late life. Thus, under the most favorable scenario, if we were to discover and intervene in the genetic causes of maximum life span, we would also find the key to reducing the disabilities and dysfunctions of old age.

From an evolutionary point of view, there seems to be no obvious reason that human beings should live beyond age 30 or 40 years. We see from population studies of animals in the wild that aging rarely exists. From the standpoint of species survival, it is hard to see what biological advantage any species would gain from having aged organisms around. What follows from this evolutionary argument is that there is no intrinsic biological necessity for aging and thus no reason that extension of maximum life span would be impossible.

Is it conceivable that aging is genetically determined in some absolute way, such as through a "death gene" or "death hormone" that dictates an absolute limit on life? Those who believe that there is no fundamental genetic program ensuring aging and death for the good of the species point to studies of population biology showing that animals in the wild exhibit survival curves very similar to human populations.

Cutler, for example, argues that aging is merely a passive or indirect result of biological processes, whereas maximum life span is a positive or direct result of evolution. From this evolutionary perspective, it follows that the rate of aging and maximum life span can change, and change relatively quickly.

According to one optimistic view, most of the decremental changes associated with aging are not the result of any preprogrammed, built-in requirement for decline but are the result of environmental causes, including potentially preventable diseases, such as Alzheimer's (Cutler, 1983).

When we look at the survival curves of different species and strains of animals, it seems clear that maximum life span in nature is largely caused by very specific genetic processes rather than environmental factors. The question is thus: Would it be possible by direct intervention to alter the genetic code and thus delay the onset of age-dependent illnesses and the rate of aging itself?

Longevity and Disease

Steps toward health promotion, such as improved diet or increased exercise, can reduce the likelihood of illness and thus increase life expectancy. These steps may also reduce morbidity in later life, but not invariably so. A patient with a strong cardiovascular system who has Alzheimer's disease can live for many years in a dismal state resembling the Struldbruggs. Thus hopes for a "compression of morbidity" by health promotion strategies alone may not be convincing. The rising curve of survival into old age does nothing to alter maximum life span, the "natural death" that the Struldbruggs longed for.

Basic research on the biology of aging has been pursued by scientists in the hope of avoiding the "Struldbrugg problem": namely, having enormous numbers of frail, sick, and dependent elderly people whose lives are prolonged in a desperate condition. But do we really need to understand the biology of aging itself? Couldn't we simply concentrate research attention on eliminating the big "killer diseases" that prevent people from living out a full life span? For example, if the most prevalent diseases of later life, the big killers such as stroke, heart disease, and cancer, were eliminated, wouldn't we all live to be over 100? Unfortunately, the answer is no. Curing all these diseases would give us, on average, only a decade or so more years before some other disease would kill us.

And what if we could eliminate all diseases? Would immortality then be at hand? Alas, the answer is no. Time and chance take their toll in the form of accidents. Unless we turn our attention to the underlying vulnerability, we may change life expectancy but not maximum life span. Still worse, we might succeed in creating more and more long-living "Struldbruggs."

Research on aging could have other benefits, including the conquest or delay of ailments of old age such as cancer, arthritis, or Alzheimer's disease. Beyond curing specific diseases, some researchers are looking at interventions that could delay or actually reverse the process of aging. Here we confront very far-reaching questions about the impact of research on the biology of aging. Are we talking about moving the average life expectancy closer to the upper limit of the maximum life span—say, closer to age 120? Or are we talking about pushing that upper limit itself—say up to age 150 or 200? In either event, successful anti-aging interventions would have far-reaching consequences for human society. But until such research yields practical results, society will have to cope with the consequences of having more long-living individuals, and one of those consequences is vulnerability to disability and disease.

Epidemiology of Aging

While aging is not in itself a disease, it tends to increase susceptibility to disease. The diseases of later life are the subject of **geriatrics,** or the medical specialty of old age. Much has been learned about the major diseases of later life, and this subject is important for debates about aging, health care, and society (Blumenthal, 1983).

The discipline of **epidemiology** originally acquired its name from the scientific study of epidemics. Today, epidemiology is more broadly understood as the use of statistical techniques to study the distribution of diseases in human populations. A basic goal for the epidemiology of aging is to understand what diseases are most common among older people and to assess their impact (White et al., 1986). An example of how epidemiological data are organized is given in Table 1.1, indicating the 10 leading causes of death among older people.

Table 1.1. Death Rates for 10 Leading Causes of Death Among Older People, by Age: 1988 (rates per 100,000 population in age group)

Cause of Death	65+	65 to 74	75 to 84	85+
All causes	5,105	2,730	6,321	15,594
Diseases of the heart	2,066	984	2,543	7,098
Malignant neoplasms	1,068	843	1,313	1,639
Cerebrovascular diseases	431	155	554	1,707
Chronic obstructive pulmonary disease	226	152	313	394
Pneumonia and influenza	225	60	257	1,125
Diabetes	97	62	125	222
Accidents	89	50	107	267
Atherosclerosis	69	15	70	396
Nephritis, nephrotic syndrome, nephrosis	61	26	78	217
Septicemia	56	24	71	199

SOURCE: National Center for Health Statistics (1990d).

Major Diseases in Old Age

Today, three-quarters of all deaths of persons over 65 come from just three diseases: heart disease, cancer, or stroke. Death rates for heart disease and stroke have declined in recent decades, but they still remain the leading causes of death. If heart disease were completely eliminated as a cause of death, the average life expectancy for someone 65 years old would increase 7 years, ignoring the likelihood of death from one of the other leading causes. Though often not listed separately as a cause of death in vital statistics, Alzheimer's disease is probably the fourth leading cause of death, chiefly afflicting people over 65.

Along with diseases causing death, we also need to consider **chronic conditions** that persist for a long period, whether or not they cause death, because 80% of older people have one or more chronic conditions, such as arthritis (National Center for Health Statistics, 1982). Figure 1.1 shows the top 10 chronic conditions for people over 65. It is important to note that some conditions such as cataracts and hearing impairment can be limiting but not life threatening. Other conditions, such as hypertension (high blood pressure) and heart disease, can lead to fatal disorders.

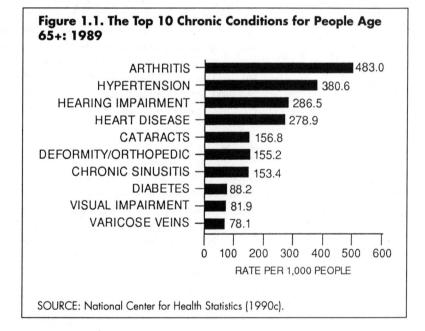

Figure 1.1. The Top 10 Chronic Conditions for People Age 65+: 1989

Condition	Rate per 1,000
ARTHRITIS	483.0
HYPERTENSION	380.6
HEARING IMPAIRMENT	286.5
HEART DISEASE	278.9
CATARACTS	156.8
DEFORMITY/ORTHOPEDIC	155.2
CHRONIC SINUSITIS	153.4
DIABETES	88.2
VISUAL IMPAIRMENT	81.9
VARICOSE VEINS	78.1

RATE PER 1,000 PEOPLE

SOURCE: National Center for Health Statistics (1990c).

Arthritis. Arthritis is the most familiar and most prevalent chronic disease of later life; it afflicts nearly half of all persons over age 65. Arthritis is basically an inflammation of the joints, also commonly known as rheumatism, and it is the most important cause of physical disability in the United States. Symptoms include red, swollen joints and muscles, and pain. Like cancer, *arthritis* is actually the name of a group of as many as 100 different syndromes, all slightly different. Rheumatoid arthritis can occur at any age, but osteoarthritis is distinctly related to old age and is aggravated by degeneration caused by wear and tear of the joints.

Degenerative joint disease in some variety is almost certain to occur in people over the age of 70. But the effect of such disease on activities of daily living varies tremendously and most people live full and active lives with it. The cause of arthritis is not known and there is no cure, but treatment of the disease to reduce symptoms can be effective. Painkilling drugs are not costly, but, for the very serious cases, joint surgery—for example, for hip replacement—can be expensive (Moskowitz and Haug, 1985).

Osteoporosis.   Osteoporosis is a condition involving deterioration or disappearance of bone tissue leading to loss of strength and, often, a fracture. The disease is most prevalent in women (4 times more common than in men), especially beyond the age of menopause. About one in four white women over the age of 65 will develop osteoporosis. When weakened by osteoporosis, bones are more likely to break, with serious consequences. It is estimated that 1.5 million fractures occur each year as a result of osteoporosis. A hip fracture, sometimes related to a fall, is one of the most common events precipitating admission to a nursing home. About half of those who survive fractures will require some form of long-term care. It is estimated that more than 12 million people in the United States have osteoporosis, and the annual cost of fractures resulting from the disorder is in the range of $7 to $10 billion.

Parkinson's disease.   Parkinson's disease is a degenerative neurological disorder characterized by a loss of control over bodily movement. It afflicts about a half million people in the United States, chiefly older people. Symptoms include tremors or shaking of the head and hands, leading to progressive loss of muscle control and the ability to walk unaided. Parkinson's disease is an age-related syndrome and its incidence increases steadily after middle life. For reasons not clear, dementia is quite prevalent among persons with Parkinson's and depression is common as well. Parkinson's appears to be caused by lack of dopamine production in brain cells, but there is no treatment that slows the progression of the disorder. Drug treatment, such as L-Dopa, however, can relieve symptoms of the disease (Mcgoon, 1990).

Cancer.   Because of successful medical interventions, older people who have cancer are living much longer than in the past, so that cancer can often become a chronic disease. In fact, cancer is overwhelmingly a disease of old age, with half of all cancers occurring in people over age 65. The incidence of malignant disease rises progressively with age, and cancer today is the second leading cause of death for Americans over 65, accounting for 21% of deaths among older people. There is no clear proof that cancer itself is related to the aging process, but the relationship among aging, cancer, and the immune system is the subject of investigation today. Different forms of cancer seem related to age but actually may be the result of longer exposure to cancer-causing chemical substances known as carcinogens: for example, asbestos or tobacco.

With growing efficacy of diagnosis and treatment, older cancer patients often face the challenge of coping with, even if not curing, a malignancy. A person diagnosed with slow-growing or controllable forms of cancer may live many years, thus increasing the cost of medical care over a longer period of time. It is also possible to prolong the period of dying for those with incurable cancer, raising questions not only about the ethics of termination of treatment but also about the cost of life prolongation.

Cardiovascular disease. The leading cause of death for people over 65 remains cardiovascular disease, which includes stroke and heart disease. Heart disease alone accounts for 43% of all deaths, while stroke accounts for another 9% of those deaths. In the past two decades, there has been a decline of almost 30% in deaths from heart disease, and the cardiovascular condition of older people shows wide variations. For example, according to a study by the National Institute of Aging, the heart of a healthy 80-year-old man performs about as well as that of a man in his twenties. But, unfortunately, about two-thirds of men in their seventies have clear evidence of coronary heart disease, so death rates remain high. The economic cost of heart disease is staggering: $117 billion during 1993, according to figures from the American Heart Association.

Stroke refers to a cardiovascular injury to the brain arising from a sudden disturbance in the blood supply. A stroke often results in some degree of paralysis, often on one side of the body, or loss of other functions, such as speech, and it can result in coma or death. While one stroke in three leads to immediate death, another one in three also causes permanent disability, such as paralysis or loss of speech. The costs for caring for impaired stroke victims are enormous to society and the family, and the loss of quality of life can be substantial for the patient (Locke, 1983).

Dementia and Alzheimer's disease. Dementia is an organic mental disorder resulting in deterioration of intellectual capacities, such as memory or the ability to think rationally. Senile dementia of the Alzheimer's type (SDAT), or Alzheimer's disease, is the most common irreversible dementia of old age, accounting for perhaps two-thirds of all dementing conditions. The proportion of people with Alzheimer's disease rises dramatically each decade over age 65. Up to 4 million Americans are now afflicted with the disease. About half the residents of nursing homes today have some form of dementia, often Alzheimer's but sometimes multi-infarct dementia resulting from accumulated damage to blood vessels in the brain.

Alzheimer's is an organic disease of the brain caused by deterioration of brain cells with characteristic plaques and tangles. The disorder typically progresses through stages from mild memory loss, through significant cognitive impairment, to very serious confusion and the loss of ability to handle dressing, bathing, or other activities of daily living (Reisberg, 1983). By the end stage of the disease, there may be incontinence, loss of speech, and inability to walk. A definitive diagnosis of Alzheimer's is difficult, and confirmation usually can be made only upon autopsy. But a mental status examination, such as the Folstein Mini-Mental Status Exam, can assess functional cognitive losses produced by the disease (Folstein et al., 1975).

Alzheimer's disease is irreversible but predictable in its course. In advanced stages, taking care of patients at home usually becomes impossible. The result is often placement in a skilled nursing home, extending potentially for many years. Even when a patient's quality of life has severely declined, it is feasible to use modern medical techniques to cure physical illness, such as pneumonia or kidney failure, and thus prolong the lives of demented patients, resulting in great expense.

In terms of the health care rationing debate, it is worth noting that acute care medical intervention can actually be less costly than long-term care provided over a period of many years for Alzheimer's patients (Cassel, Rudberg, and Olshansky, 1992). The National Institute on Aging projects that, unless a cure for Alzheimer's is found, by the middle of the next century there could be 14 million people with the disorder, costing billions of dollars a year to maintain.

Responses to the Geriatric Diseases

Interventions to eliminate specific diseases, such as cancer or stroke, can increase life expectancy but they do not raise the maximum life span of individuals. Furthermore, curing a life-threatening illness does not prevent other nonfatal diseases that may bring chronic disability.

One of the big questions about aging, health, and society is whether our health care system is capable of dealing with a growing elderly population. Many critics charge that it is not. Medicine in the United States has often neglected the dimensions of caring for and coping with people who have illnesses that cannot be cured, such as Parkinson's or Alzheimer's. That neglect is a matter of special concern for geriatric medicine. The approach of clinical medicine in most advanced countries, and certainly in the United States, focuses almost entirely on discrete causes of disease and their cures. Intrinsic causes within the organism—in other words, vulnerabilities of aging—are not well understood and are not the focus of attention. The paradox here is that, because survivorship has been increasing, the aged have become an increasing proportion of society and the remaining fatal diseases, whether cancer or Alzheimer's, are themselves linked to the process of aging itself.

Will a breakthrough in understanding the biology of aging solve this problem? There are reasons for doubt. For example, there are a whole class of age-related changes not likely to be affected by improved DNA repair, a favored mechanism for explaining biological aging. Many physical changes of old age are in the wear-and-tear category and include the decalcification of bones, uric acid incrustation in cartilage of joints, and cholesterol accumulation in blood vessels. It might be possible for geriatric medicine to develop strategies to control causes at this tissue level and to introduce rehabilitative methods that improve the clinical picture. The problem is that many of today's dramatic techniques of medicine—such as kidney transplants or bypass surgery—do nothing to affect the underlying process of aging. We can keep patients alive but do little to improve their quality of life.

An overview of geriatric epidemiology gives a concrete picture of what the "Struldbrugg" problem might look like in the future. Success in curing some forms of cancer or heart disease could raise life expectancy but leave larger numbers of people living with the burden of chronic diseases such as stroke, arthritis, or osteoporosis. A pragmatic approach to geriatric medicine might favor interventions designed to reduce the burden of age-related diseases on individuals as well as society.

Advances in medical technology and adoption of health promotion measures could bring average life expectancy closer to the theoretical upper limit of the maximum life span. But would we then be inadvertently multiplying the Struldbrugg problem? Those in favor of age-based health care rationing would cut funding from expensive life-sustaining interventions for the very old and redirect those resources toward quality of life interventions for age-related diseases. But there are serious questions about whether paying for extended long-term care is actually cheaper than any alternative we can imagine. Those questions involve the economics of health care.

Economics of Health Care

The emergence of the Struldbrugg problem in America has had an important public consequence: namely, rising health care expenditures for care of the very old. The elderly, who constitute 12% of the population, consume more than 30% of health care spending (Jacobs, 1991). This increase in expenditure has taken place against a background of escalating costs for health care in general. As a nation, the United States has gone from spending approximately 9% of gross national product on health care in 1980 to 14% in 1992. That total amounted to $838.5 billion in 1992, an increase of 11.5% over the previous year (U.S. Commerce Department, 1993). The figure is climbing at a rate twice as fast as the increase in consumer prices. The proportion of gross national product going to health care today is twice what it was in 1965 when the Medicare program was first enacted, and Medicare remains at the center of the economics of health care for aging.

Reimbursement Systems

Medicare is the chief federal government program that pays for health care for 31 million older Americans as well 3 million disabled people of all ages. Medicare is available primarily on the basis of age, in contrast to **Medicaid,** a health program funded by both the states and the federal government, which reaches only those below the poverty line. For the person who is older, Medicaid is important because it pays for a substantial portion of long-term care and nursing home care.

Medicare was created in 1965 as part of the Social Security Act. Like Social Security, it is funded from **payroll taxes** with additional funding from general revenues and premiums from beneficiaries. Overall, Medicare spending has risen much faster than the cost of living and thus presents government policymakers with a serious problem of cost control.

Medicare actually comprises two distinct programs: Part A, or hospital insurance, and Part B, supplementary medical insurance, covering nonhospital care, which primarily includes physicians' services along with limited home and outpatient services. Medicare Part A is financed by a compulsory payroll tax administered as part of the Social Security tax levied on all wages up to a specified limit. Figure 1.2 shows where money from Medicare goes.

Nearly two-thirds of the total goes to hospitals, where acute care and often high-technology care are given. If health care rationing on the grounds of age were ever to be introduced, it would probably take place in the Medicare program and would show up in the large sector of Medicare concentrated on hospitals (Inlander and MacKay, 1991).

Although Medicare expenditures have climbed dramatically, Medicare still covers only about half of the out-of-pocket medical expenses of older people: roughly the same proportion as when the Medicare program was first enacted in 1965. Part of the reason is that Medicare Part B reimburses 80% of physician's "reasonable charges." In fact, the amount reimbursed may or may not reflect actual charges in a specific geographic area. In practice, many physicians in the past have charged much more than the officially allowed Medicare rate, with the patient paying the difference. But that practice has now begun to change.

Since 1993, physicians participating in the Medicare program are limited to charging no more than 15% above the rate set for Medicare reimbursement. This law was passed because the proportion of physicians willing to accept the official Medicare reimbursement rate as full payment had declined to less than half of all doctors. It was passed in response to conditions similar to those in the Medicaid program, where some physicians in private prac-

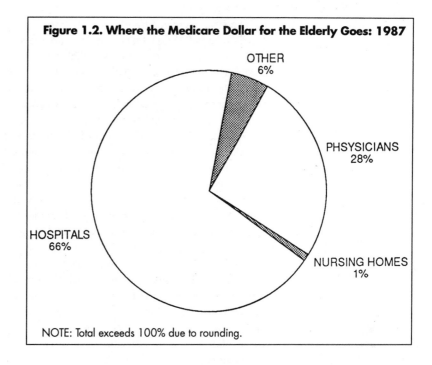

Figure 1.2. Where the Medicare Dollar for the Elderly Goes: 1987

OTHER
6%

PHSYSICIANS
28%

HOSPITALS
66%

NURSING HOMES
1%

NOTE: Total exceeds 100% due to rounding.

tice simply rejected patients on Medicaid because the reimbursement rate was too low.

The experience in both the Medicare and the Medicaid programs gives cause for concern about what might happen if cost-containment measures cut down on physician reimbursement from government insurance programs. Officials of the American Medical Association have rejected the idea of the government setting limits on the fees of doctors, and they have argued that such fee limits will inevitably bring about de facto "rationing" of health care.

Similar fears erupted after 1983 when Congress passed a law limiting payments to hospitals under Medicare. In 1983 Congress responded to the high hospital costs of Medicare Part A by introducing a Prospective Payment System: a new way of reimbursing hospitals for the cost of treating Medicare patients. Under Prospective Payment, hospitals receive a fixed amount for a specific diagnosis given to a patient, no matter how long the hospital stay or the type of service required. Over the past decade, the new Prospective Payment System appears to have held down hospital costs below what they would have been without these cost controls. But critics charge that the system resulted in higher outpatient costs and in displacing costs onto families of patients who were discharged "quicker and sicker."

The system created hundreds of diagnostic categories, or **Diagnosis Related Groups** (DRGs), that determined how much a hospital would be reimbursed for patient care. The system in effect gives an incentive to hospitals to keep their costs down and discharge patients as early as medically feasible. Despite protests and concerns about the new reimbursement system, DRGs have become an accepted fact of life in American hospitals.

In the 1980s it was widely feared, and sometimes charged, that these cost-containment measures would lead to "patient dumping" by hospitals along with widespread deterioration of patient care. Such widespread deterioration did not occur, but the 1983 law did have its intended effect in holding down Medicare Part A spending from where it would have been otherwise. Cost containment for hospital spending proved effective, but during the 1980s Medicare Part B spending for physicians tripled in size.

In part because of the success of DRGs, Congress acted to try to control costs under Medicare Part B. In 1989 Congress passed another law revising the Medicare reimbursement formula for physicians in different medical specialties. The new legislation introduced a so-called Resource Based Relative Value Scale (RBRVS) in the national Medicare program. The new Relative Value Scale means that primary care health providers—such as internists, geriatricians, and family practitioners—will be paid more for their services, while other specialists—such as some surgeons—will be paid less than they were before.

This reimbursement scheme is an effort to give more incentive to medical specialties involving prevention, health promotion, and quality of life, in contrast to the expensive technologies of life prolongation. Under this new law, doctors who spend more time with patients but do not use "high-tech" procedures will be paid more than they were previously. The aim of the new measures is to provide a more equitable system of payments reflecting skill, time, and intensity of work. But many doctors have complained that the new Relative Value Scale fee structure doesn't reimburse them adequately. In the adoption of both the Prospective Payment System and the Relative Value Scale, there was an outcry from health care providers, and others said that they worried that cost controls could compromise the quality of care or the access to care of elderly individuals (Frech, 1991).

Prospects for the Future

The escalating cost of health care has become a major problem for the elderly and for other groups in society. Will biomedical technology help solve the problem or only make it worse? Since World War II, the federal government has subsidized research and development in biomedical science to an extraordinary degree: up from $3 million to more than $11 billion today. Yet, unlike private industry, where investment in research and development leads to lower costs, advances in medical technology have led to higher costs for health care. With each new technique for life prolongation, the lives of those who are very sick and very old can be extended, but at greater and greater cost.

In the future, this picture seems likely to grow worse, for two reasons: First, health care costs, even after adjusting for inflation, have been rising at an annual rate of 5.5% since 1950 and are continuing to go up; and, second, the aging of America's population will add to these expenses because incidence of illness and disability is higher among the old. Those over age 65 spend about 4 times as much money on health care as people below that age. In terms of overall spending for health care, expenditures for those above 65 now amount to 33% of all health care spending, while people over 65 comprise only about 12% of the total population.

It is difficult to predict future levels of use of health care by an aging population. Past underestimations give cause for concern. In 1965 planners projected the cost of supplemental medical insurance under Medicare. But in 1970, only five years later, there had been a fivefold *increase* in the cost of that program. Between 1967 and 1975, the rate of use in both parts of Medicare had gone up from 367 per 1,000 enrollees to 528 per 1,000. Recently, Medicare has been growing at a rate 3 times the rate of inflation.

In light of these huge and rising costs, it is not surprising that there is fear about the prospect of an aging population in the future. In 1993 Medicare spending totaled $146 billion but it is projected to rise to more than $200 billion by 1997 and then run out of money completely, unless taxes are raised or benefits are cut. For the more distant future, the forecast is grim. Based on U.S. Census Bureau middle-range population forecasts, it is estimated that the Medicare costs for the **oldest-old** (85+) could increase sixfold by the year 2040 (Schneider and Guralnik, 1990).

The compression of morbidity theory hopes to postpone disease until a point approaching a hypothetical maximum human life span. In fact, medical expenses do rise toward the end of life. Medical costs in the final year of life now amount to approximately 18% of total lifetime medical costs. It is estimated that the Medicare program spends more than 30% of its budget on patients in the last year of life (Scitovsky, 1984). Health care spending is greatest for the oldest-old (85+). Overall personal health care spending for the oldest-old is well over $9,000 a year per person, or $2\frac{1}{2}$ times greater than for persons age 65 to 69. For nursing home care alone, the ratio is 23 times greater.

Are we then confronting the principle of diminishing returns? Prolonging the lives of elderly terminally ill patients in the last year of life at exorbitant cost might appear wasteful if we think of how the same resources could be used to improve the quality of life of other elderly people or people of other age groups. Of course, clinicians admit that it is difficult to predict just when that "last year of life" will occur, except in retrospect. Those in favor of rationing health care on grounds of age do not claim any special new power of prediction. They are willing to propose an arbitrary age limit to obtain the savings possible by rationing care based on chronological age. But such a proposal is subject to serious debate about its feasibility and its morality.

Long-Term Care

Dramatic end-of-life decisions often attract public attention in debates about the economics of health care. But a far more widespread phenomenon is taking place away from the hospital intensive care ward, in nursing homes, where growing numbers of older people spend years receiving costly care for chronic health problems. Long-term care refers to the support given to individuals suffering from chronic illness or disability that limits their ability to live independently.

How will we provide these needed services? The problem cannot be left for the future. Growing numbers of frail, chronically ill elderly are already in need of long-term care, at home or in institutions. Instead of expecting old people to die early or hoping to find the biomedical fountain of youth, we face the practical problem of how to pay for long-term care, whether furnished by families or in institutions. Opinions differ about who should bear the cost of that care.

Consider the hypothetical case of George and Martha Walton. They never expected to live into their eighties, but they're glad to be alive and glad still to be in their own home in Middletown, USA. Maintaining the house, however, has gotten harder since George had his first stroke. Martha finds herself exhausted and her arthritis prevents her from getting around the way she used to. They can't afford to hire help to come into their home. They've looked into alternative housing arrangements. But the one thing George fears most of all is that his condition will deteriorate and that he'll end up in a nursing home. They wonder, where will they turn next?

Housing Alternatives for the Elderly

George and Martha Walton are struggling with *long-term care issues,* whether they use that term or not. They live in their own home and don't want to use a long-term care facility. Their case, which is typical, shows why the distinction between long-term care services and housing for the aging is not so clear-cut. Housing for the elderly was long conceived as primarily a bricks-and-mortar affair; that is, it was mainly a matter of financing or subsidizing shelter dedicated to the aged. But increasingly it is recognized that social as well as physical concerns must be taken into account in planning for housing for the aging population (Newcomer et al., 1986).

What are the "alternative housing arrangements" that George and Martha might look into? In the past, a home for the aged might have been an option. A home for the aged is a facility typically sponsored by a church or fraternal organization and dedicated to helping the impoverished or dependent elderly. These residential facilities are less common today but commercially developed retirement communities have become attractive to the more affluent elderly (Ross, 1982; Hunt et al., 1983).

Also to be noted is a newer type of facility that has recently been growing rapidly: the life care community, sometimes called a continuing care retirement community (CCRC) (Rector, 1988). These offer a combination of housing and health care and typically provide a level of social support for those who find it difficult to live on their own. But they are often expensive: George and Martha probably wouldn't qualify. A distinguishing feature of the life care community is that residents commit to remain there for the rest of their lives and they pay a large entry fee, which can be above $100,000, in return for guaranteed support as they grow older and more frail.

If CCRCs represent the high-income end of the housing continuum, then it is also important to note the prevalence of domiciliary care facilities and board-and-care homes at the lower end (Down and Schnurr, 1991). These are homes that provide mainly custodial or personal care for elderly and disabled people who don't need the intensive medical supervision of a nursing home but do need help with activities of daily living (Eckert and Murrey, 1984).

The federal government subsidizes rental housing through the Section 202 and Section 8 housing programs for low-income elderly (Lawton, 1980). But housing programs have often looked only at "bricks and mortar" and have failed to take into account the social support needs of older people, which tend to increase with advancing age. Those needs are better taken into account through congregate housing: a residential facility providing nutrition, housekeeping, and supportive services for the marginally independent elderly (Chellis et al., 1982). Along the same lines, there has been interest in shared housing, an alternative housing arrangement involving either group residence with shared common areas or a homeowner who rents out unused rooms (McConnell and Usher, 1980; Streib et al., 1984).

All of these options are interesting but they probably won't help George and Martha Walton, who want to remain in their own home. Much of the effort at improved housing for the aging has been planned housing initiated either by government or by the private marketplace. But, in fact, more than 85% of older Americans live in unplanned housing, typically in the same home and neighborhood they had lived in before, just like George and Martha.

In fact, some neighborhoods or residential facilities have become naturally occurring retirement communities with more than half their residents over age 65. In such settings, expanded home health care and assisted living programs can offer older people an alternative to institutionalization. Whether in planned housing or in naturally occurring retirement communities, the aging of the American population means that more and more older people will face supportive housing needs in the future. Those needs will reflect a growing challenge of chronic illness in later life.

Chronic Care in Old Age

An explosion in demand for long-term care is found in all advanced industrialized countries as a larger and larger proportion of the population survives into old age. Compared with the general population, older people on average show twice as many days in which activities are restricted because of chronic conditions. The most important of these conditions are arthritis, rheumatism, and heart conditions. But there are sharp differences in the impact of such conditions among the population over age 65. Apart from people in nursing homes, the **young-old** group (age 65 to 74) have only a very small proportion—5.7%—who say they need help with everyday tasks such as household chores, dressing, or going shopping. By contrast, among the "oldest-old" (over age 85), the percentage of those needing help jumps to 40%.

Long-term care is fundamentally different than acute health care. Acute care is appropriate for conditions that result from a single cause that can be treated by medical intervention. By contrast, the chronic conditions requiring long-term care last a long time and may have varied causes. Examples of such disorders are Alzheimer's disease or other dementias and stroke leading to permanent disability. The result is an inability to perform activities of daily living (Katz et al., 1963).

What does this mean in concrete terms? Consider the case of George Walton, who has reached this point. A series of small strokes have affected him profoundly. His condition has deteriorated to the point where he needs help getting to the bathroom and even feeding himself. Martha has done the best she can, but their children, Carol and Robert, have now convinced them that the only alternative is for George to go into the local Middletown nursing home, where he can get the round-the-clock care he needs now. George and Martha are afraid to do it; they don't like the idea at all.

Nursing home can refer to any residential facility giving some degree of nursing care (Johnson and Grant, 1986). In the United States, about 80% of these facilities are proprietary: that is, operated as commercial, for-profit organizations. Most of the rest are voluntary or nonprofit, with a few run by municipal governments (American Health Care Association, 1984). Among these facilities, it is useful to identify the skilled nursing facility, which is an institution offering medical care, such as a hospital, as well as everyday personal care services to elderly or disabled people. An intermediate care facility, on the other hand, gives health-related care to patients needing a lower level of support. An extended care facility offers short-term convalescent help to patients coming from hospitals for an extended period of time.

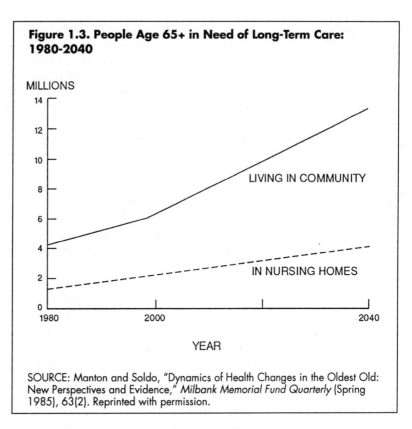

Figure 1.3. People Age 65+ in Need of Long-Term Care: 1980-2040

MILLIONS

LIVING IN COMMUNITY

IN NURSING HOMES

YEAR

SOURCE: Manton and Soldo, "Dynamics of Health Changes in the Oldest Old: New Perspectives and Evidence," *Milbank Memorial Fund Quarterly* (Spring 1985), 63(2). Reprinted with permission.

In light of George Walton's deterioration, he will probably enter a skilled nursing facility.

As shown in Figure 1.3, 1.7 million older Americans live in nursing homes, more than all those in hospitals at any one time but still less than 5% of the elderly population. The size of today's nursing home population is partly a tribute to medical technology and the success of the longevity revolution. But it may also reflect the fact that American society has failed to provide accessible alternatives to living in a nursing home: namely, long-term care based in the home or community. A sizable number of people in nursing homes don't need to be there and could probably live in community settings, if appropriate services were available. Estimates of the proportion of the nursing home population in this situation range from 10% to as high as 40%.

Why are George and Martha so fearful about entering a nursing home? Are they right to be afraid? The nursing home has been called a *total institution,* a term used to describe organizations such as prisons, mental hospitals, or boarding schools: that is, facilities that treat people like "inmates" rather than as individuals (Goffman, 1961). In a nursing home, the daily regimen is carefully organized and scheduled, so residents may lose any sense of control over their environment and easily become depressed.

A lot of criticism of nursing homes finds support in careful observational studies of life in these facilities (Gubrium, 1975), and there have been many journalistic accounts, "horror stories," that expose poor conditions in some institutions. Responsible studies have shown how the poor quality of nursing homes grew out of repeated failures in public policy to guarantee good quality long-term care (Vladeck, 1980). In light of these facts, it is understandable that so many older people today fear institutionalization.

On the other hand, it is important to remember that, just like schools or hospitals, the quality of nursing homes varies from good to bad. The stereotyped view that "all nursing homes are bad" is mistaken and does a disservice to elderly people who actually need skilled nursing care, not to mention to the untold numbers of devoted nursing home employees. Government monitoring and regulation have meant that nursing homes today are much better than in the past, and improvements continue (Kane and Kane, 1987). Moreover, there is a common misconception that, once someone is admitted to a nursing home, residence there is inevitably a life sentence. In fact, 32% of those in nursing homes stay less than a month; many return home.

How likely is it for older people to anticipate entering a nursing home? Among all people over 65, only 4% to 5% are in nursing homes at any given time. But this figure may understate the importance of nursing homes in the lives of the very old. The percentage of those who will spend a year or more in a nursing home before they die is much larger: at least one out of four people aged 65. The 4% figure that comes from citing the percentage of people in a nursing home only at a single point in time is therefore called the **four percent fallacy** (Kastenbaum and Candy, 1973).

The need for chronic care varies significantly among subgroups of the elderly. For those between 65 and 74, the chance of entering a nursing home is small: only 1 in 100. But for those over age 85, the chance goes up to 1 in 5. Specific risk factors that increase the chances for nursing home placement include mental impairment, chronic disability, advanced age, and spending time in a hospital or other health facility.

Functional Assessment

A key step in determining what kind of help people need is professional long-term care assessment. This determination frequently plays a "gatekeeping" role in deciding what services will be provided. A **multidimensional functional assessment** takes place when a geriatric professional, such as a doctor or nurse, conducts a full examination of an elderly person's physical, mental, and social condition. It focuses on **activities of daily living** as well as physical and mental health. Among the most important of these activities are feeding, toileting, transferring out of a bed or chair, dressing, and bathing

(Katz and Akpom, 1976). A comprehensive functional assessment also covers social and economic resources as well as elements such as the physical environment and even strain on caregivers. All these elements play a part in determining the kind of service an elderly person may need.

Does a failing score on an assessment test mean that it's time to enter a nursing home? Not necessarily: The key to interpreting an assessment lies in the functional emphasis; that is, asking how an impairment actually affects performance of daily tasks such as shopping, doing housework, handling personal finances, or preparing meals. A comprehensive approach to functional assessment is important because someone with, for instance, mild memory impairment or limited physical mobility may be able to live quite satisfactorily alone in an apartment as long as the environment remains safe and a neighbor or relative comes by regularly to help out. For the same reason, a physical assessment looks not only at biological organ systems but at medications being taken or the impact of sensory impairment in handling activities of everyday life.

Gerontologists have developed specialized instruments or questionnaires designed to carry out functional assessments (Kane and Kane, 1981; Gresham and Labi, 1984). A classic example is the Older American Resources and Services, known by its initials OARS, one of several widely used assessment instruments in the United States today (Duke, 1978). The OARS questionnaire gathers information on topics such as mental status, self-assessed well-being, social contact, and help from family. A second part of the instrument looks at the use of services ranging from physical therapy and meal preparation to employment training or transportation. By carefully assessing activities of daily living in this way, professionals can identify the exact type of help a client needs: for example, a walker device for people at risk of falling, a homemaker-home health aide for someone who can't prepare meals, and other kinds of help that might enable people to remain safely in their own homes.

The Continuum of Care

A 65-year-old today can expect to live, on average, for 17 more years. During those years, it is likely that health status and service needs for any individual will change, so provision for long-term care will have to reflect changes over time. Why shouldn't long-term care services take into account those changes? The idea of a **continuum of care** is based on the goal of offering a range of options responsive to changing individual needs, whether from less intense to more intense, whether at home or in an institution (Brickner et al., 1987).

The ideal of a continuum of care expresses the aim of keeping elderly people as long as possible out of nursing homes—the most expensive and service-intensive setting. The aim instead is to maintain people in the home, in independent living, or in the least restrictive alternative. If we were to take seriously the ideal of a continuum of care, it would mean spending more money to enlarge the availability of community-based long-term care services. Such a goal, however, would serve the purpose of promoting maximum independence and personal control and might also help minimize public expense (Koff, 1982; Eustis, Grenberg, and Patten, 1984). The reasons for promoting a continuum of care include both choice and economics, but it is rare to find a full continuum of care in most communities in America. There are many gaps, and the long-term care service system remains fragmented and confusing.

Health care is important, but we should not forget the importance of social care and social contact for people like George and Martha. What happens to Martha when she's left all alone after George has entered the nursing home? Who will watch out for her and her needs? If George and Martha were lucky, Middletown, USA, would have a full range of services to help them out, as a few communities already do. The kinds of formal support services delivered to the home that are shown in Table 1.2 can play a key role in enabling frail elderly to remain in their homes as long as possible (Quinn et al., 1982).

Table 1.2. Community Support Systems

Homemaker services	Light housekeeping, food shopping, and meal preparation
Meals on Wheels	Home-delivered meals supported under Older Americans Act
Congregate meals	Lunch for elderly at neighborhood sites such as churches or senior centers
Lifeline service	24-hour support system using portable emergency response
Telephone reassurance	Volunteers who call every day or so
Information and referral	Telephone inquiry office covering services available in the local community
Friendly visitors	Volunteers in regular contact with elderly who are homebound or in a nursing home

All these formal support systems provide a degree of companionship, monitoring, and concrete services for frail, isolated elderly. They also can shore up the social network of family, friends, and neighbors: that is, the totality of informal helping relationships that maintain integrity and well-being (Shaw and Gordon, 1980). Gerontologists have documented the crucial role that these natural support systems play in providing social care and their enormous role in the lives of the elderly (Cantor, 1980).

If George Walton had not needed round-the-clock care, there might have been alternatives for him other than going into a nursing home. For instance, why not provide some nursing home services on a daytime basis while he still remains at home? That, in essence, is the strategy of adult day care, which is usually offered five days a week. Patients are transported to a health facility, where they are given needed services as a group during the day and then returned to their homes at the end of the day.

Another alternative is home health care in which home care aides provide health-related tasks such as rehabilitation exercises or toileting and transferring patients who are bed-bound (Ginzberg, Balinsky, and Ostow, 1984; Portnow, 1987). Visiting nurses who can dispense medication and perform skilled nursing functions also play a critical role here. Home health services have expanded dramatically in recent years, as an alternative to institutionalization and as a means of ensuring speedier discharge from hospitals.

These forms of community-based long-term care can sometimes be more cost effective than a residential nursing home because housing costs are not involved. Most important, they offer an opportunity for those who can to remain relatively independent. The experience of other countries, such as Canada and Britain, suggests that adult day care, along with other varieties of community-based long-term care, will have to play a larger role in the United States than it has in the past (Kane and Kane, 1985).

Paying for Long-Term Care: An American Dilemma

The costs of long-term care are going up fast (see Figure 1.4). In the last 10 years, the annual growth rate for nursing home care has been more than 12%. Expenditures now stand at over $40 billion and are still climbing. Few individuals can afford to pay the complete cost of long-term care in a nursing home. Usually Medicaid pays part of the bill. Future projections of long-term care expenditures suggest that private (out-of-pocket) and Medicaid sources will continue to be the biggest source of payment for nursing homes.

Advocates for home care or other community-based care believe that staying at home costs less than entering a nursing home, just as George and Martha want. But home care is not always cheaper than institutional care. Cost estimates for home care typically fail to include the real value of housing or the value of unpaid family caregiving. Moreover, there is sharp debate about whether we ought to pay family caregivers to do what is normally done by family members for one another.

The experience of Medicaid payment for nursing home care suggests that some frail elderly people may end up being placed in nursing homes because institutional care, not community care, is the only form of long-term care paid for under the American system. When advocates for the aged propose large

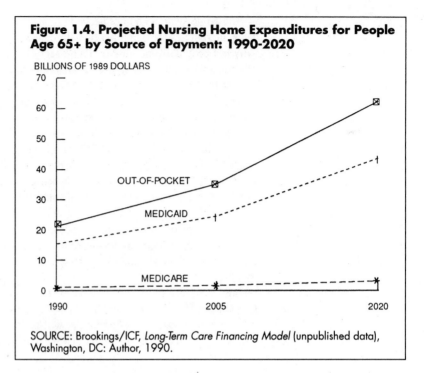

Figure 1.4. Projected Nursing Home Expenditures for People Age 65+ by Source of Payment: 1990-2020

BILLIONS OF 1989 DOLLARS

OUT-OF-POCKET

MEDICAID

MEDICARE

1990   2005   2020

SOURCE: Brookings/ICF, *Long-Term Care Financing Model* (unpublished data), Washington, DC: Author, 1990.

increases in long-term care, the question arises of who will pay for the expansion (Rivlin and Wiener, 1988). Should families provide for their own or should the cost of expanded long-term care be covered by government? Paying for long-term care remains an American dilemma.

Self-Determined Death

Our society so far has not been prepared to ration health care on the grounds of age. Nor do we seem willing to face up to the public policy problem of paying for long-term care. But at some point, decisions become unavoidable, and therefore we turn to our last option: self-determined death. Modern biomedical technology has not only enabled larger numbers of people to survive into old age, it has also forced care providers to make explicit decisions about the end of life. The result has been a continuing debate about the so-called right to die, which involves choices from forgoing life-sustaining treatment all the way to assisted suicide (Glick, 1992). In this debate, the aged occupy a central place.

Today, this debate is taking new forms as the cost of health care rises and the "oldest-old" population increases in numbers. In the future, termination of treatment decisions may become intertwined with cost-containment pressures. Instead of individuals claiming a "right to die," we may even see health care providers or policymakers suggesting that some people have a "duty to die" to stop "futile" medical treatment that uses up scarce resources.

This prospect is not just hypothetical. A case in point is the story of Helga Wanglie, who, at age 86, broke her hip and was admitted to a nursing home. As a result of complications, Mrs. Wanglie ended up on a respirator and suffered brain damage. The hospital staff felt that, due to her medical condition and advanced age, Mrs. Wanglie should not receive further life support. Her family, however, insisted that treatment be maintained, so the case wound up in court, which agreed with the family. In many other cases, providers have taken a different view and insisted on treating patients, while the family asked to end medical treatment.

Another case in which financial considerations became mixed up with termination of treatment was the 1989 legal case of *Elbaum v. Grace Plaza Nursing Home.* In this instance, Mrs. Jean Elbaum was in a persistent vegetative state (coma) and was being kept alive by tube feeding. Mrs. Elbaum had made it clear that she would not want to be kept alive under such circumstances. But the nursing home refused to honor the family's wishes. Instead, the facility provided treatment and then sued the family for payment of care provided against their wishes.

Over the past 20 years in the United States, discussion about the right to die has developed along legal and ethical lines focused entirely on individual rights and decisions; it has not focused on resource allocation issues. But both the *Elbaum* and the *Wanglie* cases, in different ways, show how end-of-life decisions may now become entangled in considerations about who will pay the bill and whether institutions should expend resources on care that is "medically futile."

The question of medical futility will involve values and will depend on the different treatments involved. A 1987 study looked at several different kinds of treatment that might be withheld from the elderly and explored the differences among them (U.S. Office of Technology Assessment, 1987). Antibiotics, respirators, cardiopulmonary resuscitation, and kidney dialysis are all very different forms of medical technology. A patient's personal decision about one kind of intervention may not hold for another kind. Similarly, a decision may be made in one way at home and differently in a nursing home or in a hospital. The setting could make a big difference in how health care personnel act and what families can expect. Perhaps the most important new developments in the right to die debate will center on the question of whether the American health care system can devise practices and forms of treatment that are both respectful of patients' wishes and also attentive to the uncertainties involved in end-of-life decisions.

The question arises of whether it is actually in the best interest of depressed or debilitated patients to have life-sustaining care terminated because of poor quality of life. The topic is controversial because the patient's best interest may or may not coincide with the interest of the family or health care providers. When subjective well-being declines and patients want to end their lives, should geriatric health care professionals treat this as a matter of self-determination or as a case of suicide prevention?

Most people are uncomfortable when economic considerations become involved with end-of-life decisions. But increasing pressure for cost containment in health care may make it difficult to keep the two matters separate. In 1990 Congress passed the Patient Self-Determination Act to uphold patients' rights. But analysts quickly noted that the law is expected to decrease costs for health care by ending unwanted care. As financial concerns become intertwined with right to die considerations, we may wonder whether "backdoor" rationing of health care could make it more difficult for elderly patients to assert their rights. It is always cheaper to say "no" to treatment than to say "yes."

Debates about costs and self-determination take place against a background of hopes and fears centered on end-of-life decisions. Our hopes are symbolized by the wonderful one-horse shay. Our fears are symbolized by the horrifying image of Gulliver's Struldbruggs, the same people who today might be hooked up to an artificial respirator or feeding tube. For increasing numbers of older Americans, self-determined death seems a way to resolve this struggle between hope and fear at the end of life.

Late Life Suicide

Self-determined death can mean many different things, ranging from termination of treatment to active euthanasia or assisted suicide. Those who favor self-determination for end-of-life decisions generally assume that it is possible to make a rational decision to end one's life: for example, to refuse further treatment and simply permit death to occur. That, at least, is the premise involved in the court decisions that uphold the right to self-determination.

But are these decisions always rational? And, if they aren't, does that fact mean that end-of-life decisions cannot be left to individual choice? The question is a difficult one. It is not possible to consider the arguments about end-of-life decisions for older people without taking into account mental health issues: specifically, depression, which is a primary cause of old age suicide. Suicide is now one of the top 10 causes of death among the old. The suicide rate for the general population is 12 per 100,000 while the suicide rate for those over 65 is 17 per 100,000: nearly 50% higher.

How can we understand old age suicide and its causes? The first great sociological investigator of suicide, Émile Durkheim, distinguished several different types of suicide. He described altruistic suicide, or self-sacrifice for the sake of the group or society (Durkheim, 1897/1951). A soldier giving up his life on the battlefield to save comrades would be an example of such self-sacrifice. This pattern could describe the voluntary death of some elderly persons in preindustrial societies facing conditions of economic scarcity. The same pattern might also apply to end-of-life decisions among elderly people today who fear becoming a burden on their families, a view heard often.

Durkheim also described a form he called anomic suicide, derived from his sociological concept of anomie, or a condition where individuals feel hopeless and cut off from any sense of meaning in life. This condition is relevant to thinking about the position of old age in contemporary society. Today, elderly people commonly experience **role loss** when they give up previous roles upon retirement, the death of a spouse, or the loss of other social positions. Rosow described old age itself in contemporary society as a roleless role: that is, a status with no clearly defined purpose or rules of behavior (Rosow, 1974; Blau, 1981). A final type of suicide described by Durkheim is egoistic suicide, where an individual may not be closely integrated into wider society—for example, among the "oldest-old," who have outlived most close relatives. In such cases, it might seem perfectly rational for people to end their lives.

As a general rule, the rate of suicide tends to go up with age and to hit a peak after age 65 in America as in other advanced industrialized countries. Estimates of suicide remain uncertain because there are 100 suicide attempts for every completed suicide. Among the elderly, however, 80% who threaten suicide actually follow through. Further, among the ill elderly, there is no way to estimate those who end their lives by noncompliance with medical treatment or other forms of self-neglect.

There are pronounced differences in suicide rates among subgroups of the elderly (Osgood, 1984), as Figure 1.5 indicates. Among ethnic groups, blacks have a suicide rate only about 60% of the average for whites, and, unlike whites, the rate does not increase in old age. For all age groups, men are much more likely to commit suicide than women, and the difference between the sexes widens with advancing age. For example, according to 1980 data, there were 66 completed suicides per 100,000 white males above the age of 85 in comparison to a rate of only 5 for white females. In fact, the highest rate of suicide in the United States occurs among older white men.

Characteristic conditions preceding late life suicides include loneliness, social isolation, diminished economic resources, the presence of illness or disability, and, above all, depression (McIntosh and Osgood, 1986). Depression is an important public health problem for the elderly and must therefore be taken very seriously by clinicians and others who work with older people. Early identification and treatment for depression remains a key measure for suicide prevention (Miller, 1979).

Subjective Well-Being and Quality of Life

In debates about end-of-life decisions, an important but sometimes ambiguous idea is conveyed by the phrase *quality of life*. Late life depression raises

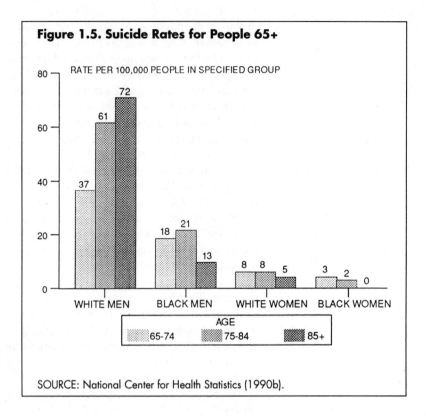

Figure 1.5. Suicide Rates for People 65+

RATE PER 100,000 PEOPLE IN SPECIFIED GROUP

AGE
65-74   75-84   85+

SOURCE: National Center for Health Statistics (1990b).

problems about how to define quality of life and opens up questions about measuring subjective well-being in old age (George, 1980). These questions have been the center of many research studies by gerontologists concerned with successful aging and life satisfaction (Larson, 1978). Broadly speaking, life satisfaction can be defined as a person's attitude toward past and present life as a whole, while morale can be defined as a specific feeling, whether optimistic or pessimistic, about the future. These psychological concepts, along with happiness and mood, are obviously important in thinking about subjective well-being in later life. But they present serious difficulties in measurement and theoretical interpretation.

Gerontologists concerned with measuring subjective well-being have made extensive use of the Life Satisfaction Index, which considers items such as zest and apathy, self-blame, attainment of life goals, and mood. The Philadelphia Geriatric Center Morale Scale has also been used to measure subjective well-being. But chronological age by itself is only weakly correlated with subjective well-being; in other words, old age by itself is not necessarily a condition for poor morale or unhappiness. Physical health, however, especially self-rated health, is a strong predictor of subjective well-being. Health problems, of course, are more common in later life. But subjective rating of one's own health is critical and reflects individual coping style rather than objective physiological function. Individual capacity for adaptation must not be ignored.

In considering depression and suicide in old age, it is important to maintain a balanced perspective. Most older people in fact enjoy good mental health and a positive attitude. A 1987 Louis Harris survey found that 72% of those over 65 report feeling satisfied with life. Even when exposed to stress, older people often show a remarkable capacity for adaptation: for example, in coping positively with bereavement or chronic illness, which are both common in later life. Adaptation reflects the capacity of the individual to cope with environmental demands and maintain subjective well-being. But when stress exceeds the capacity for coping, psychotherapy and other mental health interventions may play an important role in maintaining the capacity of those in the last stage of life to make rational decisions about the end of life (Butler and Lewis, 1982).

End-of-life choices must also take into consideration what has been learned about the process of death and dying itself. Glaser and Strauss (1965) described the dying trajectory by which a person passes from good health to progressively worse health to the point of death. In her popular book *On Death and Dying*, Elisabeth Kubler-Ross (1969) developed a stage theory of dying in which the terminally ill individual moves through stages from denial to acceptance. With respect to end-of-life decisions, it seems clear that elderly people who are experiencing a stage of denial or a condition of depression might make different kinds of "rational" decisions about terminating treatment. It would therefore be unwise simply to accept a patient's "spoken choice" at face value. On the other side, clinicians might well have a less positive view of initiating aggressive medical treatment if they were aware that an elderly patient was in a period of terminal decline and facing imminent death.

Summary

The picture of aging, biology, and health care today is a mixed one. On the one hand, optimists hope for a "compression of morbidity" in which good health can continue until late in life. On the other hand, larger numbers of elderly with physical or mental frailties are now surviving into old age. The need to make choices about treatment and life prolongation is becoming unavoidable.

Those who favor investment in basic research on the biology of aging hope that we can avoid the "Struldbrugg scenario" and instead have the "wonderful one-horse shay." The root cause of the problem is that contemporary geriatric medicine is largely symptomatic: Health care responds only after people are sick. Responding to symptoms this way is expensive and frustrating. It proceeds the same way that treatment of polio might have gone if specialists had worked to create ever more complex and refined versions of the iron lung instead of finding a vaccine to prevent the disease in the first place. In the same way, "iron lung" geriatric care is bound to be expensive and frustrating. Other medical interventions, even when successful, only make the problem worse. The dominant mode of health care has proceeded by preventing premature death. But understanding the basic biology of aging, including the goal of life span extension, is a quite different matter, as we have seen.

The American health care system, including geriatric care, spends a great deal of money on acute care conditions such as heart disease or cataracts. In that respect, Medicare simply reflects the same priorities that are favored in health care for the broader, nonaging population. In one year, 1986, for example, Medicare covered nearly 100,000 coronary artery bypass grafts, each one averaging $3,700. That year represented a 21% increase from the previous year (Fisher, 1988). That expensive high-tech procedure is fully covered by Medicare but a physical exam that could detect hypertension and recommend preventive diet or medication is not.

Medicare is a universal public insurance response to acute care for physical illness, and as such Medicare commands strong public support. By contrast, it has not proved possible to mobilize a consensus behind a universal public program for long-term care or for mental health treatment, or for such activities as early detection that might be beneficial in the long run. Medicare will not pay for regular physical examinations or for dental care. Preventive care and health promotion remain low priorities.

Changing these priorities will be difficult, and solutions to the problems of health care and aging remain elusive. Research on the basic biology of aging will continue, and no one can exclude a dramatic breakthrough that might reshape the conditions of health and sickness in later life. As costs continue to rise, there will be pressure for tough decisions, perhaps even for rationing (Mechanic, 1985). It is unlikely that overt age-based rationing will be adopted in this country, but some form of "backdoor rationing" could come as a result of cost-containment efforts. It seems likely that efforts to liberalize end-of-life decisions will also continue, but we have no way of knowing how many older people or families will decide deliberately to terminate life or where such decisions may lead us as a society. Debates about aging, health care, and society have only begun.

Why Do We Grow Old?

The popular film *Cocoon* tells the story of elderly people who gain access to a drug from outer space that can reverse the process of aging and make them young again. In the movie, the audience has the experience of seeing such famous elderly actors as Don Ameche and Hume Cronyn grow young before their eyes. The film, of course, is science fiction. But it's only the latest version of a recurrent dream as old as humanity: the search for the fountain of youth.

Is the story just a fantasy? Or can science in our time make the dream come true? Can aging be prevented? The answer isn't clear yet. But the debate about what causes aging—and whether it can be halted or even reversed—is just getting under way. That scientific debate is certain to command attention for years to come.

The dream of extending the human life span dates back thousands of years in history (Gruman, 1966). The legend of the fountain of youth is based on the search for a magical substance to prolong life. Sometimes the belief takes the shape of the so-called hyperborean theme: a conviction that people in a remote part of the earth—for example, the Asian Caucasus or the mountains of Peru—live extremely long lives. James Hilton's novel *Lost Horizon* (1933) popularized the idea of a place called Shangri-La with its secret of longevity, and a movie based on the book found wide appeal. But researchers, even in remote locations, have never succeeded in finding groups of people who live beyond the normal life span. Scientists have diligently examined the facts and failed to find any place on earth where people live beyond the maximum human life span of perhaps 110 years. The same upper limit appears in other species. In every case, there is a maximum life span (see Table 1.3).

What accounts for these clear differences in maximum life span? Comparative anatomy—the study of the structure of different species—generates some insights into this question. For example, among mammals and other vertebrates, an increase in relative brain size is positively related to an increased life span. Other factors that are correlated with life span are the measure of lifetime metabolic activity, body size, body temperature, and rate of energy use. For example, a tiny hummingbird has a rapid heartbeat and

Table 1.3. Some Organisms' Maximum Life Spans

Organism	Maximum Life Span (in years)
Tortoise	150
Human being	110
African elephant	78
Golden eagle	50
Chimpanzee	48
Horse	40
Domestic cat	30
American buffalo	26
Dog	20
Kangaroo	16
Domestic rabbit	12
House mouse	3.5
Fruit fly	25 days

SOURCE: Data from Walford (1983).

high rate of energy metabolism and it lives a comparatively short time, as if it were using up more quickly its total lifetime energy or action potential (Sacher, 1978).

Consider too the example of the chimpanzee and the human being. The maximum human life span is approximately 110 to 120 years, while the chimpanzee's is close to 50 years. The human life span, in other words, is more than twice as great. But when we look at DNA from both species, we find that the DNA is more than 99% identical. These figures suggest that, even though aging itself is a complex biological process, the rate of aging may be determined by genetic elements that may be a relatively limited part of the genetic mechanism. Calculations suggest that, if a cell is determined by around 100,000 genes, then perhaps no more than a few hundred alterations in the genetic code are needed to change the rate of aging.

Aging seems to affect all physiological functions to about the same degree, and so the total aging rate of different organisms will differ because all the parts of those organisms are aging at the same rate (Cutler, 1983). In comparison to other species of mammals, the human being has the longest life span and expends more energy per body weight over the total life span than any other mammal. Energy metabolism per body weight across the life span in humans is about 4 times greater than for most other species of mammals. Human beings have an average life expectancy and a maximum life span about twice as great as those of any other primate.

Scientists who have studied the increase in maximum human life span have concluded that a large increase in maximum life span occurred fairly recently—probably within the last 100,000 years. This rapid development means that only a tiny portion of the human genome—less than 1% of the genetic code—was likely to be involved in this increase in life span. Is it possible that the genetic and biological mechanisms determining the rate of aging are limited enough to be susceptible to intervention? Answering that question means having a comprehensive explanation or theory about aging.

Theories of Aging

The facts about aging and maximum life span among species have led many biologists to believe that there may be a single fundamental cause for the phenomenon of senescence. Theories of aging are efforts to find such a single primary process that would explain those time-dependent changes we recognize as biological aging (Adelman and Roth, 1982). At present, no single theory of aging explains all the complex processes that occur in cells and body systems as we age, but research is under way that is leading to new insights into why we grow old.

Broadly speaking, we can distinguish between two kinds of theories of aging:

(1) *Chance*: Some theories see aging as the result of external events, such as accumulated random negative factors that damage cells or body systems over time. For example, these factors might be mutation or damage to cells as the organism wears down.

(2) *Fate*: Some theories see aging as the result of an internal necessity, such as a built-in genetic program that proceeds inevitably to senescence and death.

In either case, the question remains open on whether some type of intervention is possible that would correct damage or would modify the genetic program. What interventions are feasible, of course, depends on what theory best explains the facts about aging (Ludwig, 1991).

Wear and tear theory.   The wear and tear theory sees aging as the result of chance. The human body, like all multicellular organisms, is constantly wearing out and being repaired. Each day, thousands of cells die and are replaced, while damaged component parts of cells are repaired. If we think of the body as being like a machine, it seems reasonable to imagine that, over time, the parts wear out and then the machine gradually breaks down. The wear and tear theory of aging originally goes back to Aristotle but in its current form can be ascribed to one of the founding fathers of modern biogerontology, August Weismann (1834-1914), a German biologist. He distinguished between the germ plasm cells, such as the sperm and egg, which are capable of reproducing and are therefore "immortal," in contrast to the somatic cells of the rest of the body, which die. Weismann, in his treatise *On the Duration of Life* (1882), argued that aging takes place because somatic cells cannot renew themselves, and so living things succumb to the wear and tear of existence.

What we see as aging, then, is the statistical result of "wear and tear." For instance, it turns out that the average lifetime for glassware in a restaurant follows a curve similar to that for human populations; over time, fewer and fewer glasses are left unbroken, until finally all are gone. The "life expectancy" or survival curve of glasses follows a linear path of disappearance over time. But the whole result comes about because of chance. Nothing "decrees" in advance that a specific glass will break at a fixed point in time. It's just that glasses are inherently breakable, so normal wear and tear in the restaurant will have an inevitable result. Just like everyone born in a certain year—for example, 1890—one by one, each of the "glasses" disappears until there is none left.

The result of this wear and tear can be described in mathematical terms. When we plot death rates according to age in humans, we see a predictable survival curve, a specific pattern known as the Gompertz curve. That curve shows that the likelihood of death rises exponentially with age; that is, death rates double about every eight years over the course of life. The curve is used even today by life insurance companies to construct numerical tables that display the death rate or life expectancy for different age groups in the population. These are called **life tables.** We can also draw survival curves that show the number of people surviving at any given age. Among the "old-old" (75+), we see that this survival curve drops dramatically as the death rate goes up. As more and more people survive into old age but later experience a rapid death rate, the result is an increasingly rectangular-shaped survival curve.

Some modern biological theories of aging are actually updated versions of the original wear and tear theory. For instance, somatic mutation theory notes that cells can be damaged by radiation and thereby undergo mutation or alteration in genetic characteristics (Szilard, 1959). Even without actual mutation, it is possible that over time there might be a loss of the proper differentiation of cells, itself the consequence of normal dynamic changes in DNA. According to another related theory, the so-called error accumulation theory or error catastrophe theory of aging, what we see as decremental changes of senescence are the result of chance or random events: essentially, the degradation of the genetic code (Medvedev, 1972; Orgel, 1973).

The process is similar to what would happen with a defective photocopying machine if we were to use a previous photocopy to make the next copy. With each copy, small errors accumulate. Over time, the errors eventually make the copies unreadable. By analogy, the error catastrophe theory suggests that altered proteins eventually bring on what we know as aging through dysfunction in enzyme production.

Still another view is the accumulative waste theory, which points to the buildup in the cells of waste products and other harmful substances. According to this theory, the accumulation of such waste products would eventually interfere with cell metabolism and lead to death. Although waste products do accumulate, there is little evidence that this is harmful to the organism. The key to longevity may be the extent to which the cell retains the capacity to repair damage done to DNA. In fact, DNA repair capacity is correlated with the metabolic rate and life span of different species. Some studies suggest that DNA damage in excess of repair capacity may be linked to age-related diseases such as cancer.

Autoimmune theory.   The immune system is the body's front line of defense against foreign invaders such as bacteria. The body's immune system is designed to protect and preserve its integrity, and it does this by developing antibodies to attack hostile invaders. We know that the immune system begins to decline after adolescence, and the weakening of immune function is linked to age-related vulnerability. According to autoimmune theory, with aging, the system eventually becomes defective and no longer distinguishes the body's own tissues from foreign tissues. The body may even begin to attack itself, as suggested by the rising incidence of autoimmune diseases, such as rheumatoid arthritis, with advancing age (Kay & Makinodan, 1981).

Aging clock theory.   According to this theory, aging is programmed into our bodies, like a clock ticking away from the moment of conception. One of the best examples of the aging clock in humans is the menstrual cycle beginning in adolescence and ending in menopause. One version of the aging clock theory emphasizes the role of the nervous system and endocrine system. This theory postulates that aging is timed by a gland such as the hypothalamus, the thymus, or the pituitary gland. Such a gland would act like an orchestra conductor or a pacemaker to regulate the sequence of physiological changes that occur over time. Some support for this idea is found in the fact that the hormone dehydroepiandrosterone (DHEA) is found in higher levels among younger people. It also turns out that DHEA supplements help laboratory rats live longer. The aging clock theory is a concept of programmed aging in which aging is seen as a normal part of a sequence leading from conception through development to senescence and finally to death.

The aging clock theory has stimulated current research on the role of hormones secreted by the thyroid, pituitary, or thymus glands. These include the human growth hormone, which can now be manufactured in quantity through techniques of genetic engineering. In experiments with humans, volunteers injected with growth hormone lost flabby tissue and grew back muscle, essentially reversing some manifestations of the aging process for a time. Other investigators have looked to hormones produced by the pineal gland that may help regulate the "biological clocks" that mark the natural time rhythm of the body.

Cross-linkage theory.   Connective tissue in the body, such as the skin surface or the lens of the eye, shows changes with advancing age as the tissues lose elasticity; we recognize the wrinkling of skin as the body ages. The explanation for this change lies in a substance known as collagen, a natural protein found in the body, particularly in skin, bones, or tendons. According to the cross-linkage theory of aging, the changes we see result from the accumulation of cross-linking compounds. As in the waste accumulation theory, the idea is that there is an accumulation of immobilized molecules that eventually impair cell function. Some of the cross-linking may be caused by free radicals, which are cited in several different theories of aging.

Free radical theory.   Free radicals are unstable organic molecules that appear as a by-product of oxygen metabolism in cells (Armstrong et al., 1984). Free radicals are highly reactive and toxic when they come in contact with other cell structures, thus generating biologically abnormal molecules: for example, in mutations, damage to cell membranes, or damage by cross-linkage in collagen.

Free radical damage has been related to many syndromes associated with aging, such as Alzheimer's disease, Parkinson's disease, cancer, stroke, heart disease, and arthritis. According to the free radical theory of aging, the damage created by free radicals will eventually give rise to the symptoms we recognize as aging. An important point about this theory is the fact that the body itself produces so-called antioxidant substances as a protection against free radicals. These antioxidants "scavenge" or destroy free radicals and thus prevent some of the damage to cell structures.

It turns out that the production of antioxidants is correlated with the life span of many mammals. One attraction of the free radical theory is that, if proven, it might be possible to consume antioxidant substances such as Vitamin E to retard the process of aging. Genetic engineering techniques can now be used to produce antioxidants in vast quantities, but ordinary nutrients also supply them in our diet. Vitamins A, C, and E as well as less familiar enzymes play a role as antioxidants. Animal studies to date, however, show that consumption of antioxidants produces only minimal changes in what appears to be aging.

Cellular theory.   A major finding from cell biology is that normal body cells have a finite potential to replicate and maintain their functional capacity. This potential appears to be intrinsic and preprogrammed, part of the genetic code governing cell function and replication.

One of the major milestones in the contemporary biology of aging was the discovery that cells in laboratory culture have a fixed life span. In 1961 Leonard Hayflick and associates discovered that normal human cells in tissue culture go through a finite number of cell divisions—around 50 times—and then stop (Hayflick, 1965). This maximum number of divisions is known as the Hayflick limit. The cellular theory of aging argues that aging ultimately results from the progressive weakening of a capacity for cell division, perhaps through exhaustion of the genetic material or through some other process (Hayflick, 1968). That cellular limit, in turn, may be related to the maximum life span of species (Stanley, Pye, and MacGregor, 1975).

The cellular theory of aging sees aging as somehow "programmed" directly into the organism at the genetic level. In this view, it is just as "natural" for the body to grow old as it is for the embryo or the young organism to develop to maturity. Sacher has pointed out that this program theory of aging would appear to hold true for such organisms as annual plants, such as flowers in the garden, that go through a sequential reproductive cycle ending in death and dispersal of seeds. An example in the animal world would be the Pacific salmon that swims upstream to lay eggs and then quickly ages and dies off. But does the program theory of aging also apply to higher organisms such as mammals and specifically human beings? Probably so, but not as obviously as in organisms where rapid aging is linked with reproduction.

We do know that cells taken from older organisms divide proportionately fewer times than those taken from younger organisms. As cells age in cultures in laboratories, scientists observe changes in their functions, including protein synthesis and enzyme activity. Of interest, if normal human cells are frozen at a specific point in their process of replication, when the same cells are thawed, they seem to "remember" the level of replication at which they were frozen. Furthermore, if normal cells from a donor animal are transplanted, these donor cells will not survive indefinitely in the new host. The situation is different with cancer cells, both in living organisms and in laboratory conditions. Strains of cancer cells can survive indefinitely and are thus "immortal." In normal cell differentiation, cells divide and become more specialized as the ability to live indefinitely goes down.

Is Aging Really Necessary?

The aging process may not be the result of a rigid genetic program that in itself dictates longevity. On the contrary, what we see as maximum life span may simply be the complex and indirect result of multiple traits in the organism that are intrinsically tied to normal development. In other words, it is not that the body is somehow preprogrammed to acquire gray hair, wrinkles, or diminished metabolic functions. Rather, these signs of aging are simply telltale side effects of activities of the organism.

Consider the analogy of an "aging car." Suppose a distinctive "species" of automobile were designed to burn fuel at a fixed temperature with an efficient rate of combustion. That specific rate of combustion is required for appropriate acceleration, cruising speed, fuel mileage, and so on. But, alas, when the car functions in this way over a period of time, the car also, of necessity, produces certain emission by-products that, over time, begin to clog the cylinders, reduce automotive efficiency, and lead to the breakdown and final collapse of the machine.

In the case of the human "car," it could be that burning oxygen in normal metabolism generates harmful by-products in free radicals that prove toxic to the organism. What we see here may be a basic trade-off: Oxygen is essential for life yet harmful to our eventual well-being. In this view, the human "car" is not intentionally designed to accumulate toxic emissions "in order" to collapse. But there seems to be no way for the car to function at optimum levels without the destructive by-products.

But suppose we could find some special "fuel additive" that eliminates toxic emissions. Would we then have an "immortal" car? Probably not; changing the fuel used in your car won't prevent accidents, nor would any fuel additive prevent rusting or the wearing down of springs and shock absorbers. The "human car" analogy, of course, is misleading, because an organism, unlike a manufactured object, has a capacity for repair and self-regeneration, at least up to a certain point. The whole question about why we grow old is finding out why that capacity for self-repair ultimately seems unable to keep up with the damage rate: in short, why aging and death seem to be universal.

Prolonging the Human Life Span

As we have seen, most theories of aging have depicted biological aging as an inevitable process, almost like a disease to which we must all fall victim as we live longer. But aging is *not* a disease; it is, rather, a process of change, part of which may make us vulnerable to diseases. Instead of aging being the result of a single primary process driven by a single biological clock, aging is more akin to many different clocks, each on a different schedule but each driven by the same basic process or genetic unfolding of the developmental pattern. As we have seen, some theories look upon the organism succumbing to chance events, while others favor a built-in biological clock. Yet either way, by chance or by fate, a pessimistic conclusion about aging has seemed inevitable.

Today, basic research in the biology of aging is challenging that pessimistic conclusion. Two approaches have been found that can successfully push back the maximum life span limit for a species: one based on environmental intervention through diet, the other on a genetic approach.

Environmental Approach

For more than 50 years, scientists have known of only one environmental intervention—restricting food intake—that has been proven to extend maximum life span in mammals. Dietary restriction produces gains in longevity in laboratory animals, even up to a doubling of normal life span. The existence of even one such intervention disproves the idea that maximum life span for a species is unalterable (Weindruch and Walford, 1988).

As long ago as the 1930s, it was discovered that the life span of rats can be extended by restricting food intake after weaning and continuing through life. When caloric intake is restricted, age-related deterioration also slows down and age-related diseases, such as kidney problems and autoimmune syndromes, are diminished (Bronson & Lipman, 1991). There is no deterioration until very late in a more extended life span.

More recent experimenters have repeatedly confirmed that it is possible to increase both the average and the maximum life span of laboratory rats by reducing their caloric intake. A diet where caloric intake is cut to around 60% of a normal diet will produce a 30% gain in life span. The results here approximate the gains that are produced by genetic manipulation. Furthermore, Walford and associates found that caloric restriction in mice has similar effects even when it is begun in midlife (Walford, 1983). A basic question is thus: What accounts for this dramatic, well-established impact of dietary restriction in enhancing longevity? Across different species, longevity or maximum life span appears to be related to metabolic development, including caloric intake, as well as the length of reproductive period and the ratio of brain weight to body weight.

The metabolic factor appears to be central to explaining why caloric reduction works to increase longevity. The longevity gain is achieved not because of reduction in any specific component of the diet but simply because of less total calories consumed. Some biologists believe that dietary restriction works by affecting gene activity via the endocrine system and hormones. Other explanations are possible, but the major conclusion is that dietary restriction, like genetic manipulation, can be effective in slowing the rate of aging and increasing longevity. Roy Walford, one of the premier investigators of the biology of aging, has proposed a so-called High-Low diet that incorporates high nutritional value along with low calories (Walford, 1986).

A related approach is suggested from cryobiology, or the study of organisms at low temperatures. Lowering internal body temperature can increase life span in fruit flies as well as vertebrates, such as the fence lizard, an animal that lives twice as long in New England as its cousins do in warmer Florida. Experiments with fish demonstrate that, with lower temperature, life span is prolonged in the second half of life, but it remains uncertain if this process can be extended to warm-blooded animals like humans.

Of interest, calorie restriction seems to lower body temperature a small amount, and this fact correlates with other findings about the relation between body temperature and longevity. Calorie-restricted mice have a lower average body temperature, and the temperature itself changes according to biorhythm.

It has also been found that lower temperature can significantly reduce DNA damage. Caloric restriction somehow protects genes from damage by the environment and perhaps serves to strengthen the immune system. Caloric restriction also reduces the incidence of cancer. The experimental findings on caloric reduction converge with what is known about indirect regulation of genetic expression that controls the aging process.

Do the findings on dietary reduction and longevity have importance for humans? Almost certainly, but practical implications are not yet clear. The National Institute on Aging is spending $30 million on biomarker studies in the next few years to see if this approach works in primates and later perhaps in humans (Ingram et al., 1990). In the meantime, health promotion through dietary change remains an attractive option for those concerned with increasing life expectancy.

Genetic Approach

Many lines of evidence point toward the central role of genetic inheritance in fixing the longevity for each species, though we have seen that, for any individual, length of life will be the result of both genetic and environmental factors. We often think of genetic inheritance as the element that is fixed and unalterable. But some genetic studies have shown a dramatic ability to improve maximum life span over generations.

For example, studies have been conducted on bread mold, fruit flies, mice, and nematode worms. In all of these different species, genetic manipulation has been shown to be effective in modifying maximum life span. Mutations among nematode worms as well as in bread mold have been shown to exhibit substantial increases in maximum life span. Among mice, there are large differences in average life expectancy and maximum life span among different strains due to hereditary differences. In the fruit fly, scientists have achieved an increase in average as well as maximum life span by using artificial selection as a breeding technique.

Some recent experiments have produced astonishing gains in longevity from genetic intervention. For example, Michael Rose, a population geneticist, used artificial selection to produce long-living fruit flies whose life span of 50 days is double the normal average of 25 days. Rose, in effect, has changed some genes and thus in the laboratory mimicked an increase in the evolutionary rate of change. As a result, successive generations of fruit flies passed along genes favoring prolonged youth and longevity. Thomas Johnson, a behavioral geneticist, has gone further and altered a single gene out of the roundworm's 10,000 genes. He also achieved a doubling of the worm's three-week life span (Johnson, 1990). These dramatic successes, through breeding or direct genetic intervention, point to the way that genetic determination may have changed as a result of evolutionary selection. Still other recent studies suggest that, in some populations of fruit flies, the risk of mortality may actually *decrease* with advancing age, a finding that directly contradicts much prevailing wisdom in the biology of aging (Barinaga, 1992).

Whether these findings could be applied to humans is unknown. But some major conclusions about the genetics of aging point in a few clear directions. For instance, in at least several of the species cited here, it is likely that the genes involved are those governing antioxidant enzymes, which have been at the center of several theories about the biology of aging. Second, in the species where genetic manipulation has worked, there are a small number of genes involved in determining longevity. Thus there is no reason to believe that these results won't have application to higher animal species.

Some genes may even reverse aging as specific genes are switched on or off. Scientists have already found a way to double the life of skin cells by switching off the gene that regulates production of a specific protein responsible for manifestations of aging. A similar method of genetic engineering has been used with tomatoes, permitting them to be stored and shipped without decay. The key here lies in so-called mortality genes that determine the number of times cells divide, an intervention touching on the "Hayflick limit" that is central to aging at the cellular level. Even without affecting maximum life span, it is likely that gene therapy could have major applications in the future, perhaps leading to a cure for age-related diseases such as Parkinson's, Alzheimer's, and cancer (Anderson, 1992; Freeman, Whartenby, and Abraham, 1992).

On the horizon here is the current 15-year Human Genome Project supported by the U.S. government, one of the most ambitious scientific projects ever undertaken. The Human Genome Project is intended to yield a comprehensive "map" of the entire molecular sequence of genes on the human chromosome. Advances in genetic engineering could draw on that knowledge in ways that might dramatically change what we have thought of as the process of aging and even assumptions about the maximum human life span (Watson, 1992). Such speculations, however, belong to the future.

Compression or Prolongation of Morbidity?

Biology has not yet succeeded in unraveling the mystery of aging, so it is not surprising that medical science has produced no technology or method for raising the maximum life span of human beings. Caloric reduction and genetic methods have worked with lower organisms, but they have no proven impact for human beings. Medical interventions have succeeded in raising human life expectancy, but, as we have seen, with mixed results. It is possible that further steps, such as health promotion, might succeed in postponing chronic illness. Such steps might avoid the Struldbrugg scenario in favor of the one-horse shay. Whether that can and will happen is at the center of an important debate in aging, biology, and health care: the debate over compression of morbidity.

In the readings that follow, we hear some of the major voices in the debate. On one side, James Fries and Lawrence Crapo take the optimistic position that improving life expectancy will also lead to decreasing or "compressed" morbidity: People will live longer and not be sick until the very end of their natural life span. This "sunny" view of aging is paradoxical, in a way, because it presumes that the upper limit of maximum life span remains fixed: a limitation that other biologists might reject. In support of Fries's view, we can acknowledge that some postponement of morbidity has already occurred: Declining death rates from heart disease and stroke reflect improvements in health due to lifestyle, diet, hypertension detection, and so on. But not all are persuaded by Fries's reading of the evidence on morbidity and death rates. Edward Schneider and Jacob Brody point to other diseases, such as degenerative bone and joint disease, Parkinson's, or Alzheimer's, that cannot easily be prevented or postponed by any obvious interventions. Still other conditions, such as depression or sensory losses, are not linked to causes of improved life expectancy at all, so we still remain haunted by the Struldbrugg scenario (Verbrugge, Lepkowski, and Imanaka, 1989; Olshansky, Carnes, and Cassel, 1990).

The debate over compression of morbidity shows us that scientific facts are rarely as simple as we imagine. The meaning of the facts depends on our theories and interpretations and is therefore subject to debate and social construction in different ways. As Manton reminds us in the reading that follows, different readings of the facts about illness and survival in old age today are leading us to new ways of thinking about mortality and morbidity among the elderly. Indeed, the debate about compression of morbidity is only partly empirical: What do data from epidemiology and aging tell us? But it's also a debate about health care economics: What can we expect in the future if medical technology succeeds in prolonging life still more? Finally, it is a debate about policy: How much emphasis should we give to health promotion as opposed to other steps to prepare for an aging society? Whatever our view, the compression of morbidity theory stands out as an important reminder of how the frontiers of biology will be critical for the future of an aging society.

Vitality and Aging
Implications of the Rectangular Curve

James F. Fries and Lawrence Crapo

Why do we age? Why do we die? How can we live longer? How can we preserve our youth? Questions about life, aging, and death are fundamental to human thought, and human beings have speculated about the answers to these questions for centuries. Our own age values the methods of science—the methods of gathering evidence, of observation, of experiment—above the musings of philosophy. Yet, philosophical speculation and scientific theory may interact and enhance each other. The scientific theories of Copernicus and the conception of a sun-centered solar system, of Newton and an orderly universe, of Einstein and the relationship between matter, energy, and spacetime, of Darwin and the evolution of species have influenced our notions of who we are, where we are, how we came to be here, and the meaning of life itself. Similarly, the study of health and aging may contribute a new philosophical perspective to these age-old questions about life and death.

The implications of new scientific discoveries are often not widely appreciated for many years. Scientific knowledge develops by small increments within a relatively cloistered scientific community, whose members are sometimes more interested in the basic ideas than in their social implications. . . .

So it is with the study of human aging. The ancient philosophical questions have largely fallen to those who search for the biological mechanisms that affect our vitality and that cause our death. The

study of aging as a separate scientific discipline is relatively new and is not yet the province of any single science. Independent observations have been made in medicine, in psychology, in molecular biology, in sociology, in anthropology, in actuarial science, and in other fields. There are remarkable parallels in the ideas that have emerged from these independent fields of research. It is our intention to review these parallel developments and to present a synthesis of scientific ideas about human aging that will offer insights into the fundamental questions about the nature and meaning of the life process, aging, and death.

The Incomplete Paradigm

The growth of scientific knowledge historically has been impeded by thought systems (paradigms) that worked well for a time but that increasingly failed to explain new observations. For the study of aging, the contemporary paradigm is often called the *medical model*. The medical model defines health as the absence of disease and seeks to improve health by understanding and eradicating disease. This model of life and health, while useful, has obscured a larger perspective. There are four prevalent beliefs in the medical model that have

Source: Vitality and Aging: Implications of the Rectangular Curve, by J. F. Fries and L. Crapo, 1981, New York: W. H. Freeman. Reprinted by permission of authors.

The Limiting Premises

1. The human life span is increasing.
2. Death is the result of disease.
3. Disease is best treated by medication.
4. Aging is controlled by the brain and the the genes.

---

proved to be limiting (see [the] box . . .). Certainly, few present scholars hold these beliefs literally, but these ideas nonetheless have largely defined contemporary opinion about the aging process.

These four premises seem to imply the following conclusions. If the human life span is increasing, then our scientific goal can be the achievement of immortality. If death results from disease, our objective must be the elimination of disease. If disease is best treated with medication, our strategy is to seek the perfect drug or surgical procedure. With regard to aging, the medical model suggests that we should perform basic research to understand the genetic, neurologic, or hormonal mechanisms that control the process, and then learn to modify them.

Historically, these premises, objectives, and strategies have been useful. They are still worthy and deserving of study and hope. But they are certainly incomplete, and, taken literally, they are misleading. The human life span is not increasing; it has been fixed for a period of at least 100,000 years. The popular misconception of an increasing life span has arisen because the average *life expectancy* has increased; the *life span* appears to be a fixed biological constant. Three terms must be understood. The maximum life potential (MLP) is the age at death of the longest-lived member of the species—for human beings, 115 years. The life span is the age at which the average individual would die if there were no disease or accidents—for human beings, about 85 years and constant for centuries. The life expectancy is the expected age at death of the average individual, granting current mortality rates from disease and accident. In the United States, this age is 73 years and rising.

Death does not require disease or accident. If all disease and all trauma were eliminated, death would still occur, at an average age not much older than at present. If premature death were eliminated, and it may be in large part, we would still face the prospect of a natural death.

Medical treatment is not the best way to approach current national health problems. The major chronic diseases (atherosclerosis, cancer, emphy-sema, diabetes, osteoarthritis, and cirrhosis) represent the major present health threats. They are deserving of continued medical research, and further advances are to be expected. But abundant evidence points to personal health habits as the major risk factors for these diseases. Preventive approaches now hold far more promise than do therapeutic approaches for improving human health.

Aging does not appear to be under direct control of the central nervous system or the genes. Rather, the aging process occurs in cells and in organs. The aging process is most likely an essential characteristic of biological mechanisms. The process of aging, or *senescence,* is an accumulation in cells and organs of deteriorating functions that begins early in adult life. Aging may result from error-prone biological processes similar to those that have led to the evolution of species.

So the prevailing ideas about aging are incomplete. An increasing body of new scientific information requires revision and extension of these ideas. The time for a new synthesis has arrived, heralded by a number of new discoveries that do not fit well into the old paradigm but that as yet lack a coherent paradigm of their own.

Competing Themes

Changes in our ideas about health and aging are now being reflected in our social institutions and lifestyles. Change in a prevalent system of thought is often turbulent, and such turbulence is now manifest in health by a set of new movements. Within the medical community, there has been increasing recognition of the importance of preventive medical approaches. Such technical strategies as mass screening have been promoted. New departments of preventive medicine have been developed within medical schools; previously, such efforts were largely carried out within schools of public health. These developments are not entirely successful (screening efforts have proved disappointing, and some departments of preventive medicine have not thrived), but their very creation acknowledges the ferment of new approaches to health care.

The public has asked for more active involvement in consumer choices and for more accurate information on which to base such choices. In response, a self-care movement in health has developed, which now represents a considerable social force. At its best, this movement encourages critical consumption of medical services and increased autonomy from professional dominance. At its worst, the self-care movement takes an adversary stance and would replace professional medical treatment with idiosyncratic folk remedies. Still, the growth of these movements indicates discontent with the prevailing medical orthodoxy.

Recent changes in personal lifestyles have been even more significant. Joggers organize footraces in which tens of thousands compete, and cocktail party conversations concern the number of miles run per week. The number of militant antismokers has grown, and the nonbelievers are being packed into smaller and smaller spaces in the back of the airplane. Such spontaneous social changes are very likely to have constructive effects on health, and we applaud them, but the point is that the phenomenon itself represents a profound changing of the public consciousness.

Within professional medicine, new themes are evident. There is an increased interest in long-term patient outcome as a goal and less interest in correcting the trivial laboratory abnormality that does not materially affect the patient. Benefit-cost studies are sometimes advocated as a solution to the astronomical increases in the cost of medical care. Many observers have pointed out that orthodox medical approaches have reached the area of diminishing returns. The quality of life, rather than its duration, has received increasing emphasis.

Both psychologists and physicians have recently described strong relationships between psychological factors and health, and theories explaining such relationships have been developed that emphasize life crises, helplessness, loss of personal autonomy, depression, and other psychological factors. Correction of some psychological problems, it is implied, will improve health, and indeed the circumstantial evidence that this may be true is quite convincing. Again these approaches are outside the orthodoxy of the medical model.

Two new research areas have recently been emphasized—chronic disease and human aging. Increasingly, researchers recognize the central roles that aging and chronic disease play in our current health problems. The study of aging and chronic disease is oriented toward long-term outcomes, is interdisciplinary, requires preventive strategies, seeks to demonstrate the relevance of psychological factors, and uses lifestyle modification as a major tactic. The student of aging and the student of the diseases of the aged now have a unique opportunity to harmonize the incomplete old orthodoxy and the emerging new themes.

A New Syllogism

Using new knowledge of human aging and of chronic disease, we attempt here to provide a model that harmonizes these competing and chaotic themes, one that points toward new strategies of research and of health attainment. Our theoretical structure allows predictions to be made, and the predictions are strikingly different from those traditionally expected.

Figure 1.6 shows the actual data. Quite . . . startling conclusions follow from these data. The number of extremely old persons will not increase. The percentage of a typical life spent in dependency will decrease. The period of adult vigor will be prolonged. The need for intensive medical care will decrease. The cost of medical care will decrease, and the quality of life, in a near disease-free society, will be much improved.

Adult life may be conveniently divided into two periods, although the dividing line is indistinct. First, there is a period of independence and vigor. Second, for those not dying suddenly or prematurely, there is a period of dependence, diminished capacity, and often lingering disease. This period of infirmity is the problem; it is feared, by many, more than death itself. The new syllogism does not offer hope for the indefinite prolongation of life

Figure 1.6. Human Survival Curves for 1900, 1920, 1940, 1960, and 1980

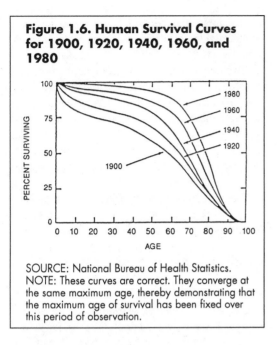

SOURCE: National Bureau of Health Statistics.
NOTE: These curves are correct. They converge at the same maximum age, thereby demonstrating that the maximum age of survival has been fixed over this period of observation.

expectancy, but it does point to a prolongation of vitality and a decrease in the period of diminished capacity.

There are two premises to the syllogism; if they are accepted, then it follows that there will be a reversal of the present trend toward increasing infirmity of our population and increased costs of support of dependency. . . . The first premise is almost certain; the second is very probable. If, after careful evaluation of the supporting data, one accepts the premises of this syllogism, then one must accept the conclusion and the implications of the conclusion.

Some Questions of Semantics

Nuances of meaning may mask the substance of a subject, and slight changes in emphasis may allow a new perspective to be better appreciated. There are problems with several of the terms often used to describe health, medical care, and aging. Among these are *cure, prevention, chronic, premature death,* and *natural death.* We will use these terms in slightly different senses than is usual.

Cure is a term with application to few disease processes other than infections. The major diseases of our time are not likely to be cured, and we have tried to avoid this term. *Prevention* is better but is unfortunately vague; this term, as we shall see, is sometimes misleading. We prefer the term *postponement* with regard to the chronic diseases of human aging, since prevention in the literal sense is difficult or impossible. *Chronic* is a term usually used to denote illnesses that last for a long period of time. It serves as a general but imprecise way of distinguishing the diseases that may be susceptible to cure (such as smallpox) from those better approached by postponement (as with emphysema). Regrettably, this important distinction cannot be based solely on the duration of the illness, since some diseases that last a long time both are not chronic conditions and might eventually be treatable for cure (such as rheumatoid arthritis and ulcerative colitis). We limit our use of the term *chronic* to those conditions that are nearly universal processes, that begin early in adult life, that represent insidious loss of organ function, and that are irreversible. Such diseases (atherosclerosis, emphysema, cancer, diabetes, osteoarthritis, cirrhosis) now dominate human illness in developed countries. We have defined *premature death* simply as death that occurs before it must, and we have used *natural death* to describe those deaths that occur at the end of the natural life span of the individual. . . .

A New Syllogism

1. The human life span is fixed.
2. The age at first infirmity will increase.
3. Therefore the duration of infirmity will decrease.

The Rectangular Curve

Survival curves for animals show a similar pattern of *rectangularization* with domestication or better

---

Figure 1.7. Theoretical Survival Curves for an Animal Become Progressively More Rectangular as the Environment Progresses from Wild to Domestic

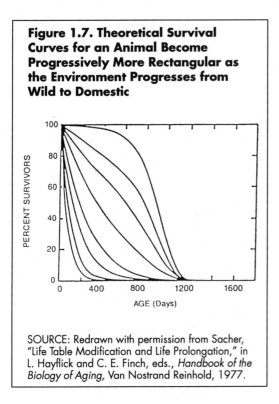

SOURCE: Redrawn with permission from Sacher, "Life Table Modification and Life Prolongation," in L. Hayflick and C. E. Finch, eds., *Handbook of the Biology of Aging*, Van Nostrand Reinhold, 1977.

rectangularization has been documented for many animals, including dogs, horses, birds, voles, rats, and flies. . . .

Figure 1.8 is drawn from the data Shock developed in 1960, and it is modified only slightly from what has been called "the most frequently shown data in the field of gerontology." The data show that many important physiological functions decline with age, and the decline is quite close to being a straight line. It is important to emphasize that these data were obtained from healthy human subjects in whom no disease could be identified that was related to the function being measured. Thus, the observed decline does not depend on disease.

Figure 1.8 is a major oversimplification of complex data. . . . The lines are not actually as straight as portrayed, and some of the data have been contested. The point is that a considerable body of

care. Old age in wild animals is very rare, as it probably was for prehistoric man living in a dangerous environment. In uncivilized environments, accidental deaths and violent deaths account for a greater proportion of deaths than the biologically determined life-span limit. For the great majority of wild animals species, there is a very high neonatal mortality, followed by an adult mortality rate that is almost as high and is nearly independent of age. In such environments, death occurs mostly as a result of accidents and attacks by predators. One day is about as dangerous as the next.

By contrast, animals in captivity begin to show survival curves much more rectangular in shape. Such animals are removed from most threats by accident or predator, and for them the second term of the equation, that of the species' life span, begins to dominate. Figure 1.7 shows theoretical calculations of this phenomenon after Sacher (1977). Such

Figure 1.8. The Linear Decline of Organ Function with Increasing Age

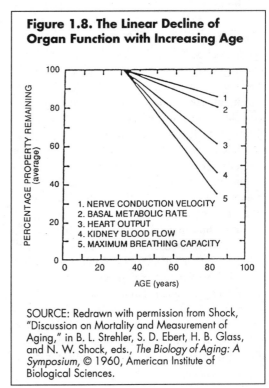

SOURCE: Redrawn with permission from Shock, "Discussion on Mortality and Measurement of Aging," in B. L. Strehler, S. D. Ebert, H. B. Glass, and N. W. Shock, eds., *The Biology of Aging: A Symposium*, © 1960, American Institute of Biological Sciences.

research supports a gradual, nearly linear decrease in organ function with age.

Normal, healthy organisms maintain an excess organ reserve beyond immediate functional needs. We have four to ten times as much reserve function as we need in the resting state. The heart during exercise can increase its output sixfold or more. The kidneys can still excrete waste products adequately if five-sixths of the functional units, the nephrons, are destroyed. Surgeons can remove one entire lung, and sometimes part of the second, and still have an operative success. Three-fourths of the liver can be removed, under some circumstances, and life is still maintained.

However, the mean level of reserve in many of our organs declines as we grow older. We seldom notice this gradual loss of our organ reserve. Only in the circumstances of exceptional stress do we need all that excess function anyway. Shock and others suggest that the decline may be plotted as a straight line.

Homeostasis and Organ Reserve
The human body may be viewed as a remarkable assembly of components functioning at various levels of organization. Systems of molecules, cells, and organs are all marvelously integrated to preserve life. The eminent nineteenth-century physiologist Claude Bernard emphasized that these integrated components act to maintain a constant internal environment despite variable external conditions. Bernard saw life as a conflict between external threats and the ability of the organism to maintain the internal milieu.

These fundamental observations have stood well the test of time. Indeed, the human organism cannot survive if the body temperature is more than a few degrees from normal, if acid-base balance is disturbed by a single pH unit, or if more than 20% of the body water is lost. Body chemicals are regulated closely, often to within 2% or 3% of an average value. A change in one direction in body constituent is often followed by a complicated set of responses that act to restore equilibrium.

Bernard also noted that living beings change from a period of development to a period of senescence or decline. He stated that "this characteristic of a determined development, of a beginning and an end, of continuous progress in one direction within a fixed term, belongs inherently to living beings."

The regulation of bodily functions within precise limits was termed *homeostasis* by Cannon (1932). Living organisms under threat from an extraordinary array of destructive sources maintain their internal milieu despite the perturbations, using what Cannon called the "wisdom of the body." Dubos (1965) has pointed out that this "wisdom" is not infallible. Homeostasis is only an ideal concept; regulatory mechanisms do not always return bodily functions to their original state, and they can sometimes be misdirected. Dubos sees disease as a "manifestation of such inadequate responses." Health corresponds to the situation in which the organism responds adaptively and restores its original integrity.

The ability of the body to maintain homeostasis declines inevitably with decreasing organ reserve. Figure 1.8 shows the decline for lungs, kidneys, heart, and nerves. The decline is not the same for all individuals, nor is the decline the same for all organs. For example, nerve conduction declines more slowly than does maximal breathing capacity. And some organs, such as the liver, intestinal lining cells, and bone marrow red cells, seem to show even less decline with age.

The important point, however, is that with age there is a decline in the ability to respond to perturbations. With the decline in organ reserve, the protective envelope within which a disturbance may be restored becomes smaller. A young person might survive a major injury or a bacterial pneumonia; an older person may succumb to a fractured hip or to influenza. If homeostasis cannot be maintained, life is over. The declining straight lines of Figure 1.8 clearly mandate a finite life span; death must inevitably result when organ function declines below the level necessary to sustain life. . . .

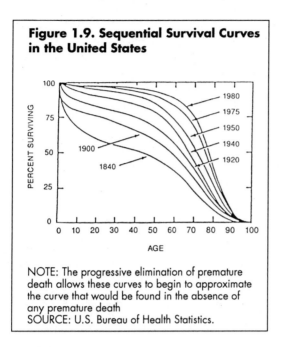

Figure 1.9. Sequential Survival Curves in the United States

NOTE: The progressive elimination of premature death allows these curves to begin to approximate the curve that would be found in the absence of any premature death
SOURCE: U.S. Bureau of Health Statistics.

Implications of the Rectangular Curve

The rectangular curve is a critical concept, and its implications affect each of our lives. The rectangular curve is not a rectangle in the absolute sense, nor will it ever be. The changing shape of the curve results from both biological and environmental factors. Many biological phenomena describe what is often called a normal distribution. This is the familiar bell-shaped or Gaussian curve. If one studies the ages at death in a well-cared-for and relatively disease-free animal population, one finds that their ages at death are distributed on both sides of the average age of death, with the number of individuals becoming less frequent in both directions as one moves farther from the average age at death. A theoretical distribution of ages at death taking the shape of such a curve in humans is shown in Figure 1.10. This simple bell-shaped curve, with a mean of 85 years and a standard deviation of 4 years, might exemplify the age at death of an ideal disease-free, violence-free human society. The sharp downslope of the bell-shaped sur-

vival curve is analogous to the sharp downslope of the rectangular curve.

In Figure 1.9, the first part of the curve becomes ever flatter, reflecting lower rates of infant mortality. Several factors prevent the total elimination of infant mortality and thus prevent the curve from becoming perfectly horizontal. These premature deaths are the result of birth of defective babies, premature disease and violent death. Improvements in medicine can lower but never eliminate the birth of defective babies and premature disease. It seems likely that the ever dominant proportion of violent deaths during early life will prove recalcitrant to change and will form an ever larger fraction of total premature deaths.

So, the rectangular curve has an initial brief, steep downturn because of deaths shortly after birth, a very slow rate of decline through the middle

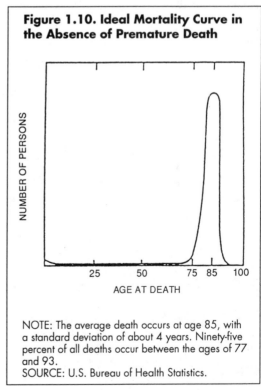

Figure 1.10. Ideal Mortality Curve in the Absence of Premature Death

NOTE: The average death occurs at age 85, with a standard deviation of about 4 years. Ninety-five percent of all deaths occur between the ages of 77 and 93.
SOURCE: U.S. Bureau of Health Statistics.

years, a relatively abrupt turn to a very steep downslope as one nears the age of death of the ideal Gaussian curve, and a final flattening of the curve as the normal biological distribution of deaths results in a tail after the age of 90. . . .

Thus, two profound characteristics of the mortality of man, the elimination of premature disease and the development of the sharp downslope representing natural death, have remained far from the public consciousness. These data have been available for many years. The first solid comments about rectangularization of the human survival curve can be found in prophetic statements in the 1920s. Many statisticians and actuaries working with national health data since that time have noted the increasingly rectangular shape of the curve, and many have speculated that it represents a natural species life limit. Entire theories of the aging process . . . have been built around the observed fact of a natural life span in man and animals. Yet, the public has remained largely ignorant of these developments.

A society in which life expectancy is believed to increase at every age and in which one becomes increasingly feeble as one grows older is a society heading for trouble. A society moving according to the curves of Figure 1.9, as our society is, is a society moving toward a world in which there is little or no disease, and individuals live out their natural life span fully and vigorously, with a brief terminal period of infirmity. . . . Dramatic changes in mortality patterns result in equally dramatic social changes.

References

Cannon, W. B. *The Wisdom of the Body*. New York: Norton, 1932.

Dubos, R. *Man Adapting*. New Haven: Yale University Press, 1965.

Sacher, G. A. Life Table Modification and Life Prolongation. In Birren, J., and Finch, C., eds. *Handbook of the Biology of Aging*, pp. 582-638, New York, Van Nostrand Rinehold, 1977.

READING 2

Aging, Natural Death and the Compression of Morbidity
Another View

Edward L. Schneider and Jacob Brody

In a compelling and articulate Special Article published in the *Journal* over three years ago, Fries[1]

Source: "Aging, Natural Death and the Compression of Morbidity: Another View," by E. L. Schneider and J. Brody, 1983, *New England Journal of Medicine* [Editorial], 309:14, pp. 854-855. Reprinted with permission of *The New England Journal of Medicine*.

outlined a set of predictions indicating that the number of very old people would not increase, that the average period of diminished vigor would decrease, that chronic diseases would occupy a smaller proportion of the life span, and that the needs for medical care in later life would decrease. Such predictions have important implications for planning the future allocation of health resources. The evidence that we will review supports quite different conclusions: that the number of very old people is increasing rapidly, that the average period of diminished vigor will probably increase, that chronic diseases will probably occupy a larger proportion of our life span, and that the needs for medical care in later life are likely to increase substantially.

Life Span and Life Expectancy

It is important to define the terms "life span" and "life expectancy" before proceeding with discussions of these concepts. Life span is best defined as the maximum survival potential of a particular species.[2] For human beings, there is documented survival of between 110 and 115 years.[3] Claims for enclaves with longevity past these ages have been demonstrated to be inaccurate.[4] Life expectancy is the average observed years of life from birth or any stated age. At present, life expectancy at birth in the United States is approximately 70.7 years in males and 78.3 years in females.[3]

Are There Biologic Limits to Life Span?

One important cornerstone to Fries' predictions[1] is that there is a genetically defined human life span that we are rapidly approaching. Hayflick and Moorhead demonstrated in an elegant series of experiments that human fetal lung fibroblasts, when placed in tissue culture, underwent a predictable and finite number of cell-population doublings and then ceased replication.[5,6] Fries[1] offers this limited in vitro replicative ability of cultured human cells as evidence for an internal cellular limit on the human life span. However, examination of several aging cell populations in vivo reveals that there is no evidence that aging of any organ or group of cells is caused by a limited number of replications. In fact, it has been amply demonstrated that some replicating cell populations have life spans that far exceed the replicative life span of the parent organism, often by several fold.[7,8]

A Natural Death?

Fries[1] suggests that the decline in function that occurs in most organs with aging can lead to "natural death" without disease. Although this fulfills Oliver Wendell Holmes' "one hoss shay" metaphor,[9] there is no documentation of its occurrence in human beings. A recent article suggested that in 30 percent of autopsies of patients over the age of 85, no acceptable cause of death was ascertained.[10] However, at autopsy, these patients had bronchopneumonia, pulmonary edema, pulmonary infarctions, and aspirations.[10] Their deaths were attributed to aging because no lesions were found of the magnitude "that would cause death in middle-aged persons."[10] Although most organs undergo functional declines with aging,[11] none is compromised sufficiently, even at extreme ages, for death to result in the absence of disease. Therefore, the compromised physiology of the elderly still requires a specific pathologic insult, such as pulmonary edema or pulmonary infarction, for death to occur.

Is the Population Rapidly Approaching a Maximum Life Expectancy?

The basis for Fries' predictions is his premise that the human survival curve will continue to "rectangularize."[1] This includes two assumptions: that death rates will remain low until a certain age (the horizontal component of the rectangle), and that the majority of deaths will occur over a short span of years (the vertical component of the rectangle). Fries predicts that this rectangularization will result in an average life expectancy of approximately 85 years in the first part of the next century.[1] We agree with Fries that chronic disease has replaced acute disease.[1] Improvements in general living conditions, diet, sanitation, and other public-health measures, as well as in the control of infectious diseases and in the reduction of infant mortality, have resulted in a gradual rectangularization of the survival curve, particularly for white women in the 20th century. However, the evidence that we will present indicates that life expectancy is increasing and will continue beyond the ninth decade if present trends persist. Fries' assertions were based on actuarial predictions that mortality rates were reaching a plateau. However, mortality rates resumed their decline in the 1970s after the plateau observed in the early 1960s.[12,13] According to recent actuarial data from the Social Security Administration,[14] life expectancy at birth may be longer than 90 years for white females by the year 2080. This is probably an underestimate, since the calculation did not take into account the rapid decline in mortality rates for the elderly that has occurred in the past 10 years.[13,15]

Of particular importance, the mortality rate of persons over age 85 is decreasing faster than that of any other older age group (i.e., 55 to 65, 65 to 75, or 75 to 85).[13] In addition, the absolute numbers of persons in this age group and the percentage of the population in this age group are increasing.[15] For the survival curve to continue to rectangularize toward a maximum life expectancy of 85 years, there must be very high, stable mortality rates in the age groups immediately below and above 85, to produce the vertical drop at the end of the survival curve. However, the observed much more rapid decrease in mortality at 85 and above, when compared with 75 to 84, indicates that there is a horizontal trend at age 85 and above, causing a "derectangularization" of the survival curve. Manton's examination of survival curves from 1940 to 1978 clearly demonstrates this trend away from increased rectangularization at 50 and older.[16] . . .

Will There Be a Compression of Morbidity?

Fries' prediction of a compression of morbidity is based on two assumptions: that rectangularization of the survival curve will continue and will result in a compression of mortality (which is opposed by the evidence presented above), and that there will be a postponement of the onset of chronic diseases. Fries suggests that this can be achieved by preventive approaches such as stopping smoking and undergoing treatment for hypertension. We strongly support preventive approaches with the goal of postponing the onset of chronic diseases, and we assume that this is occurring to a limited extent. However, this optimistic view must be tempered by two realities: the absence of evidence of declining morbidity and disability in any age group, particularly those aged 45 to 64 years,[17] and the increasing numbers of people who are reaching advanced age. If current trends continue, the fastest growing segment of the population will be those most vulnerable to chronic diseases, the group over age 85. This group has the greatest need for health care; although it represents only 0.8 percent of the overall population, 21.6 percent of this group are currently residing in nursing homes.[18] Recent evidence indicates that the incidence of one of the major chronic diseases of aging, Alzheimer's disease, may be as high as 3 percent per year for persons in the ninth decade of life and that the prevalence of the disease in persons over 80 is above 15 percent.[19]

Obviously, any compression of morbidity would have to result from a postponement of chronic diseases or a reduction of the disabilities that they produce. Interviews with members of older populations during the past decade have revealed no substantial change in the percentage reporting poor health[20] and no decline in morbidity or disability.[17] If the percentage of the elderly who are in poor health at specific ages (e.g., 60, 65, and 70) remains the same or increases and the numbers of individuals at advanced ages continue to increase, more people will spend longer proportions of their lives afflicted with chronic diseases. Unless preventive measures are extraordinarily fruitful or successful methods of treating or minimizing the impact of the chronic diseases of aging are developed, we will be faced with a burgeoning number of patients in need of long-term care.

Implications for Health Policy

If current demographic trends continue we will clearly be faced with increased numbers of people at advanced ages. The unknown variable will be the health of this group. If the health of this group in the future is not considerably different from the health of the present cohort, a huge proportion of the population will be suffering from chronic diseases. Today, health-care resources are stretched to the point at which federal entitlement programs for the health care of the elderly have become a major political issue. Increased pressures on the limited resources of our society will require difficult decisions in terms of the quantity and quality of health care for older Americans. The only approach that can forestall these consequences of increased life expectancy is for substantial inroads to be made in the prevention, treatment, or management of the common chronic diseases of aging. We write this article in the hope that Fries' seductive predictions will not be used for health-care planning and policy decisions, and that valuable resources will not be diverted from programs directed at the prevention and treatment of chronic diseases.

Notes

[NOTE: Only the notes that are included in the excerpted material appear here.]

1. Fries JF. Aging, natural death, and the compression of morbidity. N Engl Jour Med 1980; 303:130-135.

2. "Life span." *Encyclopedia Britannica.* Vol. 13. Chicago: William Benton, 1969:1098.

3. Population characteristics of the United States. Age, sex, race and Spanish origin of the population by regions, divisions, and states. Supplementary reports. 1980 census of population. Bureau of the Census, 1981.

4. Leaf A. Long-lived populations: Extreme old age. Jour Am Geriatr Soc 1982, 30:485-487.

5. Hayflick L., Moorhead PS. The serial cultivation of human diploid cell strains. Exp Cell Res 1961; 25:585-621.

6. Hayflick L. The limited *in vitro* lifetime of human diploid cell strains. Exp Cell Res 1965; 37:614-36.

7. Harrison DE. Normal production of erythrocytes by mouse marrow continuous for 73 months. Proc Natl Acad Sci USA 1973; 70:3184-8.

8. Daniel CW, Young Lit. Influence of cell division on an aging process: Life span of mouse mammary epithelium during serial propagation *in vivo.* Exp Cell Res 1971; 65:27-32.

9. Holmes OW. The deacon's masterpiece: or the wonderful "One-hoss Shay." Cambridge, Mass.: Houghton Mifflin, 1881.

10. Kohn RR. Causes of death in very old people. JAMA 1982; 247:2793-7.

11. Shock NW. Systems integration. In: Finch CE, Hayflick L, eds. Handbook of the biology of aging. New York: Van Nostrand Reinhold, 1977:639-65.

12. United States National Center for Health Statistics. The change in mortality trend in the United States. Hyattsville, Md.: National Center for Health Statistics, 1964. (Vital and Health Statistics. Series 3. No. 1). (DHHS publication no. (PHS)1000).

13. United States National Center for Health Statistics. Changes in mortality among the elderly: United States, 1940-1978. Hyattsville, Md.: National Center for Health Statistics, 1982. (Vital and Health Statistics. Analytical Studies. Series 3, No. 22). (DHHS publication no. (PHS)82-146).

14. Faber JF, Wilkin JC. Social security area population projections 1981. Washington, D.C.: Social Security Administration, 1981:42, Actuarial study no. 85.

15. Rosenwaike I, Yaffe N, Sagi PC. The recent decline in mortality of the extreme aged: An analysis of statistical data. Am J Public Health 1980; 70:1074-80.

16. Manton KG. Changing concepts of morbidity and mortality in the elderly population. Milbank Mem Fund Q 1982; 60:183-244.

17. Colvez, A, Blanchet M. Disability trends in the United States population 1966-76: Analysis of reported causes. Am J Public Health 1981; 71:464-71.

18. United States National Center for Health Statistics. The national nursing home survey: 1977 summary for the United States. Hyattsville, Md.: National Center for Health Statistics, 1979. (Vital and Health Statistics, Series 13, No. 43) (DHEW publication no. (PHS)79-1794).

19. Hagnell O, Lanke J, Rorsman B, Ojesjo L. Does the incidence of age psychosis decrease: A prospective longitudinal study of a complete population investigated during the 25-year period 1947-1972; the Lundby study. Neuropsychobiology 1981; 7:201-11.

20. Health: United States, 1979. Hyattsville, Md.: Public Health Service, 1979. (DHEW publication no. (PHS) 80-1232).

READING 3

The Sunny Side of Aging

James F. Fries

When confronting the health and medical care costs of the aging of America, there are optimists and there are pessimists. In a most curious way the "optimists" have become those who believe that life is limited and that the average life expectancy of seniors is unlikely to grow rapidly in the future. "Pessimists" are those who believe that life expectancy increases will continue, and perhaps will even increase in the future. In a thoughtful article in this issue of *JAMA,* Schneider and Guralnik[1] beat the pessimistic drum loudly and clearly. Medicare costs may rise sixfold by the year 2040 in constant 1987 dollars. Dementia might ultimately afflict 28% or more of the senior population. We might expect 800,000 hip fractures annually by the year 2040. Research funding for the conditions that will pose the largest health care problems in the next century, including osteoarthritis, osteoporosis, and Alzheimer's disease, is woefully inadequate. Schneider and Guralnik emphasize the mental senescence of Alzheimer's disease; I would add an equal concern for the problems of osteoarthritis and musculoskeletal disability.

Are they right? In large part they are. There is no avoiding the fact that the national health burden is shifting toward problems of the elderly, or that these problems will increasingly dominate the health

burdens of the next century. The overwhelming majority of health difficulties will become the physical (osteoarthritis and musculoskeletal disability) and mental (Alzheimer's disease) conditions associated with senescence. More of everything will be needed to deal with emerging problems in this area. More research, more prevention, more care, more facilities, and more money. It is already past time to admit the magnitude of the problem, as well as the inappropriateness and inadequacy of present facilities and training, and to declare war on infirmity. There can be no disagreement about this.

I, however, am an optimist. Granting that we make the necessary investments, the pessimistic future may be ameliorated by two "optimistic" trends. First, increases in longevity may slow, and, second, disability, on average, may occur later in life. There is already strong evidence that gains in life expectancy are slowing in females.[2-4] There are increasing data on the ability to move infirmity farther into the life span, shortening its overall duration. A theoretical framework for intervention into these serious problems, the compression of morbidity, is emerging.[2,5,6] Many gerontologists, including Schneider, are involved in programs with names like "Successful Aging," implying a prevalent belief that the problems are indeed accessible and that solutions are possible. The history of the next 50 years is not yet written. There are options for research and for the implementation of new interventions based on behavioral principles, on social adaptation and on the new biomedical information and techniques that will become available over this period.[2,6]

This article was supported by grant AM21393 to the Arthritis, Rheumatism, and Aging Medical Information System (ARAMIS), Stanford, Calif, and the National Institutes of Health.
Source: "The Sunny Side of Aging," by J. F. Fries, 1990, *Journal of the American Medical Association*, 263:17, pp. 2354-2355. Copyright © 1990 American Medical Association. Reprinted by permission.

The Number of Elderly

There are two numbers that, when multiplied together, yield the health or illness burden of the future. The first is the absolute number of elderly. The second is the average health of the elderly individual. The firmest estimates are for the absolute number of individuals aged 65 and older that we may expect. Here there is little room for major disagreement. The number of future elderly is driven by the number of individuals who pass 65 years of age each year. These individuals, through the next 65 years, are already born and, barring catastrophe, nearly all will reach 65 years of age. The proportion of a birth cohort that reaches 65 years of age has steadily risen. Birth cohorts in the United States increased steadily and even dramatically through 1963. These increases will be passed forward into the senior population, and it is this factor that drives the estimates for the aging of America. To be sure, there are differences in estimates of future life expectancy from 65 years of age, and the Social Security Administration's Office of the Actuary provides a range of alternative projections to encompass this uncertainty. But whether life expectancy for those aged 65 years increases to about 20 years, as we expect, or 25 years, as Schneider and Guralnik predict, this 25% difference in estimates does not account for more than a small fraction of the 600% increase in costs that Schneider and Guralnik foresee. The main issue is that there are going to be many more seniors. Even the most fervent optimist cannot but fully agree with the call for action.

The Health of the Elderly

It is not only how long seniors live that determines the overall health burden, however, it is additionally how well they live. At what average age does first physical infirmity occur? At what age is first mental impairment, on average, noted? At what average age does dependence on others become a problem? The health burden of the elderly is made up of age-dependent, fatal chronic diseases that include heart disease, cancer, and stroke, and also of a variety of nonfatal, age-dependent conditions, led by osteoarthritis, Alzheimer's disease, falls, incontinence, and others. There are well-known risk factors for the prevalent fatal diseases, and there is general agreement that, in part, because of changes in health behaviors of the public, there has been a marked decrease (now about 40% in cardiovascular disease) in age-specific risk of some major problems such as heart attack, stroke, and lung cancer in men and that these conditions have been pushed later into life.[2,7,8]

The nonfatal diseases present a new frontier, and one that now appears approachable. Our group has been carefully investigating risk factors for musculoskeletal infirmity in four large senior populations that involve thousands of subjects.[9,10] Risk factors for future infirmity include the preventable problems of lack of exercise, obesity, and the presence of chronic comorbid conditions that have risk factors themselves. Fractures, as discussed by Schneider and Guralnik, have many well-defined risk factors. Osteoporosis is amenable to prevention with exercise, estrogens, avoidance of corticosteroids, maintenance of adequate dietary calcium, and other measures.[3,10] The fall that results in the fracture is related to risk factors of bone density, muscular strength, presence of handrails, absence of household clutter, and restraint in medication use, among others. If we can put helmets on motorcyclists, we ought to be able to find some effective ways to reduce the incidence of osteoporotic fractures by prevention.

Alzheimer's disease represents a substantial exception to an optimistic view. It does not have recognized risk factors. Its prevalence increases as the number of seniors increases and as the senior population increases its average age, even though its incidence may not change. Alzheimer's disease may prove amenable to biomedical solutions, although this observer does not anticipate much success in attempting to revitalize atrophic brains and suspects that any effective biomedical interventions will have to be employed in preclinical stages of illness. Is it possible to be optimistic, even a little bit, about Alzheimer's? Perhaps. There may be some hope that nonspecific factors that influence health also influence the incidence of Alzheimer's disease, and that as these change there might be an increase in the average age of onset. Conjecture, but optimistic conjecture. We desperately need data on trends in incidence of chronic disease. Perhaps more importantly, life expectancy from 65 years of age in females has plateaued over the past decade. Despite decreasing mortality rates from specific chronic diseases, life expectancy has not improved significantly. This provides an important perspective for the individual patient. If life expectancy for females (who make up the great majority of patients with Alzheimer's disease) remains essentially constant and the age-specific incidence of Alzheimer's disease also remains constant, then the chance of Alzheimer's disease developing in a given individual does not increase. The national health burden of Alzheimer's disease increases because of the larger number of individuals at risk and the slowly increasing average age of these individuals, but the risk for the individual remains constant.

The research agenda must contain three major components. First, there must be data that support an epidemiology of morbidity. We must know what is happening to incidence rates of disability, disease, and dementia, and we need to know what is happening to mortality rates. Second, we need, as Schneider and Guralnik urge, an increased effort to understand the fundamental basis of age-associated conditions and of nonfatal chronic diseases, with the hope of discovery of biomedical solutions. Finally, we need research into prevention of chronic infirmity, research into delaying the onset of morbidity, and research into using interventions that already exist. The obvious interventions include exercise, diet, self-efficacy, and other lifestyle risk modification. It is neglect of this research arena, perhaps even more than neglect of a biomedical research agenda for age-associated disease, that limits our ability to foresee and control our future health.

Half Empty or Half Full?

Ninety-nine percent of individuals below the age of 75 years are not in nursing homes. Pretty healthy bunch. Eighty percent of those over age 85 years, with an average age of nearly 90 years, are *not* in nursing homes.[1] Half of all individuals in nursing homes are there because of chronic conditions and do not necessarily have to be there; their conditions have definable and modifiable antecedent risk factors.

It will help if we have better scientific knowledge to confront the coming problems. It will help if we have good data on the prevalence and incidence of specific types of morbidity, and good data on changes in these incidence rates over time. But managing old age better is not an issue best handled by waiting for the cure. It requires healthy lifestyles to prevent morbid disease; healthy life-styles to preserve fitness, vigor, and independence; environmental improvements to render the surroundings less hazardous; and living wills and durable powers of attorney for health care to limit inappropriate and inhumane terminal care. I hope that Dr. Schneider receives funding and that he and his colleagues find a cure for Alzheimer's disease. But aging well, with vigor and vitality toward the end of life, is already a reasonable prospect. Many seniors do it now, and more can.

Notes

1. Schneider EL, Guralnik J. The aging of America: Impact on health care costs. *JAMA.* 1990; 263:2335-2340.

2. Fries JF. The compression of morbidity: Near or far? *Milbank Q.* 1990; 67:208-232.

3. *Monthly Vital Statistics Report.* Hyattsville, Md: National Center for Health Statistics; 1989; 37:1-15.

4. Metropolitan Life. Changes in life expectancy. *Statistical Bull.* 1987; 68:10-17.

5. Fries JF. Aging, natural death, and the compression of morbidity. *N Engl J Med.* 1980; 303:130-136.

6. Fries JF. Aging, illness, and health policy: Implications of the compression of morbidity. *Perspect Biol Med.* 1988; 31:407-423.

7. Pell S, Fayerweather WE. Trends in the incidence of myocardial infarction and in associated mortality and morbidity

in a large employed population, 1957-1983. *N Engl J Med.* 1985; 312:1005-1011.

8. Horm JW, Kessler LG. Falling rates of lung cancer in men in the United States. *Lancet.* 1986; 2:425-426.

9. Lane NE, Bloch DA, Wood PD, et al. Aging, long-distance running, and the development of musculoskeletal disability: A controlled study. *Am J Med.* 1987; 82:772-780.

10. Lane NE, Bloch DA, Jones HH, et al. Long-distance running, bone density, and osteoarthritis. *JAMA,* 1986; 225: 1147-1151.

READING 4

Changing Concepts of Morbidity and Mortality in the Elderly Population

Kenneth G. Manton

There is little doubt that the aging of the population of the United States is a demographic phenomenon that holds profound implications for both private and public American institutions. In order to best adapt those institutions to serve the aging of the population, it is necessary to understand the dynamics that underlie this phenomenon. One component of those population dynamics, mortality, is of particular importance since it has implications for both individual and institutional planning. At the individual level mortality determines the number of years of life a person can expect to live past a given age—an important factor in planning career, retirement, and investment goals. At the institutional level, mortality is important since it is the prime dynamic factor determining short-run changes in the size and age structure of the elderly population. Since health and social service requirements for individuals change dramatically and rapidly after the age of 65, accurate predictions of the

changes [in] age distribution at advanced ages are especially important to social policy, . . .

Current Theories of Human Mortality and Longevity

A primary goal of a model of human mortality is to anticipate changes in mortality rates and human life expectancy. Many current models of human mortality predict that life expectancy in the U.S., with the present organization of medical science, is unlikely to increase much beyond present levels—a view that has strongly influenced forecasts of the rate of population aging and federal planning. Two mechanisms are proposed to explain this "ceiling" on life expectancy, one involving limitations on life span due to cellular processes of senescence and one involving an increased societal risk from chronic degenerative diseases. In the following we discuss basic principles of each type of model.

Biological Constraints on Human Mortality Changes

A number of theorists (Fries, 1980; Keyfitz, 1978; Hayflick, 1975) argue that mortality reductions and life expectancy increases in the U.S. popula-

Source: "Changing Concepts of Morbidity and Mortality in the Elderly Population" by K. G. Manton, 1982, *Milbank Memorial Fund Quarterly*, 60:2, pp. 183-191. Copyright © Milbank Memorial Fund. Reprinted by permission.

tion will cease in the near future because of biological constraints on the length of the human life span that are due to species specific processes of senescence. A prime implication of this perspective is that current efforts to increase life expectancy through disease control serve mainly to "rectangularize" the survival curve (Comfort, 1964). Thus, the curve describing the proportion of a cohort surviving to any given age will become nearly square with the surviving proportion remaining near 1.0 until the age range where mortality due to biological senescence occurs. Then the curve will drop rapidly to 0.0. Thus, life expectancy is increased by eliminating "premature death" due to specific diseases, so that large proportions of a cohort survive to their biologically determined life span to die a "natural death." As Fries (1980:133) concludes, "The surprising fact is that we are already approaching the limits."

The argument that senescence will soon limit life expectancy change is based upon four types of evidence. *First*, historically, the maximum human life span has not been observed to change except in populations where age documentation is poor and the literacy rate is low (Fries, 1980; Hayflick, 1975). *Second,* the risk of death seems to increase as an exponential function of age with a doubling time of about eight years, so that the likelihood of observing persons at extreme ages is small (Fries, 1980; Sacher, 1977). *Third,* standard actuarial computations indicate that the elimination of cancer and heart disease would increase the average life expectancy, at most, by 20 years (Hayflick, 1975). *Finally,* there is experimental evidence to suggest that at least certain types of human cells are internally programmed for only a limited number of reproductions (Hayflick, 1965, 1975, 1977). The weight of this evidence leads to an important conclusion—that mortality is not necessarily linked to disease processes, or, in Fries's (1980: 130) words:

The bioscientific, medical model of diseases, our prevalent model, assumes that death is al-

ways the result of a disease process; if there were no disease, there would be no death. This view is hard to defend.

Therefore, once we are close to the elimination of disease-related, premature death, then the average life expectancy in the population is unlikely to change significantly unless we discover the key to altering the basic biological aging rate of human organisms—an accomplishment viewed as unlikely at least in the near future (Fries, 1980; Hayflick, 1975).

An important corollary to the model of biological constraints on population life expectancy is the implication it holds for the age distribution of chronic disease morbidity. Two basic principles of this model (i.e., that mortality and morbidity are not necessarily linked and that changing disease risks do not alter the underlying aging rate of the organism) give rise to distinct and contradictory views on future changes of chronic disease morbidity. It is useful to present and contrast these views.

A distinctly pessimistic perspective is presented by Kramer (1980) and Gruenberg (1977; 1980: 1304-1305), who suggest that chronic disease prevalence and disability will increase as life expectancy is increased. This conclusion is reached because increases in life expectancy are viewed as not being accomplished either by reducing the incidence or by retarding the rate of progression of chronic degenerative disease, but by controlling the lethal sequelae of those diseases (i.e., primarily early terminal infections such as pneumonia). Therefore, Gruenberg (1977:3) concludes that "the net effect of successful technical innovations used in disease control has been to raise the prevalence of certain diseases and disabilities by prolonging their average duration." This will lead to what Kramer (1980) has labeled as a "pandemic of mental disorders and chronic disease."

A more optimistic appraisal is offered by Fries (1980). He argues that, in analogy to the rectangularization of the survival curve, there can be a rectangularization of the age at onset of chronic degenerative diseases. Thus, although medical science is viewed as not being effective in increasing the human life span, hope is offered that personal participation in health maintenance can help "postpone chronic illness, to maintain vigor, and to slow social and psychological involution" (Fries, 1980:134). Consequently, while the growth of the elderly population will be limited by biological constraints on the human life span, the requirements for health and social services for the elderly can be reduced by eliminating or postponing chronic disease, so that smaller portions of the life span will be affected (Fries, 1980:130). Unfortunately, the optimism with which Fries's arguments have been accepted needs to be tempered due to a critical omission in Fries's arguments. Specifically, he does not indicate how society is to deal with the increased social and health service demands currently manifest, and emerging, between the present time and the time of occurrence of his "utopian" stage where chronic disease onset can be delayed till age 85 and beyond.

Despite the differences in the degree of optimism with which Gruenberg and Fries view the future, there are several important commonalities in their perspectives. Most important is their view that chronic illness and not mortality should be the prime focus of public health efforts. Each, however, has a somewhat different perspective on how we should proceed in this effort and the difficulty in achieving significant progress. Gruenberg views chronic diseases as distinct pathological states, and emphasizes the search in epidemiological studies for preventable causes of chronic illness. Fries (1980:133) views chronic illness as a physiological process accelerating loss of organ reserve for which "postponement," rather than "cure," is likely to be effective. That is, for Fries a "cure" is achieved by delaying the age at which a disease reaches the symptomatic threshold beyond the age programmed for "natural death." Both Fries and Gruenberg suggest that alternatives to clinical treatment of chronic diseases need to be developed

in the effort to control illness and disability; Gruenberg emphasizes the importance of epidemiology and prevention, while Fries emphasizes the role of geriatric medicine and personal responsibility for self care.

In part, the differences in optimism seem to be a function of what Fries and Gruenberg perceive to be our present state of knowledge concerning mechanisms for slowing chronic disease progression. For example, though one might agree that "personal autonomy" could be the "probable final common pathway to improved health" (Fries, 1980:134)—say by better nutrition, exercise, and reduced smoking—it is not clear from Fries's exposition how such personal responsibility is to be engendered in the population. For example, we know that in certain population groups such as the Mormons mortality rates are 30 percent below the nation as a whole—largely as a consequence of a religious and social ethic that emphasizes personal responsibility for health (Lew, 1980). Though the success of such groups in improving health is well known, fostering such a health ethic nationally is a difficult task. Fries gives few directions on how such goals are to be accomplished programmatically. Indeed, though Fries argues that we are near the elimination of premature death, he acknowledges that currently 80 percent of mortality, and a higher proportion of disability, are due to chronic illness. Thus, though he suggests that "present approaches to social intervention, promotion of health and personal autonomy" (Fries, 1980:135) may serve to compress morbidity and senescence, and points to recent declines in circulatory disease mortality as possible signs of such improvement, it must be recognized that current social conditions have led to the majority of our health problems being due to what Fries views as "preventable" causes. Given the difficulties in achieving reductions in such an apparent health hazard as smoking we would be inclined to agree with Gruenberg's and Kramer's more pessimistic outlook. Furthermore, Gruenberg points out that certain chronic conditions (e.g., Down's syndrome) are genetically programmed. Consequently, there may be significant chronic morbidity that cannot be altered by personal choice. Such arguments reach a logical extreme in the thesis of P.R.J. Burch (1976) who argues that a major component of all chronic disease risks is genetically determined through individual variation in the immune system.

Fries and Gruenberg also seem to differ in their belief about future increases in life expectancy. Fries sees these as constrained by the biological processes of senescence. Gruenberg suggests an imbalance between life-saving technology and health-preserving technology so that continuing life expectancy changes presently serve to greatly increase the demand for health service. Thus Gruenberg seems to argue for further life expectancy changes. However, it seems reasonable to assume that future improvements in life expectancy will be limited since the progression of chronic diseases is unaltered. Both views posit that chronic disease morbidity and at least certain components of mortality have no necessary connection.

Societal Constraints on Human Mortality Changes

A second theoretical position is that, historically, major declines in mortality have resulted from reductions in infectious disease risk due to improvements in lifestyle, hygiene, nutrition, and other public health factors—and not due to innovations in medical technology (Omran, 1971; McKeown, 1976; McKinlay and McKinlay, 1977). Omran proposed a model of epidemiological transition in which the correlation between the economic, demographic, and public health changes of a society were described as a series of stages, with the U.S. and other developed nations having reached an "end" stage, the "Age of Degenerative and Manmade Diseases." In this end stage, mortality slowly declines (to rates below 20/1000) and eventually approaches stability at relatively low levels, while life expectancy at birth increases slowly until it

exceeds 50 years (Omran, 1971: 517). At this stage, fertility "becomes the crucial factor in population growth" and heart disease, cancer, and other chronic diseases become the prominent public health hazards—with little said about the prospects for reducing chronic disease risks. Indeed, the nature of developed industrial societies is viewed by certain authors as having positive health risks for chronic diseases due both to societal, public health factors—such as environmental deterioration or occupational stress—and to factors involving choice at the individual level, such as smoking (Dubos, 1965).

Models of societal determinants of mortality also have implications for aging changes in U.S. society because they imply that a societal health state has been reached in which major improvements in life expectancy in the near future are unlikely. In contrast to the view that life expectancy is biologically bounded, however, the potential for reductions in infectious disease and maternal mortality due to improvements in hygiene, nutrition, and sanitation is viewed as having been largely fulfilled, while societal factors relevant to chronic disease risks have recently shown either marginal improvements (e.g., smoking rates) or actual deterioration (e.g., environmental toxicological hazards). Thus, while there is nothing in the societal model to preclude the existence of a biologically determined limit, societal constraints on life expectancy are viewed as becoming operational before biological constraints. As in the biological model, medical science is argued to have little potential for increasing life expectancy through the treatment of chronic degenerative diseases. Consequently, it cannot serve to compensate for possible increases in societal risks. Often both perspectives are combined to suggest an even more limited potential for life expectancy change than could be projected under a pure biological model. Fries's optimism seems to result from his belief that societal constraints on both life expectancy increases and health improvement can be overcome.

References

Burch, P.R.J. 1976. *The Biology of Cancer: A New Approach.* Baltimore: University Park Press.

Comfort, A. 1964. *Ageing.* New York: Holt, Rinehart and Winston.

Dubos, R. 1965. *Man Adapting.* New Haven: Yale University Press.

Fries, J.F. 1980. Aging, Natural Death, and the Compression of Morbidity. *New England Journal of Medicine* 303:130-135.

Gruenberg, E.M. 1977. The Failures of Success. *Milbank Memorial Fund Quarterly/Health and Society* 55:3-24.

Gruenberg, E.M. 1980. Mental Disorders. In Last, J., ed., *Public Health and Preventive Medicine.* New York: Appleton-Century-Crofts.

Hayflick, L. 1965. The Limited *In Vitro* Lifetime of Human Diploid Cell Strains. *Experimental Cell Research* 37:614-636.

————. 1975. Current Theories of Biological Aging. *Federation Proceedings of American Societies for Experimental Biology* 34:9-13.

————. 1977. Perspectives on Human Longevity. In Neugarten, B., and Havighurst, R., eds. *Extending the Human Life Span: Social Policy and Social Ethics*, pp. 1-12. Chicago: Committee on Human Development, University of Chicago.

Keyfitz, N. 1978. Improving Life Expectancy: An Uphill Road Ahead. *American Journal of Public Health* 68:954-956.

Kramer, M. 1980. The Rising Pandemic of Mental Disorders and Associated Chronic Diseases and Disabilities. In Epidemiologic Research as Basis for the Organization of Extramural Psychiatry. *Acta Psychiatrica Scandinavica*, Suppl. 285, Vol. 62.

Lew, E. 1980. Discussion Comment in Implications of Future Mortality Trends: Follow-up to Ideas Presented at the Chicago Mortality Symposium. *Record* of the Society of Actuaries, Montreal meeting, October 20-22, 1980, pp. 1365-1366.

McKeown, T. 1976. *The Role of Modern Medicine: Dream, Mirage or Nemesis?* London: Nuffield Provincial Hospitals Trust.

McKinlay, J. B., and McKinlay, S. M. 1977. Questionable Contribution of Medical Measures to the Decline of Mortality in the United States in the Twentieth Century. *Milbank Memorial Fund Quarterly/Health and Society* 55:405-428.

Omran, A. R. 1971. The Epidemiological Transition: A Theory of the Epidemiology of Population Change. *Milbank Memorial Fund Quarterly* 49:509-538.

Sacher, G. A. 1977. Life Table Modification and Life Prolongation. In Birren, J., and Finch, C., eds. *Handbook of the Biology of Aging*, pp. 582-638. New York: Van Nostrand Reinhold.

QUESTIONS FOR WRITING, REFLECTION, AND DEBATE

1   James Fries is optimistic about postponing chronic illness until very late in life. His optimism is based on enhancing personal responsibility for health care. What would Fries say in response to health threats outside personal control—for example, environmental toxins, such as air pollution, or genetic diseases?

2   What are the arguments for, and against, the view that aging itself is a disease? Pick one side of this issue and then try writing down each of the separate arguments that can be used to rebut or oppose the other point of view.

3   What do Fries and Crapo mean by "natural death"? What is the relation between "natural death" and the "natural life span"? Should we consider the natural life span to be identical to the maximum life span?

4   In criticizing Fries and Crapo's predictions, Schneider and Brody still
    seem to support Fries's point that it would be desirable to prevent or
    postpone the chronic diseases of old age. If they all agree, then, that health
    promotion is a good idea, what is the real basis of debate between the two
    authors and Fries and Crapo? Does their disagreement matter in any
    practical way? Write your own summary of the opposing views and then
    summarize what the implications might be for practical matters such as
    medicine, health care policy, or personal decisions about diet.

5   Kenneth Manton points to the importance of "societal constraints" on
    raising life expectancy. What are some examples of such constraints and how
    do societal factors relate to personal responsibility factors? What can we
    learn from the AIDS epidemic about future steps to raise life expectancy?

6   Recent Swedish data have turned up the surprising fact that death rates
    for the oldest-old (85+) have actually been going down. Some scientific
    studies suggest that there may be no end in sight to an ever-increasing
    life expectancy (Kolata, 1992). These findings sound like good news. Are
    there any reasons to believe that these findings are *not* good news? What
    would Fries's response be to these claims?

7   The current Human Genome Project expects to produce a complete map
    of all human chromosomes. Considering the different theories of aging,
    what are some of the ways in which new genetic knowledge might change
    how we think about the causes of biological aging? What are the social
    and ethical implications of that knowledge?

8   Try writing a scenario or imaginary picture of how the United States might
    look in the year 2030 if dramatic breakthroughs in the biology of aging
    occur. In developing this picture, be sure to state the year in which it is
    suggested that a certain discovery or invention will occur, then describe
    what are the likely consequences of that discovery or invention.

FOCUS ON PRACTICE: HEALTH PROMOTION

Can we take steps to control our longevity? Today, there is a growing consumer market for life-extension products and magazines on the subject can
be found on newsstands. But claims for these life-extending products exceed
what science has proven. If intervention in the aging process is possible, what
are the implications for practice? Some environmental interventions have
already been shown to promote health and longevity. For example, the death
rate from cardiovascular disease has been cut in half in the last two decades,

chiefly because of a reduction in high-risk behaviors like smoking. Other changes in diet or exercise patterns could provide further gains in adult life expectancy. The key point is that most of the causes of lost life years today are not only environmental but are related to lifestyle choices: alcohol, tobacco, and exercise (Arking, 1991).

One promising approach is dietary. Millions of Americans have already started eating a low-fat, high-fiber diet, just as they have given up smoking. Others go further in seeking to minimize free radical damage to cells by changing their diets to include more antioxidant carotenes. Dr. Roy Walford, well known for his immunological theory of aging, has for years been eating according to a calorie-restricted diet based on findings from laboratory animals (Walford, 1986).

Walford's diet is a low-fat, high-fiber one, used in combination with regular exercise and some reliance on vitamin and mineral supplements. Naturally, no smoking and little drinking is permitted. Walford hopes to live beyond the century mark. But even if he doesn't, there is reason to believe that his diet or other diets like it would enable people to be healthier in old age, as Fries predicts for the future.

On the subject of health promotion and aging, we encounter a familiar argument between the "optimists" and the "pessimists." On the one hand, Hayflick argues that calorie-restricted, long-living mice are merely living out their fixed natural life span. In the end, the genetic program prevails and environmental interventions, like diet, can only accomplish a limited amount. If he is right, then Walford, like Ponce de León, has embarked on a vain search for the fountain of youth.

The optimists hold a different view. According to one scenario for the future, as a result of prudent nutrition and more exercise, after the year 2000, the average life span could rise from 75 up to 80 years. Then, early in the next century, through hormone replacement and genetic engineering, the maximum life span could push well beyond the current limit of 110 to 120 years. Optimists believe that a combination of lifestyle enhancement along with new technologies could provide ways to delay or even reverse aging, thus extending youthfulness and pushing back the limit of the life span itself.

Regardless of how the arguments turn out, steps to improve longevity are already becoming part of the popular culture (Brody, 1984; Dychtwald, 1986). Changes in diet and exercise, reductions in smoking, and health promotion activities of many kinds are now far more common than a decade ago. As baby boomers move into middle age, these activities are likely to spread and have an impact on longevity.

In thinking about these scenarios for the future, it is important to retain a measure of skepticism and also to focus on practical steps that are proven and feasible right now. Health promotion is based on science, not on hypothesis or hopes for the future.

The National Institute on Aging has reviewed the scientific evidence for interventions promising to increase longevity (NIA, n.d.). A number of alleged anti-aging treatments are examined, including eating antioxidant vitamins, consuming DNA and RNA supplements, using of DHEA hormone supplements, and other dietary interventions, including calorie restriction. For each of these interventions or supplements, the National Institute on Aging review concludes that there is no definite proof to support claims made on behalf of these products. But the sale of health food products containing such components, along with publication of books on life extension, is a brisk business. In some cases, the products offered are outright quackery; in other cases, they represent promising lines of scientific research that are simply not yet proven. Individuals must judge for themselves evidence on behalf of claims for anti-aging interventions. The issues remain a legitimate subject of debate among biologists and in the medical community.

Much less subject to debate are recommendations that lie in the broad area of health promotion, including the following:

- Avoid smoking
- Eat a balanced diet and maintain proper weight
- Keep up regular exercise
- Have regular health checkups to detect problems early
- Drink alcohol only in moderation
- Practice good safety habits at home and when driving
- Stay active and involved
- Allow time for rest, relaxation, and enough sleep

It is never too late to adopt better health habits; older people who adopt health promotion activities can improve their well-being even in later life (Weiss, 1988; Gross, 1991). Indeed, some researchers have concluded that about half of the declines associated with aging can be prevented by changes in lifestyle such as those cited here. The result would be a reduction in premature disability and death. Health promotion, when successful, can prevent or delay the onset of many chronic diseases in later life and so allow more of us to live closer to what has been identified so far as the maximum life span for the human species.

Suggested Readings

Arking, Robert, *Biology of Aging: Observations and Principles*, Englewood Cliffs, NJ: Prentice Hall, 1990.

Kahn, Carol, *Beyond the Helix: DNA and the Quest for Longevity*, New York: Times Books, 1985.

Rosenfeld, Albert, *Prolongevity II*, Henry Holt & Co., 1987.

Schneider, Edward L. et al. (eds.), *Handbook of the Biology of Aging* (3rd ed.), San Diego, CA: Academic Press, 1989.

Sprott, R.L., Warner, H.R., and Williams, T.F. (eds.), "The Biology of Aging," [entire issue], *Generations* (1992), XVI:4.

Warner H.R. et al. (eds.), *Modern Biological Theories of Aging*, New York: Raven Press, 1987.

Should We Ration Health Care on Grounds of Age?

To every thing there is a season, and a time
to every purpose under the heaven.
A time to be born, and a time to die . . .

—Ecclesiastes

It is no secret that we're spending lots of money on health care for the elderly: more than $120 billion on Medicare alone each year, and the figure is growing. As America's population grows older, it seems inevitable that we must spend even more. But what are we getting for all that money? Can we really afford so much health care for an aging population? These questions would have been unthinkable a few years ago. But today, more and more people are asking such questions. Some have even urged that we cut off expensive health care services for the very old, for people who have lived "too long."

Rationing health care on grounds of age is troubling to most Americans. How are we to think about the justice, or the wisdom, of spending vast amounts of money prolonging the lives of the elderly? Prolonging life seems desirable but it isn't cheap. With rising costs and new advances in expensive medical technology, decisions about life prolongation are no longer questions just for medical practitioners. The decisions quickly become questions of economics and social justice: Who will get access to expensive health care resources?

Answers to these questions are not easy to find. Some answers that have been given are disturbing and controversial. One of the most controversial is the idea that someday, perhaps soon, we are going to have to "ration" health care to people above a certain age; in effect, we will be telling older people: "You've lived long enough." Philosopher Daniel Callahan made just such a proposal, which provoked enormous debate and is examined in more detail later in this chapter. But in thinking about the issues, it is important to remember that others, such as former Colorado Governor Richard Lamm and philosopher Norman Daniels, have also called for age-based rationing of health care (Daniels, 1988; Lamm, 1993).

Precedents for Health Care Rationing

An important question in the health care rationing debate is a practical one: Has it ever happened before? How is rationing based on age likely to be introduced in America? A few examples are suggestive here.

Kidney dialysis in Britain. In Britain, for many years, kidney dialysis was routinely withheld from people above a certain age—usually 55 or 60 (Aaron and Schwartz, 1984). Doctors in Britain's National Health Service simply didn't refer such patients to clinics that offered dialysis treatment and the patients died. Some officials defended the policy on the grounds that, with limited resources, it made more sense to provide funding to improve quality of life: for example, offering ample home health care for elderly people. As the covert policy of withholding some treatment for older people became publicly known, it was abandoned (Halper, 1989).

Waiting lines in Canada. In Canada, medical care is provided by a national health insurance system, a plan many have advocated for the United States. Under the Canadian system, virtually no one is deprived of health care because of inability to pay. For some forms of care, however—certain surgical procedures that are not needed to save life—it may be necessary to wait long periods. In effect, the waiting list has replaced a market system for allocating some types of medical care (Naylor, 1991).

Life-and-death decisions. In Seattle during the 1960s, when kidney dialysis first became available, there were not enough kidney machines to take care of all the patients who could benefit. For a period then, hospitals set up special committees to decide who would have access to dialysis. The committees wrestled with life-and-death decisions and took into account such factors as severity of illness, age, compliance with medical regimen, and social contribution. Decisions by such committees were criticized and eventually Medicare reimbursement for kidney dialysis made it unnecessary to ration treatment.

Oregon rationing plan. In Oregon, the state legislature in 1990 passed legislation putting into effect a computer-based ranking of which health care problems would be covered under the state's Medicaid program. According to this ranking system, funding would be made available and services would be rationed not according to individual cases but according to a consensus reached by democratic means. The state finally obtained federal government approval for the new rationing scheme but Oregon's proposal received approval over objections that the plan would discriminate against people with disabilities (Brown, 1991).

These examples show how hard it is to get public agreement on when or how to ration scarce health care resources. Rationing policies are sometimes put into effect when a clear-cut, unavoidable scarcity exists; organ transplants would be a good example. But if all that is needed is more funding, then rationing health care seems especially open to public criticism. There is evidence that other European countries in addition to Britain have practiced some form of age-based rationing. But virtually none has ever come out publicly and acknowledged this or defended it.

Rationing as a Cost-Saving Plan

One problem with age-based rationing is knowing just how much money it would save. Most of the money spent on health care for older people doesn't go for "high-tech" care in a hospital setting. A substantial share goes for prescription drugs, medical equipment, nursing home care, and home health services. The cost of these last two categories—long-term care for the aged—is increasing rapidly as more and more people survive to advanced ages, and Callahan himself favors spending more on long-term care instead of high-technology medicine. Callahan seems to be saying that we can't afford our current health care spending for an aging population. But the rapid rise in health care costs is not primarily attributable to longevity by itself. Expensive medical technology is part of the problem, and so are increases in treatment frequency; expensive treatments for life-threatening diseases such as AIDS, heart disease, and cancer; and labor intensity in the use of health care personnel. Singling out aging alone may miss the larger picture. In any event, critics charge that Callahan's proposals, even if fully implemented, would save only $5 billion a year—not a large amount in an $800 billion health care budget.

Others have replied to Callahan's proposal by insisting that rationing of health care isn't necessary at all (Relman, 1990). They point out that the current health care system is riddled with waste and inefficiency. For example, by comparing statistics with other countries, some analysts have argued that up to *half* of all the cardiac bypass operations in the United States may not be needed. A 1992 study by the federal government's General Accounting Office found that the present health care system permits unscrupulous providers of services to defraud insurance companies at a staggering rate. It is estimated that 10%, or $70 billion, is lost to fraud and abuse every year. Still others point out that 28% of the Medicare budget is spent on patients in the last year of life (Lubitz and Prihoda, 1984). Perhaps by voluntarily avoiding unneeded care or treatment that simply prolongs dying, we could avoid rationing health care.

The problem with this last proposal is that it is simply not so easy to predict how long a given patient will live. We only know that we've spent money on the "last year of life" when life is over: that is, in retrospect. Studies of the cost of medical care at the end of life for the frail elderly confirm what doctors have privately admitted for a long time: Medical science lacks any realistic way of determining who would have died if they hadn't gotten the care they received. At bottom, we haven't got a good way of predicting when the "last year of life" will occur.

The real solution, many critics argue, is a system of national health care combined with careful cost controls to ensure that appropriate care—but not overtreatment—is provided to people at all levels throughout the health care system, not simply in the last year of life. A variety of proposals for providing more health care in a cost-effective manner have actually been put into practice in recent years. These include new forms of managed care, popular with private industry, and **case management,** practiced by community-based health service programs. Both are methods for deciding how much care to provide individuals based on some verified assessment of individual need.

Will more efficient management of health care distribution solve the problems of access and allocation in an aging society? Can we institute reforms that will avoid the specter of age-based rationing? The answer we give depends in part on what America's aging population looks like in the decades ahead. The answer to the question, "Can we afford an aging population?" involves some forecast about the health status and needs of the aging population in decades to come: for example, the likely impact of health promotion, such as reductions in smoking, or the probability of a breakthrough in understanding the biology of aging or the causes of specific diseases.

A prime factor in the rationing debate is economics, which can be defined as the science of scarcity. It is only when scarcity is at hand—when the wolf is at the door—that rationing is seriously considered. In times past, there have been societies where older people were deprived of resources, sometimes even life itself, to make way for the young. One example often cited is the Aleut (Eskimo) tribes who at the point of starvation were sometimes forced to put an elderly person out on an ice floe to die in order to have enough food for the remainder of the group. The situation was a literal case of "lifeboat ethics." Similarly, in Leningrad during World War II, hundreds of thousands of people, including the very old, died of starvation so that young children could survive.

But these life-threatening conditions that promoted rationing have become more rare as economic conditions have improved through history. Today, we face a different kind of scarcity created by the fact that medical technology can save and extend the lives of the very sick and old. Even if the technology is cheap—a penicillin shot, for example—caring for elderly people with chronic diseases—such as stroke or Alzheimer's disease—can be very expensive. As new medical technologies enable us to prolong the lives of victims of chronic diseases, the expense goes up still further: exactly the situation that brought proposals for rationing health care resources on grounds of age.

Figure 2.1 shows a large actual and projected increase in the population 85 years and older. This group aged 85+, sometimes called the "oldest-old," also has the greatest number of health problems and costs the most. If expensive health care resources were rationed on grounds of age, as Callahan proposes, then this group would probably be the group denied care.

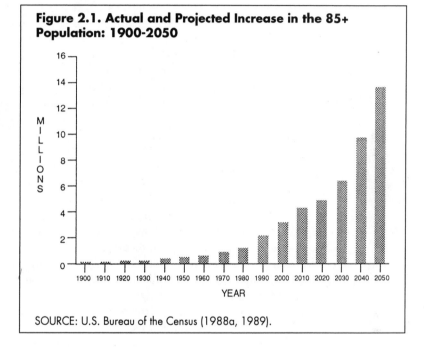

Figure 2.1. Actual and Projected Increase in the 85+ Population: 1900-2050

SOURCE: U.S. Bureau of the Census (1988a, 1989).

In his book *Setting Limits*, philosopher Daniel Callahan argues that America is spending too much on health care and he believes that health care costs for the elderly are a big part of the problem. He concludes that we should set limits on health care costs by "rationing" health care and, specifically, by withholding expensive life-prolonging medical technology from people on grounds of chronological age alone.

As medical technology advances, Callahan fears that life-extending technology will run up against the law of diminishing returns. He fears that we will end up spending more and more to achieve limited incremental gains, often with very poor quality of life, while other social needs go unmet.

But is this assumption about technology correct? Some life-extending technology—say, a penicillin shot—is actually quite inexpensive. On the other hand, keeping a patient alive and cared for in a nursing home—usually a low-technology environment—can be very expensive: $30,000 or $40,000 a year or more. If we really want to cut down on the expense created by too many old people, why wouldn't we also withhold *cheap* life-extending technologies? As long as we look exclusively at the economic aspect of health and aging, it is hard to avoid thinking of choices in terms of cost-benefit or cost-effectiveness standards (Avorn, 1984; Welch, 1991). But once we adopt those standards, don't we inevitably come to downgrade the value of life in old age? Callahan believes that society owes the elderly a decent minimum of health care, at least up to a certain age. Callahan hopes to inspire a debate and finally to encourage a social consensus in favor of his idea of a *"natural" life span.*

What is the basis of Callahan's argument? The high cost of more health care for the elderly is part of the problem. But cost alone isn't the whole story for Callahan, because he would accept paying for certain expensive procedures—say, surgical operations—for younger people. The basic principle that Callahan wants us to consider is chronological age. Callahan, like the passage from the Book of Ecclesiastes cited earlier, believes that human life has a natural rhythm or cycle. Just as there is a time to live, so too there is a time when it is appropriate to die. Callahan argues that this "natural" life span—at least the traditional 60 years and then 10 years or maybe a bit more—should be the basis for thinking about the goals of health care. He believes we should do what we can to enable people to live out a full life span, however defined, but nothing more. After that, we should not expend scarce resources on the very old. Instead, we should let them die.

Callahan is absolutely serious about his proposal, and this fact has shocked many people. Is Daniel Callahan cruel and hard-hearted, or is he instead courageous and far-sighted in willing to advocate a controversial idea? His own words, and the response of his critics, must be the basis for what the fair-minded reader will conclude.

The "notch" problem. Callahan calls for changes in public expenditure programs to carry out his plan for age-based rationing. How would this work in practice under the Medicare program? There is fear that in practice it might create a troublesome "notch problem" for people as they come near the age for cutting off health care resources. The situation could be comparable to what we now have under Medicare. If you're very sick and need care but you're only 64, you can't qualify for Medicare. As soon as you pass the magic age of 65, you become qualified. You've passed over the "notch" that separates those eligible from those not eligible. Under Callahan's plan, once you passed over another notch, you would no longer be qualified for life-extending treatment.

Why is the "notch" problem so troubling? We've probably all been in the situation of being in line at a movie theater when people are admitted and then the line is halted. How does the person feel who is the next person in line but doesn't get admitted because of the "notch"? Somehow it seems unfair for there to be an arbitrary cutoff. What would the public response likely be to a new kind of "notch" problem? Suppose a doctor notices that a patient is above the cutoff age (85 or whatever). At that point, it would no longer be possible to provide life-extending treatment.

The notch problem comes up when we try to put clear boundaries around when aging begins. In fact, Callahan takes for granted that old age is a distinct stage of life, perhaps comparable to adolescence, with certain boundaries and distinctive characteristics. But we might wonder whether aging fits that picture anymore. Some gerontologists, such as Bernice Neugarten, argue that America today is now more of an "age-irrelevant" society, that people of advanced ages—those over 70 or 80—cannot be stereotyped with any set of fixed characteristics. If America is becoming the kind of society where chronological age makes less and less difference, then Callahan's proposal would seem to face some problems in being accepted.

Euthanasia and suicide.   Another issue that comes up in considering Callahan's proposal is that of euthanasia and assisted suicide, a subject taken up in the third controversy in this book. Callahan, in other writings, makes it clear that he is against deliberately killing people or having doctors collaborate with patients who want help in ending their lives. Callahan's rationing proposal calls for holding back on treatment, not directly killing people, say, by an injection. But other critics have wondered if Callahan's argument isn't self-contradictory. Why is it acceptable to hold back treatment, when that holding back will predictably result in a patient's death, but not acceptable to cooperate with a patient who voluntarily asks for help in ending life?

It seems as if Callahan is calling for involuntary death for people above a fixed age, but at the same time he wants to prohibit acts, such as voluntary euthanasia, that people might adopt as a matter of personal choice. Is it possible that his own proposal could make more headway if instead he called for more voluntary withdrawal of treatment for people of advanced age (Battin, 1987)? And if we moved to a voluntary system, rather than the involuntary one urged by Callahan, what might be the likely consequences for society? For health professionals like doctors and nurses? For older people themselves?

The questions continue, and the debate goes on. Callahan himself has maintained his original call for age-based rationing. But he has gone further in calling for wider reform of health care. He makes it clear that, in his view, not only must health care for the elderly be rationed but other hard choices will have to be made to have a just system for all (Callahan, 1990). Whether he is right remains the subject of vigorous debate.

Why We Must Set Limits

Daniel Callahan

In October 1986 Dr. Thomas Starzl of Presbyterian University Hospital in Pittsburgh successfully transplanted a liver into a seventy-six-year-old woman, thereby extending to the elderly patient one of the most technologically sophisticated and expensive kinds of medical treatment available (the typical cost of such an operation is more than $200,000). Not long after that, Congress brought organ transplants under Medicare coverage, thus guaranteeing an even greater range of this form of life-saving care for older age groups.

That is, on its face, the kind of medical progress we usually hail: a triumph of medical technology and a newfound benefit provided by an established health-care program. But at the same time those events were taking place, a government campaign for cost containment was under way, with a special focus on Medicare. It is not hard to understand why.

In 1980 people over age sixty-five—11 percent of the population—accounted for 29 percent of the total American health-care expenditures of $219.4 billion. By 1986 the elderly accounted for 31 percent of the total expenditures of $450 billion. Annual Medicare costs are projected to rise from $75 billion in 1986 to $114 billion by the year 2000, and that is in current, not inflated, dollars.

Is it sensible, in the face of rapidly increasing health-care costs for the elderly, to press forward with new and expensive ways of extending their lives? Is it possible to hope to control costs while simultaneously supporting innovative and costly research? Those are now unavoidable questions. Medicare costs are rising at an extraordinary pace, fueled by an increasing number and proportion of the elderly. The fastest-growing age group in the United States is comprised of those over age eighty-five, increasing at a rate of about 10 percent every two years. By the year 2040, it has been projected, the elderly will represent 21 percent of the population and consume 45 percent of all health-care expenditures. How can costs of that magnitude be borne?

Yet there is another powerful reality to consider that moves in a different direction: Medicare and Medicaid are grossly inadequate in meeting the real and full needs of the elderly. The system fails most notably in providing decent long-term care and home care. Members of minority groups, and single or widowed women, are particularly disadvantaged. How will it be possible, then, to provide the growing number of elderly with even present levels of care, and also rid the system of its inadequacies and inequities, and yet at the same time add expensive new technologies?

The straight answer is that it will be impossible to do all those things and, worse still, it may be harmful even to try. The economic burdens that combination would impose on younger age groups, and the skewing of national social priorities too heavily toward health care, would themselves be good reasons to hesitate.

Source: "Setting Limits," by D. Callahan in *A Good Old Age: The Paradox of Setting Limits* (pp. 23-35) edited by P. Homer and M. Holstien, 1990, New York: Simon and Schuster. Copyright © 1987 by Daniel Callahan. Reprinted by permission.

Beyond Economics:
What Is Good for the Elderly?

My concern, however, extends beyond the crisis in health-care costs. "I want to lay the foundation for a more austere thesis: that even with relatively ample resources, there will be better ways in the future to spend our money than on indefinitely extending the life of the elderly. That is neither a wise social goal nor one that the aged themselves should want, however compellingly it will attract them. . . . Our affluence and refusal to accept limits have led and allowed us to evade some deeper truths about the living of a good life and the place of aging and death in that life" (*SL*, 53, 116).[1]

The coming economic crisis provides a much-needed opportunity to ask some fundamental questions. Just what is it that we want medicine to do for us as we age? Other cultures have believed that aging should be accepted, and that it should be in part a time of preparation for death. Our culture seems increasingly to dispute that view, preferring instead, it often seems, to think of aging as hardly more than another disease, to be fought and rejected. Why does our culture have such difficulty with this question?

Let me start by saying that "the place of the elderly in a good society is a communal, not only an individual, question. It goes unexplored in a culture that does not easily speak the language of community and mutual responsibility. The demands of our interest-group political life constitute another obstacle. . . . It is most at home using the language of individual rights as part of its campaigns, and can rarely afford the luxury of publicly recognizing the competing needs of other groups. Yet the greatest obstacle may be our almost utter inability to find a meaningful place in public discourse for suffering and decline in life. They are recognized only as enemies to be fought: with science, with social programs, and with a supreme optimism that with sufficient energy and imagination they can be overcome. We have created a way of life that can only leave serious questions of limits, finitude, the proper ends of human life, of evil and suffering, in the realm of the private self or of religion; they are thus treated as incorrigibly subjective or merely pietistic" (*SL*, 220).

In its long-standing ambition to forestall death, medicine has reached its last frontier in the care of the aged. Of course children and young adults still die of maladies that are open to potential cure, but the highest proportion of the dying (70 percent) are over sixty-five. If death is ever to be humbled, that is where endless work remains to be done. This defiant battle against death and decline is not limited to medicine. Our culture has worked hard to redefine old age as a time of liberation, but not decline, a time of travel, of new ventures in education and self-discovery, of the ever-accessible tennis court or golf course, and of delightfully periodic but thankfully brief visits from well-behaved grandchildren. That is, to be sure, an idealized picture, but it arouses hopes that spur medicine to wage an aggressive war against the infirmities of old age.

As we have seen, the costs of such a war would be prohibitive. No matter how much is spent, the ultimate problem will still remain: People will grow old and die. Worse still, by pretending that old age can be turned into a kind of endless middle age, we rob it of any meaning.

The Meaning and Significance
of Old Age

There are various sources of meaning and significance available for the aged, but it is the elderly's particular obligation to the future that I believe is essential. "Not only is it the most neglected perspective on the elderly, but it is the most pertinent as we try to understand the problem of their health care. The young—children and young adults—most justly and appropriately spend their time preparing for future roles and developing a self pertinent to them. The mature adult has the responsibility to procreate and rear the next generation and to manage the present society. What can the elderly most appropriately do? It should be the special role of the elderly to be the moral conservators of that which has been and the most active proponents of that which will be after they are no longer here. Their indispensable role as conservators is what generates what I believe ought to be the *primary* aspiration of the old, which is to serve the young and the future. Just as they were once the heirs of a society built by others, who passed on to them what they needed to know to keep going, so are they likewise obliged to do the same for those who will follow them.

"Only the old—who alone have seen in their long lives first a future on the horizon and then its actual arrival—can know what it means to go from past through present to future. That is valuable and unique knowledge. If the young are to flourish, then the old should step aside in an active way, working until the very end to do what they can to leave behind them a world hopeful for the young and worthy of bequest. The acceptance of their aging and death will be the principal stimulus to doing this. It is this seemingly paradoxical combination of withdrawal to prepare for death and an active, helpful leave-taking oriented toward the young which provides the possibility for meaning and significance in a contemporary context. Meaning is provided because there is a purpose in that kind of aging, combining an identity for the self with the serving of a critical function in the lives of others—that of linking the past, present, and future—something which, even if they are unaware of it, they cannot do without. Significance is provided because society, in recognizing and encouraging the aged in their duties toward the young, gives them a clear and important role, one that both is necessary for the common good and that *only* they can play" (*SL*, 43).

It is important to underscore that while the elderly have an obligation to serve the young, the young and society have a duty to assist the elderly. Before any limits are imposed, policies and programs must be in place to help the elderly live out a "natural life span," and beyond that to provide the means to relieve suffering.

A "Natural Life Span" and a "Tolerable Death"

Earlier generations accepted the idea that there was a "natural life span"—the biblical norm of three-score and ten captures that notion. It is an idea well worth reconsidering and would provide us with a meaningful and realizable goal. Modern medicine and biology have insinuated the belief that the average life span is not a natural fact at all, but instead one that is strictly dependent on the state of medical knowledge and skill. And there is much to that belief as a statistical fact: Average life expectancy continues to increase, with no end in sight.

There are, moreover, other strong obstacles to the development of a notion of a "natural life span." This notion "requires a number of conditions we seem reluctant to agree to: (1) that life has relatively fixed stages—a notion rejected on the ground that we are free to make of our different stages of chronological age whatever we want; biology presents no unalterable philosophical and moral constraints or any clear pointers; (2) that death may present an 'absolute limit' to life—an idea repudiated because of the ability of medicine to constantly push back the boundary line between life and death; life is an open-ended possibility, not a closed circle; (3) that old age is of necessity marked by decline and thus requires a unique set of meanings to take account of that fact—a viewpoint that must be rejected as part of the political struggle against ageism, which would make of the old a deviant, marginal, and burdensome group; and (4) that 'our civilization' would be better off if it shared some common view of 'the whole of life'—rejected as a politically hazardous notion, more congenial to authoritarian and collectivist cultures than to those marked by moral and religious pluralism and individualism" (*SL*, 40-41).

I want to argue that we can have and must have a notion of a "natural life span" that is based on some deeper understanding of human needs and possibilities, not on the state of medical technology. I offer a definition of the "natural life span" as "one in which life's possibilities have on the whole been achieved and after which death may be understood as a sad, but nonetheless relatively acceptable event.

"Each part of that definition requires some explanation. What do I mean when I say that 'one's life possibilities have on the whole been accomplished'? I mean something very simple: that most of those opportunities which life affords people will have been achieved by that point. Life affords us a number of opportunities. These include work, love, the procreating and raising of a family, life with others, the pursuit of moral and other ideals, the experience of beauty, travel, and knowledge, among others. By old age—and here I mean even by the age of 65—most of us will have had a chance to experience those goods; and will certainly experience them by our late 70s or early 80s. It is not that life will cease, after those ages, to offer us some new opportunities; we might do something we have never done but always sought to do. Nor is it that life will necessarily cease to offer us opportunities to continue experiencing its earlier benefits. Ordinarily it will not. But what we have accomplished by old age is the having of the opportunities themselves, and to some relatively full degree. Many people, sadly, fail to have all the opportunities they might have: they may never have found love, may not have had the income to travel, may not have gained much knowledge through lack of education, and so on. More old age is not likely to make up for those deficiencies, however; the pattern of such lives, including their deprivations, is not likely to change significantly in old age, much less open up radically new opportunities hitherto missing" (*SL*, 66-67).

A longer life does not guarantee a better life. No matter how long medicine enables people to live, death at any time—at age 90 or 100 or 110—would frustrate some possibility, some as-yet-unrealized goal. The easily preventable death of a young child is an outrage. Death from an incurable disease of someone in the prime of young adulthood is a trag-

edy. But death at an old age, after a long and full life, is simply sad, a part of life itself, what I would call a "tolerable death."

This notion of a "tolerable death" helps illumine the concept of a "natural life span," and together these two notions set the foundation for an appropriate goal for medicine in its approach to aging. "My definition of a 'tolerable death' is this: the individual event of death at that stage in a life span when (a) one's life possibilities have on the whole been accomplished; (b) one's moral obligations to those for whom one has had responsibility have been discharged; and (c) one's death will not seem to others an offense to sense or sensibility, or tempt others to despair and rage at the finitude of human existence. Note the most obvious feature of this definition: it is a biographical, not a biological, definition" (*SL*, 66).

The Principles and Priorities of a Plan

How might we devise a plan to limit the costs of health care for the aged under public entitlement programs that is fair, humane, and sensitive to their special requirements and dignity? Let me suggest three principles to undergird a quest for limits:

"1. Government has a duty, based on our collective social obligations, to help people live out a natural life span, but not actively to help extend life medically beyond that point. By life-extending treatment, I will mean any medical intervention, technology, procedure, or medication whose ordinary effect is to forestall the moment of death, whether or not the treatment affects the underlying life-threatening disease or biological process.

2. Government is obliged to develop, employ, and pay for only that kind and degree of life-extending technology necessary for medicine to achieve and serve the end of a natural life span; the question is not whether a technology is available that can save a life, but whether there is an obligation to use the technology.

3. Beyond the point of a natural life span, government should provide only the means necessary for the relief of suffering, not life-extending technology" (*SL*, 137-38).

What would the actual policy look like? "A full policy plan would include detailed directions, for example, for determining priorities within basic biological research, within health-care delivery, and between research and delivery. That I will not try to provide. I can only sketch a possible trajectory—or, to switch metaphors, a kind of likely general story. But if that at least can be done in a coherent fashion, avoiding the most flagrant contradictions, it might represent some useful movement" (*SL*, 141-42).

Three elements of health policy emerge from my position: "The first is the need for an antidote to the major cause of a mistaken moral emphasis in the care of the elderly and a likely source of growing high costs of their care in the years ahead. That cause is constant innovation in high-technology medicine relentlessly applied to life-extending care of the elderly; it is a blessing that too often turns into a curse. . . . No technology should be developed or applied to the elderly that does not promise great and inexpensive improvement in the quality of their lives, no matter how promising for life extension. Incremental gains, achieved at high cost, should be considered unacceptable. Forthright government declarations that Medicare reimbursement will not be available for technologies that do not achieve a high, very high, standard of efficacy would discourage development of marginally beneficial items" (*SL*, 142, 143).

"The second element is a need to focus on those subgroups of the elderly—particularly women, the poor, and minorities—who have as yet not been well served, for whom a strong claim can be entered for more help from the young and society more generally. . . . The elderly (both poor and middle-class) can have no decent sense of security unless there is a full reform of the system of health care. It may well be that reforms of the sweeping

kind implied in these widely voiced criticisms could more than consume in the short run any savings generated by inhibitions of the kind I am proposing in the development and use of medical technology. But they would address a problem that technological development does nothing to meet. They would also reassure the old that there will be a floor of security under their old age and that ill health will not ruin them financially, destroy their freedom, or leave them dependent upon their children (to the detriment of both)" (*SL*, 142, 147).

"The third is a set of high-priority health and welfare needs—nursing and long-term care, prevention—which would have to be met in pursuit of the goals I have proposed. . . . Beyond avoiding a premature death, what do the elderly need from medicine to complete their lives in an acceptable way? They need to be as independent as possible, freed from excess worry about the financial or familial burdens of ill health, and physically and emotionally positioned to seek whatever meaning and significance can be found in old age. Medicine can only try to maintain the health which facilitates that latter quest, not guarantee its success. That facilitation is enhanced by physical mobility, mental alertness, and emotional stability. Chronic illness, pain, and suffering are all major impediments and of course appropriate targets for medical research and improved health-care delivery. Major research priorities should be those chronic illnesses which so burden the later years and which have accompanied the increase in longevity" (*SL*, 142, 149).

Euthanasia and Assisted Suicide
Some might view my position as an endorsement of euthanasia and assisted suicide. My position "is exactly the opposite: a sanctioning of mercy killing and assisted suicide for the elderly would offer them little practical help and would serve as a threatening symbol of devaluation of old age. . . . Were euthanasia and assisted suicide to be legalized, would there be a large and hitherto restrained group of elderly eager to take advantage of the new

opportunity? There is no evidence to suggest that there would be, in either this country or in any other. But even if there might be some, what larger significance might the elderly in general draw from the new situation? It would be perfectly plausible for them to interpret it as the granting of a new freedom. It would be no less plausible for them to interpret it as a societal concession to the view that old age can have no meaning and significance if accompanied by decline, pain, and despair. It would be to come close to saying officially that old age can be empty and pointless and that society must give up on elderly people. For the young it could convey the message that pain is not to be endured, that community cannot be found for many of the old, and that a life not marked by good health, by hope and vitality, is not a life worth living. . . .

"What do we as a society want to say about the elderly and their lives? If one believes that the old should not be rejected, that old age is worthy of respect, that the old have as valid a social place as any other age group, and that the old are as diverse in their temperaments and outlooks as any other age group, an endorsement of a special need for euthanasia for the old seems to belie all those commitments. It would be a way of legitimizing the view that old age is a special time of lost hopes, empty futures, and personal pointlessness. Alternatively, if it is believed that old age can have a special value, that it can—with the right cultural, economic, and political support—be a time of meaning and significance, then one will not embrace euthanasia as a special solution for the problem of old age, either for the aged as individuals or for the aged as a group. It would convey precisely the wrong symbolism. To sanction euthanasia as a special benefit for the aged would signal a direct contradiction to an effort to give meaning and significance to old age" (*SL*, 194, 196, 197). We as a society should instead guarantee elderly persons greater control over their own dying—and particularly an enforceable right to refuse aggressive life-extending treatment.

Conclusion

The system I propose would not immediately bring down the cost of care of the elderly; it would add cost. But it would set in place the beginning of a new understanding of old age, one that would admit of eventual stabilization and limits. The elderly will not be served by a belief that only a lack of resources, better financing mechanisms, or political power stands between them and the limitations of their bodies. The good of younger age groups will not be served by inspiring in them a desire to live to an old age that maintains the vitality of youth indefinitely, as if old age were nothing but a sign that medicine has failed its mission. The future of our society will not be served by allowing expenditures on health care for the elderly to escalate endlessly and uncontrollably, fueled by the false altruistic belief that anything less is to deny the elderly their dignity. Nor will it be aided by the pervasive kind of self-serving argument that urges the young to support such a crusade because they will eventually benefit from it.

We require instead an understanding of the process of aging and death that looks to our obligation to the young and to the future, that recognizes the necessity of limits and the acceptance of decline and death, and that values the old for their age and not for their continuing youthful vitality. In the name of accepting the elderly and repudiating discrimination against them, we have succeeded mainly in pretending that with enough will and money the unpleasant part of old age can be abolished. In the name of medical progress we have carried out a relentless war against death and decline, failing to ask in any probing way if that will give us a better society for all.

"There is little danger that the views I advance here will elicit such instant acclaim (or any acclaim, for that matter) that the present generation of the elderly will feel much of their effect. That could take two or three decades if there is any merit in what I say, and what I am looking for is not any quick change but the beginning of a long-term discussion, one that will perhaps lead people to change their thinking, and most important, their expectations, about old age and death" (*SL*, 10).

Note

1. Daniel Callahan, *Setting Limits: Medical Goals in an Aging Society* (New York: Simon and Schuster, 1987). References may appear in this text with the notation "*SL.*"

READING 6

The Pied Piper Returns for the Old Folks

Nat Hentoff

I expect that the sardonic Dean of Dublin's Saint Patrick's Cathedral, Jonathan Swift, would appreciate Daniel Callahan's *Setting Limits*—though not in the way he would be supposed to. Swift, you will recall, at a time of terrible poverty and hunger in Ireland, wrote *A Modest Proposal.* Rather than having the children of the poor continue to be such a burden to their parents and their nation, why not persuade the poor to raise their children to be slaughtered at the right, succulent time and sold to the rich as delicacies for dining?

What could be more humane? The children would be spared a life of poverty, their parents would be saved from starvation, and the overall economy of Ireland would be in better shape.

So, I thought, Callahan, wanting to dramatize the parlous and poignant state of America's elderly, has created his modern version of *A Modest Proposal.*

I was wrong. He's not jiving. . . .

Source: "The Pied Piper Returns for the Old Folks" by N. Hentoff, *The Village Voice* (April 26, 1988). Reprinted by permission of the author and *The Village Voice.*

Callahan sees "a natural life span" as being ready to say goodbye in one's late seventies or early eighties. He hasn't fixed on an exact age yet. Don't lose your birth certificate.

If people persist in living beyond the time that Callahan, if not God, has allotted them, the government will move in. Congress will require that anybody past that age must be denied Medicare payments for such procedures as certain forms of open heart surgery, certain extended stays in an intensive care unit, and who knows what else.

Moreover, as an index of how human the spirit of *Setting Limits* is, if an old person is diagnosed as being in a chronic vegetative state (some physicians screw up this diagnosis), the Callahan plan mandates that the feeding tube be denied or removed. (No one is certain whether someone actually in a persistent vegetative state can *feel* what's going on while being starved to death. If there is a sensation, there is no more horrible way to die.)

What about the elderly who don't have to depend on Medicare? Millions of the poor and middle class have no other choice than to go to the government, but there are some old folks with money. They, of course, do not have to pay any attention to Daniel Callahan at all. Like the well-to-do from time immemorial, they will get any degree of medical care they want.

So, *Setting Limits* is class-biased in the most fundamental way. People without resources in need of certain kinds of care will die sooner than old folks who do not have to depend on the government and Daniel Callahan. . . .

Callahan reveals that once we start going down the slippery slope of utilitarianism, we slide by— faster and faster—a lot of old-timey ethical norms. Like the declaration of the Catholic bishops of America that medical care is "indispensable to the protection of human dignity." The bishops didn't say that dignity is only for people who can afford it. They know that if you're 84, and only Medicare can pay your bills but says it won't pay for treatment that will extend your life, then your "human dignity" is shot to hell. . . .

It must be pointed out that Daniel Callahan does not expect or intend his design for natural dying to be implemented soon. First of all, the public will have to be brought around. But that shouldn't be too difficult in the long run. I am aware of few organized protests against the court decisions in a number of states that feeding tubes can be removed from patients—many of them elderly—who are not terminally ill and are not in intractable pain. And some of these people may not be in a persistently vegetative state. (For instance, Nancy Ellen Jobes in New Jersey.)

So, the way the Zeitgeist is going, I think public opinion could eventually be won over to Callahan's modest proposal. But he has another reason to want to wait. He doesn't want his vision of "setting limits" to go into effect until society has assured the elderly access to decent long-term home care or nursing home care as well as better coverage for drugs, eyeglasses, and the like.

Even if all that were to happen, there still would be profound ethical and constitutional problems. What kind of society will we have become if we tuck in the elderly in nursing homes and then refuse them medical treatment that would prolong their lives?

And what of the physicians who will find it abhorrent to limit the care they give solely on the basis of age? As a presumably penitent former Nazi doctor said, "Either one is a doctor or one is not."

On the other hand, if the Callahan plan is not to begin for a while, new kinds of doctors can be trained who will take a utilitarian rather than a Hippocratic oath. ("I will never forget that my dedication is to the society as a whole rather to any individual patient.") Already, I have been told by a physician who heads a large teaching institution that a growing number of doctors are spending less time and attention on the elderly. There are similar reports from other such places.

Meanwhile, nobody I've read or heard on the Callahan proposal has mentioned the Fourteenth Amendment and its insistence that all of us must have "equal protection of the laws." What Callahan aims to do is take an entire class of people—on the basis only of their age—and deny them medical care that might prolong their lives. This is not quite *Dred Scott,* but even though the elderly are not yet at the level of close constitutional scrutiny given by the Supreme Court to blacks, other minorities, and women, the old can't be pushed into the grave just like that, can they?

Or can they? Some of the more influential luminaries in the nation—Joe Califano, George Will, and a fleet of bioethicists, among them—have heralded *Setting Limits* as the way to go.

Will you be ready?

Letting Individuals Decide

Terrie Wetle and Richard W. Besdine

Setting Limits is disturbing in several ways. First, there is the premise that we are justified in setting public policy that determines a "natural life span" for an entire cohort of the population. Referring to the Nazi concept of the *Untermensch,* Callahan notes the evils that result from the political deter- mination that a life is dispensable, but he sets aside the concern far too easily that the elderly—or any other age group, for that matter—would interpret his "natural life span" policy as devaluation of life in old age.

A second concern is whether the program could be applied consistently and fairly. Noting that a policy to limit public payment for life-sustaining care on the basis of age would lead to a two-tiered system in which wealthy older people could still buy such care, Callahan still does not believe that "a society would be made morally intolerable by that kind of imbalance." It was just such an imbal- ance between those who could pay for care and those who could not that led to the enactment of Medicare and Medicaid 25 years ago.

Many distinctions on which the proposed pro- gram would depend are not made clearly or reli- ably. For example, the distinction between inter- ventions that prolong life and those that relieve suffering is perhaps easy to make conceptually and in situations, but not at the bedside or in that vast middle ground where the majority of cases are found. An 80-year-old man with excruciating ab- dominal pain and fecal vomiting due to adhesions obstructing his small bowel will have his suffering relieved quickly and best by surgery to release the obstruction. In the process, his life may also be saved. We wonder whether Callahan would urge morphine rather than surgery for such a patient.

Callahan uses the treatment of diabetes to define the rules of his game further. Considering insulin a life-prolonging rather than a symptom-relieving treatment, he states that a diabetic using insulin before the end of his policy-defined natural life span would be "grandfathered" into a continuation of that medication, whereas the person who ac- quires diabetes after the cutoff age would not be provided such treatment. Similarly, dialysis would be continued indefinitely if it was initiated before the cutoff date, but it would not be provided for late-onset renal disease. Thus, the patient whose diabetes or renal failure develops before the cutoff age and who begins treatment promptly is given preference over the person healthy at that age but in whom illness develops later. This is a peculiar logic.

Much of the book, it seems, is based on the premise that such a policy would save the tax- payer money and allow a reallocation of resources. It is not clear, nor is evidence provided, that the policy actually would accomplish these goals. In fact, it is possible that certain "life-prolonging" interventions also improve function, resulting in the decreased use of other expensive forms of care.

Certainly, the book is worth reading, but with a critical eye. Care must be taken to avoid facile applications of its arguments in support of neg-

Source: "Letting Individuals Decide," by T. Wetle and R. W. Besdine, 1988, *New England Journal of Medicine,* 319(7): pp. 452-53. Reprinted with permission of the *New England Journal of Medicine.*

ative views of older people. Although Callahan has warned against the tyranny of individualism throughout his career, perhaps aging and health care are one arena in which an acute focus on the individual is most appropriate. The decision to provide or withhold life-prolonging interventions may still be best left to the individual patient, family, and care provider.

READING 8

Aim Not Just for Longer Life, but Expanded "Health Span"

Daniel Perry and Robert Butler

Most Americans instinctively recoil at the thought that their government would try to save money by pulling the plug on life-sustaining care when it is needed by older people. In this case, their instincts are correct.

To determine a person's access to medical care solely on the basis of that person's age is clearly unfair, unworkable and unnecessary. It is wrong to blame the elderly for rising hospital expenses and physicians' fees that are driven principally by other factors or to require older Americans to pay for the failure of government and industry to find a more humane and workable policy to curb health care costs.

President Reagan signed into law the most sweeping Medicare expansion in that program's 22-year history, indicating the nation's strong commitment to providing health care to the elderly. The new catastrophic care program will cost about $31 billion over five years. Even that amount will seem small when compared to proposals for insuring

Source: "Aim Not Just for a Longer Life, but Expanded 'Health Span'," by D. Perry and R. Butler, *The Washington Post* (December 20, 1988). Reprinted by permission of the authors.

Americans against the costs of long-term care, the next major health care issue to face Congress and the Bush presidency.

As the curtain rose on Congressional debate over long-term care, some came forward to argue that the United States could save billions by simply denying lifesaving medical interventions to people over a certain age—say 65 to 75. But there is a better way to control costs of providing health care to the elderly: work to eliminate the very afflictions of old age, which are costing billions in health care, long-term care, and lost productivity. By attacking diseases associated with aging—such as Alzheimer's disease, stroke, osteoporosis, arthritis and others—the need for many costly medical procedures, lengthy hospital stays and financially draining long-term care could be ended or reduced.

Why not start with a real commitment to scientific research that could extend the healthful middle years of life and compress the decline of aging into a very short time?

Why not redirect federal research efforts to aim for scientific and medical discoveries to reduce frailty, improve health status and increase independence in older people? It's a far better goal—and more realistic—than rationing medical treatment.

At present, however, aging research is not where the U.S. government is placing its biggest bets. Most people don't believe much can be done to change aging. Therefore, research funds generally go elsewhere.

There is every reason to fear spiraling health costs if effective ways to lengthen healthy years and delay the onset of debilitating age are not found before the baby boomers become the biggest Medicare generation in history.

Americans already are paying billions because medical science lacks the ability to cure, prevent or postpone many chronic maladies associated with aging. And national investment in research to avoid these costs is minuscule when compared to the billions spent for treatment.

Of the $167 billion a year spent on health care for people over age 65, far less than one half of 1 percent of that amount is reinvested in research that could lead to lower health care costs for chronic diseases and disabilities. That is a poor investment strategy for a nation soon to experience the largest senior boom in history.

Tinkering with changes in the health care delivery system can save some money, but these savings will not equal the long-term benefits of dramatic medical and scientific changes that alter the way people experience old age.

If scientists do not find a way to treat Alzheimer's, for instance, by the middle of the next century, there will be five times as many victims of this disease as there are now simply because of the demographic shift that is occurring. Incontinence, memory loss and immobility are the main factors driving long-term care and high health costs to the elderly. If no advances occur in these and other conditions of aging, up to 6 million older Americans will be living in nursing homes, instead of the 1 million who are there today.

Unfortunately, there may be no way to prevent aging per se. However, there are conditions that occur only as a person ages. Many of these can be prevented. The risk of suffering a chronic disease such as arthritis or osteoporosis is very slight at middle age. But from the forties onward, that risk doubles exponentially about every five years until someone in the mid-eighties has about a one-in-three chance of having dementia, immobility, incontinence or other age-related disabilities.

If medicine could delay the beginning of decline by as few as five years, many conditions and the costs they incur could be cut in half. The ability to re-set biological clocks to forestall some of the decline of aging may be closer than anyone realizes, thanks to new knowledge in immunology and in the molecular genetics of aging.

Answers may be near. Help for immobility, osteoporosis and incontinence can be achieved with only a modest extension of present technologies. If the U.S. doubles its present meager $30 million for osteoporosis research, by the year 2010 this condition could be eliminated as a major public health problem, which now affects 90 percent of all women over 75.

Learning how to postpone aging could help lower health care costs and improve the health of older Americans at the same time. The goal here is not just longer life span but extended "health span," with fewer problems caused by chronic disease.

A Tough Choice on Health Care Costs

William B. Schwartz and Henry Aaron

Daniel Callahan, an ethicist and author of the book *Setting Limits,* has stirred sharp debate over his proposal for slowing the rise in health care costs by eliminating life-extending care for most people over the age of 75.

Mr. Callahan's recommendation has attracted attention because other vaunted panaceas for soaring health care costs, such as health maintenance organizations and other competitive mechanisms, are having little effect.

But Mr. Callahan's proposal suffers from two major shortcomings. First, it almost certainly would not be acceptable to patients, health care providers, or, one suspects, anyone else. Second, it would do almost nothing to slow the rise in costs of medical care.

Mr. Callahan's idea is something less than thoroughly reasoned. He provides no analysis of current costs and offers no estimate of the savings he hopes to achieve. In fact, the impact on costs would be minimal.

In 1986, people aged 75 or older constituted less than 5 percent of the United States population. Because per capita medical costs for the very old run about three times the national average, such costs account for about 15 percent of annual health care spending. Abruptly eliminating half of the services used by this group—a Draconian cut, because even Mr. Callahan has not proposed denying routine care or ignoring life-threatening illness in the aged who are otherwise healthy—would reduce total spending by only about 7 percent.

In recent years, health care spending has risen by 5.5 to 6 percent annually after adjusting for inflation. Thus, a sudden cut in services to the elderly would reduce current outlays by no more than the costs typically grow in a little more than a year—a significant amount but not enough to materially slow the steady climb in health care costs.

Most of the growth in health care spending results from scientific advances—open heart surgery, organ transplants, magnetic resonance imaging, clot-dissolving agents to prevent heart attacks—that are applied to the general population, not just the few who are 75 or older.

Indeed, a simple calculation shows that even if all fruits of future medical progress were denied to the elderly, the nearly 5 percent annual growth rate in medical costs would be slowed by less than half a percentage point.

If cutting care to the elderly won't contain health care costs, what will? The United States is not the first developed country to face this question. The British health care system, which has rationed health care for years, shows that age is only one of many social, medical and economic factors invoked to contain costs.

For example, visible suffering commands far more resources than private pain. The grotesque swollen joints and massive bleeding of hemophiliacs have caused the British to reject all restrictions on therapy. But because angina pectoris, or chest pain from coronary artery disease, causes silent and invisible suffering, Britain spends less than one-fifth as much as the United States does on coronary artery surgery.

Many other basic societal values also determine what services the British withhold. Services dependent on equipment allocated by bureaucrats located far from the point of treatment are rationed far more than are those dependent on resources readily available in hospitals. A case in point: many major British hospitals lack a CAT scanner, now widely acknowledged to be vital in modern diagnosis.

Simple fear also shapes rationing decisions. The dread of cancer has led the British not to stint on radiotherapy or chemotherapy even for cases in which the treatment is designed only to relieve pain rather than to prolong life.

Aggregate costs of therapy is a further key factor. Bone marrow transplants, averaging $50,000 to $100,000 a patient, are provided as often in Britain as in the United States, largely because only a few patients require them.

In contrast, some British patients must wait five years for hip replacements because the thousands of people with arthritic hips would impose burdensome costs on the health care system if all were treated.

One British expert, asked what would happen if a high-cost curative drug became available for a common form of metastatic cancer, responded, "I wake up screaming at such a prospect" and expressed the opinion that many people would go untreated.

If the American public ever gets serious about containing health care costs, rationing of treatment will likely proceed along lines similar to those in Britain, not simply on the basis of age. But Americans are unlikely to be as willing as the British to accept reduced quality of care. Americans, promptly informed by the media of each new medical advance, are quick to demand the new treatment.

How will we resolve the conflict in the basically incompatible goals of controlling costs while maintaining quality? Some real economies can be achieved by increased efficiency, but no matter what, a significant reduction in the growth of medical spending will require the sacrifice of beneficial services not by just the very old but by all of us.

Efficient Allocation of Health Care to the Elderly

Lawrence DeBrock

Source: "Efficient Allocation of Health Care to the Elderly" by L. DeBrock in *Set No Limits*, edited by R. Barry and G. Bradley, 1991, Chicago: University of Illinois Press. Copyright 1991 by the Board of Trustees of the University of Illinois. Reprinted with the permission of the University of Illinois Press.

As front pages of newspapers continue to remind us, public policy toward the aged is a very sensitive and important policy issue. While policy-makers wrangle with the issues of what to do and how to pay for the resulting programs, constant budget pressures have caused many analysts to scour the landscape for relief. Some have called for a re-evaluation for our programs for the elderly.[1] Make no mistake about the well-placed motives of these observers. Their attack is not on the elderly per se, but on the size of public expenditures directed to that group. . . .

The combination of rapid growth in health-care expenditures in the United States coupled with the changing demographics has led some individuals to conclude that society must intervene in the allocation decisions of the medical marketplace. Proposals for rationing services are not new, and the forms of rationing involve economic and noneconomic criteria.[4] Those calling for intervention, of which Daniel Callahan may be the most obvious, believe that we as a society must make some hard rationing decisions about the use of our limited resources. In that regard, they are 100 percent correct. All goods are subject to the laws of scarcity and therefore *must* be rationed. What can be questioned, however, is the nature of the allocation mechanism suggested. To evaluate fully the soundness of the age-based criterion, all costs, benefits, and implications must be examined. . . .

Moral Hazard

When a population is at risk of a harmful event, but the occurrence of this event is not universal, society has long recognized the advantage of pooling risk. In other eras, when a neighbor's house burned down, farmers would interrupt their own work to provide labor and material to replace the lost structure. Today, we are more than happy to pay insurance companies for the service they provide in finding other individuals to help us share the risk of one of our houses burning down. Loss of health is just one of many things against which we can buy insurance.

Unfortunately, the existence of insurance often leads to a serious inefficiency called moral hazard. Moral hazard refers to situations where the existence of the insurance against some event makes the event more likely to occur. Put differently, if some-one else (an insurance company or a government agency) is paying for some event, you are more likely to overconsume. . . .

By the end of the 1970s, the issue of cost containment became more important to the private sector. . . . This demand side movement was the impetus for the growth of CMPs (competitive medical plans). Led most notably by the emerging health maintenance organizations (HMOs), CMPs offered insurance policies that returned some notion of the relative value of the resources to those parties directly involved in the allocation process. . . .

The common principle linking the CMPs is the inherent cost-containment mechanisms. The actual application of pressure on costs comes from one or all participants in the transaction. Some plans force the provider to bear the risk by paying a group of doctors (the HMO providers, for example) a fixed fee regardless of the health-care services that will be eventually supplied. Some plans force the consumer to be more sensitive to costs by strict application of nontrivial copayments, returning to price as a rationing device. Some plans use a third party, the insurance company's management utilization review team, as a device for alerting the two principal decision-makers, the patient and the provider, of the real costs of the health-care procedures. Someone in authority reviews utilization patterns by providers of the health care. Again, such systems vary in nature, but all have the characteristic of making some decision-maker the party at risk. Such systems have been shown to be quite effective in restricting utilization on the margin.[12]

Consider the example of Medicare's prospective payment system (PPS). Faced with extreme cost increases in a time of already severe budgetary pressures, the federal government made a significant policy change in 1983. Using the diagnosis-related group (DRG) classification system, the government determined a fixed price to be paid for a given incidence of medical care according to the most appropriate DRG. If the hospital could provide the service at a cost below the PPS rate, the residual could be kept as profit. If the hospital spent

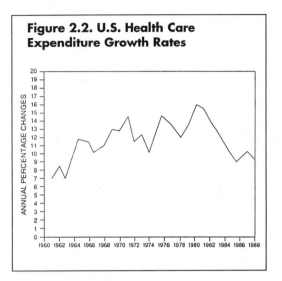

Figure 2.2. U.S. Health Care Expenditure Growth Rates

Figure 2.3. Medicare Hospital Days (per 1,000 enrollees)

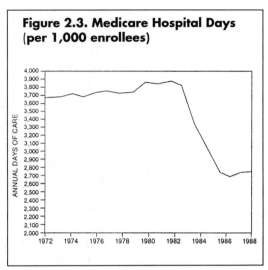

more on the patient than the PPS amount, the excess came from hospital funds. Note the economic significance of this mechanism. The provider is now the party at risk for each resource expended. Allocation decisions will be more efficient as they will be based on marginal values and costs.

PPS has been in place long enough to have produced early signals of its success as a cost-containment device. While the data are not sufficiently rich at a micro level to permit a thorough statistical study, we do have some simple evidence. Figures 2.2 and 2.3 offer some confirmation that cost containment is working under the PPS regime instituted in 1983. Figure 2.2 presents a picture of the percentage change in national health care expenditures.[13] While the general trend line is not dramatic, it is clear that the annual change in health-care expenditures began to slow in the early 1980s. This corresponds with the introduction of PPS for Medicare and the emergence of CMPs in the private insurance market. Even more dramatic evidence of the effect of capitation payments (i.e., PPS) comes from the data on hospital days for the elderly. Figure 2.3 shows that the number of Medicare hospital days of care per 1,000 aged enrollees dropped pre-

cipitously with the introduction of PPS.[14] Again, the cost-containing incentives provided by such a system should be apparent. . . .

Conclusion

The United States has high quality health care, and we spend a large amount for this service. Many argue that we spend too much on health care. We have demonstrated the real possibility of overspending due to moral hazard. Recent trends toward cost containment promise more efficient outcomes.

Our future spending patterns will undoubtedly grow. This growth will not just be a result of increasing population. Rather, much of the growth will come because we will be getting richer. Wealthier people buy an increasingly larger amount of health care. Microeconomic models that provide theoretical justification of the logic behind such a prediction are numerous. . . . As nations grow more wealthy, they devote a larger percentage of their budgets to health. . . .

Callahan and others take the position that health care markets are somehow tight and that we are going to have to make hard decisions about rationing to be able to provide a minimum level of health care. . . . While the resources devoted to health care are certain to continue to rise, this increase is a natural outcome. It is a reflection of consumer preferences and incomes, as is true of other sectors of spending.[30]

There is nothing special about spending 12 percent of our national income on health care. Given our income elasticity, we can expect national health-care expenditures to be over 15 percent of GNP by the turn of the century. Again, this is not a matter of concern; there is no critical threshold level, no magic percentage limit on health-care expenditures.

This is not the place to put on rose-colored glasses, however. Just as it is clear that health-care expenditures will become an increasing part of our budgets, it is also clear that a solution to the moral hazard problem must be forthcoming. As society takes on more responsibility for the health-care obligations of the elderly, such expenditures could become socially inefficient. The scale of these inefficiencies could indeed be enormous.[31]

What Callahan and his supporters have correctly perceived is the need for *some* policy intervention in the rationing of health care. Society has deemed health care to be, in some sense, a merit good: a privilege owed to everyone in our society. However, in handling the process of making this care available to those not able to access it by their own means, we must be careful to avoid exacerbating the moral hazard problems. Some decision-maker in the allocation process must understand the true resource costs of the health-care procedure in question: some decision-maker must be made the party at risk.

I have tried to make it clear that the question of "resource availability" is wrong-headed. We as a society will have a continually increasing appetite for health-care services. The interesting question is not whether this increase in demand for health care is bad or good. Rather, the question is how to guarantee that the allocation mechanism is both equitable and efficient.

If we were able to solve the moral hazard problem while setting up our social aid programs, we would have no reason to be concerned about the size of health-care expenditures. Consider this simple analogy. We as a society have an ever-increasing appetite for leisure activity. Such expenditures are income elastic; we use them at a greater rate as we get richer. No one is calling for government intervention to ration this industry as its spending takes up more and more of our national income. Why? Because this is a market that "works." The health-care market has demonstrated well-established market failures, and policy-makers have intervened. If we operated these regulatory programs "perfectly," market failures would be mitigated and the outcome would approach the efficient solution. Conversely, a poorly devised intervention scheme results in even more inefficiency than does an unchecked market failure.

Callahan's proposed age-based rule has only one attraction: it is one of the simplest rationing rules one could follow. . . . From an economic standpoint, it should be clear that some form of rationing of resources is a necessity. This is the case in all markets. Regardless of the ethical, moral, and constitutional issues involved with age-based rationing, such a rationing rule has nothing to do with efficiency. Rather than attempt to make decision-makers more aware of the real cost of resources used, such a program would try to limit health care by fiat, by strict application of an arbitrary threshold.

The future will involve hard policy decisions. . . . I have tried to convey the message that the rationing scheme should be centered on efficiency. The key to efficiency lies in making certain that those in a position of deciding care levels— providers, patients, and insurers—have the proper incentives. That is, these allocation makers should be aware that health-care resources are limited and do involve real social cost. Balancing such social costs with social benefits should be the goal of the intervention mechanism, not some single-minded goal of reducing expenditures by simply lopping off one tail of the distribution of users.

Notes

[NOTE: Only the notes that are included in the excerpted material appear here.]

1. For purposes of this paper, the term elderly will be used interchangeably with the term aged; both terms refer to people 65 years of age and older.
4. See, for example, Evans (1983) and Strauss et al. (1986).
12. As should be obvious, the restriction in utilization might have implications for quality of care. Economists argue that providers have the proper incentive to offer the correct level of care for at least two reasons. First, the majority of consumers have alternative choices among health care packages, and second, the very real threat of malpractice litigation forces providers to pay close attention to proper procedures.
13. Data for Figure 2.2 come from Kowalczyk, Freeland, and Levit (1988).
14. Data for Figure 2.3 come from Latta and Keene (1990).
30. As a point of reference, various studies have estimated the income elasticity for automobiles to be greater than

3.0 while that of owner-occupied housing is greater than 1.5.
31. In fact, many of the doomsday scenarios used as evidence to support radical rationing programs are not caused by demographics or technology but are just prime examples of moral hazard. This moral hazard and the spending problems it generates would exist even if our elderly population was not on the growth path we foresee.

References

Evans, R., "Health Care Technology and the Inevitability of Resource Allocation and Rationing Decisions," Parts I and II, *Journal of the American Medical Association* 249 (1983): 2047-53, 2208-19.

Kowalczyk, George I., Mark S. Freeland, and Katharine R. Levit, "Using Marginal Analysis to Evaluate Health Spending Trends," *Health Care Financing Review* 10 (Winter 1988): 123-29.

Latta, Viola B., and Roger Keene, "Use and Cost of Short-Stay Hospital Inpatient Services under Medicare," *Health Care Financing Review* 12 (Fall 1990): 91-99.

Strauss, M. et al., "Rationing of Intensive Care Unit Services. An Everyday Occurrence," *Journal of the American Medical Association* 255 (1986): 1143-46.

QUESTIONS FOR WRITING, REFLECTION, AND DEBATE

1 Is Callahan right in his suggestion that our modern American culture thinks of aging as "hardly more than another disease"? Does it make sense to talk about aging as a "disease" whose cause might be identified and then perhaps even "cured"? How do we decide whether something is a disease? Following Callahan's own argument, would it be a good idea to promote anti-aging research if this might reduce the expenses of geriatric care?

2 Antibiotic therapies like erythromycin today are very inexpensive. According to Callahan's own argument, would they have to be withheld from the very old just because they are "life-extending"? Or is it only expensive therapies that should be withheld? What happens if a cheap therapy helps people to survive an illness but then it turns out to be very expensive to take care of them?

3 How do we know when "rationing" starts taking place? During World War II, everyone knew that butter, gasoline, and other commodities were being rationed. But some critics argue that rationing of health care is *already* going on in America. Is it possible for resources to be "rationed" without public knowledge of it? As a hypothetical exercise, assume that you are a journalist who has just discovered that a local hospital routinely makes decisions about health care based on the age of the patients. Write a short newspaper article bringing public attention to the practice.

4 Hentoff argues that Callahan's proposal is class biased—that is, it discriminates against the poor—because people with money can purchase any amount of medical care they want. Is this argument convincing? Is there any alternative to this arrangement? Does Hentoff's point, if valid, destroy Callahan's argument?

5 At the end of his article, Hentoff argues that the Callahan proposal deprives an entire class of people of the "equal protection of the laws" and he cites the *Dred Scott* case in which the U.S. Supreme Court approved slavery. Is age-based rationing a kind of discrimination like slavery? In what ways is age discrimination like, or unlike, race discrimination? Assume that you are a lawyer arguing this case before the U.S. Supreme Court. Write a "brief" based on Hentoff's general idea and offer your strongest possible arguments to convince the justices.

6 Wetle and Besdine, like Hentoff, cite the case of the Nazis and their program of killing off certain groups of people who were judged unworthy to live. Is it fair to judge Callahan's proposal by comparing it to what the Nazis did? Assume for a moment that you are Daniel Callahan and write a "letter to the editor" defending yourself against this charge of being like the Nazis.

7 Schwartz and Aaron offer economic calculations to suggest that Callahan's proposal, if adopted, won't really save much money as long as rationing is limited to people over age 75. If their figures are right, should Callahan be willing to lower his age limit to 70 or 65? Why or why not?

8 In his article, DeBrock argues that some kind of rationing scheme, perhaps through the marketplace, is inevitable. The only question, he believes, is what rationing scheme is "efficient." If efficiency is the real criterion, then, on DeBrock's own economic grounds, why wouldn't it simply be most "efficient" for society to let unproductive elderly people die?

9 What are the ethical dilemmas involved in becoming a case manager who has to decide who will get served and who will not? What can be learned

from considering the activities of gatekeepers in other domains—for example, college admissions officers or case workers in the welfare system? Imagine that you are a gatekeeper and that you're faced with a situation where it might not be possible to provide a health care service needed by an elderly person. Write a memorandum to your boss giving arguments on why the service should be provided.

FOCUS ON PRACTICE: CASE MANAGEMENT

Traditionally, human service fields such as nursing or social work have attracted people inspired by a goal of providing quality care to individual patients according to high standards of professional practice. But cost containment in the health care system changed the world in which service providers operate. Increasingly there is a shift from patient-centered values to organizational demands: that is, away from an ethic of patient welfare toward a new imperative for organizational accountability and justifying money spent.

The new imperative is accompanied by a redefinition of traditional tasks in nursing or social work to highlight the "gatekeeping" function. New positions in health care have names like "Hospital Discharge Planner" or "Case Manager." But the shift in definition of responsibility is clear. Human service providers are increasingly held responsible not only for individual patient welfare but for allocating organizational resources most efficiently.

When reimbursement rules decree that a patient must leave the hospital for home care, how will this be accomplished? When approval for home care depends on the cooperation of available family members, how will that cooperation be secured? When demand for service exceeds what insurance provides, how will professionals carry out their screening and assessment tasks? These questions have all become part of a new debate about the ethics of case management (Kane and Caplan, 1992).

Callahan and other proponents of age-based rationing argue that rationing should be done by standards that are publicly explicit and justified, and also that rationing should be done at the highest level in the resource allocation process: for example, through global budgeting in national health care. Only in that way, they argue, can we be sure that rationing will be fair and equitable.

But the current health care system doesn't match this ideal picture. The current system is facing cutbacks of funding, and the idea of rationing holds some appeal. One pattern that has already emerged is "backdoor rationing," which happens when gatekeepers tighten up on the access people have to the system. One way to see how backdoor rationing takes place is to look at geriatric case management.

A recurrent complaint about services and programs for the elderly in the United States has been that the services and programs are fragmented and confusing for older people seeking access. One response to this problem has been case management: that is, having a single provider or practitioner put together all the services needed by an individual, regardless of who provides the services. Such an approach is especially helpful for frail or homebound persons who often aren't able to put together the complex entitlements and services required (Applebaum and Austin, 1990).

Case management, as commonly defined, includes determination of level of care and eligibility, needs assessment, development of a care plan, and coordination and monitoring of services. In theory, the case manager would fulfill many of the best features of a good social worker and nurse practitioner. But a case manager isn't just a broker or an advocate acting for the client. In fact, a case manager commonly acts as a gatekeeper, because the case manager is responsible for needs assessment and may be employed by a public social service agency. These divided loyalties can create a problem (Callahan, 1989).

The gatekeeping function begins with an assessment of need, and the case manager will typically rely on screening instruments to conduct that assessment. The scores on an assessment instrument then become the basis for someone deciding how much help, for instance, a homebound person will receive or whether Medicare will reimburse for services given. As funding becomes tight, the standards for assessment and screening become tighter too.

Gatekeeping through case management can become a way of saying no to people who want or need services that will be denied to them. Elderly people who fail to measure up to some standards can be denied access to services, not because of a publicly announced decision to "ration" service but because of "backdoor" rationing reflected in the assessment and case management procedure.

Of interest, there is little empirical research to support the idea that case-managed long-term care actually saves money (Kemper, 1990). But efficiency and cost control have been motives for adopting case management in many localities (Capitman, 1988). Similar administrative methods, such as managed care, have become popular among health care planners seeking to contain the escalating costs of health care paid for by private industry. For the same reason, health maintenance organizations (HMOs) play a key role in plans for national health reform.

The controversy about age-based rationing, inaugurated by Daniel Callahan and taken up by his critics, has created a vigorous debate. The ethical principles—justice, rights, the greatest good for the greatest number, and so on—are clear and understandable. But when we come to "backdoor rationing," the whole picture becomes murky and confusing. Should we speak about "rationing" when health care providers control access through case management? What about through prices—for example, admitting patients on the basis of ability to pay? These are some of the troubling questions raised by practices of "backdoor rationing" in our present society, where strong opinions are expressed against Callahan's proposal yet access to scarce resources still remains constrained. The questions raised by the public debate about rationing scarce health care resources according to age are bound to provoke strong opposing views. Yet the problems that gave rise to the proposal are likely to be with us for some time to come.

Suggested Readings

Barry, Robert L., and Bradley, Gerard V. (eds.), *Set No Limits: A Rebuttal to Daniel Callahan's Proposal for Limited Health Care for the Elderly*, Chicago: University of Illinois Press, 1991.

Binstock, Robert H., and Post, Stephen G. (eds.), *Too Old for Health Care? Controversies in Medicine, Law, Economics and Ethics,* Baltimore, MD: Johns Hopkins University Press, 1991.

Homer, Paul and Holstein, M. (eds.), *A Good Old Age? The Paradox of Setting Limits*, New York: Simon & Schuster, 1990.

Menzel, Paul, *Strong Medicine: The Ethical Rationing of Health Care*, Oxford, 1989.

Sagan, Leonard, *The Health of Nations*, New York: Basic Books, 1987.

Smeeding, Timothy M. (ed.), *Should Medical Care Be Rationed by Age?* Rowman & Littlefield, 1987.

Should People Have the Choice to End Their Lives?

It is just as neurotic in old age
not to focus upon the goal of death as it is in youth
to repress fantasies which have to do with the future.

—*Carl Jung, The Soul and Death*

The film *Whose Life Is It, Anyway?* tells the story of a patient suffering from paralysis and confined to bed (Clark, 1978). In the movie, the patient, played by Mary Tyler Moore, engages in a spirited debate with her doctor, asking for help in ending her life. She is no longer able to live as the kind of person she has always known herself to be, and so the drama of the film centers on the question: What to do?

Increasingly this kind of question is being asked not about young women like Nancy Jane Cruzan—a recent legal landmark among "right to die" cases—but about her grandmother. Over two-thirds of deaths in America occur among people over 65. More and more, the timing of death is not an event that happens according to nature but is instead a decision made by human beings.

End-of-life decisions are rapidly becoming our choice to make, whether we want to make them or not. Recent medical advances have brought with them decisions unforeseen just a few decades ago. For example, in times past a person who was unable to breathe without help would die within minutes. Today, mechanically assisted respiration or artificial nutrition and hydration (tube feeding) can sometimes sustain life for years. Medical technology that is a benefit to some can become a burden to others. The decision, in any case, is not something easily avoided.

How we understand the decisions to be made will help shape the kind of decisions we make. Consider the moral problem of *euthanasia,* a term that originally came from ancient Greek, meaning simply a "good death." The question put by the film *Whose Life Is It, Anyway?* is whether a doctor should help the patient end her life. Will the doctor, in other words, engage in active euthanasia—sometimes called "mercy killing"? The term *active euthanasia* is used here to denote some deliberate intervention to end the patient's life, such as giving a fatal dose of painkilling medication. Passive euthanasia, by contrast, means not doing something—such as withdrawing life-supporting therapy—with the result that the patient dies (Rachels, 1986). Finally, there is the option of assisted suicide, where a doctor or family member actively provides the means or carries out the instructions required for an individual to end his or her life (Wennberg, 1989).

When it comes to the morality of these acts or omissions, people will answer the ethical questions in very different ways. Some answers depend on how we ask the question and the terms that we use. Most people sharply condemn the act of involuntary euthanasia, that is, killing someone without his or her consent because one believes that person would be better off dead. But there is much more controversy about voluntary euthanasia (Kohl, 1975). Moreover, is there really a valid ethical distinction between active versus passive euthanasia, for example?

The crucial question arises at the time of termination of treatment when a life-sustaining intervention is held back (Hastings Center, 1988). If a medical treatment is terminated, does it make any difference if we withhold a treatment or withdraw that treatment once it has already started—for example, "pulling the plug" in the case of a mechanical respirator? Then again, what really counts as "treatment" anyway? For instance, would food and water be considered a "treatment" in just the same light as antibiotics is a treatment? Finally, is there any difference between direct killing in contrast to assisting someone who takes his or her own life?

These are some of the ethical issues involved in end-of-life decisions and the debate that has grown up around those decisions. As the timing of death has been displaced more and more in later life, older people obviously have a vital interest in this debate. On one side are those who argue that the right to self-determination means patients should have the means to end their lives at a time of their own choosing. On the other side are those who warn that the right to suicide or euthanasia runs grave moral risks: for example, encouraging depressed elderly people to end their lives instead of changing the conditions that gave rise to the problem. To appreciate their argument, we need to consider some facts on late life depression.

Depression

Clinical depression is the most common psychological problem among the elderly who have mental health problems (Breslau and Haug, 1983). Unfortunately, depression is not always easy to diagnose: first, because it can manifest itself in a variety of symptoms; second, because depression can be found concurrently with other mental problems, such as dementia; and, third, because some symptoms of depression are extreme instances of changes associated with normal aging such as withdrawal from activities. Further, late-onset depression may differ from the recurrent onset of depressive disorders that began earlier in adulthood (de Leo and Diekstra, 1990).

According to some estimates, as many as a quarter of community-residing elderly people show significant depressive symptoms. But advanced age alone is not necessarily a risk factor for depression, and depression is not more common among the aged than among younger adults (Blazer, 1982). For older people who are isolated, however, lack of social support may make it difficult for them to cope with depression and overcome it.

It is useful to distinguish clinical depression from the emotional "down" state that is a common, but usually temporary, response to setbacks. A 1986 Louis Harris survey found that 48% of persons over 65 felt depressed at least occasionally. Among younger people, life presents opportunities to recover from losses: For a young or middle-aged person, it is reasonable, for example, to hope that a divorce or loss of a job can be followed by a "second chance." But, for older people, such hopes can be unrealistic. Among women 65 to 74, well over a third are already widowed, and for those over 75, the proportion is nearly two-thirds. Depression following bereavement and depression among residents of nursing homes may be a reaction to the fact that it is difficult to "start over" in later life. Remarriage or return to the community is statistically less likely than for younger people.

The psychological problem is that multiple losses and the expectation of further losses can be damaging to self-esteem and can weaken healthy psychological defense mechanisms (Vaillant, 1977). Denial may no longer be possible when an elderly person faces deterioration and dependency in the course of illness (Busse and Blazer, 1980). In such cases, it is not easy to say whether an elderly patient's rejection of life-saving treatment, for instance, represents an informed choice to be respected or instead is a sign that the patient needs help for a depressive disorder.

The problem here poses a very serious ethical dilemma for elderly people and their families. For example, many doctors are intensely committed to keeping patients alive. They may therefore doubt that anyone who rejects a life-sustaining medical treatment can be fully rational. The mere fact of deciding not to continue living becomes "proof" of irrationality. But this attitude of treatment at all costs fails to take seriously the possibility that some people in the last stage of life may decide that they simply have lived long enough. Should we therefore fail to respect their decision?

The dilemma was clear in the case of Theresa Leguerrier, a resident in the Good Samaritan Nursing Home in upstate New York. In this instance, the patient was in her eighties but not suffering from any serious medical problems. One day she began to refuse food and water, expressing a wish to die of starvation. Staff in the nursing home were divided in their opinion about what to do. The nursing home administration claimed that by refusing food a resident might make the home vulnerable to legal penalty for assisting suicide. Against this view, a physician and social worker involved in the case maintained that Theresa Leguerrier was rational and competent to make her own decision in the matter. The nursing home petitioned a court to institute artificial feeding but the court eventually agreed with the patient's right to refuse treatment in this case.

Some patients who reject a treatment or behave in another way that puts life at risk—for example, those who stop eating—may be suffering from a treatable depressive disorder. They simply lack enough "tender loving care." The 1985 National Nursing Home Survey, for example, discovered that 25% of residents in nursing homes had a major depression, and this figure does not include the majority of nursing home residents who suffered some degree of mental impairment. To adopt a laissez-faire attitude—"Well, it's their choice to make"—fails to take seriously the way depressive disorders can impair judgment. Failing to identify, diagnose, or treat late life depression could consign untold numbers of older people to self-imposed death by neglect under the label of "self-determination." But to regard anyone who refuses treatment as suffering from mental illness would disregard patient autonomy.

Recent History of the "Right to Die"

To appreciate the dilemma here, it is helpful to review the recent history of "right to die" decisions in the United States. Public discussion of the ethics of death and dying began during the late 1960s. The first great stimulus came with attention to the problem of brain death: that is, a condition in which some part of the brain—either the cerebral cortex or the brain stem—had lost ability to function. The problem was that mechanical respirators could be used to keep patients in this condition alive. Most states went on to pass laws defining when "death" could be said to occur under these conditions. But defining the moment of death has turned out not to be as vexing a problem as the ethical dilemmas revolving around end-of-life choices.

The first major "right to die" case was that of Karen Ann Quinlan (New Jersey, 1976). In that case, Karen Ann Quinlan, 21 at the time, was in a coma. Her family asked court permission to discontinue "extraordinary means" or "heroic measures" for sustaining life: in this case, a mechanical respirator. Upon appeal, the New Jersey Supreme Court ruled that there was a constitutional "right to privacy" to permit withholding or withdrawing life-sustaining treatment. Karen Ann Quinlan was then removed from the ventilator and brought to a nursing home, where she remained for nine years, sustained by feeding tubes and antibiotics until her death in 1985.

The *Quinlan* case was not an isolated incident. It reflected growing public concern reflected in new legislation. The first important "right to die" law passed was the California Natural Death Act (1976), but in the years after its passage, other states were the scene of both legislation and court decisions that pushed far beyond the California law (Glick, 1992).

Under the common law—that is, widely recognized principles of law in the United States—there is a right to accept or reject medical treatment and therefore a right to refuse treatment. Many state courts, along with the U.S. Supreme Court in the *Cruzan* case, have found that a constitutional right to refuse treatment can be exercised by another person on behalf of someone who has become legally incompetent. In some cases where no family member is present, courts have relied upon a "guardian at litem": that is, a designated spokesperson who acts to represent the interests of the incapacitated person and reports to the court.

Courts have relied on two different kinds of standards to determine when it is proper to withhold or withdraw life-sustaining treatment from incompetent patients: (a) the standard of **substituted judgment** (What would this patient have wanted under these conditions?) and (b) the **best-interest standard** (What is the balance of benefits and burdens that a "reasonable person" might want under these conditions?).

The American Medical Association in 1986 issued a statement approving, in appropriate cases, the removal or withholding of life-prolonging medical treatment. The AMA stated that discontinuing all means of life-prolonging treatment was "not unethical" even if the patient's condition was not terminal but the patient was instead in an irreversible coma. This view echoed the finding of some courts, as in the case *Rasmussen v. Fleming* (Arizona, 1987).

Typical of a whole range of end-of-life decisions among the very old was the 1985 case of Claire Conroy, 84 and a nursing home resident. Her nephew, appointed as her guardian, asked a New Jersey court for permission to remove a nasogastric tube. The trial court first granted permission on the grounds that life for the patient had become too great a burden. But the New Jersey Supreme Court, reviewing the *Conroy* case, rejected that reasoning and instead defined a range of procedures incorporating tests of substituted judgment and patient's best interest.

Another case of this kind was that of Earle Spring, 77 years old and suffering from both dementia and kidney failure. The Supreme Judicial Court in Massachusetts ruled that court approval is not necessarily required before withholding treatment from an incompetent patient. But decisions in one state court may not be consistent with those in other states. In the *O'Conner* case (1988), New York's Appellate Court adopted a very strict interpretation of the idea of substituted judgment. In this case, the court insisted that there is a duty to preserve life in all cases, unless there is "clear and convincing evidence" that the patient intended to refuse treatment under a particular circumstance. In the *O'Conner* case, the New York court was fearful that, without a strict standard of proof, there could be abuse of the vulnerable elderly, for example, by family members interested in inheriting property or caregivers exhausted by the burden of care. This is a concern about geronto-cide, or the killing of the old: a practice prevalent in some primitive societies facing conditions of extreme scarcity (Simmons, 1945).

It is important to recognize that a Living Will does not answer all questions that can arise in end-of-life decisions. Consider the case of Estelle Browning of Florida (1986), who suffered a massive stroke at age 86. In a previously written Living Will, Mrs. Browning had stated that she wanted medical treatment, including artificial nutrition, withheld or withdrawn in the event that her condition was terminal and death was imminent. But did these provisions of her Living Will apply to the present condition?

Mrs. Browning was not in a coma but damage from the stroke was extensive and irreversible. But is "irreversible" the same thing as "terminal"? The court eventually agreed to permit withdrawal of Mrs. Browning's feeding tube on grounds of a right to privacy and in recognition of the substituted judgment rendered by a **proxy decision maker.** But many of the same troubling questions recurred in the case of Hilda Peter (New Jersey, 1987), a patient in a persistent vegetative state without hope of recovery but with the possibility of surviving for many years in that condition.

The most important recent case concerning the right to die is that of Nancy Beth Cruzan, a young woman who suffered brain damage following an accident and was kept alive with artificial nutrition and hydration. The Missouri court denied her parents' request to discontinue treatment, maintaining that clear and convincing evidence of Nancy's wishes was not available. In 1990 this Missouri decision was upheld, by a 5-4 vote, by the U.S. Supreme Court. But, by an 8-1 vote, the court endorsed "the principle that a competent person has a constitutionally protected liberty interest in refusing unwanted medical treatment." At the same time, the court ruled that there were legitimate state interests in preserving life and preventing potential abuse in terminating treatment. For this reason, the court judged it proper to permit states to impose a high standard of evidence in determining whether an action by a surrogate decision maker (e.g., Nancy Cruzan's parents) actually reflects the wishes of the patient.

The *Cruzan* case was the first time the U.S. Supreme Court had rendered a verdict on right to die cases. In its decision, it found a constitutional "liberty interest" that included the right to refuse life-sustaining care, including artificial nutrition as a medical treatment. A majority of the court found that an appointed proxy or surrogate decision maker, just like a competent patient, would be legally entitled to refuse treatment. Significantly, the court finally endorsed the use of **advance directives,** such as the Living Will or Durable Power of Attorney for health care. But the court also left procedural requirements to the states, ensuring that both legislation and litigation will continue for years to come.

In many ways, the recent evolution of right to die laws and court cases represents a continuation of long-held cultural ideals: above all, the idea of self-determination and protection of rights by due process of law. For a competent adult, the right to refuse medical treatment, even at risk of death, has been widely recognized in the common law tradition of America. The *Natanson v. Kline* case (1960) expressed the ideal of self-determination in these words: "Each man is considered to be master of his own body, and he may, if he be of sound mind, expressly prohibit the performance of life-saving surgery, or other medical treatment." Recent developments in the so-called right to die do not confer on anyone a right to have active euthanasia performed, nor do they confer a right to involve other people in assisting with suicide. The right to die in all cases under law has involved some variety of passive euthanasia.

But general principles and court decisions do not resolve all the issues. Where to draw the line between suicide and euthanasia remains a problem for many people. An early case, the *Perlmutter* case (1978), illustrates the point. In that case, a 73-year-old man was terminally ill but fully competent and sought to have his respirator disconnected. The Florida state attorney argued that anyone helping to disconnect the respirator could be criminally charged with assisting a suicide, an argument that was firmly rejected by the Florida Supreme Court. Today, very few people would regard withdrawing treatment from the terminally ill as equivalent to suicide. Courts have repeatedly concluded that termination of life-sustaining treatment is not homicide, suicide, or assisted suicide.

At the same time, assisting a suicide does remain a crime in most jurisdictions of the United States. This fact is important in weighing the actions of Dr. Timothy Quill, who actively assisted a terminally ill patient in committing suicide. It is also important in considering the case of Dr. Jack Kevorkian, who developed the infamous "suicide machine" designed to deliver a lethal dose of drugs to patients requesting it. His initiative, like the popularity among the elderly of the so-called suicide manual *Final Exit*, underscores that the right to die debate in America is far from over.

Consensus and Controversy: Outlook for the Future

By the time Karen Ann Quinlan finally died in 1985, public opinion in the United States had undergone a substantial change that paralleled dramatic developments in the legal sphere. We can note a clear trend in public opinion over the last two decades. Withdrawal or withholding of heroic measures—such as artificial respiration or cardiopulmonary resuscitation (CPR)—has become more acceptable to a majority of Americans, at least in the case of terminal illness. Active euthanasia, on the other hand, still remains disapproved by health care professionals and by vocal elements of the public.

Other issues still remain controversial. For example, is artificial nutrition or hydration actually to be considered in the same category as other medical treatments? The American Medical Association has claimed that there is no ethically significant difference between withdrawing food and water versus other life-supporting measures. Most medical ethicists and courts have agreed. But many lay people and professionals remain unconvinced (Solomon et al., 1993).

In a similar way, ethicists have argued that there should be no strict moral difference between withholding life-supporting treatment in contrast to withdrawing treatment once it has already begun. But, again, most families and health care practitioners remain persuaded that there is an important psychological difference: It is easier not to start a treatment than to withdraw it once already begun. Clearly, the social and interpersonal context of a decision continues to make a difference to those who are involved in end-of-life decisions.

A major step in the process came with the enactment of the Patient Self-Determination Act (PSDA), which went into effect in December 1991. This law requires hospitals, nursing homes, and other health care facilities to advise all patients at the point of admission about their right to accept or refuse medical treatment. The PSDA in effect creates new requirements for hospitals but does not create new rights for patients. Under the law, patients are specifically to be told about their right to determine in advance whether they wish life-sustaining treatment if they become ill without hope of recovery. The staff of health facilities are required to document and implement policies that respect the wishes of patients (LaPuma, Orentlicher, and Moss, 1991).

Despite this law, however, it appears that relatively few patients actually complete an advance directive document of any kind. Public opinion polls have revealed that close to 90% of American adults would not want to be maintained on life-support systems without prospect of recovery. Yet a survey by the American Medical Association revealed that not even 15% of the general public had actually completed a Living Will, and the same low proportion appears to hold true for persons over age 65.

Why is the proportion so low? It appears that physicians generally express an opinion in favor of the idea of advance directives, but they remain reluctant to open a discussion on the topic. In one study of attitudes held by older people (Stetler et al., 1992), a clear majority (61%) wanted the doctor to begin a discussion. The PSDA is unlikely to be the final answer to helping patients make end-of-life decisions. Nor will the *Cruzan* case and other court decisions put an end to the ethical debate about right to die issues, which is certain to continue for many years to come.

In the readings that follow, we hear impassioned voices in the debate over the right to die. Martin Tolchin's article describes the kinds of conditions of desperation that are leading more and more elderly people to take their own lives. Lilian Stevens gives us the voice of one of those people for whom suicide would be a welcome relief, not a symptom of mental illness. Sidney Hook, a distinguished academic philosopher, argued along much the same lines in favor of voluntary euthanasia. Along with these individual voices, there is a selection from Derek Humphry, perhaps the best known public advocate of "self-deliverance" or assisted suicide. Humphry, the president of the Hemlock Society, has been a force behind public referendums that would legalize assisted suicide and voluntary euthanasia.

Humphry's position is one that Leon Kass decisively rejects. Kass offers strong arguments for why doctors must never kill and why physician-assisted suicide is morally wrong. Kass's arguments force us to think carefully about a basic question arising in end-of-life decisions. To what extent is the decision to end one's life a purely individual matter and to what extent does it involve other people? For example, does the ending of one's life become a different matter because physicians, family members, or others participate or assist in the act of suicide? As individuals and society debate the issue in years to come, we will be preoccupied with the question of how individual choices are connected to wider social values. However we resolve the debate, this connection is a point to be pondered and discussed.

When Long Life Is Too Much
Suicide Rises Among Elderly

Martin Tolchin

Reversing a half-century trend, the suicide rate among elderly Americans steadily increased in the 1980's, according to Government records.

The 25 percent increase from 1981 to 1986, the last year for which the Government has records, brought the suicide rate among those 65 and older to 21.6 per 100,000 people, as against an overall national rate of 12.8. The trend perplexes health care experts, who note that the elderly are generally more financially secure and healthier, and they live longer than their forebears.

"There's no other group showing that kind of an increase," said Dr. John L. McIntosh, associate professor of psychology at Indiana University. "Teenage suicide peaked in 1977 and is going down."

But some experts speculate that the technological advances extending the lives of the elderly sometimes bring a quality of life that they cannot accept.

Life at What Cost?

Dr. McIntosh, who with Dr. Nancy J. Osgood wrote "Suicide and the Elderly," a 1986 review of literature in the field, said the increase in suicides among the elderly suggested that "medical technology may have created physically longer lives, but it also has created new concerns."

"People say, 'I'm going to live longer, but is that going to be the kind of life I want to live?' " Dr. McIntosh added.

Dr. Robert Butler, chairman of the department of geriatrics at the Mount Sinai School of Medicine in New York, said, "There's a much greater awareness of Alzheimer's disease and other incurable diseases, and people know they're going to become helpless and the costs are going to be great."

Dr. Osgood, associate professor of gerontology at the Medical College of Virginia, said the increase in the suicide rate reflected society's changing attitude toward suicide by the elderly.

"There's been more of an attitude that suicide is an acceptable solution to life's problems, especially those of the elderly," Dr. Osgood said.

The suicide rate of those 65 and older, long the highest of any single group, steadily declined from 1933, during the height of the Depression, to 1981, according to statistics compiled by the National Center for Health Statistics, an agency of the Department of Health and Human Services.

In 1933, the first year in which the agency collected data from all the states, the suicide rate among the elderly was 45.3 per 100,000, as against a national average of 15.9. In 1981, it was 17.1 per 100,000, as against a national average of 12.0. But from then until 1986, it steadily increased.

The suicide rate of those 15 to 24 was 13.1 in 1986, and the rate of those 25 to 44 was 15.5. Those 45 to 64 had a suicide rate of 16.7 per 100,000.

Statistics May Mislead

Of the elderly, those 65 to 74 had a suicide rate of 19.7, those 75 to 84 had a rate of 25.2, and those 85 and over had a rate of 20.8.

The Government statistics are based on death certificates that list suicide as the cause of death. But the number of elderly suicides is believed to be underestimated because older people sometimes end their lives surreptitiously, by starving themselves or not taking medication, and their deaths are seldom reported as suicides.

"An awful lot of suicide in old age doesn't get reported as suicide," Dr. Butler said.

Dr. McIntosh said, "We think older people are supposed to die, so we're not as concerned about knowing the circumstances as we are with younger people." What of other countries? Dr. McIntosh says that long-term declines in the suicide rate among the elderly had been noted in most western countries, but that he is unaware of any published material to indicate a reversal in this trend, like the reversal that has occurred in the United States.

Some health experts note the growing acceptance of the concept of "rational suicide," by which older people calmly examine their lives and decide whether they are worth living.

"The concept of rational suicide is gaining credence," said Dr. Seymour Perlin, professor of psychiatry at the George Washington University School of Medicine and [the second president of] the American Association of Suicidology.

But Dr. Perlin says "rational suicide" often masks the complicity of grown children, who tacitly agree with an ailing elderly parent, aware that his medical treatment is draining the family resources, that "you would be better off without me."

Children May Play Role
By not protesting, children encourage the parent to commit suicide, Dr. Perlin said.

"Often the neutral stance in favor of rational suicide is actually collusion, because the parent is really reaching out to the child for affirmation of a desire to live," said Dr. Perlin, who is the editor of the "Handbook for the Study of Suicide." "The concept of rational suicide thus creates an expectation of suicide."

A new study of elderly suicide by the American Association of Retired Persons notes that white males 65 and over have the highest suicide rate, 43.2 per 100,000, or nearly four times the national average. The ratio of male to female suicides in the age range of 65 to 69 is 4 to 1 but gradually increases to 12 to 1 by the age of 85.

"It's an accumulation of losses that just keeps getting worse," said Dr. Susan O. Mercer, professor of social work at the University of Arkansas, who prepared the A.A.R.P. report. "It's loss of spouse, friends, health, status, and a meaningful role in society."

"More older people are committing suicide, not out of depression, but because they just don't want to go on living," Dr. Mercer said. "They are projecting what's ahead, and just don't want to go through it. They're living longer, but the quality of life is not that great."

Decision Ends in Death
The A.A.R.P. study said that when older persons decided to commit suicide, they were likely to succeed. "The elderly can more easily commit 'covert' suicide by starving themselves, terminating life-sustaining medications or overdosing on prescribed medications," the report said. "Such suicides may also be disguised as fatal accidents." The study also found that men are more likely than women to use firearms.

The increased suicide rate of older Americans comes as their economic security has been enhanced by such Government programs as Medicare and Social Security. The percentage of those 65 and over living below the poverty level has declined to 12.2 percent in 1987, from 35.2 percent in 1959. The current poverty level is defined by the Federal Government as $5,671 for an individual 65 or older, and $6,152 for those under 65.

At the same time, medical technology has brought steady increases in longevity, from an expected life span of 62.9 years for those born in 1940 to 74.7 years for those born in 1985.

For an Ill Widow, 83, Suicide Is Welcome

Lilian Stevens

A close friend, an 83-year-old widow in rapidly declining health, plans to commit suicide within a couple of months.

She finds travel difficult but made the effort to come from another city to tell me. Blocked arteries have left her vulnerable to a stroke that, unless fatal, would doom her to the horror of vegetating in a nursing home.

When I suggested that surgery might prolong her active life, she replied that, even if successful, it would leave her too weakened to make continued activity possible.

Still suffering from the aftereffects of surgery two years ago, she said: "I think people at this advanced age should review their prospects very carefully before accepting major surgery, as I should have done. I simply forgot that one's recuperative powers at this stage of life aren't what they were 10 or 20 years ago."

She sees no justification for becoming a burden to herself, her friends and society. She wishes only to leave the scene as quietly as possible.

In contemplating her own death, she recalls her father's declining years. He was a highly intelligent man who survived a major stroke and spent four years paralyzed and speechless.

Tragically, he retained enough sensibility to realize his condition and to beg, by emphatic gestures, for release. He repeatedly pointed to a drawer of a cabinet that her mother opened to find a gun. She bitterly regrets that neither she nor her mother could summon the courage to grant him this gift. His last three years in a nursing home were agony for them all. Her mother died senile, also in a nursing home.

Haunted by those memories and those of close friends who have suffered the humiliation of complete helplessness, she feels quite unable to face a similar fate.

She says she has known for years that she would end her life when it became insupportable. She considered suicide when her husband died 14 years ago, but out of an old-fashioned sense of duty decided that she should continue her volunteer activities, using her knowledge and long experience.

One of her chief interests was the serious threat to her local environment. She wishes now that she had included an effort toward legislation that would permit a decent suicide in situations such as hers.

Following her visit, after considerable thought, I wrote her, expressing my deep concern and asking reassurance.

I asked: "What about society's condemnation of suicide? Have you really considered that?"

She replied: "Oh yes. I realize that many people can't accept the taking of life under any circumstances, either from religious scruples or reverence for tradition. But I think the Almighty will forgive our attempts to solve the mysteries of the universe and to determine our role in it. I'm sure everyone who really knows me will understand my viewpoint.

"Eventually society will come to terms with situations like mine, not only for humanitarian reasons but out of economic necessity. There have been repeated warnings that the alarming increase in our numbers versus the declining birth rate will soon force severe cutbacks in Government support of radical surgery and extended care. Those costs are already an unjustifiable burden upon the younger generations and those to come.

"Many doctors agree with me, and their number is increasing. Some act out of mercy, but until the law becomes similarly enlightened and sensitive, they're at great risk.

"My fondest hope is that everyone who realizes the urgency of the situation—and particularly those with families—will exert pressure for legislation that will enable physicians to comply with their patients' wishes. In a civilized era, a gentle, peaceful death could be accomplished by a simple injection.

"In all other ways a law-abiding citizen, I am now obeying what I consider to be a higher law. The alternative would be unendurable. I simply haven't the courage to spend years dying by inches in a nursing home. I've earned the rest that only 'turning out the light' will give."

She hopes to find a sure, quick, painless method of release. For her sake, I hope that she will have been able to accomplish it in a humane manner.

In Defense of Voluntary Euthanasia

Sidney Hook

A few short years ago, I lay at the point of death. A congestive heart failure was treated for diagnostic purposes by an angiogram that triggered a stroke. Violent and painful hiccups, uninterrupted for several days and nights, prevented the ingestion of food. My left side and one of my vocal cords became paralyzed. Some form of pleurisy set in, and I felt I was drowning in a sea of slime. At one point, my heart stopped beating; just as I lost consciousness, it was thumped back into action again. In one of my lucid intervals during those days of agony, I asked my physician to discontinue all life-supporting services or show me how to do it. He refused

Source: "In Defense of Voluntary Euthanasia," by S. Hook, *The New York Times* (March 1, 1987). Copyright © 1987 by The New York Times Company. Reprinted by permission.

and predicted that someday I would appreciate the unwisdom of my request.

A month later, I was discharged from the hospital. In six months, I regained the use of my limbs, and although my voice still lacks its old resonance and carrying power I no longer croak like a frog. There remain some minor disabilities and I am restricted to a rigorous, low-sodium diet. I have resumed my writing and research.

My experience can be and has been cited as an argument against honoring requests of stricken patients to be gently eased out of their pain and life. I cannot agree. There are two main reasons. As an octogenarian, there is a reasonable likelihood that I may suffer another "cardiovascular accident" or worse. I may not even be in a position to ask for the surcease of pain. It seems to me that I have already paid my dues to death—indeed, although time has softened my memories they are vivid enough to justify my saying that I suffered enough to warrant dying several times over. Why run the risk of more?

Secondly, I dread imposing on my family and friends another grim round of misery similar to the one my first attack occasioned.

My wife and children endured enough for one lifetime. I know that for them the long days and nights of waiting, the disruption of their professional duties and their own familial responsibilities counted for nothing in their anxiety for me. In their joy at my recovery they have been forgotten. Nonetheless, to visit another prolonged spell of helpless suffering on them as my life ebbs away, or even worse, if I linger on into a comatose senility, seems altogether gratuitous.

But what, it may be asked, of the joy and satisfaction of living, of basking in the sunshine, listening to music, watching one's grandchildren growing into adolescence, following the news about the fate of freedom in a troubled world, playing with ideas, writing one's testament of wisdom and folly for posterity? Is not all that one endured, together with the risk of its recurrence, an acceptable price for the multiple satisfactions that are still open even to a person of advanced years?

Apparently those who cling to life no matter what, think so. I do not.

The zest and intensity of these experiences are no longer what they used to be. I am not vain enough to delude myself that I can in the few remaining years make an important discovery useful for mankind or can lead a social movement or do anything that will be historically eventful, no less event-making. My autobiography, which describes a record of intellectual and political experiences of some historical value, already much too long, could be posthumously published. I have had my fill of joys and sorrows and am not greedy for more life. I have always thought that a test of whether one had found happiness in one's life is whether one would be willing to relive it—whether, if it were possible, one would accept the opportunity to be born again.

Having lived a full and relatively happy life, I would cheerfully accept the chance to be reborn, but certainly not to be reborn again as an infirm octogenarian. To some extent, my views reflect what I have seen happen to the aged and stricken who have been so unfortunate as to survive crippling paralysis. They suffer, and impose suffering on others, unable even to make a request that their torment be ended.

I am mindful too of the burdens placed upon the community, with its rapidly diminishing resources, to provide the adequate and costly services necessary to sustain the lives of those whose days and nights are spent on mattress graves of pain. A better use could be made of these resources to increase the opportunities and qualities of life for the young. I am not denying the moral obligation the community has to look after its disabled and aged. There are times, however, when an individual may find it pointless to insist on the fulfillment of a legal and moral right.

What is required is no great revolution in morals but an enlargement of imagination and an intelligent evaluation of alternative uses of community resources.

Long ago, Seneca observed that "the wise man will live as long as he ought, not as long as he can." One can envisage hypothetical circumstances in which one has a duty to prolong one's life despite its costs for the sake of others, but such circumstances are far removed from the ordinary prospects we are considering. If wisdom is rooted in knowledge of the alternatives of choice, it must be reliably informed of the state one is in and its likely outcome. Scientific medicine is not infallible, but it is the best we have. No rational person would forego relief from prolonged agony merely on the chance thought a miraculous cure might presently be at hand. Each one should be permitted to make his own choice—especially when no one else is harmed by it.

The responsibility for the decision, whether deemed wise or foolish, must be with the chooser.

Final Exit
The Practicalities of Self-Deliverance
and Assisted Suicide for the Dying

Derek Humphry

The Most Difficult Decision

This is the scenario: you are terminally ill, all medical treatments acceptable to you have been exhausted, and the suffering in its different forms is unbearable. Because the illness is so serious, you recognize that your life is drawing to a close. Euthanasia comes to mind as a way of release.

The dilemma is awesome. But it has to be faced. Should you battle on, take the pain, endure the indignity, and await the inevitable end which may be weeks, or months, away? Or should you resort to euthanasia, which in its modern language definition has come to mean 'help with a good death?'

Today the euthanasia option comes in two ways:

Passive euthanasia. Popularly known as "pulling the plug," the disconnection of life-support equipment without which you cannot live. There is unlikely to be much legal or ethical trouble here so long as you have signed a Living Will and a Durable Power of Attorney for Health Care, documents which express your wishes.

Active euthanasia. Taking steps to end your life, as in suicide, handling the action yourself. Alternatively, and preferably, getting some assistance from another person, which is assisted suicide. (Remember, assisted suicide is still a felony. . . .)

If you are not on life-support equipment, then the first option is not available to you because there

Source: Final Exit: The Practicalities of Self-Deliverance and Assisted Suicide for the Dying by D. Humphry, 1991, Eugene OR: The Hemlock Society and Dell Paperbacks, 1992. Reprinted by permission of the author.

is no 'plug' to pull. Roughly half the people who die in Western society currently are connected to equipment. You may be one of the other half who are not. If you wish to deliberately leave this world, then active euthanasia is your only avenue. Read on, carefully.

(If you consider God the master of your fate, then read no further. Seek the best pain management available and arrange hospice care.)

If you want personal control and choice over your destiny, it will require forethought, planning, documentation, friends, and decisive, courageous action from you. This book will help, but in the final analysis, whether you bring your life to an abrupt end, and how you achieve this, is entirely your responsibility, ethically and legally.

The task of finding the right drugs, getting someone to help (if you wish that), and carrying out your self-deliverance in a place and in a manner which is not upsetting to other people is your responsibility.

If you have not already done so, sign a Living Will and have it witnessed. Get the one that is valid for your particular state. This document is an advance declaration of your wish not to be connected to life-support equipment if it is adjudged that you are hopelessly and terminally ill.

Or, if you are already on the equipment because of an attempt to save you which failed, a Living Will gives permission for its disconnection. By signing, you are agreeing to take the fatal consequences.

But remember, a Living Will is only a request to a doctor not to be needlessly kept alive on support equipment. It is not an order. It may not be legally enforceable. But as your signed 'release,' it is a valuable factor in the doctor's thinking about how to handle your dying. The Living Will gives the doctor protection from lawsuits by relatives after your death. . . . .

A Check List

If you are now comfortable with the decision to die because of the advanced and unbearable state of your terminal illness, and have considered those problems raised in this book which relate to your circumstances, you should review the following list:

1. Be sure that you are in a hopeless condition. Talk it over with your doctors one more time.
2. If the urge to die is coming from physical pain, ask for pain medications to be increased. If asking is not succeeding, then insist. Be noisy.
3. Will your doctor help you die? He or she might. It is worth trying. Negotiate frankly but diplomatically. You must respect a physician's decision if he or she refuses.
4. Do this in your home if you can. Check yourself out of the hospital if it is physically possible. A hospital cannot forcibly keep you, but it may require you to sign a release in which you accept responsibility for whatever happens.
5. Give cautious advance warning to those family and friends close to you that you plan, sometime in the near future, to end your life because of your suffering. Do not disclose the planned actual time except to those who will be beside you.
6. Make sure you have absolute privacy for up to eight hours. A Friday or Saturday night is usually the quietest time; there are generally no business transactions until Monday.
7. If you have someone beside you during your self-deliverance, to avoid risk of prosecution remind the assister to not touch you before death and to be discreet in speaking to anyone afterwards.

8. Leave a note of explanation as to why you are ending your life, together with your Living Will documents.
9. Make sure that a Will dealing with your financial affairs is with your executor.
10. Consider whether there are any life insurance policies which will be affected by the manner of your death. Leave them where they can be easily found.
11. Leave instructions about disposal of your body, whether you want burial or cremation. Leave guidance on the funeral or memorial service, if any.
12. Tell those around you the complimentary things which have been left unsaid due to the strain of illness. The appropriate "I am grateful for what you've done" or similar remark will help comfort those left behind after you have gone.
13. Be careful about the contents of your stomach.
14. Make sure you have not built up a tolerance to any medication that you are taking regularly. If possible, stop using any regular medications and allow time for your system to clear, probably several days.
15. Do not take the telephone off the hook or disconnect an answering machine. Any changes will only alert callers to something unusual happening. Turn the bell down or put a blanket over the telephone if you do not want to hear it.
16. Make the preparations for your end extremely carefully and with consideration for others. Leave nothing to chance. . . .

Euthanasia Involving Doctors & Nurses

Justifiable Euthanasia

A great many doctors believe in justified euthanasia but, given the criminal risk, say nothing about it. There are only a handful of America's half-million physicians who have publicly acknowledged their belief in the ethical rightness of aid-in-dying. To acknowledge their belief publicly offers a risk of being branded—and perhaps investigated—as a practitioner of this compassionate option.

Since 1978 I have spoken—by invitation only—to several hundred meetings of medical men and women. Usually I am invited because their patients have been asking awkward questions about help with death. As a rule, after my talk, statements and questions come almost exclusively from opponents and doubters. Supporters remain silent, presumably because of fear of internal political problems. Then, during the coffee break, a man or woman will say to me privately that they agree with my views. "It goes on, anyway," they invariably add. In the next few days I am apt to get supportive notes in the mail from a few others.

Those doctors at meetings who feel free to speak up because they support the status quo almost always raise two points:

1. They have never (in 20 or 40 years) been asked by a patient to be helped to die.
2. There is no need for euthanasia because modern medicine has the answers to unbearable suffering.

My answer to the first point is that patients are not stupid. They can usually detect whether a doctor is likely to sympathize with their intended suicide. Perhaps they put out a feeler through the nursing staff. Or they might be using such subjective criteria as the doctor having a name which sounds Jewish or Irish and concluding that there would be opposition on religious grounds. (The patient might or might not be right.) Usually the patient assesses from the bedside manner whether a certain physician is approachable.

The second point, pain control and good nursing, requires a much more detailed answer. Certainly, modern pharmaceutical developments have provided us with wonderful analgesics, which, with shrewd management, control terminal pain in about 90 percent of cases. Having read the little amount of literature available on pain management and attended conferences to listen to world experts,

my conclusion is that there is about ten percent of pain that is not yet controllable. We have to care about those people who fall within that margin. It could be me or you.

But even more important than that ten percent, are the other forms of suffering which are not physically painful. I am left with a very distinct and uncomfortable impression that most doctors do not fully appreciate the symptoms of terminal illness that a patient is feeling. Even if they do appreciate them, can they do much about them? Probably not. This is what may be propelling the patient towards a request to be helped to die and thus deserves respect. . . .

Professional Reasons to Help

There are plenty of reasons why a physician should help a suffering terminally ill patient to die. Here are some of them:

- Physicians know better than anyone else approximately when the patient will die, and the manner of death. If the patient is asking for euthanasia and it clearly is not justified, or is too early, the physician is in the best position to advance arguments to this effect.
- Only physicians have lawful access to lethal drugs, know the techniques for their administration, and can avoid toxicological mistakes caused by tolerance and interaction.
- Physicians are trained to observe criteria before acting. The Dutch experience has shown careful procedures and preparations are essential in acts of euthanasia.
- Certain patients, such as those with ALS or cancer of the throat, cannot swallow and need skillful injections to end life.

Social Reasons to Help

- By the time the end of life is reached, some people have no one to assist them to die. Widows have often outlived their close relatives and friends, for instance.

- Sometimes relatives of the patient have too many emotional problems to be able to help. Issues of guilt, unfinished business, even financial debt, may confuse the person to whom the patient is turning for assistance.
- The patient is certain to be afraid of doing it alone for fear of botching it, then having to live on with the stigma and perhaps physical damage.
- The role of the physician is both to cure and to relieve suffering. When cure is no longer possible and the patient seeks relief through euthanasia, the help of physicians is most appropriate.
- Alone at this crucial time, the physician is the independent broker, the one not involved emotionally or historically, and possessing the technology and skill to end the patient's life with certainty and gentleness. It has to be a carefully negotiated death, with both patient and doctor sharing the responsibilities it entails.

Reasons Not to Help

It would be judicious and fair for a physician to decline to help if one or more of the following circumstances prevails:

- Helping another person to die offends the physician's moral and ethical codes.
- The physician hardly knows the patient and/or mutual respect is lacking.
- The physician is not fully conversant with the patient's medical status. This is not the time for hasty, ill-considered actions which may be regretted later.
- There remain other treatments which offer a positive chance of recovery or remission. (But this is hardly the time to think about experimental medicine.) The patient has the right of ultimate choice so long as it is an informed decision.
- The patient who is asking for assistance in suicide is clearly depressed and so not rational. That depression may be treatable. Bear in mind that the prospect of death would throw most people into the doldrums, so first wait and see if it passes. If not, treat it with appropriate drugs and also check to see if some other circumstances, such as family stress or financial worries, are causing the unhappiness. If doubt remains about the patient's rationality, after getting consent, call in a psychologist or psychiatrist for an evaluation.

READING 15

Neither for Love Nor Money
Why Doctors Must Not Kill

Leon Kass

Source: "Neither for Love Nor Money: Why Doctors Must Not Kill" by L. Kass, *The Public Interest* (Number 94, Winter 1989), pp. 26-37, 42-45. Copyright © 1989, The Public Interest. Reprinted by permission of *The Public Interest* and the author.

Contemporary Ethical Approaches

The question about physicians killing is a special case of—but not thereby identical to—this general question: May or ought one kill people who ask to be killed? Among those who answer this general question in the affirmative, two reasons are usually given. Because these reasons also reflect the two leading approaches to medical ethics today, they are especially worth noting. First is the reason of *freedom* or *autonomy*. Each person has a right to control his or her body and his or her life, including the end of it; some go so far as to assert a right to die, a strange claim in a liberal society, founded on the need to secure and defend the unalienable right to life. But strange or not, for patients with waning powers too weak to oppose potent life-prolonging technologies wielded by aggressive physicians, the claim based on choice, autonomy, and self-determination is certainly understandable. On this view, physicians (or others) are bound to acquiesce in demands not only for termination of treatment but also for intentional killing through poison, because the right to choose—freedom—must be respected, even more than life itself, and even when the physician would never recommend or concur in the choices made. When persons exercise their right to choose against their continuance as embodied beings, doctors must not only cease their ministrations to the body; as keepers of the vials of life and death, they are also morally bound actively to dispatch the embodied person, out of deference to the autonomous personal choice that is, in this view, most emphatically the patient to be served.

The second reason for killing the patient who asks for death has little to do with choice. Instead, death is to be directly and swiftly given because the patient's life is deemed no longer worth living, according to some substantive or "objective" measure. Unusually great pain or a terminal condition or an irreversible coma or advanced senility or extreme degradation is the disqualifying quality of life that pleads—choice or no choice—for merciful termination. Choice may enter indirectly to confirm the judgment: if the patient does not speak up, the doctor (or the relatives or some other proxy) may be asked to affirm that he would not himself choose—or that his patient, were he *able* to choose, *would* not choose—to remain alive with one or more of these stigmata. It is not his autonomy but

rather the miserable and pitiable condition of his body or mind that justifies doing the patient in. Absent such substantial degradations, requests for assisted death would not be honored. Here the body itself offends and must be plucked out, from compassion or mercy, to be sure. Not the autonomous will of the patient, but the doctor's benevolent and compassionate love for suffering humanity justifies the humane act of mercy killing.

As I have indicated, these two reasons advanced to justify the killing of patients correspond to the two approaches to medical ethics most prominent in the literature today: the school of autonomy and the school of general benevolence and compassion (or love). Despite their differences, they are united in their opposition to the belief that medicine is intrinsically a moral profession, with its own immanent principles and standards of conduct that set limits on what physicians may properly do. Each seeks to remedy the ethical defect of a profession seen to be in itself amoral, technically competent but morally neutral.

For the first ethical school, morally neutral technique is morally used only when it is used according to the wishes of the patient as client or consumer. The implicit (and sometimes explicit) model of the doctor-patient relationship is one of *contract*: the physician—a highly competent hired syringe, as it were—sells his services on demand, restrained only by the law (though he is free to refuse his services if the patient is unwilling or unable to meet his fee). Here's the deal: for the patient, autonomy and service; for the doctor, money, graced by the pleasure of giving the patient what he wants. If a patient wants to fix her nose or change his gender, determine the sex of unborn children, or take euphoriant drugs just for kicks, the physician can and will go to work—provided that the price is right and that the contract is explicit about what happens if the customer isn't satisfied.[2]

For the second ethical school, morally neutral technique is morally used only when it is used under the guidance of general benevolence or loving charity. Not the will of the patient, but the humane and compassionate motive of the physician—not as physician but as *human being*—makes the doctor's actions ethical. Here, too, there can be strange requests and stranger deeds, but if they are done from love, nothing can be wrong—again, providing the law is silent. All acts—including killing the patient—done lovingly are licit, even praiseworthy. Good and humane intentions can sanctify any deed.

In my opinion, each of these approaches should be rejected as a basis for medical ethics. For one thing, neither can make sense of some specific duties and restraints long thought absolutely inviolate under the traditional medical ethic—e.g., the proscription against having sex with patients. Must we now say that sex with patients is permissible if the patient wants it and the price is right, or, alternatively, if the doctor is gentle and loving and has a good bedside manner? Or do we glimpse in this absolute prohibition a deeper understanding of the medical vocation, which the prohibition both embodies and protects? Indeed, as I will now try to show, using the taboo against doctors killing patients, the medical profession has its own intrinsic ethic, which a physician true to his calling will not violate, either for love or for money. . . .

Assessing the Consequences

Although the bulk of my argument will turn on my understanding of the special meaning of professing the art of healing, I begin with a more familiar mode of ethical analysis: assessing needs and benefits versus dangers and harms. To do this properly is a massive task. Here, I can do little more than raise a few of the relevant considerations. Still the best discussion of this topic is a now-classic essay by Yale Kamisar, written thirty years ago.[4] Kamisar makes vivid the difficulties in assuring that the choice for death will be *freely* made and adequately *informed,* the problems of physician error and abuse, the troubles for human relationships within families and between doctors and patients, the difficulty of preserving the boundary between voluntary and involuntary euthanasia, and the risks to the

whole social order from weakening the absolute prohibition against taking innocent life. These considerations are, in my view, alone sufficient to rebut any attempt to weaken the taboo against medical killing; their relative importance for determining public policy far exceeds their relative importance in this essay. But here they serve also to point us to more profound reasons why doctors must not kill.

There is no question that fortune deals many people a very bad hand, not least at the end of life. All of us, I am sure, know or have known individuals whose last weeks, months, or even years were racked with pain and discomfort, degraded by dependency or loss of self-control, isolation or insensibility, or who lived in such reduced humanity that it cast a deep shadow over their entire lives, especially as remembered by the survivors. All who love them would wish to spare them such an end, and there is no doubt that an earlier death could do it. Against such a clear benefit, attested to by many a poignant and heartrending true story, it is difficult to argue, especially when the arguments are necessarily general and seemingly abstract. Still, in the aggregate, the adverse consequences—including real suffering—of being governed solely by mercy and compassion may far outweigh the aggregate benefits of relieving agonal or terminal distress.

The "Need" for Mercy Killing

The first difficulty emerges when we try to gauge the so-called "need" or demand for medically assisted killing. This question, to be sure, is in part empirical. But evidence can be gathered only if the relevant categories of "euthanizable" people are clearly defined. Such definition is notoriously hard to accomplish—and it is not always honestly attempted. On careful inspection, we discover that if the category is precisely defined, the need for mercy killing seems greatly exaggerated, and if the category is loosely defined, the poisoners will be working overtime.

The category always mentioned first to justify mercy killing is the group of persons suffering from incurable and fatal illnesses, with intractable pain and with little time left to live but still fully aware, who freely request a release from their distress—e.g., people rapidly dying from disseminated cancer with bony metastases, unresponsive to chemotherapy. But as experts in pain control tell us, the number of such people with truly intractable and untreatable pain is in fact rather low. Adequate analgesia is apparently possible in the vast majority of cases, provided that the physician and patient are willing to use strong enough medicines in adequate doses and with proper timing.[5]

But, it will be pointed out, full analgesia induces drowsiness and blunts or distorts awareness. How can that be a desired outcome of treatment? Fair enough. But then the rationale for requesting death begins to shift from relieving experienced suffering to ending a life no longer valued by its bearer or, let us be frank, by the onlookers. If this becomes a sufficient basis to warrant mercy killing, now the category of euthanizable people cannot be limited to individuals with incurable or fatal painful illnesses with little time to live. Now persons in all sorts of greatly reduced and degraded conditions—from persistent vegetative state to quadriplegia, from severe depression to the condition that now most horrifies, Alzheimer's disease—might have equal claim to have their suffering mercifully halted. The trouble, of course, is that most of these people can no longer request for themselves the dose of poison. Moreover, it will be difficult—if not impossible—to develop the requisite calculus of degradation or to define the threshold necessary for ending life.

From Voluntary to Involuntary

Since it is so hard to describe precisely and "objectively" what kind and degree of pain, suffering, or bodily or mental impairment, and what degree of incurability or length of anticipated remaining life, could justify mercy killing, advocates repair (at least for the time being) to the principle of volition: the request for assistance in death is to be honored because it is freely made by the one whose life it

is, and who, for one reason or another, cannot commit suicide alone. But this too is fraught with difficulty: How free or informed is a choice made under debilitated conditions? Can consent long in advance be sufficiently informed about all the particular circumstances that it is meant prospectively to cover? And, in any case, are not such choices easily and subtly manipulated, especially in the vulnerable? Kamisar is very perceptive on this subject:

> Is this the kind of choice, assuming that it can be made in a fixed and rational manner, that we want to offer a gravely ill person? Will we not sweep up, in the process, some who are not really tired of life, but think others are tired of them; some who do not really want to die, but who feel they should not live on, because to do so when there looms the legal alternative of euthanasia is to do a selfish or a cowardly act? Will not some feel an obligation to have themselves 'eliminated' in order that funds allocated for their terminal care might be better used by their families or, financial worries aside, in order to relieve their families of the emotional strain involved?

Even were these problems soluble, the insistence on voluntariness as the justifying principle cannot be sustained. The enactment of a law legalizing mercy killing on voluntary request will certainly be challenged in the courts under the equal-protection clause of the Fourteenth Amendment. The law, after all, will not legalize assistance to suicides in general, but only mercy killing. The change will almost certainly occur not as an exception to the criminal law proscribing homicide but as a new "treatment option," as part of a right to "A Humane and Dignified Death."[6] Why, it will be argued, should the comatose or the demented be denied such a right or such a "treatment," just because they cannot claim it for themselves? This line of reasoning has already led courts to allow substituted judgment and proxy consent in termination-of-treatment cases since *Quinlan*, the case that,

Kamisar rightly says, first "badly smudged, if it did not erase, the distinction between the right to choose one's own death and the right to choose someone else's." When proxies give their consent, they will do so on the basis not of autonomy but of a substantive judgment—namely, that for these or those reasons, the life in question is not worth living. Precisely because most of the cases that are candidates for mercy killing are of this sort, the line between voluntary and involuntary euthanasia cannot hold, and will be effaced by the intermediate case of the mentally impaired or comatose who are declared no longer willing to live because someone else wills that result for them. In fact, the more honest advocates of euthanasia openly admit that it is these nonvoluntary cases that they especially hope to dispatch, and that their plea for *voluntary* euthanasia is just a first step. It is easy to see the trains of abuses that are likely to follow the most innocent cases, especially because the innocent cases cannot be precisely and neatly separated from the rest.

Everyone is, of course, aware of the danger of abuses. So procedures are suggested to prevent their occurrence. But to provide real safeguards against killing the unwilling or the only half-heartedly willing, and to provide time for a change of mind, they must be intrusive, cumbersome, and costly. As Kamisar points out, the scrupulous euthanasiasts seek a goal "which is *inherently inconsistent*: a procedure for death which *both* (1) provides ample safeguards against abuse and mistake; and (2) is 'quick' and 'easy' in operation." Whatever the procedure adopted, moreover, blanket immunity from lawsuits and criminal prosecution cannot be given in advance, especially because of ineradicable suspicions of coercion or engineered consent, and the likelihood of mixed motives and potential conflict, post mortem, among family members.

Damaging the Doctor-Patient Relationship

Abuses and conflicts aside, legalized mercy killing by doctors will almost certainly damage the doctor-patient relationship. The patient's trust in the doctor's wholehearted devotion to the patient's best interests will be hard to sustain once doctors are licensed to kill. Imagine the scene: you are old, poor, in failing health, and alone in the world; you are brought to the city hospital with fractured ribs and pneumonia. The nurse or intern enters late at night with a syringe full of yellow stuff for your intravenous drip. How soundly will you sleep? It will not matter that your doctor has never yet put anyone to death; that he is legally entitled to do so—even if only in some well-circumscribed areas—will make a world of difference.

And it will make a world of psychic difference too for conscientious physicians. How easily will they be able to care wholeheartedly for patients when it is always possible to think of killing them as a "therapeutic option"? Shall it be penicillin and a respirator one more time, or perhaps just an overdose of morphine this time? Physicians get tired of treating patients who are hard to cure, who resist their best efforts, who are on their way down—"gorks," "gomers," and "vegetables" are only some of the less than affectionate names they receive from the house officers. Won't it be tempting to think that death is the best treatment for the little old lady "dumped" again on the emergency room by the nearby nursing home?

Even the most humane and conscientious physician psychologically needs protection against himself and his weaknesses, if he is to care fully for those who entrust themselves to him. A physician friend who worked many years in a hospice caring for dying patients explained it to me most convincingly: "Only because I knew that I could not and would not kill my patients was I able to enter most fully and intimately into caring for them as they lay dying." The psychological burden of the license to kill (not to speak of the brutalization of the physician-killers) could very well be an intolerably high price to pay for physician-assisted euthanasia, especially if it also leads to greater remoteness, aloofness, and indifference as defenses against the guilt associated with harming those we care for.

The point, however, is not merely psychological and consequentialist: it is also moral and essential. My friend's horror at the thought that he might be tempted to kill his patients, were he not enjoined from doing so, embodies a deep understanding of the medical ethic and its intrinsic limits. We move from assessing the consequences to looking at medicine itself. . . .

But there is a difficulty. The central goal of medicine—health—is, in each case, a perishable good: inevitably, patients get irreversibly sick, patients degenerate, patients die. Unlike—at least on first glance—teaching or rearing the young, healing the sick is *in principle* a project that must at some point fail. And here is where all the trouble begins: How does one deal with "medical failure"? What does one seek when restoration of wholeness—or "much" wholeness—is by and large out of the question? . . .

Although I am mindful of the dangers and aware of the impossibility of writing explicit rules for ceasing treatment—hence the need for prudence—considerations of the individual's health, activity, and state of mind must enter into decisions of *whether* and *how vigorously* to treat if the decision is indeed to be for the patient's good. . . .

Ceasing medical intervention, allowing nature to take its course, differs fundamentally from mercy killing. For one thing, death does not necessarily follow the discontinuance of treatment; Karen Ann Quinlan lived more than ten years after the court allowed the "life-sustaining" respirator to be removed. Not the physician, but the underlying fatal illness becomes the true cause of death. More important morally, in ceasing treatment the physician need not *intend* the death of the patient, even when the death follows as a result of his omission. His intention should be to avoid useless and degrading medical *additions* to the already sad end of a life. In contrast, in active, direct mercy killing the physician must, necessarily and indubitably, intend *primarily* that the patient be made dead. And he must knowingly and indubitably cast himself in the role of the agent of death. . . .

The enormous successes of medicine these past fifty years have made both doctors and laymen less prepared than ever to accept the fact of finitude. Doctors behave, not without some reason, as if they have godlike powers to revive the moribund; laymen expect an endless string of medical miracles. It is against this background that terminal illness or incurable disease appears as medical failure, an affront to medical pride. Physicians today are not likely to be agents of encouragement once their technique begins to fail.

It is, of course, partly for these reasons that doctors will be pressed to kill—and many of them will, alas, be willing. Having adopted a largely technical approach to healing, having medicalized so much of the end of life, doctors are being asked—often with thinly veiled anger—to provide a final technical solution for the evil of human finitude and for their own technical failure: If you cannot cure me, kill me. The last gasp of autonomy or cry for dignity is asserted against a medicalization and institutionalization of the end of life that robs the old and the incurable of most of their autonomy and dignity: intubated and electrified, with bizarre mechanical companions, helpless and regimented, once proud and independent people find themselves cast in the roles of passive, obedient, highly disciplined children. People who care for autonomy and dignity should try to reverse this dehumanization of the last stages of life, instead of giving dehumanization its final triumph by welcoming the desperate goodbye-to-all-that contained in one final plea for poison.

Notes

[NOTE: Only the notes that are included in the excerpted material appear here.]

2. Of course, any physician with personal scruples against one or another of these practices may "write" the relevant exclusions into the service contract he offers his customers.
4. Yale Kamisar, "Some Non-Religious Views Against Proposed 'Mercy-Killing' Legislation," *Minnesota Law Review* 42: 969-1042 (May, 1958). Reprinted, with a new preface

by Professor Kamisar, in "The Slide Toward Mercy Killing," *Child and Family Reprint Booklet Series,* 1987.

5. The inexplicable failure of many physicians to provide the proper—and available—relief of pain is surely part of the reason why some people now insist that physicians (in-stead) should give them death.

6. This was the title of the recently proposed California voter initiative that barely failed to gather enough signatures to appear on the November 1988 ballot. It will almost certainly be back.

QUESTIONS FOR WRITING, REFLECTION, AND DEBATE

1   In the early 1980s, when Sidney Hook was close to death, he asked the doctor to discontinue life support, but the doctor refused. Hook recovered and went on to publish his autobiography as well as other writings before he died in 1989. Are these examples of later productivity sufficient to justify the doctor's refusal to honor Hook's request? If not, is there any other reason to justify the doctor's refusal?

2   A main point in Sidney Hook's argument for voluntary euthanasia is that he dreads imposing a burden on his family. Is this a convincing reason for encouraging infirm older people to end their lives? Imagine that you are Sidney Hook's son or daughter and then proceed to write a detailed letter to your "father" explaining why you agree, or disagree, with Hook's fear about becoming a burden on the family.

3   Are Derek Humphry's reasons that a physician should help a terminally ill patient to die convincing? Would exactly the same reasons apply if the patient were not terminally ill but instead suffering from a chronic condition—for example, the aftereffects of a stroke—that diminished the quality of life?

4   Humphry believes that, if a person is clearly depressed and not rational, it is a good reason not to help end that person's life. Is it possible for someone to be deeply gloomy about life yet still be rational and therefore decide to commit suicide? Imagine that you have just received a letter from an old friend expressing such gloomy thoughts in favor of suicide. Write a detailed letter to be sent to the friend giving your reasons for agreeing or disagreeing with the conclusions reached.

5   Is there really a difference between a doctor going along with a request to terminate treatment, when that will inevitably result in a patient's death, in contrast to a doctor intentionally giving a deadly drug? What about the case of withdrawing artificial nutrition or hydration from a patient?

6   Kass offers a "slippery slope" argument against allowing doctors to engage in mercy killing. In other words, he believes that, once we set a

precedent and get used to idea of deliberate killing, there will be no way to stop the practice from expanding. Is Kass's fear of the danger a realistic one or is it exaggerated? Are there steps that could be taken to avoid the dangers here?

7 Assume that you have been asked by your employer, the chief of a nursing home, to draft a statement of policy by the facility expressing what the nursing home should do in cases where a resident says he or she no longer wants to go on living. In developing your policy statement, be sure to give guidance to doctors, nurses, and social workers on how they should act when they come in contact with such a situation.

FOCUS ON PRACTICE: ADVANCE DIRECTIVES

The ethical dilemmas of end-of-life decisions have increasingly led to demands by the public for a greater measure of control in how those decisions are made. One practical response to this problem has been the spread of so-called advance directives, or written statements, prepared well before a serious illness arrives, in which an individual can state the choice to be made when a decision is necessary (Collins, 1991). A general written statement specifying or limiting treatment would be a Living Will. A legal instrument that names another individual to make the actual decision would be a Durable Power of Attorney for health affairs.

A Living Will permits an adult of sound mind to stipulate the kind of life-prolonging treatment to be provided: for example, "I desire food and fluids but no cardiopulmonary resuscitation." A Living Will is an official legal document and should be prepared on a standard form, although a simple written declaration of preference may also suffice. Different states have different legal requirements about witnesses and other rules under which a Living Will may be acceptable.

A Durable Power of Attorney is also a witnessed legal document. But in this instance an individual need not specify all the details about treatment to be given or withheld. Instead, the individual designates someone else—called a proxy or health care agent—to make those decisions in the event the person is incapacitated. Again, as with Living Wills, different states have varying rules and regulations applying to power of attorney documents and their acceptability for health care decision making.

It is sometimes asked: Which is better, a Living Will or a Durable Power of Attorney? Living Wills were the first type of advance directive to become popular, but health care powers of attorney have turned out to be more flexible. The exact kind of document required will depend on state laws, which have become a critical factor in light of the *Cruzan* decision. Such variations in law from state to state can of course be a problem because it is unclear whether one state will always honor a directive from another state.

It is important to note that only a small minority of Americans—less than one in five—have actually prepared any kind of written advance directive. But the number is growing, especially among older people. When end-of-life decisions must be made in the absence of a written directive, the decision about discontinuing treatment is typically made by the family and health care providers in consultation. It is rare that such decisions end up being made by a court, which is a cumbersome way to proceed. Written advance directives can be helpful in keeping such cases out of the legal system and in the hands of those closest to patients.

Advance directives may not be the complete solution to end-of-life decision problems. For example, in a study of patients on kidney dialysis, it turned out that 61% said they wanted the doctor or proxy decision maker to have "leeway" to disregard their own previously expressed preferences. Instead of simply following a Living Will, they wanted decision makers to take into account circumstances and the patient's best interest.

Some critics have argued that the move toward advance directives may end up making refusing treatment easier only for those who have filled out the necessary "paperwork." Those who have not completed the proper legal documents—for instance, persons without the necessary information or education—may find themselves lacking the rights theoretically granted them by law.

Other critics argue against advance directives because people might change their minds about end-of-life decisions. Why shouldn't people be able to change their minds about forgoing treatment should conditions change? It is common for older people to say, "I would never want to live in an old age home," and yet, after living for a time in a retirement residence or nursing home, it is not unusual for the same people to discover that life is quite satisfactory there. The same point could hold about chronic illness. People fear that they would be unable to go on living with an extreme disability, yet adaptation to loss and disability commonly does take place.

These problems of uncertainty about the future, excess paperwork, or the fact that people can change their minds may not be arguments against using advance directives. Instead, they may suggest a need to improve the way advance directives are used in practice: for example, to strengthen communication between health care professionals and patients and not simply to treat written directives as another form of "red tape." The need for better communication also suggests that advance directives can be an occasion for family members to share with one another their own reasons and expectations about end-of-life decisions. Used in this way, advance directives can help older people and their families better approach end-of-life decisions. Advance directives do not solve all problems but, at their best, they can be a useful tool to ensure that providers know and respect the wishes of patients of all ages.

Suggested Readings

Annas, George J., *The Rights of Patients: The Basic ACLU Guide to Patients' Rights,* Totowa, NJ: Humana Press, 1992.

Kapp, Marshall B., *Ethical Aspects of Health Care for the Elderly: An Annotated Bibliography*, Westport, CT: Greenwood, 1992.

Moody, Harry R., *Ethics in an Aging Society*, Baltimore, MD: Johns Hopkins University Press, 1992.

Waymack, Mark H., and Taler, George A., *Medical Ethics and the Elderly: A Case Book*, Chicago: Pluribus Press, 1988.

Should Families Provide for Their Own?

When problems in old age arise, most people turn to their families for help. The vast bulk of care for the frail elderly, perhaps 80%, is furnished by families and other private individuals (Shanas, 1979). But the American family itself is changing at the same time that American society is witnessing changes in the proportion and character of the aging population (Bengtson, Rosenthal, and Burton, 1990; Cantor, 1992). Families are facing new challenges to give care and help as well as bearing the cost of long-term care for elderly members (Brubaker, 1987).

Let's go back to the Walton family as they struggle to cope with their long-term care problems. For several years, the Waltons' daughter, Carol, has been juggling her time between her job, her children, and the time she felt she had to give to helping her mother and father. After George Walton started going downhill, he and Martha started seriously thinking about the Middletown nursing home. The problem was, he couldn't afford to go in as a private-pay patient but he and Martha had too much money in their bank account to qualify for Medicaid. At that point, their son Robert insisted that he knew a lawyer who could arrange for them to receive Medicaid. The Waltons didn't like it but they went along with what the lawyer advised and eventually George was able to qualify for Medicaid to cover nursing home costs.

After George Walton went into the home, the problems didn't end for the Waltons. It turned out that Martha Walton's forgetfulness got so bad that Carol and Robert were worried about Martha staying in the house alone. Eventually, she ended up moving in with Carol's family. These days, Carol still feels caught between the demands that are made on her: She feels like she has three jobs—one at work, one as a mother, and one taking care of Martha. The arrangement isn't ideal for anyone but at least she feels she's doing right by her mother.

Aging and the American Family

The image of the lonely older American abandoned by family is for the most part a false one. The fact that older people have a rich and **extended family** life is documented by recent statistics on the subject. For example, more than half of Americans above age 65 are married and nearly four-fifths of them have children. An equivalent proportion have at least one brother or sister, and three-quarters are grandparents. By all evidence, these older people remain in contact with other family members.

Caregiving responsibility for the elderly has already become a major and predictable part of the life cycle of Americans (Glick, 1977). Among married couples, the primary caregiver tends to be the spouse if available and healthy (Stephens and Christianson, 1986). But a big problem for old-old couples is that, with advancing age, older spouses themselves are more and more likely to be impaired. In that event, older people typically turn for help to adult children, who are the chief caregivers for older men or women who are no longer married (Brubaker, 1985).

Some patterns of caregiving over the life span are illuminated by the **exchange theory of aging,** which is based on the idea that interaction in social groups is based on the reciprocal balancing of rewards depending on actions performed (Dowd, 1975). Thus parents care for children and spouses care for one another both because of moral obligation and because they know they can count on mutual support and reciprocal exchange of help in time of difficulty (Dowd, 1984).

Many different kinds of family members can be involved in caregiving (Hays, 1984), but responsibilities still tend to be divided according to gender, as Figure 4.1 demonstrates. The overwhelming amount of care for aged relatives is still provided by women, typically wives, daughters, or daughters-in-law, who must balance the burden of care for the aged with the demands of employment and their own children and family. This task for middle-aged women has given rise to the term *sandwich generation* to describe the impact of such parent-care responsibilities on women in the middle (Brody, 1985, 1990). The average American woman in the middle years will spend more years with elderly parents than years spent caring for children under age 18 (Watkins, Menken, and Bongaarts, 1987). For many women during those years, time will be spent in caregiving. Among those 45 to 54 years of age, for example, 17% have some responsibility for a disabled older parent (Stone and Kemper, 1989). Like child care, this issue is attracting interest from business in discussions about corporate elder care (Work/Family Elder Directions, 1988). Along with other equity issues raised by family caregiving, we need to keep in mind that the burden of care is overwhelmingly borne by women: a fact to consider when we shortly come to review the subject of gender and aging.

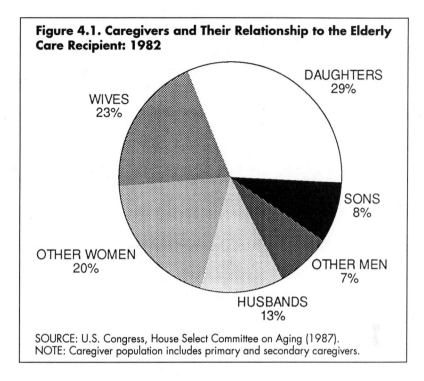

Figure 4.1. Caregivers and Their Relationship to the Elderly Care Recipient: 1982

DAUGHTERS
29%

WIVES
23%

SONS
8%

OTHER WOMEN
20%

OTHER MEN
7%

HUSBANDS
13%

SOURCE: U.S. Congress, House Select Committee on Aging (1987).
NOTE: Caregiver population includes primary and secondary caregivers.

In cases of extreme frailty or dependency, the burden on family members may prove exhausting, leading to "burnout" and perhaps elder abuse or neglect (Stone, Cafferata, and Sangl, 1987). Alzheimer's disease and other varieties of dementia would be a case in point. As the disease progresses and the patient's behavior becomes more extreme, caregiving burden and stress can become almost impossible in a home setting (Springer and Brubaker, 1984; Corbin and Strauss, 1988). These conditions have led gerontologists to speak of family caregivers themselves as the "hidden victims" of the disease (Zarit, Orr, and Zarit, 1985).

The portrait of caregiver burden, however, should not be exaggerated. Many caregivers remain in their role for a long time and never "burn out." There is a normalcy to family caregiving, especially between spouses, that makes it seem nonextraordinary to those who render care. Moreover, significant help for caregiver burden does exist. Social supports, especially the **informal support** of family or friends, can prove crucial to people under stress. Family members may benefit from respite care: that is, temporary care for dependent older people to allow the caregiver some time off. Such programs can relieve some of the strain involved in efforts to delay placing a demented relative in a nursing home (Klein, 1986; Montgomery, 1989).

Mutual self-help groups, such as those sponsored by the Alzheimer's Association, have also proved very effective for caregivers (Mace and Rabins, 1981). In all these cases, the provision of formal human services can work in a complementary way with what the family does: not to replace it but to support it (Litwak, 1985).

Abandonment or Just Living Alone?

Four out of five older people have at least one living adult child, and relationships with adult children usually involve frequent contact. Nearly half of seniors report that they presently live or expect to live in proximity to their children. Three-quarters of those with living children have a child who could reach them in less than 30 minutes (Shanas, 1980). Significantly, more than 40% are in daily contact with their children and another 20% are in contact once a week. Thus, even when families are spread out geographically, this distance does not imply that families are broken up or that the young have abandoned the old.

Nonetheless, a clear trend toward independence in living arrangements among the elderly has been visible and increasing in recent years. For instance, in 1960 only one-fifth lived alone; by 1984 the proportion had increased to one-third. Sharing a household in an extended family has also dropped significantly in recent years. In 1960 40% of older people were residing with their adult children, but by 1984 the proportion had dropped to 22% (U.S. Congressional Budget Office, 1988). By the mid-1980s, almost half of women over the age of 75 were living alone.

Do these figures show the breakdown of family for elderly relatives? As a description of actual family behavior, the stereotyped picture of the isolated elderly is wrong in two ways. First, the image of the three-generation family living happily under one roof in the past is mistaken. In Europe and America, multigenerational living arrangements were never very common even in agrarian societies centuries ago (Laslett, 1972). Idealizing the three-generation or extended family living under one roof is part of the **"world-we-have-lost" myth** (Laslett, 1971) in which we mistakenly believe that family life has disintegrated and that older people were better off in an idealized "golden age" of preindustrial society (Stearns, 1982). Western societies have tended toward a separate residence for the nuclear family (only parents and children) for a long time.

In the second place, families today typically remain in close and frequent contact. This pattern has been called "intimacy at a distance" and it reflects the common desire by older people to live independently from grown children yet still remain in close enough proximity to have regular contact. When illness or need arises, a spouse, adult children, or other relatives are typically the first sources of help.

But in refuting the stereotype of the abandoned elderly, we need also to recognize that conditions are different with respect to living arrangements of older people in comparison to the pattern of a century ago. One big reason for change is simply demographic. Today, unlike in the past, there are vastly larger numbers of older people who survive into advanced age and who thus require sustained help with activities of daily living. In cases of debilitating chronic illness such as stroke or Alzheimer's disease, these elderly people may live many years in conditions of dependence that exceed the capacity of family caregivers. Other older people may have never been married or may simply outlive available family members. The result is that we must increasingly rely on government to provide what families are no longer in a position to give.

Family Responsibility

The development of social welfare programs such as Social Security and Medicare has meant that health care and income support for the aged have become a societal responsibility rather than a family obligation. But in the United States, unlike other advanced industrialized countries, long-term care has remained an exception to that trend (Buchanan, 1984). Government has been reluctant to provide long-term care, and families remain an important source of both hands-on care and financial support. When it comes to long-term care needs, elderly people first rely on spouses; **spousal responsibility** is deeply embedded in our culture as a matter of both ethics and law. If a spouse is not available to provide care, other family members and other generations then become responsible.

In some cultures, such as the Chinese, Confucian teachings inculcate filial piety or strong reverence for parents, including the duty to support them over one's own children (Cowgill, 1986). In the United States, **filial responsibility**—that is, responsibility for care of the aged by adult children—is treated ambiguously as a matter of law, custom, and ethics (Schorr, 1961; Callahan, 1985; Post, 1989). In fact, half the states do have laws on the books that could compel children to give financial support to aged parents, but these laws have rarely been enforced (Garrett, 1980; Lammers and Klingman, 1986), perhaps because of deeply conflicting public attitudes toward filial responsibility (Seltzer and Troll, 1982).

In fact, however, filial responsibility continues to be practiced as a matter of ethics or custom, and gerontologists have documented rich intergenerational ties in American families (Pfeifer and Sussman, 1991). The unresolved question is how government programs should act in taking into account both spousal and filial caregiving duties and financial responsibilities, which in fact continue to play a prominent role in family life today.

Medicaid and Long-Term Care

The American health care system provides near-universal coverage for acute diseases among the old under Medicare. The same system provides for separate financing and administration of acute care and long-term care, however (Hellman and Hellman, 1991). About half of the money spent on long-term care in nursing homes comes from some branch of government, chiefly Medicaid (Stevens and Stevens, 1974). Medicaid is a joint government program, supported by federal and state funds, created in 1965 to provide health care for the poor. Over the years, however, it has become the primary government mechanism to pay for care for the aged and disabled (Spiegel, 1979). Medicare pays only 2% of those nursing home costs, while Medicaid pays 36%. Medicaid is a large and expensive program, and the cost is growing rapidly. In fiscal year 1991, Medicaid outlays were $95 billion, up 31% from the previous year.

Although created as a health care program for poor people, such as people on welfare, Medicaid has in fact become a key factor in nursing home coverage for middle-class elderly people. While three-fourths of Medicaid recipients are low-income parents with children, these families receive only about a quarter of total Medicaid dollars. In 1990 two-thirds of what Medicaid spent went to institutional care for the elderly, disabled, or mentally retarded (Kent, 1992). In 1990 27% of all Medicaid expenditures went to cover nursing home costs.

Financing Long-Term Care

Do families have the financial capacity to bear the cost of long-term care (Cohen et al., 1987)? Long-term care already consumes a larger portion of the private health care dollar for the elderly than any other type of expenditure. The cost of a year in a nursing home today can range between $25,000 and $50,000 or more in different parts of the country ("Paying for a Nursing Home," 1989). Few individuals or families can afford that cost on an extended basis. If individuals enter a nursing home as a "private-pay" patient, after only three months nearly 70% of residents have reached the poverty level, and within a year 90% are impoverished.

In the likely event that long-term care costs exceed savings, those who face such costs have few options. One option is to qualify for Medicaid to cover nursing home expenses. But Medicaid is a **means-tested entitlement** program: that is, it makes use of eligibility rules, based on income and assets, to determine whether people qualify for Medicaid coverage. A nonmarried nursing home applicant for Medicaid can keep nonexempt assets of only $2,000 or less. Married couples, taking advantage of recent changes in the law, can keep between $13,000 and $66,000 in such assets, excluding the value of a home. Thus all but a limited portion of a spouse's assets are assumed to be available to pay for the partner's long-term care (Tilly & Brunner, 1987).

Many of those who do not qualify for Medicaid still do not have enough assets to pay for long-term care themselves. They face a cruel choice: struggle to provide home-based care or do what is necessary to obtain Medicaid. To qualify for Medicaid, it is necessary to "spend down" lifetime accumulated financial assets to become impoverished and thereby eligible for medical assistance (Liu and Manton, 1991). Under regulations of the Medicaid law, spouses of those thus impoverished may obtain some protection but other generations lose accumulated life savings. One major problem with Medicaid financing of long-term care is that it introduces serious inequities across families, age groups, and social classes (Arling et al., 1991).

According to public opinion surveys, 82% of the general public recognizes that they cannot afford to pay the cost of long-term care either at home or in a nursing home. They also know that they cannot rely on the family alone: 86% want the government to help pay for long-term care instead of leaving it entirely up to the family. Significantly, in an era of strong sentiment against taxes, more than two-thirds say they would be willing to pay for a long-term care program with increased taxes (data from a Louis Harris Survey reported in *Older American Reports*, April 1, 1988).

But despite such clear public sentiment, a universal public insurance program for long-term care is still not available in America. On the contrary, Medicaid has become the public program of last resort to pay nursing home costs. In fact, Medicaid is the fastest growing component of state budgets and is increasingly becoming an old-age program; nearly 40% of all Medicaid benefits go to the elderly, chiefly for nursing home care, as Figure 4.2 demonstrates.

The growing burden of Medicaid on the government has prompted a search for more affordable alternatives. For years, aging advocates have sold the idea of home care to legislators and to the public with the argument that home care is more humane, in keeping with people's preferences to stay at home, and also more cost effective. Unfortunately, the facts are not so clear. National demonstration projects and other studies have shown that home care may be more desirable but it doesn't necessarily save money. One reason may be the so-called **woodwork effect,** or latent demand (Fama and Kennell, 1990). Government policymakers are afraid of people coming "out of the woodwork" to demand services that families would have provided otherwise or that weren't provided before (Arling and McAuley, 1983). Once the government is willing to pay, people may ask "someone else" to pick up the tab.

It is often said that older people should only go into a nursing home as a matter of their own choice, not for the convenience of the family. But when the bulk of hands-on care is given by family members, it is not so simple to say that the legitimate interests of the family are to be disregarded (Dill et al., 1987). The reality is that virtually no one enters a nursing home as a matter

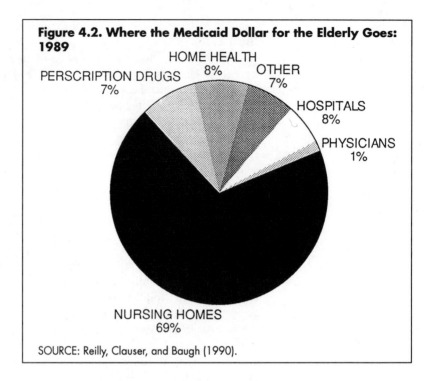

Figure 4.2. Where the Medicaid Dollar for the Elderly Goes: 1989

HOME HEALTH 8%

PERSCRIPTION DRUGS 7%

OTHER 7%

HOSPITALS 8%

PHYSICIANS 1%

NURSING HOMES 69%

SOURCE: Reilly, Clauser, and Baugh (1990).

of choice. People go into nursing homes, by and large, as an act of desperation, when everything else fails and when the family has no other alternative. We need to keep that fact in mind when considering the role of financial incentives for Medicaid and nursing home admissions.

Medicaid Planning

As older people and their families have become more aware of the cost of long-term care, middle-class families have found ways of qualifying for Medicaid without complying with the harsh spenddown requirements imposed by Medicaid. Financial planners in recent years have been joined by a new group of specialists: **elderlaw** attorneys who specialize in law and aging. Both attorneys and financial planners urge a variety of strategies to enable middle-income families to qualify for Medicaid coverage of nursing home costs. The heart of these strategies comes down to divestment planning, that is, appearing to be poor by taking advantage of legal loopholes to "avoid the Medicaid trap" (Budish, 1989).

The following are some of the key strategies elderlaw attorneys recommend:

- Transfer assets at least 30 months ahead of applying for Medicaid
- Transfer assets between husband and wife
- Seek protection from a court order
- Keep assets in a form exempt from Medicaid
- Set up a trust account

It is not known exactly how many middle-class older people presently take advantage of loopholes in the Medicaid law to appear impoverished and thus protect their family wealth. But the numbers are large enough to have sustained a rapidly growing body of "elderlaw" attorneys, who have now established their own association, the National Elderlaw Academy. As Medicaid divestment planning has become more widespread, the practice has attracted criticism from those who argue that the practice is like deception used by some poor people to qualify for welfare payments or like schemes by rich people who dodge taxes through loopholes.

Regardless of whether such practices are technically "legal," the critics argue that they are socially immoral and that Medicaid planning is too. This moral criticism is another way of insisting that taxpayers in general should not pay to protect the inheritance wealth of affluent families (Freedman et al., 1983). Indeed, it is not possible to understand what is at stake in the debate about Medicaid and family responsibility without seeing the importance of inheritance and the intergenerational transfer of assets (Dobris, 1989; Langbein, 1991).

Gerontologists agree that family abandonment of the elderly is a myth and that families already *do* take care of their own by giving their time and effort, sometimes to the point of exhaustion. But there is disagreement about whether families *ought* to go further and make use of a portion of their assets to pay for long-term care costs.

Similarly, gerontologists have documented how informal supports *do* enable frail elders to remain at home when the only alternative for them might be entering a nursing home. But once again, there is strong disagreement about whether families should be paid in cash by the government for giving the kind of hands-on care that they customarily give. Knowledge of the facts is essential for debating the issue. But values and choices in the debate are not settled by facts alone (Stone, 1991).

In the readings that follow, strong opinions are expressed about whether people ought to take advantage of Medicaid eligibility laws and whether it's right for government to pay family members. On one side of the debate is Alexander Bove, a prominent elderlaw specialist who believes that families should realistically plan ahead for nursing home costs by transferring their assets to qualify for Medicaid. This approach, he argues, is not immoral or illegal; indeed, it is no different than planning ahead to minimize taxes. On the other side of the debate, Andrew Bates finds transfer of assets to be a very troubling practice at the borderline of legality and social morality. Bates echoes a widely shared opinion. It seems wrong for some families to preserve an inheritance while others are forced to impoverish themselves to pay for long-term care expenses. In his article, Stephen Moses focuses directly on the phenomenon of impoverishment due to nursing home expenses. Moses moves the debate away from moralistic rhetoric and urges us instead to look carefully at the facts about paying for long-term care. Finally, in the piece by Gunhild Hagestad, we hear a different perspective on the debate about family caregiving. Here, too, equity or fairness is an issue and there is a major question about the role of women who assume the burden of caregiving. It's not just "families" who provide for their own but, overwhelmingly, women who provide that care. The legal and financial debate about **Medicaid spenddown** must take into account this other form of inequity that ought to command our attention when we think about steps to provide better care for elderly people.

The Medicaid Planning Handbook

Alexander A. Bove, Jr.

The Morality of Medicaid Planning: Is It True That "Only the Suckers Pay"?

An article written in late 1989 by a nationally known if not acclaimed financial columnist viciously attacked the practice of Medicaid planning as shameful and "offensive" behavior on the part of the public and advisors alike. The gist of the article was that this type of planning—creating "artificial poverty"—is ultimately paid for by the public. The columnist argued that the Medicaid

Source: From *The Medicaid Planning Handbook* by Alexander A. Bove, Jr. Copyright © 1992 by Alexander A. Bove, Jr. By permission of Little, Brown and Company.

program is designed to help the "poor" and that it is positively immoral for advisors like me to show readers like you (who presumably are not poor) how to protect your home and life's savings if you or a family member should be faced with the need for expensive long term care.

Our columnist and the righteous others who agree with her seem to be totally ignorant of two critical facts. First, the very law which they claim we are abusing tells us clearly that we are expected to pay for nursing home costs only for a specified period of time (thirty months). After that, the Medicaid law provides that the government will pay, unless we are foolish enough to pass up the opportunity to stop paying. Clearly, arranging assets in a way allowed by the law to qualify for Medicaid is no more immoral than arranging assets to legally qualify for income tax or estate tax savings.

Second, a truly fair and objective analysis of the *whole* picture would reveal that even in the case of the most aggressive Medicaid plan, it is not the planners who are immoral but the system itself.

Think about it. We have a system that will pay every penny of the medical bills of a multimillionaire who has cancer, while stripping a working, middle-class elderly couple of virtually everything they own if one or both have to enter a nursing home. Where is the morality there? And if someone were to show the elderly couple how they could legally protect their home and a little savings, where is the immorality in that? Is it more moral to be a millionaire with cancer than a middle-class old man with Alzheimer's disease?

Use of the argument of morality to denigrate Medicaid planning is without foundation and is put forth only by those few who refuse to address the larger and more important underlying question: How do we as a nation take care of our elderly? And not just the elderly who are "fortunate" enough to be stricken with the right illness (one that will be paid for by the Medicare part of our system).

The Medicaid laws (and those who speak out against Medicaid planning) have overlooked one indisputable fact: a person does not *choose* to develop Alzheimer's disease or multiple sclerosis or paralysis (where costs are *not* paid) over cancer or blood disease or chronic kidney disease (where costs *are* paid). Our health care system has become some sort of morbid lottery whereby the illness you happen to get will determine whether you go bankrupt or not.

In my opinion, it is only a matter of time before these inequities will be recognized and the system will pay for all of us who need care, regardless of our financial situation. In the meantime, however, there are ways to avoid the risk of bankruptcy if you happen to draw the wrong illness. . . .

As to the final word on morality, perhaps that must come from within each of us when we are faced with the choice between Medicaid planning or bankruptcy. If, like our friendly columnist, you feel you should pay until virtually everything is gone, you do have that choice. . . . However, at least you will be aware of your other options. . . .

The Way It Is

In the beginning there were the Green family and the Benson family. Herb Green and Rob Benson knew each other well, as they had worked almost side by side with the same company for nearly thirty years. Both families consisted of a husband and wife in their late sixties and two adult children. Both families owned their own homes and had a comfortable amount of savings. And, coincidentally, both families were stricken with catastrophic illness at about the same time.

There was one major difference, however. Herb's illness, costly as it was, did not affect the financial security of his family, while Rob's illness, which in fact was less costly to treat than Herb's, left Rob's family almost bankrupt. Here are their stories.

Herb Green worked most of his life at Boston Edison and retired at age sixty-five. After the children left for college, Herb's wife, Mary, resumed her teaching position with the city of Medford, just outside Boston, and worked there until she retired, also at sixty-five. Subsequently, a routine physical disclosed that Herb had prostate cancer that was at an advanced stage. Extensive tests and then chemotherapy and radiation treatments were prescribed. Ultimately, surgery was required, as well as extensive follow-up treatment that included at-home visits by nurses. Treatment would continue for the rest of Herb's life, with costs running into the hundreds of thousands of dollars, all to be paid by the Medicare program together with the Green's supplemental health insurance coverage. As a result, the Greens retained the security of their home and virtually every penny of their savings.

Rob Benson also retired at sixty-five, but his wife, Betty, continued to work at that age, intending to retire later with extra benefits. Shortly after Rob's retirement, Betty began noticing that Rob was becoming increasingly forgetful. At first his behavior was almost humorous and cute, but as the condition worsened, Betty became frightened and fearful, not only for Rob's safety but also for her own security. She took Rob to specialists for several tests, and he was finally diagnosed as having Alzheimer's disease. The doctor told Betty there was no meaningful treatment and that she must simply keep an eye on him and care for him at home as long as she could.

Betty took care of Rob for about a year (she had to retire from her job before she had planned to), but eventually the task was more than she could handle. Even the part-time nurses she hired to care for Rob at home were not enough. He needed constant care and supervision. Finally, she resigned herself to the fact that Rob would have to enter a nursing home.

When Rob was placed in the home, Betty was required to complete forms that disclosed every detail of their financial information, such as savings, investments, life insurance, retirement income, and so on, not only for the nursing home but also for their state's Department of Public Welfare, which administers the Medicaid program. Shortly after Betty completed these forms, the department sent a notice to Betty advising her that all of Rob's pension income would have to be spent on his care. In addition, Betty would have to spend all but about $66,000 of their savings toward Rob's care before she could expect any help from the state and federal government. It didn't take Betty long to figure that at a cost of $48,000 per year for Rob's nursing home, in about three years she would have spent about $150,000 of their savings on Rob's care and would then be down to the required sixty-odd thousand dollars she was "allowed" to keep. "But then," Betty thought, "what if *I* get sick?" And Betty's concern was well placed. If she does get sick, then there goes not only the rest of the family's money but probably their home as well. . . .

Such is the state of our system and a stark illustration of the difference between *Medicare* (the Green family case) and *Medicaid* (the Benson family case). Those lucky enough to be stricken with the right type of illness can retain their financial security; the others are forced into bankruptcy. There are, however, steps that can legally be taken to protect a family's financial security in the face of a long term illness.

In fact, in many respects the Medicaid laws are like the tax laws—you can get the advice of experts and take maximum legal advantage of the laws and pay much less, or you can ignore them or fail to get proper advice and pay much more. The critical difference, however, between the tax laws and the Medicaid laws is that ignorance of the Medicaid laws can cost you everything you own. . . .

Case . . .

Harry and his wife, Sally, have a condo in Florida, jointly owned and valued at $200,000, and they rent an apartment in Vermont. Their other assets are nominal. They live on pensions received by each of them. Although they maintain a residence in Florida, their roots and their children are in Vermont. Harry is ill and is slated to enter a nursing home in Vermont before the year's end.

Solution. If Harry enters a nursing home in Vermont, he cannot at the same time be considered a Florida resident. The value of the condo in Florida would be fully countable for Vermont Medicaid purposes. If Harry and Sally have definitely decided not to place Harry in a Florida nursing home, the condo presents a bit of a problem, but not an insurmountable one.

It is quite possible for Harry and Sally to have different domiciles, so that Harry could have a Vermont residence and Sally a Florida residence. It is also permissible for Harry to make transfers to Sally without jeopardizing his Medicaid eligibility, so long as Sally does not, within the succeeding thirty-month period, subsequently transfer those assets to another person. Therefore, Harry can deed over his half of the Florida condo to Sally.

In the subsequent determination of her spousal resource allowance, Sally would claim an *exemption* for the Florida condo as it is *her* residence (assuming she continues to maintain a Florida domicile), and, therefore, Harry should immediately qualify for Medicaid. At some future date, Sally can plan for the disposition of the Florida condo, either through a trust or through a deed to the children with a reserved life estate, *without* affecting Harry's Medicaid eligibility.

Result. The couple has preserved the Florida condo, even though it is situated out-of-state.

Case . . .

Jack and his wife, Mabel, have recently sold their jointly owned home and now rent an apartment for $1,000 per month. They live off the income from the $250,000 proceeds of the sale and have no other assets and only nominal income. Jack is ill and about to enter a nursing home.

Solution. First, they should investigate the possibility of purchasing the apartment they live in. If they could purchase it for, say, $150,000, this would immediately protect that amount of funds for Mabel. The balance of $100,000 is very likely to be allowed to her in full (perhaps after a hearing) as her spousal resource allowance, since it is her primary source of income. . . . They should consider approaching the landlord to arrange a *prepayment of rent* under their nonassignable lease. . . .

Result. Most if not all of the couple's savings have been preverved.

Case . . .

Brenda, age fifty-nine, and her husband Eddie, age sixty-six, rent an apartment in Manhattan and have a home on Cape Cod that they have used during the summers. The jointly owned Cape Cod home is worth about $225,000 (no mortgage), and they have about $160,000 in joint savings, mostly from Eddie's earnings. Eddie is suffering from an illness that is likely to lead to his institutionalization in the near future. Brenda has been advised that

if she does nothing, she will lose the Cape home plus all but about $66,000 of their savings.

Solution. Brenda and Eddie can move into the Cape Cod home and immediately treat it as their principal residence. This will render the full value of the residence exempt and, therefore, noncountable as an asset for Medicaid purposes. Next, and before Eddie enters the nursing home, Brenda should take a major portion of their savings, say $125,000, and purchase an annuity contract that will pay her a fixed monthly income for the rest of her life. For instance, at her age, for $125,000 Brenda could purchase an annuity that would pay her about $950 per month for her life with a fifteen-year term certain. This means that if she died within the first fifteen years, the $950 per month would be paid for the balance of the fifteen-year period to a beneficiary Brenda would name when she purchased the annuity (for example, her children). (If Brenda were concerned about providing for her husband, she could purchase a "joint and survivor" annuity, which would pay a little less per month, but would continue payments for *both* their lives and could *still* contain the fifteen-year term-certain option.)

The effect of the purchase of the annuity would be to convert the fully countable savings into *noncountable income* for Brenda. That is, although the income to Brenda would count against her $1,500 maximum monthly income allowance, the $125,000 used to purchase the annuity would no longer be a countable asset. The thirty-month waiting period will not apply to the purchase of the annuity because it is a transfer for full consideration (she got something of equal value in return).

Brenda would *also* be entitled to one-half the remaining $45,000 savings as her spousal resource allowance (or, in some states, all of it, since it is less than $66,500) and the balance of the savings could easily be used to improve their home, purchase an automobile, and so on.

Result. They have saved their home and most or all of their savings, while insuring Brenda an income for life.

Middle-Class Medicaid

Andrew Bates

Golden Girls

With the dramatic surge in the elderly population during the past couple of decades, it's not surprising that there's now a cottage industry of attorneys and financial planners specializing in "elder law." Sounds pretty innocuous, as does the specialty called "Medicaid estate planning." What this really means, however, is helping middle- and upper-income seniors shelter their assets—no matter how great—so they can qualify for Medicaid coverage. It's a practice—and a perfectly legal one—that puts extra pressure on the already financially strapped Medicaid program by squandering precious resources on those who should not have taxpayers financing their care.

Because Medicare covers only the cost of short-term, acute care, paying for long-term care has always been a problem for the elderly. But until the recent explosion of medical costs, old folks were typically able to pick up their own tabs, with the help of their children. In the past decade, however, the cost for nursing home care has soared; it now averages between $25,000 and $30,000 a year. The pressure for loopholes has thus intensified. More and more elderly patients are taking advantage of flaws in the Social Security Act, which enable them to avail themselves of government-subsidized care *and* save their assets for their heirs.

Several recent studies suggest that only 10 percent to 25 percent of nursing home patients have

Source: "Middle-Class Medicaid" by A. Bates, *The New Republic* (February 3, 1989), pp. 17-18. Reprinted with permission of *The New Republic*.

impoverished themselves on medical bills ("spent down," in health care vernacular) to qualify for Medicaid. Even these relatively low figures, which are based on the numbers of patients who start as private pay and end up on Medicaid, overestimate the extent of "spend down" by failing to account for the artificial "impoverishment" that's occurring.

The lawyers who exploit Medicaid loopholes are neither obscure nor shady. The American Bar Association sponsors seminars about where the loopholes are and how to exploit them. Senior citizens can even get advice on Medicaid estate planning from many state Medicaid offices. Boston attorney Harley Gordon, whose *How to Protect Your Life Savings from Catastrophic Illness and Nursing Homes* has sold over 200,000 copies and landed him appearances on talk shows throughout the country, is at least blunt about his agenda: "Every city in America has thousands of lawyers whose job it is to help wealthy people and corporations avoid as much tax as legally possible. What I do is the same thing. Only I help the little people." "Little people" in Gordon's mind means the same as in Leona Helmsley's: the typical recipient of his and others' advice are individuals with between $100,000 and $400,000 in liquid assets.

How does Medicaid planning work? In most states, a single individual cannot qualify for Medicaid until her "countable assets" have been reduced to about $2,000. (For married couples, the rules are more lenient: depending on the state, the spouse can keep anywhere from about $13,000 to $66,000 in assets and from $1,000 to $1,600 a month for personal maintenance needs.) Since virtually all cash and securities have to go to pay nursing home bills, the theory is to convert "countable" liquid assets into exempt assets. The largest shelter in Medicaid estate planning is your home, so elder gurus advise you to pay off your mortgage, remodel your kitchen, or build on. If you don't own a home, buy one.

To spend the rest of your disposable income, pay off your debts, buy a car (the more expensive the better, of course, since it's all exempt), or, in most states, buy personal property—clothing, furniture, jewelry—of any value. Take a vacation. Or, as financial planners Ira Schneider and Ezra Huber advise in *Financial Planning for Long-Term Care*, "An applicant could spend all of his or her assets on something 'frivolous,' such as a ninetieth birthday celebration of Ziegfield Follies proportion."

Not surprising, Medicaid officials say that Medicaid planning is being driven not by the elderly, but by heirs desperate to preserve their inheritance. In doing so, heirs face an ethical dilemma, since Medicaid recipients have more trouble getting into top-quality nursing homes than private-pay patients, and nursing homes with mostly private-pay patients provide much better care than those facilities dependent on Medicaid patients. To avoid having to choose between inheritance and consigning Mom and Dad to second-rate care in understaffed nursing homes, Medicaid planning gurus often recommend that the patient retain enough money to pay privately for at least six months to get into a top-notch nursing home. The elderly patient then "spends down" to qualify for Medicaid, yet at the same time remains in the high-quality, well-regarded nursing home. It's the best of all worlds: Mom and Pop get top-notch care, the kids get the full inheritance, and taxpayers foot the bill.

Although there is little empirical data on the precise extent of asset sheltering by the elderly and their attorneys, Medicaid officials throughout the country say that the practice is widespread. For instance, Massachusetts Medicaid workers have reported that roughly 30 percent to 50 percent of

Medicaid applications from affluent Boston suburbs involve the sheltering of assets.

The policy implications of this trend are enormous. Taxpayer dollars are being used to preserve the assets of the middle-class and fairly well-to-do elderly, while Medicaid dollars for poor women and children and the elderly poor are scarce. In addition, with the vast majority of their patients on Medicaid, many nursing homes are in desperate shape financially. Since Medicaid reimbursement covers only about 80 percent of the full cost of care, nursing homes have to charge more from private-pay patients—those middle- to upper-income elderly who, either misinformed or highly principled, aren't inclined to make the rest of us pay their medical bills. For those covered by private insurance, this cost is passed on in the form of higher premiums.

In an effort to crack down on such abuses, states such as New York and Connecticut are developing "public-private" solutions that would allow individuals to retain some of their assets and still qualify for Medicaid. Under the Connecticut venture, for example, an individual buys an experimental policy that pays nursing home bills up to a fixed amount, say, $100,000. Once the coverage runs out, Medicaid kicks in automatically. At first glance, these programs seem to be a palatable compromise. The problem is that unless the federal Medicaid eligibility requirements are tightened, there's little incentive to buy three years' worth of private insurance when one can qualify for Medicaid almost immediately.

What to do? The inspector general of the Department of Health and Human Services laid the groundwork for a feasible solution in two major studies released in 1988 and 1989. Congress should tighten many of the loopholes in the Social Security Act, strengthening the transfer of assets rules so that patients could not artificially impoverish themselves to qualify for Medicaid. Congress should also allow families to retain and manage property while their parents are on Medicaid. In return, as a condition of eligibility for such public assistance, the government would require a lien (which would equal the total amount of Medicaid benefits paid) be placed on the recipient's property and assets. But Congress hasn't followed through on these recommendations.

Recovery on estates should be made mandatory so that heirs cannot, in the words of one analyst, "reap the windfall of Medicaid subsidies." With the exception of Oregon, however, most states have proved reluctant to recover expenses from the estates of deceased Medicaid recipients. Recovery programs are politically unpopular but they save states money that can then be plowed back into Medicaid budgets. Congress could provide an in-centive to states to build up effective recovery programs by reducing federal Medicaid payments to those that fail to do so.

If the elderly and their heirs don't like these tougher rules, that's too bad. If seniors want to avoid liens on assets and estate recovery after their death, they should purchase private long-term care insurance by using the equity built up in their homes (which can cover the average senior citizen's medical bills) or insisting that their heirs contribute to the cost of care. Like it or not, it is not the birthright of upper-income and middle-class Americans to have their medical bills paid by the rest of us. At least not yet.

READING 18

The Fallacy of Impoverishment

Stephen Moses

The debate over how to solve the long-term care financing crisis has reached a new and perilous stage: stalemate. Big government solutions are out of favor, but private sector initiatives appear inade-

This paper is based on research conducted by the Office of In-spector General of the Department of Health and Human Ser-vices and published in *Medicaid Estate Recoveries* (OAI-09-86-00078), June 1988 and *Transfer of Assets in the Medicaid Program: A Case Study in Washington State* (OAI-09-88-01340), May 1989. . . . The views expressed herein are those of the author. Neither the Office of Inspector General nor the Department of Health and Human Services reviewed the paper in draft and no endorsement by them should be inferred. [The author was] . . . project director for the studies cited above. *Source:* "The Fallacy of Impoverishment" by S. Moses, *The Gerontologist,* Vol 30, No 1, 1990, pp. 21-25. Copyright © The Gerontological Society of America. Reprinted with permission.

quate. When a problem seems intractable, wise counsel is to check your premises. Is there a missing piece in the long-term care financing puzzle? Does a false assumption underlie the deadlock on this issue?

Conventional wisdom holds that eligibility for Medicaid, the nation's single largest financier of long-term care, requires the spenddown of assets and income to impoverishment. Federal and state laws, regulations and policies seem to say that a person must spend down to the poverty level or below before qualifying. If this is true, elderly people and their heirs should seek private risk-sharing protection aggressively, but they do not. If it is false, private sector options such as long-term care insurance are severely handicapped—people only insure against real risks.

This paper describes research that casts doubt on the belief that Medicaid requires impoverishment. It also explores the broader social and policy ramifications of such a finding.

Background

Although originally intended to ensure access to mainstream health care for the poor, Medicaid has become the major payor of nursing home care for the middle class (Rymer, Burwell, Adler, & Madigan, 1984, p. 122). The program funds 44% of America's nursing home costs (Letsch, Levit, & Waldo, 1988) and is the principal payor for over 63% of patient days (Dean, personal communication, Oct. 20, 1989). Nevertheless, from the enactment of the Medicaid statute in 1965 until 1981, no federal rules existed against transferring assets to qualify for assistance. People who needed nursing home care could give away their property in order to qualify for Medicaid.

In 1981, Congress took the first step to limit this practice with the Boren-Long amendment. This statute allowed states to restrict asset transfers made for the purpose of qualifying for Medicaid. But Boren-Long did not apply to exempt property. Inasmuch as Medicaid exempts the home, and 70% of the net worth of the median elderly person is in a home (U.S. Bureau of the Census, 1986), Boren-Long excluded large amounts of property from the transfer restrictions.

Congress corrected this shortcoming and developed a more comprehensive approach in 1982 with the Tax Equity and Fiscal Responsibility Act (TEFRA). The TEFRA authorized states to (1) restrict asset transfers within 2 years of Medicaid nursing home eligibility, (2) place liens on the property of living recipients, and (3) recover from the estates of deceased recipients. Each of these procedures was optional for state Medicaid programs. Nevertheless, the expressed intent of Congress was "to assure that all of the resources available to an institutionalized individual, including equity in a home, which are not needed for the

support of a spouse or dependent children will be used to defray the cost of supporting the individual in the institution" (U.S. Code, 1982, p. 814).

In 1985, a draft report of the Health Care Financing Administration revealed lax state enforcement of the TEFRA asset control authorities (Moses & Duncan, 1985). For example, transfer of assets rules were fraught with loopholes, only one state (Alabama) fully used the lien power, and although 18 states recovered from estates, most did so with very little success. Based only on telephone inquiries to state Medicaid programs and a valid random sample of cases in Idaho, this report speculated that estate recoveries could leap from $36 million nationally per year to $535 million if all states followed the asset control methodologies of Oregon's exemplary program. Although it remained unpublished, the report was released to the Office of Inspector General (OIG) of the Department of Health and Human Services and to the General Accounting Office (GAO). Both the OIG and the GAO began national studies of Medicaid estate recoveries in 1986.

OIG and GAO Medicaid Estate Recovery Studies

Office of Inspector General (1988)

The OIG sent a 17-page questionnaire to all 50 state Medicaid programs probing their policies and practices on transfer of assets, liens, and estate recoveries. The objective of the study was:

to find out exactly what States have done since 1982 to implement TEFRA's asset control authorities . . . to determine the extent and effectiveness of Medicaid estate recovery programs throughout the country . . . to report on "best practices" . . . [and] to examine State Medicaid eligibility policy with regard to transfer of assets and liens, because estate recoveries are obviously moot if no property is retained in recipients' possession that can be recovered after their deaths (OIG, 1988, p. 2).

Both the Health Care Financing Administration and the Office of Management and Budget approved the OIG's survey instrument in advance. All 50 states and the District of Columbia responded. The study team did extensive telephone follow-up with Medicaid eligibility and estate recovery staff in three-fourths of the responding programs.

The OIG found very weak enforcement of asset transfer restrictions: "The States report that Medicaid eligibility rules permit knowledgeable individuals to transfer or shelter property from Medicaid resource limitations in a manner reminiscent of income tax avoidance" (p. ii). Three pages of quotations from Medicaid eligibility staff across the country supported this conclusion. For example: "People are starting to use a lot of fancy footwork to avoid losing the 'family fortune'" (Maryland). "Many, many, many attorneys call on a daily basis looking for 'loopholes.' There are lots of welfare specialists who help people avoid welfare resource limits" (Minnesota). "We recover from people who are not clever enough to transfer their property, and everyone else goes scot-free" (California).

Only two states had implemented TEFRA's lien provisions to secure property for estate recovery. Most states found the lien authority too restrictive to administer cost effectively. For example: "Liens are too difficult to administer because of Federal restrictions. Other property retention techniques, such as aggressive identification of assets, reversing illegal transfers, and challenging every possible resource shelter, are more effective under the circumstances" (Oregon, p. 20). Commenting on the ineffectuality of transfer of assets and lien rules, the OIG observed, "States cannot recover what is not there" (p. 23).

Twenty-three states and the District of Columbia recovered $42 million from the estates of Medicaid recipients in 1985, according to the OIG. But most states were very inefficient at recoveries.

Even under the existing restrictive laws, regulations, and policies, the OIG concluded that "if all States recovered at the same rate as the most effective State (Oregon), national recoveries would be $589 million annually" (p. 46).

General Accounting Office (1989)

The GAO study sought to "assess the extent and effectiveness of state efforts to reduce program costs by using the estates of Medicaid nursing home recipients or their surviving spouses to recover all or part of the costs of care paid for by Medicaid" (GAO, 1989, p. 14). The agency reviewed 200 randomly selected nursing home cases in Oregon and seven other states. Oregon was chosen "to identify the key elements of a successful estate recovery program because it reported annual recoveries per nursing home recipient more than twice those reported by any other state" (p. 14). It recovered "about $10 for every $1 spent administering the program . . ." (p. 3). Projections of potential estate recoveries in the other states were based on their use of Oregon's policies and procedures.

The GAO found that ". . . two-thirds of the amount spent for nursing home care for Medicaid recipients who owned a home could be recovered from their estates or the estates of their spouses. If implemented carefully, estate recovery programs can achieve savings, while treating the elderly equitably and humanely" (p. 3). The six states GAO studied that lacked recovery programs "could recover $85 million from recipients admitted to nursing homes in fiscal year 1985" (p. 4). Only "about 14 percent of the Medicaid nursing home residents in the eight states GAO reviewed owned a home . . ." (p. 4). The GAO did not account for the discrepancy between this percentage and the well-known statistic that three-quarters of elderly people own their homes (Rivlin & Wiener, 1988, p. 123). One presumes that people are either selling their homes and "spending down" before going on Medicaid or they are effectively transferring or sheltering the home's value.

Thus, both the OIG and the GAO studies confirmed that large amounts of private resources ($589 million nationally and $85 million in six states, respectively) pass to heirs each year instead of being used for long-term care costs or to reimburse Medicaid. Additionally, for reasons discussed in the next section, the OIG and GAO projections may be vastly underestimated.

Medicaid Asset Shelters

Assets that do not remain in an estate until the death of a Medicaid recipient are obviously not recoverable and would not show up in studies like the OIG's and GAO's. Therefore, the extensive anecdotal evidence of asset transfers and shelters discovered by the OIG in its estate recovery study raised another serious question. If people are jettisoning property before they apply for Medicaid nursing home care, how could we possibly know how much money is diverted from private to public long-term care costs? The OIG conducted further research that bears on this question (OIG, 1989). It found that people initially denied but subsequently approved for Medicaid nursing home benefits in Washington state for 1 year possessed $27.5 million in assets at the time of their denial. These assets had to be disposed of before they could qualify for assistance. Over 80% of the assets had been sheltered: 59% were transferred to a spouse, 11% were transferred to adult children, and 11% were retained as exempt. Only 8% were consumed for long-term care. The remainder was of uncertain disposition.

To account for the magnitude of these figures, the OIG interviewed 32 professional advisers on Medicaid eligibility. These people described a network of private "elder law" attorneys, publicly funded legal services attorneys, social workers, and even Medicaid staff who counsel families on how to qualify an infirm elder for Medicaid while preserving income and assets. The sheltering techniques recommended by such advisers included: interspousal and other legal transfers, trusts, purchase of exempt assets, "intent to return" to the

home, life estates, joint tenancy with right of survivorship, gift and estate planning, durable power of attorney, guardianships, divorce, relocation, care contracts, and nonsupport suits. One attorney, whose bag of tricks is highlighted in the OIG report, guaranteed Medicaid eligibility within 30 days for a $950 fee. . . .

Finally, the OIG observed that "financial abuse of the elderly, according to study respondents, is 'commonplace,' 'bigger than anyone thinks,' 'rife.' We heard many stories about people forced onto Medicaid when their income or resources were taken" (OIG, 1989, p. 11).

Medicaid Asset Spenddown

A common understanding, often referenced in the literature, is that half or more of all nursing home patients on Medicaid were private pay until they spent down to poverty (Branch et al., 1988, p. 649; Burwell, Adams, & Meiners, 1989, p. 2; Davis, 1984, p. 3; DHHS, 1987, p. 19; Dobris, 1989, p. 10; NAIC, 1987, p. 2). Tragically, many people actually do sell their homes and spend their life savings on nursing home care before they qualify for Medicaid. Evidence is mounting, however, that such draconian measures are both unnecessary and less common than previously supposed. Impoverishment is not the only path to Medicaid nursing home eligibility, according to the OIG work. Financially sophisticated people who are accustomed to dealing with attorneys, accountants, and financial planners can find ways to protect their assets and still qualify for Medicaid. Others, with less financial savvy, often lose what little they have before they learn how the system works (OIG, 1988, p. ii).

Very little is known about the magnitude of asset spenddown. For example, Branch reported how fast people would become impoverished *if* they spent down in nursing homes (Branch et al., 1988). He did not tell us how often or to what degree they actually do spend down. Several recent studies have found that spenddown is actually much smaller than previously believed (Burwell, Adams, & Meiners, 1989; Liu & Manton, 1989; Liu, Doty,

& Manton, 1989; Spence & Wiener, 1989). Like the Branch study, however, these studies assume that people who had significant assets at one time, but ended up on Medicaid, must have had catastrophic care costs. None of them develop the possibility that assets were transferred or sheltered in order to qualify for nursing home assistance. Nevertheless, the techniques to transfer and shelter assets, and the counseling to learn them, are readily available, according to the OIG.

Spousal Impoverishment

Impoverishment of the spouse at home caused by institutionalization of a disabled husband or wife used to be a serious problem. Medicaid rules allowed only a few hundred dollars of income per month to be shifted from an institutionalized to a community spouse who had little or no separate income (Neuschler, 1987, pp. 48-49). The new community spouse "minimum monthly maintenance needs allowance" was designed to solve that problem at considerable public expense. We should keep in mind, however, that the same people whose income and resources will now be protected may live in homes they own free and clear. Their problem is not poverty per se, but rather cash flow.

Medicare Catastrophic Coverage Act

The Medicare Catastrophic Coverage Act of 1988 changed Medicaid long-term care eligibility in several ways that affect asset shelters and estate recovery potential. Some of the changes, such as more generous treatment of community spouse income and resources, will make Medicaid benefits easier to obtain. This could mean that more assets will remain to be recovered from estates or, alternatively, that people will have longer to find ways to protect the assets. Other changes, such as mandatory and lengthened transfer of assets restrictions, make eligibility somewhat more difficult. This could lead to liquidation of assets and greater spenddown or, alternatively, to wider use of better planning and qualifying techniques. Most of the methods used to shelter or transfer assets legally in the past are still intact. The basic condition remains unchanged: families can preserve significant assets while qualifying elders for Medicaid nursing home care. Without estate recovery programs, these assets pass unencumbered to noncontributing heirs and Medicaid shoulders the full brunt (minus mandatory contributions to cost of care) of the long-term care costs.

Implications

Medicaid requires impoverishment. Few scholarly papers or popular articles on long-term care financing say otherwise or explain further. Yet, impoverishment is neither a sufficient nor a necessary cause of Medicaid eligibility. Two-thirds of the elderly poor in America are not covered by Medicaid (Holahan & Cohen, 1986, p. 99). On the other hand, people with median and even higher income and resources often qualify for the program's most expensive benefit (nursing home care) while preserving the bulk of their assets for heirs (Neuschler, 1987, p. 20; OIG, 1988; OIG, 1989).

Looming in the background of last year's "catastrophic" debate was the question: what shall we do about *long-term care* costs? That predicament is front and center now. Most of the work done by the federal government on this issue has encouraged the development of private risk-sharing solutions. Private sector answers, however, have been much slower to develop than anticipated. This is a puzzle, because most of the obstacles to market-based solutions do not seem insurmountable. Experts on long-term care financing have assumed that Medicaid is not a major impediment.

In light of the findings discussed here, however, consider that elderly people are often unclear about catastrophic long-term care risks. They deny their personal jeopardy and do not plan ahead to protect privately against financial catastrophe. They do not plan to rely on public assistance either, but once they get sick, welfare is their only option. Under today's system, they can avoid paying insurance premiums (often in excess of $100 per month) or risk-sharing membership fees, wait to see if they are stricken by a long-term debilitating illness, and still receive nursing home care paid for by Medicaid while preserving their assets for heirs. Because of the shame felt by families forced to qualify their elders for welfare, the negative aspects of Medicaid nursing home care—dependency, loss of income, access and quality problems, institutional bias, and stigma—often go uncommunicated to others.

Therefore, the elderly population perceives no urgent need to purchase insurance, join a Social/Health Maintenance Organization or Continuing Care Community, convert the equity in their home, or save toward long-term care costs. Without a compelling need among consumers to buy (low demand), sellers of such services lack sufficient reason to invest in the necessary research, development, and marketing of private protection (low supply). This in itself could explain why the impact of private-sector long-term care financing options has been disappointing.

Conclusion

A plan to eliminate this impasse between public and private long-term care financing options is quite simple conceptually: give middle class elderly people a clear choice between access to public funding of long-term care or preservation of their estates—not both. The rudiments of such a plan are evident in the OIG report's (1988) recommendations:

- Change Medicaid rules to permit families to retain and manage property while their elders receive long-term care.
- Strengthen the transfer of assets rules so that people cannot give away property to qualify for Medicaid.
- Require a legal instrument as a condition of Medicaid eligibility to secure property owned by applicants and recipients for later recovery.

- Increase estate recoveries as a nontax revenue source for the Medicaid program while steadfastly protecting the personal and property rights of recipients and their families. (p. ii)

Underlying these recommendations is the belief that we should eliminate the indignities and inequities associated with qualifying for nursing home assistance. We should not pressure people to divorce, impoverish their spouses, liquidate their property, or hire estate planners in order to qualify. Elderly people, financially independent all their lives, but stricken by catastrophic illness in their most vulnerable years, should not be compelled to rely on welfare because of temporary cash flow problems. To correct such deficiencies in the existing program, however, we would have to pay for the solution. We can do this by closing the loopholes in transfer of assets restrictions, requiring legal encumbrances on property as a condition of eligibility, and mandating cost-effective estate recoveries as a prerequisite for federal financial participation. Alternatively, we could offer middle class seniors a line of credit secured by their estates with which to purchase home or nursing care and get them off welfare entirely.

If implemented, these recommendations would increase Medicaid estate recoveries substantially. But this new nontax revenue is not the most important aspect of the recommendations. We would also be sending a message to America's senior citizens and their families: If they do not or cannot protect themselves privately against the risk of catastrophic long-term care costs, their government will provide the necessary care. But, if they own property, they must understand that it will be recovered—when it is no longer needed for the livelihood of their immediate dependents—to pay for publicly funded care and ensure that the same benefits will be available for others. Only the remainder after reimbursement of costs will pass to their heir and beneficiaries. So if they do not want to encumber their estate, then they or their heir should purchase protection in the private market-place.

If we send this message, we can expect the demand for private risk-sharing products to increase. Greater demand means more suppliers, increased competition, better products, leaner pricing, thriving new industries and, therefore, increased employment and tax revenues.

The last piece in the puzzle is to explain how seniors will pay for private risk sharing. The experts say older people lack the cash flow to purchase private long-term care protection (Rivlin & Wiener, 1988). Yet people over 65 possess more than $800 billion in home equity (Rivlin & Wiener, 1988, p. 131). Seniors are "house rich" and "cash poor." Home equity conversion experiments intended to solve this problem have failed. These experiments have failed, however, because Medicaid pays for nursing home care *and* exempts the home. Why encumber the house to buy insurance you may not need when the government will pay for your care if you need it and save the house anyway? When people know they can save the house or get Medicaid, but not both, they will be more likely to seek home equity conversion to provide the cash flow to purchase private protection. This change could make home equity conversion economically viable as private enterprise.

Finally, faced with the potential loss of their inheritances, adult children of elderly people will contribute voluntarily toward long-term care insurance premiums or other forms of financial protection for their parents. They have the cash flow and their aging parents have the assets. Both parties have an intense interest in preserving the estate, including the family home. Under the current system, the adult children of elderly people reap a windfall from Medicaid for ignoring the risk of catastrophic costs.

The proper role of government in this arena is to help those who cannot help themselves. It is not to transfer wealth from tax payers to indemnify heirs. If we make long-term care assistance more readily available than now, but require a payback from estates, middle class elderly people will have better access to care and stronger reasons to seek nonwelfare protection. In time, they will be freed entirely from the indignity of legal maneuvering to qualify for public assistance.

References

Branch, L. G., Friedman, D., Cohen, M., Smith, N., & Socholitzky, E. (1988). Impoverishing the elderly: A case study of the financial risk of spenddown among Massachusetts elderly people. *The Gerontologist, 28,* 648-652.

Burwell, B., Adams, E., & Meiners, M. (1989). *Spend-down of assets prior to Medicaid eligibility among nursing home recipients in Michigan* (contract 500-86-0016). Washington, DC: SysteMetrics/McGraw-Hill for the Health Care Financing Administration.

Davis, C. (1984). *Long-term care financing and delivery systems: Exploring some alternatives* (conference proceedings). Washington, DC: Health Care Financing Administration.

Department of Health and Human Services (DHHS) (1987). *Report of the task force on long-term health care policies.* Washington, DC: U.S. Government Printing Office.

General Accounting Office (1989). *Medicaid: Recoveries from nursing home residents' estates could offset program costs* (GAO/HRD-89-56). Washington, DC: U.S. Government Printing Office.

Holahan, J. F., & Cohen, J. W. (1986). *Medicaid: The trade-off between cost containment and access to care.* Washington, DC: The Urban Institute.

Letsch, S. W., Levit, K. R., & Waldo, D. R. (1988). National health expenditures, 1987. *Health Care Financing Review, 10,* 109-122.

Liu, K., & Manton, K. (1989). The effect of nursing home use on Medicaid eligibility. *The Gerontologist, 29,* 59-66.

Liu, K., Doty, P., & Manton, K. (1989). *Medicaid spenddown of disabled elderly persons: In nursing homes or in the community?* (unpublished paper prepared under Cooperative Agreement No. 18-C-98641/4-02). Washington, DC: Health Care Financing Administration.

Moses, S. A., & Duncan, J. (1985). *The Medicaid estate recoveries study* (unpublished report). Seattle, WA: Health Care Financing Administration.

National Association of Insurance Commissioners (NAIC) (1987). *Long-term care insurance: An industry perspective on market development and consumer protection.*

Neuschler, E. (1987). *Medicaid eligibility for the elderly in need of long term care.* Washington, DC: National Governors' Association.

Office of Inspector General (1988). *Medicaid estate recoveries* (OAI-09-86-00078).

Office of Inspector General (1989). *Transfer of assets in the Medicaid program: A case study in Washington State* (OAI-09-88-01340).

Rivlin, A. M., & Wiener, J. M. (1988). *Caring for the disabled elderly: Who will pay?* Washington, DC: The Brookings Institution.

Rymer, M., Burwell, B., Adler, G., & Madigan, D. (1984). *Grants and contracts report, short term evaluation of Medicaid: Selected issues* (contract no. HHS-100-82-0038). Washington, DC: Health Care Financing Administration.

Spence, D. A., & Wiener, J. M. (1989). *Medicaid spend-down in nursing homes: Estimates from the 1985 national nursing home survey* (unpublished draft). Washington, DC: The Brookings Institution.

U.S. Bureau of the Census (1986). Household wealth and asset ownership: 1984 (Current Population Reports Series P-70, No. 7). Washington, DC: Author.

U.S. Code (1982). *Congressional and Administrative News,* 97th Congress—Second Session, Legislative History (Public Laws 97-146 to 97-248, Vol. 2). St. Paul: West.

READING 19

The Family
Women and Grandparents as Kin-Keepers

Gunhild O. Hagestad

Concern is growing over the strain experienced by families who provide care for their ill or impaired elderly members. It is frequently argued that families in an aging society must be prepared to assume more of a care load than was the case for families in the past. We do not really have the historical data to judge if such statements are accurate, but it is important to keep in mind that before improved living conditions and medical advances produced rectangular survival curves, illness and death were encountered in all phases of family life—and at a time when there were far fewer outside institutional facilities and programs to alleviate their pressures. Families have always been expected to experience and absorb the shocks of illness and bereavement. The main difference between today's families and those of the past is not likely to be in the total *amount* of care and concern they expend, but the *focus* of them.

Infants and young children have always been regarded as vulnerable and dependent. But now, after childhood, these attributes are linked nearly exclusively with old age. Never before in human history has the experience of human frailty and the loss of a family member been so clearly linked to one group: the old. Perhaps part of the sense of burden associated with their care stems from the fact that the illness and loss are represented by *parents*—individuals who for decades were perceived as pillars of strength and support. . . .

Effects of "The Mortality Gap"

Women in the United States currently outlive men by about seven to eight years. The world of the very old is a world of women, both in society and within families. Men and women also spend the latter part of their lives in differing living arrangements and relationships. Most older women are widows liv-

Source: "The Family: Women and Grandparents as kin-keepers," by G. O. Hagestad in *Our Aging Society* edited by Alan Pifer and Lydia Brente, 1986 New York: Norton. Reprinted by permission of the author.

ing alone; most older men live with their wives. For example, among individuals over the age of seventy-five, two-thirds of the men are living with a spouse, while less then one-fifth of the women are.

These contrasts between older men and women have strong implications for the rest of their family members. First of all, the oldest members of a family are likely to be women. Women are also more likely to have great- and great-great-grandchildren. In societies where historical events have made sex ratios even more imbalanced than in this country, the three oldest generations may be populated only by women. For example, a German study found that many five-generation families contained three generations of widows.

Differences in widowhood and remarriage mean that men tend to maintain a significant horizontal, intragenerational relationship until the end of their lives; women do not. Consequently, women draw more on their intergenerational relationships for help and support in old age. At the time when men face serious impairment, they are likely to have a wife to care for them, while frail and ill older women are typically widows who turn to younger generations for help. This may be one reason why women, throughout their adulthood, invest more time and energy in intergenerational ties than men do. . . .

New Forms of Interdependence
. . . Over the last century, economic needs have given way to emotional needs as the main family "glue," especially in relationships among adults. Over the same time period, we have seen a shift in emphasis from the needs of the family as a group to the needs and wishes of individuals. Individual choices, such as the decisions about when to marry and leave the family, were once guided by the needs of the family unit as a whole. The twentieth century, with its pension and health-care plans, has "freed" generations from many of these economic interdependencies.[12] It is commonly argued that, as a result, family ties are seen as more *voluntary* in nature.[13] Kin connections are seen as a latent po-

tential, from which active and viable relationships may or may not develop.

Even though we have a good deal of cultural ambiguity regarding relationships between young and old in the family, members of our society still share some key values and norms about family responsibilities and interconnections.[14] Surveys that have compared the attitudes and expectations of parents and children have often found that children are more ready than parents to state that the younger generation should provide help to needy elderly parents. It has also been found that the old are the most receptive to formal, non3family services, while the young are those most in favor of family-provided help. Researchers attribute such contrasts to "youthful idealism" on the part of the young. The middle-aged and the old, on the other hand, are often responding on the basis of actual care-taking experiences. Recently, a number of writers have argued that with the growth of societal supports for the old, an increasingly important function of the family will be to serve as mediators between bureaucracies and the aged,[15] and the modern families not only meet needs, they identify needs, so that other institutions can address them.

While pension systems and health plans have lightened the economic pressures for most families, there is still a steady flow of intergenerational support, and the majority of the states have enacted so-called "family responsibility" laws, statutes that establish relatives' responsibility for family members who are indigent, needy or dependent. But recent research and public debate indicate that enormous complexity still remains in sorting out rights and obligations among family members in an aging society.

Kin-Keeping and Its Costs
There is a rather extensive literature showing that women are kin-keepers, and that their preparation for this role starts early in life. Kin-keeping tasks include maintaining communication, facilitating contact and the exchange of goods and services, and monitoring family relationships. These func-

tions are often performed for the husband's kin as well as for the women's own family line. Even when they are not the initiators and orchestrators of family get-togethers, old women may nevertheless facilitate family contact by serving as the "excuse" for bringing kin together. The mother-daughter connection has emerged as the pivotal link, both in the maintenance of family contact and in the flow of support.

Daughters have been found to be the linchpin of widows' support systems. When aging parents live with offspring, eight out of ten are mothers, and two-thirds of them are living with a daughter. It is estimated that when older family members are in need of constant care, 80 percent of such care is provided by kin, usually by wives and daughters.[17] It is interesting to note that the same clear trends, identifying women as carrying an extensive and complex load of family caring, have emerged in studies of welfare states. Although Norway eliminated family-responsibility laws following the introduction of a "law for comprehensive care" which covered the young as well as the old, the care provided by Norwegian women has been described as "the hidden welfare state."[18]

It has been common, especially in the popular press, to suggest that women's involvement in the world of work will make them spend less time and effort on kin-tending. There is little evidence to support such a claim. Indeed, there are indications that an opposite trend is occurring. A growing number of women may be adjusting their work plans and work schedules to accommodate the needs of elderly parents[19]—much as they formerly planned around the needs of their children. Recent research found that employment significantly reduced caregiving to aging parents among sons, but this was not a statistically significant trend for daughters.[20]

There seems to be good reason to worry about what Betty Friedan has called "the superwoman squeeze"—the overload experienced by middle-generation women who provide support for both children and parents, in addition to facing the demands of the workaday world.[21] A growing num-

ber of writers express concern that our current social expectations regarding family help to the elderly are unrealistic—even dysfunctional, given recent demographic and social change. One asks: "At what point does the expectation of filial responsibility become social irresponsibility?"[22]

It is quite possible that as a result of dramatic and rapid demographic change—particularly the enormous increase in the proportion of people who survive to advanced old age and face chronic health problems—we are finding that old attitudes and expectations about family care for impaired members simply do not work. The main casualties of this situation are likely to be middle-aged and young-old women, who face unmanageable burdens or strong feelings of guilt. It is important, however, to regard such conclusions cautiously; in devoting so much attention to the sick and the needy old, we may go too far in equating "old" with "needy." . . .

During recent decades, ideology has stressed equality between the sexes in their family roles. Yet, as we have seen, demographic and social changes have in many ways created very different family worlds for men and women. An increasing proportion of men have only precarious vertical ties, both up and down generational lines, while women's intergenerational ties are more varied, complex, and durable than ever before in human history.

Families are social arenas in which historical changes take on personal and shared meanings. They are also groups that meet critical human needs, and settings where biographies are written and rewritten as lives unfold, take on structure, and become interwoven. This [reading] has reviewed some of the recent demographic and social changes that have transformed family life. Siblings, parents and children, grandparents and grandchildren, now look forward to decades of shared biographies. Altered patterns of mortality have not only created relationships of unprecedented duration, but have also made the timing of family deaths more predictable. As the number of children per family has decreased, differences in life experiences among siblings have become reduced, and a greater proportion of family relationships are conducted across generational lines rather than with generational peers. Trends in fertility and mortality have resulted in increasingly "top-heavy" families, and family care-giving has become more and more focused on very old members. Multigenerational families have become more common, which means that a wider spectrum of kinship roles and relationships are open to family members.

Finally, many of these recent changes have affected men and women quite differently, in some ways creating sharper contrasts between their family and social worlds.

Notes

[NOTE: Only the notes that are included in the excerpted material appear here.]

12. John Modell, Frank F. Furstenberg, Jr., and Theodore Hershberg, "Social Change and Transitions to Adulthood in Historical Perspective," *Journal of Family,* Winter 1976, pp. 7-32.

13. Matilda White Riley, "The Family in an Aging Society: A Matrix of Latent Relationships," *Journal of Family Issues,* Sept. 1983, pp. 439-54.

14. Lillian E. Troll, Shiela J. Miller, and Robert C. Atchley, *Families in Later Life* (Belmont, CA: Wadsworth Publishing Co., 1979).

15. [Ethel] Shanas and Marvin B. Sussman, eds., *Family, Bureaucracy, and the Elderly* (Durham, N.C.: Duke University Press, 1977).

17. Troll, et al., op. cit.

18. Kari Waerness, "The Invisible Welfare State: Women's Work at Home," *Acta Sociologica,* supplement 1978, pp. 193-207.

19. Elaine M. Brody, "Aged Parents and Aging Children," in P.K. Ragan, ed., *Aging Parents* (Los Angeles: University of Southern California Press, 1979), pp. 267-88.

20. Eleanor Palo Stroller, "Parental Caregiving by Adult Children," *Journal of Marriage and the Family*, Nov. 1983, pp. 851-58.

21. Betty Friedan, *The Second Stage* (New York: Summit Books, 1981).

22. Brody, op. cit.

QUESTIONS FOR WRITING, REFLECTION, AND DEBATE

1 Elderlaw attorneys such as Alexander Bove often argue that transfer of assets is perfectly right because it is permitted by law. Is this reply a convincing one? Imagine that you are an elderlaw attorney who has been suddenly questioned about your practice by a reporter from a local newspaper. Write a detailed statement defending your practice to be distributed to the newspaper.

2 Alexander Bove defends transfer of assets by arguing that Medicare treats physical illnesses differently than Alzheimer's disease or similar impairments. Is this argument a persuasive one? If Medicare were amended to provide full coverage for Alzheimer's and related disorders, would that mean that transfer of assets was not justified?

3 Critics such as Andrew Bates sometimes charge that for older people to deliberately transfer assets to qualify for Medicaid is a form of "middle-class welfare." Is this charge a fair one? Write each of the arguments in

favor and against this charge. Then look over what you've written and produce a rebuttal for each argument.

4   Some who favor the idea of transfer of assets from aged parents to adult children to qualify for Medicaid argue that elderly people have a "right to leave an inheritance." Is this a "right" that ought to be encouraged or discouraged either by Medicaid or by the tax system? Who would benefit, and who would be harmed, if we were to expand that practice? Who would benefit, and who would be harmed, if we were to limit it?

5   Many believe that frail elderly people should be able to select anyone, including a family member, to provide services to which they are entitled and have the government pay for that care. Are there any valid reasons for prohibiting the hiring of family members to perform home care services? Write a draft letter to your congressional representative suggesting why you think this practice should be permitted or why you believe such a practice is mistaken.

6   Assume you are an assistant to a U.S. senator responsible for drafting an expanded version of a national health care law to cover the whole range of long-term care, from community to the nursing home. Write a "bill" containing the kinds of services that might be provided to the public under the new law, including the types of conditions covered. Then write an accompanying memorandum for the senator suggesting ways the new services could be paid for: that is, what combination of taxes and fees would cover the full package of long-term care services.

7   Gunhild Hagestad points out what most families would immediately recognize: namely, women end up handling most caregiving for frail elderly people. Is this fact about gender differences something that government ought to be concerned about or is it an issue best left for families to work out for themselves? If government were concerned to correct this apparent unfairness in the burden of caregiving, how could the government step in to make things fairer?

FOCUS ON PRACTICE: LONG-TERM CARE INSURANCE

Many middle-income elderly people and their relatives have been following the debate over Medicaid coverage of long-term care with great anxiety. Those who don't have enough financial resources to pay for an extended stay in a nursing home or who have a strong desire to pass along an inheritance have had to face the dismaying prospect of bankrupting themselves to qualify for Medicaid. Today, however, families who want to plan ahead for long-term care costs have a new option: purchasing private long-term care insurance. More than 100 insurance companies now offer these policies, and interest in this type of insurance is growing (Sloane, 1992). According to figures from the Employee Benefit Research Institute, the number of policies in force grew from 815,000 in 1987 to an estimated 2.5 million by 1993.

Private long-term care insurance covers nursing home care and sometimes other community-based services. The best of long-term care insurance pays for such medically necessary services for a period of one year or as long as a lifetime, but typically with a maximum period of coverage. Good policies are guaranteed renewable and need not require a prior hospital stay, as Medicare does.

Long-term care insurance is bought mainly by people above age 55; half the current policyholders are in their sixties. The age when a policy is first purchased is very important because the periodic premium paid, though level once purchased, rises sharply with age at purchase. For example, the same policy that goes for $250 a year at age 50 would cost up to $2,000 a year at age 70. But as companies include such insurance in benefit programs, it is likely that more younger people will participate, and group rates may bring costs down. At present, private long-term care insurance provides only 2% of total funding for long-term care in the United States. Less than 4% of the older population are covered by such policies (U.S. General Accounting Office, 1991).

Because long-term care is an expensive and widespread problem for older people, one might wonder why more people do not buy private long-term care insurance. One reason is that older people and their families mistakenly believe that Medicare will cover long-term care expenses. Another reason is that many policies are simply not affordable when purchased at an advanced age. The best estimates are that only a tiny proportion of the older population can afford to buy private long-term care insurance (Families USA, 1990; Rivlin and Wiener, 1988). Further, many consumers, as well as state governments, lack confidence in the products on the market.

There are many exclusions and limitations that make it complicated to evaluate comparable insurance products on the market. For example, insurance companies generally will not write insurance for preexisting conditions—an exclusion that covers many chronic diseases. There is also the problem of "*adverse selection*": the fact that insurance companies avoid people who look like bad risks. Still another problem is that long-term care policies generally pay a fixed dollar amount for each day of care covered. This fixed dollar approach is different than that of Medicare, which pays a percentage of customary or reasonable fees, regardless of inflation. Without inflation protection, a person buying long-term care coverage at age 60 may find the policy inadequate when it is needed, say, at age 80.

Private long-term care insurance is now left entirely to regulation by state governments. States differ widely in the level and quality of regulations that they apply. Without some kind of federal regulation, many states appear unlikely to implement standards for long-term care insurance to protect vulnerable consumers: for example, to provide protection from forfeiture of the policy should a payment be missed.

As government funding to pay for long-term care becomes explicitly income based or means tested, as it is under Medicaid, it is natural that middle-class elderly people will look to private insurance to protect themselves. Another option might be to organize a form of public long-term care insurance funded by some combination of tax revenues and individual contributions for those at risk. But until that happens, older people and their families will need to be familiar with all practical options for covering long-term care costs (Boyd, 1990), and long-term care insurance is one of those options.

Suggested Readings

Biegel, David E., and Blum, A., *Aging and Caregiving: Theory, Research, and Policy*, Newbury Park, CA: Sage Publications, 1990.

Finch, Janet, *Family Obligations and Social Change*, Cambridge, MA: Basil Blackwell, 1989.

Kane, Rosalie, and Kane, Robert, *Long-Term Care: Principles, Programs, and Policies*, New York: Springer, 1987.

Linsk, Nathan, and Keigher, Sharon, *Wages for Caring: Compensating Family Care of the Elderly*, New York: Praeger, 1991.

Rivlin, Alice M., and Wiener, Joshua M., *Caring for the Disabled Elderly: Who Will Pay?* Washington, DC: Brookings Institution, 1988.

Troll, Lillian E., Miller, Sheila J., and Atchley, Robert C., *Families in Later Life*, Belmont, CA: Wadsworth, 1977.

Social and Economic Outlook for an Aging Society

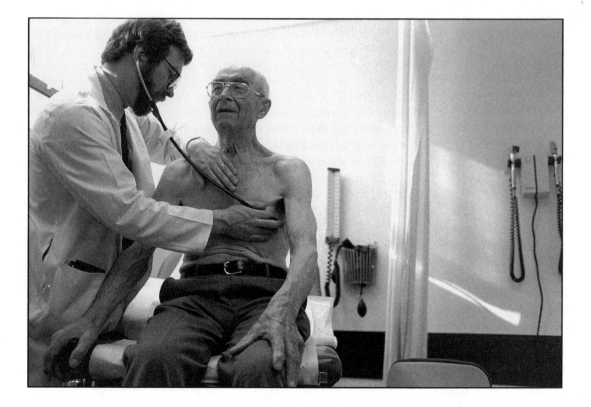

In centuries past, when few people survived to old age, it wasn't essential for society to give much thought to planning for old age. Traditional societies throughout history had only a small proportion of people who were old. But today, larger numbers of people are living longer, and population aging raises new questions about roles and responsibilities in an aging society.

Because government has assumed a role in providing older people with income, health care, and social services, more resources are now going to the elderly than in the past. That fact prompts unavoidable questions. How has government expenditure affected the condition of older people? What about resources needed by other age groups? What has been the effect of age-based political advocacy in shaping government response to aging in America?

It is tempting to make generalizations about the status of older people, but generalizations overlook dramatic differences within the elderly population. Those called "old" are divided by social class, ethnicity, and gender. How should we take into account those differences? How can government best target resources to the most vulnerable or least advantaged groups among the elderly?

With increased life expectancy, more people spend a larger part of their lives in old age, and retirement income therefore becomes a major consideration. How will individuals plan and provide for retirement? In the past, Social Security has decisively improved the economic well-being of older Americans. What are its prospects for the future? There are still disputes about whether Social Security fairly treats subgroups among the elderly. But there is no dispute that Social Security, along with private pensions, has given older people more freedom to retire at earlier ages. Will this freedom endure or will we someday look back on the late twentieth century as the "golden age of the golden years" (Weinstein, 1988)?

In the next few decades, we will see a continued and very rapid aging of the American population as the baby boomers enter the retirement years. To cope with this huge demographic shift, we have already begun to rethink some major institutions of our society. For instance, by early in the next century, the age of eligibility for retirement under Social Security will gradually be raised by two years. With larger numbers of older people eligible for Social Security and Medicare, these programs already claim a major share of the federal budget. Questions have therefore been raised about whether age or need should be the basis for entitlement. It is not surprising that these questions provoke intense controversy.

Other issues of an aging society are also claiming our attention, such as the meaning of work and leisure in the later years. Why do we encourage older people to withdraw from productive roles after a certain age? The fact that retirement is common, indeed nearly universal, today should not make us take the practice for granted.

These issues about the diversity of the aging population, the role of government, and the future of work and retirement all provoke vigorous debate.

An understanding of basic concepts of aging in society can help us ask the right questions and be familiar with the key facts involved in the debates. Understanding the facts and clarifying our values can be vital in shaping what the aging society of the future will be like for all of us.

The Varieties of Aging Experience

People often speak about "aging" as if it were a universal human experience. But describing broad trends and discussing those in later life as a group may obscure marked differences among people within a given generation. Some of these differences are apparent when we look at the experience of aging as it varies with social class, racial and ethnic groups, and gender.

Social Class

Social class is a key factor influencing the condition of old age in all societies. The concept of social class denotes a pattern of social **stratification** of society whereby people possess unequal shares of wealth, status, or power. For example, the president of a corporation is likely to enjoy material and social advantages that an assembly line worker for that corporation will not possess; in turn, that same employee will have advantages that a homeless person is lacking. This familiar contrast underscores the crucial role of work in shaping social class. But the occupational system is not the whole story. Especially for older people, who typically are no longer in their working years, we need to look at other factors that reveal patterns of social stratification. The impact of social class in old age depends largely on accumulated advantage or disadvantage built up over the previous course of life, and a **life-course perspective** is therefore important.

Streib identifies four key elements that influence class position in aging: occupation, income, property, and education (Streib, 1985). In this listing, economic elements are prominent and it is easy to see how savings or assets like home ownership and private pensions determine wealth and income in later life. But a role is also played by less tangible factors such as educational attainment and family support networks that provide transfers among households. These intangible elements, often linked to social class, can influence the resources available to elderly people. A good example is occupational status. A retired governor or judge may still command prestige even if available income is reduced, and status often can be converted into power; for instance, the retired official might get better access to health care or other special treatment not available to less favored people who lack "connections."

Yet old age does not simply reproduce a pattern of social class accumulated in earlier years. Consider what happens when a person of high social class—

such as a physician or prominent writer—becomes ill or impoverished to the point where living conditions are seriously degraded. This is a case of downward mobility leading to status discrepancy: Current status is perceived as inconsistent with social class. Such a movement is not unusual among groups of elderly people who outlive their economic resources: for example, when widowhood or expensive illness causes a drastic depletion of assets. As a general rule, after the point of retirement, income tends to decline with the result that the oldest-old (85+) are also on average likely to be the poorest old.

It is a mistake, however, to equate old age with poverty and economic vulnerability. Until quite recently, the aged in most societies have formed a large share of the poor. Yet at the same time, the richest people are also more likely to be old: The average age of millionaires is 60 and one survey turned up the fact that the median age of the richest people in the United States is 65 (Louis, 1968). Significantly, about half the millionaires in the United States are women, perhaps reflecting the role of inheritance in conditions when women typically outlive men. One clear conclusion here is that social class, along with age, gender, and other factors, interact in complex ways, so that a person can be privileged in one respect and disadvantaged in another.

Race, Ethnicity, and Aging

The study of race and ethnicity in aging has become more important in recent years (Gelfand and Baresi, 1987; Markides and Mindel, 1987; Markides, Liang, and Jackson, 1990). Today, whites comprise 90% of people over 65. But whites are only 83% of those under age 55, so we will see more minorities among the older age groups. The minority aging population, especially Hispanic and Asian elderly, is growing faster proportionally than whites. By 2025, 15% of those over 65 are expected to be members of minority groups. In one state, California, it is expected that nearly 40% of the aged will be minorities (Torres-Gil and Hyde, 1990). The result of these population changes will be felt throughout the 1990s and into the new century, as the aging population becomes less white and less English speaking than it was before. Services for the aging, such as those provided under the **Older Americans Act,** were developed with a white, middle-class population in mind (Jacobson, 1982). These services will now need to take more into account differences in language, customs, and racial or ethnic background.

Any study of race and ethnicity presents serious problems. For example, not every distinctive ethnic group is generally thought of as a "minority group" (e.g., Irish Americans). Nor is a minority group necessarily limited to one definable ethnic or racial group (e.g., Hispanics with their many nationality subgroups). Then, too, the term *ethnicity* itself is often used loosely. Ethnic groups can be defined by a common ancestry or history, with shared culture such as religion, language, or national heritage (Schermerhorn, 1970). The idea of minority group, which puts the emphasis on social disadvantage or discrimination, may therefore be more useful in discussing how different subgroups experience aging. Finally, the *Harvard Encyclopedia of Ethnic Groups in America* lists literally hundreds of distinct ethnic subgroups deserving of consideration. But in this discussion, we will focus on four: black or African Americans, Hispanics, Asian Americans, and Native Americans.

African Americans are the largest minority group among the aged. Blacks in comparison to whites face a lower life expectancy at birth and also in most decades of life. An interesting pattern, however, is the so-called **crossover phenomenon**; once they reach their late seventies, blacks actually are likely to live longer than whites. For instance, mortality from heart disease is higher for blacks than whites from ages 65 to 84 but then the death rate becomes lower above age 85 for reasons that are not understood.

As a group, black Americans face many disadvantages attributable to racism and prejudice (Jackson, 1988). Not all African Americans are disadvantaged to the same degree. For instance, some are quite well off at retirement, especially those who have had a college education and a professional career. Here we see how different systems of inequality—race and social class—interact in ways that make it difficult to engage in simple generalizations or stereotypes. Nonetheless, one large generalization is proper here, and it points to the effect of history on the present older generation. Today's older African Americans entered old age bearing the results of accumulated disadvantage attributable to growing up with segregated schools and facing racial discrimination in the job market. Any judgment about public policy and aging must take into account that accumulated disadvantage in understanding the vulnerabilities among subgroups of the aged.

On the positive side, government benefit programs have had a favorable impact on the well-being of older blacks. Nine out of ten older blacks receive Social Security: a proportion comparable to the rest of the older population. But 25% receive Supplemental Security Income, reflecting a higher poverty rate.

Use of nursing homes by older blacks presents a puzzling pattern. As a group, older African Americans experience more functional impairment from chronic illness, yet at most ages they are far less likely than whites to be admitted to nursing homes. Is this disparity accounted for by effects of the crossover phenomenon or by discrimination in long-term care facilities or by some other factor, such as family caregiving patterns (Stoller and Gibson, 1994)? This last possibility points to a source of strength among black families: namely, reliance on an extensive network of informal support, such as aunts or godfathers (Dilworth-Anderson, 1992). An appraisal of the condition of minority groups among the aged must always take into account both strengths and vulnerabilities.

The Hispanic aged encompass many subgroups including Mexican Americans, Cubans, Puerto Ricans, and those from other countries in Central and South America (Applewhite, 1988). Traditional Hispanic cultures tend to encourage respect for older persons, with women in key caregiving roles (Coles, 1974). We need to be cautious, however, in lumping together different nationality groups. It would be a mistake, for example, to overlook differences between Puerto Rican elderly (Zambrana et al., 1979) and Chicano elderly (Maldonado, 1979). Compared with the general older population, elderly Hispanics are more likely to be poor and in need of long-term care services. In short, the elderly Hispanic population is quite definitely a group at risk (Lopez and Aguilera, 1991). In meeting their needs, they are also more likely to rely on informal supports than on formally organized services. This tendency may give rise to an assumption by service providers that Hispanics, and other minorities "take care of their own" (Gratton, 1987). But that assumption cannot be an excuse for neglect by formal service providers. Research has identified significant barriers to information and services, such as the poor quality of health care available, lack of transportation, and lack of materials translated into Spanish.

Like Hispanics, Asian Americans are divided into subgroups according to many different countries of origin, predominantly Chinese, Japanese, Korean, and Filipino. Older Asian Americans, like other minorities, have faced discrimination over the course of their lives (Fujii, 1976). In addition, elderly Asian American immigrants face difficulties in reconciling their cultural heritage with American life (Cheung, 1989). Today's older immigrants must cope with the fact that the status and traditional roles of the elderly are often eroded when children and grandchildren adopt the values of the dominant culture (Yee, 1992). As a result, Asian American elderly commonly experience family strains when the comparative status of the elderly is diminished (Koh and Bell, 1987). In East Asian societies influenced by Confucian religion, the obligation to honor one's parents in old age is taken seriously, despite modernization and industrialization (Palmore, 1975; Kim, Kim, and Hurh, 1991). But American attitudes toward filial piety are likely to be very different in this respect.

Native Americans or American Indians constitute a relatively small proportion of the total aged population but they suffer from major disadvantages (Block, 1979). These problems are partly offset by a rich cultural heritage and the role of family support (Murdock and Schwartz, 1978). When the elders of the tribe take on the role of "cultural conservator" of old ways, they can actually enhance their prestige and play constructive roles as grandparents helping the next generation to a better future (Weibel-Orlando, 1990).

All those who are old today carry with them the accumulated advantages and disadvantages of entire lifetimes that have gone before. For example, the impact of the civil rights movement on desegregating schools only began to be felt after the 1950s and 1960s. Thus today's older blacks carry with them the effects of prejudice that limited their life chances many decades ago. One effect of that accumulated disadvantage is found in poor health status. Another example is the American ideal of the "melting pot," which once was understood to mean that immigrants of all ethnic groups were encouraged to assimilate to the dominant culture and discard their old one. More recently, we have come to celebrate ethnic differences more openly. But today's elderly still carry with them the impact of earlier policies. For instance, the children of elderly Native Americans were long discouraged from maintaining traditional languages or tribal ways (Stoller and Gibson, 1993).

Racial and ethnic differences in aging are important when we look at major public policy questions such as the future of work and retirement. If we take ethnicity seriously, we may be forced to ask just what retirement means for different subgroups within the aged population (Gibson, 1987; Zembek and Singer, 1990). Older blacks, for instance, may respond to poor employment prospects by defining themselves as "retired." Those who qualify for disability benefits in the absence of any pension would not be officially labeled as "retired" yet they would withdraw from the labor force. Finally, among many minority groups, there is a pattern of exchange of services among kinship groups over the life course—in effect, noncompensated productivity. But that pattern of productivity doesn't show up on official statistics about work and retirement. Ethnic differences like these will have to be more seriously explored as society considers what leisure and "productive aging" may mean in the future (Allen and Chin-Sang, 1990).

Gender and Aging

The role of gender in aging deserves special consideration, not least because so many more women survive into old age than men. Indeed, the sex ratio, or proportion of men to women in the population, declines dramatically each decade after age 65. This is primarily a phenomenon of the advanced industrialized countries. In the United States today, there are 84 men per 100 women between ages 65 and 69, but only 39 per 100 for those over age 85. The typical fate is for men to die earlier but for women to survive with chronic diseases.

The experience of growing old is different for men and women in our society in many ways, some obvious, others less so. For instance, there is a distinct double standard in growing older because physical signs of aging bring more severe consequences for women than for men (Bell, 1989). Media images celebrate youth and sexuality in younger women, so that older women become virtually invisible in general society. Yet in the family division of labor, older women typically play a vital role of "kin-keeping" through social networks and caregiving (Rosenthal, 1985). The family caregiving role taken on by women often has the consequence of removing them from the paid labor force so that lower accumulated pension benefits are the result.

In gender roles, we can see a pattern similar to what was noted among minority groups: namely, cumulative disadvantage means diminished economic security in retirement. For instance, retirement income for older women is on average only about 55% of what it is for comparable men, and nearly three out of four older Americans who fall below the poverty line are women (U.S. Senate, 1991). The "feminization of poverty" in old age in fact has many causes, including sex discrimination, patterns of economic dependency, and widowhood (Smolensky, Danziger, and Gottschalk, 1988).

Part of the reason for higher poverty rates among older women relates to longevity and living arrangements. Statistically, women tend to marry older men, and women's longevity is greater. Thus women are much more likely than men to live alone in old age. Among those aged 65 to 75, up to 80% of men are married and living with their spouses; for women in this group, the figure is only 52%. Among those over the age of 75, the proportion of men with a still living spouse declines a bit—to 67%, but still the vast majority of these elderly men have a spouse. For women, however, the number of those over 75 who are living with a spouse has dropped sharply to 24% (U.S. Bureau of the Census, 1988b). Thus, while most older men are married, nearly half of all women over age 65 are widowed, but there are differences according to age and ethnicity, as Figure 5.1 indicates. Of all seniors living alone, four out of five are women (U.S. Senate, 1989, p. 110).

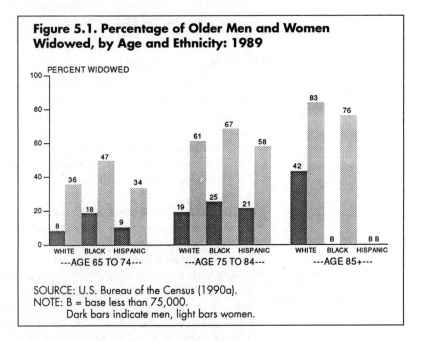

Figure 5.1. Percentage of Older Men and Women Widowed, by Age and Ethnicity: 1989

SOURCE: U.S. Bureau of the Census (1990a).
NOTE: B = base less than 75,000.
    Dark bars indicate men, light bars women.

Although widows receive Social Security benefits at age 60 based on their husband's earnings record (O'Grady-LeShane, 1990), spousal benefits under private pensions are typically much worse. Only 3% of American women receive a benefit from their deceased husband's pension. Older divorced women, even those who were long married, are even worse off. Typically they receive nothing from their ex-husband's pension and can therefore easily be plunged into poverty (Crooks, 1991).

Divorce and widowhood both have a disproportionate effect on women. Widowhood generally means a drop in income (Lopata, 1979; Holden, Burkhauser, and Myers, 1986); two-thirds of older widows live in poverty (U.S Bureau of the Census, 1986). A consequence of no-fault divorce has been to undermine the economic well-being of women after divorce (Weitzman, 1985). Older women who were long married suffer the most in economic terms after divorce. In essence, displaced homemakers receive no compensation for years of investment in a marriage, and it is far more difficult for the woman than for a former husband to "start over" in a career or a new marriage. A dramatic increase in the number of older divorced women today could mean serious socioeconomic problems in the decades ahead (Uhlenberg, Cooney, and Boyd, 1990).

Another factor relates to gender differences in employment. Among people over age 65, there are more than twice as many men as women receiving private pensions. Moreover, there have been persistent patterns of pay inequity. Those facts reflect past and present sex discrimination. But other patterns of behavior are also at work, including the fact that in the cohort of older women today there are fewer women with significant experience in the paid labor market. With more women in the labor market accumulating pension rights on their own, the economic position of women could improve in the future. Finally, it must be noted that women frequently leave the workforce to take care of small children or elderly relatives, reducing the opportunity to increase income with experience or to guarantee eligibility for a pension. For example, 72% of those caring for frail elderly are female (Stone, Cafferata, and Sangl, 1987).

Older women's economic problems remain unresolved, but some positive steps have been taken. For example, mutual self-help groups for widows have shown great effectiveness in helping isolated older women. The Widow-to-Widow Program is one outstanding example of this kind of mutual self-help group (Silverman, 1986). Another step toward improving the lives of older women is organized advocacy such as that demonstrated by the Older Women's League (OWL), founded in 1980 to address issues faced by middle-aged and older women. Earlier phases of the feminist movement focused on issues more relevant to younger groups, such as abortion or day care—but often failed to give adequate attention to the problems of older women (Lewis and Butler, 1972). In recent years, there has been more attention given to displaced homemakers, to women's pension rights, and to the physical and mental health concerns of older women.

Double Jeopardy

Patterns of inequality involving race and gender can reinforce one another. An older person who is simultaneously a member of two (or more) disadvantaged groups presents the issue of so-called **double jeopardy** (Dowd and Bengtson, 1978; Minkler and Stone, 1985). The reasons are understandable. If women earn less than men and if minorities are subject to prejudice over a lifetime, it would not be surprising to see older minority women suffering multiple disadvantages with respect to health status, income, housing, and so on. Figure 5.2 shows the disadvantage of being old, black or Hispanic, and female.

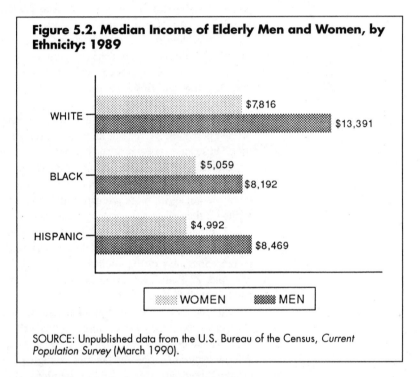

Figure 5.2. Median Income of Elderly Men and Women, by Ethnicity: 1989

WHITE — WOMEN $7,816 / MEN $13,391
BLACK — WOMEN $5,059 / MEN $8,192
HISPANIC — WOMEN $4,992 / MEN $8,469

WOMEN   MEN

SOURCE: Unpublished data from the U.S. Bureau of the Census, *Current Population Survey* (March 1990).

Empirical proof of the double jeopardy hypothesis has not been convincing to everyone. Others have pointed out that old age, instead of widening disadvantage, may perhaps even serve as a leveling influence; in other words, the elderly are more alike in their economic and social circumstances than younger people are. Clearly, more research is needed to clarify how the multiple disadvantages of aging, gender, and minority status affect different groups in later life. Yet, whatever explanation is accepted, the facts about differential disadvantage among subgroups of the elderly remain a potent challenge for public policy in an aging society (Davis and Rowland, 1991).

Aging in a Diverse Society

Given the diversity and heterogeneity of today's older population, it may not make much sense to speak of the "elderly." It may make more sense to distinguish between two broad groups in the 65+ population: the "ill-derly" and the "well-derly." The first group of older people tends to be poor and subject to chronic illness, while the second group tends to be well off both physically and financially (Cook and Kramek, 1986). These two groups have been described as the "two worlds of aging" (Crystal, 1982).

As Figure 5.3 reveals, the rate of poverty among the aged tends to vary dramatically according to different characteristics. We see here for example that the poverty rate among married men of all races is less than 6%. For older black women living alone, it is 60%—more than 10 times greater. The poverty rate for the oldest-old (85+) and for women living alone is much higher than average. In general, higher poverty rates are found among older women, minorities, and those with chronic illnesses: all groups that could be candidates to be those least advantaged.

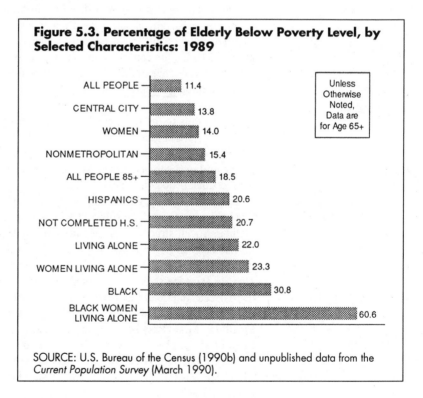

Figure 5.3. Percentage of Elderly Below Poverty Level, by Selected Characteristics: 1989

Unless Otherwise Noted, Data are for Age 65+

ALL PEOPLE	11.4
CENTRAL CITY	13.8
WOMEN	14.0
NONMETROPOLITAN	15.4
ALL PEOPLE 85+	18.5
HISPANICS	20.6
NOT COMPLETED H.S.	20.7
LIVING ALONE	22.0
WOMEN LIVING ALONE	23.3
BLACK	30.8
BLACK WOMEN LIVING ALONE	60.6

SOURCE: U.S. Bureau of the Census (1990b) and unpublished data from the *Current Population Survey* (March 1990).

The differences in economic well-being among subgroups of the elderly are important to keep in mind when we come to consider debates about age versus need in distributing benefits and entitlements. For example, the great strength of social insurance programs like Social Security or Medicare has been universality and egalitarianism. Everyone is treated alike. Growing old is seen as part of a universal human experience, like birth and death, a great leveler. The aged are thought of as being "our future selves," and Americans are not reluctant to pay into a Social Security system from which we all hope one day to benefit.

When we focus on heterogeneity and diversity, however, a different reality comes into view. There are sharp differences between male and female, white and minority. How then should universal programs, like Social Security or the Older Americans Act, take account of such differences? For example, if average black life expectancy is lower than it is for whites, does that mean the age of eligibility for Social Security should be reduced for blacks? If we did that, would we then have to do the same for men, who live, on average, less than women? But then, what about the fact that women on average have lower earnings and income in retirement, or a higher poverty rate? Should that mean we should revise Social Security to give more to women in contrast to men?

The Social Security system does redistribute income, in modest ways, toward lower income people, regardless of gender or ethnicity. But the redistributive function in Social Security is balanced by other elements in the system. Much more controversial is the question of how to take into account women's experience in family roles and how those characteristic gender differences influence Social Security.

An important lesson here is that some degree of redistribution and targeting of benefits to the most needy can be acceptable and feasible as long it remains within certain bounds. But as the long controversy over race and affirmative action shows, once we begin targeting benefits too explicitly or giving preference to one group over another, then principles of "need" versus "universalism" do come into conflict.

Issues of ethnicity, gender, and aging need to be kept in balanced perspective so that those who are subject to double jeopardy do not appear as mere victims. Social structures of inequality are not that simple. For one thing, individuals can be both privileged and disadvantaged at the same time. A good example is the elderly white widow played by Jessica Tandy in the film *Driving Miss Daisy*, who continued to enjoy advantages, in comparison to her African American chauffeur, by virtue of her race and wealth. At the same time, she faced a certain measure of discrimination as a Jew and as a woman. Finally, as Miss Daisy became very old and frail, she maintained the advantages of social class but encountered other problems based on stereotyped images of old age. What we see in any concrete case, such as the story of Miss Daisy, is that gender, race, and social class interact in complex ways (Dressel, 1988).

Furthermore, it is striking how many older people who have confronted disadvantage are still able to cope, to find meaning in life, and to be productive. In helping individuals age successfully, certain institutions have played a special role in providing cultural resources for self-esteem. One example is the black church, which has been a critical informal support system for the well-being of aged blacks in America (Walls and Zarit, 1991). The "triumph of survivorship" is represented at one level by the crossover in life expectancy among older black women. It is also represented at another level by the possibility that old age can be a time to celebrate independence and self-affirmation, a time, for example, when older women can find an unexpected opportunity to come into their own at last (Martz, 1987; Thone, 1992). Clearly, both race and gender are linked to social structures of inequality over the life course. But a full account of the varieties of aging experience must also acknowledge the adaptive strength of aging as well.

In years to come, America's aged population will reflect the diversity of American society. An important issue at the end of the twentieth century is our ability to equitably accommodate an influx of immigrants, most of whom are Asian or Hispanic. The 8 million immigrants who came to America during the 1980s represent a figure comparable to the number who came to these shores early in this century. Most of those in this immigrant group are young, but as they age in decades to come they will make the older population far more diverse than it is today.

Finally, there are unresolved questions about the meaning of ethnicity in relation to citizenship and national identity. In the last decade of the twentieth century, we have seen the breakup of large multiethnic nation-states, most notably the former Soviet Union and the former Yugoslavia. The question is whether different racial and ethnic groups can live together in the United States without disintegrating tensions. Can we do better than other societies? The verdict isn't in yet. But America's history has been one of a society produced by successive waves of immigrants and guided by a political ideal of equal treatment under the law. Increasing ethnic diversity and a growing population of the elderly will present a challenge for decades to come and will demand thoughtful attention to the varieties of aging experience.

The Economic Status of Older People

We have noted how economic circumstances vary sharply among different subgroups of older Americans. We now need to focus directly on the question: How has the economic condition of older people as a group fared in recent decades? One of the most controversial questions today is whether older people have been doing better than other age groups in our society. But answering that question is not as simple as it may seem.

At first glance, older people as a group have done reasonably well. Since the early 1980s, older people have seen a faster growth in income than have the nonelderly in America (Radner, 1987; Smolensky et al., 1988). The rate of poverty among the aged has been drastically cut, and the value of some assets, like the market value of a home, has brought a dramatic rise in net worth.

But here it is important to distinguish between two very different economic concepts: income versus wealth. Income denotes available money or its equivalent in purchasing power, while wealth denotes all economic resources of value, whether they produce cash or not. But wealth and income are not the same and are not necessarily connected to each other. For example, an elderly person might continue to live in a home that has substantially increased in market value to a point where that person can no longer afford to maintain the home while receiving only a modest fixed income.

Older people tend to have more assets of all kinds than younger people and they receive more favorable public benefits and entitlements than other age groups. On average, however, older people have lower incomes than other adults in America, as demonstrated in Figure 5.4 and Table 5.1. If public entitlements, such as Medicare, are converted into cash value, would the economic status of older people move closer to that of younger people?

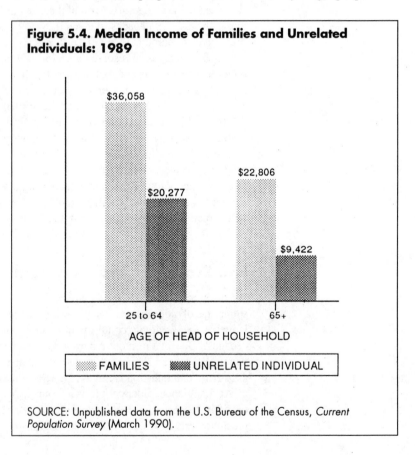

Figure 5.4. Median Income of Families and Unrelated Individuals: 1989

$36,058

$20,277

$22,806

$9,422

25 to 64   65+

AGE OF HEAD OF HOUSEHOLD

FAMILIES   UNRELATED INDIVIDUAL

SOURCE: Unpublished data from the U.S. Bureau of the Census, *Current Population Survey* (March 1990).

Table 5.1. Median Income of Families and Unrelated Individuals: 1989

Type of Unit and Age	Median Income
Families:	
Head 25 to 64	$36,058
Head 65+	$22,806
65 to 74	$24,868
75 to 84	$19,520
85+	$17,600
Unrelated individuals:	
25 to 64	$20,277
65+	$ 9,422
65 to 74	$10,821
75 to 84	$ 8,684
85+	$ 7,947

SOURCE: Unpublished data from the U.S. Bureau of the Census, *Current Population Survey* (March 1990).

There is a further, more important point to be noted here. Both the assets and the income of older people have a much wider range than is seen in other age groups; that is, there are more extremes of wealth and poverty among the old. The key point is that we need to look behind statistics about average economic well-being (Quinn, 1987) and we also need to look at the difference between assets and cash income.

Sources of Retirement Income

Retirement income policy in the United States has often been described as a three-legged stool. The three components are Social Security, private pensions, and individual savings and other assets that yield income (Greenough and King, 1976). Some older people also have earnings from employment, but in the last three decades, there has been a clear decline in the contribution of earnings to the income of older people. In this discussion, we will focus only on Social Security, pensions, and assets. Figure 5.5 indicates the relative importance of these different income sources for households over age 65.

It is interesting to note trends in sources of income. As Social Security has grown to become a larger portion of income for older people, earnings from employment have sharply diminished. For instance, in the late 1960s, earnings were still the leading income source for married couples over age 65, but by 1976, earnings had been surpassed by Social Security. Another trend has been the rising importance of assets and private pensions. Between 1978 and 1984, income from assets, such as savings accounts, increased dramati-

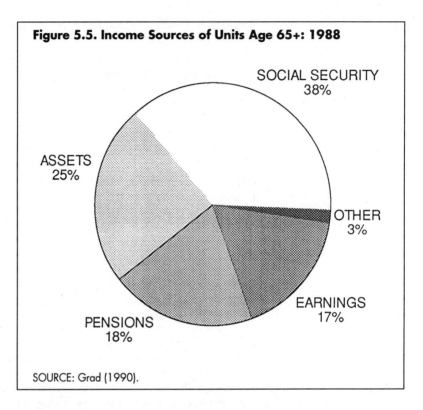

Figure 5.5. Income Sources of Units Age 65+: 1988

SOCIAL SECURITY
38%

ASSETS
25%

OTHER
3%

EARNINGS
17%

PENSIONS
18%

SOURCE: Grad (1990).

cally from 18% to 27% of elderly income while pensions grew modestly from 14% to 16%. Similar trends were seen in sources of income for unmarried older people, except that for them Social Security was even more important.

Social Security.   Today, Social Security is the biggest source of income for people over 65 in the United States. Nine out of ten older American households rely on Social Security for some portion of income, and three out of ten older households depend on it for four-fifths or more of their total income; but 13% get *all* their income from Social Security. It is clear that Social Security is vitally important for the poorest elderly.

At present, approximately 95% of the American workforce is covered by Social Security, and the trend in recent years has been toward universal coverage. Social Security payments go to 29 million retirees (age 62 and over) along with 7 million survivors (widows and children) and 4.6 million disabled workers of all ages. In effect, 16% of the U.S. population, comprising the retired elderly, the disabled, as well as family dependents, receive payments from Social Security.

To be eligible for full income benefits under Social Security, it is necessary to be 65 years old (or 62, for partial benefits under an early retirement option) and it is also necessary to have a wage-earning history in a job covered by

Social Security or to be married to a spouse with such a history. In other words, *both* chronological age *and* a record of earnings plus employer contributions are necessary to qualify.

Social Security is intended to provide a replacement for a percentage of earnings in prior employment, but the percentage differs depending on income level. For example, in 1990 the average income level for all workers was estimated at $21,179, and an average retired worker would receive a Social Security benefit equal to 43% of 1990 earnings, or around $750 a month. Someone earning the maximum amount taxable under Social Security would in retirement get a benefit of 24% of 1990 earnings, or only $1,020. This example shows how the earnings-replacement formula is tilted in favor of lower income workers. For many decades to come, it is expected that the Social Security system will maintain a **replacement level** of 42% for an average level worker, with higher or lower percentages for low-income or higher income retirees.

The principle of individual equity would insist that people get back an amount proportional to whatever they contributed. Conversely, the principle of social adequacy would give lower income retirees a larger replacement percentage to compensate for the fact that they are much less likely than wealthier people to have adequate assets or private pensions in retirement. Social Security, as it has evolved over time, incorporates both principles of equity and adequacy and tries to achieve a compromise between the two. As we shall see, many debates about the fairness of Social Security have come about because of this compromise between two opposing values.

Pensions.   A pension is a contractual plan by an employer to provide regular income payments to employees after they have left employment, typically at retirement. Pensions are thus a form of deferred compensation. This fringe benefit became widespread only in the years after World War II. Over the years, the proportion of private sector workers covered by private pension plans grew from 25% in 1950 to a peak of 50% in the mid-1980s. By contrast, 90% of state and local government employees are covered by civil service pensions. But pensions are far from universal among older Americans: Today, only 45% of households over age 65 have private pension income (Andrews, 1985) and that proportion is declining, a worrisome trend for the future well-being of an aging population.

There are basically two different types of pension plans available today. One is the **defined benefit plan,** which promises a specific or defined amount of pension income for the remainder of life. The company then is responsible for setting aside funds to cover the benefits promised. Another type of pension is the **defined contribution plan.** Employers, employees, or both contribute money, but the amount of pension income depends on how much is contributed to the fund over the years and on how successfully it is invested. In the past, most workers eligible for pensions, chiefly employees of large companies, have been enrolled in defined benefit plans. The current trend is to offer only a defined contribution plan, which means that retirees in the future could face less economic security than retirees enjoy today.

Employers in the United States are not required to offer a pension plan to employees, but if they do they must satisfy certain legal requirements. A major step in protecting workers and retirees came with passage of the Employee Retirement Income Security Act, known as ERISA, in 1974. ERISA regulates private pension plans in the United States and provides protection against loss of benefits to retired workers. Protection is not absolute, however. A pension plan can be terminated if a company goes out of business or is merged with another company. Even employers with pension plans aren't required to include those who work less than 20 hours a week, a crucial omission in light of the tremendous growth of part-time employment in the United States in recent years.

Equally ominous is the financial outlook for the Pension Benefit Guaranty Corporation (PBGC), a federal agency established to protect pensions when companies cannot meet their obligations. The PBGC has a deficit of $2.3 billion and will confront up to $50 billion in underfunded obligations in the future for bankrupt or financially ailing companies. Some analysts fear that the pension insurance fund could become the next "savings and loan" burden for taxpayers.

A key point to understand about pensions is **vesting,** or the period of time required for an employee to be on the job before being legally eligible to collect the pension. If an employee leaves a job before being vested in the plan, then the worker is not entitled to receive benefits. Until recently, most pension plans required at least ten years of employment for full vesting. But legislation following adoption of ERISA reduces this to only five years, a move likely to help workers in our increasingly mobile society. Critics have urged a system of portable pensions, where the employee can, in effect, take a pension from one job to another. Pension **portability,** it is argued, would not only improve equity but would also promote flexibility and better use of middle-aged or older workers, who might then be more inclined to move to new opportunities.

Private pension coverage is often designed to be coordinated with Social Security coverage, sometimes in ways that present retirees with an unpleasant surprise. For instance, many private pension plans unilaterally reduce the amount of the pension by whatever Social Security benefits a retiree gets, a practice that in the future may be limited to a loss of up to half the total pension promised. Social Security benefits are indexed for inflation, meaning that income automatically increases when the cost of living does, but private pensions usually have not been fully indexed. As a result, pension income may be quite sufficient early in retirement but become inadequate as inflation diminishes its real value over time.

An increasingly important feature of private pension income is the option for **early retirement benefits**: that is, pension eligibility at age 55 or 60. A 1986 study by Hewitt Associates, a benefits research company, found that 32% of companies of all sizes offered some variety of early retirement plan. But early retirement may be a growing trend. In recent years, there has been more pressure for layoffs and "downsizing" the workforce, so early retirement benefits are sometimes enriched to give older workers an inducement to leave early, thereby saving jobs for those who remain. This trade-off between early retirement and jobs for younger workers is not always fully voluntary, however, and it also poses significant hidden risks that may need to be considered carefully. For example, employees who have opted for early retirement may face reduction in employer-sponsored retiree health benefits at a later date. Some organizations have offered early retirement packages and been surprised when large numbers of employees took advantage of the option and abruptly left key departments without experienced personnel.

Individuals whose employers do not provide pension benefits and those who are self-employed can set aside savings to provide pensions for themselves. It has long been possible to do this through an annuity, which is an investment vehicle sold by life insurance companies permitting one to defer taxes on accumulated earnings. Congress has also created a number of mechanisms providing a tax incentive for people to save for their own retirement. One of these is the Individual Retirement Account or IRA, in which the person can accumulate money on a tax-deductible and tax-deferred basis until retirement. The Tax Reform Act of 1986 tightened eligibility for IRA contributions, which are now limited to taxpayers with incomes below $25,000 ($40,000 for couples). The so-called Keogh plan and the 401(k) plan have the same basic purpose but they are not limited to people below a certain income limit.

Assets and savings. Older people accumulate assets over a lifetime; here again, the condition of old age reflects the consequences of the entire life course. Some assets are tangible, like home ownership; others are financial, like entitlement to a pension based on years of work. Assets are second only to Social Security as a source of income for older people; around one-fourth of income is based on assets. As a group, older households own many more assets and have more accumulated wealth than nonelderly households, at least until household members are roughly 80 years old.

The total value of all assets, including real estate, savings, or personal property, is called the net worth of an individual or family. Figure 5.6 shows the median net worth of households based on the age of the householder. In this instance, "median" indicates that half the people are above and half are below the average figure cited here. Thus half of all householders under age 35 have a net worth of $6,078 or higher, while among people in their late

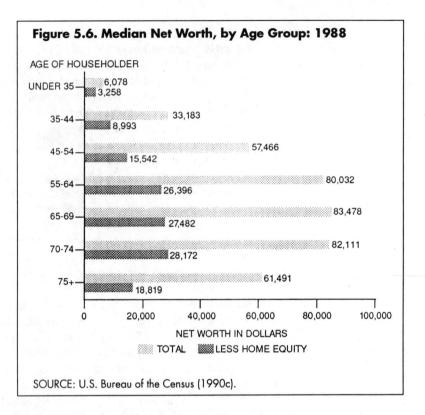

Figure 5.6. Median Net Worth, by Age Group: 1988

AGE OF HOUSEHOLDER

UNDER 35 — 6,078 / 3,258

35-44 — 33,183 / 8,993

45-54 — 57,466 / 15,542

55-64 — 80,032 / 26,396

65-69 — 83,478 / 27,482

70-74 — 82,111 / 28,172

75+ — 61,491 / 18,819

NET WORTH IN DOLLARS

TOTAL   LESS HOME EQUITY

SOURCE: U.S. Bureau of the Census (1990c).

sixties, half have a net worth above $83,478. Among all households with a head over age 65, the median net worth was $73,471 in 1988 compared with the median net worth for all households of all ages, which was $35,752.

When we look at Figure 5.6, we see that the overwhelming majority of assets for those over 35 are in the form of home equity: the market value of a home, exclusive of mortgage debt. Approximately 75% of people over age 65 are homeowners, and the vast majority of these people own their homes outright. Two-fifths of the assets of elderly households are in the form of home equity, which amounts to a staggering total of $1.1 trillion, or 30% of the total U.S. home equity. Typically, today's older homeowner bought a home years ago and has enjoyed a dramatic appreciation in its market value.

Because so much wealth is represented by elderly home ownership, there has been repeated interest in the possibility of home equity conversion, that is, enabling older people to convert the accumulated value of a home into a regular monthly income (Scholen and Chen, 1980). One way of doing this is through a reverse mortgage, where a bank guarantees a monthly income to a homeowner for the remainder of life but claims ownership of the home upon death. To date, very few older people have participated in reverse mortgages, so home ownership remains an important part of assets but not a contribution to income for older people.

The importance of home equity may lead us to exaggerate the net worth of elderly households in average statistics. About 70% of the elderly's assets are represented by home ownership. Thus, when we subtract that home equity, it turns out that the median net worth of all households over age 65 is only $23,856 (1988 data). These assets are chiefly interest-bearing savings and checking accounts, with much smaller amounts of assets in the form of stocks and bonds or other real estate.

Just as general well-being differs dramatically according to social class, gender, and ethnicity, so does the distribution of assets, as Figure 5.7 illustrates. Note that the median net worth for older men and women as such does not differ appreciably. But there is a dramatic difference between married couples and the average for all households, including single people, another testimony to the importance of marriage as a factor for financial well-being in later life.

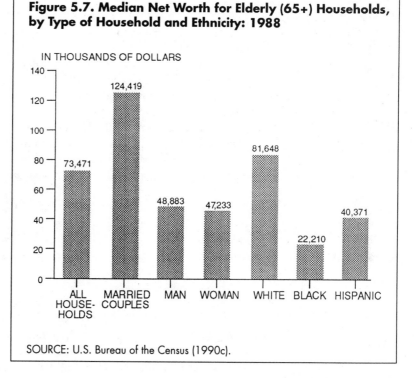

Figure 5.7. Median Net Worth for Elderly (65+) Households, by Type of Household and Ethnicity: 1988

IN THOUSANDS OF DOLLARS

SOURCE: U.S. Bureau of the Census (1990c).

Racial and ethnic differences are also dramatic. The median net worth of white householders is 3 to 4 times greater than that of older blacks. Once again, average figures can be misleading. We need to look behind the averages to acknowledge differences in economic status that reflect the varieties of the aging experience.

Overall Financial Health of Older Adults

The turbulent American economy of the last two decades has had important effects on the well-being of America's elderly. Older people who live disproportionately on fixed incomes from pensions and annuities are affected more severely by inflation than other groups. Fortunately, in the past couple of decades, government policies and economic trends have reduced the erosion of buying power through inflation. For example, 86 federal programs increase their benefits for the old based on some index for inflation (Clark et al., 1985). The largest of these programs of course is Social Security, indexed for inflation since the early 1970s and therefore providing a measure of protection for older people who rely on it. On the economic front, although the United States experienced high inflation rates during the 1970s, since the early 1980s, inflation has been moderated. In recent years, however, a low inflation rate has been accompanied by historically low interest rates, which has sharply diminished the income of the elderly, who rely on interest from savings more than do other groups.

Nevertheless, the overall economic position of older Americans has improved substantially in the past two decades. Improvements in pension coverage and indexing of Social Security are the main reasons for this improvement in income, while rising home equity is the main reason for the gain in assets. Income from earnings has declined as more older Americans have left the labor force for retirement.

Despite the good news, the stereotype that most older people are affluent is mistaken. When we look behind the average figures, we see two things: first, an enormous variation among subgroups of the aging with respect to economic circumstance and, second, a large group of older people who have been brought above the poverty line but are still near-poor. The insidious feature of old age poverty is that it lasts longer and is more likely to be permanent than poverty among younger people. The elderly poor have fewer chances for remarriage or finding better jobs. For all these reasons, income and services for the elderly poor have enormous importance, and so has the question of how to target those benefits to those who are least advantaged.

The concept of accumulated disadvantage helps explain the disparity in income among different subgroups of the aging population. For instance, Gibson found that older African American women had typically had disadvantaged work lives in which opportunity was constricted by prejudice (Gibson, 1983). In previous decades, black women too often ended up confined to the secondary labor market, where a job such as household maid would pay low wages with negligible fringe benefits and poor security. By contrast, a white male would be much more likely to find employment in the primary labor market: for instance, in a managerial or unionized position offering job security and the opportunity to accumulate pension benefits or other assets for old age (Crystal and Shea, 1990).

The change in the economic circumstances of older Americans can be both a source of pride in the success of government programs, chiefly Social Security, and also a challenge for the future of those programs. These matters have become items of broad public controversy and are likely to continue to provoke vigorous debate.

Public Policy on Aging

We have already seen some of the many ways in which action by government has had a decisive effect on the well-being of today's generation of elderly, and that fact in itself marks an important historical change. When today's older Americans were born—say, those born before 1930—the U.S. government gave no special attention at all to issues of old age. Yet by the 1970s, a prominent political scientist took note of the "graying of the federal budget." Trends since then have amply confirmed his point (Hudson, 1978). Today, more than 30% of the total federal budget is spent on the aged and the percentage is rising each year.

History and Scope of Government Policies

Action by both state and federal government on behalf of older people has a long history in the United States, but for the most part early government action was limited to paying pensions for war veterans or their widows (Achenbaum, 1978). Until the twentieth century, the aged population was small and the role of government was quite limited. The big change came during the Great Depression of the 1930s with the passage of the Social Security Act (1935), which still remains the cornerstone of U.S. policy on aging. The expansion of Social Security to families (1939) and the provision of early retirement benefits (1956) were important changes in the law. During the post-World War II period, Social Security showed slow but steady expansion in its coverage. Later revisions of Social Security in 1977 and 1983 helped put the program on a more secure financial foundation and are the basis for how Social Security functions today.

Like the depression of the 1930s, the decade of the 1960s was one of social upheaval and pressure for political change. Public policy in aging reflected that pressure and resulted in another expansion of the federal government's role in helping older people. One of the major turning points was the Great Society legislation of the 1960s, which included steps such as the federalization of old age assistance and landmark laws such as Medicare and Medicaid (1965). During the 1970s, there was some retreat from federal commitments to all social programs (Estes, 1989). The 1980s, continuing the same trend, were also a period of cutbacks: Cost-containment measures for Medicare were enacted in 1983 and efforts to expand Medicare further were repealed

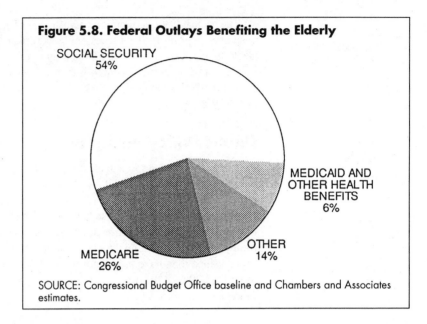

Figure 5.8. Federal Outlays Benefiting the Elderly

SOCIAL SECURITY
54%

MEDICAID AND
OTHER HEALTH
BENEFITS
6%

OTHER
14%

MEDICARE
26%

SOURCE: Congressional Budget Office baseline and Chambers and Associates estimates.

(1989). Still, the bulk of federal funding goes for Social Security and Medicare, as Figure 5.8 indicates.

Another area of concern in federal legislation has been retirement. Today, there are more than 40 million private sector workers who participate in 800,000 pension plans in the United States. Those plans represent retirement security for millions of workers, and the safety of pension funds is critical. Steps to protect pensions culminated in the Employee Retirement Income Security Act of 1974, which was strengthened in 1986. Retirement benefits came under further federal protection in 1984 and 1990. In addition, the federal government is directly involved in providing pension income through civil service retirement, military retirement, and the railroad retirement system.

Federal legislation has been responsive to older workers as well as retired persons. The general trend has been to protect the rights of older workers against arbitrary dismissal on grounds of age. The key breakthrough was the Age Discrimination in Employment Act of 1967, which gave protection to older workers; it was significantly expanded in 1978. By 1986 a long campaign to eliminate mandatory retirement was finally successful in eliminating legal prohibitions against hiring and retention of employees on the basis of age.

Still another area of federal government activity has been the direct provision of social services. In the first essay in this book, we discussed the Section 8 and Section 202 housing laws. The 1978 Congregate Housing Act brought housing and social services for the aged together, an important step for long-term care policy. The enactment of comprehensive social service

Table 5.2. Key Federal Legislation on Aging

Social Security Act	1935
Expansion of Social Security Benefits (for spouses and children)	1939
Early Retirement Benefits under Social Security (men added in 1961)	1956
Medicare and Medicaid	1965
Older Americans Act	1965
Age Discrimination in Employment Act	1967
Older Americans Act Amendments (creating the National Aging Network)	1973
Employee Retirement Income Security Act (ERISA, Amended 1986)	1974
Congregate Housing Services Act	1978
Social Security Amendments	1983
Medicare Prospective Payment System	1983
Retirement Equity Act	1984
Abolition of Mandatory Retirement	1986
Medicare Catastrophic Coverage Act (Repealed 1989)	1988
Older Workers Benefit Protection Act	1990

programs was made possible by the Older Americans Act (OAA) in 1965. There has been inadequate funding for OAA programs, just as there has been for comprehensive social services under Title XX of the Social Security Act. Still, the OAA has provided a strong stimulus for planning and advocacy on behalf of the aged in ways that involve every level of American government. Table 5.2 gives a comprehensive summary of the high points of federal legislation on aging in the twentieth century.

The aging network. Another element in public policy deserving of attention is a component of government specifically created for the purpose of serving older people and advocating on their behalf. The Older Americans Act, first passed in 1965 and amended in 1973, created a national **aging network** of services for older people, such as nutrition programs, senior citizen centers, and information and referral services. A key element of the aging network is local Area Agencies on Aging (AAA), generally based in city or county government with responsibility for planning and organizing services to older people in that region. Each state also has a State Agency on Aging designated to engage in planning and disbursement of federal funds under the Older Americans Act. At the federal level, the U.S. Administration on Aging coordinates Older Americans Act programs and provides a focal point for advocacy.

Among the key service programs under the Older Americans Act are senior centers, which have grown from the first, founded in 1943, to more than 10,000 today (Krout, 1989). Despite that growth, Older Americans Act programs such as senior centers or nutrition services reach only a tiny proportion of Americans over 65: at most, 5% to 10%. Yet the professionalized aging network provides a vehicle for planning and advocacy at all levels of government that would otherwise be lacking.

Those who criticize the professionalized aging network do so from contrasting perspectives. Analysts on the political left argue that human service programs, such as those created by the Older Americans Act, provide a meager response to "social problems" that doesn't do anything about the underlying causes of the problems faced by older people (Olson, 1982; Estes et al., 1984; Minkler and Estes, 1984). These analysts favor a political economy approach that attacks discrimination, unemployment, and oppression in capitalist society. By contrast, analysts on the conservative side tend to see the current aging service system as wasteful social spending by the welfare state (Rabushka and Jacobs, 1980). Others believe older Americans are being helped at the expense of young people (Peterson and Howe, 1988) and they dispute arguments made by advocates for the aged.

Aging interest groups.   There is no dispute that there has been a remarkable expansion in the role of the federal government in helping older people. The government went from paying virtually no attention to aging in 1930 to a situation today where more than $3 out of every $10 spent by the federal government will go to older Americans. This increase in the budget has come about primarily for two reasons: (a) population aging, meaning that there is a larger proportion of older people in the population, and (b) the enactment of programs to protect income and provide health care to the elderly. But why did government respond as it did? To understand what happened, we need to appreciate the important influence of aging-based interest groups in shaping public policy in America (Van Tassel and Meyer, 1992).

America from the beginning has always thought of itself as a "young" country, and in earlier centuries, old age was not the focus of much government interest. The Great Depression that began in 1929, however, made Americans willing to think in new ways about the role of government. One result was the expansion of government social welfare in the New Deal period of the 1930s. During the early years of the Great Depression, Social Security did not exist and older people were among the poorest in America. It is not surprising that older Americans at the time banded together to advocate for their own interests. One of the first groups established was the Townsend Movement, founded in 1934 to eliminate old age poverty and stimulate the economy (Holtzman, 1963). Some scholars believe that the Townsend Movement was influential in the passage of the Social Security Act in 1935, marking the birth of a federal government policy on aging.

Another group also active at the time was End Poverty in California (EPIC), an advocacy group led by novelist Upton Sinclair. A similar group was the colorfully named "Ham and Eggs Movement," also based in California, which urged a pension for those over 50 who were unemployed (Putnam, 1970). The passage of Social Security and the end of the Great Depression caused these age-based movements to go into eclipse. During the 1940s and 1950s, Social Security grew in modest but important ways, though not in response to political pressure or social change.

It was not until the 1960s that age-based movements again appeared in America. Today, the most prominent of these is the American Association of Retired Persons (AARP), which is the country's largest voluntary organization of older people (Schurenberg and Luciano, 1988). Founded in 1958 as an outgrowth of the National Retired Teachers Association, AARP today is open to anyone over the age of 50. AARP provides a range of services and benefits to members, such as health and life insurance, prescription drugs, and travel services. Its magazine, *Modern Maturity*, is one of the most widely read periodicals in America.

AARP is joined by other important **aging interest groups,** such as the National Council on Aging, the Gerontological Society of America, and the American Society on Aging: all prominent professional or academic societies. A different history marked the National Council of Senior Citizens, which is a membership group coming out of the labor movement. Many of these groups have joined forces as part of an umbrella body called the Leadership Council of Aging Organizations, based in Washington, D.C., and devoted to promoting the concerns of older people. Still another prominent aging interest group today is the National Committee to Preserve Social Security and Medicare, whose 5 million members helped to repeal the Medicare Catastrophic Coverage Act of 1988. This whole collection of national interest groups, along with parallel organizations at the state level, such as the "Silver-Haired Legislatures," has been called the "gray lobby" (Pratt, 1976, 1982; Hess and Kerschner, 1978). There are currently more than 1,000 aging interest groups lobbying all levels of government (Day, 1990).

Somewhat distinguished from the Gray Lobby is the group the Gray Panthers, founded in 1970 by activist Maggie Kuhn with the goal of fighting against ageism on an intergenerational basis (Jacobs and Hess, 1978). The Gray Panthers have sometimes criticized mainstream aging organizations as the establishment-based "aging enterprise," or cadre of professionals who earn their living by providing services to dependent elderly clients (Estes, 1979; Moody, 1988). Still, the professionalized aging network remains an achievement of successful advocacy through "interest group liberalism" (Binstock, 1972).

The arguments raised by the Gray Panthers and other critics of the Gray Lobby raise a point debated today. To what extent should age-based advocacy groups press for laws or benefits to help the elderly alone as opposed to those that help people of all ages? For every person over 65 who is disabled, there is a younger person with similar disabilities who could benefit from home health care. When Medicare was created in 1965, many people believed it was the first step toward creating a national health insurance program (Marmor, 1973; Feder, 1977). But it took more than a quarter of a century until Congress seriously began debating how to create such a program to cover all age groups.

Debates about public policies on aging are intensely political and to understand them we must understand something about political attitudes in old age. It is a mistake to assume that older people are bound to be more conservative just because they are older (Cutler, 1981). A sizable body of literature in political science suggests that age in itself does not have much impact on political attitudes or behavior, and people tend to maintain their political affiliation as they age (Glenn and Hefner, 1972). There seems to be little likelihood of a "generational politics" developing in which people vote according to age lines (Heclo, 1988). On the other hand, interest in politics, and certainly voting behavior, does tend to increase with age. The most active voters are in the 65- to 75-year-old age group. Although older Americans are likely to have a disproportionate voice in elections, they do not necessarily speak with one voice.

In addition, the sheer size and diversity of aging interest groups may weaken their ability to influence public policy. For instance, AARP is larger in size than any other organized interest group in the United States. With 34 million members, it has more people than Canada. But the power of AARP, which sometimes claims to speak for the elderly, is commonly overrated. Perhaps the most striking example of its limited power is the case of the Medicare Catastrophic Coverage Act of 1988. That act was intended to help older people pay high medical bills. The act was hailed at the time as the biggest expansion of Medicare in its history and Congress expected it to be popular. But the act soon proved controversial and unpopular. AARP, against the wishes of many of its own vocal members, supported the act while the National Committee to Preserve Social Security and Medicare opposed it. In little more than a year, the catastrophic coverage act was quickly repealed in response to grassroots protests from more affluent elderly voters who disliked the higher taxes required by the law. The repeal came not because of a powerful Washington interest group but despite it.

"Gray Power" sounds impressive. Yet the skeptic might ask: Just how effective are these interest groups in the real world of politics? Political scientists who have studied the matter tend to argue that aging interest groups are not all that effective except in preventing cuts in popular programs, such as Social Security (Binstock, 1972). Critics who charge that the elderly represent an all-powerful voting bloc have a difficult time explaining recent political developments.

For instance, in the 1992 presidential election, Bill Clinton received a much higher proportion of votes from those aged 60 and over than he did from other age groups. Yet during the campaign, he openly proposed higher taxes on Social Security to reduce the federal deficit, and in his first year in office President Clinton raised taxes on Social Security while pushing huge cuts in the Medicare program. This example suggests that the political power of aging interest groups remains a highly debatable matter.

Trends in Public Policy and Aging

Whatever we may think about the effectiveness of political advocacy for the aged, there is no question that an increasing share of the federal government's expenditures have been going for the aged. But growth in programs to help older people has several explanations.

First, programs like Social Security and Medicare have grown rapidly mainly because they have been available on the basis of age alone and without means testing. These programs serve all older adults without reference to need. In fact, the beneficiaries of this spending are mostly the middle-class elderly, not the poor. Even the rich elderly collect Social Security.

The second point, related to the first, is that federal programs for the elderly enjoy broad political support. Most recipients sincerely believe that they are only getting what they are entitled to, that Social Security functions something like an annuity—with every dollar contributed in the working years being returned, with interest, during retirement. This view is in fact mistaken: Social Security does not operate like a bank account. But the huge majority of elderly, conservative or liberal, expect their due. At the same time, many younger people are only too happy to support programs that help their parents and that are expected to help younger people in their old age as well.

A third point is that programs for the elderly have developed incrementally for the most part, making it harder to see just how much they have grown over the years. Sometimes there have been dramatic breakthroughs, as when Social Security was instituted in 1935. But equally important have been the less noticed, gradual expansions of Social Security in 1939 and 1956. These small, step-by-step changes have had a large cumulative impact. Then, too, periods of growth have been offset by cutbacks like the Social Security amendments of 1983, when Congress agreed for the first time to tax Social Security benefits. But all the changes and technical details of the program have not been well understood by the general public.

Finally, the growth of benefit programs for the aged reflects the growth of the aging population itself. Population aging virtually guarantees that a growing share of resources will go to older people. Age-based entitlements make such a shift natural and inevitable, not the result of special political advocacy.

The rapid growth of federal programs serving older people over the past 20 years presents a quandary. Today's massive federal budget deficits have motivated many observers to look more carefully at old age advocacy and age-based benefits (Kutza, 1981; Torres-Gil, 1992). Furthermore, the retirement of baby boomers beginning early in the next century will dramatically increase the numbers of those eligible for Social Security and Medicare. At the same time, the population of working adults will be relatively smaller. Will we find a fiscally responsible way of maintaining benefits in the face of these population pressures? One positive answer came in 1983 when Congress decided to raise the age of eligibility for Social Security benefits by two years early in the next century. But the evolution of Social Security is by no means over. Still others advocate changing Social Security to make it fairer to women or to give incentives to people who want to continue working part-time after retirement.

Although some changes are inevitable, it seems unlikely that the general shape of federal aging programs will change dramatically. Many people have a strong interest in seeing these benefit programs continue, and the political pressure to maintain them will be intense. On the other hand, precisely because aging expenditures are so large and because other public needs are pressing, it is hard to see how age-based entitlements will remain exempt from pressure to cut costs.

Moreover, other serious questions remain. One of them concerns equity or fairness. The most successful federal aging programs have been the ones that serve all the aged, such as Social Security and Medicare. These programs have succeeded in improving the well-being of the average elderly person; indeed, they constitute America's "hidden success," a stunning example of how government can come to agreement and move decisively to solve a problem (Schwarz, 1983). But celebration of success should not obscure the fact that groups like older women and minorities continue to have high rates of poverty.

Furthermore, America's most successful programs have all been based on a presumption of need or dependency. Both Social Security and Medicare arose from a "permissive consensus" in favor of the elderly depicted as weak, needy, and dependent (Hudson, 1978). That image is what Kalish called the "failure model" of old age (Kalish, 1979). To the extent that older Americans today are healthier, better educated, and more affluent, that stereotype of "compassionate ageism" will be under challenge and so, too, the permissive consensus is likely to be eroded (Binstock, 1985).

Another issue is generational equity. The elderly are already receiving a substantial portion of the federal budget and will likely receive more as the retired population grows. At the same time, federal expenditures on children and families have decreased, and rates of homelessness, poverty, malnutrition, and poor health have increased among younger Americans. Is it fair—or wise—to continue distributing benefits on the basis of age alone, or do we need to take a more **needs-based** approach?

Another question is how the retirement income system, both private pensions and Social Security, can take account of gains in longevity and the greater vigor and productive capability of today's older people. Age-based benefit programs such as Social Security are understood to be **entitlements,** just as private pensions are forms of deferred compensation. But the idea of entitlement, of benefits owed to us as a right, is different than the idea of productivity. Productivity implies that income and benefits are provided on the basis of how much a person contributes. How is it possible to maintain the integrity of retirement income while also encouraging productivity among the older population (Moody, 1990)?

The new politics of aging in America has been deeply influenced by the economic condition of older people and especially by recent improvement in their average economic status. In the United States, as in other advanced industrialized societies, one result of higher retirement benefits has been a movement of more older workers out of the labor force through early retirement, a move that can be attractive to workers and employers alike. Today's policies in effect push many vigorous, capable "young-old" out of their productive social roles and into retirement. To be sure, older people often find a great deal of personal meaning in leisure, family life, and voluntary association with churches, community groups, and the like. But can our society afford to lose their contributions?

These issues, which depend so much on values, all provoke vigorous debate. Clearly, the improved economic circumstances of older people have already prompted some reassessment of aging programs by policymakers. This shift in mood marks a change from the past and provokes new controversies that will command attention for years to come. As we think about the future, it is important to keep in mind the key ideas emphasized in this discussion: (a) the *diversity* of the aging population, including dramatic differences in well-being among subgroups; (b) the impact of *cumulative disadvantage* whereby earlier life-course experience influences what old age will be like; and (c) the *social construction* of roles in old age, including social expectations about gender behavior and the meaning of retirement.

Population aging is an important and indisputable fact. But by itself, population aging does not dictate the shape of things to come, and it is certainly no cause to be gloomy about the coming of an aging society. For both individuals and for society, the key point to remember is that the life one leads as a younger person will affect prospects for old age (Taeuber, 1990). The social and economic outlook for an aging society, then, is not simply something to be predicted but something to be constructed. The decisions we make today will depend on thoughtful consideration of the controversies that will shape the aging society of tomorrow.

Should Age or Need Be a Basis for Entitlement?

Americans as a people have always looked to the future and expected that the next generation would do better than their parents. But in recent years, that confidence has faded in response to mounting economic problems and doubts about the future (Newman, 1993). In an era of declining expectations, disturbing questions are being raised about what the older generation is entitled to and what is fair to younger generations. Not so long ago, the elderly as a group were thought of as uniformly poor and vulnerable. That image has changed. Now it is not surprising to see older people depicted in the media as well off or even prospering at the expense of the young, especially children (Villers Foundation, 1987). This new image leads to questions about fairness in how different generations are treated.

A Tale of Two Generations

The question of generational equity can be seen in the story of two generations of the Walton family. George and Martha Walton were members of the World War II generation and proud of what they had accomplished: surviving the depression and winning the war. When George got out of the army and came back to Middletown, he and Martha were able to buy a house with a VA mortgage loan. George went to college on the GI Bill, and during the 1950s and 1960s the Waltons enjoyed prosperity. When they retired, they found it possible to sell their house and use some of the capital gains, along with George's pension, to enjoy a comfortable income in retirement. The Waltons were never rich but they were satisfied with how things turned out.

Things worked out a little differently for the Walton children. Carol and Robert were baby boomers born just after World War II and when they graduated from high school they had high hopes. Both attended college and married, but they found themselves having financial trouble putting their own kids through school in the 1980s because college tuition had risen. Unfortunately, Robert lost his job when his company was merged; Carol's oldest boy finished school but couldn't find a job and ended up moving back home with Carol and her husband. Carol felt she needed to stay at work but was forced to cut back her hours when her father, George, got sick and now she helps out her mother, Martha, a lot. Both Carol and Robert had gotten seriously into debt and haven't managed to save much. They worry a lot about the future.

Sometimes it seems as if life has not been "fair" to the Walton children and grandchildren. Some things that have happened to the different Walton generations are a matter of economic circumstance, such as rising home values or losing a job. Other things are a matter of government policy, for example, the impact of the GI bill or Social Security. Whether intended or not, it does seem that circumstances and policies affect different generations in different ways. How then can we sort out what is at stake in debates about justice between generations?

In thinking about issues of equity or fairness between "generations," it is clear that two different meanings of *generation* must be kept distinct: (a) a specific age group, such as "the elderly" (65+) or "children under age 18," and (b) a historical **cohort** consisting of a group of people born in the same year or in a certain period (Ryder, 1965). *Cohort* also describes those who experienced a specific historical event (Mannheim, 1952), for example, the "World War II Generation" or the "Sixties Generation." Corresponding to these two meanings of *generation* are two very different concerns about the fairness of distributing benefits on the basis of need rather than age. First, are the elderly today as a group receiving too much of society's resources in comparison to children? And, second, can the baby boom generation and successive cohorts count on economic security—for example, Social Security benefits—in the future?

The story of the Waltons has become familiar and it forms the background in which new questions are being raised about the benefits society provides to people based on age. At the time these trends were first recognized, the noted gerontologist Bernice Neugarten (1983) published a book titled *Age or Need?* which asked the provocative question about whether government benefit programs should be available to people on the basis of need rather than chronological age.

For many years, Americans were used to thinking of older people as the "deserving poor": that is, financially dependent for reasons beyond their control and therefore deserving of help. This assumption was the basis for many important government programs from Social Security to the Great Society. Not all older people fit this stereotype, of course, but a picture of the old as especially needy or vulnerable did become widespread: a form of "compassionate age-ism," as some called it (Binstock, 1983). But as government programs for the aged have become more expensive, another, less compassionate point of view has been heard. Critics began to depict the aged as

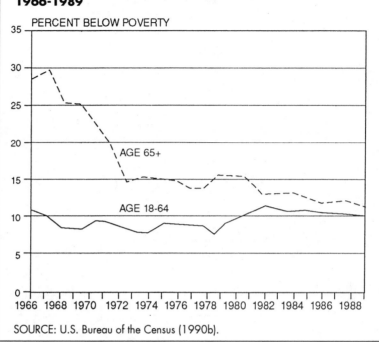

Figure 5.9. Poverty Rates of Elderly and Nonelderly Adults: 1966-1989

PERCENT BELOW POVERTY

AGE 65+

AGE 18-64

SOURCE: U.S. Bureau of the Census (1990b).

a "burden" on society and to worry about the negative impact of population aging now and in the future. Those worried about generational equity asked: Are older people today getting too much at the expense of the young?

To understand the many elements of the generational equity debate, we need to look at several trends, including the incidence of poverty among the old and the young, the relative burden of supporting a dependent aging population, and the impact of taxes and other public policies on different age groups. Finally, we will consider the question of who among the elderly are most in need of help.

Poverty Among the Old

By any measure available, there has been a dramatic reduction in the rate of poverty among older Americans in the last three decades. The trend is illustrated in Figure 5.9. A key point here is that most of the gains in income for older people took place between 1960 and 1974, long before it became common to talk about generational equity or to complain that older people were getting too many benefits. For instance, in 1960 the poverty rate of older people in America was one out of three. But the figure shows how dramatically the poverty rate has dropped for older people compared with nonelderly

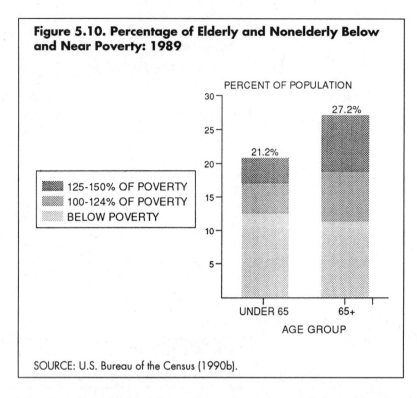

Figure 5.10. Percentage of Elderly and Nonelderly Below and Near Poverty: 1989

PERCENT OF POPULATION

125-150% OF POVERTY
100-124% OF POVERTY
BELOW POVERTY

21.2%

27.2%

UNDER 65   65+

AGE GROUP

SOURCE: U.S. Bureau of the Census (1990b).

adults. The situation is different when we look at the condition of children; today, only 12% of older Americans fall below the poverty line, while 22% of children under age 18 live in poverty.

It is important to be clear about the meaning of *poverty* in discussing this question. The official **poverty line** in 1988 defined a poverty level for unrelated individuals over age 65 (not living as a family) at $5,674, a figure slightly higher than for those under 65. According to that measurement, only one out of eight people over 65 would be officially classified as "poor." When Medicare is taken into account, the proportion of older people who are "poor" drops to only 6%. On the other hand, if we ignore all government cash transfer programs such as Social Security, then 44% of Americans over 65 would fall below the poverty line. This is another way of stating how important Social Security has been in preventing late life poverty.

But the official poverty line is not the whole story here (Cook and Kramek, 1986). If we look at the group of elderly who could be called "near-poor"— those with an income up to one and a half times the poverty line—then more than one out of four older people fall into the category facing economic hardship. Figure 5.10 shows the proportion of people under and over age 65 who fall into this "near-poor" category.

Government benefit programs and other measures have certainly reduced poverty among the aged in America. But the stereotype of the well-to-do elderly is a mistaken one as we see when we look closely at the group Timothy Smeeding calls the "'Tweeners," that is, people caught in the middle, the economically insecure lower middle class elderly. These are the "near-poor": people living on incomes between the poverty line and up to twice that level. The 'Tweeners are not well off economically but they are not poor enough to be eligible for means-tested poverty programs such as SSI or Medicaid. When people in this in-between category run into unexpected hardship—for example, a rent increase, the death of a spouse, or an expensive illness requiring long-term care—then they are extremely vulnerable.

What has happened is that many older people have been lifted out of poverty, but they still remain precariously perched in the "near-poor" category. In fact, the near-poverty rate among older people has hardly decreased at all since the 1970s. Further, the average statistics on poverty and aging also conceal some important differences among subgroups of older people. Most discussion of generational equity revolves around averages, but these can be misleading.

Condition of Children and Young People

There is clear evidence that the current generation of children are threatened by damage ranging from poor prenatal care to inadequate child care and a mediocre educational system—all creating conditions for a "generation in crisis" (Moynihan, 1986; Hamburg, 1992). International comparison shows that U.S. rates for poverty among children are higher than those of every industrialized nation in the world (Smeeding, 1990).

Do these facts about child poverty mean that government programs to help the aged are responsible for the problem? It is true that government programs to help younger poor families—such as welfare or Food Stamps—are unpopular and were reduced during the 1980s. In terms of government spending, public support for children at risk has declined sharply in recent years and means-tested benefits for families have been cut. But by contrast, social entitlement programs like Social Security or Medicare have withstood most, but not all, attacks on them much better.

But the basic cause of rising child poverty seems to have little to do with government entitlement programs. Defenders of old age programs point out that the high poverty rate among younger generations is caused mainly by family structure, unemployment, and declining wages. In all countries, children living in single-parent families have poverty rates more than double those in two-parent families.

Some commentators have blamed the declining well-being of children on the voting power of the elderly. In an influential article, demographer Samuel Preston was one of the first to worry that the political power of the elderly, along with their greater numbers, poses a threat to the well-being of children in America (Preston, 1984). But there is little evidence that the elderly as a

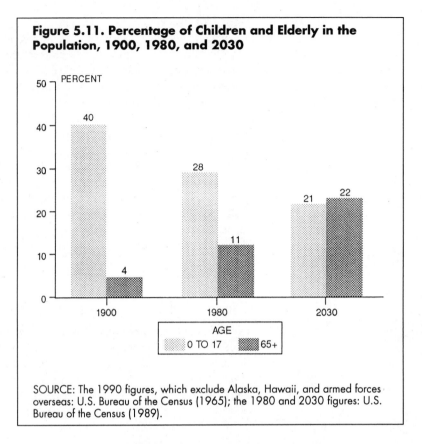

Figure 5.11. Percentage of Children and Elderly in the Population, 1900, 1980, and 2030

SOURCE: The 1990 figures, which exclude Alaska, Hawaii, and armed forces overseas: U.S. Bureau of the Census (1965); the 1980 and 2030 figures: U.S. Bureau of the Census (1989).

group have acted to swamp other age groups with their voting power (Rosenbaum and Button, 1989). Still, there is no question that children and families with children today form a smaller part of the electorate than in the past, reflecting the aging of the population, as the numbers in Figure 5.11 demonstrate.

The Dependency Ratio

The changing proportion of children and elderly in the population has prompted another question: Will we as a society be able to support such a large population of older people in the future? The support ratio, or dependency ratio, is a numerical measure of the economic burden imposed on the working population who must ultimately support people who are not in the labor force. If we look at the aged alone, we can compute the elderly support ratio by comparing the number of people over age 65 with the number in the working age group (18 to 64). Similarly, we can compute the support ratio for children by comparing the number of those under age 18 with the number in the working-age group. Figure 5.12 and Table 5.3 display how both

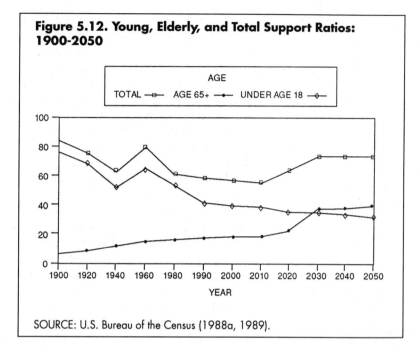

Figure 5.12. Young, Elderly, and Total Support Ratios: 1900-2050

SOURCE: U.S. Bureau of the Census (1988a, 1989).

Table 5.3. Young, Elderly, and Total Support Ratios: 1900-2050 (number of people of specified age per 100 people age 18 to 64)

Year	65+	Under 18	Total
Estimates:			
1900	7	76	84
1920	8	68	76
1940	11	52	63
1960	17	65	82
1980	19	46	65
Projections:			
1990	20	41	62
2000	21	39	60
2010	22	35	57
2020	29	35	64
2030	38	36	74
2040	39	35	74
2050	40	35	75

SOURCE: U.S. Bureau of the Census (1988a, 1989).

ratios—child dependency and elderly dependency—have changed over time, in this century and projected into the twenty-first century.

Those who are fearful about the burden of an aging population point out that when Social Security was created in the 1930s there were 50 workers to support each Social Security beneficiary. They point out with alarm that today there are only 3 workers for each beneficiary, and early in the next century the proportion will go down to 2 workers for each beneficiary.

Does this mean that the future of Social Security is gloomy? Not necessarily. The charts above show that the old age dependency ratio has risen and will continue to rise into the next century. But they also show that the support ratio for children has declined over this same period. In the post-World War II period, the support ratio for children reached a peak in 1960 but has since decreased because of smaller family sizes. As a result, when we look at the combined dependency ratio—that is, support for both young and old—we see that the combined ratio has actually declined since 1960 and is projected to continue declining until after 2010, when it begins to rise only modestly again. Thus, looking at the dependency ratio more closely, we see that the picture is more complicated than at first glance.

The key point is that different kinds of expenditures support children and the elderly. Publicly funded programs such as Social Security and Medicare support older people, while, apart from public education, children are mostly supported through private family expenditures. The overall dependency ratio suggests that, at least well into the next century, the burden of an aging population is not unreasonable. On the other hand, the cost of specific programs—such as Medicare—may pose other problems, which we have examined in previous Controversy sections. But, again, it is not an abstract dependency ratio but the means by which health care expenditures are financed and controlled that is the point at issue here.

Taxation and Generational Accounting

Discussions of generational equity usually look only at the cost of government expenditures for the elderly. But equally important is the role of the tax system with its far-reaching impact on different age groups and cohorts. Tax expenditures are distributed much less equally than are income or benefit entitlements such as Social Security and Medicare. For example, there are a number of "tax breaks"—sometimes called tax expenditures—that go disproportionately to older people at higher incomes levels. By contrast, the elderly poor (those with incomes below $5,000) get only 2% of the benefits from tax expenditures (Nelson, 1983).

A key stimulus to the generational equity debate has been a growing awareness that not all the elderly are any longer poor or needy. Taking that idea seriously might mean replacing age-based entitlement programs, such as Medicare, with those that are accessible to persons of all ages (Wisensale,

1988). A related question is whether benefits, such as Social Security, should be taxed at progressive rates to take into account the heterogeneity of today's older population.

An important new tool for analyzing the issue of generational equity has emerged in economics. It is a method called generational accounting developed by economists Lawrence Kotlikoff and Alan Auerbach (Kotlikoff, 1992). The aim of this approach is to analyze how government tax and spending policies affect different historical cohorts. Generational accounting adds up all taxes paid to federal, state, and local governments over a lifetime and then subtracts benefits received, such as Social Security, Medicare, or schooling. On that basis, it turns out that baby boomers born in 1950 will pay an average lifetime tax rate about a third higher than their parents (31% as opposed to 24%). That difference means paying $200,000 more in taxes than collected in benefits over a lifetime (Nasar, 1993).

The method of generational accounting provides a way of thinking about the long-range impact of budget decisions made today. Many controversies about Social Security can also be analyzed in terms of generational accounting. But critics have pointed out that generational accounting is based on so many uncertain predictions about the future that it may not provide guidance about today's budget or policy choices.

Power and Competition for Scarce Resources

Does the debate about generational equity imply that the old and young are locked in conflict? Here we need to look carefully at how the terms are defined. It is useful to make a distinction between the notion of *conflict* between generations as opposed to *competition* for different public programs. Conflict and competition are not the same thing. Age conflict does occur in some societies, for example, when the aging patriarch of a family controls property (Foner, 1984). Similarly, it is possible to find examples of **gerontocracy,** or the rule of society when the groups cling to positions of power as they grow older. A current instance might be Communist China with its aging party leaders. Yet even the Chinese case might better be described as not so much rule by the aged but a case where a restricted group maintains its power through incumbency and authoritarian control (Eisele, 1979).

In America, there is no real evidence of "conflict" between age groups. On the contrary, public support for Social Security and other benefit programs for the elderly remains high. But there can be competition over limited resources and the resulting political struggle may affect age groups differently: for instance, when school bond issues are voted down or when Social Security benefits are taxed. But changes in taxes or spending are not necessarily motivated by hostility among age groups, and it would be a mistake to pit age groups against one another. It would also be a mistake to overlook the fact that competition, choice, and trade-offs are simply the law of political life, as cuts in Social Security have demonstrated (Light, 1985). The fact that these changes have taken place at all is proof enough that the presumptive political power of the aged has clear limits.

Who Are the Least Advantaged Elderly?

Since the 1980s, hard questions have been asked about how to pay for these benefits and about who should receive them. Are government-funded services actually helping the vulnerable elderly? How should government target its resources to those most in need? How, in fact, do we agree on who the "least advantaged" are among the elderly (Harel, Ehrlich, and Hubbard, 1990)?

A variety of replies have been given and some answers have included the following:

- All the elderly or perhaps those above a very advanced age
- Elders in minority ethnic groups
- Older women
- Rural or inner-city elderly
- The physically or mentally frail
- Older people who are vulnerable to abuse or neglect
- Seniors in poverty

The earliest answer to the question of who was least advantaged was the reply that all elderly people should be viewed as vulnerable; in other words, age itself would be a criterion for need. This conviction originally inspired the Older Americans Act. Some said that older people, as a group, were subject to prejudice or bigotry, and their treatment could be compared with that of minority groups (Barron, 1953). Instead of racism, one could speak of **ageism,** or stereotyped prejudice against older people leading to discrimination and disadvantage (Butler, 1969; Levin and Levin, 1980). But is it helpful to think about older people as a minority group? That formulation has proved controversial, not only in gerontology but in public policy discussions (Streib, 1965).

Some have therefore suggested that the age of entitlement might perhaps be raised (Torres-Gil, 1992). For example, raising the age for Medicare eligibility from 65 to 67 would over a period of years save $75 billion and prevent bankruptcy of the system, according to a Health and Human Services Department study completed in 1992. But if the age of eligibility were raised, that change would have a negative impact on minority groups, whose life expectancy is on average lower than that of the white population.

Still another answer to the question of who is least advantaged might be the aged poor (Clark, 1988; Crystal, 1986). Indeed, most of the multiple disadvantages of the aged, regardless of gender or ethnicity, come from poverty, often a lifetime of low earning power (Nelson, 1982). Looking at disadvantage from a longitudinal or life span point of view underscores the importance of **socioeconomic status** (SES), a term sociologists use to describe what is often known as social class (Bendix and Lipset, 1966). Instead of simply describing older people as "rich," "poor," or "middle class," we can rank groups of people in terms of socioeconomic status and see how occupation, income, and educational background are interrelated.

Social class, or socioeconomic status, is one way to think about stratification or the structured inequality in the distribution of power, prestige, or wealth among older people (Dowd, 1980; Streib, 1985). Socioeconomic status over the life course tends to produce cumulative disadvantages that are perpetuated in old age. Higher socioeconomic status tends to mean higher longevity and better health as well as more income (Streib, 1984). As we have seen, gender and race, along with class, create interlocking hierarchies of privilege and disadvantage, making it more difficult to identify a single characteristic that defines the "least advantaged" among the aged.

Helping Those Most in Need

If "need" instead of age alone is to be the basis for distributing benefits or services, then how will we assess need as a practical matter? One popular method is to use a **means test**: that is, a measure of eligibility based on whether a person's income or assets fall below a certain amount. For example, Medicaid, Supplemental Security Income, and Food Stamps are all programs with a means test. By contrast, Medicare and Social Security are not means tested.

A common argument against means-tested programs is that they are stigmatizing; that is, it is embarrassing and degrading for people who are forced by necessity to make use of such programs. Even if eligible, many older people are reluctant to apply for SSI because to them it has the image of "welfare." In the past, it was customary for local governments to take care of old age poverty through a local "poorhouse" or almshouse, a familiar institution in American life dating back to colonial times (Achenbaum, 1978). Older people who descended into poverty or who had no family to care for them could be forced into the stigma of "outdoor" relief, a predecessor of today's welfare system.

Other methods of helping the least advantaged have been less stigmatizing but have also taken account of different levels of need. The tax system itself can reflect the principle of ability to pay, which is basic to the idea of progressive taxation. For example, at the local level, where property taxes are important, many local governments have circuit breaker provisions or homestead exemptions to offer tax reductions or exemptions for low-income older homeowners. Since 1983, half of Social Security benefits for more affluent beneficiaries have been subject to federal taxation. Whether through a means test or through progressive taxation, there is recognition that ability to pay for benefits differs within the older population.

Finally, it is possible to use an approach that combines elements of means testing and taxation: namely, cost sharing. Older Americans Act programs are not permitted to charge for the service, but Congress has never appropriated enough money to reach more than a small part of those who could be served by the programs. Some program administrators believe that, to expand the services, it is reasonable to charge recipients for services based on their ability to pay. For example, elderly with incomes at least 200% above the poverty line might pay a part of the cost of a service according to a sliding scale. Opponents of cost sharing fear that it would discourage use of services by those least able to pay and that it would also begin to erode broad public support for universal programs (Kassner, 1992).

The Targeting Debate

There are many different answers to the question: "Who are the least advantaged elderly?" The Older Americans Act explicitly directs that the aging service network should **target** its services to "individuals with the greatest economic or social needs, with particular attention to low-income minority individuals." That injunction has given rise to debates about targeting of benefits, including a major legal case in the federal courts (*Meek v. Martinez*) disputing what criteria should be used for allocating resources to those "most in need."

The targeting debate has provoked strong differences of opinion about how universal programs, such as the Older Americans Act, can properly give preference to some needy groups (Jacobs, 1990). The debate has some similarity with disputes about financing and distributing the benefits of Social Security. On one side are those who believe that programs are most fair and effective when they are universal and open to all. On the other side are those who believe that the least advantaged need some special consideration if they are to receive their fair share. The arguments here are reminiscent of debates about affirmative action programs. As the aging population becomes more diverse, and as long as all public expenditures remain limited, there will be controversy about age or need as a basis for entitlement.

In the readings that follow, there are sharply different views about the fairness of our social programs that help the elderly. On one side is Philip Longman, who takes aim at the politics of aging in America. The political power of the elderly, he believes, has caused us to spend too much on older people and not enough on children. Longman believes that need, not chronological age, should be the basis for giving people help from the government. By contrast, Eric Kingson and colleagues in writing their book *Ties That Bind* take a more favorable view of age-based entitlements. They argue that public benefit programs directed at the aged actually help people of all ages, among other reasons because they relieve middle-aged children of supporting aged parents. Meredith Minkler is one who believes that the entire debate about generational equity is misguided. She believes that talking about "greedy geezers" is a new kind of victim blaming that distracts our attention from the real issues of injustice arising from social class along with racial and gender inequalities. Finally, Stephanie Gould and John Palmer offer still another perspective on this debate by showing how the same kinds of generational issues arise in different countries and reflect broad changes, such as improvement in the life expectancy and well-being of older people.

Whatever we conclude about arguments on justice between generations, there is a practical question to be faced in the debate over need versus age. What factor should be primary in designating who are the least advantaged elderly? How do we decide who is most in need? In her article, Louise Kamikawa argues strongly that social class by itself is not sufficient for measuring need among older people. Race and ethnicity also should be taken into account, she believes. Kamikawa identifies a variety of entitlement programs for older people ranging from the poor, to lower middle class, and upper middle class elders. She points out that, even in programs intended for the poor or marginal elderly, it is whites, not minorities, who tend to get most of the resources. Her argument here is close to the view advanced on behalf of affirmative action programs in education or employment; that is, special consideration should be given to minority status to ensure that the results of participation are fair and equal.

In their article, Robert Hudson and Eric Kingson make the case for universality in social programs. They want to avoid as much as possible any kind of means testing or other forms of explicit targeting that could prove stigmatizing or divisive. On the contrary, they believe that the key challenge now is to maintain universalism—to make benefits or services available to everyone—while at the same time directing greater benefits to those in greatest need. The way to accomplish that, they argue, is by making the financing of government services more progressive through the tax system, while also using a targeting strategy within universal programs, much as the Older Americans Act has tried to do.

But even with additional funding financed through tax revenues, service providers will still face hard choices about how to distribute benefits to those in greatest social or economic need. The debate about who are the least advantaged will continue to be a challenge for the future.

Born to Pay

The New Politics of Aging in America

Philip Longman

We can predict few trends with any degree of certainty regarding American life in the first half of the twenty-first century. The aging of the population, however, has already built such a powerful momentum that it is hard to conceive of any likely future development that could reverse its course. Although the year 2050, for example, may seem a long way off, it is important to remember that everyone who will be over sixty-five by that time has already been born. It is reasonable to assume that mortality rates will continue to improve as medical knowledge advances. Indeed, in recent years life expectancy among the elderly has been increasing faster than for any other age group. But even if for some reason no further medical advances are achieved, the absolute growth, if not the relative growth, of the elderly population is more or less a given.

The proportion of the total population that will be elderly is only slightly less certain. As the oldest women of the baby boom generation pass beyond their prime childbearing years, the chances for a second boom are receding rapidly. To the casual observer it may seem as if the fertility rate is about to take a big jump. News magazines report a trend toward elaborate weddings. Many young women are interrupting their careers to concentrate on marriage and children. And in point of fact, the number of women giving birth each year has begun to rise. But the picture is deceptive. One reason is that the rise in the birthrate has been concentrated among women who have delayed having their first child until their thirties. Both time and, typically, economic necessity conspire against such women's ever raising as many children as their mothers did. Largely because of the trend toward deferred marriage and childbearing, the average American woman now has 1.8 children over her lifetime, whereas 2.1 are needed just to replace the population.[7]

Prevailing attitudes toward family size also argue against a significant increase in the fertility rate. In 1959, 45 percent of all Americans believed that the ideal family would include four children; today only 11 percent believe this. Over the same interval, the percentage of Americans favoring two-child families has increased from 16 to 56 percent.[8] Moreover, even if the children of the baby boomers do decide to raise large families, their relatively small numbers will ensure that the overall effect on the age composition of the population will be minimal. At least for the rest of this century, the percentage of American women who could potentially have children will continue to fall, as the baby boom generation passes beyond its prime childbearing years and is replaced by the much smaller "baby bust" generation. . . .

Thus, the baby boomers must face the prospect of becoming the largest generation of senior citizens in history, both in absolute size and relative to the number of younger citizens available to support them. By 2030, the Census Bureau projects, using cautious assumptions, more than one out of five Americans will be age sixty-five or older. Nearly one in ten will be seventy-five or older.

To some readers, it may seem that sheer force of numbers will assure the baby boomers a comfortable retirement. Today, Americans over sixty-five compose little more than 12 percent of the population. Yet they are a commanding force in American politics. Social Security, even for the wealthy, is immune to budget cuts, despite the federal budget deficits. If today's relatively small cohort of senior citizens can so effectively command public resources, why shouldn't the baby boomers look forward to an even easier time as they swell the ranks of the elderly?

So long as democratic institutions survive, the baby boomers will enjoy great political strength in old age. Politicians will bid against one another to court their vote. Entrepreneurs will organize vast pressure groups to lobby on their behalf. The baby boomers are sure to find their own curmudgeonly "spokesperson" to play the role of Claude Pepper. But while the baby boomers in old age will command far more votes and probably will enjoy far greater political influence than do today's senior citizens, they will nonetheless be forced to seek their support from a working-aged population that will be comparatively much smaller and quite likely poorer. At the same time, whatever old age subsidies they secure will have to be divided thinly because of their great numbers. The baby boomers' strength in numbers will also be their great weakness. In 1985, there were 4.9 Americans aged twenty to sixty-four available to pay benefits to each member of the population over sixty-five. By 2030, according to Census Bureau projections, this ratio will at "best" fall to 3 to 1—assuming a dramatic increase in fertility and small improvement in life expectancy—and could well fall as low as 2.2 to 1.[10]

The Twilight of Youth
While there will be many more elderly in the next century relative to the working-aged population,

there will probably also be many fewer children. This has led some observers to conclude optimistically that since the working-aged population will presumably be spending a much smaller fraction of its income for public education and other programs for the young, they will accede to paying much more for the elderly.

Several considerations argue against placing much faith in this thought. The first is that, under current spending patterns, the public cost of supporting each retiree far exceeds the amount spent on each child. Thus the savings realized by a decline in the relative number of children would probably be not nearly as large as the extra cost of providing the growing number of elderly with the same level of benefits enjoyed by today's senior citizens.

The most recent comprehensive study of the subject was published in 1977 by economists Robert Clark and J. J. Spengler. In 1975, according to their estimates, total per capita expenditures for the elderly, at all levels of government, exceeded the amount spent on children age seventeen and under—including the total spent on public education—by more than three to one. The disparity is no doubt much larger today. Social Security pensions and Medicare pensions have become much more generous, while welfare and educational programs for the young have been cut.[11]

At the federal level, according to the Office of Management and Budget, the total spent in 1983 on the population over sixty-five amounted to $217 billion, or about $7,700 per senior citizen. The amount spent per child, on the other hand, is more difficult to calculate, and the government keeps no official figures. In an article for *Scientific American,* however, Samuel H. Preston, a demographer at the University of Pennsylvania, calculated that total federal expenditures benefitting children came to $36 billion in 1984, which was about one-sixth of the total spending on the elderly. Because there are many more children than there are elderly people, the expenditure per child was about one-tenth the expenditure per older person.[12]

In our society, of course, the cost of raising children is still largely borne by individual parents. Thus the potential savings realized by a decline in the relative number of children is not fully revealed just by examining the pattern of public expenditures for the young and the old. Still, we must consider the harsh reality that most parents derive far more satisfaction and reward in spending money on their own children than in paying taxes to support the elderly in general. If parents have fewer children in the future, they will surely prefer to spend more on each child than pay higher Social Security taxes. This is especially likely since, as society grows more complex, their children will need ever more education to succeed. Single Americans also will prefer to use the money they save by not having children for purposes other than supporting the baby boomers in old age.

Finally, we must consider how working-aged Americans in the early decades of the next century will be looking to their own prospects for retirement. If fertility rates continue to decline and longevity continues to increase, today's children will face even greater difficulty in securing their own old age benefits than will the baby boomers. Before providing their parents' generation with generous old age benefits, today's children will be required by prudence to save up toward the cost of their own golden years. Thus, there is no reason to believe that a continued decline in the relative number of children will assure the baby boomers adequate support in old age, and there is good reason to believe the opposite.

Can the Baby Boomers
Pay Their Own Way?

Unable to depend on population growth to finance their future Social Security and other old age benefits, the baby boomers have an inordinately great need to accumulate assets, such as savings accounts and home equity, from which they can draw income in old age. Yet it is highly unlikely that the baby boomers as a whole will ever be able to pay their own way through retirement.

The first reason is the cost of supporting today's retirees. Members of every generation, in their middle years, have sacrificed to provide support for their elders. But prior to the adoption of Social Security, Medicare, and other old age entitlement programs, such support was typically extended only to the elderly in need, not to everyone beyond a certain age. A rich father was not likely to receive payments from his children solely because he had passed age sixty-five; indeed, any transfer was more likely to be in the opposite direction, in the form of an inheritance.

Today, the Social Security system alone costs most younger Americans more than one out of every seven dollars they earn.[13] Not only do the young support the old as a whole—regardless of need—but the ranks of the old have never been larger. Today's elderly are retiring earlier and living longer than any generation in history. The average age of retirement is now sixty-two, while life expectancy for people at that age is over seventy-seven years for men and over eighty-two years for women.[14] No matter whether one applauds or deplores Social Security, no one can deny that its cost, together with other entitlement programs for today's senior citizens, diminishes the ability of younger Americans to save toward their own retirement. Since 1939, the maximum annual Social Security tax has increased by more than 10,000 percent, from $60 to $6,006; since 1960, the tax has increased by nearly 2,000 percent.[15]

The second great obstacle to saving faced by most members of the baby boom generation is their relatively low standard of living. In the 1980s, two stereotypes of the baby boomers prevail. They are depicted either as narcissistic yuppies wallowing in discretionary income, or as victims of downward mobility—unable to afford children for the price of the wife's not working, bid out of the housing market, or burdened with unprecedented mortgage payments. There is no doubt that some baby boomers are well-to-do. The generation is so large that even the small percentage of its members who are affluent attract inordinate attention from advertisers and journalists—who tend to be yuppies themselves. But the vast majority of baby boomers are better described by the second image.

In 1984, 47 percent of all Americans aged twenty-five to thirty-four who were in the work force earned less than $12,500 a year; 70 percent earned less than $20,000.[16] The typical young American family headed by a person aged twenty-five to thirty-four consisted of a husband, a wife, and a single child under age twelve. Fewer than half owned their own homes. In most families, both husband and wife worked. Before taxes, the median income for such families, from all earners, totaled $25,157—hardly enough to buy a BMW, or even to save much toward retirement.[17]

The downward mobility of the baby boom generation is revealed by several other measures. The first is the unprecedented disparity in the wages between older and younger workers. Throughout most of American history, the premium paid for seniority was much less than it is today. Once—largely because they tended to be better educated—young men starting out earned nearly the same pay as their fathers. As recently as the mid-1950s, the median income of fully employed men in their early twenties equaled 93 percent of the amount paid to fully employed men aged forty-five to fifty-four. But by 1984, that ratio had dropped to a mere 47 percent. This income disparity is also growing among female workers. In relative terms, starting wages for persons of both sexes have probably never been lower.[18]

The change is particularly significant when one considers the baby boom generation's relatively advanced level of education. Only 65 percent of Americans aged thirty-five and older have completed high school, while nearly 86 percent of those aged twenty-five to thirty-four are high school graduates. Some 24 percent of the younger group hold college degrees, compared with only 15 of the population over thirty-five.[19] Yet this educational edge hasn't been enough to prevent each successive cohort of the baby boom from slipping farther behind in its per capita share of the nation's total income. Younger baby boomers, who came into the work force after the economy turned downward in 1973, are doing substantially worse than older baby boomers. A rising percentage of recent college graduates, moreover, are coming into the work force encumbered by enormous student loans, as student aid programs have been cut. In 1986 the median debt incurred by graduates of public colleges was $8,000; of private schools $10,000.[20]

It is still too early to tell, of course, whether the baby boomers will eventually reap the same high premium for seniority realized by today's older workers. But there are many reasons to believe that they won't. Consider, for example, the following trend line. According to a recent study commissioned by the Joint Economic Committee of the U.S. Congress, the average male worker turning age thirty in 1950 saw his income rise by 118 percent over inflation during his next ten years in the work force. Similarly, men turning age thirty in 1960 saw their real wages rise by 108 percent over the next decade. But men turning age thirty in 1970 realized almost no premium for their increased seniority. Over the next ten years, their real wages increased by a mere 16 percent.[21]

Looking to the future, the continuing decline of the U.S. manufacturing sector, the massive trade deficits, and the low wages generally paid to workers in the growing service sector of the economy all argue against the possibility that today's young workers as a whole will eventually become as upwardly mobile as were their parents in the 1950s and 1960s. In many industries, the downward mobility of the young has become institutionalized through the growth of so-called two-tier wage contracts, which exempt senior workers from sacrifice but place new hires on a permanently lower wage scale. . . .

The pressure on young families is relieved in part by the young wives who are going to work in increasing numbers. Still, even young families with two paychecks today earn little more than young families with one paycheck did in the early seventies. For young married couples, with a household head aged twenty-five to thirty-four, who *both* were in the work force, the combined median income (adjusted for inflation) in 1983 was only $3,400 higher than the amount enjoyed ten years earlier by young couples living on the husband's salary alone. Over the same period, the purchasing power of young families relying on a single paycheck declined by roughly $4,000.[23] That so many young families now depend on two paychecks to maintain even the trappings of a middle-class lifestyle is another reason not to expect any dramatic rise in the birthrate.

By another measure, net wealth, the baby boomers are also shown to be downwardly mobile. Between 1977 and 1983, for example, the average net wealth of all American households, adjusted for inflation, rose from $41,000 to $47,000. But for households headed by a person aged twenty-five to thirty-four, net wealth declined, from $18,804 to $16,651; for households headed by a person aged 35 to 44, from $44,359 to 40,710.[24]

For many baby boomers, the quest to maintain the same standard of living they knew as children requires that they go deeply and often foolishly into debt. The increase in consumer borrowing among the young is both a cause and a consequence of their general downward mobility. Between 1970 and 1983, the proportion of all families headed by a person twenty-five to thirty-four who were paying off consumer debt increased from 67 to 77 percent. Among the vast majority of young families in debt in 1983, the average amount they owed on their credit cards and installment loans was $4,781.[25] Debtors obviously have a hard time saving. In 1984, more than a third of all households headed by a person under thirty-five had no savings whatsoever on deposit with banks and other financial institutions, aside from noninterest-paying checking accounts. Only 13 percent held any assets in the form of stocks or mutual funds.[26]

Finally, the baby boomers' ability to save toward retirement has been reduced by the extraordinary inflation in real estate prices during their lifetimes. In 1949, a thirty-year-old man who purchased the median-priced house needed to commit only 14 percent of his income to meet the carrying charges. At that time, a new "Cape Cod" in Levittown went for just $7,990—no money down, $60 dollars a month. By 1983, the combination of stagnant or falling wages, high interest costs, and mounting real estate prices meant that the average thirty-year-old man needed to commit 44 percent of his income to meet the carrying charges on the median-priced house. That same year, 65 percent of all first-time home buyers needed two paychecks to meet their monthly payments.[27]

For most of today's elderly, the vast appreciation in the value of their homes provides a great measure of security. Fully 73 percent of the elderly own their homes; the average value of their home equity in 1984 was $54,667. Elderly home owners by and large were able to save more during their working years, and they can now hold on to their financial assets longer in retirement because they have been sheltered from rising housing costs. The average value of bank deposits held by persons over sixty-five exceeded $33,000 in 1984. The average value of stock and mutual fund portfolios held by the elderly that year exceeded $42,000.[28]

The baby boomers, however, faced with extraordinarily high housing costs, will find it commensurately more difficult to save for retirement, or for any other purpose—even assuming that they manage to buy a first house. Between 1977 and 1983, the percentage of families headed by a person under thirty-five who owned their own homes declined from 41 to 34 percent.[29] Moreover, while no one knows the future direction of real estate prices, it is sobering to consider that those baby boomers who do manage to buy property will eventually see its value determined by whatever the members of the very small and so far very poor baby bust generation are able and willing to pay.

Children in an Aging Society

Polls consistently show that most baby boomers have little or no faith in receiving adequate income from Social Security and other old age programs.[30]

Yet many believe that one way or another they will be able to save enough to support themselves in old age. For this to happen, the baby boomers would have to do what no other generation has done before: save up the cost of their own retirement, and, through Social Security and Medicare and other programs, pay a large share of the cost of the preceding generation's retirement as well.

Providing the baby boomers with greater tax incentives to save, such as through expanded Individual Retirement Accounts, hardly solves the problem. In 1986, IRAs cost the Treasury Department $21 billion in forgone revenue and to that extent increased the national debt and its burden on future taxpayers. Increasing savings through expansion of the private pension system entails the same dilemma. Tax subsidies for employer-sponsored pension plans increased the national debt in 1986 by more than $71 billion.[31] Moreover, as the United States moves toward a service economy, we can expect an ever smaller percentage of workers to be covered by private pension plans, which historically have been concentrated among large, unionized manufacturing industries. Between 1979 and 1983, the percentage of workers covered by such plans dropped for the first time in the postwar era, from 56 to 52 percent.[32] Although tax subsidies to support IRAs and private pensions may in the end be justified, they do not provide a panacea for the problems facing the baby boomers.

Unavoidably, then, the baby boomers' prospects for old age depend on the success of the next generation—today's children. As Frances FitzGerald has written, "Americans in their sixties and seventies are surely the first generation of healthy, economically independent retired people in history— and, in the absence of significant economic growth, they may well be the last."[33] If you believe that today's children are bound to grow up many times richer and more productive than today's workers, then logic will permit you to believe that Social Security, Medicare, and other government programs will be able to provide adequately for the baby boomers in old age. The Social Security Ad-

ministration predicts that in order for both its pension and disability funds to remain solvent over the lifetime of the baby boomers, real wages must more than double today's levels by 2015 and increase sixfold before 2060—and this is assuming that fertility rates increase rapidly as well, and that other demographic and economic trends are also extremely favorable.[34]

A dispassionate look at the hazards now standing in the way of the younger generation's prosperity should give pause, however, to anyone who would trust such an eventuality to fate. Consider first the alarming increase in poverty among today's children. Throughout American history, each new generation has grown up to be richer than the one that went before. And yet as Daniel Patrick Moynihan has asserted, the United States has now become "the first society in history in which a person is more likely to be poor if young rather than old."[35] The downward mobility of the baby boomers has been compounded with a vengeance on their children. Between 1973 and 1984, the percentage of children living beneath the poverty line increased by more than two-thirds. By 1984, more than one out of five American children under age eighteen was poor.[36]

Cutbacks in federal programs for children go a long way toward explaining this alarming trend. Between 1980 and 1986, programs for children and families suffered budget cuts of over $50 billion. Due to tighter eligibility requirements, for example, Aid to Families with Dependent Children—the government's main welfare program—served only fifty-five of every one hundred poor children in 1984, compared with seventy-five of every one hundred in 1978.[37] But other deeper, more intractable problems were also at work which have affected even children nominally born into the middle class.

Of all baby boomers, those with children have generally fared the worst. During the first two postwar decades, family income among both two-parent and female-headed families with children grew by an average of more than 6 percent a year. But between 1973 and 1984, families with children saw their average, inflation-adjusted income drop by more than 8 percent, from over $32,000 a year to $29,500, despite the enormous increase in the number of working mothers.[38]

Even white families with both parents present saw their income fall—by more than 3 percent. If the increase in Social Security and other taxes were taken into account, the decline in overall family income would be even steeper. Between 1960 and the early 1980s, the average family of four saw its tax rate rise by more than 200 percent. A family of four earning poverty-level wages in 1986 paid between 10 and 12 percent of its meager earnings in federal taxes alone, up from 2 percent in 1979.[39]

The increasing poverty among children is a national scandal in its own right. But a closer examination of its causes suggests an even greater tragedy in the future. Besides higher taxes and lower wages, the rising rates of divorce and of children born out of wedlock have also contributed mightily to the increase in childhood poverty, while also eroding the bonds between the baby boomers and their children within all economic classes. . . .

Single-parent families are currently forming at twenty times the rate of two-parent families. The potentially horrendous implications for the future are revealed by the fact that children with divorced or unwed mothers are more than five times as likely to be poor as children in two-parent homes. Even those children in single-parent homes who do escape poverty may well be emotionally and economically handicapped by their experience. How many of these children find the wherewithal to finish high school or go to college? How many will have the means or be of a mind to support their aged parents, either directly, or through Social Security and other programs? . . .

The Prophets of Crisis
Predictions of a coming war between the generations have by no means been confined to the present era. Many of the trends that are currently weakening the bonds between young and old have quietly been at work for many decades, and a few far-sighted observers could see their eventual implications. As early as 1951, in a speech before the Southern Conference on Gerontology, the economist Frank G. Dickenson warned that "the enormous growth in the number of old people in America, and their increasing demands for pensions, may lead us to expect a new sort of class war—between our younger and older citizens." Dickenson prophesied that the burden of supporting the old would grow inexorably, and that as a result "we will see workers and employers, despite their natural respect for age, standing shoulder to shoulder against hard-driven politicians who promise our senior citizens impossible pensions." [70]

Today, partisans of the senior power movement frequently attack suggestions that any real competition ever exists between the generations. In 1986, for example, the Gerontological Society of America published a study, later publicized by the House Select Committee on Aging, which argued that young and old were inevitably bound together by common interest and that any suggestions to the contrary were "intentionally divisive" and the result of an "improper frame of analysis." [71] Yet before the trends just discussed began to force the issue of generational equity, gerontologists were among the first to warn of a youthful revolt against the growing power of the elderly. Bernice Neugarten, for example, one of the country's most widely respected gerontologists, predicted in 1974 that during the rest of the decade "anger toward the old may rise . . . as a growing proportion of power positions in the judiciary, legislative, business and professional arenas are occupied by older people, as the number of retirees increases and taxes rise." [72] The next year, Robert N. Butler, who coined the term *ageism* in the mid-1960s and who for many years headed the National Institute on Aging, warned that "one unhappy aspect of the politics of aging is the pitting of one age group against another in the quest for scarce social resources. . . . The consequent resentment of younger age groups can boomerang against old people."[73]

Today's elderly probably have little to fear, despite these warnings. Indeed, throughout the remaining years of today's older people, the aging of the population will actually work in favor of more generous retirement benefits. As the youngest of the baby boomers join the work force and as the oldest gain income through seniority, their taxes are expected to swell the coffers of the Social Security trust funds for many years to come. Moreover, as life expectancy among the elderly continues to lengthen, there will be ever more middle-aged Americans seeking relief from the potentially astronomical cost of supporting their elderly parents in nursing homes or of paying for the cost of operations and catastrophic illnesses not covered by Medicare. Finally, as the percentage of households with children present continues to decline, fewer Americans will be pressing for the government to spend its money first on the needs of children. With current fertility and mortality rates, it turns out that there is no longer any stage in life when the average married couple will have more children under the age of twenty than they will have surviving parents.[74]

Instead, it is the baby boomers who need fear abandonment in old age. For it is they, along with their children, who will inherit the consequences of this spendthrift era. There are no purely technical solutions to the deficit looming everywhere in American society—in the birthrate that is below replacement level, in the declining educational performance of the nation's children relative to their counterparts abroad, in the federal budget, in the balance of trade, in the long-term financing of Social Security and Medicare. Our problem is as much cultural as it is economic. As a nation and as individuals we have committed ourselves to spending more in real resources than we will likely be able to produce over our lifetimes. Behind the abstract and bloodless debate over fiscal policy, trade, and general national decline lurk the terrifying

ethical and societal issues that have created our deficit state.

Notes

[NOTE: Only the notes that are included in the excerpted material appear here.]

7. Official estimates of the fertility rate are published by the National Center for Health Statistics' *Monthly Vital Statistics Report* (Washington, D.C.: U.S. Government Printing Office).

8. Selected Gallup poll opinion surveys, collected in *Public Opinion* (December-January 1986): 28.

10. U.S. Bureau of the Census, Current Population Reports, *Projections of the Population of the United States, 1982 to 2080* [Washington, D.C.: Government Printing Office].

11. Robert L. Clark and J. J. Spengler, "Changing Demography and Dependency Costs: The Implications of Future Dependency Ratios," in *Aging and Income: Essays on Policy Prospects*, ed. Barbara R. Herzog (New York: Human Sciences Press, 1977), 55-89.

12. Samuel H. Preston, "Children and the Elderly in the U.S.," *Scientific American* 251: 6 (December 1984): 45.

13. This figure includes the portion of a worker's wages that is forwarded to Social Security directly by his or her employer. Although advocates of Social Security sometimes argue that this tax is actually borne by the employer, economists are nearly in unanimous agreement that the funds actually come out of the worker's salary, as common sense would also confirm. . . .

14. D. P. Rice et al., "Changing Mortality Patterns, Health Services Utilization, and Health Care Expenditures, United States, 1978-2003," *Vital and Health Statistics* (Washington, D.C.: Public Health Service, U.S. Government Printing Office, series 3, no. 23, DHHS pub. no. (PHS) 83-14-7, September 1983), table 4.

15. U.S. General Accounting Office, *Social Security: Past Projections and Future Financing Concerns* (Washington, D.C.: U.S. Government Printing Office, GAO/HRD-86-22, March 1986), appendix 2, p. 80.

16. U.S. Bureau of the Census, Current Population Reports, *Money Income of Households, Families, and Persons in the United States, 1984* (Washington, D.C.: U.S. Government Printing Office, series P-60, no. 151, 1986), 121.

17. Frank S. Levy and Richard C. Michel, "The Economic Future of the Baby Boom" (Paper presented at the first annual conference of Americans for Generational Equity, Washington, D.C., 10 April 1986. Research originally prepared in December 1985 under contract with the Joint Economic

Committee of the U.S. Congress and authorized by Chairman David Obey and Vice Chairman James Abnor).

18. Louise B. Russell, *The Baby Boom Generation and the Economy* (Washington, D.C., Brookings Institution, 1982), table 4-6, and U.S. Bureau of the Census, Current Population Reports, *Money Income of Households, Families, and Persons in the United States,* selected years.

19. Bryant Robey and Cheryl Russell, "The Year of the Baby Boom," *American Demographics* 6:5 (May 1984): 21.

20. Janet Bamford, "Degrees of Debt," *Forbes*, 7 April 1986, 122.

21. Levy and Michel, "The Economic Future," 8.

23. U.S. Bureau of the Census, Current Population Reports, *Money Income of Households, Families, and Persons in the United States,* 1975, 1985.

24. John Weicher and Susan Wachter, "The Distribution of Wealth Among Families: Increasing Inequality?" Paper presented to the Working Seminar on the Family and American Welfare Policy, American Enterprise Institute, 10 November 1986.

25. Robert B. Avery, Gregory E. Elliehausen, and Glenn B. Canner, "Survey of Consumer Finances, 1983: A Second Report," *Federal Reserve Bulletin* (December 1984); Levy and Michel, "The Economic Future," 17.

26. U.S. Bureau of the Census, Current Population Reports, *Household Wealth and Asset Ownership: 1984* series P-70, no. 7, 14.

27. Levy and Michel, "The Economic Future," 13. For Levittown prices, see Kenneth T. Jackson, *Crabgrass Frontier: The Suburbanization of the United States* (New York: Oxford University Press, 1985), 236.

28. U.S. Bureau of the Census, Current Population Reports, *Household Wealth and Asset Ownership: 1984,* series P-70, no. 7, 14.

29. Avery, Elliehausen, and Canner, "Survey of Consumer Finances, 1983," *Federal Reserve Bulletin* (September 1984).

30. See, for example, Yankelovich, Skelly, and White, Inc., *A Fifty Year Report on Social Security,* 1985 (survey sponsored by the American Association of Retired Persons, Washington, D.C.). Nearly two-thirds of the respondents aged twenty-five to forty-four stated that they were "not too confident" or "not at all confident" about the future of Social Security. For a comprehensive study of public attitudes toward Social Security, see Robert Y. Shapiro and Tom W. Smith, "The Polls: Social Security," *Public Opinion Quarterly* 49 (Winter 1985): 561-72.

31. Office of Management and Budget, *Special Analyses of the Budget of the United States Government, Fiscal Year 1987* (Washington, D.C.: U.S. Government Printing Office, 1986).

32. E. S. Andrews, *The Changing Profile of Pensions in America* (Washington, D.C.: Employee Benefits Research Institute, 1984).

33. Frances FitzGerald, *Cities on a Hill: A Journey Through Contemporary American Cultures* (Simon and Schuster, 1986), 209.

34. Social Security Administration, *The 1986 Annual Report of the Board of Trustees of the Federal Old-Age and Survivors Insurance and Disability Insurance Trust Funds* (Washington, D.C.: U.S. Government Printing Office, 1986), table 10, p. 32. The number is arrived at by compounding the annual growth in real wages assumed by the system's actuaries under "Alternative I," the only model that shows both the disability and pension trust funds remaining solvent past 2030. See, for example, table 31, p. 75. Note as well that these estimates do not take into consideration the cost of financing the Hospital Insurance or Medicare trust funds.

35. Daniel Patrick Moynihan, *Family and Nation* (San Diego: Harcourt Brace Jovanovich, 1986), 112.

36. U.S. Bureau of the Census, Current Population Reports, *Characteristics of the Population Below the Poverty Level: 1984* (Washington, D.C.: U.S. Government Printing Office, series P-60, no. 152, 1986).

37. Mary Bordette (Director, Government Affairs, Children's Defense Fund), "Investing in the American Family: The Common Bond of Generations" (testimony before the Select Committee on Aging, U.S. House of Representatives, 8 April 1986).

38. Sheldon Danziger and Peter Gottschalk, "Families with Children Have Fared Worst," *Challenge* (March-April 1986): 40-47.

39. Bordette, "The American Family."

70. Frank G. Dickenson, "Economic Aspects of Our Population," in *Problems of America's Aging Population: A Report of the First Annual Southern Conference of Gerontology* (Gainesville: University of Florida Press, 1951), excerpted as "The Coming Class War—Old vs. Young," *Harper's*, July 1952, 81.

71. Eric R. Kingson et al., *The Common Stake: The Interdependence of Generations* (Washington, D.C.: The Gerontological Society of America, 1986).

72. Bernice L. Neugarten, "Age Groups in American Society and the Rise of the Young-Old," *Annals of the Academy of Political and Social Sciences* 415 (1974): 189.

73. Robert N. Butler, *Why Survive? Being Old in America* (New York: Harper & Row, 1975), 323. For other early warnings of generational conflict over equity, see Pauline K. Ragan, "Another Look at the Politicizing of Old Age: Can We Expect a Backlash Effect?" *Urban and Social Change Review* (Summer 1977): 6-12.

74. Preston, "Children and the Elderly," 48.

Ties That Bind

Eric Kingson, John Cornman,
and Barbara Hirschorn

Issues associated with the aging of America are best framed and analyzed if one bears in mind that

- the aging society is both a success and a challenge;
- the elderly population is greatly diversified;
- the relationship between individuals and generations is characterized essentially by interdependence and reciprocity;
- all generations have a common stake in social policies and intergenerational transfers that meet needs throughout the life course; and
- the nation's future *can* be changed and shaped by choices made today.

The Trends and the Challenge

More people are living longer, largely because of better sanitation, improved public health, and the control of life-threatening diseases. In 1900 life expectancy at birth was about 47 years for men and 49 years for women. . . . In 1985 it was an estimated 71.5 years for men and 78.8 years for women. About four out of five individuals can now expect to reach age 65, at which point—all things being equal—there is a better than 50 percent chance of living past 80. Moreover, for increasing numbers of elderly people, the quality of life is vastly improved over that for previous generations.

Source: Ties That Bind: The Interdependence of Generations (pp. 1-14) by E. Kingson, J. Cornman and B. Hirschorn, 1986, Arlington, VA: Seven Locks Press. Reprinted with permission.

Both the increased probability of reaching old age and the generally improving quality of life in old age can be credited to the successful advances made by past and present generations in addressing problems across the life course, notably public and private investments in research, education, public health, social policies, and economic growth. These investments were often made in policies and programs having no apparent connection with the aged as well as in those that appear to serve only the elderly. For example, although programs that have all but eliminated many life-threatening infectious diseases may have been justified previously for their benefit to children and young adults, their success also accounts for the increasing numbers who survive to old age. Similarly, although Social Security provides income directly to retirees, it also benefits younger persons in many ways.

Still, as a society we must deal with the reality that millions of older people continue to live in or near poverty and continue to be afflicted with debilitating chronic illnesses. Further, we have to recognize that the large majority of the elderly who are not poor or who are not significantly limited in their normal activities—and even many who are—wish to maintain their autonomy, to contribute as much as they can to their families and communities, even in advanced old age. Thus, we are challenged to find ways to ensure the economic well-being of the elderly; to reduce the incidence, or delay the onset, of chronic illness; to provide humane care to those who require assistance or attention on a continuing basis; and to offer opportunities for the elderly to make productive contributions to society at large.

To meet the challenge of an increasingly aging society will naturally cost increasing sums of money. Unhappily, the challenge comes at a time of painful economic uncertainty. The nation faces a seemingly intractable federal-deficit problem. Sharp budget cuts in many government programs at all levels—federal, state, and local—have particularly impaired our ability to meet the needs of poor children, and demographic changes (e.g., growth in single-parent households and increasing participation of women in the work force) are limiting the time family members can spend providing direct care to the very young or to the functionally disabled of any age. Inevitably, questions press about the quantity and quality of opportunities available to younger generations, and about the impact of the federal deficit on these opportunities.

So the challenge of an aging society extends far beyond concerns about the quality of life for the elderly. It cries for a civic commitment to improve the quality of life for *all* members of society, regardless of age. At root, the challenge is inextricably linked to the need for economic growth and for full use of the nation's productive capacity.

Diversity of the Elderly

The outstanding characteristic of the elderly, now and in the future, is their diversity. In 1984 about a fourth of elderly families reported incomes of $30,000 or more, while one-fifth reported incomes under $10,000. Among elderly individuals, about 11 percent reported incomes of $20,000 or above while 25 percent reported incomes under $5000. At the same time, a substantial portion of the elderly occupy marginal economic status. In 1984 the incomes of 5.6 million elderly (21.2 percent) were below the near-poverty thresholds ($6,224 for a single elderly person and $7,853 for an elderly couple).

Although most noninstitutionalized elderly consider themselves to be in good or even excellent health, about one-fifth report limitations on their ability to carry on at least one major activity of daily living. Persons aged 85 and over are more than four times as likely as persons 65 to 74 to need in-home and institutional long-term care.

Understanding this diversity is critical if society is to assess accurately the various impacts of policies and proposed changes on particular groups of the elderly.

Interdependence and Reciprocity

The amount and type of resources individuals give and receive vary as they grow and age, generally in this sort of pattern: 1) in childhood individuals mainly receive resources; 2) throughout the young adult and middle years, they usually give more than they receive; and 3) in later years—particularly in advanced old age—they receive more and more resources even as they continue to give them. For any society to progress and prosper, each generation must provide assistance to, and receive assistance from, those that follow.

A comprehensive social policy, therefore, must focus not on a single moment in the life course—say, childhood or old age—but rather on the positions and needs of diverse individuals as they move through their lives. From such a perspective, the reciprocity of giving and receiving that goes on over time among individuals, and between generations, becomes a commanding principle. It is the bond of interdependence that ties society together. Prior experience thus emerges as an important determinant in the quality of life at all ages.

The Intergenerational Inequity Thesis

Regrettably, the current debate over the role of government in society has produced an approach that frames policy questions primarily in terms of competition and conflict between young and old. It is grounded not in the interdependence of generations but in an assumption of intergenerational inequity, the rationale for which goes like this:

> Due to previous circumstances of the elderly and the broad-based perceptions of the elderly as both "needy" and "worthy," there has been a flow of public resources (income, health, and social services) toward the elderly, which has successfully improved their economic status and access to health care. In fact, the elderly are (or shortly will be) financially better off than the nonaged population. In light of this improved status, of large federal deficits, of the cost to younger persons of continuing present policies, and of anticipated growth of the elderly population, the flow of resources to the elderly seems "intergenerationally inequitable" and a source of intergenerational conflict.

While seemingly neutral in approach and possessing an intuitive appeal (who can be against fairness?), the argument carries with it very pessimistic views about the implications of an aging society. It would have us believe that

- programs for the elderly are a major cause of current budget deficits and economic problems;
- the elderly receive too large a portion of public social welfare expenditures to the detriment of children and other groups;
- because of demographic trends, the future costs of programs for the elderly will place an intolerable burden on younger workers; and
- younger people will not receive fair returns for their Social Security and Medicare investments.

As articulated thus far, the "intergenerational inequity" argument frames policy questions in terms of competition for scarce resources. It assumes that it is possible to measure accurately the fairness of the flows of resources between generations; that the amount of resources available for

social programs in the future will and should be comparable to or less than what is currently available; and that advances in research, education, and economic growth will not change straightline projections of the need for future health care and retirement income, nor will they change projections of our collective ability to respond. The approach evaluates costs and benefits of social policies primarily at a single point in time, measures fairness in terms of dollars rather than outcomes, and draws many of its conclusions from comparisons between broad demographic groups such as "the elderly" and "children."

Flaws and Misunderstandings

Not only are many of these assumptions based on misunderstandings, but the analytic approach itself is flawed. For example:

1. *"Intergenerational inequity" does not take into account the overall dependency ratio.* Many pessimistic arguments are based on the oft-referenced "aged dependency ratio," which measures the number of persons aged 65 and over (all of whom, for the purpose of this measure, are presumed "dependent") for every 100 persons aged 18 to 64 (all of whom are presumed to be contributing to the economy). Currently, there are 19 dependent elderly persons per every 100 persons of so-called "working ages." Using the definition above, the aged dependency ratio is projected to rise slowly to 22 persons in 2010 and then increase rather precipitously to 37 persons by 2030, leading some to conclude that the costs of programs for the elderly will be unsustainable unless drastic changes are made now.

This sounds ominous indeed, but the aged dependency ratio as described shows only part of the so-called "dependency burden." In contrast, the "overall dependency ratio," which measures the total number of persons under age 18 plus those aged 65 and over for every 100 persons aged 18 to 64, provides a very different picture. As economist Barbara Boyle Torrey points out, never at any time during the next 65 years is the overall dependency ratio projected to exceed the levels it attained in 1964. While it should be noted that the composition of governmental and private expenditures for younger and older Americans is quite different, clearly the overall dependency ratio does not paint quite so gloomy a picture about society's ability, through public and private mechanisms, to enhance the quality of life for persons of all ages.

Further, according to Brandeis University researcher William Crown, both the aged dependency ratio and the overall dependency ratio are flawed because they fail to take into account such factors as the increasing labor force participation of women, the potential for significant portions of the elderly to work longer, or the effect of economic growth. For example, when the midrange assumptions of the Social Security Administration about the growth of the economy and the size of the future U.S. population are used, real GNP per person is projected to nearly double by 2020 and triple by 2050. Barring unforeseen disasters, the economy of the future seems likely to be able to support a mix of programs for all age groups.

2. *"Intergenerational inequity" assumes that all the elderly are well off.* Having discovered that all elderly are not poor, some journalists, academics, and policymakers have gone to the other extreme and declared that all elderly are financially comfortable, thereby justifying the position that public benefits should be reduced.

Failure to recognize the heterogeneity among the elderly—even among those aged 85 and over—leads to distortions in how social problems are defined, to misunderstandings about the implications of policy options, and ultimately to poor policy. Even so, these stereotypes persist, in part because stereotypical thinking is convenient, in part because negative attitudes about the elderly and growing old exist, and in part because, for some, stereotypes further political ends such as reducing social programs.

3. *"Intergenerational inequity" sees conflict as the rule.* Conflict between generations is the exception, not the norm. Certainly, examples of conflict can be found, such as those showing the elderly voting against a school-related tax in a particular community. Care should be taken, however, not to conclude that conflict between generations is the "rule" or that the elderly are a cohesive political group intent on forcing their will against the interests of the young (or vice versa). Despite assertions of "senior power" by the press and by senior advocacy organizations themselves, political scientists such as Robert Binstock, Robert Hudson, and John Strate, who study the voting behavior of the elderly, generally conclude it is influenced far more by such things as lifelong party affiliation, social class, race, and political beliefs than by age. Opinion surveys show, too, that all age groups are willing to support programs for the elderly, particularly when given a choice between cutting defense spending or programs like Social Security and Medicare.

Considerable evidence also exists to show that the elderly are concerned about the needs of the young. In a 1983 poll commissioned by the American Council of Life Insurance, 88 percent of the elderly believed parents should feel a great deal or some responsibility to provide grown children with a college education, and 85 percent believed parents should feel a great deal or some responsibility to provide their grown children with a place to live if those children are unable to afford their own.

4. *"Intergenerational inequity" is based on a narrow view of fairness.* Equity between generations, while certainly desirable, is a very limited criterion on which to base the distribution of scarce resources among those with competing claims. Even if all parties could agree on what constitutes a fair distribution of resources among generations, achieving such a balance would not necessarily meet many of the nation's goals for social justice. For example, it would not guarantee 1) that poor citizens would be provided with minimally adequate resources; 2) that nonpoor citizens would be

protected from the risks of drastic reduction in their standards of living due to factors beyond their control; or 3) that all citizens would be afforded equal opportunity to achieve what their potentials allow. In short, as Binstock, a professor at Case Western Reserve University, has observed, the current preoccupation with equity between generations "blinds us to inequities within age groups and throughout our society."

Similarly flawed is the notion that per capita public expenditures on children and the elderly ought to be equal. Such an equation assumes that the relative needs of children and the elderly for public expenditures are identical and that equal expenditures are the equivalent of social justice. In fact, a sense of fairness based on the concept of need may require that greater per capita expenditures be directed at children than at the elderly, or that very substantial outlays of public resources be directed at certain subgroupings of children (for example, the growing number of children living in poverty), but not at others. Further, even if the aggregate needs of each group were the same, equal per capita expenditures directed at children and the elderly in the face of substantial unmet needs are not the same as social justice, nor would they result in equal outcomes.

It is sometimes argued that Social Security is unfair because today's young, as a group, will not have as high a rate of return on their "investments" in these programs as current retirees. Still others consider it "intergenerationally inequitable" that these programs do not function like private insurance programs, in which benefits are strictly related to the amount of contributions made.

The concept of fairness incorporated in such arguments is based on a misunderstanding of the multiple purposes of Social Security and Medicare. These goals include preventing economic insecurity through the sharing of risks against which very few could protect on their own, enhancing the dignity of beneficiaries, and providing stable financing. For example, to prevent economic insecurity, Social Security must provide a floor of protection

through special provisions for low-wage workers and for certain family members, thereby emphasizing social adequacy. Once this goal is accepted, it is impossible to guarantee in addition that the rate of return for all parties will be identical.

5. *"Intergenerational inequity" uses limited measures to draw broad conclusions.* Since each generation receives transfers from those that precede it and also gives transfers to those that follow, to reach accurate conclusions about equity between generations would require an examination within the context of the multiple intergenerational public and private transfers that are occurring constantly. Further, such an examination would have to answer questions like these:

How should the economic and social investments made by previous generations be valued? What about those of current ones?

Should part of what is spent on the elderly be counted as a return on *their* investments in younger generations? Should part of what is spent on children be considered an investment in future productivity?

How should investments made in research, conservation, environmental protection, and defense be allocated among generations?

Comprehensive measurement of intergenerational transfers is virtually impossible. As an alternative, analysts sometimes measure a particular resource transfer—for example, the percent of the federal budget directed at children versus the elderly. There is nothing necessarily wrong with making such measurements. What's wrong is to use them as the basis for broad and inappropriate conclusions about equity.

6. *"Intergenerational inequity" fails to recognize the common stake in social policies.* By framing policy issues in terms of competition and conflict between generations, the intergenerational inequity perspective implies that public benefits to the elderly are a one-way flow from young to old and that there is no reciprocity between generations. This simply is not the case.

7. *"Intergenerational inequity" assumes a zero sum game.* In accepting a framework that pits

young against old over the division of scarce resources, the intergenerational inequity framework assumes a "fixed pie," which apparently can only be cut from one of two places—either the elderly or the young. By doing so, the framework takes for granted, wrongly, that the federal pie cannot be increased by economic growth or more tax revenues, and/or that the slice of pie for domestic programs cannot be increased as a result of reduced defense spending.

8. *"Intergenerational inequity" distracts attention from important policy issues.* By framing issues in terms of trade-offs between young and old rather than in terms of policy goals or other trade-offs, the intergenerational inequity framework distracts attention from more useful ways of evaluating and making social policy. It also serves to deflect consideration of such important questions as 1) whether taxes should be raised; 2) whether the rapid growth and current composition of defense expenditures are in the national interest; and 3) whether new policies are needed to meet the needs of the most vulnerable citizens, regardless of age. Discussions about the unacceptably high rates of poverty among children, for instance, get obfuscated by the suggestion that declines in the elderly poverty rate are causally related to the precipitous increase in poverty among children—almost as if an increase in poverty among the elderly would somehow help children!

9. *"Intergenerational inequity" undermines the family.* Were the inequity argument to be embraced as principle and used to justify government's lack of obligation to respond to the growing pressure on families for care-giving, many families could be overwhelmed by the stresses inherent in providing care for relatives. By promoting conflict, advocacy of such a principle might even subtly weaken the bonds between generations within the family.

While those who use this approach to policy-making span the political spectrum, some proponents see it simply as a convenient rationale for an ideology that opposes all public efforts directed at meeting family and individual needs. This point of view encourages attitudes that do not fully represent either the rich mix of values in our society or the balance generally sought between private and public solutions to social problems.

In Truth, the Generations Are Interdependent

Fairer and more effective social policy, we suggest, would be based on a tacit understanding of the interdependence of generations. This approach recognizes the heterogeneity of age groups within the U.S. population, evaluates costs and benefits of social policies primarily over time rather than at just one moment in time, and stresses the importance of understanding who—indirectly as well as directly—pays for and benefits from social policies existing and proposed. Finally, the approach takes a life course perspective to help explain the seeming paradox of the autonomy and interdependence of individuals and age groups as they move through life. Consequently, it emphasizes the importance of thinking broadly about how policies directed at one age group may affect all others—at any given point in time and over time—as these groups age. And it suggests that in an interdependent and aging society, all generations have a common stake in family efforts and public policies, or intergenerational transfers, that respond to the needs of people of all ages.

The Role of Intergenerational Transfers

Intergenerational transfers are not limited to government programs and public policies that transfer income and in-kind services (e.g., Social Security, education between generations). They also include private (e.g., family care-giving, inheritances) and societal (e.g., economic growth, new technology) transfers.

To consider only transfers resulting from public policies would be to miss a major way generations assist each other. Analysis that includes the value of housework and child care along with a few other nonmoney items (e.g., imputed rent from equity in a house) as part of the contribution made by individuals in families leads University of Michigan economist James Morgan to conclude that "the family is by far the most important welfare or redistributional mechanism even in an advanced industrial country like the United States with extensive public and private income maintenance programs"; he estimates transfers within families in 1979 to be $709 billion, equivalent to 30 percent of the gross national product.

Generations also assist each other through societal intergenerational transfers. These involve, for example, the legacy (e.g., economic growth, culture, values, knowledge) older generations bequeath to younger ones as well as the improvements (e.g., economic growth, new technology) younger generations make to the benefit of older ones.

There is no guarantee that particular birth cohorts or generations (within families) will receive more than they will give through intergenerational transfers, although generally this has been the case in American society. Without intergenerational transfers, however, the very continuity and progress of society and families would cease because needs that all experience at various points in life would not be met and legacies of the past would not be transmitted.

Currently, for children, especially the very young, the family is the principal provider. This is particularly true in this country because care-giving is a special domain of the family. As a child ages, the family generally remains dominant, although formal structures (especially educational institutions) become increasingly important. Farther along the life course, society has chosen to have government play a stronger role, especially through income maintenance and health care programs. Nevertheless, the family plays a significant role in offering assistance to the elderly who are functionally disabled.

Interdependence of generations within families. Ordinary care-giving and care-receiving exchanges occur within the family every day, ranging from assisting a spouse or child with a cold to paying for a college education. These exchanges are numerous, as exemplified by findings from a Harris survey that 1) more than four-fifths of family members aged 18 to 24 run errands for parents or grandparents and help them when someone is ill; and 2) even people aged 80 and over continue to provide support to younger generations in their families, with 57 percent helping out when someone is sick and 23 percent running errands. And some of these transfers involve financial resources; Urban Institute researcher Thomas Espenshade estimates that the cost of raising a typical child in a middle-class household to age 18 is $82,400 (in 1981 dollars).

Over the course of life, many persons will also give and/or receive extra-ordinary care. This might happen, for example, if a child is born with Down's syndrome, if a spouse becomes a paraplegic following an automobile accident, or if an aged parent or grandparent develops a chronic and seriously debilitating heart ailment.

It is primarily the family that is asked to respond when serious support needs arise and, in most cases, to bear most of the long-term costs. About 80 percent of elderly persons requiring assistance in the normal activities of daily life live in private settings. Most of the service these persons receive comes from family members, who provide such care for a number of reasons, including a sense of reciprocity, of filial responsibility, and of duty based on assistance previously provided by the older family members.

The costs to families of providing such care are likely to increase in the future as a result of the aging of society—especially the growth of the very old population—and other demographic trends. One set of projections suggests that the elderly long-term care population will increase from 6.6 million persons today to over 9 million by the year

2000, to nearly 13 million by 2020, and to nearly 19 million by 2040. Further, other social trends are straining the family's capacity to function as a provider of care. These trends include 1) increased rates of divorce and childbirth to unmarried persons, resulting in growing numbers of single-parent households; 2) increased participation of women in the labor force; and 3) the growing preference for smaller families, resulting in fewer children to share care-giving.

The real issue facing the nation, then, is not how to ask families to give more care across the life course with the intent of reducing public expenditures. Rather, given demographic trends, the crucial question is what kinds of assistance should be offered to help the family continue in its traditional care-giving role.

Long-Term Views of
Social Programs

The interdependence of generations framework primarily bases its analysis on a longitudinal approach to evaluating costs and benefits of public policies. This approach examines the flow of tax payments and benefits over time. Thus, it is quite different from the cross-sectional approach emphasized by the intergenerational inequity framework, which examines the flow of tax payments and public benefits primarily at one moment in time. And it often leads to very different conclusions about who pays for and who benefits from such policies as public education, public health, investments made in research, Social Security, and Medicare. Take public education as an example. From a cross-sectional perspective it would appear that education is primarily a transfer from working persons and other taxpayers to children and youth. From a longitudinal perspective, however, although the young clearly receive a transfer in the form of education, as they age they will also contribute to the education of those who follow as well as to economic growth and tax revenue, which will benefit the current workers as they age.

Social Security. As an outstanding example both of a program in which all generations have a common stake and of the importance of taking the long-term view of a social policy, consider Social Security. It serves these goals and values:

- the widespread preference for nonpersonal means of financial support in old age—that is, for the major responsibility for financial support of older relatives to be placed outside the family;
- the desire for a dignified and stable means of support for the elderly, the disabled, and surviving and financially dependent family members; and
- the need for a rational approach for protection against basic risks such as reduction of income due to retirement, disability, or death of a breadwinner.

The common stake in Social Security is also a result of the widespread distribution of benefits and costs among persons of all ages. To understand this common stake, it is not sufficient just to examine the direct benefits at one point in time—those that go primarily (about 85 percent), but not exclusively, to retired workers and their spouses and to widows and widowers aged 60 and over. When time is "frozen" in this fashion, it may appear as if the distribution of burdens and benefits is unfair—with the young mostly paying and the elderly mostly taking. But identifying the direct and indirect benefits and the costs of Social Security over time presents a far different picture. The long-term perspective of Social Security shows that

- retirement benefits for today's younger workers will, on average, have greater purchasing power than those of today's retirees;
- Social Security introduces a critical element of stability into the retirement plans of young and

middle-aged workers because even before benefits are first received, their value is kept up-to-date with rising wages and increases in the standard of living;

- disability and survivors protection alike have tangible worth to covered workers and their families;
- by providing cash benefits to older family members, Social Security frees up younger and middle-aged family members to concentrate more financial resources on their children; and
- by enabling family members and individuals to protect themselves against some major financial risks, Social Security stabilizes family life and the society.

Summary and Recommendation

These observations do not lead to the conclusion that such transfers are flawless and should never be changed. On the contrary, because of the basic functions they serve and because demographic and economic change is an ongoing process, policies should be reviewed carefully and options vigorously debated. Of critical importance now, however, is that those who are considering changes understand both who benefits from these policies and the common stake that prevails in these intergenerational transfers.

At best, the framing of issues in terms of competition and conflict between generations is based on a misunderstanding of relations between generations and distracts attention from more useful ways of examining social problems. At worst, it is a cynical and purposely divisive strategy put forth to justify and build political support for attacks on policies and reductions in programs that benefit all age groups. In contrast, we advocate an approach that assumes the interdependence of generations and emphasizes the importance of thinking broadly about how policies directed at one age group affect all others, at any given point in time and over time,

as these groups age. Among our more important conclusions are these:

1. It is erroneous to think of Social Security as a one-way flow of resources from young to old, or of education as a one-way flow from adults to children.

2. The elderly, now and in the future, have at least two important stakes in programs that respond to the needs of children, young adults, and the middle-aged. First, they benefit directly and indirectly from education, training, and health programs that help increase the productivity of the work force. Second, it is in their political interest to pursue strategies that do not pit generations against each other.

3. Younger generations have two important stakes in programs that assist the elderly to maintain a decent quality of life. First, they will be served by those programs when they become old. Second, such programs relieve young and middle-aged family members of financial burdens and intrafamily stresses.

4. For both humanitarian and practical reasons, advocates for the elderly and others concerned with preparing for the retirement of the baby boomers have a special responsibility to support policies that respond to the needs and aspirations of the many poor and near-poor children in America. Failure to provide adequate educational, health, and employment opportunities to these children could undermine their future productivity and reduce the quality of life for the baby boomers during their retirement years.

Granted our preference for the interdependence framework, this report deals with a more basic issue—the importance of framing properly the policy debate necessary to meet the challenge of an aging society. Our single recommendation is that all those concerned understand the power of various frameworks to define the terms of this debate, and that they give careful consideration to the implications of each approach.

"Generational Equity" and the New Victim Blaming

Meredith Minkler

> This policy and reverence of age makes the world bitter to the best of our times; keeps our fortunes from us till our oldness cannot relish them. I begin to find an idle and fond bondage in the oppression of aged tyranny, who sways, not as it hath power, but as it is suffer'd.
>
> —*King Lear, I, ii, 47*

Stereotypic views of the elderly in the United States as a wealthy and powerful voting block have replaced earlier stereotypes of this age group as a poor, impotent, and deserving minority (1). Capitalizing on and contributing to these changing perceptions, the mass media and a new national organization, Americans for Generational Equity (AGE), prophesize a coming "age war" in the United States, with Social Security and Medicare as the battleground (2). Like Gloucester's young son in *King Lear,* they argue that entitlement programs for today's affluent elderly "mortgage our children's future" and contribute to high poverty rates among the nation's youth.

The framing of complex public policy issues in terms of conflict between generations, however,

tends to obscure other, far more potent bases of inequities in our society. Indeed, in Binstock's words (1, pp. 437-438):

> To describe the axis upon which equity is to be judged is to circumscribe the major options available in rendering justice. The contemporary preoccupation with . . . intergenerational equity blinds us to inequities within age groups and throughout society.

This [reading] will examine the assumptions underlying the concept of generational equity, with particular attention to notions of fairness and differential stake in the common good. Tendencies by policy makers, scholars, and the mass media to statistically homogenize the elderly and to utilize inadequate and flawed measures of poverty further will be examined and seen to contribute to the myth of a monolithic and financially secure elderly population. Finally, the false dichotomy created between the interests of young and old will be

Source: " 'Generational Equity' and the New Victim Blaming," in *Critical Perspectives on Aging*, edited by M. Minkler and C. Estes (pp. 67-79), 1991. Amityville, NY: Baywood Publishing Co. Reprinted with permission of Baywood Publishing and author.

found to illustrate a new form of victim blaming, whose employment is inimical not only to the elderly but to the whole of society.

The Making of a Social Problem

In his trenchant look at the cyclical nature of social problems, O'Conner noted that when the economy is perceived in terms of scarcity, social problems are redefined in ways that permit contracted, less costly approaches to their solution (3). Thus, while the economic prosperity of the 1960s permitted us to discover and even declare war on poverty, the recession of 1973 and its aftermath resulted in a redefinition of poverty and the subsequent generation of less costly "solutions."

The discovery of high rates of poverty and poor access to medical care among America's elderly in the economically robust 1960s and early 70s helped generate a plethora of ameliorative programs and policies including Medicare and Social Security cost of living increases (COLAs). By the mid-1970s however, amid high inflation and unemployment, Social Security and Medicare were themselves being defined as part of the problem. By implication, the elderly beneficiaries of these programs frequently were characterized by the mass media as targets of special resentment. The "compassionate ageism" which had enabled the stereotyping of the elderly as weak, poor and dependent, from the 1930s through the early 1970s, (1) gave way to new images of costly and wealthy populations whose favored programs were "busting the federal budget."

In the mid-1980s, a new dimension was added to this socially constructed problem when the rapidly increasing size of the elderly population and the costliness of programs like Social Security and Medicare were directly linked to the financial hardships suffered by younger cohorts in general and the nation's children in particular. Indeed, in a widely publicized article in *Scientific American,* Samuel Preston, then President of the Population Association of America, argued that the elderly now fare far better than children in our society (4):

In the twelve years from 1970 to 1983, he pointed out, the proportion of children and elders living in poverty was reversed, with the proportion of children under fourteen living in poverty growing from 16 percent to 23 percent and the percent of elderly poor dropping from 24 percent to only 15 percent. While public outlays for the two groups had remained relatively constant through 1979, moreover, many public programs for children were cut back in the 1980s, at the same time that programs for the politically powerful elderly were expanded. Preston's widely quoted paper went on to compare the elderly and children on a variety of parameters including suicide rates and concluded with a plea for redressing the balance of our attentions and resource allocations in favor of youth.

Following closely on the heels of Preston's analysis, the President's Council of Economic Advisors reported in February of 1985 that the elderly were "no longer a disadvantaged group," and indeed were better off financially than the population as a whole (5).

These two publications helped generate a new wave of media attention to the "costly and wealthy elderly." They further provided much of the impetus for a new, would-be national organization devoted to promoting the interests of younger and future generations in the national political process. With the backing of two prominent congressmen and an impressive array of corporate sponsors, Americans for Generational Equity (AGE) attacked head on government policies which, under pressure from a powerful gray lobby, were seen as creating a situation in which "today's affluent seniors are unfairly competing for the resources of the future elderly" (6).

The mass media, AGE, and other proponents of an intergenerational conflict framework for examining current U.S. economic problems have successfully capitalized on growing societal concern over certain facts of life which have coincided with the graying of America. These include:

• a massive federal deficit;

- alarming increases in poverty rates among children, with one in five American children now living in poverty (7); and
- a 76 million strong "Baby Boom" generation whose real incomes have declined 19 percent over the last fifteen years.

These statistics have been coupled with another set of facts and figures used to suggest that the growing elderly population is itself part of the problem:

- The elderly, while representing only 12 percent of the population, consume 29 percent of the national budget and fully 51 percent of all government expenditures for social services (8);
- Since 1970, Social Security benefits have increased 46 percent in real terms, while inflation-adjusted wages for the rest of the population have declined by 7 percent (9).

The picture presented is one of a host of societal economic difficulties "caused," in part, by a system of rewards that disproportionately benefits the elderly regardless of their financial status.

The logic behind the concept of generational equity is flawed on several counts, each of which will be discussed separately. In addition to these specific inaccuracies, however, a broader problem will be seen to lie in an approach to policy which lays out the issues in terms of competition among generations for scarce resources. Each of these problems will now be discussed.

The Myth of the
Homogeneous Elderly

Basic to the concept of generational equity is the notion that elderly Americans are, as a group, financially secure. Borrowing statistics from the President's Council of Economic [Advisors], proponents of this viewpoint argue that the 1984 poverty rate for elderly Americans was only 12.4 percent (compared to 14.4 percent for younger Americans), and dropped to just 4 percent if the

value of Medicare and other in-kind benefits was taken into account (5).

While the economic condition of the elderly as a whole has improved significantly in recent years, these optimistic figures obscure several important realities. First, there is tremendous income variation within the elderly cohort, and deep pockets of poverty continue to exist. Close to a third of black elders are poor, for example (32%), as are 24 percent of older Hispanics and 20 percent of all women aged eighty-five and above (10).

Minority elders and the "oldest old," aged eighty-five and above, not only have extremely high rates of poverty, but also comprise the fastest growing segments of the elderly population. Thus, while only about 8 percent of blacks are aged sixty-five and over, compared to over 13 percent of whites, the black elderly population has been growing at a rate double that of the white aged group. The number of black elders further is increasing at twice the rate of the younger black population (11). In a similar fashion, the "oldest old" in America—those aged eighty-five and above—are expected to double in number by the turn of the century, from 2.5 million in 1985 to some 5 million by the year 2000 (12). The very high rates of poverty in the current generation of "old old" may reflect in part a Depression-era cohort effect. At the same time, however, the heavy concentration of women in the eighty-five and over age group, coupled with continued high divorce rates and pay and pension inequities, suggest a significant continuing poverty pocket as the population continues to age (13).

The myth of a homogenized and financially secure elderly population, in short, breaks down when the figures are disaggregated and the diversity of the elderly is taken into account.

Problems in the
Measurement of Poverty

Analyses which stress the low poverty rates of the aged also are misleading on several counts. First as Pollack has noted, comparisons which stress the favorable economic status of the aged *vis-à-vis* younger cohorts fail to acknowledge the use of two separate poverty lines in the United States—one for those sixty-five and above and the other for all other age groups (14). The 1987 poverty line for single persons under sixty-five thus was $5905— fully 8 percent higher than the $5447 poverty line used for elderly persons living alone (15). If the same poverty cutoff had been used for both groups, 15.4 percent of the elderly would have fallen below the line, giving the aged a higher poverty rate than any other age group except children.

The inadequacy of even the higher poverty index also merits attention. It is telling, for example, that Molly Orfshanksy, the original developer of the poverty index, dismissed it some years ago as failing to accurately account for inflation. By her revised estimates, the number of elderly persons living in or near poverty almost doubles (16).

Discussions of the role of Social Security and other in-kind transfers in lifting the elderly out of poverty also are problematic. Blaustein thus has argued that while Social Security and other governmental transfers helped lift millions of elders out of poverty, they for the most part succeeded in "lifting" them from a few hundred dollars below the poverty line to a few hundred dollars above it (17). Indeed, some 11.3 million elders, or 42.6 percent of the elderly, live below 200 percent of the poverty line, which for a person living alone is about $10,000 per year (15).

Recent governmental attempts to reduce poverty by redefining it also bear careful scrutiny in an effort to uncover the true financial status of the elderly and other groups. The argument that poverty in the aged drops to 4 percent where Medicaid and other in-kind transfers are taken into account thus is extremely misleading. By such logic, an elderly woman earning less than $5000 per year may be counted as being above the poverty line if she is hit by a truck and has $3000 in hospitalization costs paid for by Medicaid. The fact that she sees none of this $3000 and probably incurs additional out of pocket health care costs in the form of

prescription drugs and other deductibles is ignored in such spurious calculations (14).

The continuing high health care costs of the elderly are themselves cause for concern in any attempt to accurately assess the income adequacy of the elderly. The elderly's out of pocket health care costs today are about $2400 per year—three and one-half times higher than that of other age groups, and higher proportionately than the amount they spent prior to the enactment of Medicare and Medicaid more than two decades ago (18). Contrary to popular myth, Medicare pays only about 45 percent of the elderly's medical care bills and recipients have experienced huge increases in cost sharing (e.g., a 141 percent increase in the Part A deductible) under the Reagan administration (14). Inflation in health care at a rate roughly double that of the consumer price index further suggests that the *de facto* income adequacy for many elderly may be significantly less than the crude figures imply.

Moral Economy and the Cross-Generational Stake in Elderly Entitlements

Another criticism of the logic behind intergenerational equity lies in its assumption that the elderly alone have a stake in Social Security, Medicare, and other governmental programs which are framed as serving only the aged. Arguing that the nation's future "has been sold to the highest bidder among pressure groups and special interests" (6), Americans for Generational Equity and the mass media thus cast Social Security and other income transfers to the aged in a narrow and simplistic light. For even if one disregards the direct benefits of Social Security to nonelderly segments of the society (e.g., through survivors benefits to millions of persons under age sixty-five), the indirect cross-generational benefits of the program are significant. By providing for the financial needs of the elderly, Social Security thus frees adult children from the need to provide such support directly. As such, according to Kingson et al., it may reduce interfamilial tensions while increasing the dignity of elderly family members who receive benefits (19). Research by Bengston et al., has suggested that the family is not perceived by any of the major ethnic groups in America as having major responsibility for meeting the basic material needs of the elderly (20). Rather, families are able to provide the support they do in part because of the availability of government programs like Social Security. When these programs are cut back, the family's ability to respond may be overtaxed, to the detriment of young and old alike (21).

Programs like Social Security are not without serious flaws. . . . Yet despite these problems, and contrary to recent media claims, there has been little outcry from younger taxpayers to date about the high costs of Social Security and Medicare. Indeed, in an analysis of some twenty national surveys conducted by Louis Harris and Associates over a recent two-year period, Taylor found no support for the intergenerational conflict hypothesis (22). While the elderly appeared somewhat more supportive of programs targeted at them than did younger age groups, and vice versa, the balance of attitudes in all generations was solidly on the same side. The majority of both elderly people, and young people under thirty, thus opposed increasing monthly premiums for Medicare coverage, opposed increasing the deductible for Medicare coverage of doctors' bills, and opposed freezing Social Security cost of living increases. Similarly, both young and old Americans opposed cutting Federal spending on education and student loans, and overwhelmingly opposed cutting Federal health programs for women and children (22). In short, while young and old differ significantly on questions relating to values and lifestyle, issues of government spending and legislation affecting persons at different stages of the life course appeared to evoke intergenerational *consensus* rather than *conflict*.

The strong support of younger Americans for Social Security and Medicare is particularly enlightening in the wake of recent and widely publicized charges that these programs may be bankrupt before the current generation of young people can reap their benefits. Such charges, while poorly substantiated, have made an impact: poll data suggest that today's younger workers are pessimistic about the chances of Social Security and Medicare being there for them when they retire. In light of this pessimism, how might their continued high level of support for elderly entitlements be explained?

As noted earlier this phenomenon reflects in part the fact that younger people in the workforce prefer to have their parents indirectly supported than to shoulder this burden themselves in a more direct way.

Yet on a more fundamental level, the continued support of younger generations for old age entitlements they believe will go bankrupt before their time reflects what Hendricks and Leedham describe . . . as a moral economy grounded in use value—one whose central goal is "to structure a society so as to maximize possibilities of a decent life for all." As these analysts go on to note, moral economies grounded in use value envision the public interest as "a negotiated rule structure, to which people adhere *even though it may run counter to their own immediately desired satisfactions* since it improves overall opportunities of obtaining satisfaction" (emphasis added). Further, a moral economy based on use value or individual and social utility views citizens "not as passive recipients or consumers of public policy, but as active moral agents." Within such a vision of moral economy, resource allocation would be viewed not in terms of competition between generations, but in Rawls' sense, as allocations appropriate to ourselves at various points over the life course (23). . . .

Generational equity proponent Daniel Callahan has argued that such life course perspectives are flawed in their failure to adequately address the fact that the huge demands made by unprecedented numbers of elders in recent years "threaten to unbalance any smooth flow of an equitable share of resources from one generation to the next" (24, p. 207). Yet he and other proponents of generational equity similarly evoke a notion of moral economy in support of their arguments that the purpose of old age in society should be reformulated as involving primarily service to the young and to the future—in part through an acceptance of the need for "setting limits" on government support for life-saving medical treatment for those over a given age.

Callahan indeed proposes a shifting of the existing moral economy and a questioning of some of its basic assumptions. In particular, a fundamental tenet of the existing moral economy—that health care not be rationed on the basis of age—should, he argues, be reconsidered in light of current and growing inequities in the distribution of scarce public resources for health care between young and old (24).

The strong public outcry against age based rationing, coupled with the considerable evidence of the continued popularity of Social Security and Medicare among young and old alike, suggests, however, that the older moral economy notions of what is just and "due" the old have continued to hold sway. For both young and old, it appears, elderly entitlement programs like Social Security are not simply the way things are, but the way they should be. The reality, in short, stands in sharp contrast to the rhetoric which claims that Social Security is "nothing less than a massive transfer of wealth from the young, many of them struggling, to the elderly, many living comfortably" (25). Instead, the program, firmly grounded in American moral economy, is one which all generations appear to support, and from which all see themselves as receiving some direct or indirect benefit.

Age/Race Stratification and Inter-Ethnic Equity

Arguments that young and old alike have a stake in programs like Social Security and Medicare may break down, according to some analysts, when the element of ethnicity is introduced.

Indeed, Hayes-Bautista et al. suggest that there may be strong resentment of entitlement programs for the elderly thirty to fifty years from now in age/race stratified states like California (26).

Within such states, the burden of support for the large, predominantly white elderly population is expected to fall heavily on the shoulders of a young work force composed primarily of Latinos and other minorities.

Utilizing California demographic projections as a case in point, Hayes-Bautista et al. note that unless major shifts take place in fertility and immigration patterns, and/or in educational and job policy achievements, the working age population of the future will not only be heavily minority, but also comprised of individuals whose lower total wage base will require that larger proportions of their income go simply to maintaining current Social Security benefit levels for the white elderly Baby Boom generation. Under such conditions, they argue, the nation may be ripe for an "age-race collision."

While these investigators go on to suggest policy measures that might avert such a catastrophe, the "worst case scenarios" which they and other analysts (27, 28) describe have unfortunately received far more media attention than their recommended policy solutions. It is precisely because of the popularity of these "age wars" predictions, moreover, that a deeper look at the current reality is in order.

While it is of course impossible to project attitudinal shifts in the population in the way that demographic changes can be forecasted, current national opinion poll data on the attitudes of Latinos and other minorities toward entitlement programs for the elderly are instructive.

If the hypothesis is correct that there may be substantial resentment of Social Security and Medicare in the future on the part of a large minority working class population left to shoulder this burden, one might expect hints of such resentment now. Contrary to expectation, however, opinion poll data show Hispanics, blacks and other minorities to be strongly supportive of Social Security and Medicare and indeed often more opposed than whites to proposed budget cuts in these programs (22).

The hypothesis of growing minority resentment of elderly entitlement programs also may be questioned on demographic grounds. Thus, while minorities make up only about 10 percent of the aged population today, that figure is expected to increase by 75 percent by the year 2025. [The (c)omparable increase among white elders will be only about 62 percent (29).] Elderly Hispanics, already the fastest growing subgroup within the older population, will see their numbers grow even more rapidly, quadrupling by the year 2020 (30). From 2025 to 2050, the period corresponding to the graying of the huge Baby Boom generation, the proportion of elderly within the nonwhite population is projected to increase another 29 percent, compared to only 10 percent for the white population (29). While the minority aged population will remain small numerically compared to the elderly cohort, the fact that greater proportions of working aged Latinos, blacks and other minorities will have parents and grandparents reaching old age suggests again an important phenomenon which may work against the reification of an age/race wars scenario.

A final factor which may mitigate against the likelihood of increasing minority resentment of elderly entitlement programs concerns the differential importance of programs like Social Security to the economic well-being of whites, blacks, and Hispanics. The disadvantaged economic position of elderly blacks and Hispanics relative to whites, for example, means that higher proportions rely on Social Security as their only source of income, and that far fewer have private insurance and other non-government resources to cover the costs of medical care. Under such conditions, more rather than less support for elderly entitlement programs might be expected among these economically disadvantaged minority groups, and that is indeed what the survey data appear to suggest.

Guns Versus Canes?
A common theme throughout the intergenerational equity movement is that the elderly are not only numerous but also expensive: The high cost of So-

cial Security, amounting to about 20 percent of the federal budget, is juxtaposed against a $2 trillion national debt and a massive federal deficit, with the implicit and often explicit message that the costly elderly are a central part of our economic crisis.

As Pollack has noted, however, such equations are misleading at best (14). Social Security, for example, is not a contributor to the deficit and in fact brings in considerably more money than it pays out. Indeed, throughout the 1990s, when the small Depression-era cohort is elderly, the system will bring in literally hundreds of billions more than it will spend (14).

Ironically, the nation's military budget, while a major contributor to the deficit is virtually excluded from discussions by many analysts of the areas necessary for scrutiny if we are to achieve a balanced budget. AGE President Paul Hewit indeed has spoken out against a congress which, under pressure from aging interest groups, will "weaken our national defense before it will cut cost of living allowances (COLAs) for well to do senior citizens" (6).

Tendencies by the mass media and others to overlook defense spending in discussions of the costliness of programs for the elderly continue . . . a tradition described earlier by Binstock when he noted that we are taught to think in terms of how many workers it takes to support a dependent old person, but not how many it takes to support an aircraft carrier (16). Citing an OMB fiscal analyst, Binstock further pointed out that classic political economic trade-off, "guns vs. butter," has been reframed "guns vs. canes," in reference to the perceived costliness of the aged population.

In the relatively few years since Binstock's initial analysis, a further reframing has occurred with "canes vs. kids" constituting the new political economic trade-off.

As Kingson et al. (19) have noted, such an analysis assumes a zero sum game in which other possible options (e.g., increased taxes or decreased military spending) are implicitly assumed to be unacceptable (19). It is worthy of note that such traditionally conservative analysts as Meyer and Ein Lewin of the American Enterprise Institute (31) have begun arguing in favor of cutbacks in defense spending as a means of balancing the federal budget without in the process decimating needed social programs. While favoring increased taxation of Social Security and some initial taxing of Medicare benefits, the AEI analysts appear to have come down hardest on the need for massive reductions in military spending if the United States is to cease "protecting sacred cows and slaughtering weak lambs" (31, p. 1).

Still other analysts have urged the closing of tax loopholes for corporations and the rich as a means of redressing huge national deficits. Noting that corporate taxes dropped from 4.2 percent of the GNP in 1960 to 1.6 percent in the 1980s, and that money lost to the treasury through tax loopholes grew from $40 billion to $120 billion over the period 1980-86 alone, Pollack thus has argued that tax breaks for the rich, rather than Social Security COLAs for the elderly, should be viewed as the real culprits in the current economic crisis (14).

Finally, national opinion poll data show overwhelming public support for cutting military spending and closing tax loopholes, rather than cutting programs for the elderly and other population groups as a means of addressing America's economic difficulties (32).

The "canes vs. kids" analytical framework, in short, does not appear to have wide credence in the larger society, and where a hypothetical "guns vs. canes" trade-off is proposed, the American public overwhelmingly supports the latter.

Victim Blaming Revisited

. . . The new victim blaming is particularly well illustrated in the application of a market theory perspective to determinations of appropriate resource allocations for the different age groups. Demographer Samuel Preston thus has argued that, "Whereas expenditure on the elderly can be thought of *mainly as consumption,* expenditure on the young is a combination of consumption and investment"

(4, p. 49; emphasis added) leaving aside the inaccuracies of such statements from a narrow, worker productivity perspective (since many of the elderly continue to be employed full- or part-time), the moral and ethical questions raised by such an approach are significant. While it is true that the elderly "consume" about a third of all health care in the United States, for example, such figures become dangerous when used to support claims of the differential "costs" of older generations, and the need for the rationing of goods and services on the basis of age (1).

The scapegoating of Social Security and Medicare as primary causes of the fiscal crisis has served to deflect attention from the more compelling and deep-seated roots of the current economic crisis. At the same time, and wittingly or unwittingly fueled by recent mass media and groups like AGE, it has been used as a political tool to stoke resentment of the elderly and to create perceptions of a forced competition of the aged and younger members of society for limited resources. As Kingson et al. have noted, (19, p. 4):

> . . . while the concept of intergenerational equity is seemingly neutral and possesses an intuitive appeal (who can be against fairness?), its application, whether by design or inadvertence, carries with it a very pessimistic view about the implications of an aging society, which leads to particular policy goals and prescriptions.

These "policy goals and prescriptions" as we have seen, reflect a "new victim blaming" mentality in their suggestion that we must cut public resources to the elderly in order to help youth and to avert conflict between generations.

For as noted elsewhere, to trade the victim blaming approaches of the 1980s for those of the 1960s and 70s is not a solution to problems which ultimately are grounded in the skewed distribution of economic and political power within the society (33). Ultimately, as Pollack has argued, the central issue is not one of intergenerational equity but of income equity (14). Cast in this light, inadequate AFDC payments and threatened cuts in Social Security COLAs which would plunge millions of elderly persons into poverty, are part of the same problem. Programs and policies "for the elderly," like education and health and social services "for youth" must be redefined as being in fact not "for" these particular subgroups at all, but for society as a whole. Conversely, threatened cutbacks in programs for the elderly, under the guise of promoting intergenerational equity, must be seen as instead promoting a simplistic, spurious and victim blaming "solution" to problems whose causes are far more fundamental and rooted in the very structure of our society.

Conclusion

In the short time since its inception, the concept of generational equity has become a popular framework for analysis of contemporary economic problems and their proposed solutions. Yet the concept is based on misleading calculations of the relative financial well-being of the elderly *vis-à-vis* other groups and on questionable assumptions concerning such notions as fairness and differential stake in the common good. Predictions that young people, and particularly minority youth, may be increasingly resentful of elderly entitlement programs are unsubstantiated by current national survey data which show strong continued support for these programs across generational and ethnic lines. The reframing of political economic trade-offs in terms of "canes vs. kids" indeed appears to have little credence with the public at large, despite its popularity in the mass media, and with a growing number of scholars, policy makers and new, self-described youth advocates.

Proponents of an intergenerational equity approach to policy have performed an important service in calling attention to high rates of poverty in America's children, and to the need for substantially greater societal investment in youth and in generations as yet unborn. At the same time, however, their tendency to blame the costliness of America's aged for economic hardships experienced by her youth is both misguided and dangerous. The call for intergenerational equity represents a convenient smokescreen for more fundamental sources of inequity in American society. By deflecting attention from these more basic issues, and by creating a false dichotomy between the interests of young and old, the advocates of a generational equity framework for policy analysis do a serious disservice.

References

1. Binstock, R. H. The oldest old: A fresh perspective or compassionate ageism revisited? *Milbank Mem. Fund Q.* 63: 420-541, 1983.
2. Longman, P. Age wars: The coming battle between young and old. *The Futurist* 20: 8-11, 1986.
3. O'Connor, J. *The Fiscal Crisis of the State.* St. Martin's, New York, 1973.
4. Preston, S. Children and the elderly in the U.S. *Scient. Am* 251:44-49, 1984.
5. *Annual Report of the President's Council of Economic Advisors.* U.S. Government Printing Office, Washington, D.C., 1985.
6. Hewitt, P. A Broken Promise. Brochure of Americans for Generational Equity. AGE, Washington, D.C., 1986.
7. Edelman, M. W. Meeting the needs of families and children: Structural changes that require new social arrangements. (Statement before the Consumer Federation of America.) Children's Defense Fund, New York, March 15, 1990.
8. Longman, P. Justice between generations. *Atlantic Monthly,* pp. 73-81, June 1985.
9. Taylor, P. The coming conflict as we soak the young to enrich the rich.
10. Villers Foundation, *On the Other Side of Easy Street: Myths and Facts about the Economics of Old Age.* The Villers Foundation, Washington, D.C., 1987.
11. U.S. Bureau of the Census. Current reports: Poverty in the U.S. Series P 60, No. 163. U.S. Government Printing Office, Washington, D.C., 1989.
12. Bould, S., Sanborn, B., and Reif L. *Eighty Five Plus: The Oldest Old.* Wadsworth Publishing Company, Belmont, California, 1989.
13. Minkler, M., and Stone, R. The feminization of poverty and older women. *Gerontologist* 25:351-357, 1985.
14. Pollack, R. F. Generational equity: The current debate. Presentation before the 32nd Annual Meeting of the American Society on Aging, San Francisco, March 24, 1986.

15. U.S. Bureau of the Census, *Statistical Abstract of the U.S.* (109th edition). U.S. Government Printing Office, Washington, D.C., 1989.
16. Binstock, R. The aged as scapegoat. *Gerontologist* 23:136-143, 1983.
17. Blaustein, A. I. (ed.). *The American Promise: Equal Justice and Economic Opportunity.* Transaction Books, New Brunswick, New Jersey, 1982.
18. Margolis, R. J. *Risking Old Age in America.* Westview Press, Boulder, Colorado, 1990.
19. Kingson, E., [Hirschorn], B. A., and Cornman, J. *Ties That Bind: The Interdependence of Generations in an Aging Society.* Seven Locks Press, Cabin John, Maryland, 1986.
20. Bengston, V., Burton, L., and Mangen, D. Family support systems and attributions of responsibility: Contrasts among elderly blacks, Mexican-Americans, and whites. Paper presented at the Annual Meeting of the Gerontological Society of America, Toronto, Canada, November 1981.
21. Pilisuk, M., and Minkler, M. Social support: Economic and political considerations. *Social Policy* 15:6-11, 1985.
22. Taylor, H. Testimony before the House Committee on Aging, Washington, D.C., April 8, 1986.
23. Rawls, J. *A Theory of Justice.* Belknap Press, Cambridge, Massachusetts, 1971.
24. Callahan, D. *Setting Limits: Medical Goals in an Aging Society.* Simon and Schuster, New York, 1987.
25. Schiffres, M. The Editor's Page, "Next: Young vs. old?" *U.S. News and World Report* p. 94, November 5, 1984.
26. Hayes-Bautista, D., Schinck, W. O., and Chapa, J. *The Burden of Support: The Young Latino Population in an Aging Society.* Stanford University Press, Palo Alto, California, 1988.
27. Longman, P. The youth machine vs. the baby boomers: A scenario. *The Futurist* 20:9, 1986.
28. Lamm, R. D. *Mega-Traumas, America at the Year 2000.* Houghton Mifflin Company, Boston, Massachusetts, 1985.
29. U.S. Senate Special Commission on Aging. *Aging America: Trends and Projections, 1985-86.* U.S. Department of Health and Human Services, Washington, D.C., 1986.
30. Andrews, J. Poverty and poor health among elderly Hispanic Americans. Commonwealth Fund Commission on Elderly People Living Alone, Washington, D.C., 1989.
31. Meyer, J. A., and Levin, M. E. Poverty and social welfare: Some new approaches. Report prepared for the Joint Economic Committee. American Enterprise Institute, Washington, D.C., 1986.
32. Ryan, W. *Blaming the Victim* (1st edition). Random House, New York, 1972.
33. Minkler, M. Blaming the aged victim: The politics of retrenchment in times of fiscal conservatism. In *Readings in the Political Economy of Aging,* edited by M. Minkler, and C. L. Estes, pp. 254-269. Baywood Publishing, Amityville, New York, 1984.

READING 23

The Vulnerable
Outcomes, Interpretations, and Policy Implications

S. G. Gould and J. L. Palmer

Summary of Social Outcomes

When one distills the recent information . . . on the changing material well-being of children and the

Source: "Outcomes, Interpretations, and Policy Implications" by S. G. Gould and J. L. Palmer, 1988, in *The Vulnerable*, pp. 414-440, edited by J. Palmer, T. Smeeding and B. Terry, Washington, DC: Urban Institute Press. Reprinted with permission of The Urban Institute Press.

aged in the United States and other industrial democracies, three big truths emerge: the economic experience of the two groups in the United States has diverged widely over the past fifteen years; children in the United States have much higher poverty rates than their counterparts in other countries with more or less equivalent overall standards of living; and both population groups in the United

States are extremely heterogeneous in economic status.

The first two observations, which are borne out repeatedly in the aggregate data presented in this volume, call into serious question one of the basic tenets of New Deal-post-New Deal social policy making: namely, that poverty and relative economic disadvantage are primarily associated with aging. For much of the last fifty years, elderly people were viewed as—and in fact were—far more likely than other people to be poor; in addition to their higher poverty rates, their mean-income was significantly lower and income inequality among them, significantly greater. Although living standards for all age groups rose rapidly in the prosperous postwar years, age remained, until recently, correlated with relative economic deprivation.

But beginning in the early 1970s, a dramatic shift occurred in economic trends for the young and the old. The economic status of the aged continued to improve (albeit at a somewhat slower pace than over the previous twenty-five years), despite a more rapid reduction in their labor force participation. (The median real per capita income of the aged, for example, has risen—and their poverty rate declined—by well over 50 percent in the last twenty years.) In contrast, the status of children generally deteriorated, despite major increases in the labor force participation of women with children and a sharp decline in average family size. (Between 1973 and 1985, for example, the adjusted real income of all families with children declined by nearly 7 percent, while the poverty rate among children rose by 50 percent.) As a result of this recent wide divergence in the experience of the two populations, average income (adjusted for family size) and income inequality for families with children are now more or less on a par with those of the aged, and the poverty rate among children is now well above that of the aged. (By 1986 the poverty rate for children was 19.8 percent and for the aged 12.4 percent.)

The contrast in economic experience between the two groups does not appear to soften when we integrate, into the income picture sketched above, the other economic factors (wealth, tax burdens, and in-kind transfers). . . . In contrast to the aged and families without children, families with children realized little average gain in their financial wealth in the decade preceding 1984 and thus experienced a large loss in their relative share of overall wealth, with absolute losses incurring in the lower end of the distribution. Moreover, the total tax burden on families with children is both higher and, if anything, less progressive now than it was at the beginning of the 1970s, notwithstanding the federal income tax cut of 1981 and tax reform of 1986. Although both the elderly and children benefited from the substantial growth in in-kind transfers (especially health insurance) in the late 1960s and early 1970s, the growth was far greater for the elderly—and the cutbacks, in the early 1980s, far less severe. Tax burdens for the aged were generally lower than for families with children over this period, and this disparity has increased in recent years, since social insurance benefits (which are largely untaxed) became far more important to the economic status of the aged and payroll taxes (which the aged generally do not pay) accounted for the vast bulk of the general increase in overall tax burdens.

The net result of all these factors is that the aged made even greater gains in their economic status relative to children in many respects over the past fifteen to twenty years than is reflected in money income measures alone. In fact, one study found that in 1979 aged households were on average about 10 percent to 15 percent better off than all nonaged households (including those without children) on the basis of a "full income" estimate that adjusted for family size and composition and took considerable account of taxes, in-kind benefits, and certain aspects of wealth (Smeeding 1988). A similar estimate for the mid-1980s presumably would show an even greater difference, since nonaged households with children both have a lower average adjusted income than those without children and have lost considerable ground relative to the aged since 1979. . . .

When we look more closely at income inequality in the United States, it becomes clear that the economic status of American children and aged depends much less on age per se than it does on other demographic characteristics such as race and family composition, and exposure to certain events such as unemployment of a parent, divorce, illness, and death in the family. Poverty rates for various subgroups illustrate this truth most dramatically.

Although, for example, economic gains over the past forty years have been widespread among the aged, the economic status of white men has advanced more rapidly than that of minority men and of all women. As a result, poverty rates among all aged demographic subgroups are now far lower than they were several decades ago, but range even more widely—from a low of under 5 percent for white, married men to over 60 percent for older black women living alone. In general, the poverty rate for aged women is about three times that for aged men, that of blacks about three times that of whites (Hispanics are about double), and that of single aged persons about three times that of married aged persons. These different statistical outcomes reflect different vulnerabilities to life events. Women, for example, are likely to live longer than men and thus to exhaust their savings, experience the death of a spouse, or incur substantial medical or long-term care expenses, or all of these events. Minorities are more susceptible than whites to unemployment during their working years and consequently have less private means to cushion their retirement. And so on.

As among the aged, variations in economic well-being among children in the United States are considerable. Average adjusted income, net wealth and poverty rates range widely and systematically among children depending on whether or not there is an adult male in the household, the educational level achieved by the head of the household, and the number of siblings. Race and age of the head of household are also significant, though less important, independent factors in determining the economic well-being of children.[2] Poverty rates in 1986 ranged from a low of 9.8 percent for white children in two-parent families to 67.1 percent for black children in single-parent, female-headed families. In general, the poverty rate for children in female-headed families is roughly five times that of children in two-parent families, that of children living in a household where the head of household has no high school degree roughly four times that where the head has a postgraduate level of education, and that for children with four or more siblings roughly four times that for children who have only one or no siblings (Fuchs 1986).

Since wealth is distributed much more unequally than incomes, those families with children at the lower end of the income distribution, in general, and female-headed families with children, in particular, tend to have very little of it. Despite the modest overall gain in wealth among all families with children over the past several decades, the great and growing inequality in the distribution of this wealth led to a modest absolute decline in the value of wealth holdings of white female-headed families and a large absolute decline in those of all black families. By 1983 over half of all such families had virtually no net financial wealth.

Children also face very differing degrees of volatility in their economic status as they grow up—although they are much more likely than the aged to experience increases rather than declines, because their parents are generally passing through a stage of the life cycle during which their earnings and income typically rise. But numerous events can precipitate major declines in the economic status of children, the two most serious ones being long-term spells of unemployment for the family head (which are concentrated among families with initially low economic status) and separation of parents that is not soon followed by remarriage of the wife (since the majority of single women with children receive no support or alimony from the fathers). Both of these factors have contributed to what has to be one of the most distressing facets of the extreme heterogeneity of economic well-being among children: the extraordinarily high percentage of black children who not only experience poverty at some time during childhood, but for whom it becomes a way of life. For example, a full three-quarters of all black children who were under 5 years of age at the beginning of the 1970s were poor in at least one year of the decade, and for nearly half of these children poverty was a long-term condition. In contrast, white children in the same age cohort were only one-third as likely to experience poverty at all and only one-tenth as likely to experience long-term poverty. There is no reason to believe the situation for black children has improved in the 1980s; in fact, it has probably worsened.

What accounts for the deterioration in the economic status of American children in recent years? The evidence offered in this volume indicates that changes in demography, the economy, and public policies have all played a role; but the latter two have been far more important than demographic shifts, per se, in shaping the outcomes summarized above. In essence, both the economy and public policies have treated the aged far more generously than they have children over this time period.

For children, the critical factor has been the meager and unequal growth in earnings that has characterized the economy since the early 1970s. Earnings growth, or lack thereof, accounts for virtually all of the overall stagnation in the real incomes of families with children over the past fifteen years and much of the increase in inequality and poverty among this group. The remainder of the increase in poverty and inequality among children can be attributed to reductions in the antipoverty and equalizing effects of public policies since the mid-1970s, as the real value of per capita cash and in-kind transfers to the poor has declined and the overall tax system has become less progressive (Palmer 1987). . . .

Many people have speculated about the linkages between increased earnings inequality and various structural changes occurring in our economy; but for our purposes here it should suffice to note that in contrast to children, the aged have been largely insulated from the negative effects of the economy over the past fifteen years. They depended very little on current earnings at the beginning of this period and even less so more recently, and they have also benefited much more widely from public policies that became increasingly generous over the same time period. Also, the high real interest rates and appreciation in housing values that have been characteristic of the economy in recent years have been largely a boon to the aged, who were much more likely to own their own homes and to benefit from property income than younger adults.

But there can be no doubt that the Social Security program is the major reason for the continued advances in economic well-being made by the aged over the past several decades. The program has grown enormously in importance over the past three decades as a source of income to the aged, due to both the natural maturation of the program—as a rapidly increasing share of workers retired with extensive Social Security coverage—and to legislated benefit increases. This growth was particularly strong in the early 1970s as a result of several large across-the-board increases in benefits, coupled with the institution of an automatic cost-of-living adjustment mechanism that over-compensated new retirees for inflation (until it was adjusted at the end of the decade). And because of the tilt toward lower wage workers in Social Security's benefit formula, the program's great growth fueled not only the increases in average incomes for the aged but also the major reduction in overall inequality and poverty among the aged noted earlier. Of course, Social Security was given a sizable assist in these regards by other public programs, most notably Medicare and Medicaid, which also greatly expanded their assistance for the aged. . . .

Interpretations

The opening and closing lines of a 1986 *U.S. News & World Report* cover story, entitled "Those 24-Karat Golden Years—Can They Last?" do a good job of capturing the amalgam of public concerns marshalled together in the service of "intergenerational equity:"

If the 1960s were dominated by youth, the 1980s belong to the older generation. Never before have America's elderly lived so long or been so prosperous. A massive government commitment over the past 20 years to ease the burden of aging has allowed the elderly to achieve a level of health and financial independence scarcely imaginable a generation ago. . . . But the very success of the nation's campaign to better the status of the elderly has a downside that may one day tarnish the golden agers' golden era. . . . Poverty among children has risen and many young men and women find it difficult to match the living standards of their parents. . . . As a result, tax revenues may not be enough to support the current level of benefits for a swelling elderly population. America's backbone of the middle class—and the middle aged—will be hard pressed to pass on a better life to their children. And the current generation of senior citizens may well be the last to know the golden age of growing old.

Two things are curious about this presentation of the issues. First, the opening lines would seem to be reporting on a public policy success—a government social policy that actually worked—which is surely no little cause to rejoice in this era of throw-up-your-hands social policy making. Yet by the end of the article, this very success is made to seem invidious, as if the necessary price of success in one area were failure in another. The second notable thing is the absence of any "gold standard" for the "golden age." The currency of well-being for today's elderly is all relative—to yesterday's or tomorrow's elderly, to today's and tomorrow's children and middle-aged. The article makes no effort to evaluate the well-being of American elderly against some absolute standard such as the poverty standard, or against some relatively absolute standard such as an accepted goal of federal

policy, or even against some relatively less relative standard such as their peers in other countries.

We should note that we have not distorted the contents of the article by excerpting only from its beginning and end, nor have we selected an unrepresentative example of popular discussion of this issue. Most such discussions, we have found, imply acceptance of the same assumptions: that there is some kind of cause-effect relationship between federal policies toward one group (the aged) and the well-being of another (children); and that the two groups are sufficiently homogeneous in themselves, and similar in their requirements for well-being, that their claims on the public purse can be straightforwardly compared. . . .

Although it is clear that the elderly benefit more than do children from our federal social policies, it is not at all clear that children's doing worse has enabled the elderly to do better: our poverty rates for the elderly remain on the high side among industrial nations. All we can conclude from this kind of data is that, for a variety of reasons (some of which are touched on below), the United States has been willing to tolerate a much higher degree of economic inequality among its population than have other developed countries and that that tolerance has come to encompass such a large amount of poverty among the American child population as to trigger a number of alarm bells—now ringing in the intergenerational equity debate. . . .

[We] doubt that the intergenerational equity framework will become the basis for future political decision making in the social policy arena; but . . . the policy-making process will be fraught with much more intergenerational tension than was true in the past. We suggest here that one important source of tension is a lack of clarity, in both the policy-making process itself and in public understanding of the process, about the multiple concerns to which social policies respond. That is, we view the intergenerational equity framework as lumping together and obscuring many different strands of policy concerns in such a way as to encourage "us-vs.-them" thinking, and we conclude that, if these strands could be untwined in public discussion, some of the tension could be diffused. . . .

[We] think the following simple questions do a fair job of reflecting the range of concerns that social policy should address:

- What do we, as a public, need to do for dependent populations? (What are the particular needs of all of us at different stages of life for extra-familial support and to what extent does our public philosophy or sense of collective purpose imply an obligation to meet these particular needs through public means?)
- What can we afford to spend on social policies? (What will the effect of different levels and kinds of spending be on public budgets and our economy?)
- What are we willing to spend? (To what extent are we willing to forgo our own current consumption to serve the interests of dependent populations?)

Obviously, answers to these questions are not independent of one another: our willingness to tax ourselves to support dependent populations will reflect our sense of both obligation and affordability; judgments about what we can economically afford to do will condition our sense of obligation, and so on. . . .

Nevertheless, judgments about all three questions are embedded in the actual allocation of public resources that occurs under the rubric of "social policy." As long as that allocation takes place in some kind of political harmony (as it has through much of our postwar history), disaggregating the questions and answers can remain an activity of largely academic interest. But when, as now, the allocation of resources becomes a subject of serious public dispute, failure to articulate the issues clearly can further the fragmentation of political interests.

Just such a fragmentation appears to have developed in the current public debate over intergenerational equity. In this debate the always precarious balance between principled concerns for private and collective goods has tilted in an ominously personal direction. Legitimate concerns about the responsiveness of existing policies to actual need—both of dependent groups and of society as a whole—have translated into personal fears of a breakdown in the social compact: "Will tomorrow's working generation feel the same obligation to support me as a dependent as I feel to support dependents today?" Legitimate concerns about the prospects for economic growth have raised personal doubts about the availability of resources in the future to meet obligations incurred under current policies: "Will the economy be strong enough in the future to permit levels of public support for me and my children's children comparable to the levels enjoyed by dependent groups today?" And, finally, the willingness of current and future workers to pay the cost of existing social policies has been called into question by the breakdown of the insurance "fiction" upon which political support for social programs has been premised: "Will I get a fair return on what I have contributed to the system?"

Social Policy and Economic Concerns

The issue of the affordability of public spending for social purposes has two distinct but related dimensions. The first, more abstract, involves the concern that excessive social spending will be harmful to our economic health—in particular to long-run economic growth. The second dimension, quite concrete, involves the specifics of our current and prospective budgetary health and commitments: What are the implications for other public spending and tax burdens of sustaining or altering our current social policies? As we discuss below, the budgetary picture depends very much on the future course of the economy, in general, and health care cost inflation, in particular, whereas there is no necessary linkage between the amount of public spending for social purposes (within the range likely for the United States) and future economic growth.

In thinking about these two issues, we need to keep in mind some basic facts about public spending for social welfare purposes in the United States. Total public social spending currently runs about 20 percent of our Gross National Product (GNP), and about 60 percent of total public spending. Both of these percentages have more than doubled over the past thirty years. (Most of this change took place in the first two decades, as both of these measures have been relatively stable since 1976.) Even so, the United States ranks quite low on both of these measures relative to other Western industrial democracies, as we have a rather distinctive notion of what is publicly affordable in general, and attach a lower priority to social welfare spending within our relatively smaller public sector.

This public social spending in the United States is distributed by program areas (as a percentage of GNP) roughly 7 percent cash assistance, 5 percent each for education and health, and 3 percent for the remainder (essentially food, housing and social services). The vast bulk of the total goes to the aged (through such programs as Social Security, Medicare, Supplemental Security Income [SSI], and nursing home care under Medicaid) and to children (predominantly elementary and secondary education) or families with children (through AFDC, food stamps, acute care under Medicaid)—with the aged receiving about twice as much in the aggregate and four times as much per capita as children. Due to the dominant size of Social Security and Medicare, over three-fifths of total spending for social welfare purposes—and an even larger share of that for the aged—is carried out by the federal government. The major program area at the state and local levels is education. . . .

Numerous surveys have indicated a widening gap between what the public believes the government ought to do and what they are willing to pay for. As Ladd and Lipsit (1980) observed in the wake of the 1970s tax "revolt":

Even as they endorse measures to restrict the growth of government spending and taxation, Americans remain extraordinarily supportive of a high level of government services in virtually all sectors. There are no longer significant class differences in this commitment. Thus, almost identical proportions of business managers and unskilled workers, of high-income people and those in the lowest income brackets, want to maintain or increase current spending for environmental problems, health, urban needs, education, improving the position of blacks, and so on.

Other surveys have linked these ambivalent views to American attitudes toward the federal government, which—never very positive—have taken a decided turn toward the negative over the past few decades. Poll after poll records the public's poor opinion of the federal government's performance in designing and administering social programs. In the public mind, the contradiction between cutting spending and maintaining services can be resolved by simply eliminating waste. Yet the much ballyhooed efforts of both Carter and Reagan administrations at improving program efficiency and eliminating "fraud, waste, and abuse" have produced no lasting gain in public confidence (nor, it should be noted, much in the way of savings).

This stalemate between American public opinion and the reality of American government—firmly rooted though it may be in our history—no longer seems indefinitely sustainable. At some point in the budget crunch ahead, the public is going to have to strike a balance between jettisoning some expectations of government and swallowing some more or less substantial tax increase. Our purpose here is not to try to divine the particular form the balance will take, but to assess the implications of the balancing act for the interests of children and the elderly. . . .

There is [a] theme that could strike a chord in the American public, if properly appealed to by political leaders. Growing international competition and a declining birth rate in this country could lead to an increasing awareness of the greater extent to which the national economic health in the future will depend upon how well *all* our children are prepared to assume productive economic roles. Appeals to collective self-interest may help serve to accomplish what appeals to social solidarity could not.

Beyond this critical problem of public education, the central dilemma for social policy will be to find more creative ways of balancing the interests of program targeting and program universality. The Reagan era has underscored the vulnerability of many of the means-tested social programs, especially those serving families with children; while at the same time budget constraints, rising poverty rates and a growing underclass among children, and persistent pockets of financial vulnerability among the elderly, have underscored the need for more concentration of public resources among subgroups of both of these dependent populations. Some reordering of public priorities and policies that places less emphasis on age per se is clearly in order. And because of the diversity of the problems to be addressed, a diversity of approaches will be required. There is no magic solution.

There are, however, numerous promising measures for improving the economic security of the aged in a highly targeted fashion.[8] The components of the principal means-tested programs that serve the aged—Supplemental Security Income (SSI) and Medicaid—have proven to be politically resilient; and modest liberalizations of these programs (for example, expanding Medicaid eligibility for long-term care—which is essentially not covered

at all by Medicare, and raising SSI benefits to the poverty level) could go a long way toward improving the lot of the lowest income elderly at relatively modest public cost. . . .

To help pay for such program expansions and otherwise relieve some of the budgetary pressures attending the rapid aging of the population, the affluent elderly could be required to finance more fully their own retirement and health care. This might eventually entail some across-the-board restraint in the current built-in growth of Social Security and Medicare benefits affecting today's and tomorrow's younger workers, who generally can expect to have a much higher standard of living in their retirement than the current aged and near-aged. But, if an across-the-board approach is adopted in the near future, it would undermine the achievements of the past several decades in greatly improving the economic security of the majority of the current aged and near-aged, who are highly dependent upon these two social insurance programs. What is most needed now is an approach that is targeted on the more affluent aged without unduly compromising the desirable universal features of current policies. This could best be accomplished through the tax system, by such measures as imposing income-related premiums to help finance part of Medicare, full taxation of social insurance benefits and other forms of wealth, and tighter restrictions on tax incentives for private pensions and retirement benefits for higher income retirees (especially those who retire early). Congress has taken some small steps in these directions in recent years, but considerably more could and should be done.

As with the targeting of policies for the elderly, the targeting of policies for children could be substantially improved by relatively modest adjustments to integrate better the tax and transfer systems. An expansion of the Earned Income Tax Credit (EITC), for example, could provide additional income assistance to working poor and near-poor families. . . .

These policies all have the advantage of increasing reliance on more universal approaches (in contrast to means-tested), while still providing greater assistance on balance to lower income families. However, the more extreme ones have the disadvantage of being highly redistributive—probably too much so for American tastes. In any event, they only address generalized income support needs. Consistent with our earlier observations, a complementary approach that emphasizes services supportive of families and enhanced human capital of children—particularly those "at risk"—is also required.

Here policymakers would have to be guided by both past experience and prospective experimentation regarding which policies are likely to be both politically popular and programmatically effective and to determine the relative priority to place on parents as the means of helping children or direct services to children. The former would entail such things as greater financial assistance for day care, employment and training assistance for welfare recipients, and adolescent pregnancy and parenting programs; whereas the latter would entail greater emphasis upon such things as improving education standards, child health and nutrition, compensatory preschool education (such as Head Start), programs for in-school youth at risk of failure, and more financial support for skill training and higher education for disadvantaged older youths.

If such policies are to result in a substantial improvement in the opportunities for and the abilities of today's and tomorrow's children to become more productive adults, they will require an investment of public resources far larger than has been provided in the recent past. Given the budget constraint we discussed earlier, some creative approaches to financing undoubtedly will be necessary. One possibility is use of the huge surpluses that will soon be accruing in the Social Security trust funds. If these surpluses are to be of any real benefit in easing the financial burden of the retirement of the baby boom, they must be used to enhance economic growth in the interim. One way in which this can occur is if they result in higher overall national savings (through forced public savings) and concomitant investment in physical capital than would otherwise occur. Alternatively, this could also result if some of the surplus went into human capital investment, which paid off in a more productive work force in the future. Furthermore, this approach to financing investment in America's children would reflect an explicit recognition of the mutual interdependence of well-being among all generations.[10]

Notes

[NOTE: Only the notes that are included in the excerpted material appear here.]

2. Interestingly, while the other factors have maintained their degree of importance over time, the influence of race, per se, has lessened considerably (Fuchs 1986).

8. See Palmer (1988) for background on the following discussion of possible changes in public policies toward the aged.

10. Our focus throughout this chapter, and particularly in the last section, has been primarily on federal policies. However, we should note that some of the policy initiatives discussed in the last few pages (especially those for children) would fall under the purview of state and local governments, as well as the federal government. Also, state initiatives have been gaining increasing importance during the 1980s in various areas relevant to children and the aged, such as health care for the indigent, compensatory preschool education, child support enforcement, and work-welfare policy.

References

Fuchs, Victor. 1986. "Why are Children Poor." NBER Working Paper No. 1984. Cambridge, Mass.: National Bureau of Economic Research.

Ladd, E. C. Jr., and S. M. Lipset. 1980. "Public Opinion and Public Policy." In *The United States in the 1980's,* edited by Peter Daignum and Alvin Rabushka, Palo Alto, Calif.: Hoover Institute.

Palmer, John L. 1988. "Financing Health Care and Retirement for the Aged. In *Challenge to Leadership: Economic and Social Issues for the Next Decade,* edited by Isabel V. Sawhill, Washington: D.C.: Urban Institute Press.

Smeeding, Timothy. 1985. "Full Income Estimate of the Relativre Well-Being of the Elderly and the Nonelderly." In *Research in Economic Inequality: Volume I,* edited by Daniel Slottje. Greenwich, Conn.: JAI Press.

Public Entitlements
Exclusionary Beneficence

Louise Kamikawa

In the land of "our" forefathers the notion of class has traditionally been and continues to be an overriding consideration in public policy formation. With its roots in the Northeast, this orientation—and the underlying belief system about how peoples coexist—is woven into the fabric of our social contract; class is implicitly assumed to be the major factor affecting all public and private spheres of living.

While more than a grain of truth exists in this hypothesis—and it certainly did apply in eighteenth century New England—it is anachronistic to continue to allow the subtle application of "classism" to permeate public policy in the United States of today. The focus on class—traditionally and certainly in the latter part of this century—has obviated the necessity to consider color as an essential variable in the formulation of public policy. Class and color often function in tandem with each other, but the idea that they are the same is an illusion.

In the last four decades, the elderly population has grown exponentially, outpacing any other segment of our society. This has placed greater demands on government, requiring that policy makers reevaluate the needs of this particular population. The risks and vulnerabilities incurred with old age have generated greater demands for public ser-

vice/welfare measures. Government has had to assume an increased protective role. Correspondingly, the expenditures for the elderly have resulted in the "graying of the federal budget" (Hudson, 1978; Califano, 1978; Samuelson, 1987). With the expenditures to the elderly representing a major component of all social welfare expenditures (McMillan and Bixby, 1980), public resistance and criticism have been mounting.

The combination of class-rooted public policy orientation and the recent developments regarding the elderly raises some important issues, particularly as they relate to older minorities:

1. How are beneficiaries of government intervention defined?
2. Are benefits based on need?
3. What is the impact of needs- and nonneeds-based benefits on older minorities?

This article theorizes that public policy currently targets benefits for the elderly by class and serves as "an intervening variable to ensure status maintenance in old age" (Nelson, [1980]). Moreover, using class as a public policy mechanism serves to exclude consideration of minority populations.

Social Class, Race, and Aging

There is a pervading belief that all the variables of old age are experienced fairly uniformly and that seniority is the demarcation line beyond which all

Source: "Public Entitlements: Exclusionary Beneficence" by L. Kamikawa, *Generations* (Fall/Winter, 1991), pp. 21-24. Reprinted with permission from *Generations,* 833 Market St., Suite 512, San Francisco, CA 94103. Copyright 1991, ASA.

class and status attainment variables become moot. Class variables such as family origin, education, occupational attainment, and income are all examined (Sewell and Hauser, 1975) to define an individual's status, but only to the point of his or her seniority. More alarming is that the status attainment literature on people of color is sparse and obscure and often treated as undifferentiated information, relegating its use to a limited audience. The outcome of the lack of attention to social status and stratification of the elderly is to objectify them as a social class unto themselves, thus obscuring social and economic inequalities and further exacerbating the relative negative status of people of color. Henretta and Campbell (1976) examined income variation among the elderly, finding that the factors that determine income differences are the same before and after retirement. The effect of attainment variables on income are not reduced in old age, negating the posture that all persons experience the impact of aging evenly. Studies conducted by various minority organizations (Pacific/Asian Elderly Research Project, 1977; Lacayo, 1980, for the Asociación Nacional Pro Personas Mayores; National Indian Council on Aging, 1980) not only document the disparate impact of attainment variables on older minorities but suggest that these variables have a worsening effect on that segment of the elderly population. Such variables as assets accumulation, tax policies, health insurance measures, pension policies, and other governmental interventions have served to ensure the persistence of social class differences into old age (Henretta and Campbell, 1976).

Social welfare measures for the elderly parallel those welfare measures for nonelderly, attributing approved and disapproved classes of public dependency (Titmuss, 1965). "Approved" classes receive entitlements as a right resulting from preretirement occupational status, i.e., health insurance, private pensions, Social Security, income transfers such as tax protected retirement savings, property tax relief, and tax exemptions. "Disapproved" classes receive benefits as a measurement of "pa-

ternalism" (Friedman, 1962), not right. Such programs generally are means-tested and provide a "minimal level of care and sustenance" (Nelson, 1980).

Entitlements: Class Versus Race

Although the needs of various segments of the elderly population are quite different and access to resources to meet the needs uneven, very little is done to discriminate need within the population. Since social provisions are determined by socioeconomic status, the inequalities experienced in preretirement years are sustained.

Entitlement benefits/programs, composed primarily of income maintenance interventions, are the mainstay of public efforts to support the elderly. Nelson (1980), in his analysis of benefits to the elderly, conceptualizes a three-tiered network of benefits for this population. He also identifies three separate and distinct groups of elderly recipients of these benefits/programs.

Poor elders' benefits. The first tier is composed of means-tested welfare programs, which are directed to the poorest or "marginal elderly" class (Nelson, 1980). These programs are the most invasive in establishing participation eligibility, punitive in their treatment of participants, and complex in their requirements. The continuum of benefits/programs includes Supplemental Security Income (SSI), Medicaid, Title XX, and Food Stamps.

The needs of the "marginal" elderly are absolute; many remain poor even after receiving public income transfers. The data show that minorities, women, single persons, and "old" old are disproportionately represented in this group (Tissue, 1977). Even after the passage of SSI, those older persons living at or above the poverty line had increased only 6 percent between 1973 and 1984.

The healthcare program for the poor is Medicaid, also means-tested. Thirty percent of Medicaid expenditures are directed to the poor elderly, primarily for institutional care (Nelson, 1980). The provision of service is uneven and limited. Medicaid falls under state jurisdiction, with some states like Arizona opting to formulate their own health program. Expenditures vary by states, as do the regulations, creating unevenness in the service system. The bias toward institutional care limits outlays for other medical interventions; in 1978 1 percent of all Medicaid expenditures went to home health services (General Accounting Office, 1991). The elderly poor paid more in out-of-pocket costs for healthcare than did nonelderly poor (Feder and Holahan, 1979).

Title XX of the Social Security Administration (SSA) provides the mainstay of social services to the poor, "marginal" elderly. Their participation in the Older Americans Act (OAA) programs has been minimal; the primary beneficiaries of OAA programs have been nonpoor, white, lower-middle/middle-class elderly (Estes and Newcomer, 1978). Further, when the programming has been targeted to the poor, the participation rate of minorities has been minimal and far below levels necessary to address the needs of the particular group.

Lower-middle- and middle-class elders' benefits. This second tier includes both lower-middle class and middle class; there is a perceived need based on relative deprivation as opposed to the objective need experienced by the poor elderly (Townsend, 1973). With the onset of old age and retirement, they attempt to maintain their preretirement middle class lifestyle and do so through public support. This group relies primarily on earnings-related Social Security benefits, Medicare, and the OAA program. Other private resources are minimal, generally limited to savings. Without Social Security, approximately 60 percent would fall below the poverty threshold (Ball, 1978).

All programs targeted for this class are assumed to be integrative, either improving or maintaining the standard of living and status that recipients had during their working years. Service interventions seek either to reintegrate the individual or compensate him or her for losses in linkages to the community and resources. Individual beneficiaries perceive services as a right, and the system responds to that perception.

Social Security and Medicare require no arduous or extensive eligibility process and no income or assets tests are applied. This group is not perceived to be a welfare class with the ascribed stigmas. It is apparent in their utilization patterns of Medicare; in 1970 the National Opinion Research Center reported that per capita Medicare expenditures were approximately 70 percent higher for elderly with incomes above $11,000 than for those with incomes below $6,000. The per capita outlays for hospital costs are twice as high for high-income groups than low-income groups (Davis and Schoen, 1977). Physician visits commensurately increase with income. This parallels service utilization patterns of those individuals prior to their retirement.

Middle- and upper-middle-class elders' benefits. Nelson (1980) refers to this tier as the integrated class. This group not only receives government-supported pensions, they also have private pensions, assets, and income and benefits from favorable tax policies. They are able to maintain the socioeconomic status they had during their preretirement years. With such status, they retain the roles and community relationships necessary for social integration.

Healthcare coverage is comprehensive for this class and ensures optimum availability and access to necessary services. This is provided at the cost of Medicare and Medicaid patients, as physicians and hospitals will limit Medicaid/Medicare patients to serve higher-paying, private insurance patients. It must also be noted that private insurance subscribers are provided tax subsidies that undergird their ability to pay higher costs, serving to raise healthcare costs generally. . . .

Benefits: Class Vs. Race

The application of class as a measure of analyzing public policy is a necessary, but not a sufficient, criterion for ensuring appropriateness and adequacy of intervention mechanisms for all elderly. It assumes homogeneity of experience, perception, and participation in, and benefit from, the full spectrum and hierarchy of institutions and resources. Clearly, for people of color, who are disproportionately represented among the poor and disenfranchised, the use of class as a sole criterion serves to deny access to goods and services as it assumes a similarity of color and class. Minority status implicitly places groups outside the structure as separate entities. They are treated differentially and [gain] access to class status on a fragmented basis, as reflected in our national educational crisis and our employment practices in the social order.

Public policy measures directed at the elderly clearly demonstrate this phenomenon; even in programs for the poor/marginal class, the representation of minorities is far less than their reported objective needs would indicate. Census figures show that in 1989 over 30 percent of all blacks over 65, 20 percent of Hispanics, and 14.5 percent of Pacific/Asians were poor, yet they represent less than 3 percent of all poverty programs for the elderly. Ten percent of older whites were poor in 1989, yet they consume 97 percent of those benefits outlays for the poor. For non-means-tested programs such as those of the OAA, the picture has been more severe. Programs with no income or asset tests have most consistently served all classes of white populations. Class allows the illusion that everyone is being served because the poor are included in the system. But the resources are provided from a white perspective incorporating majority values and behavior relegating the minority population to position of nonalignment and nonmembership. Moreover, service providers, predominantly white, are unable to adapt or to reconcile differences brought about by minority participation and therefore create exclusionary programs, ones allowing the status quo. As a result, minorities have been consistently underserved in the OAA programs. It has taken legislative mandates and litigation to rectify the low participation rate of minorities. Policy makers and service providers have not provided leadership in their efforts. It has taken efforts within minority groups to have an impact on the system and bring about change. But reliance on such efforts is both shortsighted and self-defeating vis-à-vis the public policy infrastructure.

Public Benefits Integration

A benefit structure based on political and subjective entitlement standards like class is not effective for all older persons. Such a structure has a serious negative impact on people of color, irrespective of their "class" standing. We can no longer abide by the hypothesis that class participation cross-cuts races. We do not have a monolithic universe of older persons. Therefore, a structure that identifies minority status as a measure for determining public policy interventions must be instituted. The objective need of all minority groups must be delineated and appropriate service measures created, and these measures must be monitored and evaluated. With the perceived limitation of resources, it will be necessary to address the needs of the most needy if we are to ensure quality maintenance for all. The high degree of deterioration of certain populations in this country is too closely paralleling what is seen in underdeveloped countries.

It may be necessary to consider a guaranteed annual income, a national healthcare program, and a reconsideration of tax policies that now favor high-income beneficiaries. We cannot continue a policy of "benign neglect"; it is becoming an observable and metastasizing cancer.

References

Ball, R., 1978. *Social Security Today and Tomorrow.* New York: Columbia University Press.

Califano, J., 1978. "U.S. Policy for the Aging—A Commitment to Ourselves." *National Journal* 10: 1575-81.

Davis, K. and Schoen, C. [1978.] *Health and the War on Poverty.* Washington, D.C.: Brookings Institution.

Estes, C. and [Newcomer], R., 1978. *State Units on Aging Discretionary Policy and Action in Eight States.* San Francisco: Administration on Aging Report.

Feder, J. and Holahan, J., 1979. *Financing Health Care for the Elderly.* Washington, D.C.: Urban Institute.

Friedman, M., 1962. *Capitalism and Freedom.* Chicago: University of Chicago Press.

General Accounting Office, 1991. "Minority Participation in AoA Programs." Washington, D.C.: Subcommittee on Aging. Senate Testimony.

Henretta, J. and Campbell, R., 1976. "States Attainment and States Maintenance: A Study of Stratification in Old Age." *American Sociological Review* 41:981-92.

Hudson, R., 1978. "The Graying of the Federal Budget and Its Consequences for Old Age Policy." *Gerontologist* 18:428-40.

Lacayo, C. G., 1980. *A National Study to Assess the Service Needs of the Hispanic Elderly.* Los Angeles, Calif.: Asociación Nacional Pro Personas Mayores.

McMillan, A. and Bixby, A., 1980. "Social Welfare Expenditures, Fiscal 1978." *Social Security Bulletin* 35:746-57.

National Indian Council on Aging, 1980. *Needs Assessment in Older American Indians.* Albuquerque, N.M.

Nelson, G., 1980. "Contrasting Service to the Aged." *Social Service Review* 54:376-89.

Pacific/Asian Elderly Research Project, 1977. *Critical Factors in Service Delivery: Preliminary Findings.* Los Angeles, Calif.

Samuelson, R., 1987. "The Elderly: Who Will Support Them?" *National Journal* 10:1712-17.

Sewell, W. H. and Hauser, R. M., 1975. *Education, Occupation and Earnings: Achievement in the Early Career.* New York: Academic Press.

Tissue, T., 1977. "The Effect of SSI on the Life Situation of the Aged." San Francisco: National Gerontological Society. Paper.

Titmuss, R., 1965. "The Role of Redistribution in Social Policy." *Social Security Bulletin* 28:14-20.

Townsend, P., 1973. *The Social Minorities.* London: Allen Lane.

READING 25

Inclusive and Fair
The Case for Universality in Social Programs

Robert B. Hudson and Eric R. Kingson

Social insurance and universality of benefits—ideas that took decades to attain respectability in the United States and that now serve as the foundation of social policy for older Americans—have recently come under attack. The concepts that governmentally sponsored programs should seek to

Source: "Inclusive and Fair: The Case for Universality in Social Programs" by R. B. Hudson and E. R. Kingson, *Generations* (Summer/Fall 1991), pp. 51-56. Reprinted with permission from *Generations,* 833 Market St., Suite 512, San Francisco, CA 94103. Copyright 1991, ASA.

provide widespread protection against economic insecurity by enabling citizens to share risks through the pooling of resources and should make all individuals in a given category eligible for program benefits are viewed by many as cornerstones of enlightened social welfare policy. As social insurance programs, Social Security and Medicare embody both these concepts; as a general-revenue-financed, non-means-tested program, the Older Americans Act (OAA) addresses only the latter. Critics, however, have come to see these approaches as having spawned programs that are inefficient, misdirected, and inequitable (Lamm, 1987; Longman, 1987; Makin, 1988).

Thus, as part of celebrating 25 years of the OAA and Medicare, we find ourselves needing to re-establish the primacy of social insurance and the principle of universality. After briefly reviewing the transformation in public perceptions that brought us to this point, we shall examine the current tensions along two key dimensions of universal programs—eligibility determination and financing mechanisms. Reasserting the centrality of social insurance and universal approaches to age-related policy, we go on to suggest that considerable targeting of benefits already occurs within universal programs and that it may be possible to direct—still without means-testing—even greater benefits to lower income elders.

Our principal conclusion is that in order to both preserve universal eligibility features and serve those with the greatest need, proponents of this approach must (1) consider non-means-testing targeting strategies and (2) advance alternatives that move toward more progressive program financing, essentially a strategy of means-testing on the financing side.

Universalism and Aging:
A Brief History

The Social Security Act of 1935 and subsequent amendments to it established universal programs, most notably social insurance programs, as the central components of age-related policy in the United States.

Universal eligibility is the feature central to the political importance of Social Security, Medicare, and the OAA—and to their remarkable successes as well. To be 60, 62, or 65 (and in the instances of Social Security and Medicare, to have been tied to the labor force or married to someone who was) renders one automatically eligible for program benefits. Contributions, age, and physical well-being set or trigger benefit receipt, but level of current income does not. Selective programs such as Supplemental Security Income (SSI) and Medicaid,

which involve testing of economic means, are important supplements to the universal programs, but their overall impact and costs are considerably less than those of the universal programs.

Expanding universalism. Following enactment and stabilization of the early Social Security program, the social insurance agenda was driven by efforts to expand coverage, broaden protections, liberalize benefits, and enact some type of national health insurance program. By the 1950s, Social Security had emerged as a highly popular program and surpassed the selective Old Age Assistance program as the principal income support of American elders (Berkowitz, 1991; Derthick, 1979).

Reformers were successful in broadening coverage and adding Disability Insurance, but by the early 1950s it was clear that population-wide national health insurance was a political impossibility, at least for the foreseeable future. It was at this point that reformers switched to a strategy of first seeking such protection for older people, a politically legitimate constituency whose financial and social well-being was widely at risk because of high healthcare costs (Marmor, 1973).

Following the Democratic landslide of 1964, social reform efforts bore fruit well beyond initial expectations. The 89th Congress, which completed its first term in October 1965, was variously described as "the Congress of fulfillment," "the most productive congressional session ever held," and as bringing "to a harvest a generation's backlog of ideas and social legislation" (Sundquist, 1968). In addition to the Voting Rights Act and the War on Poverty programs, "a dramatic expansion and extension of New Deal-style welfare state measures" took place (Ehrenreich, 1985). For older Americans, the notable entries were Medicare, Medicaid, and the OAA.

The 1965-74 period was one of extraordinary liberalization of programs for elders. Social Security saw benefit increases of 13 percent in 1968, 15 percent in 1970, 10 percent in 1971, 20 percent in 1972, and 11 percent in 1974—increases that collectively outpaced inflation from January 1965 to June 1974 by about 21 percent (Myers, 1991). The automatic cost-of-living adjustment (COLA) enacted in 1972 and implemented in 1974, ensured that benefits once received would maintain their purchasing power. Medicare coverage and expenditures grew as elders flocked to the program, and physicians found gold in the hills of what was once thought to be socialized medicine. Old Age Assistance became a part of SSI, with the country's first income guarantee; the Age Discrimination in Employment Act brought civil rights to the middle-aged and old; and the OAA brought official recognition that the old as well as the young should be afforded opportunities, access, and institutional representation within government itself.

That institutional representation—initially through the federal Administration on Aging (AoA) and the State Units on Aging (SUAs)—was more fully realized by creation of the Area Agencies on Aging (AAAs) in 1972 and was completed by development of the full-blown aging network, incorporating the service providers funded through OAA appropriations. Over the years, there has been considerable ambiguity about the mix of benefits to be provided through that network—advocacy, planning, resource pooling, system development, services integration. But never in question during those years was the understanding that those benefits were to be for all elders and, more pointedly, that all elders constituted a single, identifiable beneficiary group.

Universalism challenged. Beginning with the mid-1970s, commitments to social insurance and universalism were challenged more frequently, a political shift that sharpened during the 1980s. Of the contributing factors, most pervasive was the disenchantment with the spirit and presumed failures of Great Society programs, an almost unquestioned axiom during an unabashedly conservative decade in Washington. Assaults on universalism—couched in the increasingly pejorative term "entitlements" or worse yet, "middle-class entitle-

ments"—were a core element of the David Stockman, Martin Anderson, Ronald Reagan mindset.

Other factors also spurred criticisms of ongoing programs. Financing crises in the mid-1970s and the early 1980s—both substantially the result of a weak economy and changing demographics—put the program more in the political spotlight than it had been in decades (Achenbaum, 1986; Derthick, 1979; Kingson, 1984; Light, 1985). Federal deficits, growing healthcare costs, and concerns about the aging of the population also contributed to the new questioning of the future of social insurance and other universal programs.

The aged and their programs became prime targets in the assault on universalism for a number of reasons. First, paraphrasing bank robber Willie Sutton, that's where the universalism is. In America's reluctant welfare state, the aged, to the almost total exclusion of others, were singled out for special attention (Hudson, 1978). Thus, to question the legitimacy of older people as a public policy constituency is tantamount to questioning universal program benefits in the United States.

Precisely that questioning emerged during this period, with the growing realization of the aged's improved social and economic status. The unprecedented economic growth following World War II and expansions in public and private benefit programs substantially improved the status of new cohorts of elders. By the mid-1970s, elderly poverty had declined dramatically, and the overall economic status of the aged began to more closely resemble that of other adult age groupings (Schulz, 1988).

If the aged are not all poor and otherwise in need, how should the manner in which determination of need, level of benefits, and source of payment be modified[?] Formal means testing would constitute the most severe retrenchment and would be a direct attack on universalistic principles. To seek further targeting of universal benefits to low- or potentially low-income elders would certainly be consistent with the social adequacy goal of providing widespread protection against economic need, a goal generally acknowledged to be the dominant underlying concern of social insurance programs (Hohaus, 1960; Myers, 1985). To maintain universal benefits for all while devising more progressive financing mechanisms would be very much in keeping with some existing and frequently proposed universalistic schemes.

These types of alternatives became practical as well as theoretical ones in the 1980s. Taxation of Social Security benefits in 1983 represented a major breakthrough. To some it was codification of progressive tax policy—even if directed at beneficiaries—and was consistent with social insurance principles. To others, it represented an operationalization of the idea that some elders could afford to have their benefits reduced—in this case through taxation. The Medicare Catastrophic Coverage Act (MCCA), in addition to articulating the principle that the older population could now be appropriately expected to finance new benefits for itself, called on well-off elders to subsidize the MCCA benefits of less well-off elders. The repeal of MCCA resulted from a failure to recognize that the former group already had much of MCCA's coverage and from that group's unwillingness to foot the bill in order that lower-income elders could receive similar coverage through Medicare.

Universalism has been a bedrock principle under the OAA since 1965, albeit one where the question of targeting of benefits to the socially and economically disadvantaged and to minority elders has been a concern since the mid-1970s. More recently, the question of cost-sharing on the part of better-off elders has brought the universalism issue into yet sharper relief. Voluntary contributions to the Title III programs have been formally encouraged since 1981, but current calls for mandatory cost-sharing through self-declaration of income focus the spotlight on the question of means more than the targeting issue has.

These initiatives to reduce benefits and share costs bring the universal programs enacted during the New Deal and Great Society directly in touch with the politics, economics, and demographics of

the 1990s. Programs once designed to attract clients and to broaden benefits are increasingly concerned with aggregate program costs and with the resources as well as the needs of beneficiary groups. The question becomes how to maintain and justify the principle of universality while recognizing changes in need and well-being among different population groups.

Eligibility and Universalism

Despite all of these developing pressures, universality must be considered a first principle in social policy, and social insurance must be considered the most central expression of that principle. The alternative is to move toward selective eligibility, which requires demonstration of need. Selective programs are individually stigmatizing, socially divisive, and politically vulnerable (Skocpol, 1990). The unquestioned success of Social Security, Medicare, and, to a lesser extent, the OAA lies largely in their universal eligibility feature.

The strength of universalism derives from large numbers of persons being covered in a broad-based program and in the perception that participants are being treated fairly. Breadth of coverage is easy to see and establish. Determining what other than pure proportionality is "fair," and to whom, is a much more involved undertaking, in part because of the complexity of these programs and their multiple goals.

Thus, universal programs are often mistakenly criticized as doing little to eliminate or reduce poverty. While universal programs serve the middle class, they are particularly beneficial to those who have or would otherwise have low incomes. Certainly even greater targeting or progressivity in benefit allocation could be introduced to these universal programs, but the critical and indisputable conclusion remains that these programs cannot be somehow understood as "middle-class entitlements."

Social Security, by far the most important social insurance program, does substantially more to reduce income inequality and poverty than either the

American tax system or public assistance programs, despite the latter's being explicitly targeted to that goal (Bureau of the Census, 1988). In 1989, Social Security alone reduced pretransfer poverty levels among persons aged 65 and over from 54.9 percent to 14.4 percent with means-tested cash benefits further reducing the poverty rate to 12.9 percent (Committee on Ways and Means, 1991).

Social Security's benefit formula is the most notable targeting feature within universal programs. In keeping with the importance of the program's adequacy goals, it is designed so that lower-wage workers generally receive a proportionally larger benefit than higher-income earners. While workers with higher earnings will generally receive higher absolute benefits, the program replaces a much larger proportion of preretirement earnings for low-income as compared to high-income workers. Social Security replaces approximately 55 percent of preretirement earnings of low-income workers (those with earnings equal to one-half of the average nationwide wage throughout their careers) first retiring at age 65 in 1991, compared to about 24 percent for high-income workers who had earnings equivalent to the maximum taxable under Social Security (Myers, 1991). Other features, such as the special minimum benefit and even the COLA, are also substantially more important for lower- than higher-income workers.

Medicare's targeting features are not as substantial; in fact, the program has some decidedly negative targeting aspects. On the positive side, lower-income persons receive the same benefit package as higher-income ones, even though the former have generally paid substantially less into the program through the Part A payroll tax. Also because lower-income elders on average have a higher incidence of healthcare needs, they may make greater use of Medicare benefits (Congressional Budget Office, 1983). On the other hand, negative targeting features are found in the Part B premium and in the copayments, coinsurance, and deductibles confronting the currently ill. And, politically, the important recent lesson in Medicare appears to be that many elders believe they can insure themselves privately on a more cost-effective basis than by supporting expanded Medicare coverage for all elders.

Targeting pressures under the OAA stem from financing and delivery system characteristics that are different from those in the other two programs. Contrasted with Social Security and Medicare, the OAA is subject to a closed-ended annual federal appropriation, one that has been essentially static for a 10-year period. Yet, the act formally, if not fiscally, entitles all elders 60 and over to benefits, while calling for special targeting efforts on behalf of the economically and socially disadvantaged, especially members of minority groups. The de facto cap on federal OAA expenditures, growing numbers of disadvantaged elders, and data suggesting that many other elders do not require subsidized public services have all generated increasing pressures to target resources on vulnerable populations. These pressures are at the root of recent debates about funding formulas and other targeting options under the act (O'Shaughnessy, 1990).

Ironically, pressures on the service delivery side may be pushing AAAs operating under the act in the direction of higher-income rather than lower-income clients. While the AAA's federal dollars are essentially fixed, they see other social service agencies—both proprietary and nonprofit—entering the eldercare management and services arena, and they have reason to believe that a certain number of their clients could and would pay something for the service they are receiving. Many agencies contend that allowing them to charge (cost-sharing for the clients) would allow them to target their limited federal funds on vulnerable clients, but the organizational reality would indicate that they need new clients and revenue sources to maintain themselves as viable entities. Whether allowing cost-sharing would, in fact, heighten targeting is very much an open question (Hudson, 1991; Skinner, 1990).

Universalism and Financing

Universalism with varying degrees of benefit targeting continues to be a well-entrenched principle in these programs. However, pressures on public budgets, the growing heterogeneity of the old, and emergence of other serious social problems are placing these principles under notable strain. Whether it be calls for increased reliance on savings and private pensions in income security, development of new private insurance mechanisms in health and long-term care, or cost-sharing proposals under the OAA, critics of universalism and social insurance would have us move more toward the principle of individual reliance and, in theory, toward an expansion of means-tested programs. Notions of saving public dollars by increasing reliance on individuals and families in no way eliminates the costs of supporting elders, but simply shifts those costs from one sector to another.

But before moving in the direction of selective eligibility, policy makers should first consider options that exist on the financing side of universal programs. Reform of program financing appears especially in order when one realizes that there currently is substantially less progressivity in financing than in the distribution of benefits. This suggests that one way of preserving universal eligibility features, while simultaneously assisting those in greatest need, is to be found in increasing the progressivity of financing these programs (although the MCCA experience suggests that such approaches may test the margins of political feasibility).

To see how this might be done, we can place the three sources of public sector financing and one essentially quasi-public source potentially available along a continuum ranging from the most inclusive and universal to the least: general revenues, payroll taxation, revenues derived from the pool of those currently eligible for program benefits (e.g., Medicare premiums), and user's fees levied as services are actually accessed. Depending on their particular design, these financing mechanisms can be more or less progressive, but we would gener-ally expect general revenues to be the more progressive source, with the other three more likely to be regressive.

General revenue taxation in the United States continues to be mildly progressive, even with the lowering of marginal tax rates enacted in 1986. These revenues are used to fund most of Medicare Part B and the OAA. However, historical and cross-national experience suggests limits in the use of these revenues in financing major social programs (Heclo, 1974). Conservatives have worried that general revenues might provide a bottomless revenue source for politically popular demands, whereas many advocates have worried that the interests of social insurance beneficiaries would be submerged in debates concerning the entire spectrum of public policy. Persons on both sides may instead favor reliance on payroll taxes, which force some level of discipline between benefits and revenues. More practically, general revenues are in very short supply, and one can probably hope for little more than, for example, liberalization of the Earned Income Tax Credit, which partially offsets the regressivity of the payroll tax for low-income families with young dependents.

Payroll taxation is the principal financing vehicle for Social Security, Medicare, and other social insurance programs. Revenues are dedicated to the tasks or risks at hand, and the funds are generally "off budget" to other concerns. The funds are financed through equal tax rates on the earnings of current workers up to the maximum ceiling, thereby (1) upholding the belief that workers should contribute in order to be eligible for insurance protections and (2) reinforcing the view that benefits are an earned right.

Although payroll taxation is generally a regressive source of revenues, there are alternatives that can move it toward greater progressivity. For example, the maximum level of yearly earnings subject to the Medicare Hospital Insurance (HI) tax has recently been increased—it is now levied on earnings up to $125,000, compared to a ceiling of $53,400 for Social Security. In a similar manner, the maximum taxable earning ceiling could be raised for employers and employees under Social Security, or perhaps more simply, only for employers. A payroll tax reduction would also increase the progressivity of current funding, but such a change must be assessed in terms of effects on aggregate national savings, pressures in other budget areas, and long-term financing of the system itself.

The emerging debate about targeting has brought beneficiary-pool financing to the fore. Funding comes from all of those currently eligible for services, such as through the Medicare Supplementary Medical Insurance. Where, as in this instance, the premium is a flat one, the burden falls most heavily on lower-income beneficiaries (except in those cases where the premium is paid through Medicaid). A more progressive form of beneficiary-pool financing is found in the partial treatment of Social Security benefits as taxable income, although this can alternatively be classified as a form of general revenue financing. Ronald Reagan's insisting throughout the MCCA episode that older people pay for any Medicare expansions is a recent example of beneficiary-pool financing; the failed attempt to impose an income tax surcharge on higher-income beneficiaries would have made the proposal explicitly (and fatally) progressive. Progressive, but perhaps more viable politically, would be the alternatives of treating a larger portion of Social Security benefits as taxable income; also progressive, but perhaps no more viable politically than the MCCA surcharge, would be counting the taxpayer-financed portion of the value of Medicare as taxable income.

The user's fee is the final possibility. Here, it is not those who might use the service who help cover costs, but those who are actually using it at any point. Though the application may be very similar to beneficiary-pool financing mechanisms, there is an important conceptual distinction. A presumption often behind user's fees—whether turnpike tolls, coinsurance, or cost-sharing for services—is

that people should pay for public goods much as they do for private ones. To the extent that user's fees are relied upon very heavily as sources of financing or as mechanisms to reduce costs, ideas of collective responsibility or risk pooling are diminished or disappear.

The logic of public user's fees and cost-sharing leads in the direction of privatization. In the case of social service agencies, one can ask at what point does a publicly supported agency heavily engaged in cost-sharing become, in fact, a private agency receiving a public subsidy. Nor does cost-sharing necessarily allow greater resources to be targeted on low-income individuals. If the fees charged do no more than cover the costs of services delivered, there is no added money available. If the cost-sharing client is charged more than the cost of service, there is an added element of progressive financing but in the form of cross-subsidization, which represents more an interference in what is essentially a market system rather than an insurance feature based on notions of risk and responsibility sharing.

The Question of Fairness

Universalism and social insurance, the building blocks of America's aging policy, have come under increasing challenge. Some feel that funds are being inefficiently redistributed by government largely within the middle class; others, that the problems of those in greatest need are not adequately addressed; still others, that the financing burden is unfairly borne.

The first of these concerns, however widespread in some circles, was shown earlier to be empirically incorrect; Social Security in particular is extraordinarily effective and highly efficient in both poverty reduction *and* income maintenance. A program that can simultaneously elevate and assure is one to be highly valued.

Of the second of these concerns, we assert that targeting within universal programs provides an optimal balance among the different issues that naturally arise in benefit allocation within social programs. Weighted benefit formulas, acknowledging the bedrock welfare-state concern with adequacy, are utilized, and legitimate concerns about individual equity are also addressed. In this way, fundamental protections can be provided while still allowing a reasonable, if not always proportionate, return to higher-income participants.

Concerning financing, programs that rely heavily on regressive sources of revenues do serious harm to notions of universality. As well, certain types of beneficiary-pool financing (e.g., the MCCA approach) so limit the contributor base that the ratio of benefits received to the resources contributed is very low. In contrast, broad-based payroll-tax financing provides much larger risk pools and thus deals much more adequately with this problem. The regressivity of the current Social Security payroll tax does, however, remain problematic.

Where risk pools are broad and risks are low, payroll taxation and premiums can be kept low and proportional. Where those ratios become less favorable, the case may arise for more progressive approaches to payroll taxation and financing in general.

Melding progressivity with a payroll tax addresses shortcomings potentially associated with each of the two generally preferred financing mechanisms for social programs: general revenue and payroll taxation. Dedicating payroll tax contributions solidifies the belief that a portion of earned income is dedicated to identified work and retirement risks. Adding the progressive feature usually associated with general revenue taxes—such as further treatment of social insurance benefits as taxable income or raising the maximum taxable wage base—assures that people will contribute to social insurance according to their ability to pay and that all will continue to be eligible for the same range of benefits. This kind of financing scheme as well as the targeting of benefits combine universalism and fairness in a manner suitable to the 1990s.

References

Achenbaum, W. A., 1986. *Social Security: Visions and Revisions.* New York: Cambridge University Press.

Berkowitz, E. D., 1991. *America's Welfare State: From Roosevelt to Reagan.* Baltimore: Johns Hopkins University Press.

Bureau of the Census, U.S. Department of Commerce, 1988. *Measuring the Effect of Benefits and Taxes on Income and Poverty: 1986.* Washington, D.C.: Government Printing Office.

Committee on Ways and Means, U.S. House of Representatives, 1991. *Background Material and Data on Programs within the Jurisdiction of the Committee on Ways and Means: 1991 Green Book.* Washington, D.C.: Government Printing Office.

Congressional Budget Office, 1983. *Changing the Structure of Medicare Benefits: Issues and Options.* Washington, D.C.: Congressional Budget Office.

Derthick, M., 1979. *Policymaking for Social Security.* Washington, D.C.: Brookings Institution.

Ehrenreich, J., 1985. *The Altruistic Imagination.* Ithaca, N.Y.: Cornell University Press.

Heclo, H., 1974. *Modern Social Politics in Britain and Sweden.* New Haven: Yale University Press.

Hohaus, R. A., 1960. "Equity, Adequacy, and Related Factors in Old-Age Security." In W. Haber and W. J. Cohen, eds., *Social Security Programs, Problems, and Policies.* Homewood, Ill.: Richard D. Irwin.

Hudson, R. B., 1978. "The 'Graying' of the Federal Budget and Its Consequences for the Old-Age Policy." *Gerontologist* 18 (5):428-40.

Hudson, R. B., 1991. "Reauthorization of the Older Americans Act." Testimony before the Subcommittee on Human Resources, Committee on Education and Labor, U.S. House of Representatives, May 23.

Kingson, E. R., 1984. "Financing Social Security: Agenda-Setting and the Enactment of the 1983 Amendments to the Social Security Act." *Policy Studies Journal* 13:131-55.

Lamm, R. D., 1987. "The Ten Commandments of an Aging Society." Denver: Center for Public Policy and Contemporary Issues. Mimeo.

Light, P., 1985. *Artful Work: The Politics of Social Security Reform.* New York: Random House.

Longman, P., 1987. *Born to Pay: The New Politics of Aging in America.* Boston: Houghton Mifflin.

Makin, J. H., 1988. "Social Security: Nothing but a Ponzi Scheme." *New York Times,* October 8.

Marmor, T. R., 1973. *The Politics of Medicare*. Chicago: Aldine.

Myers, R. J., 1985. *Social Security*. Homewood, Ill.: Richard D. Irwin.

Myers, R. J., 1991. "Summary of the Provisions of the Old-Age, Survivors, and Disability Insurance System, the Hospital System, and the Supplemental Medical Insurance System." Mimeo.

O'Shaughnessy, C., 1990. "Older Americans Act: 1991 Reauthorization Issues." Washington, D.C.: Congressional Research Service. Mimeo.

[Schulz], J. H., 1988. *The Economics of Aging*. Dover, Mass.: Auburn House.

Skinner, J. H., 1990. "Cost-Sharing Amendments to the Older Americans Act and Their Potential Impact on the Black Aged." Washington, D.C.: National Caucus and Center on Black Aged.

Skocpol, T., 1990. "Sustainable Social Policy: Fighting Poverty Without Poverty Programs." *The American Prospect* 1 (2):58-70.

Sundquist, J., 1968. *Politics and Policy*. Washington, D.C.: Brookings Institution.

QUESTIONS FOR WRITING, REFLECTION, AND DEBATE

1 Some have criticized Philip Longman and others worried about generational equity for being too gloomy and pessimistic about the future of American society. Is this a valid criticism? How might Longman reply to such a charge of "pessimism"?

2 If a political conservative were to agree with Longman's picture, what would a likely conservative response to the problem be? If a political liberal were to agree with Longman's picture, what would a likely liberal response to the problem be?

3 Eric Kingson and his colleagues believe that both young and old have a "common stake" that should overcome generational differences. Using Kingson's idea, prepare a short article for a local community newspaper in which you outline ideas and examples that support the "common stake" point of view.

4 Public opinion suggests that Minkler is right when she says the public at large does not much agree with the idea of generational equity. What does this fact suggest about public opinion or about what government officials should do about programs for children and the elderly? As an exercise, try writing opinion poll questions about generational equity and rephrase the same idea in different language. Then test the two different ways of framing the issue by asking the questions of people not enrolled in a gerontology class.

5 Gould and Palmer believe that various factors in the American society and economy are responsible for the deteriorating position of children, but they do not suggest that the aged are the cause of the problem. If they

are right, why do you think older people are sometimes blamed for the problem?

6 Consider the following difficult task. Imagine that you are in charge of a "Meals on Wheels" program providing home-delivered meals to the elderly in your community. Your agency has just received a 50% budget cut for next year and now you must recommend which of the current meal recipients should continue to receive food. Write a detailed memorandum explaining how you would decide who are the "least advantaged" elderly deserving of continued service.

7 Is there a way of targeting benefits to those in greatest social and economic need that doesn't make use of factors like race, which tends to be divisive, or income, which tends to be stigmatizing? What factors might work in such an approach to targeting?

8 Assume that you are the superintendent of a school district with a larger proportion of senior citizens among the voters, who are about to be asked to approve a new school bond issue that will raise taxes. Prepare a letter to be distributed to seniors in the community in which you set forth why they should vote in favor of the school bond issue.

FOCUS ON PRACTICE: INTERGENERATIONAL PROGRAMS

Interest in intergenerational programs today is a response to changes in relations among age groups in modern society. In the past, the family or local community typically provided informal opportunities for contact across age groups, especially between the very old and the very young. But one of the consequences of modernization has been the rise of **age grading** and grouping: for example, in the educational system, which introduces bureaucratic categorization and separation of children by age (Eisenstadt, 1956). Moreover, a youth culture and popular media, combined with the rapid pace of technological change, all tend to accentuate a measure of cultural separation between young and old.

Another important tendency has been that of **age segregation**, or the separation of people of different ages who live apart. Age segregation has been promoted by trends such as migration, urbanization, and income transfer programs like Social Security that enable adult children to live apart from aged parents. Of course, the existence of separate living arrangements must *not* be confused with social distance between young and old, or with supposed "abandonment" of older parents by the young, which is very rare. Age segregation may, however, pose problems in a society where young and old are both in need of a limited pool of public resources.

It should be stressed that separate household living arrangements for the nuclear family apart from the aged have long been a feature of Western societies (Laslett, 1972). Much more recent is the rise of intentionally planned residential arrangements for older people: for instance, commercially developed retirement communities like Sun City in Arizona or Leisure World in California. Residential concentration by age is a subject that has long been debated in gerontology (Rosow, 1967; Hochschild, 1973). Some observers point to the positive features of easier social relationships in age-homogeneous communities, while others worry about the "politics of age exclusion" (Anderson and Anderson, 1978).

The challenge of the recent generational equity debate has been one factor sparking new interest in intergenerational programs that intentionally seek to bring together young and old. Such deliberate programs seem more necessary because of social trends that have made age groups socially distant from one another in everyday life. Today, many children lack the opportunity for close and frequent contact with grandparents; intergenerational programs can therefore meet a need for *age integration* (Haber and Short-DeGraff, 1990).

One example of a successful intergenerational program is the Foster Grandparent Program, a federally funded effort that recruits older people for placement in settings such as schools, day-care centers, hospitals, and homes for the handicapped. Foster grandparents provide one-on-one nurturing for children who need affection and personal attention. Foster Grandparents are trained for and supervised in their tasks. As they are drawn from the low-income elderly, they receive a modest but significant cash stipend as well as a transportation allowance and a hot meal. Evaluation studies have shown that Foster Grandparents can help reintegrate older people into society and give them meaningful and appreciated roles in helping younger generations (Ziegler and King, 1982).

Intergenerational programs have been successfully demonstrated in a wide variety of settings, including old-age institutions, such as nursing homes (Newman, Lyons, and Onawola, 1984; Melvin and Ryder, 1989). In some instances, nursing homes have also served as sites for child care programs (Sommers, 1985), sparking the idea of intergenerational day care (Kopac, 1987). Some prominent corporations like the Stride Rite Company have sponsored on-site intergenerational day care (Leibold, 1989). Schools have proved to be a particularly attractive site for intergenerational programming (Aday, Rice, and Evans, 1991). The National School Volunteers Program has led the way to recruiting thousands of older people to serve as school volunteers to tutor children in classrooms (Tierce and Seelback, 1987).

What has been the real benefit of intergenerational programs, we might ask? The benefits seem to be of two kinds: (a) direct service, where young and old serve as resources for vulnerable members of other generations, and (b) attitude change, where feelings of cultural distance between old and young are somewhat overcome. On the direct service side, elderly people with time available during the day have been a source of social contact for latchkey children (Anderson, 1989) and at-risk youth (Ventura-Merkel and Friedman, 1988). But the young, too, have shown themselves to be a valuable human resource for aging network service organizations (Firman, Gelfand, and Ventura, 1983).

With respect to attitude change, there is growing evidence that positive opportunities for contact between old and young can help reduce attitudes of ageism and prejudice on the part of the young (Peacock and Talley, 1984; Dellman-Jenkins, 1986; Dobrosky and Bishop, 1986). In some cases, for example, through oral history programs, older people can become vital resources for improving the education and cultural knowledge of young people.

These programs all represent clear benefits to participants from both generations. But apart from service provided or attitude changes, we can recognize the growing importance of intergenerational programs in renewing a caring bond between generations, a bond that supports important public policies, such as social insurance programs. By all evidence, public support for Social Security and other programs to help the elderly remains very high. But will it remain strong if a stereotype of "greedy geezers" becomes accepted? Could intergenerational programs be a means of overcoming age stereotypes of all kinds?

Intergenerational programs can perhaps help here. It is surely significant that AARP and other senior advocacy groups have now come to the forefront in vigorously supporting more government spending for children's programs. In addition, AARP and the National Council on the Aging have been active in a coalition with the Children's Defense League in supporting Generations United, a national coordinating body for intergenerational programs (Thursz, Liederman, and Schorr, 1989). This new birth of interest in intergenerational programs is part of an ongoing dialogue between young and old, a dialogue that has also come to include the debate over intergenerational equity. By overcoming stereotypes and misunderstanding, it is possible to strengthen the bonds between age groups in decades to come, thus leading to more enlightened policies for taking care of both young and old.

Suggested Readings

Bengtson, V.L., and Achenbaum, W.A. (eds.), *The New Compact Among Generations*, New York: DeGruyter, 1993.

Clark, William F., Pelham, Anabel O., and Clark, Marleen L., *Old and Poor: A Critical Assessment of the Low-Income Elderly*, Lexington, MA: Lexington Books, 1988.

Johnson, P., Conrad, C., Thomson, D. (eds.) *Workers Versus Pensioners: Intergenerational Justice in an Ageing World*, New York: St. Martin's Press, 1989.

Neugarten, Bernice (ed.), *Age or Need? Public Policies for Older People*, Beverly Hills, CA: Sage, 1983.

Wilson, Janet, *Intergenerational Readings: 1980-1992*, Pittsburgh: Generations Together, 1992.

What Is the Future for Social Security?

Social Security is the public retirement pension system administered by the federal government and it constitutes the single largest program operated by the government. The broad outlines of the system are familiar to most Americans and the program is popular. But many people wonder what future Social Security will have in this decade and into the twenty-first century. The 1983 Social Security reforms aroused anxiety but succeeded in putting the program on a much more secure footing (Light, 1985). Most responsible authorities agree that Social Security will be there in the future and some go on to point out that the rhetoric of "crisis" is much exaggerated (Marmor, 1988).

The Social Security Act of 1935 was a centerpiece of the New Deal, a response to the Great Depression at a time when only 5% of the U.S. population was over 65. This legislation was notable because it acknowledged government's role in providing income support to individuals outside the labor market. Social Security from the outset was conceived as a form of social insurance. Social Security not only helped replace income lost and thereby provided a cushion or an incentive to leave the labor force (Ball, 1978; Myers, 1985), but as a bureaucratic system it legitimized age 65 as a date when it was customary and predictable to leave the labor force (Stewart, 1982).

Today, Social Security is by far the largest domestic program of the U.S. government. The money to fund Social Security comes from a payroll tax on almost everyone who receives wages or salary. Other kinds of earnings—such as interest and dividends, partnerships, and so on—are, however, excluded from tax. The payroll tax is divided equally between employer and employee. The combined rate was 2% from 1937 until 1950 and has risen to 12.4%, with another 2.9% for Medicare Hospital Insurance. Payroll taxes are paid by 132 million workers. Both workers and employers pay 7.5% of the first $55,000 of earnings per year.

Critics have often pointed out that the Social Security payroll tax is heavily regressive: that is, a person earning $20,000 a year and someone earning

$50,000 a year both pay at the same 7.5 percentage rate. By contrast, in a more progressive tax system—such as federal income tax—the percentage rises as income goes up, so that wealthier people, at least in principle, are supposed to pay a greater percentage as well as a greater absolute amount of money in taxes. But Social Security, as a flat percentage, becomes a heavier burden for poorer people than for those earning more money.

Social Security covers 90% of those over 65, and for most it is their biggest source of income. In fact, more than 60% of older people rely on Social Security for at least half of their income. In 1960 less than 15% of the federal budget was spent on the aging; by 1991, it was more than 30%, twice as large a proportion in three decades. In 1993 Social Security (technically, Old Age Survivors and Disability Insurance, or OASDI) spent more than $300 billion, an amount larger than the entire military budget.

The large reduction in the poverty rate among older Americans that has taken place since the 1960s is partly due to the increase in social insurance benefits like Social Security. For example, in a recent year, eight of every ten older families would have fallen below the poverty line without these benefits (U.S. Bureau of the Census, 1990). As the relative income of over-65 households improved faster than for younger people, government policies began to reflect that improved status. These included a revision of the Social Security law in 1983 to tax up to half of Social Security benefits for individuals with incomes above $25,000 or couples above $32,000. At present, Social Security benefits are taxed for only about a quarter of older people: an indication that more than three-quarters of older Americans in fact have very modest incomes.

Success—and Doubts

More than a half century after its founding, Social Security remains America's most successful and perhaps its most popular domestic government program (Barrett and Cook, 1988). A recent book on Social Security summed it up by characterizing it as "the system that works," and many Americans would agree with that positive judgment.

But despite the success and popularity, Social Security has been, and still remains, the subject of debate (Achenbaum, 1986; Boskin, 1986; Berkowitz, 1987). One fundamental question concerns the purpose of Social Security: Is it a welfare program designed to prevent old age impoverishment? Or is it a social insurance system in which everyone who pays into it is entitled to benefits? Social Security as it actually exists has come to embody both purposes. On the one hand, Social Security provides a floor, or minimum income, for almost all older Americans. In this way, it mildly redistributes income

(Choi, 1991). On the other hand, Social Security is a universal program in which both poor and affluent older people receive benefits.

Any program that tries to accomplish fundamentally different goals will have its critics. Thus there are some people who even question the basic fairness and integrity of the Social Security system. For example, proponents of the generational equity idea have argued that Social Security is unfair to future generations. They argue that these future cohorts will get back less than current beneficiaries of the system. According to their view, it might be better for people to have a private pension system rather than a compulsory one like Social Security. Under one plan (Ferrara, 1985), it would be possible for people to drop out of Social Security and sign up for a so-called Super IRA, hoping to collect a better return than Social Security offers. But defenders of Social Security often point out that better returns are not at all guaranteed by the private marketplace.

A related criticism is the idea that Social Security is not stable and may not be there for future recipients because the costs will go out of control (R. Campbell, 1977; C. Campbell, 1984; Aaron, Bosworth, and Burtless, 1989). There has been much discussion about the dependency ratio: that is, the proportion of younger workers to retirees (Crown, 1985; U.S. General Accounting Office, 1986). Public opinion polls have suggested that some part of the public, particularly younger people, are worried about the future of the system, whether rightly or wrongly (Yankelovich, Skelley, and White, 1985).

In the future, the baby boom cohort will probably pay higher taxes or receive lower benefits for two reasons: First, the $25,000 income threshold for taxing Social Security is not indexed for inflation, so in the future a much larger proportion are likely to have their benefits taxed. Second, according to the Social Security changes enacted by Congress in 1983, the age of eligibility for full Social Security benefits will rise from the present 65 up to 66 and then 67 in the years after the year 2000. What that means can be seen in the fact that it takes a couple retiring today only four and a half years to recover the money they contributed to Social Security taxes. For those retiring after 2010, it will take seven and a half years. Whether this difference in cohort experience is seriously inequitable, of course, is a separate question; rising life expectancies and levels of wealth among different cohorts make equity comparisons difficult.

None of these arguments has affected the basic popularity of Social Security with the American public, as demonstrated not only by polls but by the votes of Congress in more than half a century since Social Security came into existence (Day, 1990). In this discussion, then, we take for granted that Social Security will be around for the future and will retain its political support as a public, not private, retirement system. Despite broad support, however, in recent years there have been serious questions raised about some aspects of

Social Security, and these controversies are at the center of the discussion about the future of Social Security.

Earnings Limitation

One of the most controversial features of the Social Security System is its "retirement test" or **"earnings test"** (Beck, Hager, and Roberts, 1992; Rejda, 1990). This earnings limitation is a provision of the Social Security law that discourages people in their sixties from collecting Social Security benefits while they are still working. According to present law, Social Security reduces benefits for each dollar of earnings: In 1993 those aged 62 to 64 lost $1 in benefits for each $2 in earnings above $7,680, while those aged 65 to 69 lost $1 for each $3 earned above $10,560. Beneficiaries over age 70 face no reduction in benefits.

Why was the earnings test put in place? The reason goes back to the origins of Social Security itself (Brown, 1972). Social Security was designed and intended as a program to provide income for older people in their retirement years. But is Social Security supposed to provide a minimum income for all or is it more like an annuity where you receive money from a fund based on what you put into it? If Social Security is more like an annuity, then it is hard to see why a 65-year-old person cannot retire from one job and then continue working in a new one while receiving a pension based on his or her previous position, more or less like a standard pension plan.

But Social Security does not work that way. If you work for pay after age 65, Social Security puts a limit on the amount that can be earned without losing benefits. That is why the limitation is also called a "retirement test"; it ensures that Social Security benefits will go only to people who are genuinely retired from the labor force, not those who just leave one job for another.

Many people object to the earnings test because they feel the penalty is too high. Social Security beneficiaries with income over a certain level have to pay a 50% tax rate on "excess" earnings and, in addition, also have to pay all regular federal and state income taxes. On top of that, they are required to pay Social Security taxes on their earnings, resulting in what some have termed an 80% tax rate (or even higher). Those who argue that the earnings limitation is unfair feel that they are entitled to the Social Security benefits to which they contributed. They also point out that an exorbitant tax rate, like 80%, is so high that it punishes people for working and thereby places a penalty on the service that able older people are in a position to contribute to society. They charge that Social Security ends up being like the welfare system or the agricultural subsidy system; in effect, it amounts to paying people not to work (Robbins and Robbins, 1989). Thus, on grounds both of fairness and of the need for "productive aging," some people argue for the abolition of the earnings limitation.

From the economic evidence, it is not clear how much the Social Security earnings test serves as a serious disincentive to older worker productivity (Leonesio, 1990). Other incentive elements, such as private pensions, are also part of the picture. Because of these questions, some analysts doubt whether, on balance, it is worth eliminating the earnings test (Honig and Reimers, 1989). Still, each year, bills are introduced in Congress to eliminate or to raise the retirement earning limit, and over the years the level has been gradually moved up (Dumas, 1992). But the earnings test remains a topic of bitter debate and arouses strong opinions on both sides of the question.

Surplus in the Social Security Trust Fund

Social Security is funded by payroll taxes that go into a large account called the Social Security Trust Fund (actually several such funds). But despite the name, this is not actually a big bank account where money is saved up for the future. In fact, Social Security was originally designed to operate on a **pay-as-you-go** approach; that is, each year, money collected pays for people who receive benefits in that same year. In effect, then, younger workers don't really "save up" for their own Social Security benefits; they pay for the current beneficiaries. If more money is collected from payroll taxes than is paid out that year, then the trust fund develops a **surplus.** By law, the surplus must be invested in government securities (U.S. Treasury notes). These notes in effect are promises made by the U.S. government to repay the money at a specified time in the future (Stein, 1991).

The 1983 Social Security amendments put in place payroll tax rates that would create a $5.5 trillion reserve fund by the year 2025; in other words, the tax rates are now higher than needed to pay current benefits. The surplus money in the trust fund goes to buy U.S. Treasury notes. In other words, the federal government borrows the money and promises to pay it back at a certain time, with interest. Thus Social Security can be viewed as reducing or paying for the current federal budget deficit. But that is only because the surplus trust fund money reduces the need for the government to borrow somewhere else. In essence, the "real" deficit is not reduced at all.

There has been vigorous debate about how the Social Security Trust Fund should be treated: whether as part of the budget, thus reducing the combined federal deficit, or separately. Defenders of Social Security point out that the program currently does *not* increase the federal budget deficit. On the contrary, Social Security collections actually *reduce* the federal budget deficit because the amount of money collected in payroll taxes each year exceeds what Social Security pays out. In 1993 that surplus was more than $50 billion.

Not everyone is happy with the fact that Social Security is generating this surplus. In 1990 U.S. Senator Daniel P. Moynihan opened a national debate with a proposal to cut the Social Security payroll tax and convert the system more fully to pay-as-you-go financing: in other words, take in just enough money from taxes to cover current obligations. His proposal generated some support; after all, it was a proposed tax cut. But it also generated opposition: first, because it would reduce government revenues (thereby driving up the federal deficit) and, second, because it would abandon the goal of "saving up" for the baby boom's retirement.

If the payroll tax is a burden, then we might ask, why do we need a surplus anyway? One answer can be found in the story of Joseph from the Bible, where we hear how the ancient Egyptians saved up grain during seven fat years to prepare for seven lean years. So, too, today's Social Security surplus is really a collection of "IOUs" that will eventually be needed in the twenty-first century when the baby boom generation starts to retire in large numbers, after the year 2010; 15 or 20 years beyond that point, the surplus in the Social Security Trust Fund will be exhausted. At that time, Congress will be faced with cutting benefits or raising taxes to keep the system intact.

We can imagine that in ancient Egypt at the time of Joseph, the pharaoh's advisers probably had a debate about just how much grain was "enough" to be saved during the seven fat years. So today there is a debate about how much is "enough" for the surpluses in the Social Security Trust Fund (Munnel and Blais, 1984). If we do not collect enough, then maybe today's baby boomers will not have a large surplus to draw on when their retirement comes. On the other hand, the so-called surplus may just be paying for today's expenditures in the federal budget deficit (Hambor, 1987).

Women and Social Security

Not all equity issues in Social Security revolve around distant projections for the future. Some have come to the forefront right now because of changing social conditions, such as the role of women (Crooks, 1991). A major issue arises from the fact that the traditional family assumed by Social Security at its inception in the 1930s has now changed. The Social Security program was originally planned for the one-earner family, but today more than 70% of women between the ages of 20 and 44 are in the labor force. Social Security seeks to treat both men and women fairly, but there are troublesome equity problems related to caregiving, divorce, and two-earner couples (Johnson, B., 1987).

A recurrent problem arises from caregiving responsibilities, whether for young children or for elderly relatives. When women stop working because of caregiving, this form of productivity does not get counted into their Social Security records. A basic problem here is that the Social Security system recognizes only paid work for determining benefits in the system. The non-monetized work done by women in caring for a family receives no acknowledgment. The result is that family roles have a large long-range negative effect on women's economic well-being in retirement, much more so than for men (O'Rand and Landerman, 1984).

Another equity issue arises from the higher divorce rate today than in the 1930s. Under Social Security, women who have been married less than 10 years and who were out of the labor force during those years receive no credits toward Social Security, meaning lower benefits at retirement. As a result of past reforms of the system, women who are divorced are eligible for a spousal benefit if they were married at least 10 years. Nevertheless, divorce still marks a real loss of income because the woman receives only a third of what the couple would have received had they stayed together.

Still another alleged inequity comes from the way that Social Security treats married couples. A woman automatically receives a spousal benefit equivalent to half of what her husband is entitled to when they retire. Unless married women have earned a great deal, they find that their spousal benefits are higher than the level they would get from their own work history. Social Security will give benefits to a woman for work outside the home only in case her accumulated benefits are greater than her husband's: an unlikely case, for familiar reasons. Typically, older women receive only the spousal benefit based on their husband's earnings, in effect, completely disregarding the woman's lifetime economic contribution to Social Security. As a result of the same familiar patterns, women retirees receive on average lower monthly Social Security benefits than men do. Because of the redistributive structure of Social Security, two-earner couples typically receive lower retirement benefits than one-earner couples under the present system, and some critics find that inequitable (U.S. Congress, 1983).

A variety of suggestions have been made to reform the Social Security system to take into account a woman's life cycle (Wolff, 1988). Some critics have urged that Social Security give credit for time taken out for caregiving (Buckley, 1990). For example, a child care dropout option has been proposed, whereby years spent at home caring for children are not counted in determining an average benefit level. Another suggestion is the so-called double-decker system, under which retirees would receive a fixed amount of money along with a benefit related to work history and prior contributions. Finally, some women's advocates have urged an **earnings sharing** plan, whereby it would be possible to divide the earnings of the married couple between the Social Security accounts of both spouses (U.S. Congress, 1984).

Earnings sharing is attractive because it treats marriage as a partnership of equals and it also helps improve the income position of women who may be impoverished by divorce or widowhood. The question of earnings sharing versus alternatives, however, brings us back to a fundamental question concerning the rationale for Social Security itself. Is the program to be viewed as a means for replacement of earnings or as an investment judged by equity and rate-of-return? This is the same controversial question that arises in the earnings test. There is again a conflict between different ways of thinking about fairness and adequacy, and basic social values are at stake. However these debates are resolved, it is clear that, now and in the future, Social Security will remain, among other things, a key issue for women (Forman, 1983).

In the readings that follow, we hear some very different views about the future of the Social Security system. In a wide-ranging forum discussion about Social Security, Carolyn Weaver and Lawrence Kotlikoff are worried about whether the system will remain sound and will be fair to future generations. The equity or fairness of the system remains a major problem, in their view. By contrast, in this discussion, Henry Aaron and John Rother believe that Social Security is fundamentally fair to all generations. Yet they too emphasize that the system has the capacity to change and adapt to new conditions. They recognize inequities in the system but point out that changing Social Security always means a trade-off or attempt to balance competing values.

In her article, Joan Szabo attacks earnings tests in Social Security because she believes it is unfair to older people who want to work and who can contribute much to society. Senator Daniel Patrick Moynihan, chairman of the U.S. Senate Finance Committee, believes that payroll taxes for Social Security are too high. Building up a large Social Security surplus fund is not necessary, he believes. Instead, Senator Moynihan urges us to cut the tax and return more money to workers. On the Social Security surplus, Patrick Dattalo takes a different view. While recognizing that the payroll tax might be too high for low-wage workers, Dattalo also believes that the Social Security surplus could be invested by the government in ways that might promote broader social welfare goals.

The impact of Social Security on women is another topic addressed in the readings that follow. Economist Barbara Bergmann argues that feminist thinking should be the basis for changing the Social Security system to reflect new realities of gender instead of the traditional values taken for granted when Social Security was initiated in 1935. Such changes would provide greater equity for women, she believes. By contrast, Robert Myers believes that Social Security should not be expanded to take into account all equity claims. He believes that the present system is satisfactory and represents the best approach to reconciling the competing values of equity and adequacy.

Social Security
Valuable or Outmoded?

Modern Maturity

Although the Preamble to the U.S. Constitution calls for "promoting the general welfare," there was no national system to implement this until the Social Security Act was signed in 1935 by Franklin D. Roosevelt. Since that momentous legislation—through almost six decades of hard times, war, prosperity and recession in the nation, and amidst growing support for, dwindling confidence in, endless frustration with and continuing success of the system—America has wrestled with how best to provide a measure of protection for all.

Social Security has been called "a program in search of an explanation." It smacks of socialism to some, of a sacred covenant to others, and of a bureaucratic minefield to many. Because of its effect on and importance to all Americans, MODERN MATURITY decided to make Social Security the subject of its newest feature—the Roundtable. We asked four distinguished analysts to try to explain exactly what Social Security does and if it's doing what it should. Supporters hail the program as a shining example of how efficient, dependable and moral our federal government can be in assuring the economic security of the current generation of retirees by providing survivor, disability and annuity insurance. Critics, however,

[NOTE: John Wood is the editor of this article.]
Source: "Social Security: Valuable or Outmoded?" by J. Wood, *Modern Maturity* (April-May, 1992), pp. 34-36, 84-85. Reprinted with permission from *Modern Maturity*. Copyright 1993, American Association of Retired Persons.

lambaste the system as an equally clear example of how inept, unstable and inequitable our federal government can be in carrying out those very same missions.

In the course of this conversation the panelists discussed some of the most controversial issues facing Social Security today: Should it be means-tested? Were the notch babies cheated? Is the earnings limit fair? Will the trust-fund reserve be raided? Are women, singles and minorities getting a raw deal? Are older people profiting at the expense of Baby Boomers? And many more. We hope that by the end of this forum you will have a better understanding of the past, present and future of this both venerated and vilified social-insurance concept. . . .

Definition of the System

Modern Maturity: According to one observer, the Social Security Act of 1935 marked "the founding of the welfare state." Did F.D.R. set us on the right path?

John Rother: In terms of approval, support, and willingness to pay into the system, Social Security is a brilliant success—the most popular public program in American life today.

Henry Aaron: Next to Medicare.

Laurence Kotlikoff: It's certainly a very popular program for the beneficiaries over the last 40 years, but the burden it has imposed on younger generations, and on those yet to come, has not made it popular among them. If you ask Baby

Boomers, people in their 20s, even teenagers, if they want to contribute to a system under which they will pay many times more than the benefits they'll receive over their lifetime, the answer is no.

Aaron: The assumption that any generation, as a group, will pay more in taxes than it will receive in benefits is false. Every age group will get back more money than it pays in. The real rate of return will be relatively modest for workers retiring next century, but then, the real rate of return on an average investment is relatively modest. Also, the statement about public opinion is flatly contradicted by countless polls that repeatedly indicate every age bracket overwhelmingly supports the continuation of the Social Security system. Moreover, every age bracket states it is willing, if necessary, to pay higher taxes to sustain benefits.

Kotlikoff: We need to distinguish between support among young people and what young people want. What they *don't* want is to have to pay many times over for something they don't benefit from directly. The economic facts are that although people do receive a positive rate of return, it's much lower than the economy can offer. The question is whether young people today could take their contributions, which in large part are going to older generations, invest them in the private economy, and after 30 years end up with a much higher return than they'd get through Social Security. The answer is clearly yes. People shouldn't kid themselves by suggesting that young and middle-aged people haven't been significantly burdened by a system they never voted on.

Carolyn Weaver: Although there are some substantial concerns with the way Social Security is structured, I don't think F.D.R. was wrong. He made an appropriate political choice at the time. Any social security system, if it's financed on a pay-as-you-go basis, offers huge rates of return in its early years of operation, and those rates fall over time. No wonder Social Security was so popular in the past and is subject to so much concern among younger workers today. They'll have to pay considerably more for their benefits and/or they'll have to pay considerably more for the benefits paid to the elderly than did earlier generations. The cost of generosity is rising.

Kotlikoff: If you take a 20-year-old and ask what, in today's dollars, his contributions will be to Social Security over his lifetime, the answer is about $65,000. If you ask what, in today's dollars, his benefits will be, the answer is about $12,000.

Rother: Are you factoring in the value of survivorship, disability, and benefits adjusted for inflation?

Kotlikoff: Yes. It's very clear from actuarial calculations made by a range of economists that Baby Boomers and young people are paying much more than they're getting. That doesn't mean they want to eliminate the system; we just need to accept reality.

Aaron: What you just said doesn't follow from the numbers you gave. Young people are not paying more than they're getting. If you divide benefits in future years by a large enough number, it's possible to conclude that benefits will be smaller than amounts paid in. But given plausible projections of wage growth and benefit formulas as they now exist, people will get back benefits with far higher purchasing power on an actuarial basis than the value of the taxes they're paying in. That's true for every age group, and for the indefinite future.

Confidence in the System

MM: Consider Jim and Mary Gordon, a hypothetical Baby-Boomer couple in their early 40s, who are planning their future retirement needs. One source of income they're relying on is Social Security. But what are they to make of the fact that every few years a new crisis in Social Security pops up, followed by an amendment to "solve the problem for the indefinite future," followed shortly thereafter by another crisis?

What are they to make of one such amendment that caused the "notch" problem in the first place? Or the 800 number Social Security installed that callers said was so named because that's how many times you had to dial it before you got through? Or the organizations that have been formed in recent years to "save" and "preserve" Social Security? Can you reassure Jim and Mary that they have nothing to worry about?

Kotlikoff: No—for several reasons. The Baby-Boom generation will represent an enormous group of retirees, but there are concerns about whether the system will have sufficient resources to pay their benefits. We are now accumulating a Social Security trust-fund reserve to set money aside for them, but there are concerns about whether the rest of the government's finances will worsen so the Baby Boomers have the trust fund but lose in other ways. For example, if the federal deficit continues to rise, Baby Boomers will get their Social Security benefits, but they'll have to pay much higher income taxes than retirees do now. Alternatively, Medicare growth continues unabated to such an extent that the Social Security trust-fund reserve may be tapped just to pay it off. So there are several ways Baby Boomers can end up worse off because of the way we've passed the generational buck over the past 40 years, and continue to do so.

Weaver: What should the average citizen make of periodic financing crises in Social Security? Jim and Mary should become acquainted with what Social Security is—how it works, how it's financed, and who benefits at whose expense—as well as with the underlying politics that govern any major government program.

Kotlikoff: I ask my undergraduates how much they contribute to Social Security, what they expect to get back, and if they understand the benefit formula—and they have no idea.

MM: I've done some background reading on Social Security and, frankly, I'd rather examine an insurance policy.

Weaver: It's not easy to become informed, but the stakes are high for the typical family. Making an effort to understand it is essential to sound personal financial planning.

Can I reassure Jim and Mary? If they're planning to rely exclusively on Social Security for their long-range saving, I can't provide reassurance. That's not wise strategy. I would encourage them instead to save in addition to Social Security and to diversify their portfolio. I know that's easier said than done, particularly for low-income families, but it's advice everyone should take to heart.

Kotlikoff: The national saving rate in 1990 was 2.6 percent—more than 60 to 80 percent below the rate between 1950 and 1979. No one is saving. One way to focus attention on how much Americans need to save on their own would be for Social Security to send each household an annual statement saying, "Here's what we're saving for you and here's what you should save on your own or with your employer." That would show how bad a deal they're getting in terms of their contributions and their benefits—and how much better a deal older generations are getting.

Aaron: Social Security went through an extended time of troubles from the mid-1970s to the mid-1980s. There has been no crisis, or prospect of one, since. Public-opinion polls have swung gradually in the direction of increased confidence. The elderly are far more confident than the young, but for the nation as a whole, a majority now are confident that benefits will be paid.

Rother: Social Security payments ultimately have to come from our productive capacity in the year they're paid. Therefore, we must decide what measures to take to ensure that we can keep up with the growth in our retirement obligations we know will occur. If growth continues along historical lines we should be okay; but if our productivity plateaus, Social Security may have to be adjusted because, ultimately, it's a function of what the economy can support.

How fair is the earnings limit?

If you continue to work for an employer after your Social Security benefits start, your benefits may be reduced if you earn over the "earnings limit" (also called the earnings test or retirement test). Recipients age 65 through 69 can earn $10,200 a year without penalty; benefits are then cut $1 for every $3 earned above that amount. Recipients under 65 can earn $7,440 a year without penalty; benefits are then cut $1 for every $2 earned above that amount. The limitation doesn't apply after age 70.

Those who *favor* the earnings limit say:

> Repealing the test would cost $28 billion over five years.
> Repealing the test would reduce the Social Security trust-fund reserve.
> Repealing the test would give most of the added benefits to higher-income families (those most able and likely to continue working after age 65).
> Relatively few people would be affected by repealing the test.

Those who *oppose* the earnings limit say:

> Administering the test costs $200 million a year.
> Social Security benefits are an earned right—bought and paid for over a lifetime—and should not be withheld from eligible beneficiaries for any reason.
> The test discourages retirees from working and penalizes those who must.
> Since unreduced benefits are paid to people over 70 who work, they should be paid to younger workers, too.

Aaron: We've just gone through a period of ten or 15 years of slow economic growth, in a very conservative political environment, with Social Security crises coming every two or three years. At the end of that period, what happened? The most conservative President in half a century reaffirmed his commitment to Social Security. Congress enacted a series of changes embracing the system.

What we lived through was an environment that could not possibly have been more conducive to retrenchment or to cutting back the system—but just the opposite occurred. Imagine what will happen 30 years from now when the Baby Boomers are 50, 60 and 70. Thus the idea of failing to meet commitments is fanciful. I would be more concerned that if the economy grows slowly, with low savings rates, we could adhere too rigidly to current promises. So, yes, we could end up with some undesirable social policy, not because we failed to meet commitments under Social Security, but because we met them too rigidly.

Reform of the System

MM: If Social Security ain't broke, why are we always fixing it?

Kotlikoff: We need to reform Social Security fundamentally. Not in a way that undercuts the benefits to current or near-term retirees or undermines any of the system's insurance provisions. I agree with all those goals. But in a way that resembles an individual savings and insurance system. Other countries have done this. Chile, for example, radically restructured its social security system about 15 years ago to make it more efficient, equitable and individual-based. The Polish government and other Eastern European nations may even adopt the Chilean model rather than ours.

MM: Let me get this straight: Your ideal social-insurance system is one used by Chile and endorsed by Poland?

Aaron: I find it amusing that of the two countries cited as examples of reform, one experienced inflation rates of thousands of percent per year and the other experienced decades of Communism and ultimate economic collapse.

Rother: I must take issue with the recommendation for radical change. Social Security performs very important functions. It meets real needs and will continue to meet them. As those needs change, Social Security quite properly changes with it, and I don't think that should cause Jim and Mary any degree of anxiety. It's good that the system has the flexibility to change. It's not etched in concrete, it's a living system.

Weaver: Radical reform is one of those terms the guardians of Social Security don't like to hear, but one man's radical reform is another's finetuning. The United Kingdom is an interesting example. It has moved considerably in the direction of enhancing the role of private pensions and allowing companies to contract out of Social Security. A fair number of guardians in the U.S. would consider that extreme, yet it's not in the category of the Chilean reforms. Free and open debate on reform should be encouraged rather than taking some options off the table simply because they sound radical.

Kotlikoff: The "guardians" are typically those who benefit most from the system—the older generations. Discussing Social Security is taboo because whenever the subject is raised, people get concerned about losing their benefits. We need courageous politicians to talk about reforming the system for younger people while not changing the benefits for older ones. We need the younger generations to fix up the system for themselves in a way that doesn't hurt the older ones. And we need the older generations to raise publicly the discussion of reform for the younger ones. The way the system has evolved has left us with a grossly inequitable structure that cries out for reform. And, unfortunately, Baby Boomers don't know the details of the system, so they don't know how much they're being hurt relative to others.

Rother: I can't leave that statement unchallenged. An important part of Social Security is the social nature of its insurance program. It's not an individual annuity program. It's not an individual savings program. It's a program intended to meet social needs as well as to be fair to individuals. It therefore has a redistributive element that ensures that lower-wage workers receive relatively higher returns than upper-wage workers. That's entirely consistent with the goals and nature of the program. It doesn't mean it's unfair—precisely the opposite.

Kotlikoff: I'm not disagreeing with that. It does have progressive aspects to it, but in many ways it's also very regressive. It's regressive that a two-earner couple where the spouses earn the same amount receive less in benefits than a single-earner couple where the nonworking spouse receives benefits without having contributed a single penny. It's also regressive the way we treat college graduates versus high-school graduates. People who don't go to college contribute to the system earlier and longer. Those early contributions could earn interest in a bank instead. These individuals end up paying more after adjusting for lost interest than those who contribute the same dollar amount, but in later years, even though the benefits are potentially the same. There are all kinds of inequities we need to correct, and correcting them would make the system actually *more* progressive.

Work Incentives in the System

MM: Mr. Aaron, someone once wrote that Social Security trespasses on almost every aspect of our personal lives by imposing an unnecessary straitjacket of behavioral standards: When to retire, how much to earn between 62 and 70, whether or when to divorce, whether or when—

and whom—to remarry, whether to recover from disability, which employer to select, whether to save or spend, etc. Sounds like Social Security was founded in 1984, not 1935.

Aaron: Social Security doesn't put a straitjacket on any of the things you mention. It creates a set of financial incentives, some of which make sense and some of which are debatable. As far as retirement is concerned, the majority of people in the United States seem to want to retire quite early. Social Security facilitates that. The major criticism you would find from the four of us is that the system makes early retirement too easy, not too hard. In other words, the straitjacket fits too loosely. The academic criticism is that people should be encouraged, more than they are now, to work longer.

MM: Which is precisely why Jim Gordon is so upset. He just read that with Social Security's earnings limit, 680,000 retirees lost their benefits in 1987, or had them reduced, simply because they continued to work. [See (the box): "How Fair Is the Earnings Limit?" . . .] Since Jim plans to do consulting work after he retires, he's afraid this could happen to him.

If the original intention of the earnings limit back in the '30s was to move older people out of the workforce and into retirement, freeing jobs for unemployed younger people, is the earnings limit outdated?

Aaron: More bills are put into the Congressional hopper, year in and year out, to liberalize the earnings limit than to make any other change in Social Security. Also, year in and year out, the bills are either not acted on or substantially watered down. The reason: Relaxing or removing the earnings limit increases Social Security costs. Studies have repeatedly shown that liberalizing the test has an almost imperceptible effect on the amount older people are willing to work. For that reason, Congress has been slow to increase the amount people can earn without loss of benefits, and I agree with that.

Rother: There is a case to be made for liberalizing the earnings limit, as opposed to repealing it. In terms of helping those who need to work, AARP would certainly agree with most in Congress that any additional benefits need to be financed. An outright repeal would be very expensive, but a reasonable liberalization could be done by expanding the wage base—by about $3,000 above where it is today—upon which Social Security is taxed.

Kotlikoff: The earnings test should be flat-out repealed. If not immediately, then over a span of five or ten years. A good number of working elderly arrange their work to earn just under the amount beyond which they'll start losing benefits. That suggests to me that if the earnings limit were eliminated they would work more, earn more, pay more Social Security taxes, and pay more income taxes. So I don't see any reason for us to put an additional 33 percent marginal tax on older people who want to contribute to our economy.

Weaver: The earnings test is out of date. The test penalizes the older person who wants to continue working, so it creates an obvious work disincentive. It also has the perverse effect of penalizing people only if they derive their income from employment, and not if they derive their income from interest, dividends and/or capital gains.

Aaron: I can think of few lower-priority uses of funds in the United States than to increase government spending to make physicians, lawyers and academics like ourselves, who will undoubtedly continue to work past age 62, richer.

Kotlikoff: But it's the sales clerks, not the doctors, who have to rearrange their work schedules.

Aaron: They may be who you want to help, but that's not where the money will go.

Equity of the System

MM: Mary Gordon has been following Professor Weaver's advice by reading up on Social Security. Her research, however, has uncovered three unsettling facts: (1) Mary is in the paid labor force; her neighbor Alice has never worked. Yet according to the Social Security Administration, Alice will receive more Social Security benefits than Mary because Alice's husband has paid the maximum tax for years. (2) Mary will get more if she claims spousal benefits (based on Jim's work record) than if she bases her claim on her own record. (3) If Mary's marriage lasts ten years, she'll be entitled to spousal benefits; if it ends in divorce in anything *under* ten years, she'll get zip in spousal benefits.

Professor Kotlikoff, you once wrote that the need to reform Social Security's treatment of the family has been recognized by virtually every government commission studying the subject in the last decade. Why do such inequities still exist?

Kotlikoff: Because we haven't thought of reforming Social Security for young people and have left the system unchanged for everybody over 40. Reforming the system in midstream for older people collecting benefits is politically impossible, infeasible and undesirable—from anybody's perspective. But the idea of reform-

---

Should only the needy get SS?

Means-tested programs require low income and meager assets to qualify for benefits. Social Security differs from such programs in that everyone pays into it and everyone is guaranteed a basic floor of benefits.

Those who *favor* means-testing say:

> It would make the system more equitable because at present many well-off people receive more benefits than they need while many poor people receive fewer benefits than they need.
>
> Older people aren't as needy as the public has been led to believe.
>
> Although it's true that benefits as a percentage of earnings are higher for low-income people than high-income people, their life expectancy is lower so their "advantage" is reduced.

Those who *oppose* means-testing say:

> Asking high-income people to suffer cuts in their benefits would undermine support for the system.
>
> Social Security was not designed to help only the needy but to serve as part of the base upon which everyone can build greater security.
>
> People would save less because income or assets above a certain level would disqualify them from eligibility.
>
> The present system doesn't favor the well-off. Those in the lower income brackets have a greater percentage of their income replaced by benefits than do those in the higher brackets.
>
> Means-tested programs are costly, bureaucratic and don't work.
>
> Low-income people receive lower retirement benefits than high-income people simply because they've paid less into the system. It's not because the system is unfair.

---

ing the system for *young* people hasn't been debated. We don't need to maintain an outdated, inequitable, inefficient system for the next 200 years.

Aaron: Why have these inequities persisted? The answer is money. To equalize the benefits in the first example, you can go one of two ways. You can raise benefits for the two-earner couple to what the one-earner couple gets; since millions of people would be affected, the additional cost would be several billion dollars. Or you can reduce benefits for the one-earner couple to the level of the two-earner couple; naturally, the losers would fight that proposal. Incidentally, this one-earner/two-earner contrast is diminishing in light of women's increasing participation in the labor force, so it's of less importance today.

Kotlikoff: What I think you're proposing is to just redistribute the amount of benefits so there's some equity between the two couples. If that's true, I don't see how it would require more money. It's true that certain young people who were getting a better deal would not get such a deal anymore, but I think they'd be willing to accept that to have a more equitable system.

MM: Social Security has been called "the nation's most effective anti-poverty program." But according to the 1980 census, those below the poverty line received only 9 percent of total Social Security benefits while elderly with incomes in the top 20 percent ($30,000 or more) received about 30 percent of total benefit payments. Is that really the most effective way to attack poverty in this country?

Aaron: High earners pay much more than 30 percent of all taxes but receive 30 percent of benefits. Low earners pay much less than 9 percent of payroll taxes. That means low earners receive benefits that are far larger in relation to taxes paid than do high earners.

Weaver: It's both feasible and desirable to target public resources to needy elderly people. A better system would be one in which people buy their retirement-income coverage privately and tax subsidies are used exclusively to boost the retirement incomes of low-income people. This might be achieved through a two-tiered system, where the first tier provides a flat or means-tested benefit for the elderly and the second tier involves something like a mandated IRA.

Aaron: The perception of Social Security as the nation's largest anti-poverty program is more true today than ever before. It remains the largest source of income for the elderly. Without it, the poverty rate among the elderly would be far higher than among any other age group, even if every other anti-poverty program were repealed. As a society we're not prepared to envisage destitution, and we face a choice of whether to meet needs through a host of income-tested programs or through a set of entitlements that provide benefits to the general population. Excepting Australia, every developed industrial country in the world has adopted an entitlement program; this [is] because there's reluctance to subject the population to income tests, which in virtually every case where they've been used have been associated with considerable stigma and shame.

MM: Considering the alternative—the stigma of poverty, dependency and lack of access to health care—the stigma of having to prove one's need seems relatively minor.

Aaron: We have a lot of means-tested programs in the United States today, and we know the difference between them and programs like Social Security. Apart from the disability-insurance program, Social Security administrative costs run less than 1 percent of contribution income per year. Administrative costs associated with Medicaid, for example, run more than 5 percent per year, and with Aid to Families with Dependent Children more than 10 percent. It costs something to means-test: billions every year that serve no purpose other than to deny benefits to particular groups.

We also shouldn't overlook the earned-income tax credit that allows younger working

Is the trust-fund reserve safe?

To forestall bankruptcy of the Social Security system and to begin planning for future benefits for the estimated 75 million Baby Boomers, the last of which will have reached retirement age by 2030, the 1983 Social Security Amendments shifted the program from a pay-as-you-go system to a partly advance-funded system. To bring in more funds Social Security tax rates were raised, some benefits were made subject to income tax, and benefit eligibility was pushed back for future retirees. The system is now solvent and gradually building up an enormous reserve (approximately $150 million a day), which is estimated to peak at $8 trillion by 2027.

Those who want to *protect* the trust-fund reserve say:

> The fund will promote national savings, ease the supply of credit, cut interest rates, and promote economic growth.
> If it's spent to help pay for other programs, it could deplete the money we've saved for future retirees and force us to raise Social Security taxes yet again or cut benefits.
> Building up a reserve makes the system sounder and best able to withstand crises and unanticipated economic downturns.

Those who *oppose* the trust-fund reserve say:

> The taxes being levied to build it up are too high.
> Since by law the trust-fund reserve must be invested in government obligations, they can and should be better used to help pay for other much-needed programs, such as bailing out Medicare.
> Who honestly believes the government can keep its hands off a pot of gold this size for the next 40 years?

families in need to have their payroll taxes refunded. That's a progressive mechanism that substantially cushions the impact of payroll taxes on lower-income workers. But it's a mistake for the income tax to treat pensions more favorably if they're called Social Security than if they're called private pensions.

MM: The other day Jim Gordon went to an automatic teller machine and asked for $20. The ATM malfunctioned and he got $200 instead. When he drew this to the attention of the people in line behind him, they eagerly asked the machine for $20 too, hoping for a similar windfall. All they got was the $20 they asked for and were entitled to. Some shrugged their shoulders and left, but a few hollered that they'd been cheated and stormed into the bank to protest Jim's good

fortune. This struck Jim as similar to the controversy over the "notch." Were the notch babies cheated, and should those who got notch windfalls give their money back?

Weaver: That's a wonderful analogy because nobody's been cheated, but there's plenty of reason for those who came along behind the windfall recipients to feel wronged. In 1977 Congress corrected a method of adjusting benefits that couldn't be afforded. It was Congress' mistake. Fixing it—a necessity given the enormous financing problem the system faced—created the notch. Should those who got the windfall feel any moral or political obligation to give the money back? I don't see why. They got what they were entitled to under the law.

As for the notch babies, they're being treated

equitably relative to all younger people retiring in future years. If anything, they're being treated more than equitably because of the transition rules adopted when the law was changed. [Those born between 1917 and 1921 were allowed to use either a "special transition" benefit formula or the new benefit formula, whichever resulted in higher benefits. Everyone born after 1921 was allowed to use only the new benefit formula.] Still, that doesn't alter the fact that they may be receiving lower benefits than people who retired only months before them. No wonder they're irate. But the answer certainly isn't to go back and take money away from one group of individuals or give money to another group of individuals.

Aaron: The notch babies were not cheated. No injustice was done. An error was corrected.

Rother: I find it quite regrettable that one or two so-called senior organizations have taken up the notch issue. First, they're irresponsible in terms of how they're characterizing the problem. Second, they're diverting energies that could be better used to focus on legitimate problems like health care. And third, they give all seniors a bad image because they're putting before the public a group of people seen as greedy who are demanding the same windfall others got unintentionally. That's an extremely unfortunate public portrayal, and it's something these so-called advocacy groups should reconsider.

Solvency of the System

MM: Jim Gordon is optimistic about Social Security. He cites the gradual build-up of the trust-fund reserve that will ensure there will be enough money to pay him and Mary and all the other Baby Boomers when they retire. The fund is expected to reach $8 trillion by the year 2027. But Mary isn't that certain. She just read how one politician likened it to "walking through a bad neighborhood with a diamond ring." Is it true the reserve could be raided before then by politicians or interest groups?

Weaver: Mary is definitely the one who should handle the family finances.

Kotlikoff: I agree with Mary. The trust-fund reserve could be dissipated along a number of different lines, and the dissipation may already be occurring. Non-Social Security spending has generated huge deficits. At the turn of the century the Medicare trust fund will run into the red. To meet those obligations, we'll have two choices: Raise the Medicare tax rate or tap the Social Security reserve. The politically expedient thing would be to tap the fund.

Rother: It's misleading to base future viability of Social Security benefits on the trust-fund build-up. There is no way to put money in a safe-deposit box, then take it out when you need it years later. Each year's benefits must be financed out of the economy in that year. Whether we finance it out of payroll taxes, income taxes or some other revenue, the burden will be the same with or without the fund. So the real question is, Are we structuring our finances today to promote optimal long-term growth and a strong economy? The trust-fund reserve is there to assure people the money paid into Social Security will only be used for Social Security purposes. But it's not an account in the same way a bank account is; you can't just stash the money away in it.

MM: Why not? Why can't we just hide it under a mattress, stamp "FOR FUTURE SOCIAL SECURITY RECIPIENTS ONLY" on it, and make it unlawful to touch it?

Rother: First of all, if you hide it under a mattress it won't earn interest. Nobody would stand for that. Secondly, when it came time to take the money out, it would cause a sudden increase in the money supply. Talk about major inflation!

Weaver: It's wrong to suggest the way the trust-fund reserve is used has no effect on the economic burden of Social Security or [on] government spending. The concern Mary raised is whether the reserve can be raided. Yes it can. A huge reserve fund is, and will continue to be, a tempting target for interest groups and politicians. Many groups will want to lay claim to the reserve—dual-earner couples, elderly widows, notch babies, to name a few.

Congress is also looking for politically painless ways to finance both long-term health care and Medicare. If we use the Social Security surplus in this way we'll increase the real burden of Social Security. Or if, through a mishandling of the rest of the federal budget, the surplus is spent indirectly, we'll increase the real burden of government.

Aaron: It's inappropriate to call anything that might use the trust fund "raiding." We can do a lot of things with it, provided we manage the rest of government appropriately. The key question isn't what is done with one government account or another, but whether the government household is in good fiscal order. Today it's not. We need to bring government operations into balance so revenues at least equal expenditures. If, in the process of doing that, we happen to decide we want to finance health-care reform with some of the trust fund, that should be no cause for alarm.

Kotlikoff: It can be highly misleading to zero in on just the government's overall unified budget deficit, including Social Security. We could have a unified budget surplus later in this decade and *still* be dramatically undermining the welfare of future generations.

MM: But wasn't the trust-fund reserve a moral commitment or promise to be set aside for future Baby-Boomer payments only? If so, why would anyone even consider using it for government spending?

Weaver: Congress hasn't given any clear guidance about what the purpose of the reserve fund is. Is it a large savings account held on behalf of Baby-Boom and other workers to help defray part of the cost of future benefits? Or is it a slush fund for Congress? If our goal is to increase savings and investments in anticipation of Baby-Boomer retirements, then it clearly constitutes a raid on the trust fund to go in and take what's been set aside for that purpose and use it for other purposes. On the other hand, if the reserve is just a discretionary fund for Congress, we're using an awfully regressive payroll tax to build it up.

MM: Would the trust-fund reserve be better protected if Social Security became an independent agency?

Rother: AARP has long felt Social Security would be best run under an independent governance. One reason is there have been times when the agency has been perceived to be under overtly partisan influences, and an agency as important as Social Security should be insulated from that. Another reason is a program as large and complicated as Social Security needs professional management, and for many years we've had high turnover at the top there. A more independent structure would allow a greater degree of management and stability, and would benefit the system as a whole. As to the reserve, Congress sets the rules on that.

MM: But if Social Security were independent, how could Congress touch its reserve fund?

Rother: Independent means independent from the Executive branch, not from Congress.

Aaron: What Congress giveth, Congress taketh away.

The Earnings Test Has Failed

Joan C. Szabo

Earl Tindall returned to work after being retired for several years because he wanted to stay active, he says, and because he and his wife, Nancy, needed the extra income and health benefits that his current job offers. Trying to make ends meet on Social Security and a small pension is not easy in today's economy, Nancy Tindall says.

Unfortunately, though, the job is taking its toll on the couple's Social Security benefits. The Social Security retirement earnings test requires the Tindalls to give up a portion of their Social Security benefits each year.

In 1991, the earnings test reduces Social Security benefits for working individuals aged 65 to 69 by 33 percent for every dollar they earn above $9,720. For those aged 62 to 64, the benefit reduction is 50 percent for every dollar earned above $7,080.

The Social Security earnings test does not affect individuals who are 70 or older, and it does not apply to nonearned income, such as interest or dividends from investments.

When the earnings test is combined with other federal taxes, the effective marginal tax rate for a worker earning just $10,000 a year rises to nearly 56 percent, and that rate does not include state and local taxes. Single people begin paying federal income taxes when their income is over $6,400; for a married couple, the amount is $11,300.

There is also a Social Security benefit tax that affects some of the nation's elderly. Depending on

their tax bracket, the working elderly who also are subject to the benefit tax can face a marginal tax rate that can go as high as 80.34 percent. . . . The benefit tax applies only if one-half of Social Security income plus all non-Social Security income, including income from tax-exempt bonds, exceeds $25,000 for an individual, or $32,000 for a couple. (Under current law, a maximum of one-half of Social Security benefits is subject to taxation but is not automatically included in the ordinary income of the taxpayer.)

In Earl Tindall's case, it is the earnings test that has reduced his income.

Although Tindall says he will continue to work, a number of elderly people have opted not to do so because of the high effective marginal tax rates they must pay because of the test.

The effect of the test, according to those who oppose it, is to discourage retired workers from returning to work and to encourage elderly workers to leave the work force. Those aims may have seemed beneficial in the 1930s, when unemployment was high and the law was instituted, but the outlook for the work force today is quite different.

The pool of available labor is growing more slowly as fewer young people enter the labor force. As a result, many businesses are looking more and more to retired workers to fill job openings. In particular, companies in the service, retailing, and health-care industries find retired workers especially valuable additions to their work forces.

To combat the barrier to working that many older Americans face, legislation has been introduced in both the House and the Senate to repeal

Source: "The Earnings Test Has Failed" by J. C. Szabo, *Nation's Business* (May 1991), *70*, pp. 42-43. Reprinted by permission, *Nation's Business,* May 1991. Copyright 1991, U.S. Chamber of Commerce.

the earnings test. One bill, the "Older Americans' Freedom to Work Act," would eliminate the test—and thus any loss of Social Security benefits—for people once they reach age 65.

The measure was introduced by Rep. J. Dennis Hastert, R-Ill., and has 230 cosponsors. Hastert says his bill also would benefit business. "Older workers understand the work ethic, they are invaluable in training other employees, and they are a good example to have around whether in a big or small business," he says.

A similar bill has been introduced in the Senate by John McCain, R-Ariz.

Democratic opponents of such legislation, who have defeated previous attempts to eliminate the test, argue that repeal would result in a loss of federal revenue. They cite Congressional Budget Office (CBO) estimates that repeal would cost the government $3.6 billion in the first year and $26.2 billion over five years.

Proponents of repeal, however, say the CBO estimates are based on static revenue models and do not take into account the changes that would follow from repeal of the test. Lisa Sprague, manager of employee-benefits policy for the U.S. Chamber of Commerce, says repeal would encourage more elderly Americans to work. And that change in the work force would spur the economy, say the Chamber and other business groups, which strongly support legislation to repeal the earnings test.

Repeal would actually produce more revenue for the federal government, according to a recent report, *Paying People Not to Work,* by Aldona and Gary Robbins. The two former Treasury Department economists say that if the retirement earnings test is eliminated, at least 700,000 elderly retirees would enter the labor market.

The authors state: "Our annual output of goods and services would increase by at least $15.4 billion. Government revenue would increase by $4.9 billion, more than offsetting the additional Social Security benefits that would be paid." The report was co-sponsored by the Institute for Policy Innovation, in Lewisville, Texas, and the National Center for Policy Analysis, in Dallas. Both are nonprofit research organizations.

Opponents of repeal argue that it would favor the rich. But Rep. Hastert contends that two-thirds of those who would benefit from repeal would be receiving earned income of less than $40,000 a year. In fact, lower-income workers are especially hard hit by the earnings test, according to many who want it repealed. Those with lower incomes, it is argued, have the greatest need to supplement their incomes because during their working years they probably did not save enough for retirement, they are less likely to be eligible for employer pension benefits, and are more likely to receive lower Social Security benefits.

Opponents of repeal also argue that Social Security benefits should be allocated only to those who are retired. Proponents say this argument ignores older individuals' difficulties in trying to survive solely on Social Security.

In addition to producing more federal revenue, the Chamber's Sprague says, eliminating the earnings test would free resources within the Social Security Administration, which spends a disproportionate amount of its budget and staff time monitoring retiree income levels.

The American Health Care Association, a federation of state associations that serve more than 10,000 nursing homes and long-term-care facilities, also strongly supports the repeal legislation. Nursing facilities face serious staff shortages that are expected to grow more severe as demand for care increases, says Paul R. Willging, executive vice president of the association. By expanding the labor pool with older workers, repeal could help such facilities meet staffing needs with capable employees, he says. "Older workers make wonderful nurse assistants because they are dependable, compassionate, and they bring a special understanding to their jobs, which improves the quality of life enjoyed by elderly and disabled residents in nursing facilities."

The American Association for Retired Persons continues to support liberalization of the earnings limit, says Evelyn Morton, a legislative representative for the group. This approach would increase the earnings limit so that older persons could work without facing a significant reduction in their

Social Security benefits. "We are not supporting a specific dollar figure," says Morton. "But we believe that an increase in the amount that can be earned is necessary."

READING 28

Surplus Value

Daniel P. Moynihan

On the final Friday morning of 1989, at a sparsely attended press conference, I announced that I would introduce legislation to return the Social Security Trust Funds to a pay-as-you-go basis. Since then the proposal has been pronounced dead by assorted authorities. Yet it does not die. It has acquired a kind of street life, and it is mentioned to me wherever I go. In almost forty years of political campaigns and public office of various sorts I have never seen a proposal (and a fairly abstract proposal at that) win as much support as rapidly as this has—except within the Democratic Party. . . .

By way of background, in 1977 a set of increases in the rate of Social Security contributions (under the Federal Insurance Contributions Act) was put in place that, in effect, moved us from the established pay-as-you-go system to a partially funded system. These rate increases extended over a thirteen-year period. The final one went into effect this past January 1.

Little attention was paid to this shift in policy, which by definition would create a long succession

Source: "Surplus Value" by D. P. Moynihan, *The New Republic* (June 4, 1990), *202* pp. 13-16. Reprinted with permission from *The New Republic.*

of large surpluses. On the contrary, the Reagan administration came into office in 1981 proclaiming the imminent "bankruptcy" of the Trust Funds, a scare tactic that went back to the Roosevelt-Landon campaign of 1936.

Even so, the surpluses appeared and grew. In 1987, with the Democrats once again in the majority in the Senate, I became chairman of the Subcommittee on Social Security and embarked on an extended inquiry into this wholly new development. The General Accounting Office looked into the matter for us. Authorities such as Robert J. Myers, that eminent Republican and longtime chief actuary of Social Security, offered their counsel in hearings.

A range of documents emerged with a common theme: These monies were not general revenues and were not to be treated as such. They were trust funds. If we cannot save the trust fund surpluses, the money should be returned to the 132 million employees and self-employed and six million employers who pay it. There was something like a bipartisan consensus on this issue: save the surplus or return it. . . .

Still, the question is why Democrats have such difficulty with such an elemental issue. Trust funds are being raided. Republican Senator John Heinz asserts that the word for what is going on is embezzlement. The common law is nowhere more strict than in the matter of trust funds. This is something people know; it implies a standard of conduct. That standard applies to public no less than to private trusts. Never mind technicalities.

And yet the term most often invoked to explain the party's palpable fear of the proposal is that it would not be . . . *responsible*. This is put in quite simple terms. There is a large deficit. Dealing honestly with the trust funds would increase that large deficit. Finding substitute revenues—an afternoon's exercise, if the truth be known—would open the party to the charge of taxing and spending (albeit there is no spending here, in the sense of government programs). . . .

The plain fact is Democrats ought to be attracted to a proposal to raise take-home pay—responsibly or otherwise—for the blunt reason that the United States has been experiencing an unprecedented period of stagnant wages and income. In 1989 the average factory gross wage in the United States (in 1977 dollars), $167 a week, was $20 *lower* than 1970. The median family income in 1988, at $32,191, was a mere $82 above the level of 1973 (in real terms). But given the growth in FICA taxes for that period, from $1,878 to $2,418, the net change over the fifteen years from 1973 to 1988 is *minus* $458! And it was Democrats who enacted those FICA increases, worsening an already flat period of family income extending almost the length of a generation.

Just shy of thirty years ago, I came to Washington with the Kennedy administration. I became an assistant secretary of labor, with (nominal) oversight of the Bureau of Labor Statistics. At that time *the* number in Washington was the unemployment rate, then hovering between 5 percent and 6 percent. Calendars were marked with the day the monthly report was due. The commissioner would let me see it for, oh, two minutes or so before rushing it down the hall to the secretary, who would rush it over to the president. Up a point, down a point, unchanged: whatever, the unemployment rate was too high, a statement that America could do better and should.

At times I wonder. What if, in 1961, median family income in the United States had not risen but fallen during the fifteen-odd years since the end of the Second World War? Would that not have been *the* issue on which we focused our attention and energies? As it happened, real median family income had risen almost by half since the end of the war. Then commenced an extraordinary surge: 1961, $22,000; 1962, $23,000; 1963, $24,000. And so upward, $25,000, $26,000, $27,000, $28,000, $29,000, finally in 1969, $30,000. Had we continued at this pace, median family income in 1988 would have been just under $50,000. Instead, it was stuck at $32,191—and this is the highest it's been since '73!

Women by the scores of millions have gone to work just to keep family income steady. (In 1975, 47.4 percent of women with children were in the work force. By 1988, this had risen to 65 percent.) . . .

There are soundly Democratic economic arguments for returning Social Security to pay-as-you-go. The FICA contribution is, in effect, an excise tax on labor, raising the cost to employers of hiring people—especially hiring low-skill, low-wage people. Lowering the rate would create jobs—perhaps a million new jobs over a decade. But in the end this is not what the Social Security issue is about. Nor is it about federal revenue. Of course the loss has to be made up. It is not that much at this point. Returning $55 billion in FICA taxes in calendar year 1991 translates into a $38 billion net reduction in federal "revenues" in fiscal year 1991 (after accounting for increased income tax receipts from the resulting higher income). The point, however, is that these are *not* revenues. They are insurance contributions. Once that point is agreed upon, *then* you go on to make up the "loss." But it needs to be done promptly. Once we are dependent on a $5 billion or $6 billion *weekly* surplus, it will be beyond the system's capacity for change. The Democratic Party, as they say down South, had better listen up.

Social Security's Surpluses

Patrick Dattalo

In 1983, social security, defined here as Old Age, Survivors, and Disability Insurance (OASDI), was reformed to include graduated payroll tax increases. These reforms were made to moderate the large pension liabilities expected to accrue as people born between 1946 and 1964 (the "baby boom" generation) retire. However, because these payroll tax increases were based on overly conservative assumptions about economic growth, OASDI's trust fund balances are expected to rise from $69 billion in 1990 to a peak of $494 billion in 2015 (Board of Trustees, Federal OASDI, 1990).

Under the current law, all payroll tax revenues not needed to pay benefits are invested in special-issue U.S. Treasury bonds (General Accounting Office, 1990a). As a result of these investments, OASDI's trust fund is credited with a bond (that is, an IOU from one part of the federal government to another), and in exchange the Treasury receives OASDI's cash. From the Treasury's perspective, these borrowed funds are available to finance the general operations of the federal government (General Accounting Office, 1990b).

Because social security's surpluses are a planned response to the retirement needs of the baby boom generation, borrowing these funds to finance the federal government's general operations has raised questions about the program's management. For example, New York Senator Daniel Moynihan charged that using OASDI's assets for current federal expenditures violates the

Source: "Social Security's Surpluses" by P. Dattalo, *Social Work* (July 1992) *37*, pp. 377-379. Copyright © 1992, National Association of Social Workers. Reprinted by permission.

program's integrity. According to Moynihan, "the so-called Social Security tax is not a tax. . . . These contributions are premiums paid to insurance. . . . [They] are held in trust by the [F]ederal Government, but they are not Government money" ("Bill to Cut," 1990, p. S150). Furthermore, because OASDI's assets are generated by the regressive payroll tax (in 1991, wages over $53,400 were exempt from this tax), using these funds for current federal expenditures shifts the financial burden to low- and moderate-income people (Langley, 1990).

Deliberation over how to manage social security's large trust fund balances is expected to continue when the 102nd Congress convenes in the fall of 1992. Social workers must participate in this debate because OASDI's surpluses have implications for increasing the quality of life of low- and moderate-income families. This article continues the discussion in Dattalo (1990) by assessing two recent proposals for managing the program's large surpluses and recommending additional policy directions.

Two Recent Proposals

Invest the Surpluses
One proposal for managing social security's excess funds is to invest them. Recently, Illinois Representative John Porter recommended that the surplus be used to create Individualized Social Security Retirement Accounts (ISSRAs) (General Accounting Office, 1990a). The ISSRA approach would establish a two-tier retirement system. The

first tier, similar to the existing program, would pay benefits to retirees from OASDI's trust fund. These payments would be reduced to compensate for second-tier benefit levels.

Under the second tier, workers would select the financial institution (called the "trustee") at which their ISSRA would be held. Appropriate trustees include banks, insurance companies, and other money management firms. Participation in the ISSRA program would be mandatory and early account withdrawal prohibited. Benefits would be paid directly out of the proceeds of these accounts based on contributions plus interest. Trustees would be required to follow specific investment guidelines, could not release funds until the worker's retirement, and would be liable for rule violations.

To finance the new two-tier system, payroll taxes would continue to be deposited into the Treasury. However, OASDI's trust fund balances would be maintained to cover only one year's expenses. Instead of being used to purchase government securities, surplus funds would be transferred to ISSRAs in the selected trustee institutions.

Porter's scheme helps prepay future retirement benefits and, by shrinking the size of trust fund balances, can reduce the disproportionate reliance on the payroll tax to finance the federal government. However, Porter's proposal creates increased benefit risks for retirees. Depending on the market return on ISSRAs, an individual's retirement income (ISSRA plus first-tier benefits) might be the same, higher, or lower than under the existing program. Porter's scheme also increases the federal government's administrative responsibilities, because it would need to monitor ISSRAs. Moreover, the plan does not address the large revenue shortfalls that could occur when OASDI's surpluses are no longer available to finance the federal government.

Reduce the Payroll Tax

Another recent proposal for managing social security's surplus funds is to eliminate them by cutting the payroll tax (known as FICA). The best-publicized, albeit unsuccessful, efforts to cut the payroll tax have been made by Senator Moynihan. For example, one unsuccessful attempt was a Senate bill introduced by Senator Moynihan in January 1990 ("Bill to Cut," 1990). Another unsuccessful attempt by him was an amendment to the Senate's 1992-96 federal budget that he proposed in April 1991 ("Amendment No. 74 to Allow," 1991).

Senator Moynihan has recommended that the payroll tax be cut from 15.3 percent (employee and employer combined) to 15.02 percent in the first year after legislative approval and then reduced to 13.1 percent the next year. Under this proposal, rate increases are deferred until 2012 (14.2 percent), 2015 (15.3 percent), 2020 (16.9 percent), 2025 (18.3 percent), and 2045 (19.1 percent). These FICA changes would allow OASDI benefits to be paid while maintaining a reserve of 150 percent of annual outgo ("Amendment No. 74 to Allow," 1991).

Abolishing OASDI's surplus through payroll tax cuts helps prevent cross-financing between trust funds and the rest of the federal budget. In addition, a reduction in payroll taxes allows attention to the current consumption needs of low- and middle-income people. Because lower-income people spend more of their after-tax income than higher-income people, a reduction in FICA can provide a stimulus to a sluggish economy (General Accounting Office, 1990b). Furthermore, like Porter's scheme, Moynihan's tax cuts ignore the large federal revenue shortfall problems that could be created when the surpluses are no longer available.

Future Policy Directions

Both the Porter and the Moynihan plans for managing social security's surpluses raise as many questions as they seek to answer. It is difficult to address all of the questions being posed about OASDI's surpluses, but an effective solution should help redistribute the burden of financing government and anticipate the costs of future retirement benefits by increasing the likelihood that the surpluses are saved.

Redistributing the Burden of Financing the Federal Government

From 1950 to 1989, corporate taxes declined from 4.9 percent of the gross national product to 1.8 percent, individual taxes increased slightly from 7.6 percent to 8.8 percent, and the payroll tax grew substantially from 2 percent to 6.6 percent (General Accounting Office, 1990b) (Figure 6.1). As a result of these changes in the relative contribution of various federal taxes, lower-income people are being taxed more and higher-income people are being taxed less.

One way to rebalance the relative contribution of various federal taxes is to raise the effective top rates for both personal and corporate taxes. Rate increases for upper-income levels should be complemented with tax decreases for lower-income brackets by, for instance, expanding the earned income tax credit (EITC). In 1975, a refundable EITC was adopted by the federal government to lighten the burden of the social security payroll tax on low-income families with children (Mikesell, 1991). In 1991, families with children that earned less than $21,250 qualified for the EITC. The maximum amount was $1,977 for families with one child and $2,820 for those with two or more children (General Accounting Office, 1991).

The EITC is one step toward providing financial relief to low-income families. However, because it varies little by family size and therefore is insensitive to the income needs of larger families, this credit does little more than neutralize the effects of the payroll tax. Furthermore, the credit is denied to people without children. To allow EITC to move beyond simply offsetting FICA, Congress should consider varying the credit according to a wider range of family sizes and expanding eligibility to financially needy people without children.

Saving the Surpluses

Increases in the upper-income rates for personal and corporate taxes and expansion of the EITC can help redistribute the burden of financing the federal

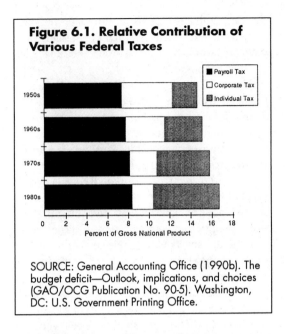

Figure 6.1. Relative Contribution of Various Federal Taxes

SOURCE: General Accounting Office (1990b). The budget deficit—Outlook, implications, and choices (GAO/OCG Publication No. 90-5). Washington, DC: U.S. Government Printing Office.

government. However, within the context of large budget deficits, the greater availability of additional individual and corporate revenues alone does not guarantee the saving of social security's excess reserves. Currently, federal law requires that OASDI's trust funds be invested in U.S. Treasury securities (General Accounting Office, 1990a). One supplemental strategy to help ensure that the surpluses are saved is amending social security's law to allow the purchase of nonfederal securities (for example, state and local government credit instruments and community loan funds) (Dattalo, 1990).

The purchase of nonfederal securities helps ensure that there is no payroll tax surplus, and consequently no funds are available to underwrite the federal government's budget. Although investing OASDI's excess reserves outside the federal system would create additional congressional responsibilities (for example, ensuring that high-risk credit instruments are avoided), state and local public pension funds have successfully addressed similar issues (Roeder, 1988). Therefore, given the current concerns over how social security is being managed, Congress should seriously consider expanding the program's investment options by adopting state and local pension fund management practices.

Conclusion

Social security's large account balances represent a planned attempt to provide funding for the retirement of the baby boom generation. However, the size of these surpluses has attracted considerable attention, and there is growing pressure to use this money for current federal expenditures. Although debate continues, current proposals fall short of addressing concerns over the management of OASDI's assets. An effective solution should help redistribute the burden of financing government and anticipate the costs of future retirement benefits by increasing the likelihood that the surpluses are saved. Greater attention to OASDI's assets provides an opportunity to focus attention on the payroll tax's regressive impact on low- and middle-income people and to use at least some of these assets for long-term investments to achieve social welfare goals.

References

Amendment No. 74 to allow for a Social Security tax cut. (1991, April 23). *Congressional Record,* pp. S4899-4905.

Bill to cut Social Security contribution rates. (1990, January 23). *Congressional Record,* pp. S149-154.

Board of Trustees, Federal Old-Age, Survivors and Disability Insurance. (1990). *The 1990 annual report.* Washington, DC: Social Security Administration.

Dattalo, P. (1990). Social security surplus: A housing policy opportunity. *Social Work, 35,* 346-349.

General Accounting Office. (1990a). *Social Security—Analysis of a proposal to privatize trust fund reserves* (GAO/HRD Publication No. 90-22). Washington, DC: U.S. Government Printing Office.

General Accounting Office. (1990b). *The budget deficit—Outlook, implications, and choices* (GAO/OCG Publication No. 90-5). Washington, DC: U.S. Government Printing Office.

General Accounting Office. (1991). *Mother-only families* (GAO/HRD 91-62). Washington, DC: U.S. Government Printing Office.

Langley, P. A. (1990). A new controversy: Social security, the deficit, and taxes. *Families in Society, 71,* 307-308.

Mikesell, J. L. (1991). *Fiscal administration—Analysis and applications for the public sector.* Pacific Grove, CA: Brooks/Cole.

Roeder, R. G. (1988). *Financing retirement system benefits.* Chicago: Government Finance Officers Association.

The Housewife and Social Security Reform
A Feminist Perspective

Barbara R. Bergmann

If we were to ponder the list of major complaints which are currently being voiced concerning the present set-up of the social security system—the "inequity" in benefits between one- and two-earner couples, the treatment of the divorced spouse, the "wasted" social security taxes of the working wife—we would find that virtually all of them, in one way or another, involve the housewife. It is the system's method of provision for the housewife— in some instances its lack of provision—that is at the heart of almost all of the complaints.

Paradoxically, it is the *decreasing* number of full-time housewives that has pushed the problem of their treatment under social security onto center stage. As long as most adult men were husbands and most adult women were housewives, the system's provision for a wife through a benefit which was supplementary to her husband's benefit seemed straightforward to most people. The spouse benefit, which gave a married male retiree 50% more than an unmarried male retiree with the same earnings record, was advantageous to the vast majority of men and the vast majority of women. True, the system's treatment of the working wife was no less anomalous and the system's treatment of the divorced wife was only slightly more shabby than it is today. But working wives and divorced wives were less numerous, and there was little public concern about their problems.

Along with the rise in the labor force participation of married women, the fall in the marriage rate, and the increase in the divorce rate, has come a trend of feminist thinking concerned with the economic, social, and psychological relations between men and women and with the institutions through which those relations are policed and expressed. Feminists now seek redress for what they perceive as previous neglect of women's satisfaction and well-being. They ask that women's interests be more faithfully represented in discussions of issues and that institutional structures be revamped to serve those interests. Whether this wave of feminist thought has been an important part of the cause of these social trends or is in reality more of an effect is something we need not debate here. What needs to be understood, however, is that feminist ideas have a considerable contribution to make to the discussion of issues like social security reform, and in fact are indispensable to a cogent discussion of any set of issues in which gender roles figure prominently. Of course, feminist thought has done more than provide an intellectual framework for the discussion of reform. It has been a source of political action to get the issue of reform onto the national agenda and will be needed to mobilize enough political power to enact reforms.

Source: "The Housewife and Social Security Reform: A Feminist Perspective," by B. R. Bergmann, in *A Challenge to Social Security: The Changing Roles of Women and Men in American Society*, edited by R. Burkhauser and K. Holden, 1982, pp. 229-233. New York: Academic Press. Reprinted with the permission of the Institute for Research on Poverty, University of Wisconsin-Madison.

The role of and treatment of the housewife, which is really the major bone of contention in social security reform, has, of course, a major place in feminist thought. Betty Friedan's book, *The Feminine Mystique* (1963), which was influential in initiating the current wave of feminism in the United States, centered on the disadvantages to women of assuming the housewife's role. All feminists believe that women should not be forced into assuming it, and that alternative choices should be available. Many feminists, such as the present writer, go further and believe that the disadvantages of the role of housewife are so great that it would be better if younger women were to avoid entering the role even temporarily and if the "option" to assume the role were to disappear.

There is a second strand of feminist thought concerning housewives, which derives from the solidarity which feminists feel with all women, housewives included. . . . This solidarity expresses itself in a concern to alleviate injuries (physical and psychological as well as financial) inflicted on housewives by their husbands and by the institutions of society. This second strand is not logically contradictory to the first; it is possible to love the sinner (the housewife herself) while hating the sin (playing the role). Nevertheless, the two strands do tend to cut different ways in terms of policy. Moreover, individual feminist thinkers differ in the emphasis they place on each.

These two strands of feminist thought inspire two kinds of complaints against the social security system—that some housewives are treated too well and that some housewives are treated not well enough. The housewives who are treated too well are those married to retired men, who are enabled by the system to live at a higher standard than retired working wives whose family had comparable total covered earnings. The housewives who are treated not well enough are those whose dignity is scanted by treatment as a dependent, or those whose marriages end, and whose husbands retain all rights to social security (and private pensions) earned during the marriage.

The solidarity-with-housewives strand of feminist thought results in attitudes which emphasize the housewife's productiveness and give dignity to the position of housewife. It results in policy suggestions which would have the effect of making the woman who becomes and remains a housewife safer, more comfortable, less subject to financial shipwreck, more able to hold up her head as a productive member of society. The most characteristic product of this line of thought is the suggestion that housewives be awarded social security credits for the homemaking work they do. Some credit schemes would require the household to pay taxes in return for the credit; others would not. One merit of homemaker credits in the eyes of the solidarity-with-housewives advocates is that it makes housework and "paid work" more alike, thereby raising the status of housework psychologically and financially. A second merit, of course, is that in the case of divorce the homemaker would keep her credits, and thus would be more financially independent than is the case now.

Earnings sharing, whereby social security credits for paid work are shared between spouses, would also give housewives earnings credits under their own names. In the event of divorce there would be no cases in which the housewife would lose all social security protection, as can happen under present arrangements. While earnings sharing is probably much easier to implement than homemaker credits, it does not go as far in protecting and dignifying housewives. Most earnings-sharing schemes call for sharing 100% of the earnings credit, and no more. For one-earner couples who retire still married, sharing 100% rather than 150% of earnings credit would result in lower pensions than the present spouse benefit or the proposed homemaker credit would provide.

One may also view the two-tiered system (or the double-decker system), in which entitlement is given to all persons of a certain age, regardless of work history, as a protective measure for the housewife and as a potential substitute for the 50% spouse benefit. Homemaker credits are based on the idea that housework should be counted as paid work in figuring pensions. Earnings sharing is based on the idea that housework earns one the right to share the pension entitlement due to the paid work of one's spouse. On the other hand, the two-tiered and double-decker schemes are based on the idea that a pension should be given to all people who reach a certain age, regardless of work history. These two schemes are not based on a concept of the value of housework; rather they are based on the assumption that work history should be less important in determining a person's pension than it now is. This attitude increases the housewife's dignity as a person, if not as a worker. The two-tiered system can also be thought of as bringing the position of the husband closer to the present position of the housewife, instead of moving the position of the housewife towards that of the husband by giving her work a market value, which is the case with homemaker credits.

The role-avoidance strand of feminist thought on the housewife suggests that the concerns of the working wife should get priority over those of the housewife because the wife with a job outside the home works harder than the housewife. The housewife and her family should not get higher benefits than two-earner families who have contributed the same amount to the social security system. This line of thought leads to an advocacy of the abandonment of the 50% spouse benefit. The role-avoidance theme is probably inconsistent with the proposal for untaxed homemaker credits, but not necessarily with any of the other forms of reform that have been mentioned. The role-avoidance strand of thought suggests that it may be detrimental to the long-run interests of women to make the housewife's position a great deal safer and more comfortable [than] it is now. However, none of the proposals for earnings sharing or a two-tier system would accomplish this in any significant degree and thus do not provoke feminist opposition.

Most informed feminists would probably choose one or another of these two programs of social security reform:

1. The sharing between spouses of earnings credits plus the elimination of the 50% spouse benefit
2. The same as 1 plus the provision of a substantial tier or deck of benefits unrelated to work history with concomitant scaling back of benefit dollars awarded per dollar of earnings credit

The first program is more "antihousewife" than the second. While it would insure that housewives get a share of benefits earned by their spouses, it would mean that there would be less to share. The second plan makes the pension less dependent on work history, and so favors those with little or no work history—the housewife, par excellence.

Feminist thought on the housewife is not only a useful guide in organizing our thoughts about social security reform, it is indispensable if certain mistakes are to be avoided. The history of thought on social policy demonstrates that women and their concerns have tended to slip out of sight, even in cases where gender roles are central to the policy being debated. Where the women involved are housewives, the tendency to ignore them is apparently almost irresistible. An egregious example occurred in the debate on welfare reform. When social scientists approached this issue, they apparently forgot that most of the adult clients of the present system are women who stay home with their children—housewives or housewives manqué. This forgetfulness resulted in the concentration of research and thought on the issue of work incentives, with little attention to child-care issues. It also resulted in proposals to expand the number of clients to include anyone of low income, with little attention paid to ways of getting adequate resources to the existing clients of the program. Some of the leading thinkers on welfare reform have recently become interested in social security reform, and once again the problematic issues connected with the housewife are being ignored. . . .

Instead of keeping up with feminist thought, social scientists have been busy learning the antifeminist "new home economics," which is for the most part a fatally oversimplified theory of the traditional form of family life. It is the passing away of this traditional form which is occasioning the need for the very reforms we are studying. A familiarity with feminist thought and attitudes is necessary at a minimum as a corrective to ingrained and unexamined sexist attitudes concerning issues which have gender roles at their core, as social security reform does. This does not mean that only women or only feminists are fit to deal with these issues. It does mean, however, that social scientists of both genders and all persuasions need to understand what the feminists are saying.

Incremental Change in Social Security Needed to Result in Equal and Fair Treatment of Men and Women

Robert J. Myers

In continuing contemporary discussion of the treatment of men and women in various aspects of our social and economic life, one of the major topics is social security. This paper will examine that subject in depth: its basic nature, past developments, and various proposals.

Nature of OASDI and Medicare

To judge whether or not the social security program provides equal treatment by sex, one must first understand the basic nature of the current program: Old-Age, Survivors, and Disability Insurance and

Source: "Incremental Change in Social Security Needed to Result in Equal and Fair Treatment of Men and Women" by R. J. Myers, in *A Challenge to Social Security: The Changing Roles of Women and Men in American Society*, edited by R. Burkhauser and K. Holden, 1982, pp. 235-245. New York: Academic Press. Reprinted with the permission of the Institute for Research on Poverty, University of Wisconsin-Madison.

Medicare. OASDI and the hospital-insurance portion of Medicare (HI) are social insurance programs, whereas the supplementary medical insurance portion of Medicare is subsidized voluntary insurance (and as such will not be considered further in this paper).

A social insurance program generally is a mix of individual equity and social adequacy, with more emphasis on the latter. Specifically, "individual equity" means that each participant receives protection actuarially equivalent to the contributions or premiums paid on his or her behalf. This does not necessarily involve, in all cases, an exact return of contributions, plus interest. On the other hand, "social adequacy" means that benefits are paid to meet presumptive needs, regardless of length and amount of contribution payments.

Frequently, individuals say that OASDI and HI are improperly structured, because they contain a mix of what they refer to as "insurance" and "welfare." By these phrases, they mean individual equity and social adequacy, although frequently they misuse "insurance" to mean a money-back plan. (Perhaps this view is prevalent among those in the academic community because of their familiarity with TIAA-CREF, which is a defined-contribution plan, a form not widely used throughout the private pension field.) They advocate splitting out the individual-equity and social-adequacy aspects, apparently for purposes of neatness, consistency, and public understanding. Yet most long-time students of social insurance believe that the best results can come from the skillful blending of these two elements into one system.

From the start of social security in 1935, different views have been expressed publicly on how to balance individual equity against social adequacy. Over the years, a gradual trend has occurred toward greater social adequacy and less individual equity. At times, however, this trend has been reversed, such as by the introduction of the delayed-retirement credit in 1972. Nonetheless, there are often general public pressures for instilling more individual equity, such as proposals to eliminate the retirement test and to eliminate the spouse benefit.

I believe that social security has the major role of providing a broad system of social benefits protecting against the long-term risks associated with old-age retirement, disability, and death of insured workers. Such benefits should provide a floor of economic security, with considerable emphasis on social adequacy. As such, the program will effect significant income redistribution (as does any insurance system, to a greater or lesser extent), but it should not be considered that this is its primary purpose—as some assert.

Accordingly, I believe that too much emphasis should not be laid on individual-equity considerations—i.e., on whether people exactly get "their money's worth." I am satisfied that there must be some consideration of individual equity. I believe that, as long as there is not too great a discrepancy between the amount an employee participant pays

and the value of the protection furnished, the program is properly balanced.

History of Equal Treatment of Men and Women under Social Security

There have, in the past, been a number of instances where different (unequal) treatment by sex was introduced by OASDI. Interestingly, the original 1935 act had completely equal treatment by sex, essentially because benefits were provided only for retired workers.

Beginning with the 1939 act, which introduced auxiliary and survivor benefits, the sexes were treated differently. Husbands and widowers were protected on the basis of the wife's earnings record *only* if dependency could be proved. Also, benefits to children were payable on behalf of women workers under much more restrictive conditions than were applied to male workers. Further, for a time, women had a lower minimum retirement age for reduced benefits and, for a much longer period, had more favorable conditions as to insured status and computation of retirement benefit amounts (because these were calculated for a shorter period of time—namely, the number of years after 1950, or age 21 if later, and up to age 62 rather than 65 as for men, although for both sexes earnings credits after age 61 could be utilized).

Over the years, owing to both legislative changes and court decisions, virtual equality of treatment of the sexes has now been achieved. The only exceptions are for relatively minor matters—such as that widows can waive payment of federal benefits based on military service before 1957 (so as to count such service under OASDI), but widowers cannot do so. Incidentally, the House version of the 1977 act provided complete equality of the sexes in all respects. However, this provision was dropped in conference, and instead a study by the Department of Health, Education, and Welfare was requested, which resulted in the report *Social Security and the Changing Roles of Men and Women*. . . .

Criticism of Present Treatment of Men and Women

A number of critics assert that the social security system unfairly discriminates against women. The very foundation for their belief is that the program was constructed almost half a century ago, at a time when the roles of men and women in our society were completely different from those that obtain at present. They seem to assume that no married women worked in the paid labor market in the mid-1930s whereas now (or certainly in the near future) the reverse is the case. This is not true, of course, although admittedly there has been a rapidly growing trend of employment of married women and of women reentering the paid labor force after their children have grown up or after widowhood. But this trend was anticipated by the original planners of the social security system, and the benefit structure was developed taking it into account.

Some people assert that, even though the benefit provisions might apply equally in all respects between men and women, equal treatment is still not present because women have both lower wages and more breaks in service, as a result of unfair discrimination in the marketplace. The solution to this problem should not be sought from OASDI. Rather, the remedies should come through altering the underlying causes. (Moreover, this argument has no validity when HI is considered, because all insured persons receive exactly the same benefit protection.)

Other people are concerned about what they believe to be the unfair treatment of two-worker families compared to one-worker families under OASDI. Any such unfairness is equally present when the one-worker family consists of a male worker and spouse or when it consists of a female worker and spouse, so there is no question of unequal treatment by sex. In this discussion, "worker" is used to refer only to workers in paid employment in the labor market outside the home.

As to relative treatment of one-worker and two-worker families, consider what the problem is stated to be by those who believe there is one. Usually, very simplistic assumptions are made, such as that the husband and wife are the same age and both retire at age 65 and that the one-worker family and the two-worker family have the same total combined earnings, but in the two-earner family the earnings are split equally. The total of the two primary benefits for the latter family is generally smaller than the primary benefit plus the spouse benefit for the former family. For example, for the cohort of persons attaining age 62 or becoming disabled or dying before age 62 in 1980, Average Indexed Monthly Earnings (AIME) of $1000 produce a primary benefit of $432.60 in the early part of 1980, so that the combined primary and spouse benefit for both, retiring at age 65, is $648.90. In contrast, an AIME of $500 produces a primary benefit of $272.60, so that the total benefit for the two workers in a two-worker family is $545.20, or 16% less than the benefits for the one-worker family. Because both families paid the same amount of social security taxes, it is then argued that the two-worker family is treated unfairly.

The weaknesses of the argument are that it is based solely on the individual-equity principle and that the advantages accruing to the two-worker family are not considered. The argument for individual equity is faulty because in many other instances it can be shown that one person is not receiving as good an "actuarial" deal from OASDI as another. This is inevitable in a system that, desirably, is founded primarily on social-adequacy principles. If individual equity were the overriding aim of social security, there would be no need for a governmental program, because the private sector could just as readily handle it. Therefore, just because complete individual equity is not present in a particular situation is no reason why an injustice is present and why a change should be made. Moreover, I would argue that, although the one-worker family and two-worker family have the same total income, from an economic standpoint they are not really in equivalent positions. The one-worker family actually has a higher real income, because of the greater time at home of the "non-worker" spouse and the resulting increased productivity for home-consumption items (and thus the lessened need for expenditures). As a result, in keeping with the principle that benefits should be somewhat greater as earned income increases, there is no reason to be disturbed about the one-worker family versus the two-worker family.

Still further, it could be argued that the two-worker family with each having equal earnings is unduly advantaged as compared with a one-person, one-worker family with the same total earnings. Although both families contribute the same, the total benefits for the former are $545.20, or 26% more than the benefit of $432.60 for the latter. Once again, this absence of individual equity is nothing to be disturbed about!

But is the two-worker family in any sense receiving less than its fair share? The two-worker family in fact receives more insurance protection for its "investment" than does the one-worker two-person family with an equal income. If one worker in such a family retires before the other, then benefits will be paid to that worker. On the other hand, in the one-worker family, no benefits are payable to the nonworker unless the worker retires. Also, child survivor benefits are payable in the event of the death of *either* spouse in a two-worker family, but only on the death of one spouse (the worker) in the one-worker family. Further, prior to retirement, both spouses in the two-worker family have disability insurance, whereas in the one-worker family only the working spouse does.

Finally, I think that an important social principle requires that a nonworking spouse who is taking care of the home and raising the children have an OASDI benefit. Then, if such a spouse also has a benefit based on earnings outside the home, it is only fair that the larger of the two available benefits should be paid—without consideration of the taxes that were or were not paid.

Proposed Solutions and Their Weaknesses

Several proposals have been made . . . to remedy what are believed to be either the unequal or inequitable treatment of women under OASDI. Little discussion has been given to the similar situation under HI, but this too should be considered.

Those who believe that gross inequities are involved recommend what might be called sweeping structural changes. There are three general types of such proposals—earnings-sharing credits, wage credits for homemakers, and the "double-decker" approach. All of these proposals would, to one extent or another, provide social-benefit protection for the "nonworking" wife (or full-time home-maker), but so too does the present spouse benefit. Which approach is best depends upon many factors, some objective and some subjective. Among these factors are cost, administrative feasibility, public understanding, and (very important) the problems involved in any transition required from the existing provisions.

Before discussing each of these proposals in turn, I want to clear up one matter. It is frequently argued that it is degrading for persons who have made a life career as a homemaker to receive OASDI and HI benefits on the basis of dependency. As I see it, a straw-person has been set up by terming these auxiliary benefits as "dependent benefits." The law does not contain (and never has contained) the designation of these auxiliary benefits as "dependent benefits." Nor, for that matter, has there ever been any dependency requirement for wives and widows. The various types of spouse benefits are now payable as a right on the basis of legal status (although 10 years of marriage is required for divorced spouses); they are not based on proof of dependency.

Now consider the proposals which have been made to solve what is said to be the inequitable treatment of two-worker families compared to one-worker families. These proposals have usually been quite simplistic. They have not considered all the complex situations that can arise, including not only those mentioned previously, but also termination of the marriage through divorce or death. Separation, too, can cause serious problems under these proposals.

Usually involved are either equally splitting the combined earnings records of the couple (earnings sharing) or providing wage credits for homemakers. The earnings-sharing approach, even though superficially attractive, would create other anomalies and inequities. If all benefit rights, both accrued and expected, were preserved for present participants, the costs involved would be very high. If such rights are not preserved, there would be grave, divisive political and social problems. Furthermore, regardless of how an earnings-sharing plan was instituted and phased in, there would be tremendous administrative problems and difficulties in explaining the program to the public (in a system which is already having troubles with public relations).

The earnings-sharing proposals would result in giving higher benefits to two-worker families by *reducing* the benefits for one-worker families. In some ways, this could be viewed as taking benefits away from men to give them to women. However, in actuality, what is involved is taking benefits away from certain women (traditional homemakers) and giving them to other women (married women working in the paid labor market).

Some might say that such a result would be good, while others would say that this would be bad. In my opinion, if one group is to be favored over another (but not to an unfairly great extent), it should be the traditional homemaker, because otherwise we *may* be endangering the familial structure of the nation and its future development. And, once again, I question whether we should care so much about apparent individual equity in a social-insurance program that we create divisive situations of benefit losses. I strongly believe that any

resulting gain in individual equity is not worth the loss, especially a loss bound to shake the public's confidence in the viability and integrity of the system. If the OASDI system had just now been initiated, it might have been possible to develop a satisfactory earnings-sharing plan. However, with OASDI having been in operation for over 40 years, it just is "not possible to get from here to there!"

Some have said that earnings sharing would eliminate the alleged demeaning nature of the present program. I fail to see any difference in this respect between getting *earnings credits* from a spouse's earnings record and getting *benefit rights* from a spouse's earnings record. Some might point out that, in the case of divorces, the earnings credits would always be available under earnings sharing, but that benefit rights would not be if the marriages lasted less than 10 years. The answer to this, essentially, is that such a requirement should be reduced to 5 years (the House version of the 1977 amendments). The absence of deferred-benefit rights for very short marriages broken by divorce does not seem vital, because the individuals involved will almost certainly obtain OASDI benefit rights in other ways.

Concern has also been expressed over the unfair treatment of homemakers under OASDI. It has been argued that homemakers should receive earnings credits for their home work which reflects the value of the services they render, because the present basis of OASDI benefits as "dependents" is degrading. Although this proposal has considerable appeal, it involves insurmountable problems of administration and/or costs. If it is offered on a voluntary basis, few will elect it—and those who do so will be the high-cost cases (i.e., women who are near retirement age or who have eligible children and are in very poor health). If it is on a compulsory contributory basis, great difficulties will arise in devising an equitable method of determining the earnings to be attributed—and then also in collecting the applicable taxes, which could be heavy financial burdens for many families. If a homemaker-credit plan is on a compulsory non-contributory basis, with the credits financed from the general treasury, a large cost is involved.

Another proposal intended to solve the alleged discrimination of OASDI against women is the so-called double-decker approach. This is by no means new, having been discussed first some 40 years ago. A flat benefit would be paid to all persons who are eligible by reason of age or other demographic condition, to be financed from general revenues. The second deck would provide wage-related benefits, financed by payroll taxes.

Although there is a certain appeal to this approach, I do not favor it. Under some circumstances, the benefit level of the first deck could become too high, and thus too costly, because of the absence of fiscal constraints (such as are inherent in earmarked, highly visible payroll-tax financing). Under other circumstances, there might be pressures to make the first deck subject to a needs test, which would be undesirable because it would discourage private savings and private pension plans.

Solutions Through Incremental Change

Despite the foregoing discussion, I believe that certain changes should be made to alleviate the problems of homemakers under OASDI. These involve such matters as the distribution of OASDI benefits between spouses, more consistent and equitable treatment with regard to termination of benefits because of marriage or remarriage, and computing average earnings by taking into account child-care years.

At present, a retired worker and a spouse who has not worked in the paid labor market can receive, at their choice, either a combined benefit check or two separate ones. In the latter case, the amounts of the checks will not be equal, being larger for the retired worker than for the spouse. I propose that, when spouses are living together, the total family benefit amount should be divided equally between them. This would apply in all cases of retirement benefits when an auxiliary spouse benefit is payable, including those cases in which both spouses are eligible for benefits on their own earnings and those in which children's benefits are payable. There would, of course, be no cost effect on OASDI.

At present the marriage (or remarriage) of a beneficiary can in some instances terminate benefits. Marriage after age 60 is not a terminating event, and neither is marriage between two survivor beneficiaries. However, when a survivor beneficiary under age 60 marries a retired worker, the survivor benefit terminates, and any subsequent benefit eligibility is based on the benefit of the new spouse as long as that spouse is living. Also, when a young survivor beneficiary (with eligible child or children) marries any person (other than certain categories of beneficiaries), her or his benefit rights end. Considering that, currently, there are widely different ethical and moral views about living together without benefit of marriage, it is unfair to penalize those who hold to tradition. Accordingly, both marriage and remarriage should be eliminated as causes of termination of benefit rights. Such a change would have a favorable effect for others beside homemakers (e.g., child student beneficiaries). There would be the continuing cost control for OASDI in that individuals can, in essence, draw only the largest of any benefits to which they are entitled, so that overlapping of benefits will not occur.

Also, as mentioned previously, the duration-of-marriage requirement for a divorced spouse to be eligible for benefits on the earnings record of the insured worker should be reduced from 10 years to 5 years.

Persons who do not engage in paid gainful work while caring for their young children can be at a disadvantage under the present benefit-computation methods. This is so because the average earnings used in the calculations are determined over a long period. This period should be shortened somewhat by allowing "child-care drop-out years"—years to be skipped in making the calculation—for periods during which the individual takes full care of a preschool child at home or a child under age 16 in school. The number of child-care drop-out years should be limited to, say, 20 years. Thus, over the long run, the average earnings for retirement cases would be computed over not less than 15 years (and not more than 35 years, as at present).

A problem in connection with child-care drop-out years is how to define such years so that the provision can be properly administered and well understood by the public. It may perhaps be the case that, although the principle is good, it is not operable. In lieu thereof—but only partially solving the problem—the period for computing the AIME could be shortened somewhat (say, for retirement benefits, from 35 years ultimately to 25 or 30 years).

Provisions for child-care drop-out years are contained, to a limited extent, in P.L. 96-265, enacted on June 9, 1980 (which deals with changes in the DI program). This law *reduces* the normal drop-out years for computing the Primary Insurance Amount for disabled-worker cases from the previous uniform 5 years to less than this for persons disabled in the year in which age 46 is attained or in an earlier year (e.g., 4 years for ages 42-46, 3 years for ages 37-41, 2 years for ages 32-36, 1 year for ages 27-31, and none for ages 26 and under). Child-care years with respect to children under age 3 can be used to "build up" the drop-out years to a maximum of 3 years (i.e., this is applicable only to those disabled at ages 36 and under). A child-care year is defined as one in which a child under age 3 was living in the same household as the individual substantially throughout the entire year, during which time the individual did not engage in *any* outside employment.

Persons who are widowed before age 60 will probably be at a disadvantage, because the indexing of the deceased spouse's pension in the deferred period (from age at widowhood to age 60) is now by prices, rather than by wages. This could be remedied by indexing the deceased worker's earnings record by wages up to the earlier of (a) when the worker would have attained age 60; or (b) when the survivor beneficiary attains age 58. This will produce a larger widow's or widower's benefit and is quite logical. (Under the present unusual economic conditions, a larger benefit would not result—but it is to be hoped that such conditions will not prevail over the long run.)

If it is felt imperative to solve the putative "equity" problem between one-worker and two-worker families, the best approach is to provide an *additional* "working-spouse" benefit for the spouse who has the smaller primary benefit. This benefit would be 25% of the smaller of (a) the spouse's own primary benefit, or (b) the benefit coming from the other spouse's earnings record. This provision was contained in the Republican alternative bill put forth when the House of Representatives was considering the 1977 amendments. The principal drawback is that it involves substantial additional cost—an estimated long-range cost of approximately 0.8% of taxable payroll.

Conclusion

I have a moderate philosophy of social security. I hold that the existing program—and especially its scope and level of benefits—is more or less proper and adequate. In contrast, holders of an expansionist philosophy feel that the benefit level particularly should be increased significantly, so as to provide for the full economic needs of covered workers. The other extreme, the contractionist or laissez faire proponents, oppose governmental social insurance and support only a limited public assistance program. They feel that individuals should provide for their own economic security through the private sector (or at least have the opportunity of opting out of social security and using this alternative).

I believe that a moderate social security program is not just desirable, it is essential. Such a program must meet presumed social needs and therefore must be primarily based on principles of social adequacy rather than individual equity. This is the kind of social security program we now have.

There is no need for radical changes in the structure of the program to solve existing problems. In fact, many things which are seen as problems by some individuals are not really problems at all.

I realize that, in intellectual circles, the defense of the status quo is often assailed on the grounds that change is always desirable and that criticism is always constructive. However, change is not always necessarily beneficial, and even when it may be beneficial in some ways, the net effect produced may be harmful. Further, although those advocating radical change in the structure of social security may see the system's problems as serious, I believe the "solutions" examined in this volume would, on balance, be damaging to our whole social security system. Who can say that the repudiation of the Ten Commandments, which have borne the test of time, would be desirable for the sake of change?

QUESTIONS FOR WRITING, REFLECTION, AND DEBATE

1   What are the key differences between the American population as it is now in contrast to how the U.S. population was in 1935 when Social Security was first introduced? Should these differences call for changes in the Social Security system in the future?

2   Critics of Social Security argue that the program does not adequately help the least advantaged elderly. Imagine that you are a staff assistant to the U.S. Commissioner on Social Security and have been asked to prepare a memorandum on this issue. Write your memorandum and examine what the evidence is for, or against, this belief.

3   Sometimes those asking for elimination of the earnings test for Social Security argue that it is unfair to penalize them for being productive to society by continuing to work. After all, they have "earned" their Social Security benefits by prior contributions. What are the strengths and weaknesses of this argument?

4   Those who believe that it is wrong to have a large surplus in the Social Security Trust Fund say they are unhappy with the fact that money in the trust fund is invested in Treasury certificates. In that respect, they say, it simply funds the federal budget deficit. Is this claim correct? Are there alternatives to investing Social Security funds in Treasury certificates?

5   Imagine that you are chair of the United Taxpayers Association of America and your organization is about to take a position on the question of changing the payroll tax rate for Social Security. Prepare a draft version of the "position paper" you will offer to your membership to adopt. Outline in detail the reasons you think it is in the interest of taxpayers to keep the Social Security tax the way it is or to change it to a different level.

6 One proposal to make Social Security more fair to women is to give credit for the work mothers and housewives do at home. Is this proposal fair to women who work outside the home?

7 Imagine that you are president of the local chapter of the National Association of Women. Prepare a detailed statement to be the basis of a public petition campaign aiming to make Social Security more fair to women. Highlight the key arguments to be used to convince the public to sign the petition.

FOCUS ON PRACTICE: PRERETIREMENT PLANNING

We have seen that Social Security, despite its broad popularity, continues to be the subject of debates about its fairness and adequacy in providing retirement income to older Americans. Yet Social Security by itself was never intended to provide a complete source of income for people in retirement. It offers a "floor" to which other sources, such as savings and employer pensions, along with earnings from employment, may be added.

In the past, Social Security was a relatively clear and predictable source of income. But today the picture is more complicated for several reasons: (a) the age of eligibility for full Social Security benefits will gradually rise from 65 to 67 after 2010 (Shaver, 1991); (b) changes in tax laws mean that for some beneficiaries up to 85% of Social Security will be treated as taxable income; (c) with more defined contribution plans, pension income will be less predictable. As a result, retirement decisions demand a greater measure of self-reliance than in the past (Underwood, 1984).

The result of all these factors is that retirement in the years to come will involve more careful financial planning than it did in the past. Social Security benefits and private pensions, taken together, constitute a very important part of the assets of older people. One study found that, for three-quarters of men in their sixties, retirement income wealth from Social Security or pensions was greater than all other wealth, including even home equity (Quinn, 1985). Therefore decisions about retirement—such as assignment of pension survivor rights or choosing whether to accept an early retirement offer—constitute some of the most important financial decisions a person will make over the course of life.

Retirement itself has become a longer and more important part of the life course. In 1900 around 3% of an average man's lifetime was spent in the retirement years, but by 1980 that proportion had increased to 20%: between 10 to 30 years. For those who retire early, the number of years in retirement can even approach the number of years in the workforce. Yet while we prepare for the world of work through schooling, few people give comparable attention to planning or preparing for retirement.

Retirement does not simply signify empty time but can signify lifelong learning, travel, a second career, or opportunities for new roles such as volunteering. But taking advantage of opportunities and achieving secure retirement income demand a degree of planning and preparation. Herein lies the rationale for preretirement planning as an educational practice with benefits for both workers and employers.

Preretirement planning is becoming more and more common today. The National Council on Aging, AARP, and Retirement Advisors, Inc., are a few of the more prominent groups marketing their own retirement planning packages. Today, brokerage firms, outplacement consultants, and other financial groups are increasingly entering the field as well. A professional body, the International Association of Preretirement Planners, seeks to promote improved retirement education. The growth of interest in the field is illustrated by the increase in membership of that group from 150 in 1983 to more than 750 by the end of the decade.

Around a third of major corporations offer some kind of formal program to their workers for preretirement planning (Morrison and Jedriewski, 1988), but the proportion is probably higher among *Fortune* 500 companies. Current preretirement planning programs typically cover issues such as financial planning, housing options, use of leisure time, and adjustment to the retirement role. Participants may engage in clarification of their own values and also receive factual knowledge during a class that meets 12 to 16 hours over a period of weeks (Giordano and Giordano, 1983).

Some recent trends in preretirement planning include the following (Dennis, 1989):

- Individualized instruction and counseling
- Use of educational technology, such as computer software, to model financial decisions
- Attention to special needs of women in retirement
- Recognition of options for positive growth and productive aging, such as second careers and voluntarism

Despite this broadening of perspective and improvement of pedagogical method, however, unanswered questions remain. After three decades of experience with preretirement planning programs, it is now clear that there are major problems with preretirement planning as it currently exists. Some of these problems include the following:

(1) Low participation rate.   A study by AARP revealed that less than a quarter of workers over age 40 reported that their employers were offering any kind of preretirement planning program (American Association of Retired Persons, 1986). Most retirement planning programs are offered by large corporations, so those who are self-employed or work for small businesses are much less likely to participate. One study found that only 10% of those with access to preretirement planning actually participated in a program (Campione, 1988).

(2) Need for earlier planning. Employers fail to offer, and employees fail to acquire, preretirement planning information earlier in workers' careers. It is harder to start accumulating retirement savings if you begin at 60 than at 35.

(3) Reaching the least advantaged. Programs typically reach only the more educated and well-off older people for whom financial planning makes sense. But poor people need education about benefits and entitlements for which they may be eligible, particularly those forced to retire early because of ill health. Minority group members report that preretirement planning is not relevant to their needs and concerns (Torres-Gil, 1984). Early retirement among minorities, instead of being a sign of wealth, is often a sign of disability (Stanford, Happersett, and Morton, 1991).

(4) Vulnerability of older workers. Early retirement incentive plans are increasingly being used as a tool for staff reduction and "downsizing" by major corporations. It is not unusual for older workers to be forced to make irrevocable choices under a tight deadline and with minimum information or help in planning. In these circumstances, educating and protecting the rights of older workers becomes of paramount concern. Choices about work and retirement reflect the cumulative advantage or disadvantage experienced by workers of different social classes over the course of a lifetime (Crystal, Shea, and Krishnaswami, 1992).

In summary, it is clear that preretirement planning has established itself as a valuable educational strategy for helping older people achieve greater security in and control over their lives. But preretirement planning and consumer education continue to be limited to the more advantaged older workers. By itself, preretirement planning cannot change the distribution of power or wealth, nor can it create new opportunities for the last stage of life. Thinking about these questions demands a more far-reaching assessment of the role of work and retirement in later life.

Suggested Readings

Achenbaum, W. Andrew, *Social Security: Visions and Revisions*, 1985.
Kohler, Peter A., et al. (eds.), *The Evolution of Social Insurance, 1881-1981*, New York: Cambridge University Press, 1986.

Marmor, Theodore R., and Mashaw, Jerry L. (eds.) *Social Security: Beyond the Rhetoric of Crisis*, Princeton, NJ: Princeton University Press, 1988.

Myers, Robert J., *Social Security* (3rd ed.), Homewood, IL: Richard D. Irwin, Inc., 1985.

U.S. Department of Health and Social Services, *Social Security Handbook*, Washington, DC, 1988.

Does Retirement Make Sense?

In all industrialized countries since World War II, there has been a decline in labor force participation among older men and women. Does that trend represent progress or is it a sign of problems (Schnore, 1985)? For society, this steady decline in labor force participation represents a loss of productivity by older people, a group who, on average, are living longer, are better educated, and are in better health than ever before. Individuals who withdraw from the workforce often face many years without any clearly defined purpose in society (Sheppard, 1990). As the cost of Social Security and private pensions continues to rise, it is understandable that people are asking whether retirement makes sense.

But the question: "Does retirement make sense?" is actually two different questions. First is the question of whether retirement is a sensible or wise choice for some specific individual, for example, a person who is considering taking early retirement, which is an option to retire before some conventional age for retirement. Second, there is the question of whether the systematic practice of retirement in our society is good policy; that is, is it a practice that makes sense for the economy or the good of society as a whole (Blau, 1985)?

Retirement, as Rosow (1967) observed, means entering a "roleless role." It signifies the withdrawal of individuals from work during the later period of life. Whether a person reduces his workload gradually or stops working abruptly, retirement often leads to new options in later life: leisure pursuits, voluntary action, part-time employment, even a second career. Typically, retirement is accompanied by reliance on pension income instead of salary as the primary means of support. In the previous discussion of preretirement planning, we stressed the importance of individual decision making. To put the emphasis on individual differences here is certainly valid. But that emphasis fails to take into account an important point: namely, that people of any age have a personal choice about retiring only if they can count on enough income to support themselves without working. A younger person who wins the lottery might have that choice, but for most people retirement is not an option until much later in life. For some middle-aged or older workers, the source of retirement income is an adequate pension provided by an employer. Other people can choose to retire only if there is a social or institutional policy to support the choice: that is, to pay those no longer in the workforce. In that respect, retirement is very much an issue for public policy debate (Munnell, 1991).

That point leads to the second question about whether American society in the future *ought* to continue the familiar kind of retirement policy that has become common in the post-World War II period (Clark, 1988). As we saw in debates about generational equity and the future of Social Security, critics have raised disturbing questions about whether in the coming century we as a society can or ought to maintain retirement as we have known the practice in the past. That questioning has already resulted in some important changes; for example, in 1986 the common practice of mandatory retirement was abolished by law and in the future the age of eligibility for Social Security will rise from 65 to 67. In this discussion, we will look at how retirement as an institution has evolved up to the present and then review some of the concerns put forward by those who doubt whether retirement makes sense for the future.

Today, people tend to take retirement for granted and assume it is a natural and appropriate pattern for later life. But in fact retirement as a social practice or institution is historically quite recent. We need to understand the origins of retirement as an institution and to better appreciate how work and retirement are now being transformed by changes in the American economy. Instead of taking for granted retirement as a natural phase of life, we need to consider current trends that will determine what work and retirement may mean in the twenty-first century.

History of Retirement

Widespread retirement by workers only became possible after the industrial revolution of the nineteenth century. It was Prussian Chancellor Otto von Bismarck who first introduced age 65 as the basis for a pension. By the early twentieth century, many European countries began to institutionalize retirement through government pension systems. The United States followed with Social Security in 1935, a development that made leaving the labor force much more attractive to people. For example, in 1890 68% of men over 65 were in the labor force. But that number dropped to 54% in 1930. In 1950, after improvements in Social Security, it dropped further to 46% and has continued to decline to 17% in 1989. Table 7.1 and Figure 7.1 show the major trends over the past 40 years.

Several points are clear from the data presented. First, beyond age 65, the overwhelming majority of both men and women are retired from work,

Table 7.1. Civilian Labor Force Participation Rates for Older People, by Age and Sex: 1950-1989 (annual averages)

Year	Men 55 to 64	Men 65+	Women 55 to 64	Women 65+	Total 55 to 64	Total 65+
1950	86.9	45.8	27.0	9.7	56.7	26.7
1955	87.9	39.6	32.5	10.6	59.5	24.1
1960	86.8	33.1	37.2	10.8	60.9	20.8
1965	84.6	27.9	41.1	10.0	61.9	17.8
1970	83.0	26.8	43.0	9.7	61.8	17.0
1975	75.6	21.6	40.9	8.2	57.2	13.7
1980	72.1	19.0	41.3	8.1	55.7	12.5
1985	67.9	15.8	42.0	7.3	54.2	10.8
1989	67.2	16.6	45.0	8.4	55.5	11.8

SOURCE: 1950-1980 data: U.S. Department of Labor, Bureau of Labor Statistics (1985); 1985 data: U.S. Department of Labor, Bureau of Labor Statistics (1986); 1989 data: U.S. Department of Labor, Bureau of Labor Statistics (1990).

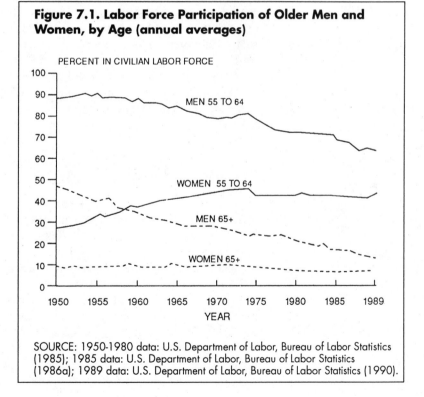

Figure 7.1. Labor Force Participation of Older Men and Women, by Age (annual averages)

SOURCE: 1950-1980 data: U.S. Department of Labor, Bureau of Labor Statistics (1985); 1985 data: U.S. Department of Labor, Bureau of Labor Statistics (1986a); 1989 data: U.S. Department of Labor, Bureau of Labor Statistics (1990).

though a small minority continues in the labor force. Second, among older men, the trend has clearly been away from work and toward retirement, and the decline in labor force participation applies equally to men in their fifties. Early retirement has become a major phenomenon in its own right (Dworaczek and Wong, 1989). Third, for women over age 65, labor force participation has not changed much in recent years. In fact, women in the 55 to 64 age bracket have counteracted the male trend in that they have joined the work force in larger numbers. The earlier discussion of gender and aging illuminates some reasons for these contrasting trends. Older men tend to have earned higher pension and Social Security benefits, while older women must face a longer life span with lower average income expectations.

What is the cause of the trends that are identified here? Some insight comes from one of the first major longitudinal studies of work and retirement, the Cornell Study of Occupational Retirement carried out between 1952 and 1962 (Streib and Schneider, 1971). That study helped challenge previously accepted but mistaken beliefs, such as the idea that retirement has a negative effect on people's health or that it causes feelings of worthlessness. The Cornell study did not find evidence supporting the idea that retirement causes ill health; yet that notion continues to persist (Ekerdt, 1987). The study did document a drop in cash income upon retirement but a large majority of retirees still reported that their income was sufficient, and around a quarter even felt their standard of living was better than earlier. Overall, the Cornell study clearly showed that retirement is not at all a negative event for most people, and subsequent studies have confirmed its main findings (Palmore et al., 1985; Parnes et al., 1985). These results help explain the trend toward earlier retirement seen in the figures cited above. Older people retire for many different reasons, but we should not overlook the growing appeal of retirement leisure as a desirable option.

Origins of Late Life Leisure

Retirement has come to mean an expansion of leisure time in the last stage of life. But leisure can be defined in different ways. Here it is important to emphasize that leisure should be viewed not merely in a negative sense as time away from work but as free time perceived in a positive sense and containing opportunities for recreation, relaxation, personal development, and service to others (Kaplan, 1979).

Retirement as a form of leisure is only possible with a certain degree of wealth. From a historical standpoint, widespread retirement first became possible when the industrial economy was productive enough to support sizable numbers of nonworking adults. At the same time, the economy no longer needed so many workers in the labor force and companies believed that older workers were not as quick or as productive as the young. Governments, corporations, labor unions, and older workers themselves found retirement to be a desirable policy and it soon became the normal practice (Graebner, 1980).

Since 1900 the average life expectancy for Americans has risen from around 47 years to 76 years today. With longer lives, people have spent increased time in education, work, and retirement. But when we look at the different uses of time over the life course during the twentieth century, it is clear that the most significant trend has been the growth in the amount of leisure time spent in retirement. Table 7.2 shows how time use has changed in this century.

Table 7.2. Life Cycle Distribution of Education, Labor Force Participation, Retirement, and Work in the Home: 1900-1980

	Year					
Subject	1900	1940	1950	1960	1970	1980
Number of years spent in activity:						
Men						
Average life expectancy	46.3	60.8	65.6	66.6	67.1	70.0
Retirement/work at home	1.2	9.1	10.1	10.2	12.1	13.6
Labor force participation	32.1	38.1	41.5	41.1	37.8	38.8
Education	8.0	8.6	9.0	10.3	12.2	12.6
Preschool	5.0	5.0	5.0	5.0	5.0	5.0
Women						
Average life expectancy	48.3	65.2	71.1	73.1	74.7	77.4
Retirement/work at home	29	39.4	41.4	37.1	35.3	30.6
Labor force participation	6.3	12.1	15.1	20.1	22.3	29.4
Education	8.0	8.7	9.6	10.9	12.1	12.4
Preschool	5.0	5.0	5.0	5.0	5.0	5.0
Percentage distribution by activity type:						
Men						
Average life expectancy	100	100	100	100	100	100
Retirement/work at home	3	15	15	15	18	19
Labor force participation	69	63	63	62	56	55
Education	17	14	14	15	18	18
Preschool	11	8	8	8	7	8
Women						
Average life expectancy	100	100	100	100	100	100
Retirement/work at home	60	60	58	51	47	40
Labor force participation	13	19	21	27	30	38
Education	17	13	14	15	16	16
Preschool	10	8	7	7	7	6

SOURCE: U.S. Bureau of the Census (1984—median years of school for persons 25 years or older, 1940-1980); Best (1981, p. 8—1900 estimates of median years of school for persons 25 years or older); National Center for Health Statistics (1990a—life expectancy data); U.S. Department of Labor, Bureau of Labor Statistics (1986b).
NOTE: Data may not add to 100 percent due to rounding.

The figures in Table 7.2 show that, while life expectancy increased by just over 50% since 1900, the period spent in retirement increased dramatically. Work now accounts for a smaller percentage of a man's life than it did in the year 1900. By contrast, for women, the big change has been a dramatic increase in the number of years spent in the paid workforce. But for both men and women, years in retirement constitute a larger and growing portion of life.

How did this pattern come to be? Free time, along with higher wages, was always a potential by-product of industrialization and economic progress. But there always exist trade-off choices: free time versus higher wages. In this century until the 1930s, the workweek and the workday gradually became shorter throughout the industrialized world. Subsequently, free time has also spread, but it has not come from reduction of the workweek. Instead, free time has taken different forms over the life cycle: increased vacation time but above all later entry into the workforce for the young and earlier retirement for the old (Hunnicutt, 1982).

In the 1920s, there was actually a "shorter hours movement," which still remains an unexplored chapter in liberal reform movements of this century. The shorter hours movement of the 1920s was followed by the "share-the-work" plan during the depression. Instead of a consumer society, these critics favored shorter working hours and more leisure as a vehicle for self-development. This goal of self-development favored by reformers had much in common with ideas that would later be advocated by writers such Fred Best, Willard Wirtz, Gosta Rehn, Max Kaplan, and others. They are among those who have advocated work sharing, flextime, phased retirement, worker sabbaticals, recurrent education, lifelong learning, and life cycle planning. When we ask: "Does retirement, as it currently exists, make sense?" we are asking whether that humanistic goal of self-development is still a possibility. That debate has barely begun.

In the past, economic forces quickly foreclosed any debate. During the 1920s, influential leaders of American business saw a combined threat to economic prosperity from overproduction and spreading leisure time. These leaders were pessimistic. They feared that consumer markets were becoming oversaturated and that workers would take rising productivity in the form of free time rather than continuing to work. Declining working hours along with declining production spelled declining profits and slowed economic growth. The leisure of the working man was seen as a threat. Against this view were the "optimists" who argued that consumption demands could be driven higher, primarily through advertising and marketing techniques to stimulate new purchasing power.

In fact, it was the consumer view that triumphed, as the emergence of the Affluent Society in America after World War II came to testify. But the consumer society of rising demand and stable working hours was supported in turn by actions of the government itself. The stimulus for government action came, of course, in the Great Depression. With the New Deal and World War II, the American government took on new responsibility for managing the economy to moderate the business cycle and ensure aggregate demand. These were the principal achievements of Keynesian economics in its heyday.

The passage of the Social Security Act, and later the spread of private pensions, marked the ratification of the institution of a fixed retirement age, typically age 65. Based on public policy, leisure would be displaced into later life, while enlarging the period of education in early life, presumably as preparation for work. Purchasing power for goods and services would be maintained by transfer payments—Social Security—disbursed in such a fashion as to keep older people out of the labor market. Work would then be compressed into the middle period of life.

With the establishment of a standard 40-hour week by 1945, the movement toward a shorter workweek lost popularity. Productivity gains were channeled into higher wages and fringe benefits; free time gains were channeled into longer vacations and, above all, earlier retirement. Free time available in old age has increased by about five years during the twentieth century, chiefly from gains in life expectancy but also from earlier retirement.

The spread of leisure in retirement is related to a debate about Social Security: namely, the earnings limitation. The earnings test shows that Social Security's function was always in part to remove older workers from the labor market, and the earnings test has indeed had this effect. Because Social Security always had the intention of removing people from the labor force, there are those who suggest that retirement is somehow forced on people and therefore is not really leisure (Hunnicutt, 1982, p. 103).

This view reflects a debatable assumption that work is desirable and meaningful for the majority of people. But in fact just the opposite seems true (Terkel, 1985). Most people are eager to leave their jobs and, contrary to a popular stereotype, retirement is not dangerous to one's health. What is wrong with retirement is not that work is always better but that the abundance of free time in late life is not adequately structured for any larger social purpose or meaning. Except for displaced workers or elite groups who leave their jobs reluctantly, people generally prefer to retire rather than continue working at jobs that are unsatisfying (Boaz, 1987).

Overall, then, most people applaud the fact that the amount of time devoted to leisure and recreation activities has increased in America during this century. The average workday and workweek have dropped, longer vacations have become common, and early retirement has become a common practice. But there are a few dark clouds on this pleasant horizon. First is a phenomenon sometimes described as "the overworked American." A larger segment of the population has been drawn into paid work as more and more married women have entered the labor force and as many workers take on second jobs to maintain their standard of living (Schor, 1991). One result of that trend is that people have less time for volunteer activities of all kinds.

Second, there has been a recent decline in the percentage of workers enrolled in pension plans. If that trend continues, it throws into doubt whether future cohorts of older people will enjoy early retirement at levels comparable to those today (McGoldrick and Copper, 1989). Third, there are concerns about the base of economic productivity that supports a sizable old age population devoted to leisure pursuits (Kleiler, 1978; Koretz, 1992). These concerns range from the future financing for Social Security to international economic competitiveness and the quality of the present and future workforce (Fogarty, 1982).

Changes in the American Economy

The idea of the three boxes of life, including a secure and predictable period of retirement, has always depended on an economic foundation. But the American economy is in the midst of far-reaching changes that will affect what retirement looks like in the future. Since the early 1980s, the U.S. economy has lost more than 5 million jobs, and the trend continued with the prolonged recession of the early 1990s. These changes in the job market were not simply part of the familiar back-and-forth swing of the business cycle. Instead, job losses reflect a long-range trend as thousands of companies engage in "downsizing," permanently letting go of employees, including white-collar and management jobs. Some labor market specialists estimate that in the 1990s a quarter of the U.S. workforce is still threatened by downsizing (Sherman, 1993). A new postindustrial American economy accompanied by international competition has reshaped American society (Eitzen and Baca-Zinn, 1988).

From a human resources point of view, the biggest change is the loss of security or predictability in the labor market: a change that has serious consequences for middle-aged or older workers. In the first place, such older workers face a leveling off in their careers as they compete for a diminishing number of good jobs (Morgan, 1981). Still worse, when companies downsize and eliminate middle-management positions, older workers find themselves pushed aside. Others opt for early retirement rather than face unemployment. In the early 1990s, blue chip corporations such as IBM, General Motors, and Sears were drastically cutting their workforces. Increasingly, big companies can no longer guarantee employment or a predictable work life based on the patterns of the past.

This volatility of the labor market is harder for older workers to cope with than it is for younger workers. Older workers have lower unemployment rates than younger workers, but when older workers are displaced from work it takes much longer to find another job. Many give up trying and become "discouraged workers"; that is, they are not even counted as part of the official unemployment rate. Others declare themselves "retired," so that retirement itself becomes a disguised form of unemployment. Indeed, one of the prime reasons for adopting the Social Security system in the United States during the Depression was to reduce the level of official unemployment by creating a way of drawing older people out of the labor market and thus opening up jobs for young people.

Looking at the labor force as a whole, long-range changes are clearly visible. In 1979 total manufacturing jobs constituted 23% of the labor force, but by 1992 the proportion had shrunk to 17%. Meanwhile, jobs in the service sector rose from 19% to 27% (U.S. Department of Labor, 1993, reported in Uchitelle, 1993). But the service sector jobs on average paid substantially less and offered fewer benefits than older jobs in manufacturing. Job growth is increasingly found not in big corporations but in small companies that can move quickly and flexibly. Typically the new jobs are much less likely to offer full fringe benefits or pension coverage. Indeed, the proportion of American workers covered by pensions peaked at around 50% in the late 1980s and has been in decline since then, thus raising the ominous prospect that future cohorts may not enter retirement with the same level of private pension support enjoyed by retirees today.

Furthermore, in recent years, the pattern of retirement income has been changing. During the 1950s and 1960s, the most common type of retirement programs were defined benefit programs that guaranteed to pay a specified level of income in retirement. In the 1980s, this guaranteed approach to retirement income has begun to change in two ways: First, fewer employers offered pensions as part of a fringe benefit package. Second, there is a trend toward defined contribution plans in all major industrial sectors and for all firms with pension plans. This trend may reduce the effects of an aging workforce by reducing barriers to job mobility for older workers (Clark, 1990). Displaced workers or others who wanted to move to new jobs would not lose pension coverage by doing so.

When we look at government, we see the same long-standing pattern of incentives for moving older employees out of the labor force (Quinn, 1990). But there is a serious question about whether that practice is financially sustainable in the future. The most striking example is military personnel, who can retire after 20 years of service and receive half of their salary for the remainder of their lives. Between 1960 and 1976, military retirement benefits increased from 6% to 25% of the total U.S. military budget, reflecting increased numbers of war veterans. These military commitments amount to nearly half of the federal government's pension debts, and the Pentagon expects to spend an increasing amount to fund these pensions. Estimates are that the cost will grow from just over $11 billion in 1992 to $296 billion by 2041.

Similar patterns of early retirement are common for state and local government, especially for police and firefighters. State and local governments, faced with budget problems, have begun using early retirement as a staff reduction technique. Early retirement gives short-term savings but turns out to be a very expensive proposition in the long run. There are now large costs extending into the future for inadequately funded pension plans of state and municipal governments. The same problems occur on both the local and the national levels. Federal civil service pension plans other than for the military are underfunded by more than $1 trillion. The Pension Benefit Guaranty Corporation now insures the private pensions of 40 million American workers. But unfunded liabilities—promises without money to support them—have been growing astronomically. Some observers fear that unfunded pension coverage could be the next "savings and loan" financial disaster in the making.

The American economy, whether in government or private industry, has found retirement a convenient practice for managing the labor force (Schulz, 1988). On the positive side, widespread retirement has meant an expansion of leisure and opportunities for self-fulfillment in later life. On the negative side, the practice of retirement entails large costs, both in funding required for pension systems and also in the loss of the accumulated skills and talents of older people.

Critics of retirement as it exists today have pointed to the rigidity of retirement practices: for example, the fact that retirement is typically an all-or-nothing proposition. Would it not be better to have some form of flexible or phased retirement, in which employees gradually reduce their work hours or take longer vacations? Such an approach might enable older workers to adjust better to retirement, while permitting employers to make gradual changes instead of coping with the abrupt departure of an employee. Retirement could be radically redefined in the future (Schmahl, 1989).

Earlier criticism of mandatory retirement at a fixed age led to legal abolition of the practice, for the most part, in 1986. The same kind of criticism has been leveled at the practice of age discrimination in employment (Levine, 1989). The Age Discrimination in Employment Act forbids older workers from being limited or treated in any way that would harm their employment possibilities. Still, most observers admit that age discrimination in the workplace remains widespread (Montgomery, 1991). The negative stereotypes of older workers have caused employers to be reluctant to hire or train older people (Yankelovich, 1986). Sometimes such discrimination against older workers is based on mistaken ideas, such as the false belief that older workers are less productive. In fact, empirical studies have not shown older workers to be less dependable in their job performance, nor are their absenteeism rates higher (Stagner, 1985).

Interest in the potential productivity of older workers has stimulated the growth of industrial gerontology, a field concerned with recruitment, performance appraisal, retraining, and redesign of jobs to permit older workers to be more productive (Marbach, 1968; Rhine, 1984). Managing an older workforce will clearly be a challenge for the future (Dennis, 1988). There is also much support for the idea of work life extension: that is, adaptations of retirement rules or employment practices to enable older people to become more productive (Doering, Rhodes, and Schuster, 1983). In favor of this idea is the fact that three-quarters of employed people over 65 are in white-collar occupations in service industries, which are less physically demanding than agriculture or manufacturing jobs. As a result, it is sometimes argued, older people can remain in productive jobs now longer than in the past. In addition, some analysts point to declining numbers of young people entering the work-force, thus anticipating a labor shortage later in the 1990s. That development, if it occurred, might stimulate a need for older workers and a reversal of the trend toward early retirement (Clark and Barker, 1981).

Against this prediction, however, there is the fact that the U.S. economy has lost jobs even while it was coming out of recession in the early 1990s. The much-anticipated labor shortage has not materialized and the shape of the labor market of the year 2000 remains a matter of much debate (Johnson et al., 1987). In any case, there is the continuing movement toward a postindustrial economy in which information systems and telecommunication technology bring rapid shifts in methods of production: for example, widespread reliance on computers and word processing in office jobs. Without retraining, it is hard to see how older people will be in a position to take up jobs that might become available in the future.

Finally, there is a question about whether this concern with work life extension is a valid concern for either older people or society as a whole. Why shouldn't the economic surplus from improved productivity be taken in the form of leisure time either over the course of life or in retirement years? The assumption that old age is unsatisfactory unless people continue to work seems an uncritical application of the work ethic that originally inspired capitalist ideology, as sociologist Max Weber first argued. While those older people who love their work may find that outlook compelling, the declining labor force participation rate for most older people does not speak in favor of work as more desirable than alternatives. A substantial body of literature in gerontology suggests that late life leisure has important meaning and de-serves attention as an activity in its own right (Kleemeier, 1961; Teague and MacNeil, 1992). The question: "Does retirement make sense?" cannot be given a clear answer unless we understand what the alternatives are now or might be in the future. That is one reason the question remains subject to debate.

In the readings that follow, we hear different voices in that debate. Robert Morris and Scott Bass argue that under today's new conditions we are obliged to think again about the meaning of retirement and, in particular, to design social institutions that can make use of the contributive capacity of older people. Steven Sandell, an experienced labor economist, turns the debate in a different direction by focusing on economic facts and trends. What will be the supply of and demand for older workers during the 1990s and beyond?

Does a policy to promote work life extension for older people make sense under these labor market conditions?

Making better use of the talents of older people would represent a new social policy goal for American society. In their article, Rhonda Montgomery and her colleagues remind us that all social policies depend on shared assumptions and values. What are these assumptions and values? On the positive side, older workers may be considered entitled to a justified reward in the form of retirement leisure. On the negative side, older workers may be considered useless or less valuable than younger workers. It is interesting that both the positive and the negative assumptions just cited would probably lead us to encourage early departure from the labor force by older people. But both assumptions can be called into question, and different social policies might result. As we think about alternative social policies, we want to ask especially about the relevance of chronological age. A 30-year-old who is uninterested in working might be judged "lazy." But a 70-year-old with the same outlook might be judged "retired."

Age is not the only factor involved in the value judgments we make. A key assumption in debates about work and retirement is the idea that people are somehow ethically better if they continue to be active and productive. In fact, this moral valuation of work and productivity has deep roots in American culture in the Puritan ethic: the idea that hard work is a virtue in itself. David Ekerdt's article highlights what he calls the "busy ethic" and shows that for many Americans both work and retirement are characterized by the same style of activity and productive engagement, whether in a paid job or not. But the "busy ethic" is not the only image of human fulfillment. Nancy Osgood's article provides us with a historical view of how the concept of leisure has changed over the centuries. Just as paid work is not the only form of productivity, so recreation or relaxation are not the only forms that leisure might take. Down through the ages, philosophers and social thinkers have dreamed about what a society might look like if the burden of work were lifted from humankind. Today, that dream has come to pass. In the twentieth century, with mass retirement as a normal social institution, we have been witnessing an experiment in what happens when vast numbers of people are given leisure in their later years. The experiment goes on and the results are debatable. In fact, controversies about work and leisure demonstrate that we have not yet agreed upon the key social values at stake when we consider the question: "Does retirement make sense?"

Toward a New Paradigm About Work and Age

Robert Morris and Scott A. Bass

The late twentieth century is witness to a rapidly maturing American society, the consequences of which are not yet fully realized. For some years the phrase "the graying of America" has been popular, referring to the growing numbers of older citizens; but the phrase does not clarify the major change in the fabric of American society and culture that the concept of maturing entails. For the most part Americans are still influenced by the relative youthfulness of their nation. They share a confidence that the frontiers of opportunity are still wide open and the belief that their destiny will continue to be unique. This helps explain the continuing buoyancy, changeability, and cultural experimentation that have made us the envy of so many in less privileged parts of the world.

This openness to social change and experimentation is seen in our resilience in coping with new patterns of family life, sexual mores, and relationships. But our economic views are slower to change; in this area, static nineteenth-century concepts prevail. Prime examples are the beliefs that the Industrial Revolution made work by older people either unnecessary or undesirable and that by age 60 individual abilities decline too much to fit into a fast-moving world. In reality, however, the abilities and capacities of older people have im-

proved dramatically over the past 100 years. This has created a tension between the popular views about the need for workers and about when people want to or should retire. This tension in the economic sphere, in turn, may propel us into new and unfamiliar forms of economic as well as social relationships with widespread repercussions.

One way of approaching this subject is to consider the common beliefs about who belongs in the labor pool. In the nineteenth century all males from perhaps age 12 to death or decrepitude were considered potential workers, as were young girls and women until marriage. Married women were not encouraged to work. Beginning in the late nineteenth century the labor pool was constricted by child labor laws and the belief that more education was needed in an industrial nation; the pool slowly shrank to those between ages 14 (and then 16, and then 18) and old age. Pensions began to fix the upper end of the pool at around age 65, which fit the physical realities of the times. The consequences were obscured by the vast influx of immigrants who were absorbed into the labor pool. In times of war, when many males were absent from work, women increasingly began to find permanent places in the labor force.

After World War II the components of the labor force settled into the age range 18 or 22 to 65. Up to half of college-aged youth entered college, which became a prerequisite for economic advancement. The labor force was further depleted by the largest standing army in American history: between 2 and 3 million men plus a large number

Source: "Toward a New Paradigm About Work and Age" by R. Morris and S. A. Bass from *Retirement Reconsidered: Economic and Social Roles for Older People*, edited by R. Morris and S. Bass, 1988, pp. 3-4, 7-14. Used by permission of Springer Publishing Company, Inc., New York, 10012.

in civilian support positions. An improved economy encouraged many workers to begin retirement as early as age 62 or 60. The labor shortfall was filled by married women entering the workplace in very large numbers.

This oversimplified excursion into the past suggests that our ideas about who belongs in the workforce are quite malleable; they respond to forces we understand only imperfectly and can identify only after the fact. The retirement age has remained relatively fixed, although the physical and intellectual vigor of the elderly has so improved that the physiological and psychological age for removal from an economic role is probably better set at 75 than 65. From a nineteenth-century workforce of males aged 16 to 70 with relatively few women, heavy immigration, and a small standing army, we went to a mid-twentieth-century workforce aged 18 to 62 with many women, a large standing army, and controlled immigration. The world of the early twenty-first century may consist of a workforce made up of adults between the ages of 24 and 70 or 75. In such a context, work for a large number of 65-to-75 year olds is not improbable.

Industrial Change: Beginnings of Surplus Labor and Leisure

During the 19th century, the Industrial Revolution gained momentum. While there were mass dislocations of people, and laborers were not treated kindly, the net effect over time was to increase the demand for labor. The aged were not given special attention, except through the Poor Laws and the poorhouses and asylums developed under those laws. This same pattern carried over to America. Respectable American opinion in the nineteenth and early twentieth centuries held that there was work for all who would work, and personal or family charity for those who could not, including the displaced aged. The fact that, periodically at least, there were conditions when labor power was in surplus, when there were more adults than the economy required, was ignored. Work to the end

of one's days was an economic and socially imposed standard.

By 1900, Simon Patten, professor of economics at the Wharton School, developed the thesis that America was entering a period when all people's needs could be met with less and less manpower. He anticipated a time when there would be an excess of labor, when working time could be drastically reduced, and when adults would have large amounts of leisure time at their disposal. His concern with this coming situation was focused on how to prepare people psychologically for a constructive social use of the new leisure. In many ways he was a prophet of the view that our 20th-century economy would be one with many "surplus" people, at least in relation to the production of goods.

During most of these centuries, the aged as a group did not play a central role in the evolution of ideas beyond those of the original biblical injunctions: work and family obligations. However, with the twentieth century the capacity of the American economy to produce more goods with less labor was matched by a major change in the demographic nature of its population. Life expectancy grew rapidly as infant mortality declined. Other improvements in health care meant that the elderly became not only more numerous but more healthy, vigorous, and able-bodied. The first policy approach to this evolution was the enactment by many states of old age pension laws and, during the Depression of the 1930s, the national Social Security Act with its provision for almost universal retirement income. Public policy provided an income base to help the no-longer-needed older worker leave the labor force.

Change in the Late Twentieth Century

An income-oriented economic approach was welcomed by all at first as solving most problems of old age. But by the 1970s, several probing questions had been raised by quite different interest groups. For advocates of the elderly, the absence of significant roles to which the nonworking, retired aged could move if they wished led to demands that forced retirement at 65 be abandoned. The same groups began to search for alternative meaningful roles for the able aged, especially as retirement incomes encouraged earlier retirement at 62, 60, or even 55. By now, many of the aged were too vigorous to be comfortable doing nothing. This led to rapid growth in education for personal enrichment in retirement and to many new ways to use leisure time, such as by travel and sports. At the same time, the goods-producing dynamism of a consumer society left many significant functions ill attended to. A growing concern with self-gratification produced so strong a dislike for taxation as a way to help the sick and disadvantaged that many public services that characterize a modern industrial society, including health and welfare, began to suffer labor shortages.

To make the contemporary picture even more confused, family functions changed. The driving economy found uses for so many young and middle-aged adult women that the functions once performed by wives at home shifted to restaurants, laundries, and the like, creating a demand for more low-paid workers.

The increase in single-parent working families and families with two working parents increased exponentially the demand for childcare services. However, the older social functions of grandparenting had also been eroded as aged parents established their independent lives apart from their children. This did not produce a break in family psychic and social ties, but it meant less inclination for family members to provide care for children, the sick, and the feeble aged and to perform other household duties as a family obligation. The interaction among these forces is too complex to elaborate here. Suffice it to note that while the aged were no longer so necessary for the goods producing economy, the community and welfare service economy did not directly benefit from the large new surplus labor created by a tradition of early retirement and independent life for the elderly.

By the 1970s economic concerns began to arise about the growing dependency ratio, with the fear that it would create an unbearable burden on the shrinking workforce.

While there is argument about the existence of this dependency shift, its iteration exemplifies the new concern with economic roles for the aged, which matches the concern about the social roles of grandparenting, consumption, or leisure. It captures an interlocking set of concerns about family responsibility, intergenerational obligation, productivity, and taxation; it is reconsidered below at some length.

In the 1980s public perception about the elderly began to shift, especially at the level of national policy making. Retirement with security, even comfort, became a divisive issue in debate over the use of national resources and government budget allocations. More and more the elderly are being viewed from a labor and manpower perspective: those who are made redundant by industry at age 50 or 55 and those who retire voluntarily at age 60 or 65 are seen as surplus labor who may have a role to play if the national economy is not stagnant. But what role? The many unanswered questions that are raised with increasing persistence have the potential for challenging many traditional ways of organizing national and local life.

A few examples can be identified. The threat of intergenerational conflict has arisen as various age groups argue their interests against others—advocates for children, for example, claiming the elderly benefit too generously under present laws. Such conflict, if it really grows, could endanger the sense of community and national solidarity on which public well-being depends. The Social Security Act, foundation for all social provision, was sustained by a consensus now threatened by the conflict.

There is widespread discussion over the best ways to use increased productivity: whether workers should consume more leisure or should work even harder to produce more goods. Workplace patterns are already shifting as new kinds of industry begin to replace heavy industry. Part-time and temporary work is increasing rapidly and in 1986 was estimated to represent 27% of all employment. Such work is often low-paid and insecure, carrying little or no social benefits such as health insurance. Better pay in better jobs demands more years of education or training. The increase in part-time work fits very well the needs and interests of many older and retired workers, but it also means less total annual income for workers so employed. This in turn encourages pressure to redistribute income through higher pay for less work, for everyone regardless of productivity.

The educational system faces a crisis in maintaining its position as the ratio of school and college-aged youth declines for a decade or two. One possible replacement for a dwindling young student body is the new population of elderly students, whose interests and patterns of activity do not fit the conventional educational patterns of most colleges and universities. Interests of the aged are also ambiguous and unsettled, sometimes leaning to cultural self-improvement, sometimes veering to training for a second career.

Finally, the pattern of family relationships and responsibilities seems to be changing as individuals seek to build family ties while at the same time living independent lives. This is especially unclear as policy makers debate the proper boundary for collective and governmental responsibility for children, the sick, and the aged as against family responsibility.

Employment patterns, changing income patterns over the life cycle, the uses of leisure consumption versus goods production, the function of the educational system, and patterns of family relationship are all being shaken up by the maturing of the society both demographically and economically. But this time we seem able to produce material goods without full use of all labor, a situation that did not exist in the past.

. . . [We] are aware that it is much easier to conceptualize a public issue than it is to act on it in a complex society. Those issues that we explore will not be easy to resolve. A mature society is one that also has its own rigidities of social, political, and economic organization to match the stiffening joints of personal old age. Employers and unions find it most difficult to change patterns of production and employment, especially when so much of that work must now compete with industry in other countries. Attitudes and ways of behaving are deeply ingrained. Even 50 years in which the elderly of an affluent society found it easy to retire from work to leisure is enough time to make it difficult to reconsider the conventional age of retirement as being too early, not too late. The psychological barrier or difficulty arises not only in free-market nations but also in planned economies, where the customary retirement age is already 55 to 60, lower than in the United States.

Future Scenarios

Despite these resistances to change, the authors believe that the scale of change that the new demography and the new economy combine to force is so urgent that we must look carefully at the available options. They are limited. We could visualize a world in which more and more people work less and less. That world would force us to confront most directly the meaning of living itself. If work is not needed (the very term may have to be redefined), what do people do with their lives?

Seek hedonistic pleasure? Engage in new active forms of social organization?—but to what ends? Seek to find fulfillment entirely (or nearly so) in family relationships alone? Try to remake the world? —but in what directions? And how will workers react to sharing income with the retired when the few can produce enough goods for all without more labor?

An alternative scenario would read that a surplus of people is temporary, that the labor of most people will be required to maintain the society we define for ourselves, and that this includes the aged who are now retired without work expectation. This approach requires that we consider the potential of technological change and the consequences of the nation's entering more fully than ever a world economy. How will our wages and income be sustained at present levels? Will the new information economy require more low-paying than high-paying jobs? If so, what will the consequences be for the standard of living in the future?

A third scenario, and one we think is most probable, involves a slow redefinition of work and leisure, where dissatisfied able-bodied older individuals place pressure on societal institutions, such as churches, government, schools, family, and corporations, to find flexible ways of accommodating them in meaningful and productive ways. This will involve the identification of labor and tasks that provide personal satisfaction, independence, and flexible use of time. Work will become a matter of choice rather than obligation, although it may become a necessity for the well-being of society. These new roles will emerge after completion of a primary career and may require preparation or training for new careers, which may provide less economic return than a previous career but more personal satisfaction. Such a change in work patterns may involve tension, even conflict, with older people being accused of displacing younger workers or of wage rate "busting" or of unfair appropriation of the benefits of a surplus economy. Nonetheless, the discontent that the elderly often experience in long periods of non-productivity may well combine with the economy's need for constructive use of all manpower resources to crystallize in new collective action to sustain a healthy world economy.

Information Bases for
Making Policy Choices

Half a dozen policy issues are the foci around which much debate is being conducted as the maturing American society begins to confront the changes in all its institutions that the new demog-

raphy of its population is forcing. These changes are in the nature of a low, rolling swell of change, not a sudden sharp shift.

Retirement: The questions about retirement involve both personal and cultural attitudes about withdrawal from work, as well as the formal policies of government and industry that encourage either early retirement or retention in productive work. Practical policy questions such as these arise: age discrimination in the workplace; the age at which retirement benefits can be drawn; the generosity of retirement benefits and discharge bonuses; the means of providing medical protection for retirees (by employer extension of medical insurance or by wider national insurance?); whether re-training programs should be designed for older workers as well as for youth and who should finance them. Should education and training concentrate on training older workers for new or second careers or on upgrading skills of the older employed workers to facilitate their retention in jobs they now hold?

Social Benefits: Aside from medical protection, especially for long-term illness, a major issue is presented by women in the workforce. By and large they accumulate less benefits than do their male counterparts. They retire with less security, or are compelled to continue work longer than men, while at the same time performing household duties for family members without much relief. Can the total of employment and social benefits be better designed for fairness to both men and women?

Intergenerational Equity: The relative improvement in the economic position of the elderly has not eliminated poverty among the aged, but it has raised serious doubts that national resources are being fairly shared between the needy young and the old. The issue directs attention to the larger share of caring for children that still falls on family members. At the heart of this issue is not so [much] the conflict between youth and old age as changing expectations about the responsibilities of government, families, and voluntary associations. Another dimension is whether the commonly shared problems of youth and age—affordable housing, health care, and income for the most poor—can be handled on any basis that is not categorical and age-dependent.

Leisure Versus Work: Retirement policies of government, of industry, or of individuals involve a tradeoff between work and leisure. It is a matter of policy just how much leisure can be afforded, by society and by individuals.

Labor-Force Requirements: Future decisions concerning the elderly will be influenced by public decision about just how much active manpower society requires at each phase of its evolution. Does economic development require the labor of all its able-bodied, more so than in the past? Will machine technology and economic developments require more manpower (womanpower) or less? Is it in society's interest to reorder the workplace to allow for shared work or part-time work or flexible work schedules and if so, at what level of compensation?

Service Requirements: What changes in the health and welfare services are required by an aging population[?] The increased demand for medical care is not followed by recognition that long-term social supports are required in increasing volume by a small but growing segment of the older population. Such supports seem to exceed the capacity of families to fill them. How can advance arrangements be made by individuals against this risk, and whence will come the manpower to provide such care? How much of this care must be given in large institutions? And if it is to be given to the elderly where they live, what is necessary to overcome widespread public reluctance to live next to severely disabled people?

Such issues are clearly interrelated, but each can also be approached piece by piece. There are numerous demonstrations and promising ideas afloat, but none has sufficiently broad and wide support or consensus to lead to widespread action by either government or voluntary associations. . . .

While many of the answers to such questions are speculative, the work option can be examined with some empirical foundation.

READING 33

The Labor Force by the Year 2000 and Employment Policy for Older Workers

Steven Sandell

Source: "The Labor Force by the Year 2000 and Employment Policy for Older Workers" by S. Sandell from *Retirement Reconsidered: Economic and Social Roles for Older People*, edited by R. Morris and S. Bass, 1988, pp. 107-115. Used by permission of Springer Publishing Company, Inc., New York, 10012.

Employment prospects for older workers in the year 2000 are an area of speculation. While the exact nature of employment opportunities is difficult to predict, the loss of jobs by some older workers is a certainty in a dynamic economy. It would be counterproductive for the nation to attempt, in advance, to keep jobs that could be done substantially more cheaply or efficiently by technologically advanced equipment or by producers with foresight. By the same token, it would be irresponsible not to provide training opportunities, new jobs, and income support for older Americans in need.

This [reading] first examines labor force trends and presents specific occupational and industrial projections for the end of the century. Then older workers' employment problems are examined to provide a basis for policies to improve their employment prospects.

Population and Labor Force Trends

Over the past century, labor force participation rates among persons aged 65 and over have declined as more people could afford to retire and retirement became socially acceptable. . . . Recently, labor force participation of persons aged 55 to 64 has also declined. Because of this reduced participation and the effects of the baby boom, the proportion of the labor force that is over 45 has been declining since 1960. It will only begin to rise again after 1990, as the increased numbers in the over-45 population offsets the lower labor force participation rates in that age group.

The relative importance of older persons (defined as 55 and over) in the labor force will decline through the remainder of the century. Regardless of popular conceptions to the contrary, it is important to remember two points. First, the rise in the average age of workers is due to the aging of the baby boom group and not to an increase in the size of the group commonly identified as older workers (those over 55). Second, the population is not the labor force. The proportion of the population over 55 is affected by the dramatic increases in longevity for persons beyond their 65th birthdays. Since most people over 65 are not working, this population increase is not affecting the composition of the labor force.

While the reasons for the declining labor force participation of older persons are the subject of a vast literature, it is important to note that the reduction is primarily due to voluntary decisions by older persons. The increased affluence of older Americans, often channeled through public and private pension benefits, is perhaps the most important factor behind this trend. The current pattern of retirement before age 65 is a product of the general affordability of retirement, individual desires, and social acceptance of retirement. Dramatic declines in labor force participation occur at age 62 and again at age 65 because of eligibility for Social Security and pension benefits.

There is little reason, if current pension benefit structures remain in place, to expect dramatic change in retirement ages. The real value of retirement benefits may be less for the baby boom generation than for people retiring during the remainder of this century. Retirement ages may rise slightly. But only if the current pattern of long-term attachment to a particular employer disintegrates—and with it the concomitant pattern of increased salaries and pensions with longevity—will there be a dramatic change in retirement patterns. Only if there is more flexibility in the labor market, something that may be nascent, will there be more people working later in life.

Table 7.3 compares the industrial distribution of all persons and those 65 and older. Although the pattern for both groups is generally similar, some differences exist. For example, only 3% of all workers, compared to 9% of workers above age 65, were in agriculture. The age patterns reflect retirement patterns by industry as well as the job openings existing when people first entered the job market. Retirement patterns, in turn, reflect the availability of jobs and pension arrangements.

Projections of the industrial and occupational distribution for the turn of the century are presented in Tables 7.4 and 7.5, respectively. The best projections available, from the Bureau of Labor Statistics, are for 1995 (see Personick, 1985; Silvestri & Lukasiewicz, 1985). These are compared with the actual industrial and occupational distributions for 1984. The differences seem to be minor.

Table 7.3. Employment by Industry, 1981

Industry	65 and over	All ages
All industries (in thousands of persons)	3,119	107,348
Distribution (in percents)	100.0	100.0
Agriculture	9.2	3.0
Mining	0.4	1.0
Construction	3.8	6.4
Manufacturing—durables	6.1	13.4
Manufacturing—nondurables	5.6	8.8
Transportation	3.2	6.3
Trade—wholesale and retail	23.6	20.5
Finance, insurance, and real estate	6.1	5.9
Services	37.8	29.5
Public administration	4.2	5.2

SOURCE: Congressional Budget Office (1982).

Table 7.4. Employment by Major Industrial Sector, 1984 and 1995

	Employment (in thousands)		Percent distribution	
	1984	1995[a]	1984	1995
Total	106,841	122,760	100.0	100.0
Agriculture	3,293	3,059	3.1	2.5
Nonagriculture	103,548	119,700	96.9	97.5
Government	15,984	17,144	15.0	14.0
Federal	2,807	2,800	2.6	2.3
State and Local	13,177	14,344	12.3	11.7
Private	87,564	102,556	82.0	83.5
Mining	651	631	.6	.5
Construction	5,920	6,636	5.5	5.4
Manufacturing	19,779	21,124	18.5	17.2
Durable	11,744	13,216	11.0	6.4
Nondurable	8,035	7,908	7.5	6.4
Transportation, communication, and public utilities	5,500	6,304	5.1	5.1
Trade	24,290	28,272	22.7	23.0
Finance, insurance, and real estate	6,296	7,397	5.9	6.0
Services	23,886	31,170	22.4	25.4
Private households	1,242	1,023	1.2	.8

SOURCE: [Data from] Personick (1985).
NOTE: a. Projection.

Table 7.5. Employment by Broad Occupational Group, 1984 and 1995

Occupation	Number (in thousands)		Percent	
	1984	1995[a]	1984	1995
Total Employment	106,843	122,760	100.0	100.0
Executive				
administrative and managerial workers	11,274	13,762	10.6	11.2
Professional workers	12,805	15,578	12.0	12.7
Technicians and related support workers	3,206	4,119	3.0	3.4
Salesworkers	11,173	13,393	10.5	10.9
Administrative support workers, including clerical	18,716	20,499	17.5	16.7
Private household workers	993	811	.9	.7
Service workers, except private household workers	15,589	18,917	14.6	15.4
Precision production, craft and repair works	12,176	13,601	11.4	11.1
Operators, fabricators, and laborers	17,357	18,634	16.2	15.2
Farming, forestry, and fishing workers	3,554	3,447	3.3	2.8

SOURCE: [Data from] Silvestri and Lukasiewicz (1985).
NOTE: a. Projection.

A Context for Public Policy Toward Older Workers

Comparing the current pattern of older workers' employment to projections of the industrial and occupational structure of the future economy is of little value for predicting older workers' employment problems at the turn of the century. Older workers, even if they lose their jobs, will be able to adjust if the economy is strong and the jobs are available, the workers have transferable skills, and age discrimination is prevented. Prior knowledge of exactly what the jobs will be and who will hold them is not possible for either private planning or public policy.

While it is important to dispel some of the crisis atmosphere surrounding the discussion of older workers' employment and the future of retirement, there are real problems and a need for new policy directions (Sandell, 1987). If in the next century the nation is to use older workers' skills and experience effectively, the development of new retirement and employment policies must begin today.

Although knowledge of specific industrial and occupational opportunities for older workers in the year 2000 is neither possible to project nor by itself important information for developing policies, it is essential to establish a context for discussing the problems and important policy issues concerning older workers. To understand the problems as well as the policy solutions in the area of the older worker, it is useful to keep in mind some prototypical older workers.

- There are average persons, mainstream individuals whose earnings normally increase over their working years, peaking in their fifties and leveling off at the end of their working lives, prior to an anticipated period of retirement.
- Average persons can experience unanticipated midlife events, such as major health or disability problems or the loss of a longheld job, that disrupt the average pattern.
- There are disadvantaged people who may have struggled all their lives. They have histories of

intermittent employment and low earnings and often have severe labor market problems as they reach old age.

Policies to improve the employment prospects of older Americans must be geared to their specific backgrounds and needs. . . . I will emphasize the situation of older persons with particular employment problems.

The most serious employment problems are faced by older persons who are seeking work. Older workers with jobs often receive above-average pay. In considering policies to alleviate the employment problems of older displaced workers, as well as other unemployed older workers, several conclusions from recent research should be emphasized (see National Commission for Employment Policy, 1985; Sandell, 1985).

First, older workers are significantly less likely than younger workers to lose their jobs or become displaced. Although workers 45 and over are about 31% of the labor force, they are only about 20% of job losers. Greater seniority probably affords older workers protection against dislocation or job loss in general compared to their younger counterparts. However, when job loss does occur, the results can be devastating, sometimes making the difference between economic hardship and a secure retirement.

Second, the consequences of job loss are more serious for older workers than younger ones in specific ways. Older workers stay unemployed longer; they experience a greater drop in pay when they find a new job; and they are more likely to leave the labor market altogether.

Third, while age discrimination is an important cause of these problems, other factors contribute significantly. Characteristics such as education and previous work experience are related to the employment consequences of losing one's job. For example, the fact that older men have, on average, lower education and poorer health than younger men makes the average duration of their job search longer. The greater drop in pay for older workers who lose their jobs is largely due to their greater loss of seniority and firm-specific skills, which were useful on the old job but which the new employers are not willing to pay for (Shapiro & Sandell, 1987). For example, workers who were aged 60 when they lost their jobs averaged more than 11 years of job tenure; these workers experienced an average wage loss of 6%. Workers who were 45 to 49 averaged 6 years of job tenure when they lost their jobs; their wages fell by an average of 3%.

The fourth important finding is that drops in pay, duration of unemployment, and the likelihood of premature retirement are greater when there are adverse conditions in the local and national economy. Regional decline probably causes more severe problems than industry or occupation alone for dislocated workers seeking new work at wages comparable to those of their previous job. In other words, if the local economy is relatively strong and unemployment rates are generally low, dislocated workers are more likely to find new work with other employers at comparable wages. This is especially true if the worker's industry is basically healthy locally and it is only the worker's employer that is having difficulty.

A fifth finding is the documentation of the important relationships among job loss, labor-market conditions, and induced retirement (Shapiro & Sandell, 1984). Older job losers are much more likely to retire than are older workers of the same age who have not lost their jobs. For example, when the national unemployment rate was 6%, almost 30% of 60-year-old male job losers retired; by contrast, less than 10% of all males aged 60 who were still employed retired at that time.

High unemployment rates disproportionately increase the number of older job losers who retire early. For example, although an estimated 18% of all 60-year-old male job losers retire when the economy is at 4% unemployment, almost one-half (44%) of 60-year-old job losers retire when the economy is at 8% unemployment. Moreover, once retired, these workers tend to stay retired.

Although this retirement may be considered voluntary in the sense that workers prefer retirement to searching for or accepting jobs, the retirement is induced by economic conditions. The workers would not have retired if they had not lost their jobs or if conditions had proved more propitious for finding a new one. As a result, job loss and high unemployment have significant long-term costs for the economy—not just the loss of potentially productive workers, but also increased Social Security, private pension, and other payments.

Conclusions and Recommendations

In the tradeoffs that inevitably must be made in developing national economic policy, federal policy makers should recognize the often hidden, but substantial, long-term costs to the economy and to older individuals that result from induced retirement caused by high unemployment. . . . The federal government should establish a new priority for employment in the development of its overall economic policies.

Three additional conclusions are useful in policy planning for the year 2000 (Sandell, 1985):

1. It is undeniable that age discrimination exists in the labor market and that vigorous enforcement of the Age Discrimination in Employment Act by the Equal Employment Opportunity Commission is essential.
2. Many of the labor market problems of older Americans—job losers or not—are grounded in causes other than age discrimination. So even if age discrimination were completely eliminated from the labor market, many older workers would continue to experience employment problems.
3. Employment policies and programs must treat these other important causes of labor market problems directly.

Although employer actions are critical to improving the employment situation of older workers, many older workers have a need for training and other services that cannot be adequately addressed by employers alone. Thus government has

an important training and employment role to play. As a general rule, older workers can be successfully served by existing public job and training programs as long as proper attention is paid to older individuals' needs.

Comprehensive Employment Training Act (CETA) programs were generally successful in training and placing older workers in private sector employment. Although older eligible persons were less likely to participate in CETA than younger adults, a substantial part of the difference is accounted for by factors other than age, such as the fact that many older eligible individuals were retired and had no interest in taking further training for employment. The experience of older workers who are served under the Job Training Partnership Act (JTPA) can also be successful.

Older workers who lose their jobs often face special difficulties. Training programs, such as those funded under JTPA, should provide special assistance to older job losers, with an emphasis on systematic assessment of their strengths in terms of job experience and long-developed skills, so that training can be provided to minimize loss of wages in new employment. Older workers who are eligible and desire training should be given equitable access to JTPA regular training programs (Title II) and to those established for displaced workers under Title III.

Many older job losers wish to work part-time or in new occupations. They often have experience, skills, and talents that go unused because they have difficulty finding appropriate work. Specialized placement services for older workers have proved to be successful in a number of areas of the country.

There are many examples of employer programs and age-neutral personnel practices that other companies can adapt to combat age discrimination and to increase employment opportunities for older workers, especially those who are approaching conventional retirement age. . . . Employer actions that simultaneously meet company-specific business needs and the training and employment needs of older workers are critical to the improvement of their employment opportunities. Federal agencies such as the Department of Labor and the Administration on Aging, as well as state and local governments, should promote the adoption of innovative employer-sponsored programs and practices for older workers through the dissemination of information on successful efforts in this area.

In the next century some older workers, especially those who lose their jobs, will have serious labor market problems. However, government and the private sector can institute policies that will not only help older workers, but will benefit those businesses that hire them.

References

Congressional Budget Office. (1982). *Work and retirement: Options for continued employment of older workers.* Washington, DC: U.S. Government Printing Office.

National Commission for Employment Policy. (1985). *Older workers: Prospects, problems and policies.* Washington, DC: U.S. Government Printing Office.

Personick, V. A. (1985). A second look at industry output and employment trends through 1995. *Monthly Labor Review, 108*(11), 26-41.

Sandell, S. H. (1985, July 24). Statement on displaced older workers. In *Hearing before the Select Committee on Aging, House of Representatives, U.S. Congress* (Comm. Pub. No. 99-528). Washington, DC: U.S. Government Printing Office.

Sandell, S. H. (Ed.). (1987). *The problem isn't age: Work and older Americans.* New York: Praeger.

Shapiro, D., & Sandell, S. H. (1984, December). *Economic conditions, job loss and induced retirement.* Paper presented at the Industrial Relations Research Association Meeting, Dallas, TX.

Shapiro, D., & Sandell, S. H. (1987). Older job losers' reduced pay: Age discrimination and other explanations. In S. H. Sandell (Ed.), *The problem isn't age: Work and older Americans* (pp. 37-51). New York: Praeger.

Silvestri, G., & Lukasiewicz, J. M. (1985). Occupational employment projections: The 1984-95 outlook. *Monthly Labor Review, 108*(11), 42-53.

READING 34

Social Policy Toward the Older Worker

Assumptions, Values, and Implications

Rhonda J. V. Montgomery, Edgar P. Borgatta, and Karl D. Kosloski

Source: "Social Policy Toward the Older Worker: Assumptions, Values, and Implications" by R. J. V. Montgomery, E. P. Borgatta and K. D. Kosloski. Reprinted from *The Aging of the American Work Force*, edited by R. Montgomery and J. Owen, 1990, pp. 19-30. By permission of Wayne State University Press. Copyright © 1990 by Wayne State University Press, Detroit, MI, 48202.

The role of the older worker is coming under increasing scrutiny by employers, unions, policymakers, and researchers. Among the developments which have stimulated this interest are a changing demographic makeup of the work force, due to shifts in birth rates and increased length of life for most persons; medical advances, with accompanying increases in medical costs, primarily associated with older persons; compression in the upper ages among workers in some industries; and the trend toward earlier retirement among certain groups of workers.

Some observers see an increase in the proportion of older workers as cause for alarm, others as a burgeoning resource. Before it is possible to make a pronouncement on whether there is a coming "crisis" in the workplace or whether dramatic shifts in policy are necessary, it is useful to consider not only where we are as a society with respect to a defined role for the older worker but also how we got there. We will look at examples that illustrate the implicit value system that appears to underlie present social policy with respect to older workers. We will then suggest possible policy initiatives that are consistent with both the new demographics and attitudinal changes toward the older worker.

The Present Role of the Older Worker

An Aging Society

The American population is changing demographically, with persons generally surviving longer. At the turn of the century, less than one in every ten Americans was 55 years old or older. Presently, the figure is one in five. By the beginning of the next century, the size of this segment of the population will increase yet another 20 percent, from 47 million to roughly 55 million, and by the year 2010, according to the Census Bureau (1983), fully 25 percent of the population will be 55 years old or over.

The aging of the population roughly parallels the aging of the baby boomers, that cohort born from the mid-1940s to the early 1960s. Almost one-third of the current U.S. population (nearly 75 million) was born during this period. Due to their large numbers and increasing life expectancy, the baby boomers are expected to be the dominant age cohort well into the next century.

The effect of the population bulge caused by this cohort is heightened by a smaller than expected succeeding cohort, often referred to as the "baby bust" generation. While the fertility rate soared during the two decades from 1945 to 1964, reaching a high of 3.7 in 1957, it dropped to a low of 1.7, substantially below the replacement rate, in 1976 (U.S. Bureau of the Census, 1982). Partly as the result of these demographic shifts, the average age of the population has been steadily increasing.

The major concern here is the change produced in the dependency ratio (the number of dependents in society supported by each working member). There are various ways of computing this ratio (see, e.g., Adamchak and Friedmann 1983), but no matter how it is conceptualized, two considerations should not be overlooked. First, as the proportion of older adults increases, there is a corresponding reduction in the number of dependent young, which tends to offset, at least in part, the impact of the older group. The exact tradeoff in costs at the individual and societal levels is, as yet, unknown. Second, there are conditions other than changing fertility rates that affect the dependency ratio. These include perturbations in the economy, legislation affecting Social Security and Medicare, and restrictive public and private policies that reduce the ability of older workers to adapt to changing conditions.

In short, demographic shifts in the population structure produce a population with a higher proportion of older persons. Though the implications of this shift for good or ill are not yet apparent, there has been much debate of the merits of alternative solutions to the "problems" created by an aging society.

An Aging Work Force

Since the composition of the work force is determined, in part, by the composition of the larger population from which it is drawn, the median age of the labor force is slowly increasing. It is important to bear in mind that much of the increase is because the baby boomers are aging, not because older workers are staying in the work force longer. At the beginning of this century, more than two-thirds of American men aged 65 and over were employed. In 1960, the proportion had dropped to roughly one-third (Back 1969); by 1979 the proportion was 19 percent and dropping (Smedley 1979); the figure is expected to fall below 10 percent by the year 2000 (Fullerton 1987).

American workers are opting for retirement at an earlier age. In 1966, 38 percent of workers retired before age 65 under Social Security; by 1976 the number had increased to 66 percent (*U.S. News & World Report* 1978). And even though recent amendments to the Age Discrimination in Employment Act of 1986 remove the age-70 cap in the law and prohibit mandatory retirement based on age for most workers, the trend toward earlier retirement continues. . . .

Currently, labor force participation begins to decline as early as age 45 for both men and women, as health problems and early retirement options begin to thin the ranks of the employed (Sandell 1987). However, the trend toward earlier retirement is particularly pronounced for males. The parallel for women is not direct, since the labor force participation of women has been changing. Work rates for women below the age of 55 continue to rise, and the work rates of older women remain relatively unchanged (Clark 1988).

As Kutscher and Fullerton point out in their paper [in the book from which this reading was drawn], the median age of the post-World War II labor force reached its apex in 1962, at 40.6 years. With the entry of the baby boom generation, the median age dropped dramatically. Since then, it has been increasing steadily. In spite of this increase, however, voluntary decisions by older workers to leave the work force are more than offsetting the effect of the aging of the baby boomers, and the median age of 1962 is unlikely to be matched in the foreseeable future.

Planners wonder whether society will have the ability to finance such a retirement level without a negative impact on the economy and the standard of living. The most frequently invoked scenario, related to the dependency ratio, is that as the average age of workers increases and older workers depart prematurely, fewer workers will be left to support an increasing proportion of retirees. As a result, workers will eventually be unable to afford to retire, and the work force will be inundated with older workers.

Objective data do not support this view. The greatest disparity in the dependency ratio occurred in the early 1960s, when there were over 150 nonworkers for every 100 workers. Since then the ratio has steadily declined, in large part because of increasing labor force participation by women. This trend is expected to continue for the next twenty years before slowly reversing itself. Even when it does, however, the ratio of nonworkers to workers is not expected to exceed 115 nonworkers for every 100 workers. So even when the baby boomers reach retirement age, the dependency ratio is expected to be much more favorable than in the 1960s and 1970s (Sandell 1987). This relatively optimistic view of the future must be tempered somewhat by the expectation that older dependents will be more expensive than younger dependents. High-tech medical advances that increase the length of the dependency period will contribute substantially to health care costs for this group.

Thus the notion of an aging work force is somewhat of a misnomer at present. Although certain sectors have older than average work forces (e.g., the auto industry), this phenomenon largely is caused by union-negotiated work and seniority rules, rather than demographic change. Age compression in industry should not be confused with demographic shifts in the population. Since they have different causes, they are likely to have different solutions. For the most part, aging trends within the general population are being offset by trends toward earlier retirement. The result has been a less rapid aging of the work force. In a similar fashion, increased participation by females in the labor force appears to have forestalled an economically debilitating dependency ratio. Indeed, Adamchak and Friedmann, in their analyses of differing conceptions of the dependency ratio, conclude: "Whatever the reasons for the revolt against the alleged increases in 'dependency' loads resulting from population aging and the institutionalization of retirement, *the argument cannot be justified on the basis of a demonstrable increase in dependency load employing any appropriate measure*" (p. 336).

Intergenerational Tension

A number of analysts have raised the specter of intergenerational conflict as a logical consequence of the present support for older Americans. Groups such as Americans for Generational Equity (AGE), with the ostensible purpose of protecting the economic rights of younger Americans, have been cited as evidence that battle lines are being drawn. Impetus for such movements is fueled by such inflammatory statements as this: "The baby boomers are paying an unprecedented proportion of their incomes to support the current older generation in retirement, and they will expect today's children to support them in turn. The likely result, unless many fundamental trends are soon reversed, will be a war between young and old" (Longman 1987, p. 2).

In reality, the prospect of such intergenerational conflict seems remote. For example, the tradition of intrafamilial responsibility for informal caregiving appears as strong as ever (Brody 1985; Shanas 1979). In addition, private transfers of money are more likely to proceed from old to young than vice versa (Gibbs 1988). In fact, it has been contended that the whole "intergenerational inequity" argument is based on a series of false assumptions such as the belief that all the elderly are well-off, that allocation of federal monies is a zero-sum game, that conflict is the rule rather than the exception, and that there is no common stake between generations (Kingson et al. 1986).

Other factors that have nothing to do with economic support also promote negative attitudes toward the old by the young. For example, there are prevailing myths that older workers "wear out"; that their knowledge becomes superannuated or even obsolete; that they are accident-prone, forgetful, and so on. One of the achievements of modern social gerontology has been the successful challenging of such myths. Indeed, it might be argued that the heightened awareness of gerontological issues has created a renewed sense of egalitarianism and an advocacy by some policymakers of the view that older workers must be given an opportunity to remain in the workplace. Given their retirement patterns, however, older workers show little sign of wanting or needing such an opportunity.

Implicit Values in Contemporary Social Policy

Some Historical Notes on Retirement

On the face of it, then, there would seem to be no compelling need for a radical revision of the role of the older worker based solely on demographic trends. This is consistent with Graebner's (1980) observation that the aging of the general population occurs too slowly to account for such historical movements in any more than a general way.

According to Graebner, formal occupational retirement emerged in the American workplace for three main reasons. First, retirement was an assault on the system of permanence that employees attempted to build into their positions, as exemplified by tenure in teaching, seniority on the railroad, and the spoils system in civil service. Retirement served to lessen the "right" of individuals to such occupational permanence.

Second, retirement weakened the effort of "personal influence" and personal relationships in institutions. In other words, a worker's ability came to be more important than his or her family and social connections. Prior to the institutionalization of retirement, public and private corporations were assumed to be providing for the welfare of their older workers; that is, income, status, and activity were to be dispensed to older workers as part of the job. Unfortunately, provision of these gratifications was never uniform. With retirement, these functions were transferred to senior citizens' groups, nursing homes, and retirement communities.

Third, says Graebner, "retirement has historically been sanctioned as a form of unemployment relief; older workers have been retired to create places for younger ones" (p. 266), a policy most blatant in the railroad industry, but applied to other occupations experiencing technological unemployment. To note this function of retirement is not to minimize the discrimination inherent in the process; however, the process is, in large part, implicitly accepted among all age groups.

From Graebner's perspective, certain social and economic values were instrumental in the eventual institutionalization of a retirement role; and, extending this line of reasoning, shifting values will most likely be responsible for any changes in the perceptions or operationalization of this role. In order to explain the renewed interest in the older worker in America, Graebner again points to the economy: "Mandatory retirement was established over the course of the last century because it served real and perceived needs; it is now being dismantled because it is increasingly seen as economically counterproductive for the firm and the nation; because the proposed alternatives seem to offer substantial benefits; and because it is generally accepted that mandatory retirement can be eliminated without significant social dislocation" (p. 250).

From this perspective, the role of the older worker can be seen as being influenced by social values that are based, at least in part, on economic considerations. According to Graebner, it would be a distinct mistake to interpret recent legislation removing mandatory retirement ages as a belated victory for older workers who want to continue working but have been barred by arbitrary age discrimination. Rather, such a change in policy became possible only when those in positions of power in corporate America decided that current retirement policies were too expensive and inefficient in their utilization of the labor supply. In short, in order to understand the role of the older worker,

it is important to identify which values are presently being represented and whose values they are.

Conventional Policy Development and Implicit Values

To illustrate where we are, as a society, with respect to a defined role for the older worker, it may be useful to examine certain contemporary policies and practices in the workplace, raise questions about the values reflected, and ask whether or not these are the values that should be implemented. The purpose of this exercise is not to engage in a systematic analysis of current policy, but to begin such an endeavor by focusing on several current practices and the implications *of* these practices. Then it may be possible to begin a dialogue about which values we as a society would like to support and the policies and practices that could be implemented to achieve these goals.

For the past few decades, there has been a movement in labor and industry toward the practice referred to as "30-and-out." Implementation of this policy was a victory for the worker who had spent long years at physically exhausting labor and was given an opportunity to retire before literally working himself to death. The "30-and-out" policy has been most conspicuous in the older manufacturing industries, where modernization has led to a decrease in the labor force and where there are few new opportunities for younger workers.

The benefits of the "30-and-out" policy are numerous and clearly transcend the original goal of assuring at least some time for retirement for laborers. For example, "30-and-out" tends to make room for younger workers and for promotion of those in the middle years. It has the potential to create an orderly influx of new members into the labor organizations and assure the continued need and support for such organizations. The practice also reinforces the societal belief that retirement is an earned right which workers may exercise even before reaching the age qualifying them for Social Security. For its part, industry has benefited to the extent that those in the system for a shorter time command lower salaries and fewer benefits.

On the surface, then, "30-and-out" would appear to be a practice that is desirable. However, careful scrutiny raises questions about the long-term costs of such a practice and the values that are being reinforced. For example, if an individual is capable of continued work and is not prepared for a reduction in income, this practice may be limiting his or her opportunities. Such a person is not only restricted from working but is less well able to prevent economic dependency in the future. In principle, "30-and-out" may appear to be a humane provision; in practice, it threatens the older person's access to continued employment. If there are not enough jobs to go around, the notion of full employment can be maintained if some groups are defined as outside the work force. Those groups could be the young, women, or minorities. And at various times in various ways, many groups have been prohibited access to employment. It may be convenient to treat the group of old people in this way.

It may be argued that legislation was passed in 1986 to prevent forced retirement in most employment settings. However, the law does not prevent enticements to retire such as bonuses and what are often referred to as "golden parachute" packages. Furthermore, the statistics reported above show that the average retirement age has been and continues to be below that required for Social Security eligibility. In reality, then, while there may be virtues associated with retirement, "30-and-out" and related policies may create expectations within society about who should retire and when, thereby placing a limitation on all future income for these persons.

It is the latter aspect of retirement (i.e., a limitation on future income) that may be problematic for individuals and society. As long as individuals live only a few years beyond retirement, initially adequate pensions will probably remain adequate as time passes. However, as larger numbers of persons live longer and the retirement period is extended, it becomes questionable whether existing pension programs will be able to meet the needs of individuals over their retirement life, particularly if inflationary pressure is substantial and there is no provision for cost of living allowances. When people outlive pension resources, government or other resources will be called upon to meet unmet needs, including substantial health care costs. In either case, the public purse will be drawn upon to pay for perhaps unanticipated consequences of early retirement, since these individuals will not be in a position to contribute to their own care.

In addition to the practice of "30-and-out," there are other private and public policies that encourage elders to leave the work force to make room for others. For example, persons who work part-time are limited in how much they can earn before their Social Security benefits are reduced for the period in which they are most likely to continue working, i.e., the years right after formal retirement. Further, recent changes in the tax law require recipients of Social Security to pay taxes on their benefit payments if they secure employment that raises their income over a designated maximum. The stated purpose of this practice is to ensure that elders with sufficiently high incomes are not equal beneficiaries of a tax transfer system. Another consequence of this law is that older workers are "penalized" for going into the work force. This set of circumstances is also mirrored by recent changes in federal employees' benefit packages. Essentially, a federal employee who elects to earn and then draw Social Security benefits after leaving government service is penalized for such an action. The message given by current practices is clear, whether intended or not: older persons should leave the work force.

Is this the message that we want current policy to send? Once this initial question is asked, a series of other questions emerges, all of which deserve serious consideration if we are to create policies concerned with older workers in a proactive way.

Do we want workers to leave the work force at ever earlier ages? Are older persons the most appropriate group economically to force out of the work force? Do we need to force a selected subgroup out of the labor force? If not, will we need to do so in the future? Are there alternative ways of achieving full employment?

A second employment practice that is intricately tied to retirement and older worker policies is the pervasive and growing tendency to hire part-time employees. The benefits of this practice to employers are clear. They gain scheduling flexibility and major savings because part-time employees are frequently paid low hourly wages and usually are not provided key benefits. From the perspective of older workers, such jobs can be viewed favorably because they allow retired persons to supplement their retirement income on a flexible schedule. One might be tempted to assert that this practice reflects an increasing value placed on older persons. However, in reality, it reflects underlying values similar to those described earlier. Specifically, older persons are employed as marginal participants in the labor market, and often the jobs are available only because other persons are unable or unwilling to take them.

Apart from the question of whether this is the value we want to foster, there are questions related to the long-term consequences of these practices for retirement policy. Older persons are not the only group employed as part-time help without benefits. Women, youths, minorities, and those with lower levels of education are also employed in such a manner. When these persons progress through their work lives to retirement age, they arrive there with no planned retirement benefits except for minimal Social Security coverage—and even that assurance continues to be questioned. Hence the savings incurred by these service industries are likely to be at a substantial cost to the public purse. If large numbers of these marginal workers live extended lives, it is likely that minimal Social Security benefits will need to be supplemented by government programs.

The Future Role of the Older Worker

Value-Driven Policy Development

All too often, when policy analysts and policymakers address difficult issues, they approach their task as one of fine tuning rather than one of asking more basic and difficult questions about which values are being supported by a policy and whether or not they should be supported. This reluctance to raise questions about values stems directly from the fact that many social issues are complex, involve a diverse set of values, and may be conflicting. The employment and retirement of older workers is one such issue. Debate concerning the rights and privileges of older persons as workers and retired citizens will not only reflect differences in values among different interest groups but will also reveal conflicting values among individuals.

In a brief presentation it is not possible to develop new directions for policy with regard to the older worker. However, we will suggest a few ways in which values can be stated in a forthright and direct way.

First, let us emphasize the simple notion that older persons are people like everyone else, and should not be treated any differently merely on the basis of age—that is to say, there should be no discrimination. Such a statement is more easily accepted as a generality than in application. It implies that older persons who wish to work should be judged on the basis of their qualifications, and the process of determining qualifications may create some costs. This value is now reasonably well incorporated in our federal legal system, and is reflected at other levels of government as well.

However, the other side of the coin is that older persons also should not be treated preferentially. For some, this is a position that is harder to accept. To hire without prejudice, it may be necessary to test persons' ability to do tasks. This adds administrative costs, but is fairer than making the prejudicial assumption that older persons will learn more slowly, perform more slowly, and lack the energy and alertness of young people. On the other hand, in many cases there are rewards for seniority that are routinized and may be applied without having any bearing on the efficiency of a given individual. If rewards were to be distributed on the basis of merit rather than seniority, assessment procedures would be necessary, and such procedures would add cost. It is a two-way street, and both practices, although less arbitrary and prejudicial, would add to operating costs.

In the area of retirement policies, one of the major politically sensitive issues is whether Social Security should be treated as a universal benefit or as a form of insurance. Presumably, the latter view was a prominent notion at the initiation of the program, and is evident in its title, Old Age and Survivors Insurance (now called Retirement Survivors Disability Health Insurance, or RSDHI). Many changes have occurred in the program over the years, including coverage by SSI for those not eligible by earnings, which bring the program closer to a notion of a universal entitlement. Consideration will need to be given to the question of whether the system should be moved fully to a universal entitlement. If this conclusion is reached, then attention will need to be given to how to make it work. If it is designed to provide baseline support only, then the assumption that people should get benefits on the basis of payments into the system would need to be negated. Similarly, the fiction that the payments are not a tax would need to be dispelled. Consequences of moving in such a direction would lead to other questions of consistency. For example, with the RSDHI program there are two parallel tax collection systems, and they could be combined. Presumably, the less regressive tax system would be the one to survive.

If clarification of the Social Security system were to occur, it could well have consequences for savings for retirement. On this score, again, policy has not been generated by broad reflection and planning, but has arisen out of historical circumstances. There is no reason why a parallel retirement savings plan as a form of insurance cannot

exist, run either by the government or by the private sector. The principle has been established with Individual Retirement Accounts (IRAs), and could be generalized further by being made a required benefit of employment.

What is unique about the IRAs is that they constitute a notion equivalent to immediate vesting. One of the great problems that has been created for older workers is that retirement benefits have not been treated as other forms of compensation, i.e., as belonging to the worker just as wages do. Pension benefits have often been associated with funds controlled by industry or unions, and thus have been subject to many forms of abuse, ranging from actual criminal exploitation of the funds to control of workers by control of access to benefits. If pension benefits are truly a part of wages, the worker should have access to them in the form of immediate vesting and transportability.

The previous sentence may be a strong statement, but it is one that should be considered. The point is that policy development rarely, if ever, begins with such a direct statement. Most often a problem becomes apparent, and then solutions are considered within the context of the political and power structures that exist. This does not necessarily lead to good policy reflecting thoughtful consideration of values.

In sum, changes may well be on the horizon with regard to the role of older workers in America. However, it would be a mistake to view these changes as the inevitable result of demographic and economic forces in the marketplace. Such a model is not only overly simplistic and shortsighted: it has a more insidious effect. It suggests that society in general, and policymakers in particular, are somehow not responsible for the present role of the older worker in the workplace. The view presented here suggests otherwise: that social policy directly shapes roles and expectations. Unfortunately, the values shaping policy are often implicit and ill-considered. Thus the challenge confronting us is not how to respond to forces largely beyond our control. Rather, the challenge is how to develop policy on the basis of explicit statements about how we, as a society, intend to meet the economic and social challenges awaiting us now and in the years to come.

References

Adamchak, D., and E. Friedmann. 1983. "Societal Aging and Generational Dependency Relationships: Problems of Measurement and Conceptualization," *Research on Aging* 5: 319-38.

Back, K. 1969. "The Ambiguity of Retirement." In *Behavior and Adaptation in Late Life,* edited by E. W. Busse and E. P. Pfeiffer, pp. 93-114. Boston: Little, Brown.

Brody, E. 1985. "Parent Care as a Normative Family Stress," *The Gerontologist* 25: 19-29.

Clark, R. 1988. "The Future of Work and Retirement," *Research on Aging* 10: 169-93.

Fullerton, H. 1987. "Labor Force Projections: 1986-2000," *Monthly Labor Review,* September, pp. 19-29.

Gibbs, N. 1988. "Grays on the Go," *Time,* February 22, pp. 66-75.

Graebner, W. 1980. *A History of Retirement.* New Haven: Yale University Press.

Kingson, E., B. Hirshorn, and J. Cornman. 1986. *Ties That Bind: The Interdependence of Generations.* Washington, D.C.: Seven Locks Press.

Longman, P. 1987. *Born to Pay: The New Politics of Aging in America.* Boston: Houghton Mifflin Co.

Sandell, S. 1987. "Prospects for Older Workers: The Demographic and Economic Context." In *The Problem Isn't Age,* edited by S. Sandell, pp. 3-14. New York: Praeger.

Shanas, E. 1979. "Social Myth as Hypothesis: The Case of the Family Relations of Old People," *The Gerontologist* 19: 3-9.

Smedley, L. 1979. "The Patterns of Retirement," *AFL-CIO American Federationist* 86: 22-25.

U.S. Bureau of the Census. 1982. *Population Profile of the United States: 1981.* Current Population Reports, Series P-20, No. 374. Washington, D.C.: U.S. Government Printing Office.

———. 1982. *America in Transition: An Aging Society.* Current Population Reports, Series P-23, No. 128. Washington, D.C.: U.S. Government Printing Office.

U.S. News & World Report. 1978. "Work beyond Age 65? Most Would Rather Not." April 3, pp. 50-55.

READING 35

The Busy Ethic
Moral Continuity Between Work and Retirement

David J. Ekerdt

There is a way that people talk about retirement that emphasizes the importance of being busy. Just

[This research was] supported in part by the Medical Research Service of the Veterans Administration and by grants from the Administration on Aging (90-A-1194) and the National Institute on Aging (AG02287). The author thanks Raymond Bosse, Thomas Cole, and Linda Evans for helpful comments. *Source:* "The Busy Ethic: Moral Continuity Between Work and Retirement" by D. J. Ekerdt, 1985, *The Gerontologist,* 25, pp. 166-171. Copyright © The Gerontological Society of America. Reprinted by permission.

as there is a work ethic that holds industriousness and self-reliance as virtues so, too, there is a "busy ethic" for retirement that honors an active life. It represents people's attempts to justify retirement in terms of their long-standing beliefs and values.

The modern institution of retirement has required that our society make many provisions for it. Foremost among these are the economic arrangements and mechanisms that support Social Security, private pensions, and other devices for retirement financing. Political understandings have also been reached about the claim of younger workers on employment and the claim of older people on a measure of income security. At the same time, our cultural map of the life course has now been altered to include a separate stage of life called retirement, much as the life course once came to include the new stage of "adolescence" (Keniston, 1974).

Among other provisions, we should also expect that some moral arrangements may have emerged to validate and defend the lifestyle of retirement. After all, a society that traditionally identifies work and productivity as a wellspring of virtue would seem to need some justification for a life of pensioned leisure. How do retirees and observers alike come to feel comfortable with a "retired" life? In this paper I will suggest that retirement is morally managed and legitimated on a day-to-day basis in part by an ethic that esteems leisure that is earnest, occupied, and filled with activity—a "busy ethic." The ideas in this paper developed out of research on the retirement process at the Normative Aging Study, a prospective study of aging in community-dwelling men (Bosse et al., 1984).

The Work Ethic in Use

Before discussing how the busy ethic functions, it is important to note a few aspects about its parent work ethic. The work ethic, like any ethic, is a set of beliefs and values that identifies what is good and affirms ideals of conduct. It provides criteria for the evaluation of behavior and action. The work ethic historically has identified work with virtue and has held up for esteem a conflation of such traits and habits as diligence, initiative, temperance, industriousness, competitiveness, self-reliance, and the capacity for deferred gratification. The work ethic, however, has never had a single consistent expression nor has it enjoyed universal assent within Western cultures.

Another important point is that the work ethic historically has torn away from its context, become more abstract and therefore more widely useful (Rodgers, 1978). When the work ethic was Calvin-

ist and held out hope of heavenly rewards, believers toiled for the glory of God. When 19th century moralists shifted the promise toward earthly rewards, the work ethic motivated the middle class to toil because it was useful to oneself and the common weal. The coming of the modern factory system, however, with its painful labor conditions and de-emphasis on the self-sufficient worker, created a moral uncertainty about the essential nobility and instrumentality of work that made individuals want to take refuge in the old phrases and homilies all the more. As work ideals became increasingly abstract, they grew more available. Rodgers (1978) pointed out that workingmen now could invoke the work ethic as a weapon in the battle for status and self-respect, and so defend the dignity of labor and wrap themselves in a rhetoric of pride. Politicians of all persuasions could appeal to the work ethic and cast policy issues as morality plays about industry and laziness. Thus, despite the failed spiritual and instrumental validity of the work ethic, it persisted in powerful abstraction. And it is an abstract work ethic that persists today lacking, as do many other of our moral precepts, those contexts from which their original significance derived (MacIntyre, 1981). While there is constant concern about the health of the work ethic (Lewis, 1982; Yankelovich & Immerwhar, 1984), belief in the goodness of work continues as a piece of civic rhetoric that is important out of all proportion to its behavioral manifestations or utilitarian rewards.

Among persons approaching retirement, surveys show no fall-off in work commitment and subscription to values about work (Hanlon, 1983). Thus, assuming that a positive value orientation toward work is carried up to the threshold of retirement, the question becomes: What do people do with a work ethic when they no longer work?

Continuity of Beliefs and Values

The emergence of a busy ethic is no coincidence. It is, rather, a logical part of people's attempts to manage a smooth transition from work to retirement. Theorists of the life course have identified several conditions that ease an individual's transitions from one status to another. For example, transitions are easier to the extent that the new position has a well-defined role, or provides opportunities for attaining valued social goals, or when it entails a formal program of socialization (Burr, 1973; Rosow, 1974). Transitions are also easier when beliefs are continuous between two positions, that is, when action in the new position is built upon or integrated with the existing values of the person. Moral continuity is a benefit for the individual who is in transition, and for the wider social community as well.

In the abstract, retirement ought to entail the unlearning of values and attitudes—in particular, the work ethic—so that these should be no obstacle to adaptation. Upon withdrawal from work, emotional investment in, and commitment to, the work ethic should by rights be extinguished in favor of accepting leisure as a morally desirable lifestyle. Along these lines, there is a common recommendation that older workers, beginning in their 50s, should be "educated for leisure" in preparation for retirement. For example, the 1971 White House Conference on Aging recommended that "Society should adopt a policy of preparation for retirement, leisure, and education for life off the job . . . to prepare persons to understand and benefit from the changes produced by retirement" (p. 53).

But the work ethic is not unlearned in some resocialization process. Rather, it is transformed. There are two devices of this transformation that allow a moral continuity between work and retired life. One—the busy ethic—defends the daily conduct of retired life. The other—an ideology of pensions—legitimates retirees' claim to income without the obligation to work. As to the latter, a special restitutive rhetoric has evolved that characterizes pensions as entitlements for former productivity. Unlike others, such as welfare recipients, who stand outside the productive process, whose idleness incurs moral censure, and who are very grudgingly tendered financial support (Beck, 1967), the inoccupation of retirees is considered to have been *earned* by virtue of having *formerly* been productive. This veteranship status (Nelson, 1982) justifies the receipt of income without work, preserves the self-respect of retirees, and keeps retirement consistent with the dominant societal prestige system, which rewards members primarily to the extent that they are economically productive.

The Busy Ethic:
Functions and Participants
Along with an ideology that defends the receipt of income without the obligation to work, there is an ethic that defends life without work. This "busy ethic" is at once a statement of value as well as an expectation of retired people—shared by retirees and nonretirees alike—that their lives should be active and earnest. (Retirees' actual levels of activity are, as shall be explained, another matter altogether; the emphasis here is on shared values about the conduct of life.) The busy ethic is named after the common question put to people of retireable age, "What will you do (or are you doing) to keep yourself busy?", and their equally common reports that "I have a lot to keep me busy" and "I'm as busy as ever." Expressions of the busy ethic also have their pejorative opposites, for example, "I'd rot if I just sat around." In naming the busy ethic, the connotation of busyness is more one of involvement and engagement than of mere bustle and hubbub.

The busy ethic serves several purposes: it legitimates the leisure of retirement, it defends retired people against judgments of obsolescence, it gives definition to [the] retirement role, and it "domesticates" retirement by adapting retired life to prevailing societal norms. Before discussing these functions of the busy ethic, it is important to emphasize that any normative feature of social life entails endorsement and management by multiple parties. There are three parties to the busy ethic.

First, of course, are the subjects of the busy ethic—older workers and retirees—who are parties to it by virtue of their status. They participate in the busy ethic to the degree that they subscribe to the desirability of an active, engaged lifestyle.

When called upon to account for their lives as retirees, subjects of the busy ethic should profess to be "doing things" in retirement or, if still working, be planning to "do things." Retirees can testify to their level of involvement in blanket terms, asserting: I've got plenty to do, I'm busier than when I was working. Or they can maintain in reserve a descriptive, mental list of activities (perhaps exaggerated or even fictitious) that can be offered to illustrate a sufficient level of engagement. These engagements run heavily to maintenance activities (e.g., tasks around the house, shopping) and involvement with children and grandchildren. Obviously, part-time jobs, volunteering, or major life projects ("I've always wanted to learn how to play the piano") can be offered as evidence of an active lifestyle. Less serious leisure pursuits (hobbies, pastimes, socializing) can also contribute to a picture of the busy life as long as such pursuits are characterized as involving and time consuming. In honoring the busy ethic, exactly what one does to keep busy is secondary to the fact that one purportedly *is* busy.

A second group of parties to the busy ethic comprises the other participants—friends, relatives, coworkers—who talk to older workers and retirees about the conduct of retired life. Their role is primarily one of keeping conversation about retirement continually focused on the topic of activity, without necessarily upholding ideals of busyness. Conversation with retirees also serves to assure these others that there is life after work. Indeed, apart from money matters, conversation about retired life *per se* is chiefly conversation about what one does with it, how time is filled. Inquiries about the retiree's lifestyle ("So what are you doing with yourself?") may come from sincere interest or may only be polite conversation. Inquiries, too, can be mean-spirited, condescending, or envious. Whatever the source or course of discussion, it nonetheless frequently comes to assurances that, yes, it is good to keep busy.

The third group can be called institutional conservators of the busy ethic, and their role is more clearly normative. These parties hold up implicit and explicit models of what retired life should be like, models that evince an importance placed on being active and engaged. Prominent institutional conservators of the busy ethic are the marketers of products and services to seniors, the gerontology profession, and the popular media. More shall be said about these later.

Returning to the purposes that the busy ethic serves, its primary function is to legitimate the leisure of retirement. Leisure without the eventual obligation of working is an anomalous feature of adulthood. Excepting the idle rich and those incapable of holding a job, few adults escape the obligation to work. Retirement and pension policies, however, are devised to exclude older adults from the labor force. In addition, age bias operates to foreclose opportunities for their further employment. How can our value system defend this situation—retirement—when it is elsewhere engaged in conferring honor on people who work and work hard? The answer lies in an ethic that endorses leisure that is analogous to work. As noted above, leisure pursuits can range from the serious to the self-indulgent. What legitimates these as an authentic adult lifestyle is their correspondence with the *form* of working life, which is to be occupied by activities that are regarded as serious and engaging. The busy ethic rescues retirement from the stigma of retreat and aimlessness and defines it as a succession to new or renewed foci of engagement. It reconciles for retirees and their social others the adult obligation to work with a life of leisure. This is the nature of continuity in self-respect between the job and retirement (Atchley, 1971).

In an essay that anticipates some of the present argument, Miller (1965) took a stricter view about what justifies retirement leisure. Mere activity is not meaningful enough; it must have the added rationale of being infused with aspects of work that are culturally esteemed. Activity legitimates retirement if it is, for example, economically instrumental (profitable hobbies), or contributes to the general good (community service), or is potentially productive (education or skill development). Whether people in fact recognize a hierarchy of desirable, work-correlative activities at which retirees can be busy remains to be determined. What Miller's essay and the present argument have in common, nonetheless, is the view that what validates retirement, in part, is activity that is analogous to work.

The busy ethic serves a second purpose for its subjects, which is to symbolically defend retirees against aging. Based on the belief that vigor preserves well-being, subscription to the norm of busyness can recast retirement as "middle-age like." Adherence to the busy ethic can be a defense— even to oneself—against possible judgments of obsolescence or senescence. To accentuate the contrast between the vital and senescent elder, there is an entire vocabulary of pejorative references to rocking chairs and sitting and idleness. As an illustration, a recent piece in my local newspaper about a job placement service for seniors quoted one of the program's participants, who said: "I am not working for income. I am working for therapy, to keep busy. There is nothing that will hurt an elderly person as much as just sitting alone all day long, doing nothing, thinking about nothing." It is appropriate to note here that, in scope, the busy ethic does not apply to all retirees. The busy life is more likely to be an expectation on the conduct of the "young-old" retiree, or at least the retiree who has not been made frail by chronic illness.

A third purpose of the busy ethic is that it places a boundary on the retirement role and thus permits some true leisure. Just as working adults cycle between time at work and time off, retirees too can have "time off." Because the busy ethic justifies some of one's time, the balance of one's time needs no justification. For example, if the morning was spent running errands or caring for grandchildren, one can feel comfortable with napping or a stretch of TV viewing in the afternoon. The existence of fulfillable expectations allows one to balance being active with taking it easy—one can slip out of the retirement role, one is allowed time offstage. Being busy, like working, "pays" for one's rest and relaxation.

The busy ethic serves a fourth function, and this for the wider society by "domesticating" retirement to mainstream societal values. It could be otherwise. Why not an ethic of hedonism, nonconformity, and carefree self-indulgence as a logical response to societal policies that define older workers as obsolescent and expendable? Free of adult workaday constraints, retirees could become true dropouts thumbing their noses at convention. Or why not an ethic of repose, with retirees resolutely unembarrassed about slowing down to enjoy leisure in very individual ways? Retirees do often describe retirement as a time for sheer gratification. In response to open-ended questions on Normative Aging Study surveys about the primary advantages of retirement, men overwhelmingly emphasize: freedom to do as I wish, no more schedules, now I can do what I want, just relax, enjoy life. Such sentiments, however, do not tend to serve drop-out or contemplative models of retired life because retirees will go on to indicate that their leisure is nonetheless responsibly busy. The busy ethic tames the potentially unfettered pleasures of retirement to prevailing values about engagement that apply to adulthood. For nonretirees, this renders retirement as something intelligible and consistent with other stages of life. Additionally, the busy ethic, in holding that retirees can and should be participating in the world, probably salves some concern about their having been unfairly put on the shelf.

The active domestication of retirement is the province of the institutional conservators of the busy ethic. The popular media are strenuous conservators. An article in my local newspaper last year bore the headline, "They've retired but still keep busy," which was reprised only a few months later in another headline, "He keeps busy in his retirement." Both articles assured the reader that these seniors were happily compensating for their withdrawal from work. It is common for "senior set" features to depict older people in an upbeat fashion, though in all fairness the genre of newspapers' lifestyle sections generally portrays everybody as occupied by varied and wonderful activities regardless of age. The popular media are also staunch promoters of aged exemplars of activity and achievement—Grandma Moses, Pablo Casals, George Burns, and so on through such lists (Wallechinsky et al., 1977). A current National Public Radio series on aging and creativity bears the perceptive title: "I'm Too Busy to Talk Now: Conversations with American Artists over Seventy."

Marketers, with the golf club as their chief prop, have been instrumental in fostering the busy image. A recent analysis of advertising in magazines designed specifically for older people found that the highest percentage of ads in these magazines concerned travel and more often than not portrayed older people in an active setting such as golfing, bicycling, or swimming (Kvasnicka et al., 1982). Calhoun (1978) credited the ads and brochures of the retirement home industry, in particular, with promoting an energetic image of older Americans. This industry built houses and, more importantly, built a market for those houses, which consisted of the dynamic retiree. While few retirees ever live in retirement communities, the model of such communities has been most influential in the creation of an active, if shallowly commercial, image of the elderly. One writer (Fitzgerald, 1983), visiting Sun City Center in Florida ("The town too busy to retire"), reflected:

> Possibly some people still imagine retirement communities as boarding houses with rocking chairs, but, thanks to Del Webb and a few other pioneer developers, the notion of 'active' retirement has become entirely familiar; indeed, since the sixties it has been the guiding principle of retirement-home builders across the country. Almost all developers now advertise recreational facilities and print glossy brochures with photos of gray-haired people playing golf tennis, and shuffleboard. (p. 74)

The visitor noted that residents talked a great deal about their schedules and activities. The visitor also noted how their emphasis on activities was an attempt to legitimate retirement and knit it to long-standing beliefs and values:

> Sun Citians' insistence on busyness—and the slightly defensive tone of their town boosterism—came, I began to imagine, from the fact that their philosophies, and, presumably, the [conservative, work ethic] beliefs they had grown up with, did not really support them in this enterprise of retirement. (p. 91)

The gerontological community has been an important conservator of aspects of the busy ethic. Cumming and Henry (1961) early on pointed out the nonscientific presuppositions of mainstream gerontology's "implicit theory" of aging, which include the projection of middle-aged standards of instrumentality, activity, and usefulness into later life. This implicit, so-called "activity theory" of aging entailed the unabashed value judgment that "the older person who ages optimally is the person who stays active and manages to resist the shrinkage of his social world" (Havighurst et al., 1968, p. 161). Gubrium (1973) has noted the Calvinistic aura of this perspective: "Successful aging, as the activity theorists portray it, is a life style that is visibly 'busy' " (p. 7). Continuing this orientation over the last decade, gerontology's campaign against ageism has, according to Cole (1983), promoted an alternative image of older people as healthy, sexually active, engaged, productive, and self-reliant.

Institutional conservators of the busy ethic are by no means monolithic in their efforts to uphold ideals of busyness. Rather, in pursuing their diverse objectives they find it useful to highlight particular images of retirement and later life that coalesce around the desirability of engagement.

Sources of Authority

The busy ethic is useful, therefore, because it legitimates leisure, it wards off disturbing thoughts about aging, it permits retirees some rest and relaxation, and it adapts retirement to prevailing societal norms. These benefits to the participants of the busy ethic are functional only in an analytic sense. No one in daily life approves of busy retirements because such approval is "functional." It is useful at this point to ask why people ultimately assent to the notion that it is good to be busy.

The busy ethic has moral force because it participates in two great strong value complexes—ethics themselves—that axiomatize it. One, of course, is the work ethic, which holds that it is ennobling to be exerting oneself in the world. The other basis for the busy ethic's authority is the profound importance placed on good health and the stimulating, wholesome manner of living that is believed to ensure its maintenance. The maintenance of health is an ideal with a deep tradition that has long carried moral as well as medical significance. Haley (1978), for example, has pointed out how Victorian thinkers promoted the tonic qualities of a robust and energetic lifestyle. The preservation of health was seen to be a duty because the well-knit body reflected a well-formed mind, and the harmony of mind and body signified spiritual health and the reach for higher human excellence. Ill, unkempt, and indolent conditions, by contrast, indicated probable moral failure. Times change, but current fashions in health maintenance still imply that a fit and strenuous life will have medical benefits and testify as well to the quality of one's will and character. Thus, admonitions to older people that they "keep busy" and "keep going" are authoritative because they advocate an accepted therapy for body and soul.

Correspondence with Behavior

One crucial issue is the correspondence between the busy ethic and actual behavior. It is important to mention that not all self-reports about busy retirements are conscious presentations of conformity to a busy ethic. There are retirees who by any reckoning are very active. But in the more general case, if people believe it is important to keep busy, should they not therefore *be* busy by some standard or another?

This paper's argument in favor of the busy ethic has implied that belief is not necessarily behavior. On one hand, the busy ethic may—as any ethic should—motivate retirees to use their time in constructive or involving pursuits. It may get them out of the unhealthful rocking chair or away from the can-of-beer-in-front-of-the-TV. On the other hand, the busy ethic can motivate people to *interpret* their style of life as conforming to ideals about activity. An individual can take a disparate, even limited, set of activities and spin them together into a representation of a very busy life. It would be difficult to contradict such a manner of thinking on empirical grounds; "engagement" is a subjective quality of time use that simple counts of activities or classifications of their relative seriousness or instrumentality are not likely to measure. Indeed, gerontologists should be wary about the extent to which the busy ethic may shape people's responses on surveys about their leisure, frequency of activities, and experience in retirement.

In posing the question, "How busy do retirees have to be under such a set of values?", the answer is they don't objectively have to be very busy at all. Just as with the work ethic, which has been an abstract set of ideals for some time (Rodgers, 1978), it is not the actual pace of activity but the preoccupation with activity and the affirmation of its desirability that matters. After all, all of us are not always honest, but we would all agree that honesty is the best policy. The busy ethic, like the work ethic and other commonplace values, should be evaluated less for its implied link with actual behavior than for its ability to badger or comfort the conscience. The busy ethic, at bottom, is self-validating: because it is important to be busy, people will say they are busy.

Conclusion

The busy ethic is an idea that people have about the appropriate quality of a retired lifestyle. It solves the problem of moral continuity: how to integrate existing beliefs and values about work into a new status that constitutes a withdrawal from work. The postulation of a busy ethic is an attempt to examine sociologically people's judgments of value and obligation regarding the conduct of daily life—their expectations of each other and of themselves.

To be sure, there are other superseding expectations on the conduct of retirees. Writing about the duties of a possible retirement role, Atchley (1976) has noted that a stability of behavior is expected, as well as self-reliance and independence in managing one's affairs. Such normative preferences are fairly vague and open-ended. Rosow (1974) surveyed the prospects for socialization to later life, in which the retirement role is nested, and found that behavioral prescriptions for older people are open and flexible, and norms are limited, weak, and ambiguous. Even admonitions to be active carry virtually no guidance about the preferred content of such activity. Perhaps this is just as well. Streib and Schneider (1971), summarizing findings from the Cornell Study of Occupational Retirement, pointed out that the vagueness of retirees' role expectations may protect retirees from demands that they might be disinclined to fulfill or from standards that diminished health and financial resources might not allow them to meet.

The busy ethic, too, comprises vague expectations on behavior. It is a modest sort of prescription—less a spur to conformity and more a way to comfortably knit a new circumstance to long-held values. Social disapproval is its only sanction. Not all retirees assent to this image of retirement, nor do they need to. Judging by the ubiquity of the idea, however, subscribers to the busy ethic are probably in the majority; one cannot talk to retirees for very long without hearing the rhetoric of busyness. The busy ethic also legitimates the daily conduct of retired life in a lower key than has been claimed by some gerontologists, who propose that work substitutes and instrumental activity are essential to indemnify retirement. While some retirees do need to work at retirement to psychologically recoup the social utility that working supplied (Hooker & Ventis, 1984), for most it is enough to participate in a rather abstract esteem for an active lifestyle and to represent their own retirement as busy in some way.

To conclude, the busy ethic, as an idealization and expectation of retired life, illustrates how retirement is socially managed, not just politically and economically, but also morally—by means of everyday talk and conversation as well as by more formal institutions. Drawing its authority from the work ethic and from a traditional faith in the therapeutic value of activity, the busy ethic counsels a habit of engagement that is continuous with general cultural prescriptions for adulthood. It legitimates the leisure of retirement, it defends retired people against judgments of senescence, and it gives definition to the retirement role. In all, the busy ethic helps individuals adapt to retirement, and it in turn adapts retirement to prevailing societal norms.

References

Atchley, R. C. (1971). Retirement and leisure participation: Continuity or crisis? *The Gerontologist, 11,* 13-17.

Atchley, R. C. (1976). *The sociology of retirement.* New York: Halsted Press.

Beck, B. (1967). Welfare as a moral category. *Social Problems, 14,* 258-277.

Bosse, R., Ekerdt, D. J., & Silbert, J. E. (1984). The Veterans Administration Normative Aging Study. In S. A. Mednick, M. Harway, & K. M. Finello (Eds.), *Handbook of longitudinal research. Vol. 2, Teenage and adult cohorts.* New York: Praeger.

Burr, W. R. (1973). *Theory construction and the sociology of the family.* New York: John Wiley.

Calhoun, R. B. (1978). *In search of the new old: Redefining old age in America, 1945-1970.* New York: Elsevier.

Cole, T. R. (1983). The 'enlightened' view of aging: Victorian morality in a new key. *Hastings Center Report, 13,* 34-40.

Cumming, E., & Henry, W. H. (1961). *Growing old: The process of disengagement.* New York: Basic Books.

Fitzgerald, F. (1983, April 25). Interlude (Sun City Center). *New Yorker,* pp. 54-109.

Gubrium, J. F. (1973). *The myth of the golden years: A socio-environmental theory of aging.* Springfield, IL: Charles C Thomas.

Haley, B. (1978). *The healthy body and Victorian culture.* Cambridge, MA: Harvard University Press.

Hanlon, M. D. (1983). Age and the commitment to work. Flushing, NY: Queens College, City University of New York, Department of Urban Studies (ERIC Document Reproduction Service # ED 243 003).

Havighurst, R. J., Neugarten, B. L., & Tobin, S. S. (1968). Disengagement and patterns of aging. In B. L. Neugarten (Ed.), *Middle age and aging: A reader in social psychology.* Chicago: University of Chicago Press.

Hooker, K., & Ventis, D. G. (1984). Work ethic, daily activities, and retirement satisfaction. *Journal of Gerontology, 39,* 478-484.

Keniston, K. (1974). Youth and its ideology. In S. Arieti (Ed.), *American handbook of psychiatry. Vol. 1, The foundations of psychiatry.* 2nd ed. New York: Basic Books.

Kvasnicka, B., Beymer, B., & Perloff, R. M. (1982). Portrayals of the elderly in magazine advertisements. *Journalism Quarterly, 59,* 656-658.

Lewis, L. S. (1982). Working at leisure. *Society, 19* (July/August), 27-32.

MacIntyre, A. (1981). *After virtue: A study in moral theory.* Notre Dame, IN: University of Notre Dame Press.

Miller, S. J. (1965). The social dilemma of the aging leisure participant. In A. M. Rose & W. Peterson (Eds.), *Older people and their social worlds.* Philadelphia: F. A. Davis.

Nelson, D. W. (1982). Alternate images of old age as the bases for policy. In B. L. Neugarten (Ed.), *Age or need? Public policies for older people.* Beverly Hills, CA: Sage.

Rodgers, D. T. (1978). *The work ethic in industrial America: 1850-1920.* Chicago: University of Chicago Press.

Rosow, I. (1974). *Socialization to old age.* Berkeley, CA: University of California Press.

Streib, G. F., & Schneider, C. J. (1971). *Retirement in American society: Impact and process.* Ithaca, NY: Cornell University Press.

Wallechinsky, D., Wallace, I., & Wallace, A. (1977). *The People's Almanac presents the book of lists.* New York: William Morrow.

White House Conference on Aging. (1971). *Toward a national policy on aging: Proceedings of the 1971 White House conference on Aging, Vol. II.* Washington, DC: U.S. Government Printing Office.

Yankelovich, D., & Immerwhar, J. (1984). Putting the work ethic to work. *Society, 21* (January/February), 58-76.

READING 36

Life After Work

Nancy J. Osgood

Work: Past, Present, and Future

Work in Classical and Preindustrial Society

Work has not always been exalted as the noblest of institutions. To the ancient Greeks, who forced

slaves to do their work for them, work was nothing more than a curse (Tilgher, 1930). Leisure was the highest aim in life. As Aristotle noted: "We should not be able only to work well but to use leisure well; for as I repeat once more, the first principle of all action is leisure. Both are required, but leisure is better than work and its end" (DeGrazia, 1962, p. 15). The Greeks classified work and other obligations as nonleisure, unlike many today who classify leisure as nonwork. To the Greeks, leisure was the noblest activity, and music, the arts, and contemplation were the highest of all activities, exemplifying the human aspect that was most godlike and that most distinguished humans from other animals (DeGrazia, 1962). Work, on the other hand, was seen as brutalizing the mind, rendering one unfit to consider truth or practice virtues (DeGrazia, 1962, p. 115).

Like the ancient Greeks, the Hebrews viewed work as a trial and tribulation, Adam's punishment for the fall. They placed no intrinsic value or meaning on work. It was merely necessary toil that had to be endured as punishment.

How was the nature and meaning of work changed since early days? What place will work hold in our lives as we enter what Daniel Bell (1973) has called the postindustrial society? . . .

In *The Coming of Post-Industrial Society,* Bell presents a detailed analysis of the distinguishing features of postindustrialism. Postindustrial society is, above all, a knowledge-based, service-oriented society whose major hallmarks are the increasing bureaucratization of science and specialization of intellectual work.

The supremacy of mind over body is one of the cornerstones of Bell's postindustrial society. As the acquisition and utilization of knowledge and information achieves a larger place in our society, new modes of life that depend on cognitive and theoretical knowledge inevitably result in individual self-enhancement and self-expression.

Writers describing modern day America have suggested that we are in the midst of a value revolution in which the Protestant work ethic, appropriate in earlier days of industrialization but sorely outdated today, is being replaced by a new system of hedonistic values that emphasize fun, consumption, play, and instant pleasure as ends in themselves. Yankelovich (1974) suggests that today success is defined differently than it was 50 years ago. As he points out, from World War I until recently, most Americans defined achievement in terms of material things. Mizruchi's study of success values conducted 20 years ago (1964) also

confirmed that materialism was a dominant measure of success in former times. Today, Yankelovich suggests, self-fulfillment and quality of life are more important than higher earnings. If the motif of the past was "keeping up the Joneses," today it is "I have my own life to live. Let Jones shift for himself" (1974, p. 81). Self-actualization has become a major value in today's society as more and more individuals resist the standardization, regimentation, and specialization characteristic of work in industrial society. Today many are choosing to work part time (roughly 45 percent of all Americans according to Eli Ginzberg) or to find jobs in which they can "do their own thing," be more creative, and "express themselves," even if it means a cut in pay. Fifty million Americans now participate in some form of amateur art activity, a further testimony to the move toward "doing your own thing." . . .

Since 1900, the percentage of a man's life spent in work activities has declined from 66.6 percent to 58.4 percent, the bulk of the reduction due to the institutionalization of retirement. The percentage of a man's total life spent in retirement has increased nearly 150 percent since 1900, from 6.5 percent to 16.8 percent (McConnell, 1980, p. 69). Best [1978] presents an interesting analysis of dramatic changes in the proportion of life spent in work through the centuries in a recent article in *The Futurist.* He states that work absorbed about 33 percent of the average person's life span in primitive times (before 4000 B.C.), 29 percent during the agriculture era (4000 B.C.-1900 A.D.), and about 14 percent during the agricultural era (past 1900 A.D.). In the twentieth century, work time for U.S. males as a proportion of their overall working and sleeping lifetime was cut almost in half between 1900 and 1970, from 23.7 to 13.4 percent (1978, p. 5).

The drastic reductions of work life for U.S. males is a result of several factors besides the institutionalization of retirement. Drastically reduced workweeks coupled with longer vacations and more holidays are a factor. As Best (1979) points out, the average workweek has declined over the last century from about 60 hours in 1870 to 39 hours today. . . .

Wilensky (1961), in his oft quoted article, "The Uneven Distribution of Leisure: The Impact of Economic Growth on 'Free Time,' " presents an interesting historical analysis of changes in the amount of time spent in work, comparing the present century not only to the 1900s but also to earlier centuries. Figures presented by Wilensky convincingly indicate that we are only barely beginning to achieve the amount of leisure time enjoyed by the Romans and by primitive agriculturists. In the old Roman calendar, nearly 109 of the 355 days, or one-third, were designated as non-work days (p. 109). It is only when we compare work time today with hours spent in work during the late 1800s and early 1900s, when industrialization was at its peak, that we can correctly conclude that the amount of time spent working has been significantly reduced. It is probable, however, that during the next century we may more nearly approximate the work-leisure distribution enjoyed by our ancestors in earlier centuries.

Other significant changes in the organization and structure of work have also been occurring since 1900. Due to the increased length of time spent in education preparing for the jobs characteristic of our new knowledge-based scientific society and to trends toward earlier retirement, workers enter the labor force later and exit earlier now than they did in 1900. The effect is a compression of work into the middle years of life. . . .

Another change is the adoption of the four-day week. Between 1973 and 1977, according to the Bureau of Labor Statistics, the number of U.S. workers on a four-day workweek increased by more than 50 percent, although such workers still represent only 1.4 percent of the U.S. labor force. Another change is the increase in part-time work. Almost nonexistent at the turn of the century, part-time work includes 17 million persons, mostly women. Both of these changes allow more leisure for the American worker and more flexible integration of work and play. . . .

The New Leisure Society

These changes in the organization and structure of work and leisure reflect the larger values of the society and impact on other social institutions, particularly on the family, education, and economic institutions. Roberts (1970), Bacon (1975), Dumazedier (1967), Parker (1976), and others have recently suggested that we are entering a new leisure age, characterized by a new leisure ethic or fun morality. The conceptualization of our society as a new leisure society implies more than simply an increase in the amount of time for leisure. These writers are referring to a major value change, a shift in the way we view work and leisure in our lives. Signs of change can be seen in increased worker dissatisfaction with jobs, absenteeism, part-time work, and midcareer job changing. The new leisure ethic emphasizes leisure as the central life interest, replacing the former centrality of work. Leisure is the most important social institution through which we achieve identity and self-expression, not through work. Finally, leisure has the most important effect on how we structure the other domains of our life (family and work, for example). Leisure is viewed as an end in itself rather than as subordinate to work.

Dumazedier, probably the best known exponent of this argument, suggests that the growth of leisure has nurtured:

a new social need for the individual to be his own master and please himself. . . . What used to be considered idleness when confronted with the requirements of the firm is now defined as dignity, what used to be called selfishness when confronted with the requirements of the family is now perceived as respect for the personality of one of its members. Part of what used to be considered sinful by religious institutions is now recognized as the art of living (1974, p. 42). . . .

The development of the new leisure ethic has been made possible primarily by improved technology, which has resulted in shorter workweeks, retirement, pension plans, and relative affluence for large numbers. Two other conditions necessary to the development of such an ethic, according to Dumazedier (1967), are the disappearance of rituals governing social activities and a clear line of demarcation between labor and other activities.

Many writers (Kaplan, 1960; Wilensky, 1964) suggest that modern society is moving in the direction of a fusion of labor and leisure in which work is becoming more like play and play more like work. With this idea in mind, Gregory Stone (1972) has asserted "more and more we play at our work and work at our play." Riesman explains this fusion in terms of the changing U.S. character from inner-directedness to other-directedness. He writes: "The other-directed person has no clear core of self to escape from; no clear line between production and consumption; between adjusting to the group and serving private interests; between work and play" (1953, p. 185). . . .

The historical relationship of work and leisure can be diagrammed as a circular one. In the beginning, there was fusion and integration. Work and leisure were part of the whole and not distinct, observable units of behavior. The Greeks identified leisure as a behavior distinct from and superior to work. The shift was from the fusion of work and leisure to leisure as a priority. With the Industrial Revolution, the gradual change from leisure as a priority to work as the ultimate goal was complete. However, change was inevitable, and gradually work was demoted as leisure achieved prominence. This change reached its peak during the late 1960s and 1970s, when leisure and "doing your own thing" were exalted. . . .

Fourastié writes that "to choose one's leisure will be to choose one's life" (quoted in Dumazedier, 1974, p. 148). If Fourastié is correct, we are currently embarking upon a happier era in the history of civilization. But not all students of leisure agree that the increased amount of leisure time is a positive phenomenon. Another Frenchman, Tocqueville, writing at an earlier time, expressed his fears about the tyrannizing effect of mass affluence resulting from industrialization:

> I seek to trace the novel features under which despotism may appear in the world. The first thing that strikes the observation is an innumerable multitude of men, all equal and alike, incessantly endeavoring to procure the petty and paltry pleasures with which they glut their lives. Each of them, living apart, is as a stranger to the fate of all the rest; his children and his private friends constitute to him the whole of mankind (1945, p. 10).

Since Tocqueville made his classic statement, numerous others have expressed similar concern over the negative effects of leisure in our mass society. Hedonism, says Daniel Bell (1973), is one of the cultural contradictions of capitalism. Capitalism fosters hedonism through its emphasis on consumption, but the hedonistic individual becomes a less dedicated worker and family worker, thereby jeopardizing future ability to produce and consume. Others have criticized our mass culture for providing spurious gratification, reducing the level of cultural quality and civilization and encouraging totalitarianism and dehumanization by creating a passive public responsive to mass persuasion. . . .

As we approach a new era of labor-leisure relationships, one more closely approximating the situation of ancient Greek and Roman civilizations in which work and leisure were merged and in which leisure enjoyed an exalted status, certain questions are suggested.

Will leisure be a liberating or an alienating social institution?

What new norms will develop to structure labor-leisure relations?

How will new values regarding work and leisure affect other major social institutions, particularly the family, educational, and economic institutions?

What new patterns of social organization and social structures will characterize the new leisure society?

What new cultural values and individual lifestyles will result from these fundamental changes in the structure and organization of work and leisure?

In what ways will patterns of production and consumption be altered in this new society and with what effects?

In the new society, what social institution, if any, will restore the authority of a common code of ethics and social discipline formerly provided by the family, then by work?

How will the new leisure ethic affect our conceptions of aging and retirement in the future? . . .

Retirement makes available a range of options in all life sectors; work role is not necessarily the only one. Continuity theory postulates the inevitability of retirement as a normal noncrisis concomitant of our industrial society and emphasizes the necessity to adapt successfully to that condition, involving as it does a change in roles. Those who view retirement as one of the most disturbing crises of their lives, it is claimed, probably had difficulty adapting to other role changes. Adaptive flexibility and a sense of well-being in the middle years of life predict the probable display of these same characteristics in later years. In fact, the entire life cycle may be conceptualized as a process in which success predicts success. Proponents of the continuity theory maintain that for retirees there is a range of options. If life has meaning only when one contributes to it, such a contribution need not be measured in economic or occupational terms. Most retirees, in fact, adapt successfully (Bultena and Wood, 1969; Streib and Schneider, 1971).

Most recent research has indicated that for most people retirement has become a normal, expected part of the occupational cycle. Retirement is not necessarily a traumatizing crisis. If the financial disadvantages of retirement could be eliminated and inflation controlled, people would look for-

ward to retirement in an even more positive sense. The decision to retire is a function of the individual's income, health, family status, and prospects for life after retirement—in other words, what the individual is retiring to as well as from is also important. Hard, dirty, or hazardous work is a factor affecting early retirement, as are increased private and public pension programs and increased social security benefits. . . .

Many researchers whose findings lend support to the continuity theory have found that work is no longer a central life interest for men in U.S. society. Rather, work represents only a means of earning the money necessary to pursue leisure or family activities. For many blue collar and white collar workers, as well as professionals, work has become an alienating and dissatisfying experience. In their study of the meaning of work to individuals, Friedman and Orbach conclude that "work does not seem to take precedence over other life areas for most workers" (1974, p. 613). Blauner's review of attitudes of U.S. workers (1964) revealed that many are alienated from their work and see no purpose in it. Similarly Williams and Wirths (1965) found that the world of work was the central element in lifestyle for only 15 percent of their subjects, echoing much earlier findings by Dubin (1956), who found that for three out of four industrial workers, work was not a central life interest. . . .

The studies reviewed here discount the belief that work is currently the most important social institution in our society and that loss of the work role results in a severe crisis of identity for the individual. What these and other recent studies reveal is the changing nature and meaning of work, leisure, and retirement in U.S. society. As retirement becomes a more widespread phenomenon in our society, norms develop around the role of retiree, and more role models are available, thus facilitating socialization and smooth transition into the role. As we enter the new leisure age, which Kaplan (1975) and others describe, and as leisure assumes greater importance and credibility as a legitimate source of personal identity, one suspects that attitudes toward and effects of retirement upon individuals will undergo profound change.

References

Bacon, W. 1975. "Social Caretaking and Leisure Provision." In *Sport and Leisure in Contemporary Society,* edited by S. Parker, mimeograph. London: Polytechnic of Central London.

Bell, Daniel. 1973. *The Coming Post-Industrial Society.* New York: Basic Books.

Best, F. 1978. "Recycling People: Work Sharing Through Flexible Life Scheduling." *The Futurist* 12 (February):5-16.

Best, F. 1979. "The Future of Retirement and Life Time Distribution of Work," *Aging and Work, 2* (Summer): 172-81.

Blauner, Robert. 1964. *Alienation and Freedom.* Chicago: University of Chicago Press.

Bultena, Gordon, and Vivian Wood. 1969. "The American Retirement Community: Bane or Blessing?" *Journal of Gerontology* 24 (January):209-18.

DeGrazia, S. 1962. *Of Time, Work, and Leisure.* New York: Twentieth Century Fund.

Dubin, R. 1956. "Industrial Worker Worlds: A Study of Central Life Interests of Industrial Workers." *Social Problems* 3 (January):131-42.

Dumazedier, J. 1974. *Sociology of Leisure.* New York: Collier-Macmillan.

———. 1967. *Toward a Society of Leisure.* Amsterdam: Elsevier.

Friedman, Eugene, and Harold Orbach. 1974. "Adjustment to Retirement." In *American Handbook of Psychiatry,* edited by Silvano Arieti, pp. 609-45. New York: Basic Books.

Kaplan, Max. 1975. *Leisure: Theory and Policy.* New York: John Wiley.

———. *Leisure in America.* New York: Wiley.

McConnell, S. R. 1980. "Alternative Work Patterns for an Aging Work Force." In *Work and Retirement: Policy Issue,* edited by P. Ragan, pp. 69-86. Los Angeles: University of Southern California, Ethel Percy Andrus Gerontology Center.

Mizruchi, Ephraim H. 1964. *Success and Opportunity.* Glencoe, Illinois: Free Press.

Parker, Stanley. 1976. *The Sociology of Leisure.* New York: International Publishers Service (G. Allen).

Riesman, David. 1953. *The Lonely Crowd.* New York: Doubleday.

Roberts, K. 1970. *Leisure.* London: Longman.

Stone, Gregory P. 1972. "American Sports: Play and Display." In *Sport: Readings from a Sociological Perspective,* edited by E. Dunning, pp. 47-65. Toronto: University of Toronto Press.

Streib, Gordon, and Clement J. Schneider. 1971. *Retirement in American Society: Impact and Process.* Ithaca, N.Y.: Cornell University Press.

Tilgher, Adriano. 1930. *Work: What it has Meant to Men Through the Ages.* Translated by D. Fischer. New York: Harcourt, Brace.

Tocqueville, Alexis de. 1945. *Democracy in America.* New York: Vintage Books.

Wilensky, Harold L. 1964. "Mass Society and Mass Culture: Interdependence or Independence." *American Sociological Review* 29 (April):173-97.

———. (1961). "The Uneven Distribution of Leisure: The Impact of Economic Growth on 'Free Time.' " *Social Problems* 9 (Summer):32-55.

Williams, Richard H., and Claudine Wirths. 1965. *Lives Through the Years.* New York: Atherton Press.

Yankelovich, D. 1974. *The New Morality: A Profile of American Youth in the 70's.* New York: McGraw-Hill.

———. 1979. "The Future of Retirement and Lifetime Distribution of Work." *Aging and Work* 2 (Summer):31-45.

QUESTIONS FOR WRITING, REFLECTION, AND DEBATE

1 The French poet Baudelaire once said, "Work is less boring than pleasure." Was Baudelaire right? Write a short discussion of Baudelaire's statement as you think it applies to the question of work versus leisure among older people. If possible, give examples of actual people you've known during their retirement years.

2 Imagine you've become the marketing director for a new $100 million residential complex called "Retirement City, USA," located in Florida.

Your job is to produce a new brochure describing the benefits of retirement in this unique residential environment. The idea is to attract a new group of retirees who are looking for a distinctive lifestyle. Prepare a draft of the brochure highlighting the points that would be most attractive to potential residents of "Retirement City, USA."

3 The words we use to describe the same action can make a big difference in how we see it. For instance, what is the real difference between "leisure," "free time," and "recreation"? Are the distinctions here just a matter of "semantics"?

4 Imagine a single middle-aged individual who stays at home all day long. What is the difference between describing that person as "on a sabbatical," "on vacation," "unemployed," or "taking early retirement"? Does the individual's age make a difference in what term might be most appropriate?

5 Assume that you've just read a long editorial in a local newspaper that calls on senior citizens to avoid the "rocking chair" approach to retirement living. You find the editorial profoundly disturbing. Write a long letter to the editor of the paper identifying the reasons that you think retirement makes sense today and in the future.

6 Based on your observation of family members or people you've seen in the workplace, what are the biggest problems middle-aged or older workers would face if they were forced to change jobs and go into a completely new field? Are there steps that could be taken to make such changes easier for people?

7 Some people believe that, if there are not enough jobs to go around for everyone, it makes more sense to encourage older people to retire and "get out of the way" to make room for the young. What are the arguments for and against this approach to older people in the labor force? What are the costs and benefits of encouraging or discouraging early retirement?

FOCUS ON PRACTICE: PRODUCTIVE AGING

As we have seen, the question, "Does retirement make sense?" is a complicated one. Indeed, for both individuals and society, the choice between work and retirement is in many ways a false choice. The real question may involve how to enable older people to lead lives of greater productivity, whether in employment or in retirement. Interest in this question about productive aging has grown in recent years (Butler and Gleason, 1985; Bass and Caro, 1993).

New Research Findings

Prospects for productive aging in the future are strengthened by new findings that most older people are in good health, active, and vital and that they are committed to contributing to the welfare of others. In 1991 Louis Harris and Associates, with support from the Commonwealth Fund, carried out a representative national survey of 3,000 adults over age 55 to investigate their involvement in productive activities such as work, volunteer roles, and caregiving for a sick or disabled spouse, other relatives, neighbors, or friends. The Commonwealth-Harris survey showed that 38 million older Americans—more than 70% of those 55 or older—were actively contributing to society through work, volunteerism, or caregiving. In the "young-old" category (ages 65 to 74), the survey found that 62% considered themselves in good to excellent health, 59% stressed the importance of helping other people, and 63% were "very satisfied with life." These findings are in stark contradiction to myths that depict older Americas as dependent, depressed, and isolated.

The Commonwealth study found that Americans over 55 represent a great overlooked national resource. The total value of their contribution to society is the equivalent of nearly 12 million full-time workers and the equivalent of 7.1 million full-time workers in caregiving activities alone. The study determined that men play a bigger role as volunteers and caregivers than they are usually credited with. These roles included helping sick or disabled relatives as well as helping children or grandchildren. Another interesting finding was the underestimated vitality of those above age 75. Health problems do increase in this group and do inhibit some activities (Herzog et al., 1989). But even among the old-old, over half reported themselves in excellent or good health, 23% were volunteering through organizations, and 22% were involved in caregiving for family or neighbors. Finally, the Commonwealth study confirmed that, along with current productive roles, older people are eager to be even more actively involved: 31% were not employed but wanted to be. A similar picture emerged for volunteers, confirming the importance of the older volunteer activities previously documented (Chambre, 1987). This rise in the number of able elders has positive implications for an aging society that deserve consideration (Hudson, 1987).

An organized vehicle for productive aging already exists in the variety of programs sponsored by the government. Some of these involve paid employment. The two largest federal programs are the Senior Community Service Employment Program (SCSEP), created under Title V of the Older Americans Act, and the Job Training Partnership Act (JTPA). SCSEP supports part-time, government-subsidized jobs for low-income people over age 55 who are placed in local community service agencies. SCSEP provides only minimal training for those eligible, but the JTPA program has a 3% set-aside reserved exclusively for older workers. JTPA has worked closely with private industry councils representing employers, and the program includes job search and placement help. The latter service can be especially helpful for older workers trying to get back into the workforce, as shown by the successful experience of Project ABLE in Chicago, a model employment agency specializing in older workers.

The Commonwealth survey showed that a great part of productive aging lies in volunteer contributive activities, and here, too, organized efforts can enhance productive roles for older people. The Office of Older American Volunteer Programs (OAVP) is the largest of the operating units within ACTION, the federal agency that coordinates volunteer activities. One of the older volunteer programs run by ACTION is the Senior Companions Program, which is similar to Foster Grandparents but is directed toward impaired adults needing help to continue living in their own homes. Another is the Service Corp of Retired Executives (SCORE), a program by the U.S. Small Business Administration to enlist retired business executives for volunteer roles as counselors and advisers in business management for small firms. The largest ACTION-sponsored initiative is the Retired Senior Volunteer Program (RSVP), offering community volunteer service opportunities in day-care centers, nursing homes, libraries, and adult education programs.

Another challenge for productive aging lies in the workplace, not so much in delaying retirement but in making better use of older workers. The aging of the American workforce, along with dramatic restructuring of many industries, will constitute a challenge for the future. It is estimated that by the year 2000 one-third of the U.S. workforce will consist of middle-aged or older workers over the age of 40. This "graying of working America" poses a challenge for the American economy (Sheppard and Rix, 1977). In the past, companies have relied on younger workers to bring in new skills and knowledge key to raising productivity. If the American economy is to prosper in the future, managers will have to pay more attention to making use of older workers who will constitute a large proportion of the workforce during a period when technological change will be accelerating (Kieffer, 1983).

Experience in industry over many years has demonstrated that middle-aged and older workers can be trained or retrained to acquire new skills as previous skills or knowledge become obsolete (Davies and Sparrow, 1985). The potential for retraining is called "plasticity." The positive experience in older worker retraining serves to contradict the common prejudice that "you can't teach an old dog new tricks." It is important to remember, however, that psychological studies have also shown that older people typically demonstrate some declines in motor performance and slowing of comprehension as new information is acquired. Such effects sometimes discourage older workers who may themselves come to believe the stereotype. But modest changes in teaching techniques can serve to offset most of these problems.

Industrial training has shown the power of the discovery method of training, which proves most successful with older workers (Belbin and Belbin, 1972). In this method, trainees discover for themselves how to carry out a task to be learned. They make decisions actively and then receive immediate corrective feedback. The method has been used successfully in operations such as post office mail sorting, stone masonry, and machine work (Belbin and Downs, 1966). It has also been used in fields such as data processing and interpretation of engineering designs (Belbin, 1969), examples that are encouraging because of the dramatic growth of jobs in the postindustrial information economy of the future.

The volatility of the American economy and the aging of the baby boom generation make it difficult to predict the shape of an aging society in the twenty-first century. But the vitality of the aging population today already constitutes a positive sign for the future if there is greater attention to the potential of productive aging. Community service employment, second careers, volunteer opportunities, and retraining of older workers will all be part of the picture.

Suggested Readings

Atchley, Robert C., *The Sociology of Retirement*, New York: Schenkman, 1976.

Bass, Scott, and Caro, Francis J. (eds.), *Toward a Productive Aging Society*, Westport, CT: Auburn House, 1993.

Bluestone, Irving, Montgomery, Rhonda, and Owen, John (eds.), *The Aging of the American Work Force*, Detroit: Wayne State University Press, 1990.

De Grazia, Sebastian, *Of Time, Work and Leisure*, New York: Doubleday, 1964.

Graebner, William, *A History of Retirement: The Meaning and Function of an American Institution,* New Haven, CT: Yale University Press, 1980.

Miletich, John J., *Retirement: An Annotated Bibliography*, Westport, CT: Greenwood, 1986.

Sandell, Steven H. (ed.), *The Problem Isn't Age: Work and Older Americans,* New York: Praeger, 1987.

Aging as Human Experience: A Life Course Perspective

From the dawn of civilization, people have acknowledged a human life course: that is, a successive series of stages from infancy through old age (Boyle and Morriss, 1987). The time between birth and death has been organized or structured in distinctive ways. The simplest concept of the life course has been a division into two stages: childhood and adulthood. As societies become more complex, they tend to develop a greater number of life stages.

In general, traditional societies have expressed their concepts of aging and the life course through symbols, rituals, and myths that are parts of a shared cultural heritage. By contrast, modern societies, especially after the industrial revolution, have tended to treat the stages of life in a more rationalized way and have endeavored to manage or control transitions from one stage to the next. The emergence of gerontology as the scientific study of aging is itself an example of this tendency.

In the modern world, the final stage of life is viewed less in terms of symbolic meaning and more as a result of causal factors shaping the entire course of life, such as social class, formal education, and occupational experience. The life course perspective shows us how the last stage of life is the result of all the stages that came before. Therefore the quality of life in old age and even the meaning of old age itself are no longer simply accepted as matters of destiny, but are viewed as matters of individual choice or social policy. Whether older people are dismissed as "uncreative" and whether they feel satisfaction and meaning in their lives will depend upon social institutions that could give new structure and purpose to the last stage of life. The meaning of old age in the future is up to us.

Stages on Life's Way

From early childhood, human beings are socialized to think about what it means to "act your age," a process described as *age differentiation*. Different roles or behavior are considered appropriate depending on age. When is it no longer appropriate for a toddler to wet the bed? When is a teenager permitted to date or to drive? When should adults get married or retire from work? Riley and Foner (1972) put forward a comprehensive theory of age stratification in an effort to determine how a person's position in the age structure affects behavior or attitudes. In age stratification theory, **age grading** refers to the way that people of different ages are assigned different roles and positions in society (Streib and Bourg, 1984).

People come to define themselves, at least in part, in terms of their specific life stage. Age identification is partly an acknowledgment of chronological age, or years since birth, but it is more too. Subjective assessment of age depends on recognition of broader age norms, which themselves change over time (Breytspraak, 1984). For example, how old is "middle age"? When does "old age" begin? As we look across different cultures and back through history, we will see that there are no simple answers to these questions.

One way that age identification takes place is through important life events or transition points such as graduation from school, first job, marriage, or retirement (Chiriboga, 1982). People in every culture have widely shared expectations about the "right time" for an event to happen. In Western society, for example, marriage at age 13 or retirement at age 30 would be "off time," while graduation from college at 21 or retirement at 65 would be "on time." We have a shared **social clock** concerning the appropriate age for life events (Helson, Mitchell, and Moane, 1984). Certain life events, such as a confirmation or a marriage ceremony or the retirement dinner, are rites of passage (Van Gennep, 1960). These rituals mark the passage from one status to another and reinforce shared norms about the timing of life events.

While some traditional rites of passage are no longer observed in our society, age-based transitions are fundamental elements in the psychology of adulthood and aging. In this discussion, we will look at the historical origins of ideas about aging and life stages and then consider the contemporary life course perspective as a way of understanding how these ideas are changing today.

Historical Ideas of the Life Course

Western cultural ideas about the life course derive from two principal sources: the Judeo-Christian tradition expressed in the Bible and the Greco-Roman world of antiquity. Ancient Hebrew religious literature displays an ambivalent view of aging. On the one hand, old age is venerated as a reward for righteous living: for example, the Fifth Commandment to honor one's parents contains a promise of long life. On the other hand, there is a realistic dread of frailty and a fear that children will reject aged parents (Isenberg, 1992). The Book of Job even questions the belief that old age brings wisdom and recognizes that the wicked can live just as long as the righteous.

The Greek and Roman view of late life also contains a basic ambivalence. In the first great work of Western literature, Homer's *Iliad*, there is worship of youth in the figure of the young, strong warrior Achilles. Youth orientation was also present in the Greek celebration of the Olympics and the idealization of young bodies in sculpture. But youth culture is not the whole story. Even in Homer's poem, the aged Nestor is revered for his wisdom. In the philosophical tradition, Plato and Aristotle took opposing views on aging. For Plato, late life offered a possibility of rising above the body to attain insight into the true nature of reality. On the other hand, Aristotle saw middle age as the summit of life, a time when creative intellectual judgment was at its peak. The contrast between creativity in youth and the wisdom of age still colors our debates about cognitive processes in adult development.

Ancient ideas about the life course express a profound conflict in human existence. One of the greatest Greek tragedies is the three-part Oedipus cycle, the last part written when its author, Sophocles, was 90 years old himself. In this story, Oedipus becomes king because he solves the famous riddle of the Sphinx: "What creature walks on four legs in the morning, two legs at noon, and three legs in the afternoon?" The answer is the human being at successive stages of the life course from infancy (four legs) until old age, when two legs require a third, or a cane, for support. The Oedipus story is also the drama of a young man struggling against his father and then in ignorance killing him: a parable of generational conflict. Freud's description of the "Oedipus complex" would put the emphasis on Oedipus's sexual involvement with his mother and the guilt it provokes. But the third part of Sophocles's story follows King Oedipus into old age, when at the end of long exile he at last finds peace and redemption.

Intergenerational conflict was a prominent theme in the ancient world (Bertman, 1976). In Rome, one source of conflict was the fact that fathers held supreme authority over their children. Perhaps partly in compensation for such power, Roman comic plays often ridicule the old and express hostility toward old men who take up young lovers, a theme often repeated in medieval literature. Clearly, competition for resources between age groups existed long before it was called the "generational equity debate," and that uncertainty about what is "age appropriate" (e.g., sex among the elderly) is part of a tradition that goes back to antiquity (Falkner and de Luce, 1992).

Greek and Roman ideas were also fundamental in elaborating how we think about the biological aspects of the life course. The Greek medical writer Hippocrates described four ages of life that match the four seasons of the year. Similar ideas were developed by the Roman physician Galen and by the astronomer Ptolemy. Ptolemy developed an idea of seven ages of life, which would have great influence during the Middle Ages. One of the most important ancient writers was Cicero (106-43 B.C.), author of the essay "On Old Age" (or *De Senectute*), which offers a realistic account of the gains and losses of aging. Cicero was a Stoic philosopher whose work was inspired by a conviction that the mind can prevail over the body. Thus he saw old age not exclusively as a time of decline and loss but as an opportunity for cultivating wisdom. Cicero is one of the first and most eloquent proponents of an ideal of "successful aging" (Baltes and Baltes, 1990). The belief in cognitive development over the life span is central to his argument.

By 400 A.D. the Roman Empire was in decline and Christianity had triumphed. During the Middle Ages, Christian civilization took over many ideas about the life course from classical tradition. But now the image of multiple stages of life was balanced by the metaphor of life as a journey, a spiritual pilgrimage. St. Augustine's *Confessions*, written during his own midlife transition, introduced the practice of autobiography or life review, a genre that later became popular after 1600 with the Protestant Reformation and the modern celebration of individualism.

During the Middle Ages, a spiritual outlook on the life course was predominant. From that standpoint, no single stage of life could be superior to another. Just as the natural life cycle was oriented by the recurrent cycle of the seasons, so the individual soul would be oriented toward the afterlife (Burrows, 1986). In this way, elements of ancient natural philosophy were balanced by the spiritual outlook of religion. The human life course as both cycle and journey was endowed with transcendent meaning and wholeness (Cole, 1992).

With the coming of the Reformation and the Renaissance, ideas about the life course changed into forms we recognize as fundamentally modern. Writing in this epoch, Shakespeare expressed again the traditional idea of the "Seven Ages of Man":

> All the world's a stage
> And all the men and women merely players.
> They have their exits and entrances;
> And one man in his time plays many parts,
> His acts being seven ages. (*As You Like It*, Act 2, scene 7)

Shakespeare's sentiment anticipates the modern concept of the life course. The periods of life are merely "roles" acted out on the wider stage of society, and the role losses of old age appear as the final act of the drama. A theatrical metaphor replaces the language of a cosmic cycle or a spiritual journey.

During Shakespeare's time, drawings and engravings depicted the stages of life in a new way. The traditional image of a completed circle changed into a new kind of image: a rising and falling staircase, where middle life occupies the peak of power. That image promoted the idea of life as a "career" in which individuals could exercise control over later life: for example, through extended education, good health care, and capital accumulated through savings. This Protestant and capitalist image of the life course as a process under human control had an enormous influence on modern ideas about aging. During the sixteenth and seventeenth centuries, the stages of the life course became demarcated in ways that we recognize today (Kohli, 1986). For example, childhood became a period of life in its own right, separate from adulthood and old age (Aries, 1962). By the twentieth century, retirement became well established, thus reinforcing the idea of old age as a distinct phase of life.

Life Course in the Modern World

The reshaping of the life course in modern times depended strongly on the impact of the educational system and the workplace. In the nineteenth century, the rise of public schools began to lengthen the period of formal education and introduce credential requirements for some types of work. The United States, as a self-consciously "modern" nation, took the lead in many of these progressive developments that reshaped ideas about the life course (Fischer, 1977; Achenbaum, 1978). By the twentieth century, adolescence was recognized as a distinct phase of life and became more prolonged, and middle age became an important period of the life course (Neugarten, 1968).

The industrial revolution brought new demographic, economic, and family life patterns as well as new cultural ideas about age-appropriate behavior (Hareven and Adams, 1982). As late as the nineteenth century, high infant mortality rates and infectious disease patterns meant that death could strike at any age. But with advances in sanitation and modern medicine, death became increasingly displaced into later life. With falling birthrates in the twentieth century, the modern family life cycle became established as well. As birth and death came under human control, so the shape of the modernized life course itself became an object of inquiry.

Life span developmental psychology.   When the behavioral sciences took the life course as an object of scientific study, neither aging nor the stages of life were seen any longer as part of a cosmic order of meaning (Cole and Gadow, 1986). One sign of this trend is the growth of life span developmental psychology, describing the process of psychological change over the entire span of life. One of the most influential developmental psychologists has been Erik Erikson, who offered a stage theory inspired by Freud's psychosexual theory but allowing for social influences and changes in adulthood. Erikson depicts psychological development as a series of **developmental tasks**: that is, challenges that require people to resolve recurrent conflicting tendencies in the human personality. For middle age, Erikson posits a conflict between stagnation versus generativity: roughly, the idea of being trapped by old habits versus going beyond self-absorption in order to nurture the next generation (Kotre, 1984). For old age, Erikson sees a conflict between ego integrity versus despair: that is, acceptance of one's life as opposed to feeling hopeless and depressed about limited remaining time.

There has recently been great interest in adult psychological changes such as the midlife crisis, a time when those in middle age confront the fact of mortality and the limits of youthful dreams (Jacques, 1965). Many of these "passages" or psychological changes of middle age have been popularized by journalists, but questions have been raised about just how universal such "passages" actually are (Braun and Sweet, 1984).

One of the most interesting of the stage theories of middle and later life was put forward by psychologist Daniel Levinson, who found life transitions characteristically associated with ages such as 30, 40, or 50 (Levinson, 1978). Like Erik Erikson's stage theory of development, Levinson's theory is attractive but neither theory has yet been proven by empirical scientific evidence. Even if evidence were available, there would remain a question of *why* such distinct stages of development occur in a specific sequence or pattern. Some sociologists argue that the whole linear pattern of life stages—the modernized life cycle—actually reflects structures of socialization tied to dominant institutions such as the school or the workplace (Dannefer, 1984). For example, retirement exists as a separate phase only because society needs to make way in the workplace for younger workers.

Role of mass media.   Another important vehicle for socialization today is the mass media, especially television, which serves as an important means of transmitting images of aging. As a rule, older people are not visible on television in anything like their proportion of the actual population. In the world of television, there are clear gender stereotypes as well; older women are far less likely to be depicted, and, when they are, the image is usually negative or comic (Davis and Davis, 1985).

Beyond stereotypes, electronic media have a latent effect both more subtle and more pervasive for our idea of the life course. Television occupies a perpetual present dominated by novelty and juxtaposition of momentary images (Meyrowitz, 1985). The effect of a medium demanding immediate response is to weaken any sense of continuity over the life course and to undercut any authority or meaning for old age (Moody, 1988). Traditional cultures tend to prize their older members as links in a historical chain reaching back to the ancestors. But the contemporary culture of television puts all age groups on an equal footing. The result is the "disappearance of childhood" and finally of old age too (Postman, 1982).

Media images of aging, like myths of the past, are of course oversimplified and based on fantasy. Advertisers that seek the gray market of older consumers present idealized images of good health and vigorous activity; the old are presented as slightly gray versions of younger or middle-aged people. By contrast, some feature-length films are able to express deeper mythic images of the last stage of life. These images range from the quest for rejuvenation through the fountain of youth (*Cocoon*) to psychological self-fulfillment of the aged hero returning home (*Wild Strawberries* and *The Trip to Bountiful*). At its best, film can present images of the older person as a genuine hero (*Driving Miss Daisy*) triumphing over circumstance.

Modernization theory.   How can we make sense of the contradictory images of aging found in modern culture? One influential theory about aging that tries to do so is modernization theory. According to this view, the status of the elderly declines as societies become more modern. The status of old age was low in hunting and gathering societies but rose dramatically in stable agricultural societies, where older people controlled the land. With the coming of industrialization, it is said, modern societies have tended to devalue older people. The modernization theory of aging, in effect, suggests that the role and status of the elderly are inversely related to our technological progress. Factors such as urbanization and social mobility tend to disperse families, while technological change tends to devalue the wisdom or life experience of elders, leading to a loss of status and power (Cowgill and Holmes, 1972). Some investigators have found that key elements of modernization were in fact broadly related to the declining status of older people in different societies (Palmore and Manton, 1974).

This account strikes a responsive chord because it echoes the "golden age" picture, which describes the old as honored in preindustrial societies (Stearns, 1982), another version of the "world-we-have-lost" syndrome (Laslett, 1965). But the truth is more complex than modernization theory suggests, and in fact the theory has been criticized (Haber, 1983; Quadagno, 1982). As we have seen already, in primitive, ancient, and medieval societies, the elderly were always depicted and treated in contradictory ways: sometimes abandoned, sometimes granted power. The real history of old age includes variations according to race, gender, social class, and culture. Image and reality have never entirely coincided.

At the core of the history of old age, there has always been ambivalence: resentment and guilt, honor and oppression. The psychological basis for the ambivalence is understandable. Why shouldn't adults feel guilt and dread at the sight of vulnerable old age stretching before them? And why shouldn't they harbor ambivalent feelings toward those who accumulate power and wealth over a long lifetime? We see the same ambivalence today: Older people as a group receive substantial benefits from the welfare state yet they are sometimes depicted, perhaps unfairly, as selfish or unconcerned about other generations. The truth is different than what all the images convey.

A decisive change with industrialization has been a growing rationalization and bureaucratization of the life course itself: a greater rigidity among the "three boxes of life" of childhood, adulthood, and old age (Bolles, 1981). At the same time, as we have seen, mass media and rapid flux in cultural values have begun to erode any special qualities linked to different life stages. A further change has been expanded longevity, which means both that more people are living to old age and that the elderly as a group are becoming a greater proportion of the total population. In that respect, the power of older people has grown by sheer numbers. Meanwhile, however, the achievement of old age has been devalued simply by becoming more familiar. Perhaps most important, old age itself has been stripped of any clear or agreed-upon meaning because the entire life course itself has changed its structure in ways that will have unpredictable but far-reaching effects on what aging may become in the twenty-first century.

The Life Course Perspective on Aging

Think about the question: What does it mean to "act your age"? Then try the following exercise. What is your typical mental image of a college student? Of a recent retiree? Of a grandmother? Of a first-time father? Hold those images in mind and then consider the following facts:

- Each year, a half million people over 60 are studying on college campuses.

- Retirees from the military are typically in their forties or fifties.

- In some inner-city neighborhoods, it is not at all unusual to meet a 35-year-old grandmother whose own daughter is a pregnant teenager.

- It is no longer surprising for men in second marriages to become a father for the first time over age 40 or 50.

Roles such as "student," "retiree," "grandmother," or "first-time father" are no longer linked to our stereotyped images of age. A change is taking place that raises questions about what old age will be like in the future.

When we read about aging in the Bible or in works by such writers as Shakespeare or Cicero, we might imagine that "old age" is a fixed stage of life, always part of the natural pattern of things, like birth or death. But the study of aging as a historical phenomenon reveals that at various times society has held different views about the stages of life, about when old age begins, and about what it involves (Minois, 1989). At the end of the twentieth century, it has become clearer than ever that human aging is ambiguous and far less "natural" than might have been imagined in earlier epochs. We can most fruitfully understand old age not as a separate period of life but as part of the total human life course from birth to death.

Increasingly the study of aging is seen from this **life course perspective**: in other words, looking at old age as one phase of the entire course of life. We distinguish here between the *span* of a lifetime, the total number of years we live, and the *course* of life, which refers to the meaningful pattern seen in the passing of time. Gerontology as the study of aging is enriched and broadened by the life course perspective. Instead of merely describing the limited characteristics of old age, we shift the time framework to include all the phases of life, from childhood, adolescence, and adulthood right up through the last period of old age. Longitudinal research, which follows individuals over long periods of time, is one manifestation of the life course perspective.

As we look back over the twentieth century, we can see how new life stages have emerged. Because of increases in longevity, on average a person will spend at least one-fourth or perhaps one-third of adulthood in retirement

(Kohli, 1987). Thus new distinctions are made between the **young-old,** the **old-old,** and now the **oldest-old.** Along with increases in longevity has come uncertainty about what it means to grow older or to "act your age" at any point in life.

A good example here is the changing meaning given to time spent in parenthood. In the 1830s, demographers estimate that around 90% of a woman's years after marriage were spent raising dependent children (Gee, 1987). But by the 1950s, that proportion had dropped to 40%, giving rise to what some observers dubbed the "empty nest" syndrome: an extended post-parental period of life that occurs after adult children have grown up and left home (Lowenthal and Chiriboga, 1972). It should be noted that women's lives have greater variability than men's because of the impact of their roles and responsibilities in primary groups such as the family (Rindfuss, Swicegood, and Rosenfeld, 1987). The impact of gender on the life course is a complex subject that will become more and more important in an aging society (Rossi, 1985).

Another change has been the postponement of child rearing, with the rise in occurrence of the later life family and its smaller family size. As a result, people are spending more of their lives in their roles as adult children of aging parents than as parents themselves (Brubaker, 1985). What does it mean, in psychological and social terms, when a "child" is 50 or 60 years old, or even older? Even to ask these questions shows that the human life course has changed in ways that are still not fully recognized.

Both paid employment and active parenting now occupy a smaller proportion of the total life span than in previous historical periods. In the past, work and family responsibilities were central to the definition of adulthood. What becomes of a society where these roles no longer take up such a large proportion of life? What sources of meaning replace them?

Ages and Transitions

In responding to these questions, we need to see how the psychology of life span development is related to stages of life and to age norms. When we look at how children or adolescents make transitions from one stage to another, we can see that many behavioral or psychological problems come about because of the difficulties of preparing for transitions. The transition from adolescence to adulthood is typically marked by events such as marriage, parenthood, and employment (Hogan and Astone, 1986). While schools, job orientation, or marriage counseling help people make transitions to adulthood, there are few social institutions that help people with the transitions of the second half of life.

In many respects, life course transitions in adulthood have become more closely related to chronological age and therefore more predictable than was true earlier in history (Winsborough, 1980). For example, as mortality has moved further into advanced old age, events such as the death of a spouse or of parents are now predictable markers of later adulthood. But in cultural terms, we now have no consensus about age norms as opposed to life events linked to specific ages (Chudakoff, 1989). Are older widows today comfortable about dating? How much obligation should people at the point of retirement feel to take care of their own elderly parents? A 70-year-old newlywed or a 60-year-old "child" makes us uncertain about what the transitions and age norms are of later adulthood.

The value of thinking in terms of age transitions is that we can see adult development as more open ended than people have often tended to see it in the past. As a result, the meaning of old age is less fixed and the choices are more varied. We can contrast this wider social freedom with stereotypes that still persist about human development in the second half of life. The most pervasive view of adulthood is not based on positive development at all but assumes continuous deterioration and decline: After youth, it's all downhill. This pessimistic age-as-decline model gives priority to biological factors and is the basis for the widely shared prejudice called "ageism." We are better off appreciating how social class, life history, and social institutions and policies create considerable variation in the experience of aging. Although aging is negative for some people, for others it opens the door to meaningful new roles and activities.

Social class.   The pathway through the stages in life depends very much on social class, which is strongly related in turn to the number of years spent in the age-graded educational system. Socioeconomic position predicts not only how long people remain in school but also, for instance, whether they will be "late" parents, that is, with a first child born after age 30. These earlier life events in turn have long-lasting effects on old age. For example, we have seen that, among women, entering the labor force at the beginning of childbearing is correlated with diminished income later in life. Gender differences in old age poverty are explainable partly as the result of life course choices made many decades earlier.

Midlife transitions are more complicated and less predictable than the transition from adolescence to adulthood. A basic rule of accumulated advantage or disadvantage still holds true, however: In sum, "the rich get richer and the poor get poorer." For example, early education and entry into a favorable occupation is converted during middle age into increased wealth in the form of home ownership and pension vesting (Henretta and Campbell, 1976). Thus the impact of a similar threat to well-being, such as job loss, will differ from person to person depending on accumulated social and economic resources. Individual adaptive psychological capacity plays a role too in coping with changes of later life.

Life history.   The adult life course is not a smooth or predictable movement from one step to another. History plays a profound role in shaping lives. For example, a large historical event like the Great Depression caused a dramatic and unexpected drop in income and status for vast numbers of people (Elder, 1974). This recognition of the influence of historical events has stimulated new interest among sociologists in using interviews and oral history to understand how social forces affect people's lives (Bertaux, 1981).

Along with large historical events that affect whole cohorts, there are also unpredictable or **nonnormative life events,** such as getting divorced or losing a job. Events such as these can dramatically change pathways into later life. For instance, a longitudinal study of the impact of nonnormative life events on income during the 1970s showed that around one-third of people experienced an unexpected but very significant drop in income (Duncan, 1988). A setback like that can affect an individual's financial status during retirement.

Research has also shown that large negative life events, such as widowhood or job loss, can cause a dramatic downturn in personal health. Negative life events induce a psychosomatic response to stress, and life events become risk factors that predict the onset of illness (Holmes and Rahe, 1967). But the impact of life events on physical or mental health is not a simple process. The same stressful life event—for example, bereavement—will have different effects on different people depending on the total psychosocial picture (George, 1980). For example, was the event expected and anticipated? What kind of personal or family resources are available to cope with mourning and readjustment? Social support from family and friends can help older people cope with stress and maintain self-esteem.

Social institutions and policies.   If the structure of the life course and psychological development are shaped by social forces, then it is reasonable to think that some of the negative features of old age may be due, at least in part, to institutional patterns that could be changed. A good example is the pattern known as **learned helplessness,** or the dependency and depression induced by reinforcement from the external environment (Seligman, 1975). It has been suggested that the depression and disengagement often seen in old age may come from social practices.

Social policies and institutions that care for dependent elderly may unwittingly reinforce excess dependency (Baltes and Baltes, 1986). For instance, in nursing homes, learned helplessness may be intensified by diminished locus of control when residents feel manipulated by forces beyond their personal control. As a result, nursing home residents may become more withdrawn, may fail to comply with medical treatment, and therefore may become fatalistic and depressed. The institutional structure responsible for such dependency can be changed, however. In an important experiment with nursing home residents, psychologists introduced small steps to increase locus of control, for example, allowing elderly residents to choose activities or giving them responsibility for taking care of plants. The result was a dramatic improvement in morale and even a decline in mortality (Rodin and Langer, 1980). But without such interventions working against dependency, it is all too common for elderly people in ill health to lose self-esteem as they experience declining control (Rodin, Timko, and Harris, 1985).

Social policies and institutions define boundaries at each stage of the life course. The educational system defines the transition from youth to adulthood, and retirement defines the transition from middle age to old age. Bureaucratic institutions, from a local school system to the Social Security Administration, always favor rule-governed, predictable procedures, so it is not surprising that with the rise of bureaucracy came a greater emphasis on defining life stage by chronological age. Like progression through the school system, the late life transition to retirement seems more orderly than midlife transitions because retirement is regulated by employment policies and pension coverage. The timing of retirement today is becoming less predictable than in the past, however, because of turbulence in the U.S. labor market as well as the disappearance of mandatory retirement. Other emerging trends include the prospect of joint retirement for two-earner couples and the option of interrupting retirement to return to work in the event of economic need. Finally, health and disability problems can cause unanticipated life transitions.

An orderly pattern?   The life course perspective presents a complex picture that includes elements of both predictability and disorder (Hagestad and Neugarten, 1985). On one hand, we see increasing bureaucratization, for example, rising educational credential requirements for entry-level jobs. But credentials are no guarantee of success, and the labor market brings about wide heterogeneity in life chances. The same fluidity appears in marriage and family structures; up to half of new marriages may end in divorce. With remarriage and blended families more common, there is a greater variety of kinship relations, which in turn can present uncertainty in later life. For example, what obligations does a stepdaughter have to an aged relative?

In this new environment, earlier expectations favoring fixed, orderly life stages now seem increasingly improbable. Research on the life course has shown that age norms or age-based expectations vary substantially not only as a matter of individual differences but because of historical changes in the labor market, the family, and government policies. The decline of job guarantees and security in marriage are matched by the shrinking of pension benefits in favor of defined contribution plans or IRAs: all signs of the rise of individual flexibility in contrast to life course predictability. The linear life plan was perhaps too rigid; but it also offered a degree of security.

Aging in postindustrial society. Successive cohorts who will grow old in the twenty-first century face different life chances and even a changing structure of the life course itself. Some major changes in recent decades include a lengthening of adolescence, greater volatility in marriage because of divorce rates, postponement of childbearing among higher income couples, and lengthening of time spent in retirement. Biomedical technology now permits greater control of events at the beginning and end of the life course, from fetal monitoring to life prolongation.

What is true about end-of-life decisions now holds for more and more transitions across the life course: Major events of life are no longer seen as parts of a predictable or natural pattern. The adult life course is becoming highly individualized and therefore a matter of social or individual choice. Familiar social institutions like marriage or employment can no longer be counted on for security throughout adulthood, and therefore the last stage of life, old age itself, becomes less predictable.

Time orientation is a major element in how we think about aging and the life course (Hendricks and Peters, 1986). Just as industrialization imposed time schedules on workers to improve efficiency in the workplace, so the life course has became "scheduled" by differentiated life stages. The factory and the assembly line had their parallel in the linear life plan, or three boxes of life. But that mode of organization has itself become outdated. In a postindustrial "information economy," the pace of life is speeding up, while more flexible modes of production require a more flexible life course.

Earlier assumptions about a shared "social clock" or timetable for life events have been thrown into question for a variety of reasons. One is variation by social class and occupation. The career timetable of a medical student, for instance, will be quite different than that of an immigrant agricultural worker. As individual lives are shaped in different ways by occupation, class, ethnicity, and culture, so the "expected life history" (Bortner, 1979) will be constantly subject to further variations. The volatile postindustrial economy demands multiple job changes and makes every career unpredictable. Thus individuals at any age may be called upon to rewrite their biographies. Reinventing oneself gets more difficult, however, as the resume gets longer.

There are deep structural reasons that advanced industrial societies have prolonged the period of life devoted to education, sometimes until the mid-twenties or beyond. The knowledge explosion and pressure for specialization put a premium on added years of schooling, and the job market has fewer places for those without advanced skills. Our postindustrial economy is increasingly based on "knowledge industries"; emerging fields such as fiber optics, computer software, or biotechnology favor cognitive flexibility at all ages. This trend underscores the importance of adaptability and lifelong learning but also poses a distinct challenge for an aging society. Middle-aged and older workers may be at a disadvantage in the fast-moving labor market;

for instance, in creative branches of advertising, an employee is viewed as "old" if over the age of 40.

The new economic landscape has implications for the shape of the life course (Roth, 1983). Older workers will have to invest more time in training and retraining for a changing job market. If retirement, the defining institutional feature of old age, is to remain economically feasible, then retraining for displaced workers and displaced homemakers will become imperative in the future.

One role for middle-aged and older people could be mentoring: that is, guiding the next generation in the capacity of teacher, coach, or counselor. This idea is attractive for two reasons. First, it encourages intergenerational relationships, and, second, it takes advantage of generativity and wisdom: the virtues to be cultivated in the second half of life in Erikson's idea of life span development. Mentors, however, will have to develop up-to-date work skills and attitudes if their advice is to be respected by younger workers.

Summary: A new map of life.   We can think of the stages of life as a kind of "map" of unknown territory through which we must move. Until recently, some regions of the territory, such as midlife crisis, were completely "unmapped" and unacknowledged. Other regions, such as adolescence, have only been built up or cultivated over the last century, although now they seem familiar and predictable. The symbolism of the stages of life was persuasive in traditional societies where a map could be understood to depict a common "space" that was stable and enduring, the same for each generation. This familiar ideal of life stages reappears in popular forms of life span development psychology, such as the theories of Erikson and Levinson. The ideal seems to correspond to a fundamental and universal fact about human psychology: the need to define the predictability of life (Marris, 1975). Now, however, it may be time to call into question this whole approach to the life course. Perhaps the metaphor of a "map" is mistaken.

At the end of the twentieth century, we no longer have confidence in a shared timetable for the course of life. We need a new "map of life" corresponding to the changed conditions of demographic circumstances, economics, and culture in a postindustrial society (Laslett, 1991). The timing of major life events has become less and less predictable at all levels of society. In upper socioeconomic groups, for example, a woman with a graduate degree and career responsibilities may delay having a first child until age 35 or later; in other parts of society, teenage pregnancy rates have soared.

The meaning of "aging" has also changed but in contradictory ways. Perhaps medicine will permit us to compress morbidity and displace some aspects of aging until later and later in life. Yet economic forces move in the opposite direction from biology. Changes in the job market can make previous skills irrelevant. In science and engineering, knowledge becomes obsolete within five or ten years, so life experience counts for less than exposure to the latest technical advances. A full account of aging and the life course will have to consider changes in family life, biology, and economics.

The changing structure of the life course has profound implications for the issues discussed previously in this book. Martin Kohli, for example, has analyzed the evolution of retirement in terms of what he calls the "moral economy" of the life cycle. The idea of a moral economy embodies our expectations of what is fair or right; for instance, stay in school and you'll get a good job; senior citizens have a right to retirement income; and so on. The modernized life course represented one powerful version of "moral economy" with its characteristic distribution of work and leisure according to chronological age. But ideas such as generational equity or productive aging call into question this linear life plan. Debates about justice between generations or the future of retirement ultimately raise questions about the quality of life in old age and the meaning of aging itself.

There is now increasing evidence that the life course is becoming "de-institutionalized": more fragmented, disorderly, and unpredictable (Held, 1986). The rigidity of the linear life plan represents a kind of "structural lag" where social institutions fail to keep up with new demographic realities, such as the rising level of health and contributive capacity among the young-old (Riley and Riley, 1986). As proponents of productive aging have argued, we therefore fail to take advantage of the potential of the added years of longevity. More broadly, the linear life plan can be criticized as socially and spiritually inadequate because it cannot reflect changing social meaning at different stages of life (Cole, 1989). To overcome the limitations of the old "map," we need to develop more flexible ideas about the positive social contributions that can be made by the old and about the meaning of life's final stage. Without such new understanding, there is a risk that older people may be dismissed as "uncreative" or that people will lose any shared sense of the positive meaning of survival to old age.

Traditional societies, as we have seen, often held ambivalent views about old age. We should not sentimentalize the status of old age in the past. But in the past, those who had lived a full life span could at last assume a high degree of shared values and experience across the generations simply because the pace of social change was slower. With rapid change of fashions and ideas, it is not surprising that the old get stereotyped as "behind the times" and therefore lacking in creativity or wisdom. That judgment may be unfair but it remains a challenge to gerontology. Creativity and wisdom obviously depend on cognitive development over the whole life course. But whether we cultivate such qualities or make use of them in older people will depend, in the end, on imaginative policies and institutions. The challenge of a modern yet aging society is somehow to nurture the special cognitive strengths of age in an environment that prizes change, novelty, and flexibility. That challenge is what is at stake in debates about creativity and meaning in the last stage of life.

Does Creativity Decline With Age?

> We shall not cease exploring
> And the end of all our exploring
> Will be to arrive where we started
> And know the place for the first time.
>
> —T. S. Eliot, The Four Quartets

There is a widely shared view that people become less creative as they grow older. Albert Einstein won a Nobel prize for his contribution to quantum theory, a creative breakthrough that appeared in published form when he was only 26 years old. He later remarked that "a person who has not made his great contribution to science before the age of thirty will never do so." Was Einstein right? Does creativity decline with age?

The question about age and creativity is an important one for individuals, of course, who worry about becoming irrelevant in a fast-paced world. The question is also important for society. The French demographer Alfred Sauvy, for example, feared that an aging society would result in a "population of old people ruminating over old ideas in old houses" (Sauvy, 1976). In coming decades, the U.S. population will become older. The workforce will be aging in a period when companies are being pushed to become more creative and introduce new methods to improve competitive performance. Can we expect middle-aged and older workers to exercise creativity and initiative or can we expect them to resist new ideas? What will happen to American inventiveness and scientific creativity as the average age of scientists goes up (Stephan and Levin, 1992)? These questions are disturbing for those who see in an aging America the "specter of decline" (Pifer and Bronte, 1986; Moody, 1988). The debate about age and creativity is important for America's future.

The Nature of Creativity

A number of social scientists, perhaps with one eye on their own advancing years and the other on a changing society, have tried to determine whether creativity declines with age. They have faced a number of practical obstacles in their research, the most basic being an acceptable definition of "creativity." Other types of cognitive function, notably intelligence, are much easier to pinpoint.

Creativity, Intelligence, and Wisdom

More often, creativity has been related to intelligence. Specifically, creativity is linked with **fluid intelligence,** which is intelligence applied to new tasks or the ability to come up with novel or creative solutions to unforeseen problems (Horn, 1982). Some believe the key to fluid intelligence is divergent thinking, a nonlinear approach to problem solving in which many different patterns or solutions are considered.

The other side of the coin is **crystallized intelligence**, which reflects accumulated past experience and socialization (Horn, 1982). Whereas fluid intelligence denotes a capacity for abstract creativity, crystallized intelligence may signify the acquisition of practical expertise in every life—in short, wisdom.

Some components of wisdom have long been familiar. Philosophers going back to Socrates have argued that wisdom lies in a balanced attitude toward what we think we know: knowing what one does not know but, at the same time, refusing to be paralyzed by doubt (Meacham, 1990). Another key feature of wisdom would seem to be the ability to transcend bias or personal needs that may distort one's perception of a given situation (Orwoll and Perlmutter, 1990). Wisdom, then, involves more than cognitive development alone; it requires a degree of detachment and freedom from self-centeredness that has been described as "ego transcendence" (Peck, 1968). It is possible that older people, if they develop a degree of detachment, might be in a position to achieve such wisdom. But, of course, no one has suggested that wisdom is a universal or inevitable result of chronological age alone. Something more is required than merely living a certain number of years, but psychologists do not agree about what that "something more" might be.

Some psychologists have wondered if there is a trade-off between creativity and wisdom, with one declining and the other increasing with advancing age. A survey of specialists in business revealed that wisdom and creativity were typically seen to be in opposition to one another.

Other psychologists argue that the cognitive processes involved in wisdom, intelligence, and creativity are all basically the same but are put to different uses by different kinds of people. Wise people, we might say, have a high tolerance for ambiguity because they appreciate how difficult it is to make reliable judgments. They see the world "in depth." By contrast, the creative person seeks to go beyond whatever is given in the immediate environment to create something new. Yet genuine creativity need not be identified with novelty for its own sake, as contemporary Western societies often do. In some societies of the East—for example, India, China, or Japan—old age is viewed as an appropriate time for spiritual exploration and artistic development. Late life disengagement is balanced by opportunities for personal growth and creativity. "A Confucian in office, a Taoist in retirement," went the Chinese proverb, so retirement roles might include meditation or traditional landscape painting. In the Hindu doctrine of life stages, later life was a time culminating in spiritual insight and wisdom.

What happens when a creative artist grows older and also develops a measure of wisdom applied to the creative process itself? Part of the answer may be found by looking at those creative artists who continued to be productive in old age. One of the greatest examples was the Dutch painter Rembrandt, whose style changed and deepened as he grew older. The aged Rembrandt practiced looser brush work and became more preoccupied with the inner world of the people he painted. Another example is the impressionist Monet, who continued to paint his famous water lilies even after he was confined to his home in his seventies. Frail health also plagued Matisse, who was forced to give up painting in favor of creating colored cardboard "cutouts" that distilled a lifetime of artistic experience into simple, powerful designs. It is as if the older artist is able to discard mere technical achievement in favor of some essential and elemental quality of art. We see a similar development of "late style" in old age among poets like Goethe and W. B. Yeats. All these examples suggest that many of the greatest creative minds experienced a change or at least a deepening of their creative style in the last stage of life that could be attributed to an accumulation of wisdom.

Measures of Cognitive Function

Intellectual creativity is difficult to define or measure but psychologists have had long experience in measuring human intelligence. The **Wechsler Adult Intelligence Scale** (WAIS) is the most influential measure of global or general intelligence in use today. The WAIS includes a verbal scale and a performance scale, which are combined to assess IQ. The verbal part focuses on learned knowledge including comprehension, arithmetic, and vocabulary, while the performance part measures ability to produce a solution to puzzles involving blocks or pictures. There has been debate about whether intelligence actually declines with age but there is general agreement that people perform worse on intelligence tests as they grow older. The WAIS shows stability for verbal skills but declines with age on performance subtests (Sattler, 1982). This persistent difference between the two components has been found so often that it is even called the **classic aging pattern.**

Some leading researchers have cautioned against taking the classic aging pattern too seriously. They question what is actually being measured by IQ tests. In other words, they challenge the very validity of IQ tests as a measure of the "real" intelligence of older adults. Perhaps test performance should not be equated with real differences in intelligence at all. This controversy has a familiar ring. It is the same kind of challenge that has been heard in recent years about the use of IQ tests and Scholastic Aptitude Tests when those tests show poorer scores for some minority groups. Again, some critics have argued that "intelligence" is a more complex, multidimensional capacity than we had previously realized (Gardner, 1985).

Interest in the validity problem, or trying to measure "real" intelligence, has helped stimulate psychologists to ask whether there are any positive cognitive developments that may come with age. The long debate about IQ and aging has resulted in greater appreciation for the fact that conventional methods of measuring intellectual abilities have not always been sensitive to the skills actually used by adults in coping with the demands of everyday life. This recognition has led some psychologists to become interested in devising new testing methods, such as an age-relevant intelligence test.

Tests to measure intelligence or creativity with age are seeking to capture something very elusive. Everyday intelligence is a multidimensional capacity involving much more than logic or information processing alone. Everyday intelligence—what we sometimes call "common sense"—involves pragmatic and social judgment, which is more than abstract reasoning alone (Cornelius, 1990). What is involved is something akin to "everyday problem solving" (Cornelius and Caspi, 1987) or "expertise in life planning." Some of these same cognitive capacities are likely to be present in what we call "wisdom." The wisdom of later life probably includes several distinct attributes; among them are reflective judgment in the face of uncertainty, the art of "problem finding" (as opposed to solving an already given problem), the capacity for integrated thought about one's life, and, finally, intuition, or the ability to use emotion and affect to achieve understanding of a concrete situation. These qualities are obviously difficult to measure on a test.

Paul Baltes, perhaps the leading psychologist investigating wisdom today, has actually tried to develop a psychological test to measure the level of wisdom. Baltes and his associates presented adult test subjects with questions such as this one: "A fourteen-year-old girl is pregnant. What should she, what should one, consider and do?" In scoring the test, Baltes was not looking for any specific answer but instead was trying to measure how wise people go about dealing with difficult questions. Baltes went on to define wisdom as an expert knowledge system derived from experience and capable of dealing with pragmatic problems. That definition is quite similar to the commonsense understanding of wisdom as consisting of good judgment in response to uncertain problems of living. If we follow this approach, we can understand why wisdom, potentially at least, might increase with age. The reason goes back to the distinction between fluid intelligence, which operates by the mechanics of information processing, as opposed to the content-rich, pragmatic knowledge of crystallized intelligence.

Steps toward defining or measuring wisdom are still in the early stages but the effort holds promise.

Aging and Creativity

Efforts to measure creativity and wisdom take place in the context of a strong debate about the causes and meaning of the measurable decline in IQ scores with age. Basically, the debate comes down to a difference between those who think of themselves as "realists" and those who take a more optimistic view. On the optimistic side, some psychologists speak of the "myth of the twilight years." They suggest that intelligence actually need *not* decline in later life at all (Baltes and Schaie, 1974). But other, equally expert psychologists bitterly reject this conclusion (Horn and Donaldson, 1977). These "realists" contend that declines in fluid intelligence in the classic aging pattern are empirical facts to be accepted no matter how unpleasant. Although we might find individuals who do not exhibit the pattern, the "realists" insist that such cases do not refute an overall decline in average performance.

Taking another tack, the optimists have other explanations for the classic aging pattern. One possible factor could be ill health, which does become more frequent with aging, though not universally so. A major study revealed consistent differences in IQ test performance depending on even modest declines in health status (Botwinick and Birren, 1963). Poor health and disability also tend to cause retirement and therefore probably weaken learning opportunities. It is important to note here that there are both biological changes, such as health status, and social changes, such as retirement, that may be responsible for changing cognitive abilities over the course of life. It may be possible to change these biosocial factors to such a degree that the classic aging pattern no longer holds true. The story about human cognitive potential in the later years is by no means complete today.

The Link Between Creativity and Age

Previously in this book, we pointed to the importance of different methodologies used to measure changes associated with aging. There is a basic difference between cross-sectional studies, which look at groups of young and old people at a single point in time, and longitudinal studies, which follow subjects over many years. Optimists on the subject of creativity and age point out that cross-sectional tests of intelligence may be revealing differences that do not come from age itself but from characteristics of different cohorts. A full answer would require longitudinal testing of intelligence.

One of the most extensive sources of knowledge about intelligence and aging comes from the Seattle Longitudinal Study, which followed individuals ranging from age 25 to age 81 over two decades. That investigation and others have found that the steepest average intellectual declines come after age 60. Averages conceal large differences among individuals, but even on longitudinal studies the classic aging pattern emerges. Still, research findings do challenge the idea of inevitable, global intellectual decline for all individuals. Even more important, it is possible to halt or reverse intellectual decline in older people by specific interventions, such as training and education. Cognitive interventions prove that intellectual decline in later life is by no means irreversible or inevitable (Schaie and Willis, 1987).

Generally, cross-sectional studies tend to overestimate the impact of chronological age in declining performance on IQ tests. One reason is ability-extraneous influences on IQ. For instance, young people taking IQ tests constitute a group quite familiar with test taking from recent experience in school. Studies have shown that young people as a group show far less "test anxiety" than do older people (Whitbourne, 1976). Furthermore, many older people themselves accept the prejudices of ageism and believe that, with advancing age, intelligence inevitably declines. Older people tend to be more cautious than younger people and thus they may be more reluctant to guess at the right answers on an IQ test (Birkhill and Schaie, 1975). Finally, one of the most important ability-extraneous influences could be that the current cohort of older people, on average, lack the formal schooling enjoyed by younger age groups (Granick and Friedman, 1973).

Longitudinal studies show that successive cohorts of older people are in fact improving their performance, perhaps reflecting higher educational attainment. Among older people, anywhere from 60% up to 85% of those tested remain unchanged or even improve their performance of specific test abilities. Even among those over age 80, the declines affected only between 30% and 40% of participants in the Seattle study. Very few people showed any global decline in intelligence, suggesting that people can optimize their cognitive functioning by drawing on their strengths or compensating for losses. Perhaps most important, even in their eighties and nineties, people tend to remain quite competent in familiar everyday situations, so these declines in test performance may have less significance than imagined. Both cross-sectional and longitudinal studies, however, do show the classic aging pattern with uniform decline among subjects beyond their seventies.

Studies of creativity, as opposed to cognitive function in general, have been harder to conduct. Again, the problem is defining "creativity." Some relevant studies have found a decline with age on tests of divergent thinking (Alpaugh and Birren, 1977).

Although these tests are not a completely satisfactory measure of creativity, we can rely on something even better and more valid. We can depend on strong public consensus about products that clearly demonstrate superior creativity, for example, Mozart's symphonies, Newton's theory of gravitation, or Thomas Edison's invention of electrical devices, all achievements of youth. This public consensus approach is precisely the method used by Harvey Lehman in his classic study of creativity and aging. Of interest, Lehman found that the curves of publicly acknowledged creativity followed exactly the curves of fluid intelligence: They both peaked after age 30 and declined with each subsequent decade (Lehman, 1962).

By contrast, Dennis, a critic of Lehman's work, looked at different data and found that for most people the decades of the forties and fifties were the most productive period (Dennis, 1966). Dennis's conclusions were based on quantitative measures of productivity, however (e.g., how many publications), not on qualitative measures (how important the contribution was). Therefore it is not clear that Dennis's results actually refute Lehman's findings. Still others, measuring scientific creativity, found that productivity among scientists peaked in the early forties—later than Lehman said—and then declined slowly after age 50 (Cole, 1979; Diamond, 1986). A longitudinal study of creativity among mathematicians found that those who published a great deal when young did continue to publish as they became older, at least through middle age.

Reasons and Explanations

The evidence shows that age does not necessarily mean loss of cognitive function. Nevertheless, performance on intelligence tests does decline. Psychologists speculating about the reasons cite strong evidence that declining speed with advancing age does have a negative effect on performance on intelligence tests, but the precise reasons remain unclear (Salthouse, 1985).

With advancing age, there is also a clear loss in **cognitive reserve capacity,** that is, the degree of unused potential for learning that exists at any given time. Studies of reaction time in training have shown that the speed of information processing capacity does show a definite decline with age. Older adults, for instance, do not reach the same peak of performance in reaction time as younger adults when presented with simple or complex-choice reaction tests (Salthouse, 1985). Nor do older people, regardless of reserve capacity, achieve comparable performance when trained in memory skills (Baltes and Baltes, 1990). The conclusion is clear that cognitive reserve capacity, like other physiological reserves, tends to be reduced in old age.

Optimists point out that, although fluid intelligence abilities decline, crystallized abilities tend to increase with age. In addition, declines in cognitive ability among older people can often be compensated for by the expertise acquired with aging: a phenomenon that has been called "decrement with compensation." In other words, pragmatic knowledge serves to compensate for declines in speed or in fluid intelligence. For instance, despite declines in typing speed, some older typists are able to demonstrate superior performance in typing productivity. It appears that these older typists compensated for loss of speed by reading farther ahead in the manuscript they were typing: a pragmatic response based on knowledge of how to type more effectively (Salthouse, 1984).

Psychological characteristics in life span development should not be thought of as behavior emerging entirely from the isolated individual organism. Individual behavior often reflects social conditions and socially structured transitions in the life course itself (Schooler and Schaie, 1987). For example, retirement has positive consequences for the cognitive performance of people who retire from very routine or boring jobs, while, by contrast, retirement may accelerate cognitive decline for those who have held complex jobs. It is also true that some psychological traits themselves can be intensified by life course transitions. For instance, people with flexible attitudes in middle age are less likely to experience a decline in psychological competence as they grow older than are those who could be described as being cognitively rigid in midlife (Schaie, 1984). In the future, rising educational levels for successive cohorts of elderly people are likely to make age differences in abilities through adulthood less pronounced than in the past: another shift toward "age irrelevance."

We should thus be skeptical of any broad generalizations or unqualified claims about the decline or about the stability of intelligence with aging. Experiments in training have shown that it is possible to reverse declines in intellectual functioning among older people. In the Seattle Longitudinal Study, investigators found that many participants showed a decline in mental abilities that proved reversible: 40% of these cases benefited from training and afterward achieved intelligence scores at least as high as those measured at the beginning of the 14-year study (Cunningham and Torner, 1990). Critics question, however, whether the reversal simply reflects more practice or whether it involves a genuine reversal of changes induced by aging.

In thinking about psychological changes in intelligence and creativity over the life course, we also need to distinguish normal aging from diseases that may occur with advanced age. Psychological studies with older people have demonstrated that intelligence, defined as the ability to think and learn new things, has a great measure of plasticity, or potential for growth even at advanced ages. Data from groups of healthy people between ages 60 and 80 show that they benefit from practice and show performance gains, just as younger people do. One series of studies showed that elderly people could even be trained to become memory experts (Baltes, 1990). When older people are stimulated and intellectually challenged, this capacity for learning is impressive.

These experiments suggest that the debate about a decline in creativity or intelligence with age is by no means settled. In the readings that follow, the classic positions in this debate are represented. The selection from Harvey Lehman's *Age and Achievement* gives some of his data and provides his major conclusions. Wayne Dennis, one of Lehman's strongest critics, offers an attack on the claim that creativity must decline with age. Dean Simonton's article provides an up-to-date summary of scientific studies of age and creativity in the four decades since Lehman published his book. As Simonton shows, many of Lehman's factual points have been supported over the years, but the issue turns out to be far more complicated than might have been imagined at the time of the early debate on this subject. Finally, the reading by Paul Baltes and colleagues offers the views of perhaps the most distinguished psychologist who has investigated cognitive development in later life. Baltes's later work looks at the question of what it means that some older people develop the higher levels of thinking that we call "wisdom." By turning our attention to this quality, which may be a distinctive strength of old age, Baltes and colleagues remind us that the last stage of life may have possibilities deserving special consideration and demanding new methods of scientific investigation.

Creativity in an Aging Population

It is only in the twentieth century that we have witnessed great gains in longevity and aging on a massive scale. It is only in recent decades that substantial numbers of people have experienced old age in relatively good health and with high levels of education. Therefore studies of older people in previous decades may not be a good basis for judging what older people are capable of today or in the future. We are left to take hope from examples of individual achievement.

When we look to the past, we can identify a number of creative artists who made outstanding contributions in their old age. At age 71, Michelangelo was named chief architect of St. Peter's in Rome. Titian painted some of his greatest works in his eighties, and Picasso produced drawings and paintings into his nineties. Martha Graham continued her choreography into her eighties, while Jessica Tandy won an Oscar at age 80, and Grandma Moses was still painting when she was over 100. It is possible that, with improving opportunities for the arts and lifelong learning, tomorrow's elders will take up the challenge of creativity in the later years in ways unimagined today. What was once a creative old age belonging to an elite could become an opportunity for all. As the noted art critic Ananda Coomaraswamy put it, it is not that the artist is a special kind of person, it is that each person is a special kind of artist. Viewed in those terms, the real debate about age and creativity has barely begun.

Age and Achievement

Harvey Lehman

What are man's most creative years? At what ages are men likely to do their most outstanding work? In 1921 Professor Robert S. Woodworth, of Columbia University, published this statement in his book, *Psychology: A Study of Mental Life*: "Seldom does a very old person get outside the limits of his previous habits. Few great inventions, artistic or practical, have emanated from really old persons, and comparatively few even from the middle-aged. . . . The period from twenty years up to forty seems to be the most favorable for inventiveness." (. . . p. 519) . . .

Assuming that the method by which one arrives at a conclusion is no less important than is the conclusion itself, let us see what is found when the inductive method is employed in the study of man's most creative years. Let us first examine the field of creative chemistry and attempt to answer the question whether chemists display more creative thinking at some chronological age levels than at others.

In his book, *A Concise History of Chemistry . . .*, Professor T. P. Hilditch, of the University of Liverpool, presents the names of several hundred noted chemists and the dates on which these chemists made their outstanding contributions to the science of chemistry. . . .

When the birth dates of the chemists listed by Hilditch were ascertained, insofar as data were available, it was possible to determine the ages at which the world's most renowned chemists made

their most significant contributions, both theoretical and experimental, to the science of chemistry. A sample of the findings is set forth graphically in Figure 8.1.

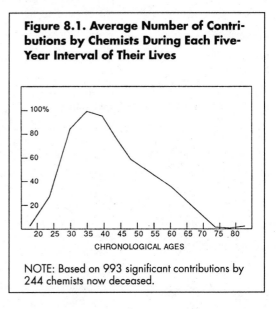

Figure 8.1. Average Number of Contributions by Chemists During Each Five-Year Interval of Their Lives

CHRONOLOGICAL AGES

NOTE: Based on 993 significant contributions by 244 chemists now deceased.

Figure 8.1 presents, by five-year intervals, the chronological ages at which 244 chemists (now deceased) made 993 significant contributions to the science of chemistry. In studying Figure 8.1 it should be borne in mind that it sets forth the *average* number of chemical contributions per five-year intervals. Full and adequate allowance is thus made for the larger number of youthful workers. . . .

Figure 8.2 presents the ages at which 554 notable inventions were made by 402 well-known in-

Source: Age and Achievement by H. Lehman, 1953, Princeton University Press. Reprinted with permission of The American Philosophical Society.

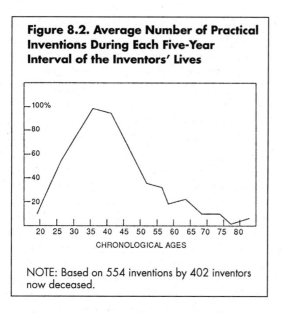

Figure 8.2. Average Number of Practical Inventions During Each Five-Year Interval of the Inventors' Lives

NOTE: Based on 554 inventions by 402 inventors now deceased.

ventors. . . . When Figure 8.2 was displayed to interested friends and colleagues, several persons immediately said, "What about Edison?" It is, of course, well-known that Thomas A. Edison was very active as an inventor throughout his entire life. Figure 8.3 reveals, however, that 35 was Mr. Edi-

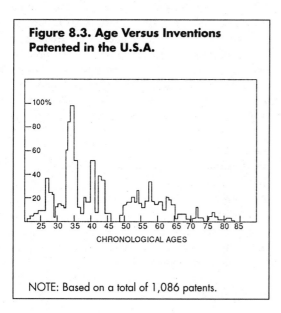

Figure 8.3. Age Versus Inventions Patented in the U.S.A.

NOTE: Based on a total of 1,086 patents.

son's most productive age. Moreover, during the four-year interval from 33 to 36, Edison took out a total of 312 United States patents. This was more than a fourth (28 per cent) of all the United States patents taken out by him during an inventive career that lasted for more than 60 years. . . .

The shape of a performance age-curve varies with a number of things: (1) the type of performance, (2) the excellence of the performance, and (3) the kind of measurement employed. This last fact can perhaps best be illustrated by use of an analogy. Thus, one might construct an age-curve setting forth the average ability of individuals within each of the several age-groups to do the ordinary high jump. At almost every age level some persons would be found who are more or less able to perform this feat. One might, therefore, test out large numbers at each age level and with the resultant data it would be quite possible to construct age-curves disclosing the *average* height that could be attained by the members of each age group.

But there are several other possible procedures which might be employed for comparing the several age groups. Thus, within each of the age groups, one might ascertain the percent of individuals able to high-jump six feet, the percent able to high-jump five feet, etc. With the obtained data it would then be possible to construct one curve that would show for each age group the per cent of individuals able to do six feet, another curve showing the per cent able to do five feet, and so on. If a number of these curves were to be constructed, it seems obvious that that curve which set forth age differences in the ability to do six feet would start its rise later and would fall off both earlier and much more rapidly than would another curve showing age differences in the ability to do, say, two feet. It is evident that very superior high jumping is likely to occur during a narrower age-range than would be found for a much lower degree of ability.

If we think in terms of actual performance, the foregoing situation seems to exist in such diverse fields of endeavor as athletics, mathematics, invention, science, chess, the composition of enduring music, and the writing of great books. For each of these types of behavior, very superior achievement seems most likely to occur during a relatively narrow age-range, and the more noteworthy the performance, the more rapidly does the resultant age-curve descend after it has attained its peak. The findings with . . . reference to sculptured works, oil paintings, and etchings suggest similarly that there is an optimal chronological age level for superlatively great success within these particular fields also. . . .

The work of the genius in his old age may still be far superior to the best work that the average man is able to do in his prime. Therefore, for the study of age differences in creativity, it is not valid merely to compare the achievements of the aged genius with the more youthful accomplishments of the average person. If one wishes to ascertain when men of genius have done their very best work, it is necessary to compare the earlier works of men of genius with their own later works. . . .

Sculpture. Effort was made to ascertain the ages at which the most noted sculptors of early Greece executed their most famous works, but this information could not be obtained. Data for Figure 8.4

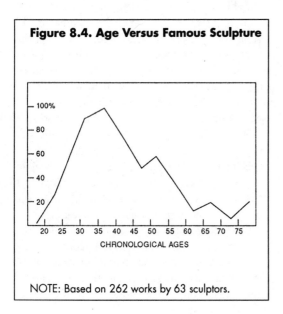

Figure 8.4. Age Versus Famous Sculpture

NOTE: Based on 262 works by 63 sculptors.

were found in Lorado Taft's *The History of American Sculpture . . .*, which attempts to list the best works of the most famous American sculptors. It seems safe to assume that Taft's list contains no age bias. From his book the dates of execution were found for 262 sculptured works by 63 sculptors now deceased. For these 262 works Figure 8.4 sets forth the average number executed during each five-year interval of the artists' lives. . . .

By means of statistical distributions and graphs [we] show the ages (1) at which outstanding thinkers have most frequently made (or first published) their momentous creative contributions, (2) at which leaders have most often attained important positions of leadership. . . .

The most notable creative works of scientists and mathematicians were identified by experts in the various specialized fields of endeavor. For such fields as oil painting, education, philosophy, and literature, a consensus of the experts was obtained by a study of their published writings. In each field listed below the maximum average rate of highly superior production was found to occur not later than during the specified range of ages. For example, item 1 of this list, chemistry, 26-30, is to be interpreted as follows: in proportion to the number of chemists that were alive at each successive age level, very superior contributions to the field of chemistry were made at the greatest average rate when the chemists were not more than 26-30. The remaining items here and those in the tabular lists that follow are to be interpreted in similar manner.

*Physical Sciences,
Mathematics, and Inventions:*
1. Chemistry, 26-30
2. Mathematics, 30-34
3. Physics, 30-34
4. Electronics, 30-34
5. Practical Inventions, 30-34
6. Surgical Techniques, 30-39
7. Geology, 35-39
8. Astronomy, 35-39

Biological Sciences:

9. Botany, 30-34
10. Classical descriptions of Disease, 30-34
11. Genetics, 30-39
12. Entomology, 30-39
13. Psychology, 30-39
14. Bacteriology, 35-39
15. Physiology, 35-39
16. Pathology, 35-39
17. Medical Discoveries, 35-39 . . .

For most types of superior music, the maximum average rate of good production is likely to occur in the thirties. Here are the maxima.

18. Instrumental selections, 25-29
19. Vocal solos, 30-34
20. Symphonies, 30-34
21. Chamber music, 35-39
22. Orchestral music, 35-39
23. Grand Opera, 35-39
24. Cantatas, 40-44
25. Light Opera and Musical Comedy, 40-44

For the study of literary creativity, fifty well-known histories of English literature were canvassed. The works most often cited by the fifty literary historians were assumed to be superior to those cited infrequently. Best-liked short stories were identified similarly by use of 102 source books, and "best books" were ascertained by study of a collation of fifty "best book" lists. As is revealed by the following tabulation, literary works that are good and permanently great are produced at the highest average rate by persons who are not over 45 years old. It is clear also that most types of poetry show maxima 10 to 15 years earlier than most prose writings other than short stories.

26. German Composers of Noteworthy Lyrics and Ballads, 22-26
27. Odes, 24-28
28. Elegies, 25-29
29. Pastoral Poetry, 25-29

30. Narrative Poetry, 25-29
31. Sonnets, 26-31
32. Lyric Poetry, 26-31
33. Satiric Poetry, 30-34
34. Short stories, 30-34
35. Religious Poetry (Hymns), 32-36
36. Comedies, 32-36
37. Tragedies, 34-38
38. "Most Influential Books," 35-39
39. Hymns by Women, 36-38
40. Novels, 40-44
41. "Best Books," 40-44
42. Best Sellers, 40-44
43. Miscellaneous Prose Writings, 41-45 . . .

Although the maximum average rate of output of the most important philosophical books occurred at 35-39, the total range for best production extended from 22-80, and for mere quantity of output—good, bad, and indifferent—the production rate was almost constant from 30-70. . . .

A very large proportion of the most renowned men of science and the humanities did their first important work before 25, and . . . in general the earlier starters contributed better work and were more prolific than were the slow starters. . . .

For most types of creative work the following generalizations have been derived. Within any given field of creative endeavor: (1) the maximum production rate for output of highest quality usually occurs at an earlier age than the maximum rate for less distinguished works by the same individuals; (2) the rate of good production usually does not change much in the middle years and the decline, when it comes, is gradual at all the older ages— much more gradual than its onset in the late teens or early twenties; (3) production of highest quality tends to fall off not only at an earlier age but also at a more rapid rate than does output of lesser merit. . . .

Item 62 in the following tabulation shows that, in proportion to the number of men who were still alive at each successive age level, presidents of American colleges and universities have served most often at 50-54. The other items in this tabulation are to be interpreted similarly.

62. Presidents of American colleges and universities, 50-54
63. Presidents of the U.S. prior to Truman, 55-59
64. U.S. Ambassadors to Foreign Countries from 1875 to 1900, 60-64
65. U.S. Senators in 1925, 60-64
66. Men in Charge of the U.S. Army from 1925 to 1945, 60-64
67. Justices of the U.S. Supreme Court from 1900 to 1925, 70-74
68. Speakers of the U.S. House of Representatives from 1900 to 1940, 70-74
69. Popes, 82-92

An analysis of age data for the most highly successful athletes reveals that their modal ages differ less from the norms for intellectual proficiency than is commonly supposed. The following comparisons are illustrative.

70. Professional Football Players, 22-26
71. Professional Prizefighters, 25-26
72. Professional Ice Hockey Players, 26
73. Professional Baseball Players, 27-28
74. Professional Tennis Players, 25-29
75. Automobile Racers, 26-30
76. Leading Contestants at Chess, 29-33
77. Professional Golfers, 31-36
78. Breakers of World Billiards Records, 31-36
79. Winners at Rifle and Pistol Shooting, 31-36
80. Winners of Important Bowling Championships, 31-36 . . .

When seven groups of earlier-born athletic champions were compared with seven groups of those more recently born, the field of sport being kept constant in each comparison, the later-born were found to be older than the earlier-born. The changes that have taken place in the modal ages of creative thinkers, leaders, and athletes all evidence the fact that these modal ages are not due solely to genetic factors. Whether the modal ages will continue to change and whether they can be subjected to some kind of human control are quite different questions.

A mere increase in man's longevity should not change greatly the modal ages at which man exhibits his greatest creative proficiency since, both for long-lived and for short-lived groups, the modal age occurs in the thirties. . . .

Possible Causes for the Early Maxima in Creativity

At present we are in no position to explain these curves of creativity that rise rapidly in early maturity and then decline slowly after attaining an earlier maximum. Undoubtedly multiple causation operates in these complex behaviors and no discovered contributing condition is likely to be of itself a sufficient or necessary cause. Nevertheless, it is profitable here to list sixteen of the factors which have been suggested as contributing to these representative functions with their early maxima, for such factors indicate possible lines for further research. Here is the list.

(1) A decline occurs prior to 40 in physical vigor, energy, and resistance to fatigue. This decline is probably far more important than such normal age changes as may occur in adult intelligence prior to outright senility.

(2) A diminution in sensory capacity and motor precision also takes place with advance in age. For example, impaired vision and hearing handicap the older individual in many cumulative ways, and writing by hand also becomes more difficult with advance in age.

(3) Serious illness, poor health, and various bodily infirmities more often influence adversely the production rates of older than of younger age groups.

(4) Glandular changes continue throughout life. It is conceivable that hormone research may some day reveal a partial explanation for the changes and especially for the early maxima.

(5) In some instances unhappy marriages and maladjustment in the sex life, growing worse with advance in age, may have interfered with creative work.

(6) The older age groups, more often than the younger, may have become indifferent toward creativity because of the death of a child, a mate, or some other dear one.

(7) As compared with younger persons, older ones are apt to be more preoccupied with the practical concerns of life, with earning a living, and with getting ahead.

(8) Less favorable conditions for concentrated work sometimes come with success, promotion, enhanced prestige, and responsibility.

(9) In some cases the youthful worker's primary ambition may not have been to discover the unknown or to create something new but to get renown. Having acquired prestige and recognition, such workers may try less hard for achievement.

(10) Too easy, too great, or too early fame may conceivably breed complacency and induce one to rest on his previously won laurels before he has done his best possible creative work.

(11) Some older persons may have become apathetic because they have experienced more often the deadening effect of non-recognition and of destructive criticism.

(12) As a result of negative transfer, the old generally are more inflexible than the young. This inflexibility may be a handicap to creative thinking, even though it is dependent on erudition.

(13) Perhaps in part because of the foregoing factors, some older persons experience a decrease in motivation which leads to a weaker intellectual interest and curiosity.

(14) Younger persons tend to have had a better formal education than their elders, they have grown to maturity in a more stimulating social and cultural milieu, and they have had less time to forget what they have learned.

(15) In some few cases outright psychosis has clouded what was previously a brilliant mind. Psychoses occur more often in the latter half of the normal life span.

(16) In other extreme cases, the individual's normal productive powers may have been sapped by alcohol, narcotics, and other kinds of dissipation. Here, as elsewhere, it is difficult to separate cause from effect. . . .

Upon the basis of all these statistics what is one to conclude? Whatever the causes of growth and decline, it remains clear that the genius does not function equally well throughout the years of adulthood. Superior creativity rises relatively rapidly to a maximum which occurs usually in the thirties and then falls off slowly. Almost as soon as he becomes fully mature, man is confronted with a gerontic paradox that may be expressed in terms of positive and negative transfer. Old people probably have more transfer, both positive and negative, than do young ones. As a result of positive transfer the old usually possess greater wisdom and erudition. These are invaluable assets. But when a situation requires a new way of looking at things, the acquisition of new techniques or even new vocabularies, the old seem stereotyped and rigid. To learn the new they often have to unlearn the old and that is twice as hard as learning without unlearning. But when a situation requires a store of past knowledge then the old find their advantage over the young.

Possibly every human behavior has its period of prime. No behavior can develop before the groundwork for it has been prepared, but in general it appears that the conditions essential for creativity and originality, which can be displayed in private achievement, come earlier than those social skills which contribute to leadership and eminence and which inevitably must wait, not upon the insight of the leader himself, but upon the insight of society about him.

Age and Achievement
A Critique

Wayne Dennis

The recent book by Lehman (1), *Age and Achievement,* seems to indicate that in many fields relatively little creative work of importance is done by persons past 45 or 50 years of age. This generalization does not hold in all fields of creativity, but the preceding sentence expresses Lehman's most striking finding.

That the production of first-rate work in poetry, art, science, and other creative areas decreases markedly with age is a matter of prime importance. If correct, it suggests that the creative worker in many fields should plan for early superannuation. If the conclusion drawn by Lehman is erroneous, the impression which it has created should be corrected with dispatch, for a conviction that early deterioration is inevitable may itself have deleterious consequences. Clearly the relationship of age to achievement is a topic in regard to which conclusions should be drawn with extreme care.

It is the thesis of this [reading] that much of the apparent decline in creative achievement revealed by Lehman's tables and graphs is due to factors other than age. We believe Lehman's data give a spurious appearance of age decrement in creativity.

Let us note first that the studies presented by Lehman are so numerous and so varied that it is difficult to do justice to them in a brief recapitulation. However, it is not incorrect to say that Lehman has been interested primarily in determining the 5 or 10 year age-period in which important creative works have most often been produced. The first step in his procedure, typically, consists in identifying important works in some field. To avoid introducing a bias of his own, he always uses a list of works drawn up by some other person. Lehman then determines the age at which each item was produced. He has done this for many creative fields, including mathematical discoveries, contributions to chemistry, lyric poems, and operas, to mention only a few. The first six chapters of his book are devoted to presenting the results of these analyses.

The graphs in these chapters almost all indicate that the production of outstanding works rises to a peak relatively early in the adult years and then declines. The age at which the peak of productivity is reached varies from field to field. It is as early as ages 22-26 for lyrics, ballads, and odes, and as late as 40-45 for novels, metaphysics, and miscellaneous prose writings. However, for a considerable number of fields the top rates for the production of outstanding works occur between ages 30 and 39.

Many aspects of these curves are worthy of attention, but we are concerned chiefly with the decrements which follow the peaks. In most instances, as presented by Lehman, the decrements are very striking. For example, . . . at ages 40-45 chemists produce, per man, only one half as many significant contributions as they produce between ages

Published on a grant from the Forest Park Foundation to the Journal of Gerontology.
Source: "Age and Achievement: A Critique" by W. Dennis, 1956, *Journal of Applied Gerontology,* pp. 331-333.

30-35. By ages 60-65 their rate of production is only 20 per cent of their peak rate. Other graphs give very similar data for other sciences. The fine arts also show a severe decrement. For example, . . . by ages 45-50 the production of orchestral music judged to be of highest merit is only about 10 per cent as great as it was 10 years earlier. By ages 55-60 the composition of orchestral music of high quality decreases to 20 per cent of the maximum rate.

Examination of such findings, page after page, creates an impression of inevitable decline. If these charts are taken at their face value, we must conclude that in most kinds of creative work the output of work of first-rate quality is greatly reduced after the thirties.

But should these charts be taken at their face value? Let us consider this question.

A major methodologic weakness in Lehman's treatment of data lies in the fact that in most instances a table or graph combines information pertaining to men of different degrees of longevity. Thus a table usually presents data for men nearly all of whom reached age 30, but only part of whom attained age 40, and still fewer of whom completed half a century of life. To equate for differences in numbers of subjects at different ages, Lehman found the mean number of important contributions per person for persons surviving each decade. We shall attempt to show that this method of treating data acts in part to produce the productivity differentials which Lehman discovers.

Let it be noted that each man whose record is used by Lehman is required to produce only one important work in order to qualify for inclusion. In most lists of outstanding works used by Lehman, each individual contributes one, or only a few items. In his collections of data, the mean number of contributions per man is often only two or three. Furthermore, the mean number of "significant" contributions per man is only slightly greater for the men who lived to age 70 than it is for the men who died relatively early.

In order to be included the short-lived man must have produced a significant work at an early age. To qualify for inclusion, a long-lived man was required to produce one significant work but this could have been done either early or late. In other words, in order to achieve a certain degree of eminence, the short-lived man must have fulfilled in a few years what the longer-lived achieved in a more leisurely fashion. We shall show that the consequence of combining data for men of different longevities is a higher average productivity in the early decades.

In this connection Lehman says . . . , "Adequate allowance for the unequal numbers of individuals alive at successive age levels was made. . . ." It seems to us that no adequate allowance can be made for the fact that all of the significant contributions of short-lived people occur in the early decades, whereas the long-lived can contribute both early and late. In tabulating entries for different decades, the twenties or thirties receive a score for each short-lived person. On the other hand, the later decades, such as the sixties, contain no entries for short-lived persons and only part of the entries for the septagenarians. When data from men of different degrees of longevity are included in the same table, the early decades have an inevitable loading which is not shared by the later decades. To give the later decades a similar loading, it would be necessary to adopt the rule of including a long-lived person only if he made a significant contribution in his later years, because, conversely, the short-lived person is included only if he made a significant contribution in the early decades of life. This is a somewhat subtle point, but one which is essential to the correct evaluation of Lehman's data.

From the point of view of the consideration presented above, a very interesting table is presented by Lehman in his penultimate chapter . . . . This table represents 1540 notable contributions to various sciences. In this case, the data for persons of different longevity are treated separately. For this reason, the criticism presented above does not apply.

The table shows that for each group the decade . . . of the thirties is most productive but the differences between the thirties and the forties are not large. The largest difference between the thirties and forties occurs among those dying in the forties. In this group ill-health may have contributed to the decrement. For longer-lived groups, even the decrements in the fifties, compared to the thirties, are not dramatic. No group in the fifties drops to the extent which is found when persons are not segregated according to longevity. In other words, this table shows that the combining of data for men of unequal longevity in other tables seems to have exaggerated the apparent age decrement. Nevertheless, even when data refer to men of equal life-spans some age decrement is still found.

This table is so significant in regard to age decrement that it is surprising that Lehman makes no reference to it when discussing the striking decrements reported in his earlier chapters. Nor are its findings adequately reflected in the summary chapter of his book. For these reasons it seems necessary here to emphasize the importance of the data which it contains.

We believe that much of this residual decrement is the product of other deficiencies in methodology. For one thing, it seems likely that the very high peaks of productivity which Lehman reports in his early chapters may be due to errors in sampling and to choosing age-intervals in such a way as to maximize the effects of sampling errors.

Many, but not all, of the curves presented by Lehman are based upon a relatively small number of entries. Thus figure 14 is the result of only 52 entries, figure 16, 30, figure 51, 53, figure 53, 67, and figure 56, 40. These entries are divided among age-intervals, usually 5-year periods, extending from age 20 to age 70 and beyond. With small numbers of entries divided among 10 or more age intervals, one would expect that, even though no true age differences are present, high values in some age-intervals would frequently be obtained through the operation of sampling errors. This fact is important because the highest age score in any body of data is taken as the peak from which decrement is mea-

sured. Therefore any exaggeration of the peak naturally results in finding exaggerated decrements.

This factor is further aggravated by the fact that Lehman did not limit himself to a fixed set of age-intervals, but apparently altered them in order to determine the particular "peak years" which seem to characterize a particular set of data. Thus, as the final chapter indicates, the step-intervals for peak years for different activities are variously reported as 22-26, 24-28, 25-29, 26-31, 30-34, 32-36, etc. The modification of age-intervals in order to find "ages of maximum productivity" would be legitimate if the findings were cross-validated against new data, but this was seldom done. Hence the extent to which "peak years" are affected by random errors of sampling is unknown.

There can be little doubt that some part of the decrements reported by Lehman are to be explained by the considerations just presented. The reader of Lehman's book will note that decrements are less precipitous in the graphs which are based upon numerous data and in the construction of which the step intervals follow the decimal system instead of being varied to maximize the peaks.

The preceding arguments have been of a mathematical or statistical sort. Those which follow are of a different kind, but, we think, no less cogent.

Lehman used as a criterion for inclusion of a work as a "significant contribution" the appearance of the work in histories of the appropriate area, or its appearance in lists of "best" books, "best" operas, etc. Perhaps, no better indices of importance are available, but it should be pointed out that these criteria may have certain weaknesses from the point of view of the study of age differences. It is possible that biographies, histories, and lists of best works contain systematic errors somewhat favoring a man's early work at the expense of his later products, and Lehman's findings may reflect these biases. For example, the art historian may be more likely to mention a painter's first significant contribution than he is to mention his last important piece of work. Likewise, an historian of science may be more likely to mention a young man's pioneering research which opened a new vista than he is to describe the subsequent painstaking investigations which were necessary to develop and validate the promise of the pioneering study. It is difficult to know to what extent an apparent age decrement may be due to the proclivities of anthologists and historians rather than to age itself.

In this connection, the possibility of a bias against the evaluation of recent contributions should be considered. It is our impression that critics and historians tend to consider the evaluation of recent contributions to be more difficult than the evaluation of more remote works. They may, therefore, suspend judgment in connection with recent contributions. Now a considerable number of Lehman's subjects were born after 1800 . . . . Their later works were recent works at the time of the preparation of the source books from which Lehman obtained his data. Unwillingness, on the part of historians and editors, to evaluate recent works would therefore lessen the number of significant works recorded for the later years of some of Lehman's subjects. Consonant with this interpretation is Lehman's report that in former centuries the decrement with age in several fields seems not to have been as great as in recent times . . . . A century or more ago the apparent decline of creativity with age was slight.

Let us note, too, that the assessment of the relative excellence of work done early and late in a man's career is made exceedingly difficult, if indeed not impossible, by the changes in standards which occur during a man's lifetime. For example, the situation in biology in 1880, when Darwin was 71, was extremely different from what it was when "The Origin of the Species" appeared in 1859 when Darwin was 50. In fact, the difference was due in large part to Darwin's own work. It seems relatively meaningless to compare biologic contributions made before and after the publication of the theory of evolution. This argument, of course, is not limited to biology. Changing standards characterize all fields, whereas judgments of quality in regard to works separated by several decades seem to imply absolute standards.

Standards for the judgment of quality are further complicated by the great increase in the number of creative workers in most fields which has taken place in recent times. Thus the best psychologist in America in 1900 was the best in a group of approximately 100. The best psychologist today, if he were ascertained, would have to be judged the best among 13,000. A psychologist living in 1900 and still living today, had 99 competitors for distinction in his youth and has 12,999 rivals (or thereabouts) in his later years. Similar, if perhaps less striking, increases in personnel have taken place in other fields. Curves for age changes in number of significant contributions do not, and probably cannot, correct for changes in standards of evaluation which occur during a lifetime.

In summary, we have presented several reasons for skepticism in regard to accepting the view that there is a decrement with age in the production of creative works of high level. We have not attempted to be exhaustive in this treatment. We submit, however, that there is a reasonable doubt that the curves presented by Lehman depict an age decline. Quality of creative work *may* decrease with age, but data presently available do not offer satisfactory evidence.

We would like to be able to suggest a method by which valid conclusions concerning changes in the quality of creative contributions with age could be reached, but we are unable to do so. All sources of data, and all methods of evaluation which we have considered seem to suffer from one or more of the difficulties discussed above. Nevertheless, it has been noted that as the methodologic difficulties in Lehman's work are reduced, the apparent decline with age becomes smaller. Whether ideal data would show no decline prior to extreme old age it is at present impossible to say, but this possibility should not be ignored.

Reference

1. Lehman, H. C.: *Age and Achievement,* Princeton University Press, 1953.

Creative Productivity
Through the Adult Years

Dean Keith Simonton

All too often the years in the latter part of life are seen as a phase of decline in creative powers. Supposedly once an individual enters his or her 40th year, society cannot and should not expect much, for the best years have been left behind. This notion is expressed cruelly in Shakespeare's words, "When the age is in, the wit is out." No wonder that many otherwise productive individuals sense a "midlife crisis" coming on as they pass into the putative region of decline and deterioration. Indeed, some commentators have aggravated matters by claiming that the downhill slide normally begins in the 30s rather than the 40s, as is evident in a little poem written by Paul Dirac, who received the Nobel Prize for Physics when only 31 years old for work he had completed when just 25:

> Age is, of course, a fever chill that every physicist must fear. He's better dead than living still when once he's past his thirtieth year. (quoted in Jungk, 1958, p. 27)

Presumably these conceptions of the superiority of youth to maturity are based on straightforward empirical observations—solid facts rather than prejudicial stereotypes. But is that necessarily so? One can always offer anecdotes about the excep-

Source: "Creative Productivity Through the Adult Years" by D. Simonton, *Generations* (Spring 1991), pp. 13-16. Reprinted with permission from *Generations*, 833 Market St., Suite 512, San Francisco, CA 94103. Copyright 1991, ASA.

tional accomplishments of youth, such as Newton's *annus mirabilis* that reportedly occurred before his 24th year, but such instances can always be balanced by stories of phenomenal achievements by personalities in advanced age; for example, Copernicus saw his treatise on the heliocentric system published as he lay on his deathbed in his 70th year. So what is required is not the compilation of anecdote and counteranecdote, but rather the systematic investigation of how creative productivity changes over the life span.

Interestingly enough, scientific inquiries on this very question have been going on for over a hundred years (e.g., Beard, 1874; Quetelet, 1835/1968). The classic study in this area is Harvey C. Lehman's (1953) well-known *Age and Achievement,* in which the connection between creative productivity and chronological age is examined for virtually every endeavor under the sun. Although Lehman's work suffered from a number of methodological problems—not surprising for such a pioneer effort—recent years have seen a resurgence of investigations that exploit more sophisticated techniques. Indeed, the fact that so many children of the baby boom generation are now entering the latter half of life may have made this a hot issue in life-span developmental psychology. Accordingly, despite the existence of several published reviews of the most current literature in the past few years (see, especially, Simonton, 1988, 1990a, 1990b), the burst of activity has already rendered these surveys somewhat obsolete!

An updated summary of key findings is thus in order.

Let us begin with one solid empirical generalization that was first promulgated in 1835 and that remains robust today. If one plots the number of creative products, such as articles, paintings, or plays, as a function of a creator's chronological age, the output rate first increases rather quickly, attaining a peak in the late 30s or early 40s of life; thereafter, productivity gradually declines. It is the latter portion of the age curve, naturally enough, that seems to shatter the hopes of those wanting to continue creativity in the final half of life. Indeed, ever since Beard (1874), this downward tendency has led to pessimistic expectations about the utility of advanced maturity. Nevertheless, while the observed age curve has been replicated hundreds of times, more detailed theoretical and empirical analyses reveal that the picture is not as bad as first meets the eye. Six considerations, discussed below, are paramount.

Exceptions Expected

It cannot be stressed too much that the typical age curve is merely a statistical average of hundreds of separate age curves for individual creators. Like any statistical summation, the result is far from deterministic; no creative person is forced to have his or her career trajectory follow the exact same course. Rather, these averaged age curves can be taken to represent merely the probability of creative output at particular stages in a human life. Because we are dealing solely in probabilities, "exceptions to the rule" must be necessarily expected, not categorically denied. This point takes on special force when we introduce a central finding of the recent empirical literature: The generalized age curve is not a function of chronological age but rather it is determined by *career age* (e.g., Simonton, 1991, in press). People differ tremendously on when they manage to launch themselves in their creative activities. Whereas those who get off to an exceptionally early start may—if circumstances to be discussed later are held constant—

find themselves peaking out early in life, others who qualify as veritable "late bloomers" will not get into full stride until they attain ages at which others are leaving the race. It is for this reason that some creative personalities have failed to reach the acme of their achievements until near the close of their lives.

Magnitude of Decline

But to make matters simpler, let us now suppose that we are confining our analysis to individuals who all initiated their creative activities at the same chronological age, such as the mid-20s, thus taking the respective career ages of these individuals as identical—what then? Notwithstanding the general occurrence of an age decrement in productivity in the final decades of life, the magnitude of this decline is seldom so substantial that an individual must become devoid of creativity at life's close. On the contrary, the average rate of output in the seventh decade of life falls to around half the rate seen at the career optimum in the 30s and 40s (Simonton, 1988). Consequently, even an octogenarian can expect to produce many notable contributions to a chosen creative endeavor. Indeed, even though a 50 percent decrement may look depressing, the drop by no means necessitates the last decade of a typical career to suffer in comparison to the first decade of that same career. Quite the contrary: Creators in their 60s and 70s will most often be generating new ideas at a rate exceeding that of the very same creators in their 20s (e.g., Dennis, 1966). In fact, toward the end of life the postoptimum decrease in output decelerates, so that rather than a plummeting we witness a leisurely asymptotic approach to the zero productivity level (Simonton, 1984). Of course, those persons who experience severe disabilities may exhibit a "terminal drop," but such an unfortunate happenstance is far from normal so long as a creator's health holds out. As a consequence, it is easy to list impressive accomplishments by people who were well along in years, yet not necessarily late bloomers (Lehman, 1953, chap. 14).

Variation Across Disciplines

The overall age curve described earlier is not only the statistical average of hundreds of separate career trajectories that can depart from the norm in manifold ways, but in addition the generalized trend represents a kind of rough summary of age curves that vary substantially across disciplines (Simonton, 1988). Especially noteworthy is the realization that the expected age decrement in creativity in some disciplines is so minuscule that we can hardly talk of a decline at all. Although in certain creative activities, such as pure mathematics and lyric poetry, the peak may appear relatively early in life, sometimes even in the late 20s and early 30s, with a rapid drop afterwards, in other activities, such as geology and scholarship, the age optimum may occur appreciably later, in the 50s even, with a gentle, even undetectable decrease in productivity thereafter (e.g., Dennis, 1966). Expressed in precise terms, whereas in some endeavors the last decade of life may see output rates only 10 percent as high as witnessed at the career maxima, in other endeavors the productivity seen in the closing years may remain quite near the magnitude of output reached in the supposed productive prime.

The occurrence of such interdisciplinary contrasts endorses the conjecture that the career course is decided more by the intrinsic needs of the creative process than by generic extrinsic forces, whether physical illness, family commitments, or administrative responsibilities. This conclusion is bolstered further by the fact that the distinctive age curves for various disciplines tend to replicate across different nationalities and historical periods (Lehman, 1962; Simonton, 1975). Now clearly, if creativity in some domains can persist until the final days, it becomes obvious that we cannot speak of broad decrements in psychological functioning required for creative output (Simonton, 1988). Significantly, a theoretical model that quite accurately predicts such interdisciplinary differences in the career trajectories does so solely by taking into consideration the information-processing requirements of distinct fields (Simonton, 1989a).

Admittedly, for creators whose aspirations fall into fields that feature early career optima, these empirical findings may still look discouraging. A lyric poet, after all, will yet be "over the hill" at a relatively youthful age. Even so, nothing prevents a person from switching fields in order to preserve creative vitality. By carefully designed midcareer changes, individuals may resuscitate their creative potential (cf. Root-Bernstein, 1989).

Quantity or Quality

One critical question lies lurking in the preceding discussion, namely, whether we are speaking of quantity or quality when publicizing the age trends. Lehman's (1953) classic summary of his extensive empirical findings has often been attacked for excessive reliance on tabulations of only those creations recognized as notable or influential, ignoring the much larger body of potential contributions that underlie the few works that are thus singled out (Simonton, 1988). Dennis (1966), in particular, argued that, whereas tabulations of famous contributions may exhibit sharp declines in the later years, truly exhaustive tallies display far more gradual decreases. Therefore, if we choose to reject the judgments of posterity and focus on strictly behavioral measures, the age decrement in creativity is much less substantial.

This criticism has two deficiencies, however. First, if the term "creative" is to have any genuine meaning, it must ultimately be tied to real social value, and thus mere behavioral productivity is largely irrelevant. Second, and more profound, empirical studies actually demonstrate that quality of output across the life span is strongly associated with quantity of output (e.g., Over, 1989; Simonton, 1977, 1985). In other words, those periods in a creative career in which an individual is generating the most total works tend to be, on the average, the same periods in which the most successful pieces emerge. In fact, if one calculates the ratio of creative products to the total number of offerings at each age interval, one finds that this "quality ratio" exhibits no systematic change with age. As a consequence, the success rate is the same for the senior colleague as it is for the young whippersnapper. Older creators may indeed be producing fewer hits, but they are equally producing fewer misses as well. Hence, on a contribution-for-contribution basis—that is, by determining the probability that a particular product will prove influential in a given domain of cultural endeavor—we cannot speak of an age decrement at all! This probabilistic connection between quantity and quality, which has been styled the "constant probability of success" principle (Simonton, 1988), strongly implies that an individual's creative powers remain intact throughout the life span.

Individual Variation
Individuals vary immensely in what may be termed *creative potential* which may be roughly defined here as the maximum number of attempted contributions an individual is capable of making given an unlimited life span (Simonton, 1988). The primary behavioral manifestation of this variable is the sheer rate at which ideas are generated throughout the career: The higher the creative potential, the faster the output per annum. Now because this individual difference variable is independent of the age of career onset (Simonton, in press), it provides yet another factor that can enhance the creativity of the later years. In particular, given a set of persons having all launched their careers at the same chronological age, that subset of individuals who score high on this attribute will tend to generate possible contributions at a more prolific rate in the closing years and thus, according to the constant-probability-of-success principle, manage to produce more truly notable works as well. The age curves do not really differ for those highest in creative potential, but rather the curves function at a larger scale; thus a person with exceptional potential will be producing at rates in the final years that can surpass the productivity of an individual with lower potential who is operating at his or her career peak. Consequently, predictions about the expected creativity in the last decade cannot be made

without reference to substantial cross-sectional variation in both the age at which the career commences and the individual's total creative capacity (see, e.g., Over, 1982a, 1982b).

A Secondary Peak
In all of the preceding points we continued to speak of an age decrement in the last years of life, the main thrust of the arguments being that certain factors can intervene to impede the seemingly inevitable decline. Yet empirical research actually suggests that creative productivity can undergo a substantial renaissance in the final years, especially toward life's close. For example, some time after the late 60s a resurgence in output often appears (Simonton, 1988). This secondary peak, to be sure, is not nearly so pronounced as that appearing in the so-called prime of life. Even so, its very existence contradicts the supposed inevitability of the downhill slide.

This contradiction gains even greater force when we consider the recent demonstration of the swan-song phenomenon, or "last works" effects (Simonton, 1989b). After subjecting 1,919 works by 172 classical composers to detailed quantitative scrutiny, one striking pattern emerged: As the composers neared their final years, when death was becoming more than an abstract contingency, they began to create compositions that were more concise, with simpler and more restrained melodic lines; yet these compositions scored extremely well in esthetic significance, as judged by musicologists, and eventually joined the popular mainstays of the classical repertoire. It is as if each composer, when seeing the end approaching fast on life's horizon, put the utmost into everything undertaken, with the knowledge that among the current works-in-progress dwelt a last artistic testament. Whatever the motivation, the mere fact that dying creators can pull off such feats provides another argument on behalf of the theory that the general decline in output need not be synonymous with a deterioration in creative powers.

The foregoing six points by no means exhaust all that might be said on this critical life-span developmental issue (cf. Simonton, 1988, 1990b). But these empirical findings should enable us to appreciate that the final phase of life can be, and often is, a period of phenomenal creativity. At the very least we should understand how it can come to pass that certain creators manage to leave posterity with monumental creations that would have been sorely missed had their late-life endeavors been summarily dismissed. Thus in the arts, Cervantes could complete Part II of *Don Quixote* at age 68, Verdi compose *Falstaff* in his 80th year, and Titian paint *Christ Crowned with Thorns* when approaching 90 years of age. And turning to science, Laplace finished his *Celestial Mechanics* at age 79, Humboldt put out the last volume of his *Cosmos* when 89, and, most remarkably, the chemist Chevreul took up the study of gerontology in his 90s and published his last scientific paper when 102! Nor are such examples restricted to a bygone era, as the recent example of Elizabeth Layton well exemplifies: At the age of 68, she combated thoughts of suicide by taking up artistic expression, propelling herself on an enterprise of distinctive creativity at an age when most would be contemplating retirement.

The important implication of these examples is that the career trajectory reflects not the inexorable progression of an aging process tied extrinsically to chronological age, but rather entails the intrinsic working out of a person's creative potential by successive acts of self-actualization.

References

Beard, G. M., 1874. *Legal Responsibility in Old Age.* New York: Russell.

Dennis, W., 1966. "Creative Productivity between the Ages of 20 and 80 years." *Journal of Gerontology* 21: 1-8.

Jungk, R., 1958. *Brighter Than a Thousand Suns* (trans. J. Cleugh). New York: Harcourt Brace.

Lehman, H. C., 1953. *Age and Achievement.* Princeton, N.J.: Princeton University Press.

Lehman, H. C., 1962. "More about Age and Achievement." *Gerontologist* 2(3): 141-48.

Over, R., 1982a. "Does Research Productivity Decline with Age?" *Higher Education* 11: 511-20.

Over, R., 1982b. "Is Age a Good Predictor of Research Productivity?" *Australian Psychologist* 17: 129-39.

Quetelet, A., 1835/1968. *A Treatise on Man.* New York: Franklin. (Reprint of 1842 Edinburgh translation of original 1835 publication.)

Root-Bernstein, R. S., 1989. *Discovering.* Cambridge, Mass.: Harvard University Press.

Shakespeare, W. "Much Ado about Nothing." In R. M. Hutchins, ed., *Great Books of the Western World.* Chicago: Encyclopedia Britannica, 1952, p. 520.

Simonton, D. K., 1975. "Age and Literary Creativity: A Cross-Cultural and Transhistorical Survey." *Journal of Cross-Cultural Psychology* 6(3): 259-77.

Simonton, D. K., 1977. "Creative Productivity, Age, and Stress: A Biographical Time-Series Analysis of 10 Classical Composers." *Journal of Personality and Social Psychology* 35(3): 791-804.

Simonton, D. K., 1984. "Creative Productivity and Age: A Mathematical Model Based on a Two-Step Cognitive Process." *Developmental Review* 4: 77-111.

Simonton, D. K., 1985. "Quality, Quantity, and Age: The Careers of 10 Distinguished Psychologists." *International Journal of Aging and Human Development* 21(4): 241-54.

Simonton, D. K., 1988. "Age and Outstanding Achievement: What Do We Know after a Century of Research?" *Psychological Bulletin* 104(2): 251-67.

Simonton, D. K., 1989a. "Age and Creative Productivity: Nonlinear Estimation of an Information-Processing Model." *International Journal of Aging and Human Development* 29: 23-37.

Simonton, D. K., 1989b. "The Swan-Song Phenomenon: Last-Works Effects for 172 Classical Composers." *Psychology and Aging* 4: 42-47.

Simonton, D. K., 1990a. "Creativity and Wisdom in Aging." In J. E. Birren and K. W. Schaie, eds., *Handbook of the Psychology of Aging,* 3d ed. New York: Academic Press.

Simonton, D. K., 1990b. "Creativity in the Later Years: Optimistic Prospects for Achievement." *Gerontologist* 30(5): 626-31.

Simonton, D. K., 1991. "Career Landmarks in Science: Individual Differences and Interdisciplinary Contrasts." *Developmental Psychology* 27(1): 119-27.

Simonton, D. K., in press. "The Emergence and Realization of Genius: The Lives and Works of 120 Classical Composers." *Journal of Personality and Social Psychology.*

Wisdom
One Facet of Successful Aging?

Paul B. Baltes, Jacqui Smith,
Ursula M. Staudinger, and Doris Sowarka

Since its origin as a science, the field of gerontology has included the search for positive features of human aging. . . . This quest was symbolized in the motto adopted by The Gerontological Society of America in the 1950s: "To add life to years, not only years to life." The current agenda of gerontological work bears witness to the unbroken continuation of this pursuit. . . .

The Search for Positive Aspects of Aging

. . . We do know . . . from cognitive training research . . . that many older adults, in principle and if they are spared from brain-related diseases, possess the capacity to engage in further efforts toward their own development by acquiring new cognitive skills or by nurturing their past strengths. The careers of top artists and experts in various professional fields illustrate this assertion. . . . Furthermore, there is some evidence that older adults may be superior in some tasks of cognitive reasoning associated with questions of social and practical intelligence and the integration of affect into cognitive reasoning. . . .

Skeptics argue, however, that such evidence is not enough to continue pressing the view that human aging includes a major reservoir for further development and true "peak" performance (e.g., Salthouse, 1985). The argument made, for example, is that solid replications are rare and that there is no empirical evidence that older adults *on the average* are better than younger adults on any task that has been brought under tight control in the laboratory. In addition, it is proffered that there is no evidence that older persons hold the "world record" in any domain of life. It is open to question whether some fields of the arts may be such an exception. . . . Thus, skeptics can argue that the case for truly superior performances of older adults, especially in the domain of the mind, has not been made.

Our approach to this state of affairs is twofold. On the one hand, and here we join with similar positions, . . . we interpret the existing empirical body of research as insufficient, especially because extant measures and criteria of performance quality are youth-oriented. We suggest that any cognitive task on which older adults perform as well as young adults, or where occasional superiority of older adults has been demonstrated, should be seen as carrying novel and important information that warrants further amplification. At present, the pool of tasks used in cognitive aging research has not been developed with adequate attention to the possible strengths and uniqueness of old age.

On the other hand, we also argue for the fundamental significance of rare exceptions to the generally obtained pattern of late-life decline or stability. If even one older adult were to perform at near-peak levels of functioning, we claim this would imply that positive functioning in old age is possible in principle. That such high levels of functioning have not been attained for most older adults in the present times may simply reflect the state of an "underdeveloped culture" with its lack of medical and cultural success in achieving an "optimized" state of old age. Cultural evolution, in other words, has not yet reached late life and, therefore, awaits another critical test: the construction of a world in which reaching old age entails the possibility of continued, albeit possibly only select, growth.

Research directed toward understanding the nature and manifestation of wisdom and wise judgment is a testing ground for the search for what may be possible in principle. This choice of research focus is not unreasonable because wisdom has been highlighted as a facet of adult cognitive and intellectual functioning that reflects extensive knowledge and expertise . . . and, therefore, could be expected to have long life as one necessary precursor. . . . In reviews on the nature of exceptional performances, . . . it has persuasively been shown that a long-term investment involving decades and thousands of hours of practice is required to acquire an expertise. Thus, wisdom may be the prototype of an area of cognitive functioning in which older adults, because of their age, have the opportunity to hold something akin to a world record. . . .

Conceptualization of Wisdom (Berlin Work)

A Dual-Process Framework of Intelligence

In our general theoretical framework of lifespan intelligence, the knowledge-based "pragmatics" of intelligence are juxtaposed with the basic "mechanics" of intelligence. . . . This heuristic distinction between the content-free mechanics and the knowledge-rich pragmatics of intelligence is similar to and extends the original conceptual framework of the Cattell-Horn theory of fluid-crystallized intelligence. . . . While we expect aging loss in the "hardware-like" mechanics of intelligence, especially if measured near limits of functioning, . . . we proceed from the assumption that some late-life advances are possible in the "software-like" pragmatics of intelligence which involves the application of knowledge. Thus, the hallmark of positive cultural evolution and positive life-long development is the possibility of growth (advances) in the knowledge-based pragmatics.

Within this dual-process distinction between the mechanics and pragmatics of life-span intelligence, wisdom is considered one of the adulthood prototypes of growth in the pragmatics of intelligence (another prototype may be associated with various forms of professional specialization . . .). The specific substantive domain related to wisdom encompasses knowledge about the conduct of life and the human condition; that is, knowledge about the course, variations, dynamics, and conflicts of life. We assume that the concept wisdom is reserved for high levels of knowledge in this domain. Therefore, we characterize wisdom as an expert knowledge system. . . .

Theoretical Definition of Wisdom and Its Operationalization

Table 8.1 summarizes our approach to defining wisdom. Our analysis starts from an everyday conception of wisdom as entailing "good judgment and advice about difficult but uncertain matters of life". . . . From this everyday meaning of the term and using a conceptual approach offered by cognitive psychology, a definition of wisdom is derived for further theoretical analysis. Wisdom is defined as *expert knowledge (involving good judgment and advice) in the domain, fundamental pragmatics of life.* This domain encompasses knowledge about life matters: for example, knowledge about the

Table 8.1. Wisdom: A Working Framework

Theoretical Definition

An expert knowledge system in the domain, fundamental life pragmatics (life planning, life management, life review).

Functional consequence: Exceptional insight into human development and life matters, exceptionally good judgment, advice and commentary about difficult life problems.

Family of Five Criteria

1. Rich factual knowledge about life matters
2. Rich procedural knowledge about life problems
3. Life-span contextualism: Knowledge about the contexts of life and their temporal (developmental) relationships
4. Relativism: Knowledge about differences in values and priorities
5. Uncertainty: Knowledge about the relative indeterminacy and unpredictability of life and ways to manage

variations and conditions of life-span development, human nature and conduct, life tasks and goals, social and intergenerational relationships, and about life's uncertainties. Three contexts are singled out initially for empirical study as areas of judgment and discourse in which wisdom-related knowledge is manifested: *life planning, life management,* and *life review.* To date, we have conducted research in two of these areas: life planning and life review. We also plan to expand our current concern with "practical" aspects of wisdom to include what we have labeled . . . "philosophical" wisdom.

The definition of wisdom as an expert knowledge system permits further specification of the nature of the knowledge system. As shown in Table 8.1, a family of five criteria can be derived from cognitive psychology and life-span theory. Together, these criteria describe the nature of the wisdom-related knowledge system and its "summa-

tive" manifestation in terms of exceptional insight into life matters and good judgment and advice about difficult life problems. The five-criterion set is as follows: (1) richness of factual knowledge about life; (2) richness in procedural knowledge about life; (3) life-span contextualism; (4) relativism associated with an awareness of variations in values and life priorities; and (5) the recognition and management of life's uncertainty. . . .

To summarize our initial findings: First, and in line with our "weak" life-span prediction, older adults are among the top performers. Second, and again in line with our definition of wisdom as an expert knowledge, there are few responses judged to be wise. Third, average age/cohort differences are small, indicating much age-related stability. In addition, it seems that the entire period of adulthood is involved in the acquisition and transformation of wisdom-related knowledge. This conclusion is suggested by the fact that there is evidence for age-specific domains of wisdom-related expertise. For example, in the life planning study, young and older adults performed best when dealing with non-normative life problems specific to their own age period. . . .

Furthermore, it appears that there may be some differential age differences in the five criteria defining the wisdom construct. For example, in the life review task older adults showed a greater understanding of life's uncertainty compared to younger adults. . . .

Conclusion and Outlook

Since the birth of ancient Greek philosophy, and carried into modern times, wisdom has been considered as the peak, the capstone of knowledge about the human condition. Recently, this long-standing cultural heritage has attracted psychological researchers interested in exploring facets of successful aging and the potential for growth in late adulthood. Such an approach seems important because it pushes the boundaries of the nature of aging beyond current realities. Thus, even in the absence of sufficient and current empirical evidence demonstrating wisdom as an area of late-life potential, the basic tenet is important. Like scholarship on world utopias, the search for wisdom in old age is likely to open new vistas on what might be possible in principle if societal conditions were different.

In our own research strategy, we proceed from the assumption of a "weak" life-span hypothesis. On the one hand, we argue that not all older persons will be wise. On the other hand, we suggest that among wise persons there should be a disproportionately large number of older persons. We do not expect many older adults to out-perform young adults, in part because of limitations in the degree of cultural evolution. In our view, cultural evolution has not yet reached anything approaching a state of optimality for old age, and so the opportunities for older persons to display characteristics of wisdom are limited. However, because we define wisdom as an expert knowledge about the nature of human development and the human condition, we expect that the acquisition and maintenance of wisdom are facilitated by living longer. Such an expectation is in agreement with theories of exceptional performance. . . .

Our initial empirical findings and those of others . . . are encouraging and suggest that wisdom may become a viable topic for scientific psychological research. Wisdom seems to be a well-marked concept in language and in people's beliefs and knowledge about human behavior and its development. People can easily speak about wisdom and wise persons, and they can identify some of the salient characteristics of the phenomenon. In terms of people's beliefs about changes during adulthood and old age, . . . wisdom appears to be one of the very few attributes in our mental scenarios about aging that typify positive late-life goals and accomplishments. Furthermore, the attributes mentioned by subjects, when describing their everyday views of wisdom and wise persons, are similar to what we have specified as the essence of a theoretical definition of wisdom.

Our emerging work on behavioral indicators of wisdom as an expertise associated with knowledge and strategies of life planning and life review is also promising. The research analog based on the theory, which involves collecting thinking-aloud protocols about life dilemmas and evaluating these protocols against a family of wisdom-related criteria, seems to work. It results in reliable and seemingly meaningful findings. There are few age/cohort differences, and older adults are among the top performers. These findings are preliminary, but they are consistent with our theoretical expectations and the notion that wisdom may be a positive late-life goal which, under supportive conditions, could be attained by older adults. . . .

QUESTIONS FOR WRITING, REFLECTION, AND DEBATE

1 Lehman's data about the peak years of creativity for different fields are derived from creative people who lived in the past. Would it be reasonable to argue that his conclusions don't apply to older people today because health and life expectancy in recent decades have increased rapidly?

2 Does Dennis succeed in refuting Lehman's argument that age generally means declining creative power? What are Dennis's strongest points in his criticism of Lehman?

3 Simonton, like Lehman, assumes that in judging late life creativity we should measure how many "masterpieces" or "breakthroughs" are produced by older people. Do you think this standard is the right one for judging late life creativity? Are there other standards or definitions of creativity that would be more appropriate?

4 What are the most important points in which Simonton's article supports or modifies Lehman's conclusions about age and achievement?

5 Assume that you are Harvey Lehman today looking at the question of late life creativity. Write a statement describing how your views have changed, or been maintained, by what has happened with the aging of America in recent years.

6 Imagine that you are writing a long obituary article about "Louise Bachelard" (an imaginary name), who died recently at age 78. "Bachelard" was a famous painter whose style changed dramatically in her later years. In your obituary article, describe the ways in which the painter's creativity changed as she grew older.

7 Baltes and his colleagues give a definition of wisdom based on accumulated experience and expertise. But that definition makes no reference to character or the ethical behavior exhibited by a wise person. Does this mean that, for example, a bank robber, like Willie Sutton, could conceivably be judged to have "wisdom" if he developed good judgment on the basis of experience? Is it a deficiency or a strength that a definition of wisdom has no reference to ethics?

8 Pick an example of an older person who seems to you to have developed some of the traits of wisdom, whether in general or in some specific field of activity. Write a description of this older person in which you try to explain to a stranger why this wise older person is someone whose advice should be taken seriously.

9 Wisdom has been defined as an ability to make good judgments that are not bound by habit or rules of past experience but are uniquely appropriate for particular, novel human problems. If we adopt this definition, then the accumulated pragmatic knowledge of older people seems to have less value. How could Baltes respond to such an alternative approach to defining wisdom?

10 If we were designing classes or educational programs for older adults based on the conclusions of Simonton and Baltes, how would we orga-

nize the learning activities? How would such an older adult educational program differ from what is offered in schools and colleges today?

FOCUS ON PRACTICE: OLDER ADULT EDUCATION

We have seen that increasingly education is no longer an activity limited to the first stage of life but instead becomes part of lifelong learning that can and should be extended into later life. One obstacle to late life education is a stereotype that the elderly are too old to learn. Sometimes older people themselves accept the stereotype. But we have seen that the psychological evidence does not support the idea of a universal, global decline in intelligence or the ability to learn. While fluid intelligence does decline, crystallized intelligence based on life experience need not decline. Along with variations in individual differences, there is evidence that continued practice and involvement in learning helps to maintain the ability to learn.

What are the practical opportunities for late life learning? The range is wide, extending from learning opportunities through mass media—TV or periodicals—to planned but informal learning projects: a retired couple learning a foreign language prior to traveling abroad. In recent years, there has been a dramatic growth in organized educational programs for older people. One example of a successful program is Elderhostel, founded in 1975 as a summer residential college program for people over 60. It offers noncredit courses in the liberal arts and now attracts a quarter million participants each year at 1,000 campuses around the United States and in 40 countries overseas. Elderhostel involves no homework, papers, or grades. But it does offer an intellectual challenge for those interested in the joy of learning.

For those who do not want to travel to another community, there are tuition-free/space-available offerings at most public universities, which offer comparable opportunities. In 1962 there emerged another model of older adult education, the Institute for Retired Professionals at the New School in New York. That program involves retired people with special skills or knowledge who teach courses to one another on a mutual-aid basis. This mutual-aid model has been replicated in 150 communities around the United States and is now affiliated with Elderhostel. In the Scandinavian countries, France, Spain, and other countries, older people have created "Universities of the Third Age" bringing comparable programs to older people in those nations.

In the future, we can expect that older adult education will increase substantially. One reason is the rising level of prior education among successive cohorts of older people: an important fact because previous education is the best predictor of continued interest in lifelong learning. The median level of education for people over 65 in the year 1900 was only 8 years, while by the 1980s it had risen to 12 years (U.S. Senate, 1989). Today, younger people do have comparatively higher levels of education, but by the year 2000, predictions are for 12.4 years of schooling for persons 65 and over compared with 12.8 for persons 25 years and over (U.S Bureau of Census, 1984).

An explosion in lifelong learning among mature adults is already taking place. In 1984 there were 2.7 million people age 55 and over who had taken adult education courses, and nearly a million of these were persons 65 and over. The number of older people participating in adult education courses is growing rapidly. Older adult learning should help people continue their intellectual growth in the later years of life.

Suggested Readings

Arieti, Sylvano, *Creativity: The Magic Synthesis*, New York: Basic Books, 1976.

Ghiselin, Brewster, *The Creative Process*, New York: New American Library, 1955.

Greenbery, Reva M., *Education for Older Adult Learning: A Selected, Annotated Bibliography*, Westport, CT: Greenwood Press, 1993.

Peterson, David A., *Facilitating Education for Older Learners*, San Francisco: Jossey-Bass, 1983.

Simonton, Dean K., *Genius, Creativity, and Leadership: Historiometric Inquiries*, Cambridge, MA: Harvard University Press, 1984.

Sternberg, Robert (ed.), *The Nature of Creativity: Contemporary Psychological Perspectives*, New York: Cambridge University Press, 1988.

Does Old Age Have Meaning?

> A human being would certainly not grow to be seventy or eighty
> years old if this longevity had no meaning for the species. The
> afternoon of human life must also have a significance of its own
> and cannot be merely a pitiful appendage to life's morning.
>
> —*Carl Jung*

Old age is uniquely human. Among animal species in the wild, we never see offspring take care of the aging parents who gave birth to them. On the contrary, young animals typically abandon their parents when they themselves reach maturity, like baby birds who leave the nest to fly on their own. It is only the human being that cares for and honors the oldest members of the species, just as only human beings care for and remember their dead. In both cases we ask: Why?

Human beings live in a symbolic world of shared meaning, and the power of meaning is a life-and-death affair. For example, the experience of bravery in wartime shows that people are willing to sacrifice their lives for what outlives the individual self, whether on behalf of family, religion, patriotism, or something else. Outliving the self—what Erik Erikson called **generativity**—is not limited to acts of sacrifice (Kotre, 1984). Awareness of something transcending the individual life is a universal human capacity. Human beings contemplate aging and death, and they reach backward and forward in time to ask questions about the meaning of existence. In remembering the dead and in caring for the aged, we express our deepest convictions about the meaning of our life on earth. But it is only in the twentieth century that a sizable proportion of the population has survived to experience old age, and it is therefore natural that in our time the meaning of old age has become an issue.

The question about whether old age has meaning is both a personal question and a challenge to social gerontology. The personal question is ultimately a matter of values: What is it that makes life worth living in the last stage? This may seem like an abstract or philosophical question. But as we saw in the earlier discussion about end-of-life decisions, the question becomes a very practical one for families and mental health professionals. Whether old age has meaning is central to what we take to be **life satisfaction** or morale in old age (Kaufman, 1986). If the experience of aging threatens deeply held values—such as the desire to be independent, to have control, or to be socially esteemed—then both society and individuals will seek to avoid it or deny it as much as possible. The denial of aging and the denial of death are central problems for gerontology (Becker, 1973).

Thus there are two questions at stake here: First, does old age have a meaning for society, and, second, do individuals experience their lives as meaningful and positive in the last stage of life? Both questions of course are related, and both pose a challenge to social gerontology. A key question is whether we have a theory of aging that can explain the facts of old age, including the different societal meanings it takes on over the course of life and through history.

Theories of Aging

The problems of constructing a theory of aging for social gerontology can be compared with a similar problem in the biology of aging. The paradox of evolutionary biology is that, from the standpoint of survival of the fittest, there seems to be no reason for organisms to live long past the age of reproduction. Old age, in short, should not exist. Yet human beings *do* live long past the period of fertility; indeed, human beings are among the longest-living mammals on earth.

The meaning of old age is thus a problem even for biology. Biologists, accordingly, have proposed a whole variety of theories: somatic mutation theory, error catastrophe theory, autoimmune theory, and so on. No single theory has proved decisive but all have stimulated research enabling us to better understand the biology of aging. Similarly, the changing condition and meaning of old age has provoked a variety of theories in social gerontology. Just as with the biology of aging, there is no clear agreement that one theory is best. But two leading types of theories are worthy of examination because they demonstrate that deeply held values affect all theories of aging and that theories of aging are related to questions about the meaning of old age.

Disengagement Theory

Old age as a period when both the older person and society experience mutual separation, such as in the case of retirement from work, is the distinguishing feature of **disengagement theory.** This process of disengagement is understood as a natural and normal tendency reflecting a basic biological rhythm of life. In other words, the process of disengagement is assumed to be "functional": that is, it serves needs for both society and the individual. Disengagement theory is related to **modernization theory** (the idea that the status of the elderly decreases as society becomes more modern) because it takes the modern idea of functional efficiency—the modernized life cycle or linear life plan—to be primary or self-evident.

Disengagement theory was one of the earliest comprehensive attempts to explain the position of old age in modern society (Cumming and Henry, 1961). The theory grew out of an extensive body of research known as the Kansas City Studies of Adult Life (Williams and Wirths, 1965). The idea of disengagement presented itself not only as an empirical account based on facts but also as a theory to explain why the facts are the way they are. The theory of disengagement has been widely criticized by gerontologists (Hochschild, 1975), including those who point out that the theory evolved in the 1950s under conditions different than those in the present. There is no doubt that disengagement *does* accurately describe the behavior of many older people—a good example is the continued popularity of early retirement. But there seem to be many others, perhaps a growing number, whose behavior cannot be accurately described as withdrawal or disengagement. Therefore disengagement as a pattern of behavior can hardly be called natural or inevitable.

Another problem arises when we describe disengagement as *functional,* which can be a synonym for *useful.* The same process that might be functional or useful for an organization—for example, compulsory retirement at a predictable and fixed age—may not prove at all useful for individuals, who might prefer flexible retirement. In fact, resentment at being forced to retire at a fixed age is what led Congress to end mandatory retirement in 1986.

There is also a difficulty about what behavior is actually being described by the concept of disengagement. For example, individuals might partially withdraw from one set of activities, such as the workplace, to spend more time on other activities, such as family and leisure pursuits. Later life today, at least for older people who remain healthy, is often filled with a rich range of activities. Total withdrawal for those people is quite uncommon.

Activity Theory

At the opposite pole from disengagement theory is the **activity theory** of aging, which argues that the more active people are, the more likely they are to be satisfied with life. Activity theory assumes that how we think of ourselves is based on the roles or activities in which we engage. Activity theory also recognizes that most people in old age continue with the roles and life activities established earlier because they continue to have the same needs.

A similar point is made by the continuity theory of aging, which notes that people who grow older are inclined to maintain as much as they can the same habits, personality, and style of life they developed in earlier years (Costa and McCrae, 1980). According to both activity theory and continuity theory, any decreases in social interaction are explained better by poor health or disability than by some functional need of society to "disengage" older people from their previous roles (Havighurst, Neugarten, and Tobin, 1968).

A large body of research seems to support some aspects of activity theory. That is, continued exercise, social engagement, and productive roles all seem to contribute to mental health and life satisfaction. Other research suggests that informal activity or even merely perceived social integration are more important in promoting subjective well-being. In other words, our attitude and expectations about activity or detachment may be more important than our formal participation patterns (Longino and Kart, 1982). What counts as "activity" depends partly on how we look at things, not on external behavior alone.

If retirement or age limitations make actual participation impossible, activity theory suggests that people find substitutes for earlier roles or activities that must be given up (Atchley, 1985). A great many social activities encouraged by senior centers or long-term care facilities are inspired by the assumption that, if older people are active and involved, then all will be well. The "busy ethic" and its hostility to retirement is expressed in similar terms and the sentiment seems widely shared. For instance, *Cosmopolitan* magazine editor Helen Gurley Brown, in her self-help book for older women (*The Late Show*), writes that work is "our chloroform . . . our life . . . our freedom from pain . . . supplier of esteem." Along the same lines, essayist Malcolm Cowley in *The View from 80* expressed the ideal of the activity theory of aging when he wrote: "Perhaps in the future our active lives may be lengthened almost to the end of our days on earth; that is the most we can hope for." We will not be mistaken here in recognizing something similar to the compression of morbidity theory put forward by Fries. Many people active in middle age would express their hope for the later years in very much this way.

Despite its appeal, activity theory may have problems that deserve to be considered. For one thing, activity may be an approach more feasible for the young-old than for the old-old. Similarly, the ideal of active aging seems in many respects a prolongation of middle age rather than something special or distinctive about the last stage of life. Still another point here is that biological limitations cannot be altogether overcome by voluntary effort; no amount of health promotion can prevent Alzheimer's disease, for example. A one-sided emphasis on activity for the frail elderly may not be as helpful as companionship, dignity, and a sense of meaning in life. Finally, despite some progress in recent years, it still remains true that society places obstacles in the way of the optimistic scenario for old age. For example, remarriage is statistically more difficult for older women than for older men, and in the labor market age discrimination is a very real barrier preventing middle-aged and older people from taking up second careers. According to official statistics of the U.S. Labor Department, an "older worker" is defined as anyone over the age of 40, and age discrimination remains a reality.

Successful Aging

The ideal of activity theory in many ways anticipates the goal of **successful aging,** which involves continued optimum functioning on a variety of measures (Rowe and Kahn, 1987). According to this optimistic picture of later life, both cognitive and physical decline can be offset by vigorous exercise and engagement. "Use it or lose it!" could be the motto here, a philosophy applied to everything from "sex after 60" to lifelong learning, second or even third careers, not to mention the Senior Olympics with its image of gray-haired joggers filling the streets of retirement communities. "You're only as old as you think you are!" expresses an optimistic outlook that fits in well with an American "can-do" attitude to life. This upbeat image of later life as a period of vigor and reengagement is promoted by advertisers and coincides with the ideal of productive aging we looked at earlier.

Gerontologists have put forward the idea of "successful aging" rather recently, partly in opposition to stereotypes based on ageism and the assumption that aging must mean decline (Rowe and Kahn, 1987). But the idea of successful aging cannot be based on denial of what happens in the last stage of life. We must take full account of such deficits; successful aging seeks to optimize the capacities that remain while compensating for inevitable losses (Baltes and Baltes, 1990).

Psychological Changes

Old age is accompanied by diverse losses in health, physical and mental ability, and social networks. Those who age most successfully adjust to and compensate for their losses by putting the changes of later life into a wider perspective. This is an attitude that traditionally has been called "wisdom."

The Kansas City Study investigators found that, with advancing age, there is also a trend toward greater *interiority,* meaning increased attention to the inner psychological world (Neugarten, 1964). Individuals appear to reach a peak of interest in activity and achievement in their middle years. As they anticipate later life, they may become more detached, more inclined to "ego transcendence," as if in anticipation of role losses in later life (Peck, 1968).

Understood in this way, "disengagement" does not necessarily describe the actual behavior of individuals but may refer to a psychological attitude toward life. Furthermore, there is no reason to assume that all older people are inclined toward even an inner, psychological stance of disengagement; some may have ambivalence about their own ambitions. Perhaps the greatest example in literature of that ambivalence is the tragic fate of Shakespeare's King Lear, who tried to give up his role as king but was not quite able to withdraw from power and prestige. As a result, he brought disaster on his family. King Lear's example shows that disengagement depends on having some sense of personal meaning that is distinct from the office one holds. The ability to achieve that degree of detachment, at any age, is a matter of wide individual difference. In later life, disengagement is the preferred style for some, while continued activity remains attractive for others.

Role Changes

Psychologist Carl Jung described the psychological task of the second half of life as individuation: that is, becoming more and more our genuine individual self as opposed to carrying out the social roles required of people in middle life (Chinen, 1989). Gerontologists have spoken about this late life transition as a matter of role loss or role discontinuity. In earlier life transitions, role losses are typically accompanied by new roles that take their place: ceasing to be a child in one's family of birth, one grows up and takes on the role of parent oneself. But in old age, certain roles may be ended by widowhood or retirement.

One response to this condition is to create a new subculture based on shared values among those who are elderly. This idea has been developed by sociologists who advocate a subculture theory of aging, which depicts older people as most comfortable living with age peers who develop social practices appropriate to the group (Rose, 1965). Evidence in support of this idea has been found in some retirement communities that cultivate an intense schedule of social activities and a strong sense of belonging (Ross, 1982).

From one sociological standpoint, old age can be described as a roleless role (Burgess, 1960; Blau, 1981); once defined in this way, it is a natural step to see aging as a "social problem." But a different perspective is possible here. Other sociologists look on old age as a period when individuals maintain informal roles that are individually negotiated and perhaps continually redefined and constructed (George, 1980). In other words, the meaning of old age, subjectively experienced, would not be decisively determined by external roles, such as spouse, employee, or parent, that might typically shape behavior earlier in life. On the contrary, the development of the self in later life becomes a highly individual matter (Breytspraak, 1984). From a more philosophical point of view, old age can actually appear as an unexpected form of "late freedom" (Rosenmayr, 1984).

The Contribution of Social Gerontology

According to one popular view, the agenda for social gerontology should be the social integration of the aged (Rosow, 1967) by means of group activities, social involvement, and participatory roles of all kinds. Whether through work or leisure, the aim is always to remain with other people and to stay busy. Those who work in senior centers and nursing homes often have this outlook. But if we view the role losses of old age as an opportunity for self-development outside of conventional roles, then social integration in group activities would no longer be a compelling or all-consuming goal. Other values might assume greater importance.

We might still encourage social connections or affiliation with groups but the form would be based on individual development and uniqueness, not conforming to group norms or activities. An example of such individual development might be a creative arts program designed to encourage individual self-expression or a religious retreat designed to permit individual prayer and meditation. These last kinds of pursuits seem more in keeping with the potential for interiority and individuation that may appear in later life. Whether individual contemplation or group activity is the more desirable approach remains debatable, of course, and that is precisely the point at issue in the question about whether old age has meaning or offers some special opportunity not easily available at other stages of life.

This question makes it appropriate for gerontology to look more deeply at human activities that cultivate a shared sense of meaning in life's last stage (Cole and Gadow, 1986). Religion would be one area for inquiry. From congregation membership figures, it seems clear that older people do manifest a high degree of interest in religion. Religious practices such as prayer to obtain help from God are the most frequently cited means of dealing with stressing life events (*Mature Market Report*, July 1988, p. 7). But the pattern of religious practice does change with age. For example, Moberg (1972) found that in advanced age some religious activity outside the home tends to decline but the decline is compensated for by an increase in religious feeling. A body of research on religion and aging has long examined the question of whether religious affiliation by itself is a key to life satisfaction (Blazer and Palmore, 1976; Koenig, Kvale, and Ferrel, 1988).

This line of research has proved inconclusive partly because social science research has typically looked at behavior, such as church attendance, rather than the *meaning* of religion in the life of the individual. Inquiries about life satisfaction may be the wrong way to learn about meaning in aging (Gubrium and Lynott, 1983). At the opposite extreme from social scientists who look at religious behavior are theologians, who see aging as a spiritual journey, an idea that evokes traditional images of the stages of life (Bianchi, 1982). These ambiguous findings about religion and aging lead to recognition that research methods must capture not just outer behavior but the inner experience. Thus we find a greater appreciation for the role of the humanities in gerontology (Moody, 1988).

Conclusion: Aging in the Twenty-First Century

The life course perspective tends to view "stages of life" as social constructions that reflect structural conditions of society. As conditions change, so will our view of what is appropriate at different stages of life. Consider the weakening of age norms and beliefs about what is "appropriate" for different stages of life. In a world where retired people can go back to college or where women have a first child at age 40, it no longer makes sense to link education or work with rigid chronological ages. Indeed, one attractive strategy for an aging society might well be to introduce more flexibility for people of all ages to pursue education, work, and leisure over the entire course of life rather than link these activities stereotypically to periods of youth, middle life, and old age, as modern societies have done in the past.

It is not clear how the meaning of old age will change in contemporary postindustrial societies. On the one hand, older people in America have achieved gains in income levels, health, and political power, as we saw in thinking about the issues involved in the generational equity debate. On the other hand, as the stages of life have evolved and become blurred, the entire image of "old age" is giving way to more of an "age-irrelevant" image of the life course (Neugarten, 1982). Chronological age, by itself, loses predictive value and importance for many purposes.

Does this mean that old age itself, as a distinct stage of life, no longer has any special meaning or significance? Here we again must distinguish between a meaning that society ascribes to old age as opposed to whatever individuals find meaningful in their lives. In an age-irrelevant society, it is hard to ascribe anything special to old age. And if there is nothing special to be found in the last stage of life, does it follow that any personal meaning in old age must simply be "more of the same": that is, continuing whatever gave meaning earlier in life? These questions have no easy answers. But they suggest why the question, "Does old age have meaning?" is *both* a challenge for theories of social gerontology and also a matter of personal values or self-concept.

This discussion has identified two theories of aging—disengagement and activity—and shown how such theories actually appeal to deeply held values that point in opposite directions. More broadly, when we think about the question of whether old age has meaning, we will come back, over and over again, to two basic alternatives: continuation of midlife values into old age versus identifying something special that belongs to the last stage of life. In the readings that follow, Simone de Beauvoir represents the view of those who insist that only continuity with midlife activity makes sense, while Carl

Jung represents the view of those who insist that detachment from midlife roles is the preferred path. Erik Erikson, with his concept of "vital involvement," occupies a position somewhere between these two opposing ideas. Finally, there is the testimony of Florida Scott-Maxwell, whose journal demonstrates the importance of a personal understanding of the sources of meaning in old age (Berman, 1986). Her account underscores the validity of seeking to understand the meaning of aging through the subjective view of those who experience growing older (Gubrium and Buckholdt, 1977; Starr, 1982-1983).

The following readings can be stimulating in thinking about what such a future might be. The selection by Simone de Beauvoir offers the views of a philosopher who criticizes traditional ideals of old age as a period of tranquility or detachment. On the contrary, de Beauvoir believes that it is only continued activity and devotion to new goals that give life meaning, whether in old age or at any other time of life. Erik Erikson, one of our most distinguished psychologists, takes a somewhat different approach. Erikson sees each stage of life as a period with a special purpose or psychological task to be achieved. Old age is different than the other stages because it offers a kind of culmination to life. But Erikson believes that it is through concern for the welfare of future generations that older people find a sense of meaning in the final stage of life.

Carl Jung offers the perspective of a psychologist fascinated by the unconscious as revealed in dreams, myths, and human personality over the life span. Jung argues that the second half of life—from middle age through old age—must have its own distinctive character and psychological challenge. Maturity, in Jung's view, is properly a time for detachment and reflection as we turn inward. In the reading from Florida Scott-Maxwell, we see a selection from her personal journal, the record of turning inward in advanced age. Scott-Maxwell's rich description of her feelings and reflections proves that, even when outer activity is restricted, an older person can find a strong sense of meaning in the last stage of life.

It seems a great irony that the modernization of society has made it possible for large numbers of people to live a greater portion of their lives in old age than ever before in history, while at the same time many of the characteristic values of modern society tend to preclude finding any special meaning and purpose for this last stage. Whether modernization has reduced the power of the old is debatable but there seems to be no doubt that modernization has helped to erode traditional ideas about the "stages of life" that were based on shared meaning (Gruman, 1978). The result today is a sense of openness or uncertainty about the meaning of old age. That openness to new ideas and to different answers is disconcerting to some, exhilarating to others. The future remains unknown. Regardless of our feelings, old age in the future will be defined by individuals and by social institutions in ways we cannot now anticipate.

The Coming of Age

Simone de Beauvoir

Die early or grow old: there is no other alternative. And yet, as Goethe said, 'Age takes hold of us by surprise.' For himself each man is the sole, unique subject, and we are often astonished when the common fate becomes our own—when we are struck by sickness, a shattered relationship, or bereavement. I remember my own stupefaction when I was seriously ill for the first time in my life and I said to myself, 'This woman they are carrying on a stretcher is me.' Nevertheless, we accept fortuitous accidents readily enough, making them part of our history, because they affect us as unique beings: but old age is the general fate, and when it seizes upon our own personal life we are dumbfounded. 'Why, what has happened?' writes Aragon. 'It is life that has happened, and I am old.' . . . When we are grown up we hardly think about our age any more: we feel that the notion does not apply to us; for it is one which assumes that we look back towards the past and draw a line under the total, whereas in fact we are reaching out towards the future, gliding on imperceptibly from day to day, from year to year. Old age is particularly difficult to assume because we have always regarded it as something alien, a foreign species: 'Can I have become a different being while I still remain myself?' . . .

Thus the very quality of the future changes between middle age and the end of one's life. At sixty-five one is not merely twenty years older than one was at forty-five. One has exchanged an indefinite future—and one had a tendency to look upon it as infinite—for a finite future. In earlier days we

could see no boundary-mark upon the horizon: now we do see one. 'When I used to dream in former times,' says Chateaubriand, harking back to his remote past, 'my youth lay before me; I could advance towards the unknown that I was looking for. Now I can no longer take a single step without coming up against the boundary-stone.' . . .

A limited future and a frozen past: such is the situation that the elderly have to face up to. In many instances it paralyses them. All their plans have either been carried out or abandoned, and their life has closed in about itself; nothing requires their presence; they no longer have anything whatsoever to do. . . .

Clearly, there is one preconceived notion that must be totally set aside—the idea that old age brings serenity. From classical times the adult world has done its best to see mankind's condition in a hopeful light; it has attributed to ages that are not its own, virtues that they do not possess: innocence to childhood, serenity to old age. It has deliberately chosen to look upon the end of life as a time when all the conflicts that tear it apart are resolved. What is more, this is a convenient illusion: it allows one to suppose, in spite of all the ills and misfortunes that are known to overwhelm them, that the old are happy and that they can be left to their fate. . . .

Why should an old person be better than the adult or child he was? It is quite hard enough to remain a human being when everything, health, memory, possessions, standing and authority has been taken from you. The old person's struggle to do so has pitiable or ludicrous sides to it, and his fads, his meanness, and his deceitful ways may irritate one or make one smile; but in reality it is a very moving struggle. It is the refusal to sink below the human level, a refusal to become the insect, the inert object to which the adult world wishes to reduce the aged. There is something heroic in desiring to preserve a minimum of dignity in the midst of such total deprivation. . . .

On the intellectual plane, old age may also bring liberation: it sets one free from false notions. The clarity of mind that comes with it is accompanied by an often bitter disillusionment. In childhood and youth, life is experienced as a continual rise; and in favourable cases—either because of professional advancement or because bringing up one's children is a source of happiness, or because one's standard of living rises, or because of a greater wealth of knowledge—the notion of upward progress may persist in middle age. Then all at once a man discovers that he is no longer going anywhere, that his path leads him only to the grave. He has climbed to a peak; and from a peak there can be a fall. 'Life is a long preparation for something that never happens,' said Yeats. There comes a moment when one knows that one is no longer getting ready for anything and one understands that the idea of advancing towards a goal was a delusion. Our personal history had assumed that it possessed an end, and now it finds, beyond any sort of doubt, that this finality has been taken from it. At the same time its character of a 'useless passion' becomes evident. A discovery of this kind, says Schopenhauer, strips us of our will to live. 'Nothing left of those illusions that gave life its charm and that spurred on our activity. It is only at the age of sixty that one thoroughly understands the first verse of Ecclesiastes.' . . .

If *all* were vanity or deceit there would indeed be nothing left but to wait for death. But admitting that life does not contain its own end does not mean that it is incapable of devoting itself to ends of some kind. There are pursuits that are useful to mankind, and between men there are relationships in which they reach one another in full truthfulness. Once illusions have been swept away, these relationships, in which neither alienation nor myth form any part, and these pursuits remain. We may go on hoping to communicate with others by writing even when childish images of fame have vanished. By a curious paradox it is often at the very moment that the aged man, having become old, has doubts about the value of his entire work that he carries it to its highest point of perfection. This was so with Rembrandt, Michelangelo, Verdi and Monet. It may be that these doubts themselves help to enrich it. And then again it is often a question of coincidence: age brings technical mastery and freedom while at the same time it also brings a questioning, challenging state of mind. . . .

Freedom and clarity of mind are not of much use if no goal beckons us any more: but they are of great value if one is still full of projects. The greatest good fortune, even greater than health, for the old person is to have his world still inhabited by projects: then, busy and useful, he escapes both from boredom and from decay. The times in which he lives remain his own, and he is not compelled to adopt the defensive or aggressive forms of behaviour that are so often characteristic of the final years. . . .

There is only one solution if old age is not to be an absurd parody of our former life, and that is to go on pursuing ends that give our existence a meaning—devotion to individuals, to groups or to causes, social, political, intellectual or creative work. In spite of the moralists' opinion to the contrary, in old age we should wish still to have passions strong enough to prevent us turning in upon ourselves. One's life has value so long as one attributes value to the life of others, by means of love, friendship, indignation, compassion. When this is so, then there are still valid reasons for activity or speech. People are often advised to 'prepare' for old age. But if this merely applies to setting aside money, choosing the place for retirement and laying on hobbies, we shall not be much the better for it when the day comes. It is far better not to think about it too much, but to live a fairly committed, fairly justified life so that one may go on in the same path even when all illusions have vanished and one's zeal for life has died away.

Vital Involvement in Old Age

Erik Erikson

Elders have both less and more. Unlike the infant, the elder has a reservoir of strength in the well-springs of history and storytelling. As collectors of time and preservers of memory, those healthy elders who have survived into a reasonably fit old age have time on their side—time that is to be dispensed wisely and creatively, usually in the form of stories, to those younger ones who will one day follow in their footsteps. Telling these stories, and telling them well, marks a certain capacity for one generation to entrust itself to the next, by passing on a certain shared and collective identity to the survivors of the next generation: the future. Trust, as we have stated earlier, is one of the constant human values or virtues, universally acknowledged as basic for all relationships. Hope is yet another basic foundation for all community living and for survival itself, from infancy to old age. The question of old age, and perhaps of life, is how—with the trust and competency accumulated in old age—one adapts to and makes peace with the inevitable physical disintegration of aging.

After years of collaboration, elders should be able to know and trust, and know when to mistrust, not only their own senses and physical capacities but also their accumulated knowledge of the world around them. It is important to listen to the authoritative and objective voices of professionals with an open mind, but one's own judgment, after all those years of intimate relations with the body and with others, is decisive. The ultimate capacities of the

aging person are not yet determined. The future may well bring surprises.

Elders, of course, know well their own strengths. They should keep all of these strengths in use and involved in whatever their environment offers or makes possible. And they should not underestimate the possibility of developing strengths that are still dormant. Taking part in needed and useful work is appropriate both for elders and for their relationship to the community.

With aging, there are inevitably constant losses—losses of those very close, and friends near and far. Those who have been rich in intimacy also have the most to lose. Recollection is one form of adaptation, but the effort skillfully to form new relationships is adaptive and more rewarding. Old age is necessarily a time of relinquishing—of giving up old friends, old roles, earlier work that was once meaningful, and even possessions that belong to a previous stage of life and are now an impediment to the resiliency and freedom that seem to be requisite for adapting to the unknown challenges that determine the final stage of life.

Trust in interdependence. Give and accept help when it is needed. Old Oedipus well knew that the aged sometimes need three legs; pride can be an asset but not a cane.

When frailty takes over, dependence is appropriate, and one has no choice but to trust in the compassion of others and be consistently surprised at how faithful some caretakers can be.

Much living, however, can teach us only how little is known. Accept that essential "not-knowingness" of childhood and with it also that playful

Source: *Vital Involvement in Old Age,* by E. Erikson, 1986, New York: W. W. Norton & Co. Inc. Reprinted with permission.

curiosity. Growing old can be an interesting adventure and is certainly full of surprises.

One is reminded here of the image Hindu philosophy uses to describe the final letting go—that of merely being. The mother cat picks up in her mouth the kitten, which completely collapses every tension and hangs limp and infinitely trusting in the maternal benevolence. The kitten responds instinctively. We human beings require at least a whole lifetime of practice to do this. The religious traditions of the world reflect these concerns and provide them with substance and form.

The Potential Role of Elders
in Our Society

Our society confronts the challenge of drawing a large population of healthy elders into the social order in a way that productively uses their capacities. Our task will be to envision what influences such a large contingent of elders will have on our society as healthy old people seek and even demand more vital involvement. Some attributes of the accrued wisdom of old age are fairly generally acknowledged and respected. If recognized and given scope for expression, they could have an important impact on our social order. We suggest the following possibilities.

Older people are, by nature, conservationists. Long memories and wider perspectives lend urgency to the maintenance of our natural world. Old people, quite understandably, seem to feel more keenly the obstruction of open waterfronts, the cutting of age-old stands of trees, the paving of vast stretches of fertile countryside, and the pollution of once clear streams and lakes. Their longer memories recall the beauty of their surroundings in earlier years. We need those memories and those voices.

With aging, men and women in many ways become less differentiated in their masculine and feminine predilections. This in no way suggests a loss of sexual drive and interest between the sexes. Men, it seems, become more capable of accepting the interdependence that women have more easily

practiced. Many elder women today, in their turn, become more vigorously active and involved in those affairs that have been the dominant province of men. Some women come to these new roles by virtue of their propensity to outlive the men who have been their partners. Many younger women have made a similar transition by becoming professional members of the work force. These women seem capable of managing parenting and householding along with their jobs, particularly if they have partners who learn cooperation in these matters as an essential component of the marriage contract.

Our subjects demonstrate a tolerance and capacity for weighing more than one side of a question that is an attribute of the possible wisdom of aging. They should be well suited to serve as arbiters in a great variety of disputes. Much experience should be a precursor of long-range vision and clear judgement.

The aged have had a good deal of experience as societal witnesses to the effects of devastation and aggression. They have lived through wars and seen the disintegration of peace settlements. They know that violence breeds hatred and destroys the interconnectedness of life here on our earth and that now our capacity for destruction is such that violence is no longer a viable solution for human conflict.

Ideally, elders in any given modern society should be those who, having developed a marked degree of tolerance and appreciation for otherness, which includes "foreigners" and "foreign ways," might become advocates of a new international understanding that no longer tolerates the vicious name-calling, depreciation, and distrustfulness typical of international relations.

It is also possible to imagine a large, mature segment of the aging population, freed from the tension of keeping pace with competitors in the workplace, able to pursue vigorously art activities of all varieties. This would bring an extraordinary liveliness and artfulness to ordinary life. Only a limited portion of our adult population now has either the time or the money to be involved in activities of art expression or as appreciative supporters of the performing arts. Widespread participation in the arts is possible only if children are encouraged to develop those roots of imaginative play that arise from stimulating sensory experience. Elders learn this as they undertake to open these new doors of experience and could promote the inclusion of the arts in the educational system. The arts offer a common language, and the learning of that language in childhood could contribute to an interconnection among the world's societies.

The development of a new class of elders requires a continued upgrading of all facilites for the health care and education of people at all stages of life, from infancy to old age. Organisms that are to function for a hundred years need careful early nurturing and training. Education must prepare the individual not only for the tasks of early and middle age but for those of old age as well. Training is mandatory both for productive work and for the understanding and care of the senses and the body as a whole. Particpation in activities that can enrich an entire lifetime must be promoted and made readily available. In fact, a more general acceptance of the developmental principle of the life cycle could alert people to plan their entire lives more realistically, especially to provide for the long years of aging.

Having started our "joint reflections" with some investigation of the traditional themes of "age" and "stages," a closing word should deal with the modern changes in our conception of the length and the role of old age in the total life experience. As we have described, modern statistics predict for our time and the immediate future a much longer life expectancy for the majority of old individuals rather than for a select few. This amounts to such a radical change in our concept of the human life cycle that we question whether we should not review all the earlier stages in the light of this development. Actually, we have already faced the question of whether a universal old age of significantly greater duration suggests the addition to our cycle of a ninth stage of development with its own quality of experience, including, perhaps, some sense or premonition of immortality. A decisive fact, however, has remained unchanged for all the earlier stages, namely, that they are all significantly evoked by biological and evolutionary development necessary for any organism and its psychosocial matrix. This also means that each stage, in turn, must surrender its dominance to the next stage, when its time has come. Thus, the developmental ages for the pre-adult life stages decisively remain the same, although the interrelation of all the stages depends somewhat on the emerging personality and the psychosocial identity of each individual in a given historical setting and time perspective.

Similarly, it must be emphasized that each stage, once given, is woven into the fates of all. Generativity, for example, dramatically precedes the last stage, that of old age, establishing the contrast between the dominant images of generativity and of death: one cares for what one has generated in this existence while simultaneously preexperiencing the end of it all in death.

It is essential to establish in the experience of the stages a psychosocial identity, but no matter how long one's life expectancy is, one must face oneself as one who shares an all-human existential identity, as creatively given form in the world religions. This final "arrangement" must convince us that we are meant as "grandparents," to share the responsibility of the generations for each other. When we finally retire from familial and generational involvement, we must, where and when possible, bond with other old-age groups in different parts of the world, learning to talk and to listen with a growing sense of all-human mutuality.

The Stages of Life

Carl Jung

The nearer we approach to the middle of life, and the better we have succeeded in entrenching ourselves in our personal attitudes and social positions, the more it appears as if we had discovered the right course and the right ideals and principles of behaviour. For this reason we suppose them to be eternally valid, and make a virtue of unchangeably clinging to them. We overlook the essential fact that the social goal is attained only at the cost of a diminution of personality. Many—far too many—aspects of life which should also have been experienced lie in the lumber-room among dusty memories; but sometimes, too, they are glowing coals under grey ashes.

Statistics show a rise in the frequency of mental depressions in men about forty. In women the neurotic difficulties generally begin somewhat earlier. We see that in this phase of life—between thirty-five and forty—an important change in the human psyche is in preparation. At first it is not a conscious and striking change; it is rather a matter of indirect signs of a change which seems to take its rise in the unconscious. Often it is something like a slow change in a person's character; in another case certain traits may come to light which had disappeared since childhood; or again, one's previous inclinations and interests begin to weaken and others take their place. Conversely—and this happens very frequently—one's cherished convictions and principles, especially the moral ones, be-

gin to harden and to grow increasingly rigid until, somewhere around the age of fifty, a period of intolerance and fanaticism is reached. It is as if the existence of these principles were endangered and it were therefore necessary to emphasize them all the more.

The wine of youth does not always clear with advancing years; sometimes it grows turbid. All the phenomena mentioned above can best be seen in rather one-sided people, turning up sometimes sooner and sometimes later. Their appearance, it seems to me, is often delayed by the fact that the parents of the person in question are still alive. It is then as if the period of youth were being unduly drawn out. I have seen this especially in the case of men whose fathers were long-lived. The death of the father then has the effect of a precipitate and almost catastrophic ripening. . . .

The very frequent neurotic disturbances of adult years all have one thing in common: they want to carry the psychology of the youthful phase over the threshold of the so-called years of discretion. Who does not know those touching old gentlemen who must always warm up the dish of their student days, who can fan the flame of life only by reminiscences of their heroic youth, but who, for the rest, are stuck in a hopelessly wooden Philistinism? As a rule, to be sure, they have this one merit which it would be wrong to undervalue: they are not neurotic, but only boring and stereotyped. The neurotic is rather a person who can never have things as he would like them in the present, and who can therefore never enjoy the past either.

As formerly the neurotic could not escape from childhood, so now he cannot part with his youth.

Source: Jung, C., "The Stages of Life," in *The Structure and Dynamics of the Psyche* (pp. 12-21). Copyright 1960-1969 by Princeton University Press. Reprinted by permission of Princeton University Press.

He shrinks from the grey thoughts of approaching age, and, feeling the prospect before him unbearable, is always straining to look behind him. Just as the childish person shrinks back from the unknown in the world and in human existence, so the grown man shrinks back from the second half of life. It is as if unknown and dangerous tasks awaited him, or as if he were threatened with sacrifices and losses which he does not wish to accept, or as if his life up to now seemed to him so fair and precious that he could not relinquish it.

Is it perhaps at bottom the fear of death? That does not seem to me very probable, because as a rule death is still far in the distance and therefore somewhat abstract. Experience shows us, rather, that the basic cause of all the difficulties of this transition is to be found in a deep-seated and peculiar change within the psyche. In order to characterize it I must take for comparison the daily course of the sun—but a sun that is endowed with human feeling and man's limited consciousness. In the morning it rises from the nocturnal sea of unconsciousness and looks upon the wide, bright world which lies before it in an expanse that steadily widens the higher it climbs in the firmament. In this extension of its field of action caused by its own rising, the sun will discover its significance; it will see the attainment of the greatest possible height, and the widest possible dissemination of its blessings, as its goal. In this conviction the sun pursues its course to the unforeseen zenith—unforeseen, because its career is unique and individual, and the culminating point could not be calculated in advance. At the stroke of noon the descent begins. And the descent means the reversal of all the ideals and values that were cherished in the morning. The sun falls into contradiction with itself. It is as though it should draw in its rays instead of emitting them. Light and warmth decline and are at last extinguished.

All comparisons are lame, but this simile is at least not lamer than others. A French aphorism sums it up with cynical resignation: *Si jeunesse savait, si vieillesse pouvait.*

Fortunately we are not rising and setting suns, for then it would fare badly with our cultural values. But there is something sunlike within us, and to speak of the morning and spring, of the evening and autumn of life is not mere sentimental jargon. We thus give expression to psychological truths and, even more, to physiological facts, for the reversal of the sun at noon changes even bodily characteristics. Especially among southern races one can observe that older women develop deep, rough voices, incipient moustaches, rather hard features and other masculine traits. On the other hand the masculine physique is toned down by feminine features, such as adiposity and softer facial expressions.

There is an interesting report in the ethnological literature about an Indian warrior chief to whom in middle life the Great Spirit appeared in a dream. The spirit announced to him that from then on he must sit among the women and children, wear women's clothes, and eat the food of women. He obeyed the dream without suffering a loss of prestige. This vision is a true expression of the psychic revolution of life's noon, of the beginning of life's decline. Man's values, and even his body, do tend to change into their opposites.

We might compare masculinity and femininity and their psychic components to a definite store of substances of which, in the first half of life, unequal use is made. A man consumes his large supply of masculine substance and has left over only the smaller amount of feminine substance, which must now be put to use. Conversely, the woman allows her hitherto unused supply of masculinity to become active. . . .

The worst of it all is that intelligent and cultivated people live their lives without even knowing of the possibility of such transformations. Wholly unprepared, they embark upon the second half of life. Or are there perhaps colleges for forty-year-olds which prepare them for their coming life and its demands as the ordinary colleges introduce our young people to a knowledge of the world? No, thoroughly unprepared we take the step into the afternoon of life; worse still, we take this step with the false assumption that our truths and ideals will serve us as hitherto. But we cannot live the afternoon of life according to the programme of life's morning; for what was great in the morning will be little at evening, and what in the morning was true will at evening have become a lie. I have given psychological treatment to too many people of advancing years, and have looked too often into the secret chambers of their souls, not to be moved by this fundamental truth.

Aging people should know that their lives are not mounting and expanding, but that an inexorable inner process enforces the contraction of life. For a young person it is almost a sin, or at least a danger, to be too preoccupied with himself; but for the aging person it is a duty and a necessity to devote serious attention to himself. After having lavished its light upon the world, the sun withdraws its rays in order to illuminate itself. Instead of doing likewise, many old people prefer to be hypochondriacs, niggards, pedants, applauders of the past or else eternal adolescents—all lamentable substitutes for the illumination of the self, but inevitable consequences of the delusion that the second half of life must be governed by the principles of the first.

I said just now that we have no schools for forty-year-olds. That is not quite true. Our religions were always such schools in the past, but how many people regard them as such today? How many of us older ones have been brought up in such a school and really prepared for the second half of life, for old age, death and eternity?

A human being would certainly not grow to be seventy or eighty years old if this longevity had no meaning for the species. The afternoon of human life must also have a significance of its own and cannot be merely a pitiful appendage to life's morning. The significance of the morning undoubtedly lies in the development of the individual, our entrenchment in the outer world, the propagation of our kind, and the care of our children. This is the obvious purpose of nature. But when this purpose has been attained—and more than attained—shall the earning of money, the extension of conquests, and the expansion of life go steadily on beyond the bounds of all reason and sense? Whoever carries over into the afternoon the law of the morning, or the natural aim, must pay for it with damage to his soul, just as surely as a growing youth who tries to carry over his childish egoism into adult life must pay for this mistake with social failure. Money-making, social achievement, family and posterity are nothing but plain nature, not culture. Culture lies outside the purpose of nature. Could by any chance culture be the meaning and purpose of the second half of life?

In primitive tribes we observe that the old people are almost always the guardians of the mysteries and the laws, and it is in these that the cultural heritage of the tribe is expressed. How does the matter stand with us? Where is the wisdom of our old people, where are their precious secrets and their visions? For the most part our old people try to compete with the young. In the United States it is almost an ideal for a father to be the brother of his sons, and for the mother to be if possible the younger sister of her daughter.

I do not know how much of this confusion is a reaction against an earlier exaggeration of the dignity of age, and how much is to be charged to false ideals. These undoubtedly exist, and the goal of those who hold them lies behind, and not ahead. Therefore they are always striving to turn back. We have to grant these people that it is hard to see what other goal the second half of life can offer than the well-known aims of the first. Expansion of life, usefulness, efficiency, the cutting of a figure in society, the shrewd steering of offspring into suitable marriages and good positions—are not these purposes enough? Unfortunately not enough meaning and purpose for those who see in the approach of old age a mere diminution of life and can feel their earlier ideals only as something faded and worn out. Of course, if these persons had filled up the beaker of life earlier and emptied it to the lees, they would feel quite differently about everything now;

they would have kept nothing back, everything that wanted to catch fire would have been consumed, and the quiet of old age would be very welcome to them. But we must not forget that only a very few people are artists in life; that the art of life is the most distinguished and rarest of all the arts. Who ever succeeded in draining the whole cup with grace? So for many people all too much unlived life remains over—sometimes potentialities which they could never have lived with the best of wills, so that they approach the threshold of old age with unsatisfied demands which inevitably turn their glances backwards. . . .

I have observed that a life directed to an aim is in general better, richer, and healthier than an aimless one, and that it is better to go forwards with the stream of time than backwards against it. To the psychotherapist an old man who cannot bid farewell to life appears as feeble and sickly as a young man who is unable to embrace it. And as a matter of fact, it is in many cases a question of the self-same childish greediness, the same fear, the same defiance and willfulness, in the one as in the other. As a doctor I am convinced that it is hygienic—if I may use the word—to discover in death a goal towards which one can strive, and that shrinking away from it is something unhealthy and abnormal which robs the second half of life of its purpose. I therefore consider that all religions with a supramundane goal are eminently reasonable from the point of view of psychic hygiene. When I live in a house which I know will fall about my head within the next two weeks, all my vital functions will be impaired by this thought; but if on the contrary I feel myself to be safe, I can dwell there in a normal and comfortable way. From the standpoint of psychotherapy it would therefore be desirable to think of death as only a transition, as part of a life process whose extent and duration are beyond our knowledge.

READING 44

The Measure of My Days

Florida Scott-Maxwell

Age puzzles me. I thought it was a quiet time. My seventies were interesting, and fairly serene, but my eighties are passionate. I grow more intense as I age. To my own surprise I burst out with hot conviction. Only a few years ago I enjoyed my tranquillity; now I am so disturbed by the outer world and by human quality in general that I want to put

Source: From *The Measure of My Days* by Florida Scott-Maxwell. Copyright © 1968 by Florida Scott-Maxwell. Reprinted by permission of Alfred A. Knopf, Inc.

things right, as though I still owed a debt to life. I must calm down. I am far too frail to indulge in moral fervour.

Old people are not protected from life by engagements, or pleasures, or duties; we are open to our own sentience; we cannot get away from it, and it is too much. We should ward off the problematic, and above all the insoluble. These are far, far too much, but it is just these that attract us. Our one safety is to draw in, and enjoy the simple and immediate. We should rest within our own confines. It may be dull, restricted, but it can be satisfying within our own walls. I feel most real when alone, even most alive when alone. . . .

Age is truly a time of heroic helplessness. One is confronted by one's own incorrigibility. I am always saying to myself, "Look at you, and after a lifetime of trying." I still have the vices that I have known and struggled with—well it seems like since birth. Many of them are modified, but not much. I can neither order nor command the hubbub of my mind. Or is it my nervous sensibility? This is not the effect of age; age only defines one's boundaries. Life has changed me greatly, it has improved me greatly, but it has also left me practically the same. I cannot spell, I am over critical, egocentric and vulnerable. I cannot be simple. In my effort to be clear I become complicated. I know my faults so well that I pay them small heed. They are stronger than I am. They are me. . . .

Another day to be filled, to be lived silently, watching the sky and the lights on the wall. No one will come probably. I have no duties except to myself. That is not true. I have a duty to all who care for me—not to be a problem, not to be a burden. I must carry my age lightly for all our sakes, and thank God I still can. Oh that I may to the end. Each day then, must be filled with my first duty, I must be "all right". But is this assurance not the gift we all give to each other daily, hourly? . . .

Another secret we carry is that though drab outside—wreckage to the eye, mirrors a mortification—inside we flame with a wild life that is almost incommunicable. In silent, hot rebellion we cry silently—"I have lived my life haven't I? What more is expected of me?" Have we got to pretend out of noblesse oblige that age is nothing, in order to encourage the others? This we do with a certain haughtiness, realising now that we have reached the place beyond resignation, a place I had no idea existed until I had arrived here.

It is a place of fierce energy. Perhaps passion would be a better word than energy, for the sad fact is this vivid life cannot be used. If I try to transpose it into action I am soon spent. It has to be accepted as passionate life, perhaps the life I never lived, never guessed I had it in me to live. It feels other and more than that. It feels like the far side of precept and aim. It is just life, the natural intensity of life, and when old we have it for our reward and undoing. It can—at moments—feel as though we had it for our glory. Some of it must go beyond good and bad, for at times—though this comes rarely, unexpectedly—it is a swelling clarity as though all was resolved. It has no content, it seems to expand us, it does not derive from the body, and then it is gone. It may be a degree of consciousness which lies outside activity, and which when young we are too busy to experience. . . .

It has taken me all the time I've had to become myself, yet now that I am old there are times when I feel I am barely here, no room for me at all. I remember that in the last months of my pregnancies the child seemed to claim almost all my body, my strength, my breath, and I held on wondering if my burden was my enemy, uncertain as to whether my life was at all mine. Is life a pregnancy? That would make death a birth.

Easter Day. I am in that rare frame of mind when everything seems simple. When I have no doubt that the aim and solution of life is the acceptance of God. It is impossible and imperative, and clear. To open to such unimaginable greatness affrights my smallness. I do not know what I seek, cannot know, but I am where the mystery is the certainty.

My long life has hardly given me time—I cannot say to understand—but to be able to imagine that God speaks to me, says simply—"I keep calling to you, and you do not come", and I answer quite naturally—"I couldn't, until I knew there was nowhere else to go". . . .

I am uncertain whether it is a sad thing or a solace to be past change. One can improve one's character to the very end, and no one is too young in these days to put the old right. The late clarities will be put down to our credit I feel sure.

It was something other than this that had caught my attention. In fact it was the exact opposite. It was the comfortable number of things about which we need no longer bother. I know I am thinking two ways at once, justified and possible in a note book. Goals and efforts of a lifetime can at last be abandoned. What a comfort. One's conscience? Toss the fussy thing aside. Rest, rest. So much over, so much hopeless, some delight remaining.

One's appearance, a lifetime of effort put into improving that, most of it ill judged. Only neatness is vital now, and one can finally live like a humble but watchful ghost. You need not plan holidays because you can't take them. You are past all action, all decision. In very truth the old are almost free, and if it is another way of saying that our lives are empty, well—there are days when emptiness is spacious, and non-existence elevating. When old, one has only one's soul as company. There are times when you can feel it crying, you do not ask why. Your eyes are dry, but heavy, hot tears drop on your heart. There is nothing to do but wait, and listen to the emptiness which is sometimes gentle. You and the day are quiet, and you have no comment to make. . . .

I don't like to write this down, yet it is much in the minds of the old. We wonder how much older we have to become, and what degree of decay we may have to endure. We keep whispering to ourselves, "Is this age yet? How far must I go?". For age can be dreaded more than death. "How many years of vacuity? To what degree of deterioration must I advance?" Some want death now, as release from old age, some say they will accept death willingly, but in a few years. I feel the solemnity of death, and the possibility of some form of continuity. Death feels a friend because it will release us from the deterioration of which we cannot see the end. It is waiting for death that wears us down, and the distaste for what we may become.

These thoughts are with us always, and in our hearts we know ignominy as well as dignity. We are people to whom something important is about to happen. But before then, these endless years before the end, can we summon enough merit to warrant a place for ourselves? We go into the future not knowing the answer to our question.

· But we also find that as we age we are more alive than seems likely, convenient, or even bearable. Too often our problem is the fervour of life within us. My dear fellow octogenarians, how are we to carry so much life, and what are we to do with it?

Let no one say it is "unlived life" with any of the simpler psychological certitudes. No one lives all the life of which he was capable. The unlived life in each of us must be the future of humanity. When truly old, too frail to use the vigour that pulses in us, and weary, sometimes even scornful of what can seem the pointless activity of mankind, we may sink down to some deeper level and find a new supply of life that amazes us.

All is uncharted and uncertain, we seem to lead the way into the unknown. It can feel as though all our lives we have been caught in absurdly small personalities and circumstances and beliefs. Our accustomed shell cracks here, cracks there, and that tiresomely rigid person we supposed to be ourselves stretches, expands, and with all inhibitions gone we realize that age is not failure, nor disgrace; though mortifying we did not invent it. Age forces us to deal with idleness, emptiness, not being needed, not able to do, helplessness just ahead perhaps. All this is true, but one has had one's life, one could be full to the brim. Yet it is the end of our procession through time, and our steps are uncertain.

Here we come to a new place of which I knew nothing. We come to where age is boring, one's interest in it by-passed; further on, go further on, one finds that one has arrived at a larger place still, the place of release. There one says, "Age can seem a debacle, a rout of all one most needs, but that is not the whole truth. What of the part of us, the nameless, boundless part who experienced the rout, the witness who saw so much go, who remains undaunted and knows with clear conviction that there is more to us than age? Part of that which is outside age has been created by age, so there is gain as well as loss. If we have suffered defeat we are somewhere, somehow beyond the battle". . . .

A long life makes me feel nearer truth, yet it won't go into words, so how can I convey it? I can't, and I want to. I want to tell people approaching and perhaps fearing age that it is a time of discovery. If they say—"Of what?" I can only answer, "We must each find out for ourselves, otherwise it won't be discovery". I want to say—"If at the end of your life you have only yourself, it is much. Look, you will find".

QUESTIONS FOR WRITING, REFLECTION, AND DEBATE

1 Some critics have argued that disengagement theory may have been a fair description of some behavior in the elderly population in the 1950s, but it was a mistake to infer that the pattern was universal. According to this view, activity theory or continuity theory might well be a better description of how older people actually are today. If this view is correct, does it mean that "theories of aging" just express the way aging appears at a certain time in history? If so, how would it be possible to develop a "theory of aging" that is more general and not limited to a certain time and place?

2 Most observers agree that America as a society places a very high value on success. Does that fact suggest that the goal of "successful aging" is a proper approach to thinking about growing old in America? Are there aspects of growing older that the idea of "successful aging" may not adequately deal with?

3 Jung believed that the psychological goal of later life is to become more and more oneself as an individual. What does this goal mean in practice? Are there drawbacks to this idea that you can think of? If we adopt Jung's approach, how would we evaluate older people who remain very much as they have always been in contrast to others who dramatically change their lives, say, after retirement or widowhood?

4 Imagine that you are now 80 years old and have discovered that you may not have long to live. Your grandchildren have asked you to put down in writing a statement about what you've learned about the meaning of life, especially in the last few years. Write such a statement and in your state-

ment contrast what you believe now (as a future 80-year-old) with what you believed in the past (at what is your present age).

5   Assume that you are the activities director of a church-affiliated nursing home that prides itself on promoting the quality of life of residents. Write a memorandum for the nursing home director outlining a range of different activities that would help enhance the residents' sense of the meaning of life in the institution.

6   Is the idea of "meaning" in life something purely personal and private or does it have some wider social importance? Does discussing the question of meaning give us an understanding of older people's behavior or is it simply confusing? In addressing this question, consider other issues discussed earlier in this book, such as assisted suicide, work and leisure, and the allocation of health care resources for life prolongation.

FOCUS ON PRACTICE: REMINISCENCE AND LIFE REVIEW

As people grow older, it is not unusual for them to reminisce about the "good old days." Feelings of both nostalgia and regret are commonly part of this attitude toward the past. A common response to such reminiscence is to assume that older people are only interested in the past or, still worse, to see those who dwell on past memories as showing signs of escapism or even mental impairment. But late life reminiscence may be a normal form of **life review**, which Robert Butler (1963) defines as a natural, even universal process stimulated by awareness of approaching death:

> The life review is characterized by a progressive return to consciousness of past experience, in particular the resurgence of unresolved conflicts which can now be surveyed and integrated. . . . If unresolved conflicts and fears are successfully reintegrated they can give new significance and meaning to an individual's life. (Butler, 1974, p. 534)

Erikson sees the psychological task of late life in terms of the goal of **ego integrity,** which implies a reintegration of all aspects of each individual's life. The view of both Erikson and Butler is based on their psychological theories about the importance of finding meaning in the last stage of life. But do the facts support their theories? How important is reminiscence in old age?

Careful studies have shown that elderly people do not actually spend much more time daydreaming about the past than do people of other ages (Gambria, 1977), so it is a mistake to see life review as a universal process. On the other hand, regardless of frequency, reminiscence may have adaptive value; that is, it may promote better mental health in old age. An early study of reminiscence found that people who spend time thinking about the past are less likely to suffer depression (McMahon and Rhudick, 1967). Some psychologists who have studied life review feel it may be a psychological defense mechanism that helps some people adjust to memories of an unhappy past. In that sense, reminiscence could be described as an adaptive feature of old age (Coleman, 1974) and something to be encouraged (Brennan and Steinberg, 1983-1984). Finally, reminiscence and life review appear to help some older people bolster their self-image (Lewis, 1971). By recalling the past, older adults can bolster self-esteem and establish solidarity with age peers of their own generation. From a life course perspective, we might argue that older people will interact with younger people in ways that help the old maximize perceived power or status, as the exchange theory of aging predicts. When activity is the preferred style, then older people are likely to downplay reminiscence in favor of talking about present or future events. On the other hand, where disengagement is the preferred style, then older people may emphasize past accomplishments.

Some gerontologists recommend that, especially for older people who can no longer remain active, reminiscence and life review can have great value (Haight, 1991). For that reason, reminiscence groups have been encouraged as a program therapy among nursing home residents as well as senior center participants. Guided autobiography has also been encouraged as a unique approach to education in the later years (Birren and Deutschman, 1991). Reminiscence tied to oral history can have additional benefits for intergenerational programs.

All these methods can be useful for practitioners who work with older people. But techniques to encourage reminiscence as a form of practice must not make us forget a basic question: Is reminiscence or life review the best way of achieving a sense of meaning in old age? The response to that question cannot be a scientific answer but depends on basic values and philosophy of life, as we have seen in the readings in this section. For example, if we follow Simone de Beauvoir's view, then activity and future orientation is the best approach to finding meaning in old age. She would therefore discourage people from spending time reminiscing about the past, unless past memories can somehow contribute to improving the world. Carl Jung, on the other hand, would see great value in inwardness or interiority in old age. The purpose or meaning of old age, in his view, is not necessarily to be active but to know ourselves better and to accept ourselves as individuals. If life review can promote that goal, then Jung would encourage it.

Does the reminiscence and life review of older people have meaning for people of other ages? Clearly, there is something special about old age precisely because it is the final stage of life. The last stage includes an added dimension of awareness of finitude through foreshortened time perspective (Kastenbaum, 1983). As the pace of social change increases, older people can

no longer take for granted that values will be shared among different historical cohorts; the "Sixties Generation" and the "World War II Generation" may
be quite different, not only from one another but from "baby busters" born
after the early 1960s. The old may be perceived by others, or perceive themselves, as belonging to "the past," regardless of their subjective time orientation. Young people therefore may assume that reminiscence is something
only for the old.

In fact, the process of life review or autobiographical consciousness is not
limited to old age but occurs at transitions across the adult life course: for
instance, in self-assessment after a job loss or bereavement. The life course
perspective helps us appreciate links between subjective and objective time
orientations and therefore to see the role of life review in broader terms. The
search for meaning in life occurs not only at the end of life but every time
human beings become aware of their limited life on earth. It is perhaps for
that reason that in the Bible the Psalms include a prayer for God to help us
all learn to "number our days" and thus to cherish each passing moment for
its value whatever our age may be.

Suggested Readings

Fowler, James W., *Stages of Faith: The Psychology of Human Develop-
    ment and the Quest for Meaning*, New York: Harper & Row, 1981.
Frankl, Victor, *Man's Search for Meaning: An Introduction to Logotherapy*
    (trans. Ilse Lasch), New York: Pocket Books, 1973.
Moody, Harry R., *Abundance of Life: Human Development Policies for an
    Aging Society*, New York: Columbia University Press, 1988.
Sherman, Edmund, *Reminiscence and the Self in Old Age*, New York:
    Springer, 1991.

Appendix: How to Research a Term Paper in Gerontology

Research and writing can be intimidating to many students, especially in a field like gerontology, which is a new subject to most. But research and writing needn't be frightening. Skillful research is the key to good writing, and careful thinking is the foundation for both.

Doing the background research for a term paper in gerontology is more than half the task of actually writing the paper itself. If you're successful in the research, you end up having *other people* do your work for you! Of course, that does *not* mean plagiarism or simply copying what other people have written without giving proper credit. But the trick in writing is to save yourself the trouble of reinventing the wheel. You want to avoid floundering around trying to rediscover a fact or idea that someone else has already worked out before you. Wasting time that way is not necessary at all. In fact, it detracts from the real job of research and writing: namely, *thinking* about what others have written and *deciding* what to take and put into your own work.

The key is not to work harder but to work smarter. By building on other people's work, and giving credit to them where credit is due, you save yourself time and devote your best effort to expressing what you really have to say. The process is the same as the one that takes place in science. All science and all scholarship stand on the work of others. This point holds true for the beginning student no less than for great thinkers. Indeed, the great physicist Isaac Newton himself once said: "If I have seen further than others, it is because I have stood on the shoulders of giants."

How does this approach apply to writing a term paper? Library research for a term paper is a bit like looking for buried treasure. If you don't know *exactly* where the treasure is buried, you end up spending a lot of time digging in places where you imagine the treasure *might* be buried. You're relying on guesswork instead of careful thought. Once you have a hunch of where the treasure lies, then the actual digging takes practically no time at all. It is just the same with library research. Once you have developed your search strategy—your map for where treasure might be found—then the information sources at your fingertips will guide you quickly to where the treasure lies. The rest of the work—including writing up your findings—will actually take very little time, because you can build on the work of others.

Defining your topic.   At every stage in the research process, you need to ask yourself: What is the question I am asking? (What information am I trying to find?) You don't only ask the question once. For example, suppose you are trying to find out what percentage of people at age 60 and age 70 are retired. At first, the question may seem simple. But as you dig deeper, you find that there may be uncertainty about how to count people as "retired" instead of "unemployed" or "disabled." As you look into the statistics, you discover that, behind the solid numbers, different assumptions are involved. In effect, you ask your basic question over and over again as you look through bibliographic sources.

When you are planning your topic, you might find it helpful first to "free associate," or let your mind wander. You need to think about points related to your topic but also to think about *other* subject terms and ideas related to your topic. This process of cross-referencing is at the heart of research and creative thinking. For example, suppose you're interested in writing a paper on "retirement." Retirement is a big subject, maybe too big for one paper. Social scientists have written whole books on the subject; some have devoted their entire careers to it. But stay with the big subject for a while. Then, think about all the other subjects—the "key words"—that are related to retirement: for instance, *work, pensions, Social Security,* and so on. Each of them could also be a term paper or indeed a whole book.

As you look over all your key words, look for connections that interest you; for instance, maybe you see a connection between *pensions* and *retirement.* You might begin to put together a hypothesis or a theme: for example, "What is the relationship between pensions and retirement behavior?"

When you ask yourself research questions, it helps to write down some tentative answers. That's the first step toward making an outline, or a plan, for your work. Carrying out research is a bit like building a house. In constructing the house, it pays to put time into planning and thinking. You don't wait to draw up blueprints until you are halfway finished constructing the house. To write a term paper, you also need a plan. Write down your ideas first without worrying too much about whether your plan is adequate or complete; you're likely to change it later anyway. Then start consulting other sources.

Starting your search.   In constructing a fruitful search strategy, you face a catch-22. You can't really narrow your research question until you know the subject matter better. But you can't define the subject matter without carving it down to size with the right research question. Imagine how discouraging your task would be if you didn't realize that pension levels and retirement behavior might be related. In gerontology as in all fields, the amount of knowledge is simply too vast for you to master all of it. To make matters worse, gerontology is a multidiscipline field involving specialized subjects such as economics, biology, psychology, and so on. Without a clear plan for research, you can simply get lost.

The secret of research is to keep widening your search process while also narrowing it at the same time. For example, the topic you've picked has two key ideas: "pensions" and "retirement." Some of the references may lead you in directions that don't interest you: for instance, "pension fund investments" or "mandatory retirement." But other references will hit right on target and lead you to refine your topic even further. There lies the real process of thinking: testing your ideas against a "map" of knowledge that sums up facts about the world. The mistake that people often make is to construct, at the beginning, a search that is either too narrow or too broad.

So, what to do? By all means, carve your topic down to size. But then, as you're searching for information on your refined topic, also be willing to follow the concept to related topics. On "pension income," you might find references to "Social Security" or "IRAs" and so on. Perhaps you'll come upon a term that isn't very familiar, like *Keogh Plan*.

As you review what you find, you'll begin to see connections among concepts. But the connected concepts may or may not be exactly the ones listed in a computer printout or an abstract summary. You've got to develop a "sixth sense," constantly looking for clues. The result of this process is a more complete cross-referencing of your subject matter; in effect, you're creating a dense network of concepts that fully captures your topic and prepares you to write your paper.

A number of resources are available to help you build your network of concepts. One is the library's own classification system as well as the librarians themselves. The Library of Congress Subject Headings present you with a uniform method of classifying documents, and that can be a useful place to begin. But the real clues will come as you examine the books and journals themselves. *Don't* go to the library card catalog or start browsing through the latest issue of a periodical related to your subject. Doing that will just waste time unless you've done some preliminary planning. By all means, use the librarian to help you but don't rely exclusively on librarians. They can't be specialists in all subject matter and they help you the most if you've already done some thinking about the question you want to pursue. But *if* you've thought about your question, then a librarian can help guide you to the information sources you need.

Another resource that might be helpful is the computerized on-line database. But because searching or researching isn't a mechanical process, the computer search won't solve all your problems and may even give the illusion of completeness. Computer searches also present the student with certain dangers. There are two kinds of dangers in on-line searching. The first is summarized in a slogan familiar to computer specialists: "garbage in, garbage out." That saying means that you only get an answer to the question you ask; if your question or hypothesis is badly framed—for example, if it's too vague—then you won't get useful information. The second danger is that you may get too much information, including lots of references that are irrelevant or useless. For both dangers, the cure is the same: good strategies for searching and for eliminating what's extraneous to your search. The main message here is that you can't do bibliographic research just by looking for simple terminology, by looking up words in an index, card catalog, or computer printout. One reason is that there are so many related but distinct terms in gerontology: for example, *aged, older persons, elderly, senior citizens,* and so on. But if you can formulate a research question and remain alert to the meanings of the terms you encounter, you can find the sources that will help you answer your question. Once you find the spot you've been looking for, the buried treasure will be lying at your feet.

Eight Steps for Carrying Out Library Research

Step 1. Consult *The Encyclopedia of Aging* for the lead article on your subject. Be sure to make note of the relevant bibliography citations.

Step 2. Consult one of the handbooks on aging (from biology, the social sciences, the humanities, and so on) or a current textbook to see if there is a chapter or a section of a chapter devoted to your subject. The index can be useful here. (Be sure also to check the more detailed bibliography provided in this Appendix.)

Step 3. Review your bibliography references and organize them starting with the most recent. Look for titles that focus directly on your topic but approach the subject in a broad way. A literature review article is often an excellent way to get started. Many published articles begin with a literature review or "state-of-the-art" summary of what is known about a topic.

Step 4. Now consult some recent issues of one of the abstract volumes listed below, such as *Abstracts in Social Gerontology*, to find the most up-to-date literature on your subject. Looking at abstracts is a quick and handy way to see a summary of what's in a possible reference without wasting time reading the entire article. You get more than just a title but you quickly find out if the publication could have value for you.

Step 5 (optional). To be truly comprehensive and up to date, ask a friendly librarian to conduct a computerized search on your subject through AGE-LINE or a similar on-line database. From your previous bibliographic work, you should have a good collection of key words or authors to help the librarian focus on your topic as precisely as possible.

Step 6. By now, you are ready to go to your college library to find the most up-to-date, relevant books or articles on your tentative topic. But note: Do not judge a book by its cover or a reference by its title. Remember to *browse* through the book, looking at the table of contents, the index, the introduction, a summary chapter, and so on, maybe even sampling a few chapters in between. Don't make the mistake of reading straight through the entire text of what looks like the "perfect" book or article on your subject. Instead, zero in on the essential information and let the rest go. You can always come back later if you need to. It's good to get other points of view on your topic.

Step 7. When you are browsing through books or articles, be sure to check the bibliography or reference list for interesting titles. Using ideas in the book or article, you will then be able to "fine-tune" your topic while taking notes and picking up additional ideas that you can incorporate into your paper.

Step 8. In most cases, you will find the references you need in your local college library. But if you cannot find them, don't hesitate to request books or articles on interlibrary loan: for example, from a wider university system or from other libraries. But don't fall into the trap of the perpetual scholar who keeps searching forever and never quite finds the "perfect" reference source. In most cases, you will find what you need close to home. When writing a term paper, you have a deadline to meet.

Ending the search. At some point in this process, you are likely to find yourself coming up again and again with the same names of books, articles, or authors as you look through new information sources. Don't be discouraged by this. It does not mean you have hit a blank wall. In fact, it isn't even a sign of failure or "going around in circles." On the contrary, it may be a sign of success. If you have gone far enough in the search, it may mean that you've struck pay dirt. When you have gone really deeply into any subject area, you are bound to start seeing the same authors come up again and again.

At that point, it is time to look through the references on hand and decide which ones are high quality and which ones are relevant for your now refined topic area. Decide which ones are really the most useful to you and gather the key ideas, always giving credit but putting the ideas into your own words. When you have found the treasure you are looking for, go home and start writing.

Resources for Papers in Gerontology

Encyclopedias and Handbooks

The best one-volume reference source for gerontology is *The Encyclopedia of Aging*, published by Springer (New York: 1987). It contains more than 500 entries written by leading authorities in each field. The *Encyclopedia of Aging* is accessible to students as well as more advanced scholars, and the vast list of references makes the book extremely useful. Also worthwhile is the *Dictionary of Gerontology* by Diana K. Harris (Greenwood, 1988), a short volume easily understandable by the beginning student.

Among the most useful single-volume reference works are the series of "handbooks" focusing on aging and the biological sciences, social sciences, psychology, and human services. These include the following:

Robert H. Binstock and Linda K. George (eds.), *Handbook of Aging and the Social Sciences* (3rd ed.), San Diego, CA: Academic Press, 1990. Contains updated articles appearing in earlier editions as well as new areas. Covers the life course and social context, stratification and generational relations, work and economy, politics and policy analysis as well as applied topics of aging and social intervention.

James Birren and K. Warner Schaie (eds.), *Handbook of the Psychology of Aging* (3rd ed.), New York: Academic Press, 1990. Covers theory and measurement, influences of behavior and aging, perceptual and cognitive processes, and applications to the individual and society.

L. L. Carstensen and B. A. Edelstein, *Handbook of Clinical Gerontology*, New York: Pergamon, 1987. Covers a wide range of clinical issues for those working with older people. Its 28 chapters are divided into five broad groups: normal aging, psychiatric disorders, common medical problems, behavior problems, and social issues.

Thomas R. Cole, David D. Van Tassel, and Robert Kastenbaum (eds.), *Handbook of the Humanities and Aging*, New York: Springer, 1992. This volume covers aging through history, comparative religion, arts and literature, and contemporary topics in humanistic gerontology.

Caleb E. Finch and Edward L. Schneider (eds.), *Handbook of the Biology of Aging* (2nd ed.), New York: Van Nostrand Reinhold, 1985. Covers all aspects of biogerontology from molecular biology, cell biology, and genetics through the physiology of major organic systems of the human body.

Abraham Monk (ed.), *Handbook of Gerontological Services*, New York: Columbia University Press, 1990. This book is primarily relevant for social work and human services. It contains chapters by specialists on home and community-based services, long-term care, and social work intervention forms.

Abstracts and Databases

Each issue of *Abstracts in Social Gerontology: Current Literature on Aging* contains 250 abstracts or short summaries of the most important recent literature, cross-indexed and organized by topics, along with 250 other (unannotated) bibliographical citations. *Abstracts in Social Gerontology* is issued four times each year by Sage Publications in cooperation with the National Council on the Aging. Another important index is *Gerontological Abstracts*, which covers chiefly biology and health sciences.

AGELINE is a computerized on-line database, accessible by telephone line and modem anywhere in the world. References in AGELINE cover all aspects of the social sciences, health care, and human services. The database includes books, articles, government documents, and dissertations as well as reports on government-sponsored research in gerontology.

For references to biomedical subjects and other health-related topics, another good source is MEDLINE, produced by the National Library of Medicine. A college library or other research-oriented library will be able to provide computer search services. A librarian can access both AGELINE and MEDLINE through DIALOG, an on-line information company that provides many different databases. For more direct information, contact DIALOG Information Services, Inc., 3460 Hillview Avenue, Palo Alto, CA 94304.

A useful companion volume is the *Thesaurus of Aging Terminology: Ageline Database on Middle Age and Aging* (3rd ed.), Washington, DC: American Association of Retired Persons, 1986. See also *Age Words: A Glossary on Health and Aging*, published by the National Institutes of Health, Washington, DC.

Statistics

The conventional source for U.S. statistics would be publications of the U.S. Census Bureau: for example, *Current Population Reports*, which updates information from the 1990 census. Census documents are available in most college libraries. The Health Care Financing Administration and the special committees of the U.S. Senate and House Committees on Aging also publish periodic reports, which can often be obtained by writing to these agencies or by visiting a large library. Documents from specialized sources may be difficult to obtain in local libraries and they are not always easy to understand.

For the student, the best single source is probably the simple and comprehensive work published by the U.S. Administration on Aging, *Aging America: Trends and Projections*, Washington, DC: Office of Management and

Policy, 1991. This book is a compilation of the most recent data covering population trends, economic status, work and retirement as well as data on health and illness, federal expenditures, and international comparisons. It is clear, easy to understand, and extremely useful for the research purposes of beginners.

For statistics and interesting facts, see also Elizabeth Vierck, *Fact Book on Aging*, Santa Barbara, CA: ABC-CLIO, 1990. Useful but now somewhat outdated are the following: Frank L. Schick (ed.), *Statistical Handbook on Aging Americans*, Phoenix, AZ: Oryx Press, 1986. This handbook provides statistical data on the United States for a variety of variables but needs to be updated for the 1990 census figures. Also Paul E. Zopf, Jr., *America's Older Population*, Houston, TX: Cap and Gown Press, 1986.

Guides to Research and Information

Dorothea R. Zito and George V. Zito, *A Guide to Research in Gerontology: Strategies and Resources*, Westport, CT: Greenwood, 1988. Valuable, easy to follow, and reasonably up to date. See also Joan Nordquist, *The Elderly in America: A Bibliography*, Contemporary Social Issues: A Bibliographic Series (No. 23), Santa Cruz, CA: Reference and Research Services, 1991.

Among older works there are John B. Balkema (ed.), *Aging: A Guide to Resources*, Syracuse, NY: Gaylord, 1983; and Linna Funk Place, Linda Parker, and Forrest Berghorn, *Aging and the Aged: An Annotated Bibliography and Library Research Guide*, Boulder, CO: Westview, 1980, the latter written as a research and study tool for undergraduates. Both volumes are out of date but still valuable for learning about the field of aging to approach term paper topics.

Other Valuable Reference Works

Ronald Manheimer (ed.), *Aging Almanac,* Detroit: Gale Research, 1993. This is an up-to-date overview of different special subject areas in the field of aging. It is written for a popular audience but based on solid academic sources.

Edward Duensing (ed.), *America's Elderly: A Sourcebook*, New Brunswick, NJ: Center for Urban Policy Research, 1988; J. Chrichton, *The Age Care Source Book: A Resource Guide for the Aging and Their Families*, New York: Simon & Schuster, 1987; P. Wasserman, P. B. Koehler, and Y. Lev (eds.), *Encyclopedia of Senior Citizens Information Sources*, Detroit, MI: Gale Research Company, 1987.

M. D. Petersen and D. L. White (eds.), *Health Care of the Elderly: An Information Sourcebook*, Newbury Park, CA: Sage, 1989.

The 1968 volume by Riley and Foner, *Aging and Society: An Inventory of Research Findings*, New York: Basic Books, gives a comprehensive summary of knowledge through the late 1960s; out of date now but an important accomplishment nonetheless. See also Matilda Riley, Beth B. Hess, and K. Bond (eds.), *Aging in Society: Selected Review of Recent Research*, Hillsdale, NJ: Lawrence Erlbaum, 1983; and Sarah Beguns et al., *An Annotated Bibliography of Recent Research on the Elderly*, Monticello, IL: Vance Bibliographies, 1982.

See also Diana K. Harris, *The Sociology of Aging: An Annotated Bibliography and Sourcebook*, New York: Garland, 1985. Covers culture and society, social inequality, social institutions, and environment and aging. Special chapters cover demography, death and dying, crime and deviance, racial and ethnic groups, and many other topics. It also covers periodicals and source materials on aging.

Finally, the federal government is an important source of information. See, for example, the U.S. Senate Special Committee on Aging, *Publications List*, Washington, DC: U.S. Government Printing Office.

Textbooks

Current textbooks on aging and gerontology are a valuable source of information and further reference for students. The following is a partial list of textbooks that may prove useful:

Atchley, Robert, *Social Forces and Aging* (6th ed.), Belmont, CA: Wadsworth, 1991.

Barrow, Georgia, *Aging, the Individual and Society*, St. Paul, MN: West, 1989.

Brown, Arnold, *The Social Processes of Aging and Old Age*, Englewood Cliffs, NJ: Prentice Hall, 1990.

Harris, Donna, *Sociology of Aging*, New York: Harper & Row, 1990.

Hendricks, Jon, and C. Davis Hendricks, *Aging in Mass Society: Myths and Realities*, Boston: Little, Brown, 1986.

Hooyman, Nancy, and H. Asuman Kiyak, *Social Gerontology: A Multidisciplinary Perspective*, Boston: Allyn and Bacon, 1991.

Kart, Cary, *The Realities of Aging: An Introduction to Gerontology*, Boston: Allyn and Bacon, 1990.

Matras, Judah, *Dependency, Developments and Entitlements, a New Sociology of Aging, the Life Course and the Elderly*, Englewood Cliffs, NJ: Prentice Hall, 1990.

Important Journals and Periodicals

For an overview, see Shirley B. Hesslein, *Serials on Aging: An Analytical Guide*, Westport, CT: Greenwood, 1986. This book covers general periodicals, social gerontology, health and biomedicine, retirement and pensions, and statistics and reference tools. Includes a geographic index and list of publishers. Among specific and notable periodicals, the following can be recommended:

The Gerontologist. Washington, DC: Gerontological Society of America, bimonthly. Interdisciplinary and focused on social gerontology.

Ageing and Society. New York: Cambridge University Press, quarterly. Edited in Great Britain with an international and interdisciplinary perspective; strong on humanities and social science.

The International Journal of Aging and Human Development. Farmingdale, NY: Baywood, eight times annually. Interdisciplinary in the social sciences but articles with clinical and practical application as well.

Educational Gerontology. Washington, DC: Hemisphere, quarterly. Covers both gerontology instruction and education for older adults.

Contemporary Long-Term Care. Nashville, TN: Advantage, monthly. Covers all aspects of long-term care, with an emphasis on applied and practical problems.

Journal of Women and Aging. New York: Haworth, quarterly. The only periodical covering all aspects of gender and aging.

Psychology and Aging. Washington, DC: American Psychological Association, quarterly. Covers all aspects of adult life span development and aging, including behavioral, clinical, and experimental psychology.

Journal of Gerontological Social Work. New York: Haworth, quarterly. The leading periodical covering all aspects of social welfare policy and clinical practice in the field of aging.

Journal of Gerontological Nursing. Leading periodical that covers clinical health care issues of interest to many health care providers.

Journal of the American Geriatrics Society. A technical medical journal for geriatricians. Many articles are above the level of the beginning student, but some are accessible.

Gerontology and Geriatrics Education. Useful for educational issues, including training for the different professional fields involved in aging.

Journals of Gerontology. Gerontological Society of America, bimonthly. This periodical is actually four separate journals that cover the biological sciences, medical sciences, psychological sciences, and social sciences. Very technical and specialized; only for very advanced inquiry.

Research on Aging. A periodical covering the broad range of inquiry for gerontology in the social sciences. Accessible for the educated reader but contains mainly specialized articles.

Bibliography

Aaron, H.J., and Schwartz, W.B., *The Painful Prescription: Rationing Hospital Care*, Washington, DC: Brookings Institution, 1984.

Aaron, Henry J., Bosworth, B., and Burtless, Gary, *Can America Afford to Grow Old? Paying for Social Security*, Washington, DC: Brookings Institution, 1989.

Achenbaum, W. Andrew, *Old Age in the New Land: The American Experience Since 1790*, Baltimore, MD: Johns Hopkins University Press, 1978.

Achenbaum, W. Andrew, *Social Security: Visions and Revisions*, Cambridge: Cambridge University Press, 1986.

Aday, R., Rice, C., and Evans, E., "Intergenerational Partners Project: A Model Linking Elementary Students with Senior Center Volunteers," *The Gerontologist* (1991), 31(2): 263-266.

Adelman, and Roth (eds.), *Testing the Aging*, Boca Raton, FL: CRC Press, 1982.

Allen, Katherine R., and Chin-Sang, Victoria, "A Lifetime of Work: The Context and Meaning of Leisure for Aging Black Women," *The Gerontologist* (1990), 30: 734-740.

Alpaugh, P. K., and Birren, J. E., "Variables Affecting Creative Contributions Across the Life Span," *Human Development* (1977), 18: 461-465.

American Association of Retired Persons, *Work and Retirement: Employees Over 40 and Their Views*, Washington, DC: AARP, 1986.

American Health Care Association, *Facts in Brief on Long-Term Health Care*, Washington, DC: Author, 1984.

Anderson, L., "Brighter Afternoons for Latchkey Children," *Aging* (1989), 359: 20-21.

Anderson, W. French, "Human Gene Therapy," *Science* (1992), 256: 808-813.

Anderson, William A., and Anderson, Norma D., "The Politics of Age Exclusion: The Adults Only Movement in Arizona," *The Gerontologist* (1978), 18: 6-12.

Andrews, E., *The Changing Profile of Pensions*, Washington, DC: Employee Benefit Research Institute, 1985.

Applebaum, R., and Austin, C., *Long Term Care Case Management: Design and Evaluation*, New York: Springer, 1990.

Applewhite, S. R. (ed.), *Hispanic Elderly in Transition: Theory, Research, Policy and Practice*, New York: Greenwood, 1988.

Aries, Philippe, *Centuries of Childhood*, New York: Random House, 1962.

Arking, Robert, "Modifying the Aging Process," in Rosalie Young and Elizabeth Olson (eds.), *Health, Illness and Disability in Later Life: Practice Issues and Interventions*, Newbury Park, CA: Sage, 1991.

Arling, Greg, and McAuley, William J., "The Feasibility of Public Payments for Family Care-Giving," *The Gerontologist* (1983), 23: 300-306.

Arling, Greg, et al., "Medicaid Spenddown in Nursing Home Residents in Wisconsin," *The Gerontologist* (1991), 31(2): 174-182.

Armstrong, D., Sohal, R. S., Cutler, R. G., and Slater, T. F. (eds.), *Free Radicals in Molecular Biology, Aging, and Disease*, New York: Raven, 1984.

Atchley, Robert, *Social Forces and Aging: An Introduction to Social Gerontology* (4th ed.), Belmont, CA: Wadsworth, 1985.

Avorn, Jerome, "The Life and Death of Oliver Shay," in Alan Pifer and Lydia Bronte (eds.), *Our Aging Society*, New York: Norton, 1986.

Avorn, Jerry, "Benefit and Cost Analysis in Geriatric Care: Turning Age Discrimination into Health Policy," *New England Journal of Medicine* (1984), 310: 1294-1301.

Ball, Robert, *Social Security Today and Tomorrow*, New York: Columbia University Press, 1978.

Baltes, M. M., and Baltes, P. B. (eds.), *The Psychology of Control and Aging*, Hillsdale, NJ: Erlbaum, 1986.

Baltes, P. B., and Schaie, K. W., "The Myth of the Twilight Years," *Psychology Today* (March 1974): 35-40.

Baltes, Paul B., and Baltes, Margaret B., "Psychological Perspectives on Successful Aging: The Model of Selective Optimization and Compensation," in P. B. Baltes and M. M. Baltes, *Successful Aging: Perspectives from the Behavioral Sciences*, New York: Cambridge University Press, 1990, pp. 1-34.

Barinaga, Marcia, "Mortality: Overturning Received Wisdom," *Science* (October 16, 1992), 258: 398-399.

Barrett, Edith J., and Cook, Fay Lomax, "Public Support for Social Security," *Journal of Aging Studies* (1988), 2(4): 339-356.

Barron, Milton L., "Minority Group Characteristics of the Aged in American Society," *Journal of Gerontology* (1953), 8: 477-482.

Bass, Scott, and Car, Francis J. (eds.), *Toward a Productive Aging Society*, Westport, CT: Auburn House, 1993.

Battin, Margaret P., "Choosing the Time to Die: The Ethics and Economics of Suicide in Old Age," in Stuart F. Spicker and Stanley Ingman (eds.), *Ethical Dimension of Geriatric Care,* Dorecht: Reidel, 1987.

Beck, Melinda, Hager, Mary, and Roberts, Elizabeth, "Counting Every Penny: A Battle Over the Social Security Earnings Limit," *Newsweek* (January 27, 1992), 199: 4, 55.

Becker, Ernest, *The Denial of Death*, New York: Free Press, 1973.

Belbin, E., and Belbin, R. M., *Problems in Adult Retraining*, London: Heinemann, 1972.

Belbin, E., and Downs, S., "Teaching Paired Associates: The Problem of Age," *Occupational Psychology* (1966), 40(1): 67-74.

Belbin, R. M., *The Discovery Method: An International Experiment in Retraining*, Paris: OECD, 1969.

Bell, I. P., "The Double Standard: Age," in J. Freeman (ed.), *Women: A Feminist Perspective* (4th ed.), 1989, pp. 236-244.

Bendix, Reinhard, and Lipset, Seymour Martin (eds.), *Class, Status and Power*, New York: Free Press, 1966.

Bengtson, Vern L., Rosenthal, Carolyn, and Burton, Linda, "Families and Aging: Diversity and Heterogeneity," in Robert Binstock and Linda K. George (eds.), *Handbook of Aging and the Social Sciences* (3rd ed.), New York: Academic Press, 1990, pp. 263-287.

Berkowitz, Edward D. (ed.), *Social Security After Fifty: Success and Failures*, New York: Greenwood, 1987.

Berman, Harry J., "To Flame with Wild Life: Florida Scott-Maxwell's Experience of Old Age," *The Gerontologist* (1986), 26: 321-324.

Bertaux, D. (ed.), *Biography and Society: The Life History Approach in the Social Sciences*, Beverly Hills, CA: Sage, 1981.

Bertman, Stephen (ed.), *The Conflict of Generations in Ancient Greece*, Atlantic Highlands, NJ: Humanities Press, 1976.

Best, Fred, "Work Sharing: Issues, Policy Options, and Prospects," Kalamazoo, MI: Upjohn Institute for Employment Research, 1981.

Bianchi, Eugene C., *Aging as a Spiritual Journey*, New York: Crossroads, 1982.

Binstock, R. H., "The Oldest-Old: A Fresh Perspective on Compassionate Ageism Revisited?" *Milbank Memorial Fund Quarterly* (1985), 63: 420-451.

Binstock, Robert, "Interest-Group Liberalism and the Politics of Aging," *The Gerontologist* (1972), 12: 265-280.

Binstock, Robert H., "The Aged as Scapegoat," *The Gerontologist* (1983), 23: 136-143.

Birkhill, W. R., and Schaie, K. W., "The Effect of Differential Reinforcement of Cautiousness in Intellectual Performance Among the Elderly," *Journal of Gerontology* (1975), 30: 578-583.

Birren, James E., and Deutschman, Donna E., *Guiding Autobiography Groups for Older Adults: Exploring the Fabric of Life*, Baltimore, MD: Johns Hopkins University Press, 1991.

Blau, Zena S., *Aging in a Changing Society*, New York: Franklin Watts, 1981.

Blau, Zena S. (ed.), *Work, Retirement and Social Policy*, Greenwich, CT: JAI, 1985.

Blazer, Dan G., *Depression in Late Life*, St. Louis: Mosby, 1982.

Blazer, D. G., and Palmore, E., "Religion and Aging in a Longitudinal Panel," *The Gerontologist* (1976), 16(1): 82-85.

Block, Marilyn, "Exiled Americans: The Plight of the Indian Aged in the United States," in Donald Gelfand and Alfred Kutzik (eds.), *Ethnicity and Aging*, New York: Springer, 1979, pp. 184-192.

Blumenthal, H. T. (ed.), *Handbook of Diseases of Aging*, New York: Van Nostrand, 1983.

Boaz, Rachel F., "Early Withdrawal from the Labor Force: A Response Only to Pension Pull or Also to Labor Market Push?" *Research on Aging* (1987), 9(4): 530-547.

Bolles, Richard N., *The Three Boxes of Life and How to Get Out of Them*, Berkeley, CA: Ten Speed, 1981.

Bortner, R., "Notes on Expected Life-History," *International Journal of Aging and Human Development* (1979), 9: 291-294.

Boskin, Michael J., *Too Many Promises: The Uncertain Future of Social Security*, Homewood, IL: Dow-Jones-Irwin, 1986.

Boyd, B., "Long Term Care Insurance: It's Your Choice," *Generations* (Spring 1990), 23-27.

Boyle, Joan, and Morriss, James, *The Mirror of Time: Images of Aging and Dying*, Westport, CT: Greenwood, 1987.

Brady, E. Michael, "Personal Growth and the Elderhostel Experience," *Lifelong Learning* (1983), 7: 3, 11-13.

Braun, P., and Sweet, "Passages: Fact or Fiction?" *International Journal of Aging and Human Development* (1984), 18: 161-176.

Brennan, Penny L., and Steinberg, L. D., "Is Reminiscence Adaptive? Relations Among Social Activity Level, Reminiscence, and Morale," *International Journal of Aging and Human Development* (1983-1984), 18: 99-110.

Breslau, L. D., and Haug, M. R. (eds.), *Depression and Aging: Causes, Care, and Consequences*, New York: Springer, 1983.

Breytspraak, Linda M., *The Development of Self in Later Life*, Boston: Little, Brown, 1984.

Brickner, Philip W., et al., *Long Term Health Care: Providing a Spectrum of Services to the Aged*, New York: Basic Books, 1987.

Brody, Elaine, "Parent Care as a Normative Family Stress," *The Gerontologist* (1985), 25: 19-29.

Brody, Elaine, *Women in the Middle: Their Parent-Care Years*, New York: Springer, 1990.

Brody, Jane E., "Hope Grows for Vigorous Old Age," *The New York Times* (October 2, 1984).

Bronson, R. T., and Lipman, R. D., "Reduction in Rate of Occurrence of Age-Related Lesions in Dietary Restricted Laboratory Mice," *Growth, Development and Aging* (1991), 55: 169-184.

Brown, J. Douglas, *An American Philosophy of Social Security: Evolution and Issues*, Princeton, NJ: Princeton University Press, 1972.

Brown, L. D., "The National Politics of Oregon's Rationing Plan," *Health Affairs* (Summer 1991), 10: 28-51.

Brubaker, Timothy H., *Later Life Families*, Beverly Hills, CA: Sage, 1985.

Brubaker, Timothy H., *Aging, Health and Family: Long-Term Care*, Newbury Park, CA: Sage, 1987.

Buchanan, R. J., "Medicaid: Family Responsibility and Long Term Care," *Journal of Long Term Care Administration* (1984), 12: 3, 19-25.

Buckley, William F., "Oversight Time," *National Review* (June 11, 1990).

Budish, Armond D., *Avoiding the Medicaid Trap: How to Beat the Catastrophic Cost of Nursing Home Care*, New York: Henry Holt, 1989.

Burgess, E. W., *Aging in Western Societies*, Chicago: University of Chicago Press, 1960.

Burrows, James, *The Ages of Man*, New York: Oxford University Press, 1986.

Busse, E.W., and Blaser, D.G. (eds.), *Handbook of Geriatric Psychiatry*, New York: Van Nostrand Reinhold, 1980.

Butler, R. N., and Gleason, Herbert P. (eds.), *Productive Aging: Enhancing Vitality in Later Life*, New York: Springer, 1985.

Butler, Robert, and Lewis, Myrna, *Aging and Mental Health* (3rd ed.), St. Louis: Mosby, 1982.

Butler, Robert N., "The Life Review: An Interpretation of Reminiscence in the Aged," *Psychiatry* (1963), 26: 65-76.

Butler, Robert N., "Age-ism: Another Form of Bigotry," *The Gerontologist* (1969), 9: 243-246.

Butler, Robert N., "Successful Aging and the Role of the Life Review," *Journal of the American Geriatrics Society* (1974), 22: 529-535.

Callahan, Daniel, "What Do Children Owe Elderly Parents?" *Hastings Center Report* (April 1985), 15: 2, 32-33.

Callahan, J. J., Jr., "Case Management for the Elderly: A Panacea?" *Journal of Aging and Social Policy* (1989), 1(1/2): 181-185.

Campbell, Colin D., *Controlling the Costs of Social Security*, Lexington, MA: Lexington, 1984.

Campbell, Rita R., *Social Security: Promise and Reality*, Stanford, CA: Hoover Institute Press, 1977.

Campione, Wendy A., "Predicting Participation in Retirement Preparation Programs," *Journal of Gerontology: Social Sciences* (1988), 43(3): 91-95.

Cantor, Marjorie, "Families and Caregiving in an Aging Society," *Generations* (Summer 1992), 67-70.

Cantor, Marjorie H., "The Informal Support System: Its Relevance in the Lives of the Elderly," in Edgar F. Borgatta and Neil McCluskey (eds.), *Aging and Society: Current Research*. Beverly Hills, CA: Sage, 1980, pp. 131-144.

Capitman, J., "Case Management in Long-term and Acute Medical Care," *Health Care Financing Review* (1988), Annual Supplement, 75-81.

Cassel, Christine, Rudberg, M., and Olshansky, J., "The Price of Success: Health Care in an Aging Society," *Health Affairs* (1992), 11(2): 87-99.

Chambre, Susan M., *Good Deeds in Old Age: Volunteering by the New Leisure Class*, New York: Free Press, 1987.

Chellis, Robert D., Seagle, James F., and Seagle, Barbara M. (eds.), *Congregate Housing for Older People*, Lexington, MA: Lexington, 1982.

Cheung, M., "Elderly Chinese Living in the United States: Assimilation or Adjustment?" *Social Work* (1989), 14: 457-461.

Chinen, Allan B., *In the Ever After: Fairy Tales and the Second Half of Life*, Wilmette, IL: Chiron, 1989.

Chiriboga, David A., "An Examination of Life Events as Possible Antecedents to Change," *Journal of Gerontology* (1982), 37: 595-601.

Choi, N. G., "Does Social Security Redistribute Income? A Tax-Transfer Analysis," *Journal of Sociology and Social Welfare* (1991), 18(3): 21-38.

Chudakoff, Howard P., *How Old Are You? Age Consciousness in American Culture*, Princeton, NJ: Princeton University Press, 1989.

Clark, Brian, *Whose Life Is It Anyway? A Play*, London: Samuel French, 1978.

Clark, R., Maddox, G., Schrimper, R., and Sumner, D., *Inflation and the Economic Well-Being of the Elderly*, Baltimore, MD: Johns Hopkins University Press, 1984.

Clark, Robert, "Pensions in an Aging Society," in Irving Bluestone, Rhonda Montgomery, and John Owen (eds.), *The Aging of the American Work Force*, Detroit: Wayne State University Press, 1990, pp. 75-100.

Clark, Robert, and Barker, David T., *Reversing the Trend Toward Early Retirement*, Washington, DC: American Enterprise Institute, 1981.

Clark, Robert L., "The Future of Work and Retirement," *Research on Aging* (1988), 10(2): 169-193.

Clark, William F., et al., *Old and Poor: A Critical Assessment of the Low-Income Elderly*, Lexington, MA: Lexington, 1988.

Cohen, Marc A., Tell, Eileen, Greenberg, Jan N., and Wallack, Stanley S., "The Financial Capacity of the Elderly to Insure for Long-Term Care," *The Gerontologist* (1987), 27(5): 494-502.

Cole, S., "Age and Scientific Performance," *American Journal of Sociology* (1979), 84: 958-977.

Cole, Thomas, *The Journey of Life: A Cultural History of Aging in America*, Cambridge: Cambridge University Press, 1992.

Cole, Thomas, and Gadow, Sally (eds.), *What Does It Mean to Grow Old? Views from the Humanities*, Durham, NC: Duke University Press, 1986.

Cole, Thomas R., "Generational Equity in America: A Cultural Historian's Perspective," *Social Science and Medicine* (1989), 29: 3, 377-383.

Coleman, P. G., "Measuring Reminiscence Characteristics from Conversation as Adaptive Features of Old Age," *International Journal of Aging and Human Development* (1974), 5: 281-294.

Coles, Robert, *The Old Ones of New Mexico*, Albuquerque: University of New Mexico Press, 1974.

Cook, Fay L., and Kramek, Lorraine M., "Measuring Economic Hardship Among Older Americans," *The Gerontologist* (1986), 26: 38-47.

Corbin, J. M., and Strauss, A., *Unending Care and Work: Managing Chronic Illness at Home*, San Francisco: Jossey-Bass, 1988.

Cornelius, S. W., and Caspi, A., "Everyday Problem Solving in Adulthood and Old Age," *Psychology and Aging* (1987), 2: 14-153.

Cornelius, Steven W., "Aging and Everyday Cognitive Abilities," in Thomas Hess (ed.), *Aging and Cognition: Knowledge Organization and Utilization* (Advances in Psychology, No. 71), Amsterdam: North-Holland, 1990, pp. 411-459.

Costa, P. T., Jr., and McCrae, R. R., "Still Stable After All These Years: Personality as a Year to Some Issues in Aging," in P. B. Baltes and O. G. Brim (eds.), *Life-Span Development and Behavior* (Vol. 3), New York: Academic Press, 1980, pp. 65-102.

Cowgill, Donald O., *Aging Around the World*, Belmont, CA: Wadsworth, 1986.

Cowgill, Donald O., and Holmes, Lowell, *Aging and Modernization*, New York: Appleton-Century-Crofts, 1972.

Crooks, Louise, "Women and Pensions," *Vital Speeches* (February 15, 1991), 57: 283-285.

Crown, William H., "Some Thoughts on Reformulating the Dependency Ratio," *The Gerontologist* (1985), 25: 166-171.

Crystal, S., and Shea, D., "Cumulative Advantage, Cumulative Disadvantage, and Inequality Among Elderly People," *The Gerontologist* (1990), 30: 437-443.

Crystal, Stephen, "Measuring Income and Inequality Among the Elderly," *The Gerontologist* (1986), 26: 56-59.

Crystal, Stephen, Shea, Dennis, and Krishnaswami, Shreeram, "Educational Attainment, Occupational History, and Stratification: Determinants of Later-Life Economic Outcomes," *Journal of Gerontology* (September 1992), 47: S213-S221.

Cumming, Elaine, and Henry, William E., *Growing Old: The Process of Disengagement*, New York: Basic Books, 1961.

Cunningham, Walter R., and Torner, Adrian, "Intellectual Abilities and Age: Concepts, Theories and Analyses," in Eugene A. Lovelace (ed.), *Aging and Cognition: Mental Processes, Self-Awareness, and Interventions* (Advances in Psychology, No. 72), Amsterdam: North-Holland, 1990, pp. 379-406.

Cutler, Neal, "Political Characteristics of Elderly Cohorts in the Twenty-First Century," in S. B. Kiesler (ed.), *Aging and Social Change*, New York: Academic Press, 1981.

Cutler, Richard, "Species Probes, Longevity and Aging," in *Intervention in the Aging Process* (Part B), New York: Alan Liss, 1983.

Daniels, Norman, *Am I My Parents' Keeper? An Essay on Justice Between the Young and the Old*, New York: Oxford University Press, 1988.

Dannefer, Dale, "Adult Development and Social Theory: A Paradigmatic Reappraisal," *American Sociological Review* (1984), 49: 100-116.

Davies, D. R., and Sparrow, P. R., "Age and Work Behaviour," in N. Charness (ed.), *Aging and Human Performance*, Chichester, England: Wiley, 1985.

Davis, K., and Rowland, D., "Old and Poor: Policy Challenges in the 1990s," *Journal of Aging and Social Policy* (1991), 2: 37-59.

Davis, Richard, and Davis, Jim, *TV's Image of the Elderly*, Lexington, MA: Lexington, 1985.

Day, Christine, *What Older Americans Think: Interest Groups and Aging Policy*, Princeton, NJ: Princeton University Press, 1990.

de Leo, Diego, and Diekstra, R.F.W., *Depression and Suicide in Late Life*, Lewiston, NY and Toronto: Hogrefe & Huber, 1990.

Dellman-Jenkins, M., "Old and Young Together: Effect of Educational Programs on Preschoolers," *Childhood Education* (1986), 62: 206-208.

Dennis, Helen, *Fourteen Steps in Managing an Aging Work Force*, Lexington, MA: Lexington, 1988.

Dennis, Helen, "The Current State of Preretirement Planning," *Generations* (1989), 13(2): 38-41.

Dennis, W., "Creative Productivity Between the Ages of 20 and 80 Years," *Journal of Gerontology* (1966), 21: 1-8.

Diamond, Arthur M., Jr., "The Life-Cycle Research Productivity of Mathematicians and Scientists," *Journal of Gerontology* (1986), 41: 520-525.

Dill, Ann E. P., et al., "Coercive Placement of Elders: Protection or Choice?" *Generations* (Summer 1987), 11(4): 48-66.

Dilworth-Anderson, Peggye, "Extended Kin Networks in Black Families," *Generations* (Summer 1992), 16: 29-32.

Dobris, Joel C., "Medicaid Asset Planning by the Elderly: A Policy View of Expectations, Entitlements, and Inheritance," *Real Property, Probate and Trust Journal* (Spring 1989), 24: 1, 1-32.

Dobrosky, B., and Bishop, J., "Children's Perceptions of Old People," *Educational Gerontology* (1986), 12: 429-439.

Doering, Mildred, Rhodes, Susan R., and Schuster, Michael, *The Aging Worker: Research and Recommendations,* Beverly Hills, CA: Sage, 1983.

Dowd, J. J., "Aging as Exchange: A Preface to Theory," *Journal of Gerontology* (1975), 30: 584-594.

Dowd, J. J., *Stratification Among the Aged*, Monterey, CA: Brooks/Cole, 1980.

Dowd, J. J., "Beneficence and the Aged," *Journal of Gerontology* (1984), 39(1): 102-108.

Dowd, James J., and Bengtson, Vern L., "Aging in a Minority Population: An Examination of the Double Jeopardy Hypothesis," *Journal of Gerontology* (1978), 33: 427-436.

Down, Ivy M., and Schnurr, Lorraine, *Between Home and Nursing Home: The Board and Care Alternative*, Buffalo, NY: Prometheus, 1991.

Dressel, Paula L., "Gender, Race, and Class: Beyond the Feminization of Poverty in Later Life," *The Gerontologist* (1988), 28(2): 177-180.

Duke University, Center for the Study of Aging and Human Development, *Multidimensional Functional Assessment: The OARS Methodology* (2nd ed.), Durham, NC: Author, 1978.

Dumas, Kitty, "Budget-Buster Hot Potato: The Earnings Test," *Congressional Quarterly Weekly Report* (January 11, 1992), 50: 52-55.

Duncan, G., "The Volatility of Family Income over the Life Course," in P. B. Baltes, D. L. Featherman, and R. M. Lerner (eds.), *Life-Span Development and Behavior* (Vol. 9), Hillsdale, NJ: Erlbaum, 1988, pp. 37-358.

Durkheim, Émile, *Suicide* (trans. J. A. Spaulding and G. Simpson), Glencoe, IL: Free Press, 1951.

Dworaczek, Marian, and Wong, Helen, *Early Retirement: A Bibliography*, Monticello, IL: Vance Bibliographies, 1989.

Dychtwald, Ken (ed.), *Wellness and Health Promotion for the Elderly*, Rockville, MD: Aspen Systems Corporation, 1986.

Eckert, J. K., and Murey, Mary I., "Alternative Modes of Living for the Elderly," in I. Altman, M. P. Lawton, and J. F. Wohwill (eds.), *Elderly People and the Environment*, New York: Plenum, 1984.

Eisele, F. R., "Origins of Gerontocracy," *The Gerontologist* (1979), 19: 4.

Eisenstadt, S. N., *From Generation to Generation: Age Groups and Social Structure*, New York: Free Press, 1956.

Eitzen, Stanley D., and Baca-Zinn, Maxine, *The Reshaping of America*, Englewood Cliffs, NJ: Prentice-Hall, 1988.

Ekerdt, David J., "Why the Notion Persists That Retirement Harms Health," *The Gerontologist* (1987), 27(4): 454-457.

Elder, Glen H., *Children of the Great Depression*, Chicago: University of Chicago Press, 1974.

Erikson, Erik, *Childhood and Society*, New York: Macmillan, 1963.

Estes, Carroll, *The Aging Enterprise*, San Francisco: Jossey-Bass, 1979.

Estes, Carroll, "Aging, Health, and Social Policy: Crisis and Crossroads," *Journal of Aging and Social Policy* (1989), 1(1-2): 17-32.

Estes, C., et al., *Political Economy, Health, and Aging*, Boston: Little, Brown, 1984.

Eustis, N., Grenberg, J., and Patten, S., *Long Term Care for Older Persons: A Policy Perspective*, Monterey, CA, Brooks-Cole, 1984.

Falkner, Thomas, and de Luce, Judith, "A View from Antiquity," in Thomas Cole, David Van Tassel, and Robert Kastenbaum (eds.), *Handbook of the Humanities and Aging*, New York: Springer, 1992.

Fama, T., and Kennell, D. L., "Should We Worry About Induced Demand for Long-Term Care Services?" *Generations* (Spring 1990): 37-41.

Families USA, *The Unaffordability of Nursing Home Insurance*, Washington, DC: Author, January 1990.

Feder, Judith, *Medicare: The Politics of Federal Hospital Insurance*, Lexington, MA: D. C. Heath, 1977.

Ferrara, Peter J. (ed.), *Social Security: Prospects for Real Reform*, Washington, DC: Cato Institute, 1985.

Firman, J., Gelfand, D., and Ventura, C., "Students as Resources to the Aging Network," *The Gerontologist* (1983), 23(2): 185-191.

Fischer, David Hackett, *Growing Old in America*, New York: Oxford University Press, 1977.

Fisher, C. R., "Trends in Medicare Enrollee Use of Physician and Supplier Services, 1983-1986," *Health Care Financing Review* (Fall 1988): 12-14.

Fogarty, Michael (ed.), *Retirement Policy: The Next Fifty Years*, Chichester, UK: Gower, 1982.

Folstein, M. F., Folstein, S. E., and McHugh, P. R., " 'Mini-Mental State': A Practical Method for Grading the Cognitive State of Patients for the Clinician," *Journal of Psychiatric Research* (1975), 12: 189-198.

Foner, Nancy, *Ages in Conflict: A Cross-Cultural Perspective on Inequality Between Old and Young*, New York: Columbia University Press, 1984.

Forman, M., "Social Security Is a Women's Issue," *Social Policy* (1983), 14: 35-38.

Frech, H. E. (ed.), *Regulating Doctors' Fees: Competition, Benefits, and Controls Under Medicare*, Washington, DC: American Enterprise Institute, 1991.

Freedman, Robert M., et al., "Why Won't Medicaid Let Me Keep My Nest Egg?" [Case Study], *Hastings Center Report* (April 1983), 13(2): 23-25.

Freeman, Scott M., Whartenby, Katharine, and Abraham, George N., "Gene Therapy: Applications to Diseases Associated with Aging," *Generations* (1992), 16: 45-48.

Fries, James F., "Aging, Illness, and Health Policy: Implications of the Compression of Morbidity," *Perspectives in Biology and Medicine* (Spring 1988), 31: 3.

Fujii, Sharon, "Older Asian Americans: Victims of Multiple Jeopardy," *Civil Rights Digest* (1976), 9: 22-29.

Gambria, L. M., "Daydreaming About the Past: The Time Setting of Spontaneous Thought Intrusions," *The Gerontologist* (1977), 17: 35-38.

Gardner, Howard, *Frames of Mind: The Theory of Multiple Intelligence*, New York: Basic Books, 1985.

Garrett, W. W., "Filial Responsibility Laws," *Journal of Family Law* (1980), 18: 793-818.

Gee, E. M., "Historical Change in the Family Life Course of Canadian Men and Women," in V. Marshall (ed.), *Aging in Canada* (2nd ed.), Markham, ON: Fitzhenry & Whiteside, 1987, pp. 265-287.

Gelfand, D. E., and Barresi, C. M. (eds.), *Ethnic Dimensions of Aging*, New York: Springer, 1987.

George, Linda K., *Role Transitions in Later Life: A Social Stress Perspective*, Monterey, CA: Brooks/Cole, 1980.

Gibson, Rose C., "Work Patterns of Older Black and White and Male and Female Heads of Household," *Journal of Minority Aging* (1983), 8 (1-2): 1-16.

Gibson, Rose C., "Reconceptualizing Retirement for Black Americans," *The Gerontologist* (1987), 27: 691-698.

Ginzberg, E., Balinsky, W., and Ostow, M., *Home Health Care*, Totowa, NJ: Rowman & Allanheld, 1984.

Giordano, J. A., and Giordano, N. H., "A Classification of Preretirement Programs: In Search of a New Model," *Educational Gerontology* (1983), 9: 123-137.

Glaser, B. G., and Straus, A. L., *Awareness of Dying*, Chicago: Aldine, 1965.

Glendenning, Frank (ed.), *Educational Gerontology: International Perspectives*, New York: St. Martin's Press, 1985.

Glenn, N. D., and Hefner, T., "Further Evidence on Aging and Party Identification," *Public Opinion Quarterly* (1972), 36: 31-47.

Glick, Henry, *The Right to Die*, New York: Columbia University Press, 1992.

Glick, Paul C., "Updating the Life Cycle of the Family," *Journal of Marriage and the Family* (1977), 39: 5-13.

Goffman, Erving, *Asylums*, Garden City, NY: Anchor, 1961.

Grad, Susan, *Income of the Population 65 or Over, 1988* (Pub. No. 13-11871), Washington, DC: Social Security Administration (June 1990).

Graebner, William, *A History of Retirement: The Meaning and Function of an American Institution*, New Haven, CT: Yale University Press, 1980.

Granick, S., and Friedman, A. S., "Educational Experience and the Maintenance of Intellectual Functioning by the Aged: An Overview," in Lissy F. Jarvik, Carl Eisdorfer, and J. E. Blum (eds.), *Intellectual Functioning in Adults*, New York: Springer, 1973.

Gratton, Brian, "Familism Among the Black and Mexican-American Elderly: Myth or Reality?" *Journal of Aging Studies* (1987), 1(1): 19-32.

Greenough, William C., and King, F. P., *Pension Plans and Public Policy*, New York: Columbia University Press, 1976.

Gresham, G. E., and Labi, M. L. C., "Functional Assessment Instruments Currently Available for Documenting Outcomes in Rehabilitation Medicine," in C. V. Granger and G. E. Greer (eds.), *Functional Assessment in Rehabilitation Medicine*, Baltimore, MD: Williams and Wilkins, 1984.

Gross, Peter A., et al., *Managing Your Health: Strategies for Lifelong Good Health*, Yonkers, NY: Consumer Reports Books, 1991.

Gruman, Gerald J., *A History of Ideas About the Prolongation of Life: The Evolution of Prolongevity Hypothesis to 1800*, Philadelphia: 1966.

Gruman, Gerald, "Modernization of the Life Cycle," in S. Spicker, K. Woodward, and D. Van Tassel (eds.), *Aging and the Elderly: Humanistic Perspectives on Gerontology*, Atlantic Highlands, NJ: Humanities Press, 1978, pp. 359-387.

Gubrium, Jay, *Living and Dying at Murray Manor*, New York: St. Martin's, 1975.

Gubrium, J. F., and Buckholdt, D. R., *Toward Maturity: The Social Processing of Human Development*, San Francisco: Jossey-Bass, 1977.

Gubrium, J. F., and Lynott, R. J., "Rethinking Life Satisfaction," *Human Organization* (1983), 42: 30-38.

Haber, Carole, *Beyond Sixty-Five*, Cambridge: Cambridge University Press, 1983.

Haber, E., and Short-DeGraff, M., "Intergenerational Programming for an Increasingly Age Segregated Society," *Activities, Adaptation, and Aging* (1990), 14(3): 35-49.

Hagestad, G. O., and Neugarten, B. L., "Age and the Life Course," in E. Shanas and R. Binstock (eds.), *Handbook of Aging and the Social Sciences,* Beverly Hills, CA: Sage, 1981, pp. 35-61.

Haight, Barbara K., "Reminiscing: The State of the Art as a Basis for Practice," *International Journal of Aging and Human Development* (1991), 33(1): 1-32.

Halper, Thomas, *The Misfortunes of Other: End-Stage Renal Disease in the United Kingdom*, New York: Cambridge University Press, 1989.

Hambor, J. C., "Economic Policy, Intergenerational Equity, and the Social Security Trust Fund Buildup," *Social Security Bulletin* (1987), 50(4): 13-18.

Hamburg, David, *Today's Children: Creating a Future for a Generation in Crisis*, New York: Random House, 1992.

Harel, Z., Ehrlich, P., and Hubbard, R., *The Vulnerable Elderly: People, Services, and Policies*, New York: Springer, 1990.

Hareven, Tamara, and Adams, Kathleen (eds.), *Aging and Life Course Transitions*, New York: Guilford, 1982.

Harman, D., "Aging: A Theory Based on Free Radical and Radiation Chemistry," *Journal of Gerontology* (1956), 11: 298-300.

Louis Harris and Associates, *The Myth and Reality of Aging*, Washington, DC: National Council on the Aging, 1975.

Louis Harris and Associates, *Aging in the Eighties: America in Transition*, Washington, DC: National Council on the Aging, 1981.

Hastings Center, *Guidelines on the Termination of Life-Sustaining Treatment and the Care of the Dying*, Bloomington, IN: Indiana University Press, 1988.

Hauser, Philip M., "Aging and World-Wide Population Change," in Robert Binstock and Ethel Shanas (eds.), *Handbook of Aging and the Social Sciences*, New York: Van Nostrand Reinhold, 1976.

Havighurst, Robert J., Neugarten, Bernice L., and Tobin, Sheldon S., "Disengagement and Patterns of Aging," in Bernice L. Neugarten (ed.), *Middle Age and Aging*, Chicago: University of Chicago Press, 1968, pp. 161-172.

Hayflick, Leonard, "The Limited in Vitro Lifetime of Human Diploid Cell Strains," *Experimental Cell Research* (1965), 37(3): 614-636.

Hayflick, Leonard, "Human Cells and Aging," *Scientific American* (March 1968).

Hays, Judith A., "Aging and Family Resources: Availability and Proximity of Kin," *The Gerontologist* (1984), 24: 149-153.

Heclo, H., "Generational Politics," in J. L. Palmer, T. Smeeding, and B. B. Torrey (eds.), *The Vulnerable*, Washington, DC: Urban Institute, 1988, pp. 381-442.

Held, T., "Institutionalization and De-institutionalization of the Life Course," *Human Development* (1986), 29: 157-162.

Hellman, S., and Hellman, L. H., *Medicare and Medigap: A Guide to Retirement Health Insurance*, Newbury Park, CA: Sage, 1991.

Helson, R., Mitchell, V., and Moane, G., "Personality and Patterns of Adherence and Non-adherence to the Social Clock," *Journal of Personality and Social Psychology* (1984), 46: 1079-1096.

Hendricks, J., and Peters, C. B., "The Times of Our Lives: An Integrative Framework," *American Behavioral Scientist* (1986), 29(5): 662-676.

Henretta, J. C., and Campbell, R. T., "Status Attainment and Status Maintenance: A Study of Stratification in Old Age," *American Sociological Review* (1976), 41: 981-992.

Herzog, Regula A., Kahn, Robert L., Moergan, James N., Jackson, James S., and Antonucci, Toni C., "Age Differences in Productive Activities," *Journal of Gerontology: Social Sciences* (1989), 44: S129-S138.

Hess, Clinton, and Kerschner, P., *Silver Lobby*, Los Angeles: University of Southern California Press, 1978.

Hochschild, Arlie, *The Unexpected Community*, Englewood Cliffs, NJ: Prentice-Hall, 1973.

Hochschild, Arlie R., "Disengagement Theory: A Critique and Proposal," *American Sociological Review* (1975), 40: 553-569.

Hogan, D. P., and Astone, N. M., "The Transition to Adulthood," *Annual Review of Sociology* (1986), 12: 109-130.

Holden, K. C., Burkhauser, R. V., and Myers, Daniel A., "Income Transitions at Older Stages of Life: The Dynamics of Poverty," *The Gerontologist* (1986), 26: 292-297.

Holmes, T. H., and Rahe, R. H., "The Social Readjustment Rating Scale," *Journal of Psychosomatic Research* (1967), 11: 213-218.

Holtzman, Abraham, *The Townsend Movement*, New York: Bookman Associates, 1963.

Honig, Marjorie, and Reimers, Cordelia, "Is It Worth Eliminating the Retirement Test?" *American Economic Review* (May 1989), 79: 103-107.

Horn, J. L., "The Theory of Fluid and Crystallized Intelligence in Relation to Concepts of Cognitive Psychology and Aging in Adulthood," in F. I. M. Craik and S. Trehub (eds.), *Aging and Cognitive Processes*, New York: Plenum, 1982, pp. 237-278.

Horn, J. L., and Donaldson, G., "Faith Is Not Enough: A Response to the Baltes-Schaie Claim That Intelligence Does Not Wane," *American Psychologist* (1977), 32: 369-373.

Hudson, Robert, "The 'Graying' of the Federal Budget and Its Consequences for Old-Age Policy," *The Gerontologist* (1978), 28: 428-440.

Hudson, Robert, "Tomorrow's Able Elders: Implications for the State," *The Gerontologist* (1987), 27(4): 405-409.

Hunnicutt, Benjamin K., "Aging and Leisure Politics," in Michael L. Teague, Richard D. MacNeil, and Gerald L. Hitzhusen (eds.), *Perspectives on Leisure and Aging in a Changing Society*, University of Missouri, 1982, pp. 74-108.

Hunt, Michael E., et al. (eds.), *Retirement Communities: An American Original*, New York: Haworth, 1983.

Ingram, D. K., et al., "Dietary Restriction and Aging: The Initiation of a Primate Study," *Journal of Gerontology* (1990), 45(5): B148-B163.

Inlander, C. B., and MacKay, C. K., *Medicare Made Easy* (rev. ed.), Reading, MA: Addison-Wesley, 1991.

Isenberg, Sheldon, "Aging in Judaism: 'Crown of Glory' and 'Days of Sorrow,' " in Thomas Cole, David Van Tassel, and Robert Kastenbaum (eds.), *Handbook of the Humanities and Aging*, New York: Springer, 1992.

Jackson, J. S. (ed.), *The Black American Elderly*, New York: Springer, 1988.

Jacobs, Bruce, *Targeting Benefits for the Elderly: The Public Debate*, New York: Ford Foundation, 1990.

Jacobs, Philip, *The Economics of Health and Medical Care* (3rd ed.), Rockville, MD: Aspen, 1991.

Jacobs, Ruth H., and Hess, Beth B., "Panther Power: Symbol and Substance," *Long Term Care and Health Services Administration Quarterly* (Fall 1978): 238-244.

Jacobson, Solomon G., "Equity in the Use of Public Benefits by Minority Elderly," in Ron C. Manuel (ed.), *Minority Aging: Sociological and Social Psychological Issues*, Westport, CT: Greenwood, 1982, pp. 161-170.

Jacques, Elliot, "Death and Midlife Crisis," *International Journal of Psychoanalysis* (1965), 46: 502-514.

Johnson, Barbara B., "The Changing Role of Women and Social Security Reform," *Social Work* (1987), 32(4): 341-345.

Johnson, Colleen L., and Grant, Leslie A., *The Nursing Home in American Society*, Baltimore, MD: Johns Hopkins University Press, 1986.

Johnson, T. E., "Increased Life-Span of *Age-1* Mutants in *Caenorhabditis Elegans* and Lower Compertz Rate of Aging," *Science* (1990), 249: 908.

Johnson, W., et al., *Workforce 2000: Work and Workers for the 21st Century*, Indianapolis, IN: Hudson Institute, 1987.

Kalish, Richard A., "The New Ageism and the Failure Models: A Polemic," *The Gerontologist* (1979), 19: 398-402.

Kane, Robert L., and Kane, Rosalie A., *A Will and a Way: What the US Can Learn from Canada About Caring for the Elderly*, New York: Columbia University Press, 1985.

Kane, Rosalie and Caplan, Arthur (eds.), *Ethical Conflicts in the Management of Home Care*, New York: Springer, 1992.

Kane, Rosalie A., and Kane, Robert L., *Assessing the Elderly: A Practical Guide to Measurement*, Lexington, MA: D. C. Heath, 1981.

Kane, Rosalie A., and Kane, Robert L., *Long-Term Care: Principles, Programs and Policies*, New York: Springer, 1987.

Kaplan, Max, *Leisure: Lifestyle and Lifespan*, Philadelphia, PA: Saunders, 1979.

Kassner, Enid, "The Older Americans Act: Should Participants Share in the Cost of Services?" *Journal of Aging & Social Policy* (1992), 4(1-2): 51-71.

Kastenbaum, Robert, "Time Course and Time Perspective in Later Life," in C. Eisdorfer (ed.), *Annual Review of Gerontology and Geriatrics* (Vol. 3), New York: Springer, 1983, pp. 80-102.

Kastenbaum, Robert, and Candy, S. E., "The Four Percent Fallacy: A Methodological and Empirical Critique of Extended Care Facility Population Statistics," *International Journal of Aging and Human Development* (1973), 4: 15-21.

Katz, S., and Akpom, C. A., "A Measure of Primary Socio-Biological Functions," *International Journal of Health Services* (1976), 6: 493-507.

Katz, S., et al., "Studies of Illness in the Aged: The Index of ADL: A Standardized Measure of Biological and Psychosocial Function," *Journal of the American Medical Association* (1963), 185: 914-919.

Kaufman, Sharon R., *The Ageless Self: Sources of Meaning in Later Life*, Madison: University of Wisconsin Press, 1986.

Kay, M. M. B., and Makinodan, T. (eds.), *Handbook of Immunology in Aging*, Boca Raton, FL: CRC Press, 1981.

Kemper, P., "Case Management Agency Systems of Administering Long-term Care: Evidence from the Channeling Demonstration," *The Gerontologist* (1990), 30 (6), 817-824.

Kent, Christina, "Medicaid: End It or Mend It?" *Medicine & Health Perspectives* (December 21, 1992): 2.

Kieffer, Jarold A., *Gaining the Dividends of Longer Life: New Roles for Older Workers*, Boulder, CO: Westview, 1983.

Kim, K. C., Kim, S., and Hurh, W. M., "Filial Piety and Intergenerational Relationship in Korean Immigrant Families," *International Journal of Aging and Human Development* (1991), 33: 233-245.

Kleemeier, Robert W. (ed.), *Aging and Leisure*, New York: Columbia University Press, 1961.

Kleiler, Frank M., *Can We Afford Early Retirement?* Baltimore, MD: Johns Hopkins University Press, 1978.

Klein, S. M., *In-Home Respite Care for Older Adults: A Guide for Program Planners, Administrators and Clinicians*, Springfield, IL: Charles C Thomas, 1986.

Koenig, Harold G., Kvale, James N., and Ferrel, Carolyn, "Religion and Well-Being in Later Life," *The Gerontologist* (1988), 28(1): 18-28.

Koff, Theodore, *Long-Term Care: An Approach to Serving the Frail Elderly*, Boston: Little, Brown, 1982.

Koh, James, and Bell, William, "Korean Elders in the United States: Intergenerational Relations and Living Arrangements," *The Gerontologist* (1987), 27(1): 66-71.

Kohl, Marvin, *Beneficent Euthanasia*, Buffalo, NY: Prometheus, 1975.

Kohli, Martin, "The World We Forgot: An Historical Review of the Life Course," in Victor Marshall (ed.), *Later Life: The Social Psychology of Aging*, Beverly Hills, CA: Sage, 1986, pp. 207-303.

Kohli, Martin, "Retirement and the Moral Economy: An Historical Interpretation of the German Case," *Journal of Aging Studies* (1987), 1: 125-144.

Kolata, Gina, "New Views on Life Spans Alter Forecasts on Elderly," *The New York Times* (November 16, 1992): A-1, A-15.

Kopac, C., "Bring Together the Young and Old with Intergenerational Day Care," *Pediatric Nursing* (1987), 13(4): 227-229.

Koretz, Gene, "The Economy Throws a Shadow on the Golden Years," *Business Week* (August 17, 1992): 22.

Kotlikoff, Lawrence, *Generational Accounting*, New York: Basic Books, 1992.

Kotre, John, *Outliving the Self: Generativity and the Interpretation of Lives*, Baltimore, MD: Johns Hopkins University Press, 1984.

Krout, John, *Senior Centers in America*, New York: Greenwood, 1989.

Kubler-Ross, Elisabeth, *On Death and Dying*, New York: Macmillan, 1969.

Kutza, Elizabeth A., *The Benefits of Old Age*, Chicago: University of Chicago Press, 1981.

Lamm, Richard D., "Intergenerational Equity in an Age of Limits: Confessions of a Prodigal Parent," in Gerald Winslow and James Walters (eds.), *Facing Limits: Ethics & Health Care for the Elderly*, Boulder, CO: Westview Press, 1993, 15-28.

Lammers, W., and Klingman, D. "Family Responsibility Laws and State Politics: Empirical Patterns and Policy Implications," *Journal of Applied Gerontology* (July 1986), 5: 5-25.

Langbein, John, "The Inheritance Revolution," *The Public Interest* (Winter 1991).

LaPuma, John, Orentlicher, David, and Moss, Robert J., "Advance Directives on Admission: Clinical Implications and Analysis of the Patient

Self-Determination Act of 1990," *Journal of the American Medical Association* (July 17, 1991), 266: 404.

Larson, R., "Thirty Years of Research on the Subjective Well-Being of Older Americans," *Journal of Gerontology* (1978), 33: 109-129.

Laslett, Peter, *The World We Have Lost*, New York: Scribner, 1971 (1965).

Laslett, Peter, *Household and Family in Past Time*, Cambridge: Cambridge University Press, 1972.

Laslett, Peter, *The Emergence of the Third Age: A Fresh Map of Life*, Cambridge, MA: Harvard University Press, 1991.

Lawton, M. Powell, *Environment and Aging*, Monterey, CA: Brooks/Cole, 1980.

Lehman, Harvey, "More About Age and Achievement," *The Gerontologist* (1962), 2: 141-148.

Leibold, K., "Employer-Sponsored On-Site Intergenerational Daycare," *Generations* (1989), 13(3): 33-34.

Leonesio, Michael V., "Effects of the Social Security Earnings Test on the Labor-Market Activity of Older Americans: A Review of the Evidence," *Social Security Bulletin* (May 1990), 53: 2-21.

Levin, J., and Levin, W. C., *Ageism: Prejudice and Discrimination Against the Elderly*, Belmont, CA: Wadsworth, 1980.

Levine, Martin L., *Age Discrimination and the Mandatory Retirement Controversy*, Baltimore, MD: Johns Hopkins University Press, 1989.

Levinson, Daniel J., *The Seasons of a Man's Life*, New York: Knopf, 1978.

Lewis, C. N., "Reminiscing and Self-Concept in Old Age," *Journal of Gerontology* (1971), 26: 240-243.

Lewis, Myrna, and Butler, Robert, "Why Is Women's Lib Ignoring the Older Women?" *International Journal of Aging and Human Development* (1972), 3(3): 223-231.

Light, Paul, *Artful Work: The Politics of Social Security Reform*, New York: Random House, 1985.

Litwak, Eugene, *Helping the Elderly: The Complementary Roles of Informal Networks and Formal Systems*, New York: Guilford, 1985.

Liu, Korbin, and Manton, Kenneth, "Nursing Home Length of Stay and Spenddown in Connecticut, 1977-1986," *The Gerontologist* (April 1991), 31(2): 165-173.

Locke, S. "Neurological Disorders of the Elderly," in William Reichel (ed.), *Clinical Aspects of Aging*, Baltimore, MD: Williams and Wilkins, 1983.

Longino, Charles F., and Kart, C. S., "Explicating Activity Theory: A Formal Replication," *Journal of Gerontology* (1982), 37: 713-722.

Lopata, Helena, *Women as Widows: Support Systems*, New York: Elsevier, 1979.

Lopez, C., and Aguilera, E., *On the Sidelines: Hispanic Elderly and the Continuum of Care*, Washington, DC: National Council of La Raza, 1991.

Louis, A. M. "America's Centimillionaires," *Fortune* (1968), 77:152-157.

Lowenthal, Marjorie F., and Chiriboga, David, "Transitions to the Empty Nest: Crisis, Change or Relief?" *Archives of General Psychiatry* (1972), 26: 8-14.

Lubitz, J., and Prihoda, R., "The Use and Costs of Medicare Services in the Last Two Years of Life," *Health Care Financing Review* (1984), 5(3): 117-131.

Ludwig, Frederic, *Lifespan Extension: Consequences and Open Questions*, New York: Springer, 1991.

Mace, Nancy, and Rabins, Peter, *The 36-Hour Day*, Baltimore, MD: Johns Hopkins University Press, 1981.

Maldonado, David, Jr., "Aging in the Chicano Context," in D. E. Gelfand and A. J. Kutzik (eds.), *Ethnicity and Aging: Theory, Research and Policy*, New York: Springer, 1979, pp. 175-183.

Mannheim, Karl, "The Problem of Generations," in K. Mannheim, *Essays in the Sociology of Knowledge*, New York: Oxford University Press, 1952.

Marbach, G., *Job Redesign for Older Workers*, Paris: OECD, 1968.

Markides, K. S., Liang, J., and Jackson, J. S., "Race, Ethnicity, and Aging: Conceptual and Methodological Issues," in *Handbook of Aging and the Social Sciences*, Orlando, FL: Academic Press, 1990, pp. 112-129.

Markides, K. S., and Mindel, C. H., *Aging and Ethnicity*, Newbury Park, CA: Sage, 1987.

Marmor, Theodore, *The Politics of Medicare*, Chicago: Aldine, 1973.

Marmor, Theodore, and Mashaw, J. L. (eds.), *Social Security: Beyond the Rhetoric of Crisis*, Princeton, NJ: Princeton University Press, 1988.

Marris, P., *Loss and Change*, Garden City, NY: Doubleday, 1975.

Martz, Sandra Haldeman (ed.), *When I Am an Old Woman, I Shall Wear Purple*, Watsonville, CA: Papier-Mache, 1987.

Masoro, E. J. (ed.), *Handbook of the Physiology of Aging*, Boca Raton, FL: CRC Press, 1981.

McConnell, Stephen R., and Usher, Carolyn E., *Intergenerational House-Sharing: A Research Report and Resource Manual*, Lexington, MA: D. C. Heath, 1980.

McGoldrick, Ann, and Copper, Cary, *Early Retirement*, Chichester, UK: Gower, 1989.

Mcgoon, Dwight C., *Parkinson's Handbook*, New York: Norton, 1990.

McIntosh, John L., and Osgood, Nancy J., *Suicide and the Elderly*, Westport, CT: Greenwood, 1986.

McMahon, A. W., and Rhudick, P. J., "Reminiscing in the Aged: An Adaptational Response," in S. Levin and R. J. Kahana (eds.), *Psychodynamic Studies on Aging: Creativity, Reminiscing, and Dying*, New York: International Universities Press, 1967.

Meacham, J. A. (1990). "The Loss of Wisdom," in R. J. Sternberg (ed.), *Wisdom: Its Nature, Origin, and Development*, Cambridge: Cambridge University Press, pp. 160-177.

Mechanic, David, "Cost Containment and the Quality of Medical Care: Rationing Strategies in an Era of Constrained Resources," *Millbank Memorial Fund Quarterly* (1985), 63: 453-475.

Medawar, Peter B., *Aging: An Unsolved Problem of Biology*, London: H. K. Lewis, 1952.

Medvedev, Z. A., "Repetition of Molecular-Genetic Information as a Possible Factor in Evolutionary Change of Life-Span," *Experimental Gerontology* (1972), 7: 227-234.

Melvin, C., and Ryder, K., "Among Friends: An Intergenerational Program for Alzheimer's Patients," *Caring* (1989), 8(8): 26-28.

Meyrowitz, Joshua, *No Sense of Place: The Impact of Electronic Media on Social Behavior*, New York: Oxford University Press, 1985.

Miller, Marv, *Suicide After Sixty: The Final Alternative*, New York: Springer, 1979.

Minkler, Meredith, and Estes, Carroll (eds.), *Readings in the Political Economy of Aging*, Farmingdale, NY: Baywood, 1984.

Minkler, Meredith, and Stone, R., "The Feminization of Poverty and Older Women," *The Gerontologist* (1985), 25: 351-357.

Minois, Georges, *History of Old Age: From Antiquity to the Renaissance* (trans. Sarah Hanbury Tenison), Chicago: University of Chicago Press, 1989.

Moberg, David, "Religion and the Aging Family" [Special Issue], *Family Coordinator* (1972) 21(1): 47-60.

Montgomery, Rhonda, "Respite Services for Family Caregivers," in M. D. Petersen and D. L. White, *Health Care of the Elderly: An Information Sourcebook*, Newbury Park, CA: Sage, 1989.

Montgomery, Rhonda J. V. (ed.) [Special Issue] "The Age Discrimination in Employment Act (ADEA)," *Research in Aging* (1991), 13(4): 411-486.

Moody, Harry R., *Abundance of Life: Human Development Policies for an Aging Society*, New York: Columbia University Press, 1988a.

Moody, Harry R., "Toward a Critical Gerontology: The Contribution of the Humanities to Theories of Aging," in James Birren and Vern Bengtson (eds.), *Emergent Theories of Aging*, New York: 1988b, pp. 19-40.

Moody, Harry R., "The Politics of Entitlement and the Politics of Productivity," in Scott A. Bass, Elizabeth A. Kutza, and Fernando Torres-Gil (eds.), *Diversity in Aging*, Glenview, IL: Scott, Foresman, 1990, pp. 129-149.

Morgan, Nicole, *Nowhere to Go?* Chichester, UK: Gower, 1981.

Morrison, M., and Jedriewski, M. K., "Retirement Planning: Everybody Benefits," *Personnel Administrator* (January, 1988), 74-80.

Moskowitz, Roland, and Haug, Marie, *Arthritis and the Elderly*, New York: Springer, 1985.

Moynihan, Daniel P., *Family and Nation*, San Diego: Harcourt Brace Jovanovich, 1986.

Munnell, Alicia H. (ed.), *Retirement and Public Policy*, Dubuque, IA: Kendall/Hunt, 1991.

Munnell, Alicia H., and Blais, L. E., "Do We Want Larger Social Security Surpluses?" *New England Economic Review* (1984), 5: 5-21.

Murdock, Steve H., and Schwartz, Donald F., "Family Structure and the Use of Agency Services: An Examination of Patterns Among Elderly Native Americans," *The Gerontologist* (1978), 18: 475-481.

Myers, Robert J., *Social Security* (3rd ed.), Homewood, IL: Irwin, 1985.

Nasar, Sylvia, "The Spend-Now, Tax-Later Orgy," *The New York Times* (January 14, 1993): D-2.

National Center for Health Statistics, *Health—United States 1982*, Washington, DC: Government Printing Office, 1982.

National Center for Health Statistics, "Life Tables," *Vital Statistics of the United States, 1987*, Vol. 2, Section 6, Washington, DC: Government Printing Office, February, 1990a.

National Center for Health Statistics, *Health—United States 1989*, DHHS Pub. No. (PHS)90-1232, Washington, DC: Government Printing Office, March, 1990b.

National Center for Health Statistics, "Current Estimates from the National Health Interview Survey, 1989," *Vital and Health Statistics,* Series 10, No. 176, Washington, DC: Government Printing Office, October, 1990c.

National Center for Health Statistics, "Advanced Report of Final Mortality Statistics, 1988," *Monthly Vital Statistics Report* (November 28, 1990d), 39(7), Supplement.

National Institute on Aging, "Age Page: Can Life Be Extended?" [Public Information Document], Washington, DC, n.d.

Naylor, C.D., "A Different View of Queues in Ontario," *Health Affairs* (1991), 10(3): 111-128.

Nelson, G., "Social Class and Public Policy for the Elderly," *Social Service Review* (1982), 56: 85-107.

Nelson, Gary M., "Tax Expenditures for the Elderly," *The Gerontologist* (1983), 23: 471-478.

Neugarten, Bernice (ed.), *Age or Need? Public Policies for Older People*, Beverly Hills, CA: Sage, 1983.

Neugarten, Bernice L., *Middle Age and Aging*, Chicago: University of Chicago Press, 1968.

Neugarten, B. L., et al. (eds.), *Personality in Middle and Late Life*, New York: Atherton, 1964.

Newcomer, Robert J., Lawton, M. Powell, and Byerts, Thomas O. (eds.), *Housing an Aging Society*, New York: Van Nostrand Reinhold, 1986.

Newman, Katherine S., *Declining Fortunes: The Withering of the American Dream*, New York: Basic Books, 1993.

Newman, S., Lyons, C., and Onawola, R., "The Development of an Intergenerational Service-Learning Program at a Nursing Home," *The Gerontologist* (1984), 25(2): 130-133.

O'Grady-LeShane, Regina, "Older Women and Poverty," *Social Work* (September 1990), 35: 422-424.

Olshansky, S., Carnes, B., and Cassel, C., "In Search of Methuselah: Estimating the Upper Limits to Longevity," *Science* (1990), 250: 634-640.

Olson, Laura K., *The Political Economy of Aging*, New York: Columbia University Press, 1982.

O'Rand, A. M., and Landerman, L. R., "Women's and Men's Retirement Income Status: Early Family Role Effects," *Research on Aging* (1984), 6(1): 25-44.

Orgel, L. E., "Ageing of Clones of Mammalian Cells," *Nature* (June 22, 1973).

Orwoll, L., and Perlmutter, M. (1990). "The Study of Wise Persons: Integrating a Personality Perspective," in R. J. Sternberg (ed.), *Wisdom: Its Nature, Origin, and Development*, Cambridge: Cambridge University Press, pp. 181-211.

Osgood, Nancy, *Suicide in the Elderly*, Rockville, MD: Aspens Systems Corporation, 1984.

Paffenbarger, Ralph S., *Proceedings of the Conference on the Decline in Coronary Heart Disease Mortality* (NIH Publication No. 79-1610), Washington, DC: National Institutes of Health, 1979.

Palmore, Erdman, *The Honorable Elders*, Durham, NC: Duke University Press, 1975.

Palmore, E. B., Burchett, B. M., Filenbaum, G. G., George, L. K., and Wallman, L. M., *Retirement: Causes and Consequences*, New York: Springer, 1985.

Palmore, E. B., and Manton, K., "Modernization and Status of the Aged: International Correlations," *Journal of Gerontology* (1974), 29: 205-210.

Parnes, Herbert S., et al., *Retirement Among American Men*, Lexington, MA: Lexington, 1985.

"Paying for a Nursing Home," *Consumer Reports* (October 1989), 664-667.

Peacock, W., and Talley, W., "Intergenerational Contact: A Way to Counteract Ageism," *Educational Gerontology* (1984), 10(1-2): 13-24.

Peck, Robert C., "Psychological Development in the Second Half of Life," in B. L. Neugarten, *Middle Age and Aging*, Chicago: University of Chicago Press, 1968.

Peterson, David A., et al. (eds.), *Education and Aging*, Englewood Cliffs, NJ: Prentice Hall, 1986.

Peterson, Peter G., and Howe, Neil, *On Borrowed Time: How the Growth in Entitlement Spending Threatens America's Future*, San Francisco: ICS Press, 1988.

Pfeifer, Susan K., and Sussman, Marvin B. (eds.), *Families: Intergenerational and Generational Connections*, Binghamton, NY: Haworth, 1991.

Pifer, Alan, and Bronte, Lydia (eds.), *Our Aging Society: Paradox and Promise*, New York: Norton, 1986.

Portnow, Jay, *Home Care for the Elderly: A Complete Guide*, New York: McGraw-Hill, 1987.

Post, Stephen, "Filial Morality in an Aging Society," *Journal of Religion & Aging* (1989), 5: 15-30.

Postman, Neil, *The Disappearance of Childhood*, New York: Delacorte, 1982.

Pratt, Henry J., *The Gray Lobby*, Chicago: University of Chicago Press, 1976.

Pratt, Henry J., "The 'Gray Lobby' Revisited," *National Forum* (1982), 62: 31-33.

Preston, Samuel H., "Children and the Elderly in the U.S.," *Scientific American* (1984), 251(6): 44-49.

Putnam, Jackson, *Old Age Politics in California: From Richardson to Reagan*, Stanford, CA: Stanford University Press, 1970.

Quadagno, Jill, *Aging in Early Industrial Society*, New York: Academic Press, 1982.

Quinn, J., "The Economic Status of the Elderly: Beware the Mean," *Review of Income and Wealth* (March 1987): 63-82.

Quinn, J. F., "Retirement Income Rights as a Component of Wealth in the United States," *Review of Income and Wealth* (1985), 31: 223-236.

Quinn, Joseph F., et al., *Passing the Torch: The Influence of Economic Incentives on Work and Retirement*, Kalamazoo, MI: W. E. Upjohn, 1990.

Quinn, J., Segal, J., Raisz, H., and Johnson, C. (eds.), *Coordinating Community Services for the Elderly: The Triage Experience*, New York: Springer, 1982.

Rabushka, A., and Jacobs, B., *Old Folks at Home*, New York: Free Press, 1980.

Rachels, James, *The End of Life: Euthanasia and Morality*, New York: Oxford University Press, 1986.

Radner, D., "Money Incomes of the Aged and Nonaged Family Units," *Social Security Bulletin* (1987), 50(8): 5-21.

Rector, Rebecca, *Continuing Care Retirement Communities and the Life Care Industry: An Annotated Bibliography*, Monticello, IL: Vance Bibliographies, 1988.

Reilly, Thomas W., Clauser, Steven B., and Baugh, David K., "Trends in Medicaid Payments and Utilization, 1975-1989," *Health Care Financing Review* (1990 Annual Supplement).

Reisberg, Barry, *Alzheimer's Disease*, New York: Free Press (Macmillan), 1983.

Rejda, George E., "Reexamination of the Controversial Earnings Test Under the OASDI Program," *Benefits Quarterly* (1990), 6: 25-35.

Relman, Arnold S., "The Trouble with Rationing," *New England Journal of Medicine* (Sept. 27, 1990), 323(13): 911-913.

Rhine, Shirley H., *Managing Older Workers: Company Policies and Attitudes*, New York: Conference Board, 1984.

Riley, M. W., and Foner, A., *Aging and Society: Vol. 3, A Sociology of Age Stratification*, New York: Basic Books, 1972.

Riley, M. W., and Riley, J. W., Jr., "Longevity and Social Structure: The Potential of the Added Years," in A. Pifer and L. Bronte (eds.), *Our Aging Society: Paradox and Promise*, New York: Norton, 1986, pp. 53-77.

Rindfuss, R. R., Swicegood, C. G., and Rosenfeld, R. A., "Disorder in the Life Course: How Common and Does It Matter?" *American Sociological Review* (1987), 52: 785-801.

Rivlin, Alice, and Wiener, Joshua, *Caring for the Disabled Elderly: Who Will Pay?* Washington, DC: Brookings Institution, 1988.

Robbins, Aldona, and Robbins, Gary, *Paying People Not to Work: The Economic Cost of the Social Security Retirement Earnings Limit*, Dallas, TX: National Center for Policy Analysis, 1989.

Rodin, J., and Langer, E., "Aging Labels: The Decline of Control and the Fall of Self-Esteem," *Journal of Social Issues* (1980), 36: 12-29.

Rodin, J., Timko, C., and Harris, S., "The Construct of Control: Biological and Psychosocial Correlates," in M. P. Lawton and G. Maddox (eds.), *Annual Review of Gerontology and Geriatrics* (Vol. 5), New York: Springer, 1985, pp. 3-55.

Rose, A. M., "The Subculture of Aging: A Framework for Research in Social Gerontology," in A. M. Rose and W. A. Peterson (eds.), *Older People and Their Social World*, Philadelphia: F. A. Davis, 1965, pp. 3-16.

Rosenbaum, W. A., and Button, J. W., "Is There a Gray Peril? Retirement Politics in Florida," *The Gerontologist* (1989), 29: 300-306.

Rosenmayr, L. *Die Spaete Freiheit* [Late Freedom], Vienna: Severin, 1984.

Rosenthal, C. J., "Kinkeeping in the Familial Division of Labor," *Journal of Marriage and the Family* (1985), 47: 965-974.

Rosow, Irving, *Social Integration of the Aged*, New York: Free Press, 1967.

Ross, Jennie-Keith, *Old People, New Lives: Community Creation in a Retirement Residence*, University of Chicago Press, 1982 (1977).

Rossi, Alice (ed.), *Gender and the Life Course*, New York: Aldine, 1985.

Roth, J. A., "Timetables and the Lifecourse in Post-industrial Society," in D. W. Plath (ed.), *Work and the Lifecourse in Japan*, Albany: State University of New York, 1983, pp. 248-260.

Rowe, John W., and Kahn, R. L., "Human Aging: Usual and Successful," *Science* (1987), 237: 143-149.

Ryder, Norman, "The Cohort as a Concept in the Study of Social Change," *American Sociological Review* (1965), 30: 843-861.

Sacher, George A., "Longevity, Aging and Death: An Evolutionary Perspective," *The Gerontologist* (1978), 18: 112-119.

Salthouse, T. A., "Effects of Age and Skill in Typing," *Journal of Experimental Psychology: General* (1984), 113: 345-371.

Salthouse, T. A., "Speed of Behavior and the Implications for Cognition," in J. E. Birren and K. W. Schaie (eds.), *Handbook of the Psychology of Aging* (2nd ed.), New York: Van Nostrand Reinhold, 1985a, pp. 400-426.

Salthouse, T. A., *A Theory of Cognitive Aging*, Amsterdam: North-Holland, 1985b.

Sattler, J. M., "Age Effects on Wechsler Adult Intelligence Scale-Revised Tests," *Journal of Consulting and Clinical Psychology* (1982), 50: 785-786.

Sauvy, Alfred, *Zero Growth*, New York: Praeger, 1976.

Schaie, K. W., "Midlife Influences upon Intellectual Functioning in Old Age," *International Journal of Behavioral Development* (1984), 7: 463-478.

Schaie, K. W., and Willis, S. L., "Can Intelligence Decline in the Elderly Be Reversed?" *Developmental Psychology* (1987), 22: 223-232.

Schermerhorn, Richard A., *Comparative Ethnic Relations: A Framework for Theory and Research*, Chicago: University of Chicago Press, 1970.

Schmahl, W. (ed.), *Redefining the Process of Retirement*, New York: Springer-Verlag, 1989.

Schneider, E., *The Genetics of Aging*, New York: Plenum, 1978.

Schneider, Edward L., and Guralnik, Jack, "The Aging of America: Impact on Health Care Costs," *Journal of the American Medical Association* (May 2, 1990), 263(17): 2335-2340.

Schnore, M., *Retirement: Bane or Blessing*, Atlantic Highlands, NJ: Humanities Press, 1985.

Scholen, K., and Chen, Y. P., *Unlocking Home Equity for the Elderly*, Cambridge, MA: Ballinger, 1980.

Schooler, C., and Schaie, K. W. (eds.), *Cognitive Functioning and Social Structure over the Life Course*, Norwood, NJ: Ablex, 1987.

Schor, Juliet, *The Overworked American*, New York: Basic Books, 1991.

Schorr, Alvin L., *Filial Responsibility in the Modern American Family*, Washington, DC: Social Security Administration, 1961.

Schulz, James H., *The Economics of Aging* (4th ed.), Dover, MA: Auburn House, 1988.

Schurenberg, Eric, and Luciano, Lani, "The Empire Called AARP," *Money* (October 1988), 17: 120-146.

Schwarz, John, *America's Hidden Success*, New York: Norton, 1983.

Scitovsky, Anne, "The High Cost of Dying: What Do the Data Show?" *Millbank Memorial Fund Quarterly* (Fall 1984), 62: 591-608.

Seligman, Martin E. P., *Helplessness: On Depression, Development and Death*, San Francisco: Freeman, 1975.

Seltzer, M. M., and Troll, L. E., "Conflicting Public Attitudes Toward Filial Responsibility," *Generations* (1982), 7(2): 26-27, 40.

Shanas, Ethel, "The Family as a Social Support System in Old Age," *The Gerontologist* (1979), 19: 169-174.

Shanas, Ethel, "Older People and Their Families: The New Pioneers," *Journal of Marriage and the Family* (1980), 42(9): 9-15.

Shaver, Sheila, "Aging, the Baby Boom, and the Crisis in Retirement Income," *The Gerontologist* (December 1991), 31: 841-843.

Shaw, David L., and Gordon, Judith B., "Social Network Analysis and Intervention with the Elderly," *The Gerontologist* (1980), 20: 463-467.

Sheppard, Harold, "The 'New' Early Retirement: Europe and the United States," in Irving Bluestone, Rhonda Montgomery, and John Owen (eds.), *The Aging of the American Work Force*, Detroit: Wayne State University Press, 1990, pp. 158-178.

Sheppard, Harold L., and Rix, Sara E., *The Graying of Working America: The Coming Crisis of Retirement Age Policy*, New York: Free Press, 1977.

Sherman, Sanford, "Brave New Darwinian Workplace," *Fortune* (January 25, 1993): 51.

Shock, Nathan, "The Physiology of Aging," *Scientific American* (1962), 206: 100-110.

Shock, Nathan, Greulich, R. C., Cosa, P. T., Jr., Andres, R., Lakatta, E. G., Arenberg, D., and Tobin, J. D., *Normal Human Aging: The Baltimore Longitudinal Study of Aging*, Washington, DC: Government Printing Office, 1984.

Silverman, Phyllis, *Widow-to-Widow*, New York: Springer, 1986.

Simmons, Leo W., *The Role of the Aged in Primitive Societies*, New Haven, CT: Yale University Press, 1945.

Sloane, Leonard, "Policies for Covering Cost of Long-Term Care," *The New York Times* (January 2, 1992): 36.

Smeeding, Timothy M., "Children and Poverty: How U.S. Stands," *Forum for Applied Research and Public Policy* (Summer 1990), 5(2): 65-70.

Smolensky, E., Danziger, S., and Gottschalk, P., "The Declining Significance of Age in the United States: Trends in the Well-Being of Children and the Elderly Since 1939," in J. L. Palmer, T. Smeeding, and B. Torrey (eds.), *The Vulnerable*, Washington, DC: Urban Institute Press, 1988, pp. 29-54.

Solomon, M., et al., "Decisions Near the End of Life: Professional Views on Life-Sustaining Treatments," *American Journal of Public Health* (January 1993): 14-23.

Sommers, K., "Generation Mix: Child Care in the Nursing Home," *Nursing Homes* (1985), 34(4): 27-30.

Spiegel, Allen D., *Medicaid Experience*, Rockville, MD: Aspen Systems, 1979.

Springer, D., and Brubaker, T. H., *Family Caregivers and Dependent Elderly: Managing Stress and Maximizing Independence*, Beverly Hills, CA: Sage, 1984.

Sprott, Richard L., and Roth, George S., "Biomarkers of Aging: Can We Predict Individual Life Span?" *Generations* (1992), 16(4): 11-14.

Stagner, R., "Aging in Industry," in James Birren and K. Warner Schaie (eds.), *Handbook of the Psychology of Aging* (2nd ed.), New York: Van Nostrand Reinhold, 1985, pp. 789-817.

Stanford, E. Percil, Happersett, Catherine, J., and Morton, Deborah, J., "Early Retirement and Functional Impairment from a Multi-ethnic Perspective," *Research on Aging* (March 1991), 13: 5-38.

Stanley, Jean F., Pye, David, and MacGregor, Andrew, "Comparison of Doubling Numbers Attained by Cultured Animal Cells with Life Span of Species," *Nature* (May 8, 1975).

Starr, J. M., "Toward a Social Phenomenology of Aging: Studying the Self Process in Biographical Work," *International Journal of Aging and Human Development* (1982-1983), 16: 255-270.

Stearns, Peter N. (ed.), *Old Age in Pre-industrial Societies*, New York: Holmes and Meier, 1982.

Stein, Bruno, "Pay-as-You-Go, Partial Prefunding, and Full Funding of American Social Security," *History of Political Economy* (Spring 1991), 23: 79-83.

Stephan, Paula E., and Levin, Sharon, G., *Striking the Mother Lode in Science: The Importance of Age, Place and Time*, New York: Oxford University Press, 1992.

Stephens, S., and Christianson, J., *Informal Care of the Elderly*, Lexington, MA: D. C. Heath, 1986.

Stevens, Robert, and Stevens, Rosemary, *Welfare Medicine in America: A Study of Medicaid*, New York: Free Press, 1974.

Stewart, Alva W., *Social Security: Its Development from Roosevelt to Reagan*, Monticello, IL: Vance Bibliographies, 1982.

Stoller, Eleanor P., and Gibson, Rose C., *Worlds of Difference: Inequality in the Aging Experience*, Thousand Oaks, CA: Pine Forge, 1994.

Stone, R., Cafferata, G., and Sangl, J., "Caregivers of the Frail Elderly: A National Profile," *The Gerontologist* (1987), 27: 616-626.

Stone, R. I., and Kemper, P., "Spouses and Children of Disabled Elders: How Large a Constituency for Long-Term Reform?" *Millbank Quarterly* (1989), 67: 485-506.

Stone, Robyn, "Familial Obligation: Issues for the Nineties," *Generations* (Summer-Fall 1991), 15(3): 47-50.

Strehler, B. L., *Time, Cells and Aging* (2nd ed.), New York: Academic Press, 1977.

Streib, G. F., and Bourg, C. F., "Age Stratification Theory, Inequality, and Social Change," in R. F. Thomason (ed.), *Comparative Social Research*, Greenwich, CT: JAI, 1984.

Streib, Gordon, "Are the Aged a Minority Group?" in Alvin Gouldner and S. Miller (ed.), *Applied Sociology*, New York: Free Press, 1965.

Streib, Gordon, "Socioeconomic Strata," in Erdman Palmore (ed.), *Handbook on the Aged in the United States*, Westport, CT: Greenwood, 1984, pp. 77-92.

Streib, Gordon, "Social Stratification and Aging," in Robert H. Binstock and Ethel Shanas (eds.), *Handbook of Aging and the Social Sciences*, New York: Van Nostrand Reinhold, 1985, pp. 339-368.

Streib, Gordon, Folts, W. Edward, and Hilker, Mary, *Old Homes-New Families: Shared Living for the Elderly*, New York: Columbia University Press, 1984.

Streib, Gordon F., and Schneider, C., *Retirement in American Society*, Ithaca, NY: Cornell University Press, 1971.

Szilard, Leo, "On the Nature of the Aging Process," *Proceedings of the National Academy of Sciences USA* (1959), 45: 30.

Taeuber, Cynthia, "Diversity: The Dramatic Reality," in Scott A. Bass, Elizabeth A. Kutza, and Fernando Torres-Gil (eds.), *Diversity in Aging*, Glenview, IL: Scott, Foresman, 1990, pp. 1-45.

Teague, Michael L., and MacNeil, Richard D., *Aging and Leisure: Vitality in Later Life* (2nd ed.), Dubuque, IA: Brown and Benchmark, 1992.

Terkel, Studs, *Working*, New York: Ballantine, 1985.

Thone, R. R., *Women and Aging: Celebrating Ourselves*, New York: Haworth, 1992.

Thursz, D., Liederman, D., and Shorr, L., "Generations Uniting," *Perspective on Aging* (1989), 18(1): 3-23.

Tierce, J., and Seelback, W., "Elders as School Volunteers," *Educational Gerontology* (1987), 13: 33-41.

Tilly, J., and Brunner, D., *Medicaid Eligibility and Its Effects on the Elderly*, Washington, DC: AARP, 1987.

Torres-Gil, F., "Retirement Issues That Affect Minorities," in H. Dennis (ed.), *Retirement Preparation*, Lexington, MA: Lexington, 1984.

Torres-Gil, F. M., and Hyde, J. C., "The Impact of Minorities on Long-Term Care Policy in California," in P. Liebig and W. Lammers (eds.), *California Policy Choices for Long-Term Care*, Los Angeles: University of Southern California, 1990, pp. 31-52.

Torres-Gil, Fernando, *The New Aging: Politics and Change in America*, New York: Auburn House, 1992.

Uchitelle, Louis, "Stanching the Loss of Good Jobs," *The New York Times* (January 31, 1993): 1-3.

Uhlenberg, Peter, Cooney, Teresa, and Boyd, Robert, "Divorce for Women After Midlife," *Journal of Gerontology* (1990), 45(1): S3-S11.

Underwood, D., "Toward Self-Reliance in Retirement Planning," *Harvard Business Review* (May-June 1984): 18-20.

U.S. Bureau of the Census, "Estimates of the Population of the United States, by Single Years of Age, Color, and Sex: 1900 to 1959," *Current Population Reports*, Series P-25, No. 311, Washington, DC: Government Printing Office, July, 1965.

U.S. Bureau of the Census, "Educational Attainment in the United States: March 1981 and 1980," *Current Population Reports* Series P-20, No. 390, Washington, DC: Government Printing Office, August, 1984.

U.S. Bureau of the Census, "America in Transition: An Aging Society," by Cynthia Taueber, *Current Population Reports,* Series P-23, No. 128, Washington, DC: Government Printing Office, September, 1988a.

U.S. Bureau of the Census, "Poverty in the United States: 1986," *Current Population Reports,* Series P-60, No. 160, Washington, DC: Government Printing Office, 1988b.

U.S. Bureau of the Census, "Projections of the Population of the United States, by Age, Sex, and Race: 1988 to 2080," by Gregory Spencer,

Current Population Reports, Series P-25, No. 1018, Washington, DC: Government Printing Office, January, 1989.

U.S. Bureau of the Census, "Marital Status and Living Arrangements: March 1989," *Current Population Reports*, Series P-20, No. 445, Washington, DC: Government Printing Office, June, 1990a.

U.S. Bureau of the Census, "Money Income and Poverty Status in the United States: 1989," *Current Population Reports*, Series P-60, No. 168, Washington, DC: Government Printing Office, September, 1990b.

U.S. Bureau of the Census, "Household Wealth and Asset Ownership, 1988," *Current Population Reports*, Series P-70, No. 22, Washington, DC: Government Printing Office, December, 1990c.

U.S. Commerce Department, *1993 U.S. Industrial Outlook*, Washington, DC: Author, 1993.

U.S. Congress, House Select Committee on Aging, *Exploding the Myths: Caregiving in America,* Washington, DC: Government Printing Office, January, 1987.

U.S. Congress, House Task Force on Social Security and Women, *Inequities Toward Women in the Social Security System*, Washington, DC: Government Printing Office, 1983.

U.S. Congress, House Task Force on Social Security and Women, *Earnings Sharing Implementation Plan*, Washington, DC: Government Printing Office, 1984.

U.S. Congressional Budget Office, *Older Americans Reports*, Washington, DC: Author, April 29, 1988.

U.S. Department of Labor, Bureau of Labor Statistics, *Handbook of Labor Statistics*, Bulletin 2217, Washington, DC: Author, June, 1985.

U.S. Department of Labor, Bureau of Labor Statistics, *Employment and Earnings* (Vol. 33, No. 1), Washington, DC: Author, January, 1986a.

U.S. Department of Labor, Bureau of Labor Statistics, "Worklife Estimates: Effects of Race and Education," Bulletin 2254, February, 1986b.

U.S. Department of Labor, Bureau of Labor Statistics, *Employment and Earnings* (Vol. 37, No. 1), Washington, DC: Author, January, 1990.

U.S. General Accounting Office, *Social Security: Past Projections and Future Financing Concerns*, Washington, DC: Author, 1986.

U.S. General Accounting Office, *Long-Term Care Insurance: Risks to Insurance Should Be Reduced*, Washington, DC: Author, December, 1991.

U.S. Office of Technology Assessment, *Life Sustaining Technologies and the Elderly*, Washington, DC: Government Printing Office, 1987.

U.S. Senate, Special Committee on Aging, *Aging America: Trends and Projections*, Washington, DC: Author, 1991.

Vaillant, George, *Adaptation to Life*, Boston: Little, Brown, 1977.
Van Gennep, A., *Rites of Passage*, Chicago: University of Chicago Press, 1960.

Van Tassel, David D., and Meyer, J. E. W., *U.S. Aging Policy Interest Groups*, Westport, CT: Greenwood, 1992.

Ventura-Merkel, C., and Friedman, M., "Helping At-Risk Youth Through Intergenerational Programming," *Children Today* (1988), 17(1): 10-13.

Verbrugge, L., Lepkowski, J., and Imanaka, Y., "Comorbidity and Its Impact on Disability," *Millbank Quarterly* (1989), 67(3-4): 450-484.

Villers Foundation, *On the Other Side of Easy Street*, Washington, DC: Author, 1987.

Vladeck, Bruce, *Unloving Care: The Nursing Home Tragedy*, New York: Basic Books, 1980.

Waldo, Daniel R., Sonnefeld, Sally T., McKusick, David R., and Arnett, Ross H., III, "Health Expenditures by Age Group, 1977 and 1987," *Health Care Financing Review* (Summer 1989), 10(4).

Walford, Roy, *Maximum Life Span*, New York: Norton, 1983.

Walford, Roy, *The 120 Year Diet: How to Double Your Vital Years*, New York: Pocket Books, 1986.

Walls, C. T., and Zarit, S. H., "Informal Support from Black Churches and the Well-Being of Elderly Blacks," *The Gerontologist* (1991), 31(4): 490-495.

Watkins, S. C., Menken, J. A., and Bongaarts, J., "Demographic Foundations of Family Change," *American Sociological Review* (1987), 52: 346-358.

Watson, J. D., *Recombinant DNA* (2nd ed.), New York: Freeman, 1992.

Weibel-Orlando, Joan, "Grandparenting Styles: Native American Perspectives," in J. Sokolovsky (ed.), *The Cultural Context of Aging: Worldwide Perspectives*, New York: Bergin and Garvey, 1990.

Weindruch, R., and Walford, R. L., *The Retardation of Aging and Disease by Dietary Restriction*, Springfield, IL: Charles C Thomas, 1988.

Weinstein, M. H., "The Changing Picture in Retiree Economics" (Metropolitan Life Insurance), *Statistical Bulletin* (July-September 1988), 69: 7.

Weiss, J. C., *The "Feeling Great!" Wellness Program for Older Adults*, Binghamton, NY: Haworth, 1988.

Weitzman, Lenore, *The Divorce Revolution: The Unexpected Social and Economic Consequences for Women and Children in America*, New York: Free Press, 1985.

Welch, H. Gilbert, "Comparing Apples and Oranges: Does Cost-Effectiveness Analysis Deal Fairly with the Old and Young?" *The Gerontologist* (June 1991), 31(3): 332-336.

Wennberg, Robert, *Terminal Choices: Euthanasia, Suicide, and the Right to Die*, Grand Rapids, MI: Erdmans, 1989.

Whitbourne, Susan K., "Test Anxiety in Elderly and Young Adults," *International Journal of Aging and Human Development* (1976), 7: 201-210.

White, L., et al., "Geriatric Epidemiology," in Carl Eisdorfer (ed.), *Annual Review of Gerontology and Geriatrics* (Vol. 6), New York: Springer, 1986.

Williams, Richard H., and Wirths, Claudine G., *Lives Through the Years*, New York: Atherton, 1965.

Winsborough, H. H., "A Demographic Approach to the Life-Cycle," in K. W. Back (ed.), *Life Course: Integrative Theories and Exemplary Populations*, Boulder, CO: Westview, 1980, pp. 66-75.

Wisensale, S. K., "Generational Equity and Intergenerational Policies," *The Gerontologist* (1988), 28: 773-778.

Wolff, Nancy, "Women and the Equity of the Social Security Program," *Journal of Aging Studies* (Winter 1988), 2: 357-377.

Work/Family Elder Directions, Inc., *Elder Care Handbook*, Watertown, MA: Work-Family Elder Directions, Inc., 1988.

Yankelovich, Skelly & White, *A 50 Year Report Card on the Social Security System: Attitudes of the American Public*, Washington, DC: AARP, 1985.

Yee, Barbara W. K., "Elders in Southeast Asian Refugee Families," *Generations* (Summer 1992): 24-27.

Zambrana, Ruth E., Merino, Rolando, and Santana, Sarah, "Health Services and the Puerto Rican Elderly," in D. E. Gelfand and A. J. Kutzik (eds.), *Ethnicity and Aging: Theory, Research and Policy*, New York: Springer, 1979, pp. 308-319.

Zarit, S., Orr, N. K., and Zarit, J. M., *The Hidden Victims of Alzheimer's Disease*, New York: New York University Press, 1985.

Zembek, B. A., and Singer, A., "The Problem of Defining Retirement Among Minorities: The Mexican Americans," *The Gerontologist* (1990), 30(6): 749-757.

Ziegler, S., and King, J., "Evaluating the Observable Effects of Foster Grandparents on Hospitalized Children," *Public Health Reports* (1982), 97(6): 550-557.

Glossary/Subject Index

A

Aaron, H., 89, 95, 262, 263, 264, 265, 266, 267, 268, 270, 272, 273
  reading from, 89-90
Aaron, H. J., 72, 257
Abraham, G. N., 45
Accumulated advantage and disadvantage:
  effect on income disparities, 178
  impact of on minorities, 162
  impact with gender roles, 163
  life course perspective, 357
  wealth and assets, 175
Achenbaum, W. A., 179, 199, 244, 256, 352
ACTION, 344
Activities of daily living (ADLs) those everyday tasks that are required for people to live on their own such as: ability to feed oneself, go to the toilet, take a bath, or get out of bed, 22, 24, 25, 131
Activity theory a theory in social gerontology holding that the more active people are, the more likely they are to be satisfied with life, 333, 397-399, 402
  age discrimination and, 399
  busy ethic and, 398
  compression of morbidity theory and, 398
  continuity theory of aging and, 398
  description of, 397
  problems with, 398-399
  research supporting, 398
Adamchak, D., 321, 322
Adams, E., 145
Adams, K., 352
Aday, R., 252
Adler, G., 143

Administration on Aging (AoA), 244, 320
Adult education. *See* Older adult education
Advanced directive a legal document authorizing a decision to be made—typically withholding life-saving medical treatment—should circumstances arise when a person has lost capacity to make that decision, 105, 123-124
  See also Durable Power of Attorney for health affairs *and* Living Wills/advance directives
African Americans. *See* Blacks, aged
Age-based transitions, 349, 356
Aged, economic status of the, 169-179
  and social programs, 235, 236
  federal outlays benefiting, 180
  improvement in, 230
  overall financial health of, 178-179
  poverty, 191-193
  poverty rate, 167, 170
  public policy and, 238-241
  Social Security and advances in, 232
  versus economic status of children, 229-237
Age differentiation, 348
Aged, the:
  distinctions between groups of, 356
  diversity of, 212
  efficient allocation of health care to, 90-94
  family caregiving for, 128-130
  health of, 59-60
  independence in living arrangements among, 130
  least advantaged, 198-201
  number of future, 59
  risk factors for future infirmity of, 59
  sources of retirement income of, 171-177

who require help with ADLs, 131

Age differentiation, 348

Age discrimination, workplace, 318, 319, 326
  prevalence of, 306

Age Discrimination in Employment Act of 1967, 180,
  244, 306, 322
  call for vigorous enforcement of, 319

Age grading designation of people into categories
  based on chronological age; for example, in public
  school systems, 251, 348

Age group, 190

Age identification, 348, 349

Ageism prejudice or negative stereotypes about people based on chonological age, 198, 333
  age-as-decline model of, 357
  and discrimination against elderly, 198
  and intelligence tests, 368
  compassionate, 186, 190

AGELINE, 425

Age segregation social or physical separation of
  groups of people according to chronological age,
  251

Age stratification theory, 348
  age grading and, 348

Aging:
  and the American family, 128-131
  as human experience, 347-418
  changing meaning of, 361-362
  environment and decremental changes associated
    with, 9
  evolutionary biology of, 8, 44, 396
  federal legislation on, 181
  history and scope of government policies on, 179-
    185
  in postindustrial society, 360-361
  in the twenty-first century, 402-403
  life course perspective on, 347-418
  loss in cognitive reserve capacity with, 369
  medical model paradigm for studying, 47-48
  normal, 5
  politics of, 200-201, 202-209
  positive view of, 58-60
  primary, 5
  public policy on, 179-187
  research agenda for study of, 60
  search for positive aspects of, 387-388

secondary, 5
signs of normal, 6
successful, 58, 333, 387, 399-402
trends in public policy and, 185-187
vitality and, 47-54

Aging-based interest groups, 182-185
  American Association of Retired Persons, 109,
    183, 184, 294-295
  End Poverty in California (EPIC), 183
  Gray Lobby, 183
  Gray Panthers, 183
  "Ham and Eggs Movement," 183
  influence of in shaping public policy, 182-185
  Leadership Council of Aging Organizations, 183
  National Committee to Preserve Social Security
    and Medicare, 183, 184
  National Council of Senior Citizens, 183
  National Council on Aging, 183
  Townsend Movement, 182

Aging, biology of, 4-10
  aging versus longevity and, 8-9
  changes involved in, 5-6
  compression of morbidity theory and, 4-5, 9, 19
  free radicals and, 6
  functional capacity and chronological age, 6-7
  longevity and disease and, 9-10
  normal aging and, 5-6

Aging clock theory, 39

Aging, controversies concerning:
  age or need as basis for entitlement, 189-253
  decline in creativity with aging, 363-371
  families providing for their own, 127-155
  future of Social Security, 255-295
  giving people the choice to end their lives, 99-124
  meaning of old age, 395-415
  rationing health care on grounds of age, 71-98
  sense of retirement, 297-345
  why we grow old, 35-68

Aging enterprise, 183

Aging, epidemiology of, 10-15
  basic goal for, 10
  major disease in old age and, 10-14
  responses to geriatric diseases and, 14-15

Aging, genetic factors in:
  "death gene," 8

Bamford, J., 205

Barinaga, M., 45

Barker, D. T., 307

Barresi, C. M., 160

Barrett, E. J., 256

Barron, M. L., 198

Bass, S., 343
  reading from, 309-314

Bass, S. A., 307, 309

Bates, A., 136, 140, 152

Battin, M. P., 77

Baudelaire, C-P, 341

Baugh, D. K., 134

Beard, G. M., 382, 383

Beck, B., 330

Beck, M., 258

Becker, E., 396

Belbin, E., 345

Belbin, R. M., 345

Bell, D., 337, 339

Bell, I. P., 163

Bell, W., 162

Bendix, R., 199

Benefits, public:
  class versus race and, 240-241
  received by aged blacks, 241
  received by aged Hispanics, 241
  received by aged Pacific/Asians, 241
  received by aged whites, 241
  recommendations for integration of, 241
  See also Entitlements, public

Bengston, V. L., 127, 166, 224

Bereavement, 33, 101

Bergmann, B. R., 262, 282
  reading from, 282-285

Berkowitz, E. D., 243, 256

Berman, H. J., 403

Bernard, C., 52

Bertaux, D., 358

Bertman, S., 350

Besdine, R. W., 86, 95
  reading from, 86-88

Best, F., 302, 337

Best interest standard making health care decisions for another person based on what is thought to produce the most benefit for that person, 103

Beymer, B., 333

Bianchi, E. C., 401

"Bill to cut," 278, 279

Binstock, R. H., 183, 184, 186, 190, 214, 215, 220, 221, 223, 226, 227
  and compassionate ageism, 190
  and intergenerational equity, 220, 226
  and politics of aging, 214-215
  and rationing health care, 98

Biological clock, 42

Biological theories of aging. *See* Aging theories, biological

Biomarkers specific physiological or functional processes that tend to change with chronological age, 7, 44

Biomedical science, federal funding of, 18

Birkhill, W. R., 368

Birren, J. E., 368, 417

Bishop, J., 253

Bismarck, O. von, 298

Bixby, A., 238

Blacks, aged:
  family and informal support of, 161
  role of black churches and, 169

Blais, L. E., 260

Blanchet, M., 56

Blaser, D. G., 101

Blau, Z. S., 31, 297, 400

Blauner, R., 340

Blaustein, A. I., 223

Blazer, D. G., 101, 401

Bloch, D. A., 59

Block, M., 162

Blumenthal, H. T., 10

Board-and-care homes, 21

Board of Trustees, Federal OASDI, 278

Boaz, R. F., 303

Bolles, R. N., 354

Bongaarts, J., 128

Bordette, M., 207, 208

Boren-Long amendment, 143

Borgatta, E. P., 320

rheumatism, 22

stroke, 22, 59

top, 10, 11

Chronic illness a sickness or disability that persists over an extended period of time, often interfering with activities of daily living *See* Chronic health conditions of old age

Chudakoff, H. P., 357

Cicero, 350, 355

Cirrhosis, 48, 50

Clark, B., 99

Clark, R., 178, 305, 307

Clark, R. L., 199, 203, 298, 322

Classic aging pattern a persistent pattern on IQ tests that shows relative stability in the verbal part but decline with age on the performance part of the IQ test, 365-366, 367, 368

Clauser, S. B., 134

Clinton, B., 185

Cognitive development. *See* Intelligence tests

Cognitive reserve capacity the degree of unused capacity for learning that exists at any given time, 369

Cohen, J. W., 146

Cohen, M., 145

Cohen, M. A., 132

Cohort a group of people born within a bounded period of years, such as the Baby Boomer generation (born 1946 - 1964), xxviii, 190, 418

and impact of historical events, 358, 418

longitudinal studies of intelligence on, 368

versus age group, 190

Cole, S., 369

Cole, T., 351, 352, 401

Cole, T. R., 333, 362

Coleman, P. G., 417

Coles, R., 162

Colitis, ulcerative, 50

Collagen, 40

Colvez, A., 56

Comfort, A., 62

Committee on Ways and Means, U.S. House of Representatives, 246

Commonwealth Fund, 343

Commonwealth-Harris survey on productive aging, 343, 344

Community support systems for elderly, 26

Competitive medical plans (CMPs), 91, 92

Comprehensive Employment Training Act (CETA), older workers and, 319

Compression of morbidity the postponement of illness later and later into advanced age, 4-5, 9, 19, 33, 58

debate over, 45-46, 56

Conflict between generations, 197, 311, 323, 350

Congregate Housing Act (1978), 180

Congregate meals, 26

Conroy, C., 103

Continuing care retirement community (CCRC), 21

Continuity theory the view that in aging people are inclined to maintain, as much as they can, the same habits, personality, and style of life developed in earlier years, 340, 398

Continuum of care, 25

Cook, F. L., 167, 192, 256

Coomaraswamy, A., 371

Cooney, T., 165

Copernicus, 47, 382

Copper, C., 304

Corbin, J. M., 129

Cornelius, S. W., 366

Cornell Study of Occupational Retirement, 300, 335

Cornman, J., 211, 223, 224, 226, 227, 323

Costa, P. T., Jr., 398

Cost-sharing, 200

Cowgill, D. O., 131, 354

Cowley, M., 398

Crapo, L., 46, 47, 65, 66

Creative achievement:

age and, 372-377, 378-381, 382-386

possible causes for early maxima in creativity and, 376-377

Creativity:

aging and, 367-371

and fluid intelligence, 369

and intelligence, 364

and wisdom, 364-365

in an aging population, 371

link between age and, 367-369

nature of, 364-367

See also Intelligence

Cronyn, H., 35

Crooks, L., 165, 260

Cross-linkage theory of aging, 39-40
  free radicals and, 40
  waste accumulation theory and, 40

Crossover phenomenon the fact that life expectancy for blacks is lower than whites up until the late 1970s, when the pattern is reversed and black life expectancy exceeds that of whites, 161

Cross-sectional design, 6

Crown, W., 214

Crown, W. H., 257

Cruzan, N. J., 99, 104, 105
  See also Right-to-die cases

Cryobiology, 43

Crystal, S., 167, 178, 199, 295

Crystallized intelligence the intellectual ability to use past experience in completing tasks or solving problems *See* Intelligence

Cumming, E., 333, 397

Cunningham, W. R., 370

Cutler, N., 184

Cutler, R., 8, 9, 36

Cutler, R. G., 6, 40

D

Daniel, C. W., 55

Daniels, N., 72

Dannefer, D., 353

Danziger, S., 164, 169, 208

Darwin, C., 47

Dattalo, P., 262, 278, 280
  reading from, 278-281

Davies, D. R., 344

Davis, C., 145

Davis, J., 353

Davis, K., 166, 240

Davis, R., 353

Day, C., 183, 257

Death and dying:
  acceptance of, 414
  accidents as cause of, 9, 48
  awareness of, 416
  bereavement, 101, 358
  causes of among older people, 10

denial of, 396
dying trajectory, 33
fear of, 410
history of right-to-die and, 102
homeostasis and organ reserve and, 52
natural, 50, 55, 62
premature, 50, 62
"tolerable," 81
view of as life transition, 412
See also Treatment, termination of

de Beauvoir, S., 402, 403, 404, 417
  reading from, 404-402

DeBrock, L., 90, 95
  reading from, 90-94

Decrement with compensation, 369, 399

Defined benefit plan a retirement program that promises a specified level of pension income in return for a certain number of years of service to a company, 173, 359

Defined contribution plan a retirement plan in which pension income varies according to how much employers, employees, or both contribute to the plan and according to how successfully the funds are invested, 173, 359

DeGrazia, S., 336, 337

de Leo, D., 101

de León, P., 2, 3, 67

Dellman-Jenkins, M., 253

de Luce, J., 350

Dementia, 13-14, 58
  definition of, 13
  Earle Spring case of, 104
  See also Alzheimer's Disease

Demographic transition theory the theory that explains population aging by pointing to a decline in both birth rates and death rates following industrialization, xxviii-xxix

Dennis, H., 294, 306, 369, 371

Dennis, W., 378, 383, 384, 390
  reading from, 378-381

Department of Health and Human Services (DHHS), 145

Dependency ratio, 194-196
  and economic burden on population, 194, 203, 213, 311, 322
  and Social Security, 257

Depression (mental health), 46
  among nursing home residents, 102
  and old age suicide, 30, 31, 101-102, 108
  bereavement and, 101
  clinical, 101
  in old age, 101-102, 409
  reminiscence and, 417
  symptoms of in elderly, 101
Depression, Great, 179, 182-183, 310, 358
Derthick, M., 243, 244
de Tocqueville, A., 339
Deutschman, D. E., 417
Developmental tasks in Erik Erikson's theory of life span development, a series of psychological challenges that require resolving conflicting tendencies in the human personality, 352, 403
Diabetes, 48, 50
Diagnosis Related Groups (DRGs) distinct categories of diseases that are the basis for Medicare's financial reimbursement to hospitals, 91
Diamond, A. M., Jr., 369
Dickenson, F. G., 208
Diekstra, R.F.W., 101
Diet:
  dietary restrictions to retard aging, 43
  health promotion, 68
Dill, A.E.P., Jr., 133
Dilworth-Anderson, P., 161
Dirac, P., 382
Disability insurance, 243
Discovery method of training, 345
Disengagement:
  as attitude, 358, 399
Disengagement theory a theory of aging claiming that separation of older people from active roles in society is normal and appropriate for the benefit of both society and the individual, 396-397, 402
  and modernization theory, 397
  as early theory of old age in modern society, 397
  criticisms of, 397
  distinguishing feature of, 396
Divorce, 165, 261, 359
DNA (Deoxyribonucelic Acid), 6, 36
  biological theories of aging and, 38-39
  caloric restrictions and damage to, 44
  supplements for antiaging, 68

DNA repair:
  and age-related changes, 15
  wear and tear theory of aging and, 39
Dobris, J. C., 135, 145
Dobrosky, B., 253
Doering, M., 307
Domiciliary care facilities, 21
Donaldson, G., 367
Doty, P., 145
Double decker system, 284, 290
Double jeopardy being simultaneously a member of two categories, such as female and a racial minority, for whom old age brings special disadvantage, 166
Dowd, J. J., 128, 166, 199
Down, I. M., 21
Downs, S., 345
Dressel, P. L., 168
Dubin, R., 340
Dubos, R., 52, 64
Dumas, K., 25, 259
Dumazedier, J., 338, 339
Duncan, G., 358
Duncan, J., 143
Durable Power of Attorney for health affairs, 105
  See also Living Wills/advance directives
Durkheim, E., 30, 31
Dworaczek, M., 300
Dychtwald, K., 67

E

Early retirement benefits pension income and other benefits for which employees are eligible when they retire before some customary retirement age, 175
Earned Income Tax Credit, 247, 280
Earnings sharing a plan to permit the income of both husband and wife to be counted together in calculating Social Security benefits that apply to either spouse, 261, 283, 289
Earnings test the requirement that persons receiving Social Security must be in a substantial degree retired; that is, may receive no more than a limited amount of income from employment. (Also known as the retirement test), 258, 274
Ebert, S. D., 51

Eckert, J. K., 21

Economy (American):
    changes in, 304-307
    loss of predictability in labor market, 304
    loss of security in labor market, 304

Edelman, M. W., 222

Edison, T., 369, 373

Education, median level of:
    for people over 65, 392

Educational system:
    elderly students in, 312
    See also Older adult education

Ego integrity in Erikson's theory of human development, the view that healthy psychological attitude in old age means acceptance of one's life instead of regret or despair, 352, 416

Ego transcendence, 364, 399

Ehrenreich, J., 243

Ehrlich, P., 198

Einstein, A., 47, 363

Eisele, F. R., 197

Eisenstadt, S. N., 251

Eitzen, S. D., 304

Ekerdt, D. J., 300, 308, 328, 329
    reading from, 328-336

Elbaum, J., 29

Elbaum v. Grace Plaza Nursing Home, 29

Elder, G. H., 358

Eldercare, corporate, 128

Elderhostel, 392

Elderlaw a specialized branch of law devoted to legal and regulatory issues affecting the elderly, 134, 140

Elders:
    ability of to pursue vigorous art activities, 407-408
    as conservationists, 407
    as tolerant and appreciative, 407
    education of, 408
    potential role of in society, 407-408
    wisdom of, 407

Eliot, T. S., 363

Elliehausen, G. E., 206

Emphysema, 48, 50

Employee Benefit Research Institute, 154

Employee Retirement Income Security Act (ERISA), 174, 180

Employment:
    by industry and industrial sectors, 316
    by occupational group, 317
    policy, 314
    public service programs for, 319, 343

End Poverty in California (EPIC) Movement, 183

Entitlements government benefits automatically payable to individuals who qualify for eligibility: for example, age-based entitlements such as Social Security for covered workers
    aged-based, 185, 196, 201
    class versus race and, 239-240
    exclusionary beneficence of, 238-241
    for lower-middle- and middle-class elders, 240
    for middle- and upper-middle-class elders, 240
    for poor elders, 239-241
    means test for, 199-200
    Meel v. Martinez case and, 200
    targeting debate and, 200-201

Epidemiology the use of mathematical methods to study the distribution of disease in human populations, 10, 46

Erikson, E., 352, 361, 395, 403, 406, 416
    developmental tasks theory of psychological development of, 352
    reading from, 406-408

Error accumulation theory of aging, 38

Espenshade, T., 217

Estes, C., 179, 182, 183, 240

Ethnicity:
    aging and, 160
    and median income among groups, 166
    and national identity, 169
    as factor in targeting services, 201

Eustis, N., 26

Euthanasia, 82-83
    active, 30, 106, 113
    and rationing health care, 77
    Callahan's argument against, 77, 82-83
    defending voluntary, 111-112
    involving doctors and nurses, 114-115
    justifiable, 114-115
    moral problem of, 100

passive, 100, 113

professional reasons for, 115

reasons physicians should not engage in, 116-121

social reasons for, 115-116

voluntary, 107, 111-112, 119

Evans, E., 252

Evans, R., 91

Exchange theory of aging   the theory that interaction in social groups based on the reciprocal balancing of rewards depending on actions performed, 128, 417

Extended family   a complete range of relatives, including grandparents, aunts and uncles, and cousins, as opposed to the nuclear family, which consists of just parents and children

F

Faber, J. F., 56

Falkner, T., 350

Fama, T., 133

Families USA, 154

Family:

changes in structure of, 127, 311

extended, 128

intergenerational transfers, 217

multigenerational, 130, 152

myth of abandonment by, 128, 135

nuclear, 130

responsibility, 131

smaller size of, 356

Fayerweather, W. E., 59

Feder, J., 184, 240

Feminism:

and attention to older women, 165

Social Security reform and, 282-285

Feminization of poverty:

in old age, 164

Ferrara, P. J., 257

Ferrel, C., 401

Fertility, xxvi, xxvii, 204, 321, 396

Filenbaum, G. G., 300

Filial responsibility   the obligation of adult children to provide care for aged parents, 131, 151, 349

Finch, C. E., 51

Firman, J., 253

Fischer, D. H., 352

Fisher, C. R., 34

FitzGerald, F., 207

Fitzgerald, F., 333

Fluid intelligence   the intellectual ability to solve novel tasks or problems, 364, 388

Fogarty, M., 304

Folstein, M. F., 14

Folstein Mini-Mental Status Exam, 14

Folstein, S. E., 14

Folts, W. E., 21

Foner, A., 348

Foner, N., 197

Food Stamps, 193, 235, 239

means test for, 199

Forman, M., 262

Foster Grandparents, 344

Foster Grandparents Program, 252

Fountain of youth, 35, 67, 353

401K plans, 175

Four percent fallacy   the mistaken idea that nursing homes aren't important for older people because, at any single point in time, only 4% of those over 65 are likely to be living in a nusing home, 24

Fozard, J., 7

Frech, H. E., 18

Freedman, R. M., 135

Freeland, M. S., 92

Freeman, S. M., 45

Free radical theory of aging, 6, 40

Freud, S., 350, 352

Friedan, B., 151, 283

Friedman, A. S., 368

Friedman, D., 145

Friedman, E., 340

Friedman, M., 239, 253

Friedmann, E., 321, 322

Fries, J. F., 46, 47, 54, 55, 56, 57, 58, 59, 61, 62, 63, 64, 65, 66, 67, 398

readings from, 47-54, 58-61

Fuchs, V., 237, 231

Fujii, S., 162

Fullerton, H., 322

Functional age   a composite picture of the body's measurable performance level that is distinct from chronological age, 7

Furstenberg, F. F., Jr., 150

G

Gadow, S., 352, 401

Galen, 350

Gambria, L. M., 416

Gardner, H., 366

Garrett, W. W., 131

Gee, E. M., 356

Gelfand, D., 253

Gelfand, D. E., 160

Gender:
   and aging, 163-165
   and life course, 356
   and Social Security, 262

General Accounting Office, 73, 144, 145, 154, 204, 240, 257, 277, 278, 279, 280
   estate recovery study by, 144-145

General Motors, 304

Generational accounting, 196, 197

Generational equity, 186-187, 189-198, 298
   and poverty rate among elderly, 191
   and Social Security, 257
   and the new victim blaming, 220-228
   in ancient Rome, 350
   problems with concept of, 222-228
   taxation and, 196-197

Generations, interdependence of, 211-219
   long-term view of social programs and, 218-219
   within families, 217

Generations United, 253

Generativity   the motivation to concern oneself for nurturing the next generation or more generally concern for whatever outlives an individual
   and generational succession, 408
   and outliving the self, 395
   versus despair, 352

Genetic factors in aging, 41
   "death gene," 8
   genetic engineering, 45
   Human Genome Project, 45, 66
   mutations, 44

raising maximum lifespan, 44-45

George, L. K., 32, 300, 358, 400

Geriatric medicine:
   as symptomatic, 33-34

Geriatrics   the medical specialty treating the diseases of old age, 10

Gerontocide, 104

Gerontocracy   political rule by the elderly, 197

Gerontological Society of America, 208, 387

Gerontology, xxiii, xxx-xxxi, 348, 355, 401
   See also Industrial gerontology *and* Social gerontology

Gibbs, N., 323

Gibson, R. C., 161, 163, 178

Ginzberg, E., 27, 337

Giordano, J. A., 294

Giordano, N. H., 294

Glaser, B. G., 33

Glass, H. B., 51

Gleason, H. P., 343

Glenn, N. D., 184

Glick, H., 28, 103

Glick, P. C., 128

Goethe, 365, 404

Goffman, E., 23

Gompertz curve, 38

Gordon, H., 140

Gordon, J. B., 26

Gottschalk, P., 164, 169, 208

Gould, S., 201

Gould, S. G., 229, 250
   reading from, 229-237

Grad, S., 172

Graebner, W., 301, 323, 324

Graham, M., 371

Granick, S., 368

Grant, L. A., 22

Gratton, B., 162

Gray Lobby, 183

Gray Panthers, 183

Gray Power, 184

Greenberg, J. N., 132

Greenough, W. C., 171

Grenberg, J., 26

Gresham, G. E., 25

Greulich, R. C., 7
Gross, P. A., 68
Gruenberg, E. M., 62, 63, 64
Gruman, G. J., 35, 403
Gubrium, J. F., 24, 333, 401, 403
Guralnik, J., 19, 58, 59

H

Haber, C., 354
Haber, E., 252
Hager, M., 258
Hagestad, G., 136, 153
    reading from, 149-152
Hagestad, G. O., 149, 359
Hagnell, O., 56
Haight, B. K., 417
Haley, B., 334
Halper, T., 72
Hambor, J. C., 260
Hamburg, D., 193
Hanlon, M. D., 329
Happersett, C. J., 295
Harel, Z., 198
Hareven, T., 352
Harman, D., 6
Harris and Associates, Louis, 33, 101, 133, 217, 224, 343
Harrison, D. E., 55
Harris, S., 359
Hastert, J. D., 275
Hastings Center, 100
Haug, M., 12
Haug, M. R., 101
Hauser, P. M., xxviii
Hauser, R. M., 239
Havighurst, R. J., 333, 398
Hayes-Bautista, D., 225
Hayflick, L., 40, 41, 51, 55, 61, 62, 67
Hays, J. A., 128
Head Start, 237
Health and Human Services Department study, 198
Health care:
    case management of, 74, 96-98
    cost containment of, 90

home, 133
home care versus nursing home care, 27
rationing of, 3, 71-77
Health care allocation, efficient:
    moral hazard and, 91-92
    to elderly, 90-94
Health care, economics of, 15-20
    prospects for future of, 18-20
    reducing costs through increased efficiency, 90
    reimbursement systems and, 16-18
    scientific advances and, 89
Health Care Financing Administration, 143, 144, 425
Health care policy:
    implications of increased numbers of older people to, 56-57
Health care rationing:
    case management as form of, 74
    managed care as form of, 74
    See also Health care rationing on grounds of age
Health care rationing on grounds of age, 71-98
    arguments against, 84-94
    arguments for, 78-84, 96
    as cost-saving plan, 73-77
    attraction of, 93
    cost of, 83
    euthanasia and suicide and, 77, 82-83
    "notch" problem and, 76-77
    precedents for, 72-73
    principles and priorities of plan for, 81-82
Health maintenance organizations (HMOs), 91
    role of in plans for national health reform, 97
Health promotion, 66-68
    and maximum life span, 68
    as based on science, 67
    dietary interventions and, 67
    environmental interventions and, 66-67
    exercise and, 67
    health food products and, 68
    recommendations for, 68
    reductions in smoking and, 67
Heart disease, 10, 15, 59
    declining death rate from, 46
    free radical theory of aging and, 40
    See also Cardiovascular disease

Heclo, H., 184, 247
Hefner, T., 184
Heinz, J., 276
Held, T., 362
Hellman, L. H., 132
Hellman, S., 132
Helson, R., 349
Hemlock Society, 107
Hendricks, J., 360
Henretta, J. C., 239, 357
Henry, W. E., 333, 397
Hentoff, N., 84, 95
    reading from, 84-85
Hershberg, T., 150
Herzog, R. A., 343
Hess, B. B., 183
Hess, C., 183
Hewitt Associates, 175
Hewitt, P., 221, 223, 226
Hilditch, T. P., 372
Hilker, M., 21
Hilton, J., 35
Hippocrates, 350
Hirschorn, B. A., 211, 223, 226, 227, 323
Hispanic American elderly:
    informal supports among, 162
    subgroups of, 160-162
    views of age-based entitlements and, 225
Hochschild, A. R., 252, 397
Hogan, D. P., 356
Hohaus, R. A., 245
Holahan, J., 240
Holahan, J. F., 146
Holden, K. C., 165
Holmes, L., 354
Holmes, O. W., 4, 55
Holmes, T. H., 358
Holtzman, A., 182
Home delivered meals, 26
Home health care, 27, 133
Homeostasis, 52
Home ownership:
    home equity and net worth, 176, 206
    home equity conversion, 148, 176

Homer, 349
Homes for the aged, 21
Honig, M., 259
Hook, S., 107, 111, 122
    reading from, 111-112
Hooker, K., 335
Horm, J. W., 59
Hormones, aging and, 39, 68
    dehydroepiandrosterone (DHEA), 39, 68
Horn, J. L., 364, 367
House Select Committee on Aging, 208
Housing alternatives for elderly, 20, 21
    See also Nursing homes
Howe, N., 182
Hubbard, R., 198
Huber, E., 141
Hudson, R., 179, 186, 201, 214, 238, 343
Hudson, R. B., 242, 244, 246
    reading from, 242-250
Humboldt, 386
Humphry, D., 107, 113, 122
    reading from, 113-115
Hunnicutt, B. K., 302, 303
Hunt, M. E., 21
Hurh, W. M., 162
Hyde, J. C., 160
Hyperborean theme, 35

I

IBM, 304
Imanaka, Y., 46
Immerwhar, J., 329
Immigration, 169
Immune system, aging and, 6, 39
Income:
    median income, 166, 170, 277
    retirement income, 171
Individual Retirement Account (IRA), 175, 207, 270, 327
Individuation, Jungian concept of, 400, 401
Industrial gerontology, 306-307
Industrialization:
    and family structure, 130
    and modernization theory, 354

decline in manufacturing and, 205
   Industrial Revolution, 309, 310, 352
Inflation, 154, 178
Informal support systems   families, friends, and
   neighbors who provide help to frail elderly people,
   26, 129
Ingram, D. K., 44
Inheritance, 104, 135, 145
In-kind benefits, 170
Inlander, C. B., 16
Institute for Policy Innovation, 275
Institute for Retired Professionals, 392
Insurance:
   adverse selection of, 154
   long-term care, 148, 153-155
   moral hazard, 91
   social, 168, 227, 242-250, 285, 291
Intelligence:
   classic aging pattern of, 365-366, 367, 368
   creativity and, 364
   crystallized, 364, 388
   decline in fluid with age, 369, 392
   decrement with compensation and, 369-370
   dual-process framework of, 388
   fluid, 364, 388
   fluid versus crystallized, 367
   increase in crystallized with age, 369, 392
   measures of, 365-367
Intelligence tests, 365-367
Intergenerational conflict, threat of, 311
Intergenerational inequity thesis, 212-213
   based on false assumptions, 323
   flaws and misunderstandings of, 213-216
Intergenerational programs, 417
Intergenerational transfers, role of, 216-218
Interiority (of personality), 399, 401
International Association of Preretirement Planners,
   294
Intimacy at a distance   the phenomenon of multi-
   generational families that remain in close social
   contact even with geographic separation, 130
Isenberg, S., 349

J

Jackson, J. S., 160, 161, 343

Jacobs, B., 182, 200
Jacobs, P., 15
Jacobs, R. H., 183
Jacobson, S. G., 160
Jacques, E., 352
Jedriewski, M. K., 294
Jobes, N. E., 85
Job Training Partnership Act (JTPA), 319, 343
Johnson, B. B., 260
Johnson, C., 26
Johnson, C. L., 22
Johnson, T. E., 44
Johnson, W., 307
Jones, H. H., 59
Journals and periodicals in aging, 428
Jung, C., 99, 395, 400, 402-403, 409, 415, 417
   reading from, 409-412
Jungk, R., 382

K

Kahn, R. L., 343, 399
Kalish, R. A., 186
Kamikawa, L., 201, 238
   reading from, 238-242
Kamisar, Y., 118, 119, 120
Kane, R., 96
Kane, R. A., 24, 25, 27
Kane, R. L., 24, 25, 27
Kansas City Studies of Adult Life, 397, 399
Kaplan, M., 300, 302, 339, 340
Kart, C. S., 398
Kass, L., 107, 116, 122, 123
   reading from, 116-122
Kassner, E., 200
Kastenbaum, R., 24, 417
Katz, S., 22, 25
Kaufman, S. R., 396
Kay, M.M.B., 39
Keene, R., 92
Kemper, P., 97, 128
Keniston, K., 329
Kennedy, J. F., administration of, 277
Kennell, D. L., 133
Kent, C., 132

Kerschner, P., 183

Kessler, L. G., 59

Kevorkian, J., 105

Keyfitz, N., 61

Kidney dialysis, 124

    rationing of in Great Britain, 72, 89-90

    rationing of in Seattle, 72

Kieffer, J. A., 344

Kim, K. C., 162

Kim, S., 162

King, F. P., 171

King, J., 252

Kingson, E. R., 201, 208, 211, 223, 224, 226, 227, 242, 250, 323, 244

    reading from, 211-219

Kin-keepers:

    and effects of "the mortality gap," 149-150

    women as, 149-152, 163

    See also Caregiving, family

Kin-keeping:

    costs of, 150-152

    new forms of interdependence and, 150

    "superwoman squeeze," and, 151

    tasks of, 150-151

    See also Caregiving, family

Kleemeier, R. W., 307

Kleiler, F. M., 304

Klein, S. M., 129

Klingman, D., 131

Koenig, H. G., 401

Koff, T., 26

Koh, J., 162

Kohl, M., 100

Kohli, M., 351, 356, 362

Kohn, R. R., 55

Kolata, G., 66

Kopac, C., 252

Koretz, G., 304

Kosloski, K. D., 320

Kotlikoff, L., 197, 262, 263, 264, 265, 266, 267, 268, 269, 270, 272, 273

Kotre, J., 352, 395

Kowalczyk, G. I., 92

Kramek, L. M., 167, 192

Kramer, M., 62, 63

Krishnaswami, S., 295

Krout, J., 182

Kubler-Ross, E., 33

Kuhn, M., 183

Kutza, E. A., 186

Kvale, J. N., 401

Kvasnicka, B., 333

L

Labi, M.L.C., 25

Labor force:

    and possible labor shortage, 307

    in year 2000, 307, 314

    participation rates, 297-299, 322

    retirement as management tool for, 306

Labor force trends, 315-317

    increase in media age of labor force, 321

Lacayo, C. G., 239

Lakatta, E. G., 7

Lamm, R. D., 72, 225, 243

Lammers, W., 131

Landerman, L. R., 261

Lane, N. E., 59

Langbein, J., 135

Langer, E., 359

Langley, P. A., 278

Lanke, J., 56

Laplace, 386

LaPuma, J., 106

Larson, E., 32

Laslett, P., 130, 252, 354, 361

Late style of aging artists, 365, 371, 385-386, 405

Latta, V. B., 92

Lawton, M. P., 20, 21

Layton, E., 386

Leadership Council of Aging Organizations, 183

Leaf, A., 55

Learned helplessness a pattern of dependency and depression resulting from a social environment that reinforces passivity, 358

Leguerrier, T., 102

Lehman, H., 369, 370, 371, 372

    reading from, 372-377

Lehman, H. C., 378, 379, 380, 381, 382, 383, 384, 390, 391

Leibold, K., 252

Leisure, late life:

   beginnings of surplus labor and, 310

   importance of, 307

   increase in time devoted to, 303

   origins of, 300-304

   positive view of, 300

   retirement as form of, 300

Leisure society, new, 338-341

   capitalism and, 339

   emphasis of, 338

   improved technology and, 338-339

   reasons for, 338-339

Leonesio, M. V., 259

Lepkowski, J., 46

Letsch, S. W., 143

Levin, J., 198

Levin, M. E., 227

Levin, S. G., 363

Levin, W. C., 198

Levine, M. L., 306

Levinson, D. J., 352, 361

   theory of middle and later life transitions of, 352

Levit, K. R., 92, 143

Levy, F. S., 205, 206

Lew, E., 63

Lewis, C. N., 417

Lewis, L. S., 329

Lewis, M., 33, 165

Liang, J., 160

Liederman, D., 253

Life care communities, 21

Life course:

   changing structure of, 362

   deinstitutionalization of, 362

   developmental tasks and psychological development theory of, 352

   modernization theory of aging and, 353-354

   need for flexibility over the, 362

   role of mass media and, 353

   theory of middle and later life transitions and, 352

Life course perspective   the approach to aging as part of the totality of human life understood as a successive series of stages from infancy through old age, 347-418

ages and transitions, 356-362

definition of, 348, 355

disorderly life pattern and, 359

empty nest syndrome, 356

historical ideas of, 349-351

in the modern world, 351-354

learned helplessness and, 358

life history and, 358

life stages, 348-354, 402

longitudinal research as manifestation of, 355

nonnormative life events and, 358

paid employment, 356

parenting time, 356

postponement of child rearing, 356

social class and, 357

social institutions and policies and, 358-359

Life events, 357

   in postindustrial society, 360

   nonnormative, 358

Life expectancy, human, 60, 211, 301

   definition of, 48, 55

   increasing, 62, 64, 202

   rise in, xxxi, 5

Life-extension products, consumer market for, 66

Life review   the idea that late life reminiscence involves the return of past memories that help the individual work through conflicting feelings about the past, 350, 389

   as autobiographical consciousness, 418

   as bolster to self-image, 417

   for transitions across adult life course, 418

   late life reminiscence as form of, 416

Life satisfaction:

   definition of, 32

   in old age, 396

   versus morale, 32

Life satisfaction   a person's general attitude toward past and present life as a whole

   Louis Harris Poll, 33

   meaning of old age, 396

   Philadelphia Geriatric Center Morale Scale, 32

"Life span," 55

Life span, human:

   biologic limits to, 55

   cryobiology and, 43

Markides, K. S., 160

Marmor, T. R., 184, 243, 255

Marris, P., 361

Martz, S. H., 169

Masoro, E. J., 7

Mass media, depiction of elderly as prosperous in, 189

Matisse, H-E-B, 365

Mature Market Report, 401

Maximum life potential (MLP), 48, 55-56

McAuley, W. J., 133

McCain, J., 275

McConnell, S. R., 21, 337

McCrae, R. R., 398

McGoldrick, A., 304

Mcgoon, D. C., 12

McHugh, P. R., 14

McIntosh, J. L., 31, 108, 109

McKeown, T., 64

McKinlay, J. B., 64

McKinlay, S. M., 64

McMahon, A. W., 417

McMillan, A., 238

Meacham, J. A., 364

Meals on Wheels, 26

Means test   a requirement for a person to fall below a certain level of income or assets in order to qualify for a government benefit program, 132, 193, 199

and Social Security, 185, 269

Mechanic, D., 34

Medawar, P. B., 5

Median age, xxvi, 322

Medicaid   a government program that pays for health care expenses of people who fall below the poverty line, 16, 17, 86, 127, 179, 193, 223, 235, 236, 139, 240, 243, 248

administrative costs of, 270

as fastest-growing component of state budgets, 133

as major payor of nursing home care, 143

as means-test entitlement program, 132

description of, 16

financing long-term care with, 132-134

inadequacy of, 78

long-term care and, 27, 153

means test for, 199

Oregon's program of, 72-73

Medicaid planning, 134-139, 140-141

and Medicaid asset shelters, 145

elderlaw attorneys and, 135, 136, 140

morality of, 136-137

strategies for, 135

Medicaid spenddown   the requirement that people divest themselves of assets down to a minimal level in order to qualify for Medicaid coverage of nursing home care, 133, 136, 145-146

fallacy of impoverishment and, 142-148

spousal impoverishment and, 146

Medical futility, 29

Medicare   the federal government program that pays for health care for older people, xxvii, xxix, xxx, 16, 19, 34, 76, 84, 85, 86, 109, 131, 132, 137, 140, 154, 158, 170, 179, 185, 186, 192, 193, 196, 198, 199, 203, 204, 209, 214, 215, 220, 223, 224, 225, 227, 235, 236, 240, 243, 263, 271

baby boom generation and, 207

cost-containment measures for, 179

cost of living increases (COLAS) for, 221

coverage of organ transplants, 78

creation of, 16

expansion of, 87, 244

expenditures, 71

funding of, 16, 180, 273

growth of, 265

inadequacy of, 78

nature of, 285-286

percentage of budget spent on patients in last year of life, 73

popularity of, 225

premiums, 247

programs, 16

Prospective Payment System for, 17-18, 91-92

reimbursement for kidney dialysis, 72

Resource Based Relative Value Scale (RBRVS) of, 18

rising costs of, 58, 78

taxes, 247

universality and egalitarianism of, 168, 242, 245, 246

versus Medicaid, 16, 138

Medicare Catastrophic Coverage Act of 1988, 146, 245, 247, 248, 249 repeal of, 183, 184, 245

Medicare Hospital Insurance (HI), 285, 287
  tax, 247, 255

Medicare Supplemental Medical Insurance, 248

Medicare trust fund, 272

Medvedev, Z. A., 38

Meek v. Martinez, 200

Meiners, M., 145

Melvin, C., 252

Memory, age and, 369

Menken, J. A., 128

Merce, S. O., 109

Mercy killing, 100, 117-119
  See also Euthanasia

Merino, R., 162

Metropolitan Life, 58

Meyer, J. A., 227

Meyer, J.E.W., 182

Meyrowitz, J., 353

Michel, R. C., 205, 206

Michelangelo, 371, 405

Middle age, 348, 349, 352
  and midlife crisis, 352
  importance of flexibility in, 370

Mikesell, J. L., 280

Miller, M., 31

Miller, S. J., 150, 151, 331-332

Mindel, C. H., 160

Minkler, M., 166, 182, 201, 220, 222, 224, 227, 250
  reading from, 220-229

Minois, G., 355

Minority elderly, 160
  as least advantaged, 198
  crossover phenomenon, 161
  life expectancy, 198

Mitchell, V., 349

Mizruchi, E. H., 337

Moane, G., 349

Moberg, D., 401

Model, J., 150

Modernization theory a theory of aging that asserts that the status of the elderly must decline following industrialization and the spread of technology, 353, 397, 403

Modern Maturity, 263-273

Moergan, J. N., 343

Monet, C., 365, 405

Montgomery, R., 129, 308
  reading from, 320-328

Montgomery, R.J.V., 306, 320

Moody, H. R., 183, 187, 353, 363, 402

Moore, M. T., 99

Moorhead, P. S., 55

Moral hazard, 91

Morbidity sickness or physical illness of some kind, 5, 61

Morgan, J., 217

Morgan, N., 304

Morris, R., 307, 309
  reading from, 309-314

Morrison, M., 294

Morriss, J., 348

Mortality the rate at which death occurs, often adjusted or calculated by age, 61
  and age, 357
  and dependency, 359
  biological constraints on changes in, 61-64
  changing concept of in elderly population, 61-64
  current theories of, 61
  differences between men and women in, 149-150, 163, 164
  societal constraints on changes in, 64

Morton, D. J., 295

Morton, E., 276

Moses, A. M. "Grandma," 333, 371

Moses, S. A., 136, 142, 143

Moskowitz, R., 12

Moss, R. J., 106

Moynihan, D. P., 193, 207, 259, 262, 276, 278, 279

Mozart, W. A., 369

Multidemensional functional assessment an examination of an elderly person's physical, mental, and social condition, including the ability to perform activities of daily living, 24
  See Older Americans Resources and Services (OARS), 25

Multiple sclerosis, noncoverage of by Medicaid, 137

Munnell, A. H., 260, 298

Murdock, S. H., 162

Murey, M. I., 21

Myers, D. A., 165
Myers, R. J., 244, 245, 246, 255, 262, 276, 285
   reading from, 285-292

N

Nasar, S., 197
National Association of Insurance Commissioners (NAIC), 145
National Bureau of Health Statistics, 50
National Center for Health Statistics, 10, 11, 32, 58, 59, 108, 202
National Center for Policy Analysis, 275
National Commission for Employment Policy, 318
National Committee to Preserve Social Security and Medicare, 183, 184
National Council of Senior Citizens, 183
National Council on Aging, 183, 294
   and Children's Defense League, 253
   support of Generations United by, 253
National Elderlaw Academy, 135
National Health Service (of Britain), 72
National Indian Council on Aging, 239
National Institute on Aging, 7, 13, 14, 44, 68, 68, 208
National Nursing Home Survey (1985), 102
National Opinion Research Center, 240
Native Americans, elderly, 162
Natural Death Act, California, 103
Natural life span, 76, 80
Naturally occurring retirement community (NORC), 21-22
Naylor, C. D., 72
Needs-based benefits providing services, such as home health care, to people according to some assessment of their individual requirement rather than according to age or some other categorical basis, 187, 199
Nelson, D. W., 330
Nelson, G. M., 196, 199, 238, 239, 240
Net worth:
   definition, 175
   median net worth by age groups, 176
   median net worth by household and ethnicity, 21-22
Neugarten, B. L., 77, 190, 208, 333, 352, 359, 398, 399, 402
Neurotic, Jungian definition of, 409

Neuschler, E., 146
Newcomer, R. J., 20, 240
New deal, 230
   and Social Security, 255, 263
   impact on aged, 182
   Keynsian economics, 303
Newman, K. S., 189
Newman, S., 252
Newton, I., 47, 369, 382, 419
Normal aging the underlying time-dependent biological process of aging in each species, which may involve functional loss or susceptibility to disease but is not in itself a disease, 5
Normative Aging Study, 329, 332
Nursing homes, 60
   admissions to, 133
   and aged blacks, 161
   as last alternative for care, 134, 135
   as total institution, 23-24
   cost of care in, 140
   definition of, 22
   depression among residents of, 102
   four percent fallacy and, 24
   hip fracture as cause of admission to, 12
   likelihood of entering, 24
   quality of, 24
   reminiscence groups in, 417
   risk factors for placement in, 24
   size of population of, 23
   types of, 22

O

O'Conner case, 104
O'Connor, J., 221
Office of Inspector General, 141, 143, 144, 145, 146, 147
   estate recovery study by, 143-144
   recommendations for changes in Medicaid, 147
Office of Management and Budget, 203, 207, 226
Off time/on time, 349
O'Grady-LeShane, R., 164
Ojesjo, L., 56
Old age:
   and Jungian stages of life, 409-412

and partaking in meaningful and useful work, 405, 406

as time of relinquishing, 406

as uniquely human, 395

constant losses with, 406

defined as period of late freedom, 400, 405

defined as roleless role, 400

depression in, 409

generativity and, 395, 408

liberation of, 405

norms for appropriate behavior in, 340, 349, 402

uncertainty about meaning of, 403

vital involvement in, 406-408

wear-and-tear physical changes of, 15

Old age, meaning and significance of, 79-80, 395-415

life satisfaction and, 396

Old Age and Survivors Insurance, 327

Old Age Assistance program, 243

and SSI, 244

Old Age Survivors and Disability Insurance (OASDI), 256, 278, 287

abolishing surplus of, 279

assets of, 281

benefits for nonworking spouses, 288

inequitable treatment of women under, 288-291

investing trust funds of, 280

nature of, 285-286

unfair treatment of homemakers under, 289

See also Social Security

Older adult education, 392-393, 411

Elderhostel, 392

future increase in, 392

Institute for Retired Professionals, New School (New York), 392

numbers of people in, 393

Universities of the Third Age, 392

Older Americans Act federal law that authorizes and funds direct services such as senior centers, nutrition programs, and information and referral, 26, 160, 168, 181, 198, 200, 240, 241, 242, 243, 245, 247

and debate over cost-sharing, 200

key service programs under, 182

national aging network created by, 181-182

Title V of, 343

universal eligibility of some programs under, 245, 246

Older Americans Freedom to Work Act, 275

Older Americans Resources and Services (OARS), 25

Older Women's League (OWL), 165

Older workers. *See* Workers, older

Oldest-old people over age 85, 19, 28, 75, 222, 356

as poorest old, 160

projected increases in population of, 75

Old-old people aged 75 to 85, 356

Olshansky, J., 14

Olshansky, S., 46

Olson, L. K., 182

Omran, A. R., 64

Onawola, R., 252

O'Rand, A. M., 261

Orbach, H., 340

Oregon, plan for rationing health care in, 72

Orentlicher, D., 106

Orfshanksy, M., 223

Orgel, L. E., 38

Orr, N. K., 129

Orwoll, L., 364

Osgood, N. J., 31, 108, 308, 336

reading from, 336-341

O'Shaughnessy, C., 246

Osteoporosis, 12, 15, 58, 59, 87

definition of, 12

need for research on, 88

prevalence of, 12

Ostow, M., 27

Over, R., 384, 385

P

Pacific/Asian Elderly Research Project, 239

Paffenbarger, R. S., 5

Palmer, J. L., 201, 229, 232, 236, 250

Palmore, E. B., 162, 300, 354, 401

Parenthood, 356-357

Parker, S., 338

Parkinson's disease, 12, 14, 46

definition of, 12

dementia and, 12

free radical theory of aging and, 40

gene therapy as possible cure for, 45

possible cause of, 12

prevalence of, 12

symptoms of, 12

treatment for, 12

Parnes, H. S., 300

Patient Self-Determination Act (PSDA), 30, 106, 107

Patten, S., 26, 310

Pay-as-you-go system system for paying for the cost of Social Security whereby workers at any point in time contribute money used to pay benefits for those now retired; in effect, current workers pay current expenses rather than saving up for future benefits

"Paying for a Nursing Home," 132

Payroll tax a uniform percentage of salary or wages deducted for the Social Security and Medicare programs

Peacock, W., 253

Peck, R. C., 364, 399

Pell, S., 59

Pension Benefit Guaranty Corporation (PBGC), 174, 306

Pensions, private, 173-175, 239, 325

as deferred compensation, 173, 187

as source of retirement income, 173-175, 293, 328

decline in percentage of workers in, 304

early retirement benefits of, 175

fewer employers offering, 305

lower for older women, 163

military, 305

portability of, 174

rising costs of, 297

types of, 173

vesting of, 174

Pepper, C., 203

Perlin, S., 109

Perlmutter, M., 364

Perloff, R. M., 333

Perry, D., 87

reading from, 87-88

Personick, V. A., 315, 316

Peter, H., 104

Peters, C. B., 360

Peterson, P. G., 182

Pfeifer, S. K., 131

Phased retirement a practice in which older workers near the age of retirement gradually rather than abruptly reduce their work schedule

Philadelphia Geriatric Center Morale Scale, 32

Picasso, P., 371

Pifer, A., 363

Pilisuk, M., 224

Plasticity, 344, 370

Plato, 349

Political economy of aging, 182

Pollack, R. F., 222, 223, 226, 227, 228

Population aging a rise in the average age of the population; alternatively, an increase in the proportion of the population made up of people over age 65, xxvii, 182, 185, 187, 321, 363

age-based entitlements and, 185

American society's response to, xxx

as historically constructed, xxxii

as long-range trend, xxix

as socially constructed, xxxii

definition of, xxix

reasons for, xxviii, xxix

versus individual aging, xxviii

Population Association of America, 221

Portability (of pensions) condition where an employee can take along claims to pension accumulations after leaving one job or another

Porter, J., 278, 279

Portnow, J., 27

Post, S., 131

Postman, N., 353

Poverty index an annual level of income for a family or individual that gives the official government definition of poverty

Pratt, H. J., 183

Preretirement planning, 293-295

as commonplace, 294

as valuable education strategy for older people, 295

issues covered in, 294

major problems with, 294-295

recent trends in, 294

President's Council of Economic Advisors, 221

Preston, S., 221, 227

Preston, S. H., 193, 203, 209, 221, 227

Prihoda, R., 74

Productivity:
    among minority aged, 163
    among young-old, 187
    decrement with compensation and, 370
    of older workers, 306
Project ABLE (Chicago), 344
Proxy decision maker   someone authorized to make
    health care decisions for another person when the
    other person has lost capacity to make decisions
Ptolemy, 350
Public Health Service, 56
Public Opinion, 202
Putnam, J., 183
Pye, D., 41

Q

Quadagno, J., 354
Quality of life, 19, 30, 112
    medical emphasis on, 49
Quetelet, A., 382
Quill, T., 105
Quinlan, K. A., 103, 121
    death of, 106
    See also Right-to-die cases
Quinn, J. F., 26, 171, 293, 305

R

Rabins, P., 130
Rabushka, A., 182
Rachels, J., 100
Radner, D., 169
Rahe, R. H., 358
Raisz, H., 26
Rationing of health care, 3, 71-77
    "backdoor" rationing, 34, 97-98
Rawls, J., 224
Reagan, R., 87, 244, 248
    administration of, 223, 235, 277
    era of, 236
Rectangular-shaped survival curve   the geometric
    curve that results when we plot the death rate
    against chronological age and discover that more
    and more people suvive into old age and then expe-
    rience a high death rate, 50, 55, 62
Rector, R., 21

Rehn, G., 302
Reif, L., 222
Reilly, T. W., 134
Reimbursement systems, 16
Reimers, C., 259
Reisberg, B., 14
Reisman, D., 339
Rejda, G. E., 258
Religion:
    Bible and aging, 349
    medieval view of the life course, 351
    old age and, 401, 411
Relman, A. S., 73
Rembrandt, 365, 405
Reminiscence, 416-418
    adaptive value of, 416-417
    as normal form of life review, 416
    guided biography as, 417
Reminiscence groups:
    as program therapy
Replacement level   the proportion of salary during
    working years that Social Security pays beneficiar-
    ies, 173
Researching term papers in gerontology, 419-428
    abstracts and databases for, 425
    conducting library research, 422-423
    encyclopedias and handbooks for, 424-425
    ending the library search, 423
    defining the topic, 420
    guides to research and information, 426
    journals and periodicals for, 428
    reference works for, 426-427
    resources for, 424-428
    starting the search, 420-422
    statistics for, 425-426
    textbooks for, 427
Reserve capacity   the ability of the body to recover
    from assaults and to withstand peak-load demands
    on organic systems, 7, 52
Respite care, 129
Retired Senior Volunteer Program (RSVP), 344
Retirement, xxxi, 158
    abolition of mandatory, 298, 306
    among black aged, 163
    and availability of range of life options, 340

and expansion of leisure and opportunities for self-fulfillment, 306

and preretirement planning, 293-295

as convenient practice for managing labor force, 306

as form of leisure, 300

as longer and more important part of life, 293, 302

as roleless role, 297

busy ethic and, 328-335

cognitive changes with, 370

continuity theory and, 340

costs of, 306

deciding sense of, 297-345

earlier, 322

flexible, 306, 397

historical notes on, 323-324

history of, 298-303, 323-324, 352

institutionalization of, 337

lifelong learning and, 302

mandatory, 298, 306, 322, 324, 359, 397

phased, 302, 306

recurrent education and, 302

successful adaptation to, 340

See also Preretirement planning

Retirement Advisors, Inc., 294

Retirement communities, 21

Leisure World (California), 252

politics of age exclusion in, 252

role changes and successful aging and, 400

Sun City (Arizona), 252

Sun City Center (Florida), 333

Retirement income sources:

assets and savings, 171, 175-177

changing pattern of, 305

private pensions, 171, 173-175

Social Security, 171, 172-173

Retirement Survivors Disability Health Insurance (RSDHI), 327

Reverse mortgage, 176

Rhine, S. H., 306

Rhodes, S. R., 307

Rhudick, P. J., 417

Rice, C., 252

Rice, D. P., 204

"Right-to-die":

brain death and, 102

debate, 28-29

recent history of, 102-106

"Right to die" cases, 99

Browning case, 104

Conroy case, 103

Cruzan case, 103, 104-105, 107, 123

Natanson v. Kline case, 105

O'Connor case, 104

Perlmutter case, 105

Peter case, 104

Quinlan case, 103, 119

Rasmussen v. Fleming case, 103

Spring case, 104

Riley, J. W., Jr., 362

Riley, M. W., 150, 348, 362

Riley, M., xxx, xxxi

Rites of passage, 349

Rindfuss, R. R., 356

Rivlin, A., 28, 144, 148, 154

Rix, S. E., 344

Robbins, A., 258, 275

Robbins, G., 258, 275

Roberts, E., 258

Roberts, K., 338

Robey, B., 205

Rodgers, D. T., 329, 334

Rodin, J., 359

Roeder, R. G., 280

Role loss the process of giving up or losing previous roles, such as the role of spouse (with widowhood) or the role of worker (with retirement), 351, 400

aging as roleless role, 297, 400

and suicide, 31

Roosevelt, F. D., 263, 264

Root-Bernstein, R. S., 384

Rorsman, B., 56

Rose, M., 44, 400

Rosenbaum, W. A., 194

Rosenfeld, R. A., 356

Rosenmayr, L., 400

Rosenthal, C. J., 127, 163

Rosenwaike, I., 56

Rosow, I., 31, 252, 297, 330, 335, 401

Ross, J-K, 21, 400

Rossi, A., 356

Roth, G. S., 7

Roth, J. A., 361

Rother, J., 262, 263, 264, 265, 267, 268, 272, 273

Rowe, J. W., 399

Rowland, D., 166

Rudberg, M., 14

Russell, C., 205

Russell, L. B., 205

Ryan, W., 227

Ryder, K., 252

Ryder, N., 190

Rymer, M., 143

S

Sacher, G. A., 8, 36, 41, 51, 62

Sagi, P. C., 56

Saint Augustine, 350

Salthouse, T. A., 369, 370, 387

Samuelson, R., 238

Sanborn, B., 222

Sandell, S. H., 307, 314, 317, 318, 319, 322
  reading from, 314-320

Sangl, J., 129, 165

Santana, S., 162

Sattler, J. M., 365

Sauvy, A., 363

Schaie, K. W., 367, 368, 370

Schermerhorn, R. A., 160

Schiffres, M., 225

Schinck, W. O., 225

Schmahl, W., 306

Schneider, C. J., 300, 335, 340

Schneider, E. L., 5, 19, 46, 54, 58, 59, 66
  reading from, 54-58

Schneider, I., 141

Schnore, M., 297

Schnurr, L., 21

Schoen, C., 240

Scholen, K., 176

Schooler, C., 370

Schopenhauer, A., 405

Schor, J., 303

Schorr, A. L., 131

Schrimper, R., 178

Schulz, J. H., 244, 306

Schurenberg, E., 183

Schuster, M., 307

Schwartz, D. F., 162

Schwartz, W. B., 72, 89, 95
  reading from, 89-90

Schwarz, J., 186

Scientific American, 221

Scitovsky, A., 19

Scott-Maxwell, F., 403, 412
  reading from, 412-415

Seagle, B. M., 21

Seagle, J. F., 21

Sears, 304

Seattle Longitudinal Study, 368, 370

Seelback, W., 252

Segal, J., 26

Self-care movement, 49, 63

Self-determined death, 28-33
  late life suicide, 30-31
  subjective well-being and quality of life and, 31-33

Seligman, M.E.P., 358

Seltzer, M. M., 131

Seneca, 112

Senior centers, 182, 401

Senior Community Service Employment Program, 343

Senior Olympics, 399

Service Corp of Retired Executives (SCORE), 344

Sewell, W. H., 239

Sex discrimination, pension benefits and, 165

Sex ratio, 163

Shakespeare, W., 351, 355, 382

Shanas, E., 127, 130, 150, 323

Shangri-La, 35

Shapiro, D., 318

Shared housing, 21

Shaver, S., 293

Shaw, D. L., 26

Shea, D., 178, 295

Sheppard, H. L., 297, 344

Sherman, S., 304

Shock, N. W., 7, 51, 52, 55

Shorr, L., 253

Short-DeGraff, M., 252

Silbert, J. E., 329

Silverman, P., 165

Silvestri, G., 315, 317

Simmons, L. W., 104

Simonton, D. K., 371, 382, 383, 384, 385, 386, 391
    reading from, 382-386

Sinclair, U., 183

Singer, A., 163

Skinner, J. H., 246

Skocpol, T., 245

Slater, T. F., 6, 40

Sloane, L., 154

Smedley, L., 322

Smeeding, T. M., 193, 230

Smith, J., 387, 391

Smith, N., 145

Smolensky, E., 164, 169

Socholitzky, E., 145

Social class, 159, 168
    and life course, 348, 357
    and net worth, 177
    socioeconomic status and, 199

Social clock   shared set of expectations about what behavior is proper or "on time" for any specific chronological age, 349, 360

Social gerontology, 396
    agenda of, 401
    contribution of to successful aging, 401
    role of humanities in, 402

Social policy:
    conventional development of and implicit values, 324-326
    implicit values in contemporary, 323-326

Social programs:
    case for universality in, 242-249
    challenge to universalism of, 244-245
    expanding universalism of, 243-244
    history of universalism, aging, and, 243-245
    intergenerational, 251-253
    question of fairness of, 248-249
    universal eligibility feature of some, 245-246
    universalism and financing of, 247-248

See also Benefits, public *and* Entitlements *and* Specific social programs

Social programs, intergenerational, 251-253
    age grading and, 251
    age integration and, 252
    age segregation and, 251-252
    benefits of, 252-253
    Foster Grandparent Program, 252
    National School Volunteers Program, 252
    new interest in, 253
    Stride Rite's on-site day care, 252

Social Security, xxvii, xxix, xxx, 16, 109, 131, 158, 178, 179, 183, 184, 185, 186, 192, 193, 196, 197, 198, 203, 209, 214, 215, 220, 223, 224, 225, 226, 227, 235, 236, 239, 240, 243, 248, 251, 298, 303, 315, 322, 324, 325
    and advances in economic status of aged, 232
    and baby boom generation, 190, 206-207, 209, 257, 260, 263, 264, 265, 267, 271, 272, 273, 281
    as entitlement, 187
    as source of retirement income, 172-173, 293, 328
    child care dropout option and, 261, 291
    confidence in, 264-266
    cost of living increases (COLAS) for, 221
    criticism of present treatment of men and women under, 287-288
    cuts in, 198
    deciding whether only the needy should receive, 269
    defining system, 263-264
    description of, 255
    divorce and, 261
    earnings sharing plan advocated for, 261, 283-284, 288, 289
    federal funding for, 180
    feminist perspective of housewives and reform of, 282-285, 289-290
    high cost of, 226
    history of equal treatment of men and women under, 286
    immunity of to budget cuts, 203
    increase in benefits, 222
    long-term view of, 218-219
    need for incremental change in, 285-292
    older blacks receiving, 161

original reason for adopting, 305

part-time workers and, 325, 326

payroll tax, 200, 204, 208, 209, 227, 245, 247-248, 249, 255, 259

percentage of aged covered by, 256

popularity of and support for, 225, 253, 256-257

proposals to remedy inequitable treatment under, 288-291

purpose of, 256

questioning future of, 255-295, 298, 304

reforming, 266-267

rising costs of, 297

solvency of, 272-273

two-worker families and, 261, 287-288

universality and egalitarianism of, 168, 242, 245-246, 257

widows receiving, 164

women and, 260-262, 288

work incentives in system, 267-268

See also Old Age Survivors and Disability Insurance (OASDI)

Social Security Act, 16, 140, 179, 182, 255, 263, 303, 310, 311

amendments of 1983 to, 257

expansions of 1939 and 1956, 185

loopholes in, 141

revisions of in 1977 and 1983, 179

Title XX of, 181, 239

Social Security Administration, 56, 59, 207, 214, 275

Title XX of, 240

Social Security earnings test, 258-259, 266

effect of, 274

failure of, 274-276

Social Security surplus the excess of Social Security payroll taxes collected over the amount paid out, including excess funds accumulated from prior years

Social Security Trust Fund surplus, 237, 259-262, 265, 276-277, 278-281

and redistributing burden of financing federal government, 280

future policy directions for, 279

proposal to invest, 278-279

proposal to reduce payroll tax, 279

recent proposals concerning, 278-279

safety of, 271

saving, 280-281

suggestion of pay-as-you-go basis for, 276, 279

Socioeconomic status location of individuals within a system of stratification or social class, reflecting inequality of wealth, power, or prestige

Sohal, R. S., 6, 40

Solomon, M., 106

Somatic mutation theory of aging, 38

Sommers, K., 252

Sophocles, 350

Southern Conference on Gerontology, 208

Sowarka, D., 387, 391

Sparrow, P. R., 344

Spence, D. A., 146

Spengler, J. J., 203

Spiegel, A. D., 132

Spousal responsibilty a legal requirement that a spouse pay for the medical or long-term care expenses of a married partner, 131

Sprague, L., 275

Spring, E., 104

Springer, D., 129

Sprott, R. L., 7

Stagner, R., 306

Stanford, E. P., 295

Stanley, J. F., 41

Starr, J. M., 403

Starzl, T., 78

Staudinger, U. M., 387, 391

Stearns, P. N., 130, 354

Stein, B., 259

Steinberg, L. D., 417

Stephan, P. E., 363

Stephens, S., 128

Stereotypes:

about second half of life, 357

images of age and, 355

negative image of older workers, 306, 323

of life stages, 402

retirement as cause of ill health, 300, 303

role of television in propagating, 353

Stevens, L., 107, 110

reading from, 110-111

Stevens, R., 132

Stewart, A. W., 255

Stockman, D., 244

Stoller, E. P., 161, 163

Stone, G. P., 339

Stone, R. I., 128, 129, 135, 165, 166, 222

Strate, J., 214

Stratification a pattern of inequality among members of society; for example, stratification by social class or stratification by age, 159, 199, 225

Straus, A. L., 33

Strauss, A., 129

Strauss, M., 91

Strehler, B. L., 5, 51

Streib, G. F., 21, 159, 198, 199, 300, 335, 340, 348

Stroke, 10, 14, 15, 59, 87, 131
  costs for caring for victims of, 13
  declining death rate from, 46
  definition of, 13
  free radical theory of aging and, 40
  results of, 13

Stroller, E. P., 151

Subculture theory of aging, 400

Substituted judgment making health care decisions for another person based on an effort to determine what that person would have wanted under the circumstances at hand, 103, 104

Successful aging optimum functioning in later life as a result of offsetting or compensating for losses, 58, 333, 350, 387, 399

Suicide:
  altruistic, 30-31
  among different ethnic groups, 31
  and late-life creativity, 386
  and rationing health care, 77
  anomic, 31
  as cause of death among aged, 30, 108
  assisted, 28, 30, 82-83, 100, 107
  conditions preceding late life, 31
  contemplation of by ill widow, 110-111
  depression and, 30, 31
  egoistic, 31
  late life, 30-21
  prevention, 31
  rates for people 65 and older, 31, 32
  "rational," 109
  rise in among elderly, 108-109

types of, 30-31
  versus termination of treatment, 105

Suicide, assisted, 28, 30, 82-83, 100, 107
  check list for, 114
  practicalities of, 113-116

Sumner, D., 178

Sundquist, J., 243

Supplemental Security Income (SSI), 193, 235, 236, 239, 243, 327
  blacks receiving, 161
  means test for, 199
  Old Age Assistance program and, 244

Survival curves, 38, 50

Sussman, M. B., 131, 150

Sutton, W., 244, 391

Swicegood, C. G., 356

Swift, J., 2, 3, 84

Szabo, J., 262, 274
  reading from, 274-276

Szilard, L., 38

T

Taeuber, C., 187

Taft, L., 374

Talley, W., 253

Tandy, J., 168, 371

Targeting directing benefits or services to a specified subgroup, based on population characteristics such as poverty, ethnicity, geographic location, etc., 200
  opposed to universalism, 197

Taxation:
  and tax expenditures, 196
  general accounting and, 197
  of Social Security benefits, 200, 245

Tax Equity and Fiscal Responsibility Act (TEFRA), 143
  lien provisions of, 144

Tax Reform Act of 1986, 175

Taylor, H., 224, 225

Taylor, P., 222

Teague, M. L., 307

Telephone reeassurance, 26

Tell, E., 132

Terkel, S., 303

W

Wachter, S., 206

Waerness, K., 151

Waldo, D. R., 143

Walford, R. L., 36, 43, 67
  High-Low diet of, 43, 67

Wallace, A., 333

Wallace, I., 333

Wallack, S. S., 132

Wallechinsky, D., 333

Wallman, L. M., 300

Walls, C. T., 169

Wanglie, H., 29

War on Poverty programs, 243

Watkins, S. C., 128

Watson, J. D., 45

Wear and tear theory of aging, 37-39
  accumulative waste theory and, 38-39
  chance and, 37
  error accumulation theory and, 38
  error catastrophe theory and, 38
  somatic mutation theory and, 38

Weaver, C., 262, 264, 265, 267, 268, 270, 271, 272, 273

Webb, D., 333

Weber, M., 307

Wechsler Adult Intelligence Scale (WAIS) the most influential test of intelligence used today; it includes a verbal part and a performance part, which combine to give an IQ score, 365

Weibel-Orlando, J., 162

Weicher, J., 206

Weindruch, R., 43

Weinstein, M. H., 158

Weismann, A., 37

Weiss, J. C., 68

Weitzman, L., 165

Welch, H. G., 76

Welfare programs, 193, 203

Well-being, subjective:
  self-rated health and, 32

Wennberg, R., 100

Wetle, T., 86, 95
  reading from, 86-88

Whartenby, K., 45

Whitbourne, S. K., 368

White House Conference on Aging, 330

White, L., 10

Widowhood, 150
  differences in by age and ethnicity, 164
  impact of on economic status of women, 165
  Social Security benefits and, 164

Widow-to-Widow Program, 165

Wiener, J. M., 28, 144, 146, 148, 154

Wilensky, H. L., 338, 339

Wilkin, J. C., 56

Will, G., 85

Willging, P. R., 275

Williams, R. H., 340, 397

Willis, S. L., 368

Winsborough, H. H., 357

Wirths, C., 340, 397

Wirtz, W., 302

Wisdom:
  and ego transcendence, 364
  and modernization, 354, 362
  as facet of successful aging, 387-390
  attempts to measure, 366-367
  conceptualization of, 388-389
  creativity and, 364-365
  familiar components of, 364
  Greek and Roman views of, 349
  in older adults, 389-390
  related knowledge, 389
  requirements for, 364
  strategies of life management and, 389
  strategies of life planning and, 389, 390
  strategies of life review and, 389, 390
  theoretical definition of, 388-389
  working framework of, 389

Wisensale, S. K., 196

Wolff, N., 261

Women:
  as caregivers of frail elderly family members, 128, 149-152, 165
  as kin-keepers, 150, 163
  double standard of aging and, 163
  labor force participation of, 299, 303, 310, 313, 322
  poverty among older, 164

sandwich generation of, 128
stereotyped roles of, 353
treatment of under Social Security system, 260-261
Wong, H., 300
Wood, P. D., 59
Wood, V., 340
Woodwork effect   phrase referring to the assumption that there is latent demand for long-term care services which would not otherwise be provided or which families might have provided, 133
Woodworth, R. S., 372
Work:
aas means to afford leisure activities, 340
decline in activities of, 337
decrease in volunteer activities due to, 303
flextime, 302
future of leisure and, 312-313
history of, 336-338
in classical and preindustrial society, 336-337
in postindustrial society, 337
leisure versus, 314
life after, 336-341
reasons for drastic reductions in, 337-338
sabbaticals from, 302
"share the work" plan and, 302
"shorter hours movement" and, 302
significant changes in structure of, 338
toward new paradigm of age and, 309-314
work sharing and, 302
Workers, older:
aging society and, 321
aging work force and, 321-323
as discouraged workers, 304
context for public policy toward, 317-319
decline in relative importance of in labor force, 315
disadvantaged in fast-moving labor market, 360
discovery method of retraining, 345
displaced, 304
future role of, 326-328
incentives for removing from labor force, 305-306
intergenerational equity and, 313-314
intergenerational tension and, 323
labor force requirements and, 314
policy choices concerning, 313-314

present role of, 321-323
problems for future, 320
prototypical, 317-318
retirement of, 313
retraining, 344, 361
serious employment problems among, 318
service requirements for, 314
social benefits for female, 313
social policy toward, 320-328
value-driven policy development and, 326-328
year 2000 labor force and employment policy for, 314-320
Work ethic, 303, 307, 308, 329
Protestant, 337
See also Busy ethic
Work/Family Elder Directions, Inc., 128
Work force, common beliefs about who belongs in, 309-310
Workplace policies encouraging older workers to retire:
"golden parachute" packages, 325
part-time work, 325, 326
"30-and-out" policy, 324-325
World-we-have-lost myth   the view that family life has disintegrated in contrast to a "Golden Age" of preindustrial society when the extended family (presumable) lived under one roof, 130, 354

Y

Yaffe, N., 56
Yankelovich, D., 329, 337
Yankelovich, Skelly, and White, Inc., 206, 257, 306
Yeats, W. B., 365, 405
Yee, B.W.K., 162
Young, L., 55
Young-old   people aged 65 to 75, 22, 356

Z

Zambrana, R. E., 162
Zarit, J. M., 129
Zarit, S. H., 129, 169
Zembek, B. A., 163
Zero population growth, xxviii, xxix
Ziegler, S., 252

Of related interest. . .

Research on Aging:
A Quarterly of Social Gerontology and Adult Development
Editor: Rhonda J.V. Montgomery, *University of Kansas*
. . . a journal of interdisciplinary research on current issues, and methodological and research problems in the study of the aged.
Quarterly: March, June, September, December
Yearly rates: Institution $160 / Individual $53

Journal of Applied Gerontology
The Official Journal of the Southern Gerontological Society
Editor: William J. McAuley, *Virginia Polytechnic Institute*
and State University
. . . strives to consistently publish articles in all subdisciplines of aging whose findings, conclusions, or suggestions have clear and sometimes immediate applicability to the problems encountered by older persons.
Quarterly: March, June, September, December
Yearly rates: Institution $150 / Individual $52

Journal of Aging and Health
Editor: Kyriakos S. Markides, *University of Texas*
Medical Branch, Galveston
. . . deals with social and behavioral factors related to aging and health, emphasizing health and quality of life.
Quarterly: February, May, August, November
Yearly rates: Institution $135 / Individual $55

Abstracts in Social Gerontology: Current Literature on Aging
Published in Cooperation with The National Council
on the Aging, Inc.
. . . provides abstracts and bibliographies of major articles, books, reports, and other materials on all aspects of social gerontology: including demography, economics, family relations, government policy, health, institutional care, physiology, psychiatric dysfunctions, psychology, societal attitudes, work and retirement.
Quarterly: March, June, September, December
Yearly rates: Institution $164 / Individual $80

SAGE PUBLICATIONS, INC.
2455 Teller Road
Thousand Oaks, CA 91320

SAGE PUBLICATIONS LTD
6 Bonhill Street
London EC2A 4PU, England

SAGE PUBLICATIONS INDIA PVT. LTD
M-32 Market, Greater Kailash I
New Delhi 100 048, India